Handbook of Research on E-Services in the Public Sector:

E-Government Strategies and Advancements

Abid Thyab Al Ajeeli
University of Bahrain, Bahrain

Yousif A. Latif Al-Bastaki
University of Bahrain, Bahrain

Information Science REFERENCE

INFORMATION SCIENCE REFERENCE
Hershey · New York

Director of Editorial Content:	Kristin Klinger
Director of Book Publications:	Julia Mosemann
Acquisitions Editor:	Lindsay Johnston
Development Editor:	Christine Bufton
Publishing Assistant:	Milan Vracarich, Jr.
Typesetter:	Deanna Jo Zombro
Production Editor:	Jamie Snavely
Cover Design:	Lisa Tosheff

Published in the United States of America by
Information Science Reference (an imprint of IGI Global)
701 E. Chocolate Avenue
Hershey PA 17033
Tel: 717-533-8845
Fax: 717-533-8661
E-mail: cust@igi-global.com
Web site: http://www.igi-global.com

Library of Congress Cataloging-in-Publication Data

Handbook of research on e-services in the public sector : e-government strategies and advancements / Abid Thyab Al Ajeeli and Yousif A. Latif Al-Bastaki, editors.
p. cm.
Includes bibliographical references and index.
Summary: "This book assists its readers in recommending formulation of ICT strategies for e-government implementation and maintenance from the perspective of acknowledging the importance of e-Governance for building institutions to achieve transparency and accountability, and eventually democratic governance"--Provided by publisher.
ISBN 978-1-61520-789-3 (hardcover) -- ISBN 978-1-61520-790-9 (ebook)
1. Internet in public administration. 2. Public administration--Information technology. 3. Communication in public administration--Technological innovations.
I. Al Ajeeli, Abid. II. Al-Bastaki, Yousif A. Latif.
JF1525.A8H36195 2010
352.3'802854678--dc22
2010000633

British Cataloguing in Publication Data
A Cataloguing in Publication record for this book is available from the British Library.

List of Contributors

Table of Contents

Detailed Table of Contents

This chapter examines the nature of Web 2.0 technologies and social media and analyses their role in political campaigning, particularly in the context of the recent federal elections in America and in Australia. While broadcast television is still a dominant political player, the empirical evidence suggests that a viable campaign needs to integrate diverse communication strategies tailored to citizen's interests and the political environment. The interactive and participatory technologies of the online world are increasingly key components of such integrated campaign strategies.

This chapter presents a review of the e-Government strategies in Nigeria, the human capital development initiatives, the information and communications technology (ICT) diffusion and e-Inclusion. The global and continental ranking of the country is presented, as well as recommendations to accelerate developments towards achieving the millennium development goals.

This chapter covers the role of government which is taken into consideration in the accreditation of service providers, as well as in the settlement of e-administrative disputes and the securing of e-transactions. The necessity for self-regulation, equality of digital divide and government's recommendation for ODR tools are discussed. The current chapter identifies and explores considerable notions, concepts and debates for moving towards the development of an international dispute resolution framework online and trustful mechanism internationally.

This chapter discusses issues that play a vital role in helping citizens overcome perceived risks. It emphasizes on how trust makes citizens comfortable in sharing personal information, making online

This chapter discusses the e-health development in Australia. The Australian government has been very proactive in e-government such as e-health in the last five years. E-health is an important application for innovation of the public sector due to its sparsely populated large rural areas.

The chapter explains the process of building security awareness culture to serve e-government initiative. These initiatives together with the existing and emerging private initiatives which offer E-Services lead to dramatically increase in the number of the Internet user. It forms the infrastructure of E-Society. The level of citizen's engagement in these initiatives depends on the extent of confidence in the security system used by these initiatives.

The chapter discusses a database model which provides a systematic, logical and regular basis for the collection, collation, dissemination and mapping of strategic e-purchasing data. Selective access to this accurate and timely data will measurably improve public sector strategic e-procurement performance, accountability and administration. It will assist the public sector to be more effective and efficient in resource allocation and investment outcomes measurement, more transparent, and will encourage the development of trust, networks and social capital amongst public sector employees and their suppliers.

This chapter introduces Mobile phone Technology used widely in these days. We expect in the near future that people will have at least one mobile phone. The chapter surveys a number of systems which are designed for communication in emergency situations. Three systems will extensively be explained. These systems were developed by the chapter's authors.

This chapter discusses one of the most powerful weapons for attackers known as the Internet worm. A worm attacks vulnerable computer systems and employs self-propagating methods to flood the Internet rapidly. Since "Worm" is self-propagated through the connected network, it doesn't need human interaction or file transmission to replicate itself. The chapter provides efficient methods of detection and correction.

This chapter explains the process of justifying texts as Arabic calligraphers use to stretch some letters with small flowing curves. The keshideh instead of inserting blanks among words. The stretching is context dependent. Adequate tools supporting such writing are based on a continuous mathematical model enables intersections to be determined dynamically.

The chapter outlines that e-government webs are among the largest webs in terms of size, number of users and number of information providers. The creation of a semantic web infrastructure to meaningfully organize e-government webs is highly desirable. The chapter also points out that the complexity of existing e-government implementations provides challenges to the feasibility of semantic web creation.

This chapter describes a holistic approach for the design of e-government platforms. It defines principles for architecting a system which must sustain the entire e-government activity of a mid-level public authority (Geneva). It discusses the principles of Legality, Responsibility, Transparency, and Symmetry. These principles provide guidance to both policymakers and users.

Preface

We live in an increasingly highly sophisticated and interconnected society, where the Internet has led to tremendous improvements in efficiency, effectiveness, and better services. The Internet has in recent years become a natural part of everyday life for an increasing number of individuals' worldwide. Through computers, wireless technology, and cell phones we can communicate with one another whenever and wherever at low costs, and all the information in the world, in theory, can be available to citizens in seconds. Those who use the net on a regular basis have gradually come to expect all manner of information and services there – including the ones from the public sector.

More than 65 percent of all Internet users interact with government websites. E-Government technology saves individuals significant amount of money and time, while adding value to citizens' experience with government and better serving their needs.

The emergence of the Internet as a major technological and social force in the 1990s was accompanied by a recognition that this medium could have a transformative impact on the relationship between government agents and citizens.

Today's citizens need to develop a wide range of specialist skills and knowledge to drive performance and help their organization achieve success in a tough global market. The E-government book, I believe, is a valuable asset providing its reader with the required knowledge that enhances competitive advantage and effective change management.

The materials in the book cover an important role in almost every aspect of an organization's activities. They provide comprehensive coverage of the e-government issues faced by managers, consultants and other practitioners. The book is divided into thirty three chapters covering most daily life activities in an electronic government.

The primary objective of the book is to assist its readers in recommending the formulation of ICT strategies for their e-government and acquiring knowledge on the significance of e-Government for developing efficient and effective government systems. At the same time, acknowledge the importance of e-Governance for building institutions to achieve transparency and accountability, and eventually democratic governance.

The book also aims to assist its readers in implementing collaborative policy initiatives among the private, public, and non-profitable sectors for eliminating the global digital divide. This book will also explore the relationship among different variables and the implementation of digital initiatives for effective e-Government readiness.

The first chapter of this book shows that governments around the world have sought to improve their governing capabilities by developing and implementing strategic information and communication technologies (ICTs). The use of ICTs can provide citizens with greater access to government services, promote transparency and accountability, and also streamline government expenditures.

The research, in this chapter, provides a comparative analysis of the practices of digital governance in large municipalities worldwide in 2005. Digital government includes both e-government and e-democracy. The research is based on an evaluation of a sample (n=81) of city websites globally in terms of two dimensions: delivery of public services and digital democracy. The official websites of each city were evaluated in their native languages. Based on the analysis of 81 cities, Seoul, New York, Shanghai, Hong Kong, and Sydney represent the cities with the most effective e-governance systems.

The second chapter introduces an approach that deals with the verification of UML collaboration and sequence diagrams in respect to the objects of internal behaviors which are commonly represented by state machine diagrams. The approach is based on the translation of theses diagrams to Maude specifications. In fact, Maude is a declarative programming language, an executable formal specification language, and also a formal verification system, which permits the achievement of the approach goals.

The chapter also defines, in detail, the rules of translating UML diagrams elements into their corresponding Maude specifications. This chapter presents the algebraic structures that represent the OR-States and the AND-states in a state machine diagram, and the structure that represents the collaboration and the sequence diagrams. The chapter explains the mechanism of the execution and the verification of the translated specification, which is based on rewriting logics rules.

Chapter Three outlines that government establishments are most times, highly involved in different reorganization programs. The processes in e-Government are diversified and complex, hence the need for an appropriate training and learning strategy for governmental employees. Changing business processes and organizational structures always means that the personnel have to be familiar with the changed procedures. Consequently, the employees need to be trained to develop capacity for new responsibilities.

The chapter outlines that existing methods of learning and training do not make provision for certain category of employees such as the visually impaired. They do not provide an alternative learning platform for government of employees that are not physically challenged. Many studies have demonstrated the value of several learning platforms, including mobile learning (m-Learning), but with the problems of access barriers and streamlined participation of most learners.

The purpose of the chapter is to propose a voice-based e-Learning system, also known as voice-learning (v-Learning) as a variant of the m-Learning with particular relevance to the visually and mobility impaired learners. V-Learning makes possible ubiquitous learning in e-Government and provides additional capacity and speed of response to help facilitate change. Cost reduction is also achieved and there is no shortage of teachers.

Chapter Four handles software reuse in Component Based Software Engineering (CBSE) which covers a variety of fields, including component design, component specification, component composition, component-based framework. CBSE is quickly becoming a mainstream approach to software development and most researchers are hoping that there will be solutions to problems that led to software crisis.

The software engineering techniques specific to this discipline, in phases such as modeling, verification or validation of component based software systems still insufficient and need more research efforts. ECATNets (Extended Concurrent Algebraic Term Nets) are frameworks for specification, modeling and validation of concurrent and distributed systems.

The techniques are characterized by their semantics defined in terms of rewriting logic. The objective of this article is to propose a formal specification of software components by using ECATNets formalism. The expected benefits of this work are: It offers a formal notation for describing the different features of concurrent and distributed software components; Defining a formal unambiguous semantics to describe the behavior of the composed system.

In chapter Five, we propose a new methodology for ontology building, which is based on a set of mapping rules from a conceptual schema (Entity-Relationship) and its corresponding logical model (relational model) toward a conceptual ontology. The proposed methodology consists of three big steps, which are, the Transformation (mapping), the Formalization and the Codification.

The crucial step in the building process of this methodology is the transformation; this last concept is based on an automatic extraction of information for a conceptual model ER (such as entities, relationships, properties and cardinalities). The data stored in the database (the schema extension) are extracted and used to create instances of the ontology. At the end of this stage, we will have a complete conceptual ontology that can be used in different applications.

Chapter Six shows how people search websites for health information for self-care, and how the information provided by these e-health portals are delivered in text form. This does not cater for the needs of the visually impaired, the blind, the low-literate and those who are not computer literate. Also, the existing speech-based disease screening initiatives lack the reasoning capability to make them attain the level of an expert system.

The work, in this chapter, presents an intelligent framework for usable speech-enabled e-health system that provides speech-based health information to cater for the needs of those not catered for in graphical user interface. It also introduces rule-based reasoning techniques into speech-based disease screening systems.

Chapter Seven introduces the usage of the internet and shows how the internet capabilities, as an example, have grown over recent years in South Africa, but at a very slow rate. This is the result of several challenges facing the growth of the Internet in South Africa. These challenges are mostly related to the lack of infrastructures of the Internet, high cost of computer technology and service provider challenges.

The chapter also provides an overview of the Internet usage and its impact on E-Government in South Africa. It examines regulatory issues pertaining to the Internet. It also examines Internet growth in the business and government sectors. In the government sector, the Cape Online Strategy, is an initiative by the provincial government of the Western Cape in SA, is an example of a global trend towards greater levels of interactivity between government and citizens.

This initiative is an excellent example of how Web-based solutions can be used to deliver certain services to citizens. Another excellent example is an E-justice initiative undertaken by the Department of Justice. The initiative aims at promoting a more efficient system of Justice in SA. The chapter provides an overview of the challenges to Internet adoption in South Africa.

Chapter Eight introduces the Internet and Information and Communications Technologies (ICTs) which have long been seen as potentially contributing to a solution to the problem of voter disaffection and disengagement that has occurred in many western liberal democracies over the past couple of decades. The success of Barack Obama in the 2008 presidential campaign in the United States has highlighted the role that ICTs, in the form of Web 2.0 technologies and social media, can play in enhancing citizen's democratic participation and involvement in political campaigning.

This Chapter examines the nature of Web 2.0 technologies and social media and analyses their role in political campaigning, particularly in the context of the recent federal elections in America and in Australia. While broadcast television is still a dominant political player, the empirical evidence suggests that a viable campaign needs to integrate diverse communication strategies tailored to citizen's interests and the political environment. The interactive and participatory technologies of the online world are increasingly key components of such integrated campaign strategies.

Chapter Nine introduces Nigeria experience which has made frantic efforts towards achieving the millennium development goals (MDGs) as spelt out in the United Nations' Agenda for the world. A critical assessment of the e-Government strategies in Nigeria is important being responsible for 20% of the population of the entire African continent. This chapter presents a review of the e-Government strategies in Nigeria; the human capital development initiatives; the information and communications technology (ICT) diffusion and e-Inclusion. The global and continental ranking of the country is presented, as well as recommendations to accelerate developments towards achieving the MDGs.

Findings revealed that there are ongoing efforts in Nigeria to address the issue of poverty. The various initiatives of government include: the National/State Economic Empowerment Strategies (NEEDS/SEEDS), the Vision 2020, the National e-Government Strategy (NeGST) and a well-formulated National IT policy, to mention a few. The little hindrance encountered in the research is that the available data was only up to the year 2005 and 2006 in some cases.

However, based on the human capital development indices such as: economic empowerment and poverty reduction, education, health, employment generation, etc, it was observed that the adult literacy level of 64.2% is satisfactory and better results are expected before 2015. The life expectancy level is constant (54 years) from 2002 to 2007, which is the one of the lowest in Africa.

On school enrolment, the major problem is access and poverty. It was observed that only 25% of primary school leavers made it to the secondary school level, while about 14% of the students at this level made it to the tertiary level. Similarly, the average percentage of female enrolment in schools is 45%. The health facilities are under-funded and are grossly inadequate both in quality and quantity. There is an average of 1,700 persons per hospital bed and the ratio of physicians to the populace is about 1:6000. This calls for a state of emergency in this sector.

One major sector of the economy that is experiencing a boost is the ICT and Telecoms. The sector had brought about a teledensity growth of 0.73 to 37.05 from 2001 to 2007. Consequently, Nigeria has been named the fastest growing Telecoms nation in Africa and the third in the world, with a number of direct and indirect jobs created. Similarly, the rate of Internet diffusion is encouraging bearing in mind that the level was almost non existent in 1999. It is obvious that Nigeria would be able to bridge the divide by 2015.

Generally speaking, there are some meaningful developments in the country arising from the various poverty eradication schemes, but the resultant effect has not imparted positively on unemployment. This is the opinion of the populace and hence the need for government to restrategize, otherwise, fulfilling MDGs by 2015 may not be realistic.

Chapter Ten covers points that characterize the century as of evolution for information technology, communication technology and electronic communications. Contemporary society does business using the internet; the forthcoming 'dispute resolution space' (Katsh & Rifkin 2001), where people buy and sell regularly and even a large number of corporations have existence via an internet address. This excitement for further improvement of dispute techniques, in relation to the exploitation of those technologies used for the management of online virtual communication led to the appearance of the Online Dispute Resolution (ODR) mechanism.

The choice for settlement of disputes through the modern mechanism provides an easement for interested parties to tackle their disputes from any place and at any time through e-mails, video conferencing or chat rooms, instead of being in courtrooms. The fact that the businesses are transactions are conducted on the internet causes uncertainty, regarding the security of personal data and business secrets in combination with the lack of a framework that could have supported such a scheme.

For that reason, the role of Government is taken into consideration in the accreditation of service providers, as well as in the settlement of *e*-administrative disputes and the securing of e-transactions in general. The necessity for self-regulation, equality of digital divide and government's recommendation for ODR tools are discussed. The current chapter will identify and explore considerable notions, concepts and debates for moving towards the development of an international dispute resolution framework on-line and trustful mechanism internationally.

In Chapter Eleven, we discuss issues that play vital role in helping citizens overcome perceived risks. Trust makes citizens comfortable sharing personal information, making online government transactions, and acting on e-Government advices. Thus, trust is a significant notion that should be critically investigated to help both researchers and practitioners to understand citizens' acceptance to e-Government. Prior research in trust has focused mainly on consumer's trust in e-Commerce.

Most of the existing literatures on trust in e-government focus on technical perspective such as PKI. This chapter contributes by proposing a conceptual model of citizens' trust in e-Government. The proposed conceptual model of citizens' trust in e-government is integrated constructs from multiple disciplines: psychology, sociology, e-commerce, and HCI. The research is aimed also to develop items in order to measure the theoretical constructs in the proposed model.

The pool of items is generated based on literature review. Q-Methodology has been utilized to validate the generated measurement items. The outcome of two Q-sorting rounds resulted in developing a survey instrument for proposed model with an excellent validity and reliability of statistical results.

Chapter Twelve introduces the methods of delivering public services through SMS (SMS-based e-government) which is becoming popular in developed and developing countries as a strategy to engage more citizens in using e-government services. Current advances in SMS-based e-government applications by local authorities in developed and developing countries are investigated to determine to what extent SMS-based e-government could deliver existing Internet-based e-government services and whether these services can fulfill the actual needs of e-government services users.

The currently available SMS-based e-government services are presented as a model with six levels: Listen, Notification, Pull-based Information, communication, Transaction, and Integration levels. The model classifies the SMS-based e-government services into levels based on the direction of communication, the complexity of the services and the benefits received by citizens; the higher the level the more complex the services and the more benefits received by citizens.

The SMS-based e-government model is compared to Internet-based e-government models and typical e-government use to show SMS-based e-government can deliver almost all of the service offerings of Internet-based e-government and meet the requirements of e-government users except for downloading forms. The outcomes justify the development of SMS-based e-government services.

Chapter Thirteen shows that stakeholders are proactive in the development of e-government initiatives; public organizations should be proactive in identifying all relevant collaborators, working with them and undertaking measures to systematically engage their stakeholders. Building coalitions with both internal and external stakeholders (Pardo and Scholl, 2002) of an e-government project may help in recognizing the critical stakeholders that deserve project managers' attention. Henceforth, e-government has to rely on a broad consensus, commitment and ownership at all levels among government officials as well as the citizens.

The diversity of stakeholder interests poses considerable challenges to project managers. Stakeholder analysis may be applied to e-government projects to assist managers in identifying potential conflicts between project stakeholders at early project stages. Insights on potential stakeholder conflicts can then be used for devising and implementing communication strategies to prevent contradictory stakeholder interests and to avoid conflicts.

Empirical evidence is needed in order to validate the suggested approach. Government to government and inter agency cooperation projects may be especially well suited, as complexity rises as multiple public sector organizations seek to align their objectives to reach common goals.

Chapter Fourteen examines the rising of the knowledge of economy, enhanced by the fast diffusion of ICTs, drives a wider perspective on the divide among Countries, interpreting it more and more as the result of an asymmetry in the access to knowledge and in the readiness to apply it in order to renew the basics of their development dynamics. Looking at the Mediterranean Area, the positive correlation between the Networked Readiness Index and the Global Competitive Index developed at Global Economic Forum – INSEAD, shows that the opposite sides of the Mediterranean Sea are performing a development path at two different paces.

In the effort to face the challenge of supporting the creation of Intellectual Capital which can be able to apply, diffuse and benefit from e-business. In 2005 the e-Business Management Section (eBMS) of Scuola Superiore ISUFI – University of Salento launched the "Mediterranean School of e-Business Management".

The present work aims to offer a presentation of its genesis, its most distinctive features, operational model and action plan. The preliminary results of its activities show the role and the main challenges of the School in addressing the needs of the Mediterranean Countries towards logic of partnership for the development of their Intellectual assets.

Chapter Fifteen shows that the posting of interactive mapping is essential for the dissemination of information to the general public and in all areas. All the elements constituting a spatial object are represented by agreements with symbols. Each element is represented at the level of reality. The posting of maps on the Internet can take many forms. It can be static maps, as a picture. Interactions with the user can be included on the maps produced. These are movements and functions of the zoom presentation (display information, change of scale, global view).

At this level, it is also possible to examine, by selection of the objects represented on the map (common facilities). This level is commonly known as Web mapping. The dynamic mapping is used when information is to be renewed or if the geographical extent of the area is large. In this case, a server handles in real-time updated database to provide users with answers to their complaints. The functions proposed in this case are close to those of GIS software (acquisition, manipulation, management and processing of geographical data). In this Chapter we will explore the possibility of integrating a dynamic mapping on the Web.

Chapter Sixteen shows that the relationships among people, governments and organizations are subject to fast changes. The increasing demand for new services conducts to the need to create services from scratch and by integrating disparate and heterogeneous legacy systems. The problem is that the monolithic form as most of the systems were implemented turns the change excessively slow and expensive. Considering that some business logic portions are quite volatile and susceptible to changes and other portions are quite stable and less susceptible to changes, this chapter proposes ontology based integrated development environment (IDE) that can capture business changes and quickly implement them into computational systems.

The volatile portions are externalized as business rules and the stable portions as SOA based services. Business rules' facts and conditions are linked to services, which are discovered in the business rules development or maintenance time. The IDE aggregates a set of tools to automate the modeling of business rules in the business people's terminology and to automate the integration of services. It is based on a set of ontologies to deal with metadata related to services, vocabularies and business rules. Business rules are modeled according to OMG's Semantics of Business Vocabularies and Business Rules Metamodel.

Chapter Seventeen presents a literature discussion and empirical research that examines the factors that affect Electronic Commerce (EC) adoption in the Arab countries. The five countries that are represented in this research include Saudi Arabia, Qatar, Kuwait, United Arab Emirates and Yemen. The purpose of this research is to analyze the crucial factors affecting EC adoption among the Arab consumers. The Chapter presents the effect of risk perception, trust and consumer knowledge on their EC adoption.

The chapter also highlights consumers' knowledge mediation in affecting their perception of risk and trust towards EC adoption. Upon filtration, three hundred samples were selected for data analysis. Descriptive and inferential statistical analyses including statistical mediation technique were carried out to analyse the data. Results reveal knowledge as the most important factor that contributes to EC adoption and it mediates consumers' perception of risk and trust in contributing to their EC adoption.

The preliminary findings of this research were presented in the International Arab Conference of E-Technology held in Amman, Jordan from 14th to 16th October 2008 and subsequently published in the first issue of the International Arab Journal of E-Technology. This chapter presents the complete research with further data analysis, extended reports and discussions on issues relating to EC adoption.

Chapter Eighteen outlines that in many countries, governments have been developing electronic information systems to support in labour market in form of on-line services, web-based application as well as one-stop service. One of the most challenges is to facilitate the seamless exchange of labour market information (LMI) across governmental departments.

This chapter introduces an efficient implementation of Thailand e-government interoperability project in LMI systems using service oriented architecture (SOA) based on XML web service technology. In Thailand, Ministry of Labour (MOL) has developed Ministry of Labor Operation Center (MLOC) as the center for gathering, analyzing and monitoring LMI to assist the policy makers.

The MOL consists of four departments: department of employment, department of labor protection and welfare, department of skills development, and social security office. Those departments utilize electronic systems to manage LMI such as employment, labor protection and welfare, skills development and social security.

Provincially, MOL has 75 branches called "labor provincial office" located at 75 provinces in Thailand. Each office has developed a "Provincial Labor Operation Center or PLOC" as the operating center in the province where the information system called. "PLOC" system has been developed to analyze, monitor the localized labor information for the provincial policy-makers. Since those systems differ, it had required the process of data harmonization, modeling and standardizations using UN/CEFACT CCTS and XML NDR for achieving the common XML schema standard, with the implementation of SOA to integrate efficiently all those systems.

We apply TH e-GIF guidelines for interoperable data exchanges and the XML schema standardization. In Thailand, the first Thailand e-Government Interoperability Framework – the TH e-GIF - came into being in November 2006. This chapter illustrates main concepts of TH e-GIF, the project background and methodology as well as key leverage factors for the project.

Chapter Nineteen considers aspects relating to the role of tertiary (i.e. higher) education in improving the engagement of the public with government provided E-services. Some of the issues considered include those of tackling the digital divide – which can exist because of technical issues in provision of the actual infrastructures, financial issues limiting access to available provision and educational barriers – as well as how to develop trust in online technologies.

The challenges of the networked society include a number that can be best addressed through education. These include

i. Engagement with new technologies and new paradigms;
ii. trust in a virtual environment;
iii. Understanding of processes and engagement with online services;
iv. Mapping of existing personal paradigms to the virtual world.

Education itself faces challenges in the networked world. Tertiary education in particular is potentially vulnerable to the changes that the modern networked world brings; however, it can also gain through some of the new opportunities. Of particular note is the potential to unlock students' research skills and enable true inquiry by students within their studies – skills which should prepare them as active participants in the knowledge.

Chapter Twenty informs that policy makers in Tunisian higher education have decided to explore ways in which e-learning and e-management could be introduced to enhance university administration and teaching. In this context, the e-learning team in the Higher Institute of Informatics and Communications in Hammam Sousse (University of Sousse) has developed and deployed a number of online courses as part of a blended learning program. Various e-learning projects covering both pedagogical and technical aspects as well as doctoral research works are under way to support this activity. The deployment of e-learning courses is supervised by the Virtual University of Tunis with technical help coming from our university.

In addition to e-learning, we focus in this chapter, on e-services for the sector of higher education and student information systems accessible from the web. We discuss e-learning strategies within a national context. We therefore describe our experiments, the results achieved thus far and some lessons that we have learned. Current e-management practices have led to increased transparency and equal opportunities. Nevertheless, some drawbacks and concerns exist and will be discussed.

In Chapter Twenty-one, assessment of the main risks of software development discloses that major threats of delays are caused by poor effort/ cost estimation of the project. Low/ poor cost estimation is the second highest priority risk. This risk can affect four out of total five phases of software development life cycle i.e. Analysis, Design, Coding and Testing. Hence, targeting this risk alone may reduce the over all risk impact of the project by fifty percent.

Architectural designing of the system is a great activity which consumes most of the time in SDLC. Obviously, effort is put to produce the design of the system. It is evident that none of the existing estimation models try to calculate the effort put on designing of the system. Although use case estimation model uses the use case points to estimate the cost. But what is the cost of creating use cases? One reason of poor estimates produced by existing models can be negligence of design effort/cost. Therefore, it shall be well estimated to prevent any cost overrun of the project.

The material in this chapter proposes a model to estimate the effort in each of these phases rather than just relying upon the cost estimation of the coding phase only. It will also ease the monitoring of project status and comparison against planned cost and actual cost incurred so far at any point of time.

The electronic electoral system is covered in Chapter Twenty-two. It shows the important of these techniques to the survival of democracy all over the world. Current happenings around the world, particularly in the developing world where poor conduct of elections had left a number of countries devastated are of great concern to world leaders. Therefore, efforts are ongoing to introduce a voting system that is transparent, convenient and reliable.

This Chapter presents an overview of an integrated electronic voting (e-Voting) system comprising: the electronic voting machine (EVM), Internet voting (i-Voting) and mobile voting (m-Voting). Similarly, issues of interoperability of the integrated system are discussed as well as the needed security measures. It is, however, recommended that emphasis be directed at EVM for use within the country while others are restricted to special cases of remote voting for citizens living abroad or living with certain deformities.

Chapter Twenty-three discusses the e-health development in Australia. The Australian government has been very proactive in e-government and applications of e-government such as e-health in the last five years. E-health is an important application of e-government in Australia for innovation of the public sector, as well as due to its very sparsely populated large rural areas.

E-health development in this chapter is analyzed using Layne and Lee's (2001) e-government development model due to the similarities in the stages of development of both applications. This chapter illustrates that in Australia e-health development is mostly at the informational stage. It also indicates that e-health developments can be established in three stages of information; transaction; vertical and horizontal integration of services.

Chapter Twenty-four deals with building security awareness culture to serve e-government initiative. It shows that many countries have adopted E-Government initiatives for providing public E-Services to their citizens. These initiatives together with the existing and emerging private initiatives which offer E-Services, lead to dramatically increase in the number of the Internet user. This will form what is now known as E-Society.

All E-Government initiatives consider citizen-centered approach, where user's security and privacy is a major issue. The level of citizen's engagement in these initiatives will depend on the extent of his/her confidence in the security system used by these initiatives. This imposes the need for developing computer security packages. These packages are intended to help users protect their assets such as information, databases, programs, and computer services from any harm or damage. The level of harm or damage that could happen to assets varies from one user to another.

This variation depends on: users' awareness of possible threats, their knowledge of the source of threats, and if they are applying security controls or not. The Chapter aims to analyze current users' level of awareness and to propose possible methods in order to increase the level of users' awareness i.e. education, continuous education, and training.

The first section of chapter twenty four presents the importance of security awareness to E-Government initiatives and also presents a research idea. The second section introduces the experimental design for a more comprehensive research that we are looking to carry on in later stages and specifies the objective of this stage; third section presents results and discussions of the new proposal of methods to increase level of users' awareness.

Chapter Twenty-five presents a database model which provides a systematic, logical and regular basis for the collection, collation, dissemination and mapping of strategic e-purchasing data. Selective access to this accurate and timely data will measurably improve public sector strategic e-procurement performance, accountability and administration. It will assist the public sector to be more effective and efficient in resource allocation and investment outcomes measurement, more transparent, and will encourage the development of trust, networks and social capital amongst public sector employees and their suppliers.

The model has been successfully demonstrated through the establishment and analysis of an e-procurement data base with the Australian Department of Defense (DoD). The Australian DoD is a Federal Government Department with a FY 2008/9 spend of AU$9.3bn on products (goods and services), their support and maintenance, from almost every industry sector, on a global basis.

While the implementation of information technology is usually viewed as a means of reducing transaction costs, in practice such implementation often increases transaction costs. Public sector bureaucratic hierarchies and their governance systems contribute to transaction costs. This research provides an e-business database model so that the public sector can achieve improved procurement field mapping and strategic e-purchasing using existing data and resources at lowest transaction cost.

Chapter Twenty-six introduces Mobile phone which is one of the technologies which are widely used these days. It is available in most of the countries and all people, even children and elderly people can use it. It seems that in near future, each person will have at least one mobile phone. So it is a good choice for communication in emergency situation such as a heart attack or after an earthquake.

In this chapter, we will survey a number of systems which are designed for communication in emergency situations and then explain three systems which are developed by authors. The first one is for locating and rescuing victims after earthquakes. The second system is for calling emergency team by patients in emergency situations. The third system is for finding lost people with amnesia. In addition, we review some of related works which use mobile phones for communication in emergency.

Chapter Twenty-seven discusses one of the most powerful weapons for attackers which are the Internet worm. A worm attacks vulnerable computer systems and employs self-propagating methods to flood the Internet rapidly. Since "Worm" is self-propagated through the connected network, it doesn't need human interaction or file transmission to replicate itself. It spreads in minutes; Slammer worm infected about 75,000 nodes through the internet in about 10 minutes.

Since most of the antivirus programs detect viruses based on their signature, then this approach can't detect new viruses or worms till being updated with their signature, which can't be known unless some systems had already been infected. This highlights worms still are on the top of malware threats attacking computer system although of the evolution of worms detection techniques. Early detection of unknown worms is still a problem.

This Chapter produces a method for detecting unknown worms based on local victim information. The proposed system uses Artificial Neural Network (ANN) for classifying worm/ nonworm traffic and predicting the percentage of infection in the infected network. This prediction can be used to support decision making process for network administrator to respond quickly to worm propagation in an accurate procedure.

Chapters Twenty-eight explains how to justify texts as Arabic calligraphers use to stretch some letters with small flowing curves; the keshideh instead of inserting blanks among words. Of course, such stretchings are context dependent. An adequate tool to support such writing may be based on a continuous mathematical model. The model has to take into account the motion of the qalam. The characters may be represented as outlines. Among the curves composing the characters outlines, some intersections are to be determined dynamically.

In the Naskh style, the qalam's head behaves as a rigid rectangle in motion with a constant inclination. To determine the curves delimiting the set of points to shade when writing, we have to find out a mathematical way to compare plane curves. Moreover, as the PostScript procedure to produce a dynamic character should be repeated whenever the letter is to draw, the development of a font supporting a continuous stretching model, allowing stretchable letters with no overlapping outlines, without optimization would be of a high cost in CPU time.

In this chapter, some stretching models are given and discussed. A method to compare curves is presented. It allows the determination of the character encoding with eventually overlapping outlines. Then a way to approximate the curves intersection coefficients is given. This is enough to remove overlapping outlines. Some evaluations in time processing to confirm the adopted optimization techniques are also exposed.

Chapter Twenty-nine explains that e-government webs are among the largest webs in existence, based on the size, number of users and number of information providers. Thus, creating a Semantic Web infrastructure to meaningfully organize e-government webs is highly desirable. At the same time, the complexity of the existing e-government implementations also challenges the feasibility of Semantic Web creation.

The chapter, therefore, proposes the design of a two-layer semantic Wiki web, which consists of content Wiki, largely identical to the traditional web and a semantic layer, also maintained within the Wiki, that describes semantic relationships. This architectural design promises several advantages that enable incremental growth, collaborative development by a large community of non-technical users and the ability to continually grow the content layer without the immediate overhead of parallel maintenance of the semantic layer.

This chapter explains current challenges to the development of a Semantic Web, identifies Wiki advantages, illustrates a potential solution and summarizes major directions for further research.

Chapter Thirty describes a holistic approach for the design of e-government platforms. It defines principles for architecting a system which must sustain the entire e-government activity of a mid-level public authority (Geneva). The four principles are: Legality, Responsibility, Transparency, and Symmetry. The principles speak to policy makers and to users.

They also lead to usable and coherent architectural representations at all levels of responsibility of a project, i.e. the client, the designer and the builder. The approach resulted in deploying multipartite, distributed public services, including legal delegation of roles and the outsourcing of non mandatory tasks through *PPP* on an e-Government platform that will support a threefold increase in services yearly until 2012. In this sense, aș well as in its daily operation, the system is a success.

Chapter Thirty one describes one of the Large-scale electronic government projects that had mixed results over the past decade. A considerably large percentage of such projects effectively failed. The over-ambitious promise e-governance positively transforming public sectors in developing nations didn't fully materialize. The actual causes of e-government failures are still to be explored in more detail to improve the understanding of the phenomenon by practitioners and scholars alike.

This chapter explores also the causes of e-government failures within the context of Arab states and discusses prevailing views of such failures in earlier literature. Based on a survey of senior e-government practitioners in nine Arab countries, our findings indicate that the underlying roots of failure in e-government projects in Arab countries (which we classify in nine main categories) are entwined with multifaceted social, cultural, organizational, political, economic and technological factors.

We argue that, despite their many similarities, e-government initiatives in the Arab states would be better equipped for avoiding failure when a local 'fit' is established between leadership commitment, sustainable cross-government vision, appropriate planning, rational business strategy, suitable regulatory framework, practical awareness campaigns and rigorous capacity building for the public administrators and society at large.

Based on our findings, we argue that replicable "best practices" in a complex and developing field of e-government rarely exist. We conclude with a proposal to nurture a culture more tolerant to risk-taking and failure in the relatively new area of e-government in the Arab states. Until a local maturity level is reached, such culture should be accompanied with home-grown e-government risk management approaches as well as effective mechanisms of knowledge management to enable extracting relevant local lessons from failed projects and partial successes.

Chapter Thirty two presents a security framework architecture for electronic voting that permits the avoidance of problems occasioned by interposing computer system and technical personnel between the voter and the electoral board. The architecture is based on replicating the conventional security mechanisms and in segregating all critical functions into very simple systems that are audited, monitored and physically secured.

This concept of security architecture minimizes the number of components that must be trusted to only two, namely, the software generating the encrypted ballot and the software opening the digital ballot boxes and the envelopes there in. This addresses one of the main causes of trouble in electronic voting systems, namely, the need to trust overly-complex systems like DREs, web browsers, operating systems or Internet servers.

Chapter Thirty three outlines the importance of e-business in today's world and how it affects decision making. In today's world e-business is extremely important for many reasons. Some of which is due to the fact that it can speed the whole process of ordering up. This means that the lead time can be decreased because the ordering of products can be done much more quickly, because the Internet is a fast running wide area network.

This chapter also shows how better procurement and supply chain make sales teams more effective, the ability to outsource functions such as accounting, remote access to systems, linking management teams, in different locations, being able to locate the lowest cost supplier, improve customer services, improve collection of customer information for databases and more effective management of remote manufacturing sites.

Abid Thyab Al Ajeeli
University of Bahrain, Bahrain

Yousif A. Latif Al-Bastaki
University of Bahrain, Bahrain

Acknowledgment

The authors wish to express their sincere thanks and appreciation for all people who participated in the development and evaluation of the work in this book. The authors are especially grateful to IGI Global publishing and their representatives for administering and monitoring the manuscript and for exercising such care and skill to see the work through to publication.

Authors would also like to thank Mike Killian for communicating, correcting errors and the careful reading of various materials during the process of developing the book. Thanks also go to Miss Suhad Sameer for her reading and administering the material in this book and for communicating with various parties during the process of finalization of the materials covered by the book.

Abid Thyab Al Ajeeli
University of Bahrain, Bahrain

Yousif A. Latif Al-Bastaki
University of Bahrain, Bahrain

Chapter 1
A Global Comparative Analysis of Digital Governance Practices

Norma M. Riccucci
Rutgers University, USA

Marc Holzer
Rutgers University, USA

ABSTRACT

The literature shows that governments around the world have sought to improve their governing capabilities by developing and implementing strategic information and communication technologies (ICTs). The use of ICTs can provide citizens with greater access to government services, can promote transparency and accountability, and also streamline government expenditures. This research provides a comparative analysis of the practices of digital governance in large municipalities worldwide in 2005. Digital government includes both e-government and e-democracy. The research is based on an evaluation of a sample (n=81) of city websites globally in terms of two dimensions: delivery of public services and digital democracy. The official websites of each city were evaluated in their native languages. Based on the analysis of the 81 cities, Seoul, New York, Shanghai, Hong Kong, and Sydney represent the cities with the most effective e-governance systems.

INTRODUCTION

There has been a plethora of research in the past few decades on the significance of e-governance to the missions of public sector organizations. Governments across the globe and at every level have sought to improve their governing capabilities by developing and implementing strategic information and communication technologies (ICTs). These technologies have transformed the ways in which governments operate and transact business with their citizenries. In addition, as Keskinen (2004) points out, the use of ICTs has created new opportunities for promoting democracy.

Ensuring citizen or customer satisfaction through web-based services and computer networking has been at the top of public reform movements across the world. ICTs can also promote government accountability and transparency, increase citizen participation, reduce

DOI: 10.4018/978-1-61520-789-3.ch001

government costs, and in remote areas, help to break down barriers associated with distance, proximity or mobility. In addition, as Grimsley and Meehan (2008) point out, the use of ICTs can broader social outcomes "such as social inclusion, community development, well-being and sustainability." Interestingly enough, however, very little effort has been made to systematically examine the comparative effectiveness of governments' efforts, worldwide, to communicate and interact with their constituencies (see Wangpipatwong, et al. 2008; Backhouse 2007; Carrizales et al., 2006; Melitski et al., 2005).

The purpose of this chapter is to examine the practices of digital governance in large municipalities throughout the world. In particular, it focuses on (1) the security/privacy, (2) usability, and (3) content of city websites, in addition to (4) the type of online services currently being offered, and (5) citizen response and participation through websites established by city governments worldwide.

FROM E-GOVERNANCE TO DIGITAL GOVERNANCE

As Singh and Byrne (2005: 71) point out, the "Internet and related technologies have made a substantial impact on the way organisations conduct business...around the world." Governments, too, have made major advances in their efforts to govern more effectively to the extent they have adopted web-based and related technologies. Democracies across the globe have embraced the practice of e-governance to enhance the quality of services they provide to their citizens as well as to business communities. More recently, the reliance on digital governance has become increasingly popular (Carrizales, 2008; Asgarkhani, 2005). Digital governance includes both electronic government (e.g., the use of ICTs to deliver public services) and electronic democracy (e.g., the use of ICTs to promote citizen participation in governance).

One of the most important components of digital governance is augmenting the directional flow of information, communication, resources and services available to the public. As Asgarkhani (2005: 465) points out: "The introduction of digital governance is an attempt to reduce traditional hierarchies in governmental practices and create an environment where information flow is bi-directional. The change from a hierarchical model to a networked and technology-based framework is a fundamental change to the nature of public administration and management, which we have been familiar with in the past."

There are several motivations for governments to pursue the use of digital governance. First, and perhaps most importantly, it fosters citizen engagement and democracy. Bi-directional communication and access to a host of government services ensures citizen participation in the governance process. It further promotes greater transparency in government, which fosters public confidence in government and ultimately serves to improve the public image of government. In addition, it can reduce government costs by streamlining government structures and procedures (see, for example, Commonwealth Centre for Electronic Governance, 2001). In remote areas, digital governance works to break down barriers associated with distance, proximity or mobility. In essence it opens doors, alleviates hurdles, and promotes ownership in government to ultimately ensure unimpeded democratic governance. To be sure, some segments of any population are unable to access electronic services (e.g., they lack the skills to use or the resources to own personal computers); thus, it is important for governments to set up learning centers in community spaces or in libraries, where direct access and assistance are available to all (Asgarkhani, 2005).

In recent years, digital governance has become increasingly prevalent throughout the world. And even though a digital divide prevails, developing countries are also instituting the practice often at the local or municipal level of government. However, very little research exists on the status or effectiveness of digital governance from a comparative perspective worldwide (see Melitski et al., 2005; Holzer & Kim, 2004). This study serves as a first step in filling this gap.

RESEARCH APPROACH AND METHODOLOGY

There are a number of studies examining the effectiveness of e-governance procedures by citizens across the globe (Yang, K. & Callahan, 2005; Carrizales, 2004; Borras, 2003). Some studies pay particular attention to the public websites of government entities when examining the effectiveness of e-governance and rely on a host of criteria, including privacy, usability, and services available (see, Melitski et al., 2005; Moon, 2002; Kaylor et al., 2001; Musso et al., 2000; Weare et al., 1999). Based on these studies, we examine a sample of online services globally in terms of two dimensions: the delivery of public services and digital democracy, with particular emphasis on: (1) the security/privacy, (2) usability, and (3) content of websites, in addition to (4) the type of online services currently being offered, and (5) citizen response and participation through websites established by city governments.

In terms of the privacy and security online city services, we looked at privacy policies and authentication of users. In examining municipal privacy policies, we determined whether such a policy was available on every page that accepted data, and whether or not the word "privacy" was used in the link to such a statement. We also examined whether there was an option to decline the disclosure of personal information to third parties. The use of encryption in the transmission of data, as well as the storage of personal information on secure servers, was also examined. So, too, was whether or not city websites used cookies or web beacons.

Regarding the usability of online services, we sought to determine if sites were "user-friendly." Here, we examined whether a municipality's homepage was too long and whether webpages used consistent color, formatting, "default colors" (e.g. blue links and purple visited links) and underlined text to indicate links. Our research also examined the use of search tools as well as online forms to determine their usability in submitting data or conducting searches on public websites.

Website content is also an important feature of digital governance. Our research looked at such issues as whether the content was current, ease of navigation, and accuracy of information provided. We also examined the availability of office hours or a schedule of when agency offices were open. In addition, we looked at whether online services were "multilingual" and whether they provided access to disabled users, such as the blind or deaf.

A critical aspect of digital governance is the provision of municipal services online. Our analysis examined three different types of services: (1) those that allow citizens to interact with the municipality (e.g., forms that allow users to request information or file complaints); (2) services that allow users to register for municipal events or services online (e.g., apply for permits and licenses online ranging from building permits to dog licenses), and (3) transactional services (e.g., paying taxes online).

Finally, online citizen participation in government is a key component of digital governance. The Internet is a convenient mechanism for citizens to engage their government, and it also has the potential to decentralize decision-making. It can also promote greater ownership in government as well as accountability. Here we examine, for example, whether municipal websites allow users to provide online comments or feedback to individual agencies or elected officials. We also looked at the availability of online bulletin boards or other chat capabilities for gathering input on public issues.

For each of the five components, a more comprehensive list of the criteria for evaluating municipal websites appears in Table 1.

Each of the measures presented in Table 1 was then coded on a scale of four-points (0, 1, 2, 3) where:

0 = information about a given topic does not exist on the website;
1 = information about a given topic exists on the website (including links to other information and e-mail addresses);
2 = downloadable items are available on the website (forms, audio, video, popup boxes and other one-way transactions);
3 = services, transaction, or interactions can take place completely online (credit card transactions, applications for permits, searchable databases, use of cookies, digital signatures, restricted access).

Where appropriate, a dichotomous variable (0, 3 or 0, 1) was relied upon. The dichotomous variable in the "service" and "citizen participation" categories corresponds with values on our four-point scale of "0" or "3"; dichotomous measures in "security/ privacy" or "usability" correspond to ratings of "0" or "1" on the scale. Our instrument placed a higher value on some dichotomous measures, due to the relative value of the different e-government services being evaluated. For example, evaluators using our instrument in the "service" category were given the option of scoring websites as either a "0" or "3" when assessing whether a site allowed users to access private information online (e.g., educational records, medical records, point total of driving violations, lost property). "No access" resulted in a rating of "0." Allowing residents or employees to access private information online was a higher order task that required more technical competence, and was clearly an online service, or "3," as defined above. On the other hand, when assessing a site as to whether or not it had a privacy statement or policy, evaluators were given the choice of scoring

Table 1. Criteria for evaluating municipal websites

Privacy/ Security	
A privacy or security statement/policy Data collection Option to have personal information used Third party disclosures Ability to review personal data records Managerial measures Use of encryption	Secure server Use of "cookies" or "Web Beacons" Notification of privacy policy Contact or e-mail address for inquiries Public information through a restricted area Access to nonpublic information for employees Use of digital signatures
Usability	
Homepage, page length Targeted audience Navigation bar Site map	Font color Forms Search tool Update of website
Content	
Information about the location of offices Listing of external links Contact information Minutes of public meetings City code and regulations City charter and policy priority Mission statements Budget information Documents, reports, or books (publications)	GIS capabilities Emergency management or alert mechanism Disability access Wireless technology Access in more than one language Human resources information Calendar of events Downloadable documents
Services	
Pay utilities, taxes, fines Apply for permits Online tracking system Apply for licenses E-procurement Property assessments Searchable databases Complaints Bulletin board about civil applications	FAQ Request information Customize the main city homepage Access private information online Purchase tickets Webmaster response Report violations of administrative laws and regulations
Citizen Participation	
Comments or feedback Newsletter Online bulletin board or chat capabilities Online discussion forum on policy issues Scheduled e-meetings for discussion	Online survey/ polls Synchronous video Citizen satisfaction survey Online decision-making Performance measures, standards, or benchmarks

the site as "0" or "1." The presence or absence of a security policy was clearly a content issue that emphasized placing information online, and corresponded with a value of "1" in accordance with the rating scale above.

In developing an overall score for each municipality, we equally weighted each of the five categories so as not to skew the research in favor of a particular category (regardless of the number of questions in each category). To ensure reliability, each city website was assessed in the native language by two evaluators, and in cases where significant variation existed (+ or – 10%) on the adjusted score between evaluators, websites were analyzed a third time. Evaluators were given comprehensive written instructions for assessing the public websites.

Study Sample

To examine digital governance practices worldwide, we selected cities based on their population size, the total number of individuals using the Internet and the percentage of individuals using the Internet. The cities were chosen using the 2003 "Internet Indicators" statistics from the International Telecommunication Union (ITU), an organization affiliated with the United Nations (see International Telecommunication Union 2005). The ITU's Internet Indicators website reports on the "digital access" of 191 UN-member countries; that is, it provides an estimate of persons accessing the Internet in those countries. Because our goal was to sample at least 100 cites, we set as a cutoff point countries whose digital access was equal to or greater than 160,000. This search identified 119 countries. Because existing research shows a positive relationship between population and e-governance capacity (see, for example, Moon, 2002; Moon & deLeon, 2001) we then selected the largest municipalities in each of those countries. Based on complete, usable data, our research identified 81 municipalities from 81 different countries for inclusion in this research. Table 2 below lists the cities included by continent.

Table 2. The 81 sampled cities by continent

Africa (4)	
Cairo (Egypt)	Lagos (Nigeria)
Cape Town (South Africa)	Nairobi (Kenya)
Asia (24)	
Amman (Jordan)	Kuala Lumpur (Malaysia)
Bangkok (Thailand)	Macao SAR (Macao SAR)
Beirut (Lebanon)	Mumbai (India)
Colombo (Sri Lanka)	Nicosia (Cyprus)
Dhaka (Bangladesh)	Quezon City (Philippines)
Dubai (United Arab Emirates)	Riyadh (Saudi Arabia)
Ho Chi Minh (Vietnam)	Seoul (Republic of Korea)
Hong Kong SAR (Hong Kong SAR)	Shanghai (China)
Istanbul (Turkey)	Singapore (Singapore)
Jakarta (Indonesia)	Tashkent (Uzbekistan)
Jerusalem (Israel)	Tehran (Iran)
Karachi (Pakistan)	Tokyo (Japan)
Europe (34)	
Amsterdam (Netherlands)	Madrid (Spain)
Athens (Greece)	Minsk (Belarus)
Belgrade (Serbia and Montenegro)	Moscow (Russian Federation)
Berlin (Germany)	Oslo (Norway)
Bratislava (Slovak Republic)	Paris (France)
Brussels (Belgium)	Prague (Czech Republic)
Bucharest (Romania)	Reykjavik (Iceland)
Budapest (Hungary)	Riga (Latvia)
Chisinau (Moldova)	Rome (Italy)
Copenhagen (Denmark)	Sofia (Bulgaria)
Dublin (Ireland)	Stockholm (Sweden)
Helsinki (Finland)	Tallinn (Estonia)
Kiev (Ukraine)	Vienna (Austria)
Lisbon (Portugal)	Vilnius (Lithuania)
Ljubljana (Slovenia)	Warsaw (Poland)
London (United Kingdom)	Zagreb (Croatia)
Luxembourg City (Luxembourg)	Zurich (Switzerland)
North America (8)	
Mexico City (Mexico)	San Jose (Costa Rica)
Guatemala City (Guatemala)	San Salvador (El Salvador)
New York (United States)	Tegucigalpa (Honduras)
Panama City (Panama)	Toronto (Canada)
South America (9)	
Buenos Aires (Argentina)	Montevideo (Uruguay)
Caracas (Venezuela)	Santa Fe De Bogota (Colombia)
Guayaquil (Ecuador)	Santiago (Chile)
La Paz (Bolivia)	Sao Paulo (Brazil)
Lima (Peru)	
Oceania (2)	
Auckland (New Zealand)	Sydney (Australia)

ANALYSIS AND FINDINGS

Table 3 presents the rankings of the 81 municipalities included in this study. The overall scores reflect the combined scores of each municipality's score in the five e-governance component categories. The highest possible score for any one city website is 100.

As the data show, the city of Seoul is ranked highest with a score of 81.7, with New York following at 72.71. Shanghai, Hong Kong, and Sydney, respectively, are ranked the next highest. The data further show that the lowest ranking cities in terms of digital governance are Zagreb (12.89), Chisinau (12.15), Montevideo (11.78), Nairobi (10.43) and Tashkent (4.48). The findings suggest that these cities are at least making an effort to embrace digital governance; this is notable since developing countries certainly may have other priorities that go well beyond digital governance.

Table 4 presents data on the average scores of municipalities by continent. The overall average score for all municipalities is 33.11.

As the data show, Oceania ranked highest among continents with a score close to 50. It is followed by Europe with a score of 37.17. Asia ranks third and falls just below the overall average for all municipalities. North American and Africa rank fourth and fifth respectively, and fall below the overall average.

We also provide data on the highest ranked municipalities for each of the five components of interest in this study: (1) security and privacy, (2) usability, (3) content, (4) services, and (5) citizen participation. The highest possible weighted score for each category is 20. Table 5 presents results for security and privacy.

As the data show, Seoul is ranked highest in terms of privacy and security with a score of 17.60, followed by Sydney, Zurich, New York and Hong Kong. An interesting observation not shown in Table 5 is the large number of municipalities with a score of 0. There are 31 municipalities[1] among our sample cities that make no provision on their websites for security or privacy. This suggests that many cities across the world still have not properly understood the importance of a privacy and security policy. Yet, with the exception of a few cities (e.g., Helsinki, Oslo and Stockholm), these cities are in developing countries throughout the world.

Table 6 provides data on the highest and lowest ranking municipalities based on usability of websites. Again, the highest possible weighted score is 20.

As the data in Table 6 indicate, New York almost reaches the highest possible score in terms of usability. We found New York's websites to be very "user-friendly." For example, all pages use consistent color, formatting, "default colors" and underlined text to indicate links. There are consistent uses of navigation bars and links to the homepage on every page. The websites contain very advanced forms, allowing citizens to submit pertinent information online. The data also suggest that the lowest ranked countries have yet some progress to make in terms of the usability of their websites.

Table 7 provides data on the rankings of municipalities by the content of websites.

The data illustrate that Seoul, New York, Tallinn, Zurich, Hong Kong, and Riga are top ranked cities in the category of content. Tashkent is ranked lowest with a score of 0.42 out of a possible score of 20. It may be recalled that the criteria for content of websites included disability access, wireless technology, access in more than one language, information about the location of offices, listing of external links and contact information.

The type of online services being offered on municipal websites is also an important function of digital governance. Table 8 provides our findings here.

The highest ranked municipalities worldwide in terms of the services offered online include Seoul, New York, Singapore, Hong Kong, and Warsaw. Services were evaluated on the basis of

Table 3. Ranking of 81 municipalities

Ranking	City	Country	Score
1	Seoul	Republic of Korea	81.70
2	New York	United States	72.71
3	Shanghai	China	63.93
4	Hong Kong	Hong Kong	61.51
5	Sydney	Australia	60.82
6	Singapore	Singapore	60.22
7	Tokyo	Japan	59.24
8	Zurich	Switzerland	55.99
9	Toronto	Canada	55.10
10	Riga	Latvia	53.95
11	Warsaw	Poland	53.26
12	Reykjavik	Iceland	52.24
13	Sofia	Bulgaria	49.11
14	Prague	Czech Rep.	47.27
15	Luxembourg	Luxembourg	46.58
16	Amsterdam	Netherlands	46.44
17	Paris	France	45.49
18	Macao	Macao	45.48
19	Dublin	Ireland	44.10
20	Bratislava	Slovak Republic	43.65
21	London	United Kingdom	43.17
22	Rome	Italy	42.67
23	Berlin	Germany	42.55
24	Copenhagen	Denmark	42.54
25	Istanbul	Turkey	42.39
26	Tallinn	Estonia	41.02
27	Ho Chi Minh	Vietnam	40.75
28	Budapest	Hungary	40.40
29	Oslo	Norway	39.22
30	Auckland	New Zealand	39.05
31	Cape Town	South Africa	37.88
32	Stockholm	Sweden	36.28
33	Sao Paulo	Brazil	35.88
34	Brussels	Belgium	34.68
35	Helsinki	Finland	34.68
36	Moscow	Russia	34.62
37	Vienna	Austria	34.62
38	Jerusalem	Israel	33.04
39	Jakarta	Indonesia	33.03

continues on following page

Table 3. continued

Ranking	City	Country	Score
40	Tegucigalpa	Honduras	32.40
41	Kiev	Ukraine	31.10
42	Lisbon	Portugal	30.27
43	Vilnius	Lithuania	30.18
44	Belgrade	Serbia & Montenegro	30.03
45	Cairo	Egypt	29.49
46	Buenos Aires	Argentina	29.05
47	Quezon City	Philippines	27.78
48	Mumbai	India	27.69
49	Minsk	Belarus	26.91
50	Dubai	U.A.E.	25.12
51	Bangkok	Thailand	24.88
52	Riyadh	Saudi Arabia	24.68
53	Santiago	Chile	24.22
54	Madrid	Spain	23.24
55	Athens	Greece	23.08
56	Ljubljana	Slovenia	22.80
57	Bogota	Colombia	22.00
58	Lagos	Nigeria	21.68
59	Nicosia	Cyprus	21.16
60	San Jose	Costa Rica	20.76
61	Kuala Lumpur	Malaysia	20.35
62	Karachi	Pakistan	19.15
63	Mexico City	Mexico	18.55
64	Bucharest	Romania	18.11
65	Amman	Jordan	16.77
66	Beirut	Lebanon	16.63
67	Colombo	Sri Lanka	16.36
68	Caracas	Venezuela	16.04
69	Guayaquil	Ecuador	15.40
70	San Salvador	El Salvador	14.91
71	Lima	Peru	14.88
72	La Paz	Bolivia	14.74
73	Dhaka	Bangladesh	14.20
74	Guatemala City	Guatemala	14.12
75	Panama City	Panama	13.11
76	Tehran	Iran	12.89
77	Zagreb	Croatia	12.89
78	Chisinau	Moldova, Rep. of	12.15
79	Montevideo	Uruguay	11.78

continues on following page

Table 3. continued

Ranking	City	Country	Score
80	Nairobi	Kenya	10.43
81	Tashkent	Uzbekistan	4.48

Table 4. Average score by continent

Ranking	Continent	Score
1	Oceania	49.94
2	Europe	37.17
3	Asia	33.05
4	North America	30.21
5	Africa	24.87

Table 5. Rankings by privacy and security

Ranking	City	Country	Score
1	Seoul	Republic of Korea	17.60
2	Sydney	Australia	16.80
3	Zurich	Switzerland	16.40
4	New York	United States	16.00
5	HongKong, SAR	Hong Kong, SAR	15.60

Table 6. Rankings by usability

Ranking	City	Country	Score
1	New York	United States	19.06
2	Shanghai	China	18.75
3	Seoul	Republic of Korea	17.81
3	Sydney	Australia	17.81
5	Riga	Latvia	17.50
76	La Paz	Bolivia	7.19
76	San Salvador	El Salvador	7.19
78	Nairobi	Kenya	6.56
79	Panama City	Panama	5.94
80	Lima	Peru	5.31
81	Tashkent	Uzbekistan	4.06

Table 7. Rankings by content

Ranking	City	Country	Score
1	Seoul	Republic of Korea	16.04
2	New York	United States	14.79
2	Tallinn	Estonia	14.79
4	Zurich	Switzerland	13.96
5	Hong Kong	Hong Kong	13.75
5	Riga	Latvia	13.75
77	Amman	Jordan	1.67
77	Zagreb	Croatia	1.67
79	Guatemala City	Guatemala	1.25
80	Tehran	Iran	1.04
81	Tashkent	Uzbekistan	0.42

Table 8. Rankings by services

Ranking	City	Country	Score
1	Seoul	Republic of Korea	16.61
2	New York	United States	15.76
3	Singapore	Singapore	14.58
4	Hong Kong	Hong Kong	13.73
5	Warsaw	Poland	11.86
77	Amman	Jordan	0.68
78	Chisinau	Moldova, Rep. of	0.51
79	Zagreb	Croatia	0.34
80	Nairobi	Kenya	0.00
80	Tashkent	Uzbekistan	0.00

the online ability to perform such tasks as: paying utilities, taxes, fines; applying for permits and licenses; tracking tasks; filing complaints; determining property assessments, and accessing private information online. The cities that have made no progress here, as indicated by average scores, are Nairobi and Tashkent, with Zagreb, Chisinau and Amman closely following.

As discussed earlier, one of the most significant components of digital governance is the ability of citizens to participate and engage in the governing process via information and communication technologies. The findings for citizen participation are presented in Table 9.

As the findings show, Seoul, which is ranked the highest in overall scores (see Table 3), is ranked first in terms of citizen participation. However, there is a notable omission from the rankings in Table 9; four of the municipalities that were ranked in the top five overall, are not among the highest ranked in terms of citizen participation. New York City, which ranked second overall, had a score of only 7.09 out of a possible 20 points on citizen participation. It ranked 13 out of the sampled cities. Similarly, Shanghai, Hong Kong and Sydney, which ranked third, fourth and fifth, overall, scored the following on citizen participation:

Table 9. Rankings by citizen participation

Ranking	City	Country	Score
1	Seoul	Republic of Korea	13.64
2	Warsaw	Poland	12.55
3	Bratislava	Slovak Republic	10.91
4	London	United Kingdom	10.55
5	Prague	Czech Rep.	10.18
66	Mumbai	India	0.91
67	La Paz	Bolivia	0.55
67	Panama City	Panama	0.55
67	Bogota	Colombia	0.55
70	Chisinau	Moldova, Rep. of	0.36
70	Mexico City	Mexico	0.36
70	Montevideo	Uruguay	0.36
70	Tehran	Iran	0.36
74	Guatemala City	Guatemala	0.18
74	Guayaquil	Ecuador	0.18
74	Ljubljana	Slovenia	0.18
74	Nairobi	Kenya	0.18
78	Caracas	Venezuela	0.00
78	Santiago	Chile	0.00
78	Tashkent	Uzbekistan	0.00
78	Zagreb	Croatia	0.00

Shanghai: 8.36 (ranked 9)
Hong Kong: 2.18 (ranked 46)
Sydney: 4.73 (ranked 21)

These cities seem to place greater attention on such features as content, usability, privacy and services at the expense of citizen participation, which is the sine qua non of digital democracy.

Table 9 further shows that some cities, with scores lower than 1.0, are making little to no provisions for citizen engagement with the local governing body.

DISCUSSION AND CONCLUSION

Municipalities across the globe are making great strides to promote digital governance. This research shows, for example, that 37 cities out of 81 have total scores above the average score, 33.1, for digital governance globally (median score is 31.1). Moreover, some of these cities are

Table 10. Summary data on digital governance globally

Mean	Median	s.d.
Security/Privacy 4.17	1.2	5.24
Usability 12.42	12.29	3.34
Content 7.63	7.71	4.01
Services 5.32	4.92	3.73
Citizen Participation 3.57	2.73	3.17

in developing countries (e.g., Bratislava, Tallinn, Ho Chi Minh).

There appears to be a continued divide in terms of digital governance throughout the world. For example, although the average score for digital governance in municipalities throughout the world is 33.1, the average score in developed countries is 44.35, while the average score in developing countries is only 26.5. In addition, whereas 25 of 30 cities in developed countries are above the world average, only 11 of 51 cities in developing countries are above that average. Importantly, the financial costs may be insurmountable to some countries, particularly when other concerns (e.g., famine or drought) are priorities. Previous research also shows that there continues to be a digital divide (see, for example, Kaaya, 2004; Foley, 2005; Komito, 2005).

There are two areas where municipalities have fallen relatively short in terms of digital governance: security and privacy of websites and citizen participation (see Table 10).

It may be recalled that the highest possible weighted score in any one category is 20. Our findings suggest, for example, that while on average cities' websites may be very user-friendly, they do not ensure security and privacy, nor do they promote citizen participation. Overall, municipalities may be making some progress in terms of e-governance, and thus promoting greater transparency and efficiency in the delivery of public services. On the other hand, municipalities are falling short particularly in the area of digital democracy, which ensures citizen engagement and enhances accountability, responsiveness, performance and ultimately the legitimacy of decisions (see, e.g., Yang & Callahan, 2005). It may be that some cities are fiscally unable to promote digital governance or are ill equipped managerially to do so. Of course, some cities may simply give the impression of openness by making certain services available online, but are less committed to actually engaging the citizenry in practice. Thus, this is an area where cities still have much progress to make.

Certainly, future research might examine the extent to which policy makers are actually working toward augmenting digital democracy as a key feature of their overall digital governance endeavors.

ACKNOWLEDGMENT

The authors would like to thank several persons as well as organizations instrumental in this research, including Seang-Tae Kim, Tony Carrizales, James Melitski, Aroon Manoharan, as well as the E-Governance Institute at Rutgers University, Campus at Newark, the Global e-Policy e-Government Institute at Sungkyunkwan University, and the United Nation's Division for Public Administration and Development Management.

REFERENCES

Asgarkhani, M. (2005). Digital Government and its Effectiveness in Public Management Reform: A Local Government Perspective . *Public Management Review*, *7*(3), 465–487. doi:10.1080/14719030500181227

Backhouse, J. (2007). e-Democracy in Australia: the Challenge of Evolving a Successful Model, *The Electronic . Journal of E-Government*, *5*(2), 107–116. Retrieved from www.ejeg.com.

Borras, J. (2003). International Technical Standards for e-Government, *The Electronic . Journal of E-Government*, *2*(2), 75–80. Retrieved from www.ejeg.com.

Carrizales, T. (2004). Citizen Driven Government Performance, *Public Performance & . Management Review*, *28*(1), 123–129.

Carrizales, T. (2008). Critical Factors in an Electronic Democracy: A Study of Municipal Managers, *The Electronic . Journal of E-Government*, *6*(1), 23–30. Retrieved from www.ejeg.com.

Carrizales, T., Holzer, M., Kim, S.-T., & Kim, C.-G. (2006). Digital Governance Worldwide: A Longitudinal Assessment of Municipal Web Sites. *International Journal of Electronic Government Research*, *2*(4), 1–23.

Commonwealth Centre for Electronic Governance. (2001). Electronic Governance in Context In *Electronic Governance and Electronic Democracy: Living and Working in the Connected World*. Retrieved May 27, 2008, from http://www.electronicgov.net/pubs/research_papers/eged/chapter1.shtml#introduction

Foley, P. (2005). Does the Internet help to overcome social exclusion? *The Electronic . Journal of E-Government*, *2*(2), 139–146. Retrieved from www.ejeg.com.

Grimsley, M., & Meehan, A. (2008). Attaining Social Value from Electronic Government. *The Electronic . Journal of E-Government*, *6*(1), 31–42. Retrieved from www.ejeg.com.

Holzer, M., & Kim, S.-T. (2004). *Digital Governance in Municipalities Worldwide, 2003*. Newark, NJ: National Center for Public Productivity, Rutgers University.

International Telecommunication Union. (2005). *Internet Indicators: Hosts, Users and Number of PCs*. Retrieved March 20, 2005, fromhttp://www.itu.int/ITU-D/ict/statistics/

Kaaya, J. (2004). Implementing e-Government Services in East Africa: Assessing Status through Content Analysis of Government Websites. *The Electronic . Journal of E-Government*, *2*(1), 39–54. Retrieved from www.ejeg.com.

Kaylor, C., Deshazo, R., & Eck, V. D. (2001). Gauging E-Government: A Report on Implementing Services Among American Cities. *Government Information Quarterly*, *18*, 293–307. doi:10.1016/S0740-624X(01)00089-2

Keskinen, A. (2004). MIDEM. Models for Interactive Decision Making. *The Electronic . Journal of E-Government*, *2*(1), 55–64. Retrieved from www.ejeg.com.

Komito, L. (2005). e-Participation and Governance: Widening the net. *The Electronic Journal of e Government, 3*(1), 39-48, available online at www.ejeg.com

Melitski, J., Holzer, M., Kim, S.-T., Kim, C.-G., & Rho, S.-Y. (2005). Digital Government Worldwide: An e-Government Assessment of Municipal Web-sites . *International Journal of E-Government Research*, *1*(1), 1–19.

Moon, M. J. (2002). The Evolution of E-government Among Municipalities: Rhetoric or Reality? *Public Administration Review*, *62*(4), 424–433. doi:10.1111/0033-3352.00196

Moon, M. J., & deLeon, P. (2001). Municipal Reinvention: Municipal Values and Diffusion Among Municipalities. *Journal of Public Administration: Research and Theory*, *11*(3), 327–352.

Musso, J., Weare, C., & Hale, M. L. (2000). Designing Web Technologies for Local Governance Reform: Good Management or Good Democracy. *Political Communication*, *17*(1), 1–19. doi:10.1080/105846000198486

Singh, M., & Byrne, J. (2005). Performance Evaluation of e-Business in Australia. *The Electronic Journal of Information Systems Evaluation, 8*(1), 71-80. Retrieved from www.ejise.com

Wangpipatwong, S. Chutimaskul, W., & Papasratorn, B. (2008). Understanding Citizen's Continuance Intention to Use e-Government Website: a Composite View of Technology Acceptance Model and Computer Self-Efficacy. *The Electronic Journal of e-Government, 6*(1), 55–64. Retrieved from www.ejeg.com

Weare, C., Musso, J., & Hale, M. L. (1999). Electronic Democracy and the Diffusion of Municipal Web Pages in California. *Administration & Society, 31*(1), 3–27. doi:10.1177/009539999400935475

Yang, K., & Callahan, K. (2005). Assessing Citizen Involvement Efforts by Local Governments. *Public Performance & Management Review, 29*(2), 191–216.

ENDNOTE

1 The cities are Amman, Athens, Bangkok, Beirut, Belgrade, Bratislava, Bucharest, Caracas, Chisinau, Colombo, Dhaka, Guayaquil, Helsinki, Jerusalem, Karachi, Kuala Lumpur, La Paz, Mexico City, Minsk, Montevideo, Nicosia, Oslo, Panama City, Prague, San Salvador, Santiago, Stockholm, Tashkent, Tehran, Vilnius and Warsaw.

Chapter 2
Formal Verification of a Subset of UML Diagrams:
An Approach Using Maude

Allaoua Chaoui
University Mentouri Constantine, Algeria

Okba Tibermacine
University of Batna, Algeria

Amer R. Zerek
Engineering Academy, Libya

ABSTRACT

We introduce an approach that deals with the verification of UML collaboration and sequence diagrams in respect to the objects internal behaviors which are commonly represented by state machine diagrams. The approach is based on the translation of theses diagrams to Maude specifications. In fact, Maude is a declarative programming language, an executable formal specification language, and also a formal verification system, which permit the achievement of the approach goals. We define in details the rules of translating UML diagrams elements into their corresponding Maude specifications. We present the algebraic structures that represent the OR-States and the AND-states in a state machine diagram, and the structure that represents the collaboration and the sequence diagrams. Also, we explain the mechanism of the execution and the verification of the translated specification, which is based on rewriting logics rules.

INTRODUCTION

The Unified Modeling Language (UML) (Rumbaugh, 1999) is widely used language for the specification of object - oriented software systems, including concurrent and embedded systems. An UML model is a set of diagrams describing and documenting the structure, behavior and the usage of a software system. The UML case tools available in today markets help designers to create models and generate code automatically from specific diagrams. Nevertheless, the most of these tools do not offer methods for the verification neither for the validation of these established diagrams, and this is due to the semantics of UML, which are sometimes inadequate in respect to the desired behaviors.

DOI: 10.4018/978-1-61520-789-3.ch002

The need of formal semantics was already discussed by (France, 1998). Also, it's recognized that formal, unambiguous, yet readable account of UML semantics would be very beneficial for the language, the model verification, and in general the oriented object software development. Hence, a lot of emerged semantics approaches attended to formalize the unified notation. They focalized on the state machine diagram. Some of these approaches are purely mathematical models; some are rewriting based systems, and some are translating approaches (Crane, 2005). Generally, the translating approaches are based on the transformation of the UML models into formal pieces ready to be verified by model-checking tools. Model checking (Clarke, 1999) is well-studied technique of automatic formal verification that ensures correctness of a given specification. In literature, some approaches like (Knapp, 2002), (Latella, 1999) and (Lilius, 1999) rely on translating UML Models into languages of model-checking to analyze and verify them. The disadvantage of these approaches is that the semantics model and the verification model aren't the same, and that due to the fact that some model-checking languages like PROMELA/SPIN or SMV are not truly formal languages (Compton, 2000) (Shen, 2002).

In this work, we propose an approach to Verify UML collaboration diagrams against the behavior represented by state machines. The verification is performed after translating the UML model to a formal rewriting logic specification within the *Maude* language. Maude supports declarative programming and executable formal specifications. Inductive theorem proving, model-checking and other formal analysis are either supported by Maude and its formal environment (Meseguer, 2002).

The rest of this chapter is organized as follows; in section 2, we recall some basic definitions of UML classes, state machine and collaboration diagrams. In section 3, we present rewriting logic and Maude language. In section 4, we present the verification of UML using Maude. In section 5, we discuss features of translation and UML models elements. In section 6, we talk about the verification of the specification and the last section concludes the work and gives some perspectives.

UML CLASS, STATE MACHINE, AND COLLABORATION DIAGRAMS

The basic element for modeling oriented object systems is the active object. An active object has its own thread of control and runs in concurrency with other active objects. A UML class diagram may represent classes of active objects and associations between them.

In this paper we use a simple model of an Automatic Teller Machine (ATM), as it's represented in (Knapp, 2002). Figure 1 shows a class diagram that specifies two active classes ATM and Bank. The association between the two classes rely an instance of Bank to an instance of ATM, and vice versa. Classes define attributes, operations and

Figure 1. Class diagram

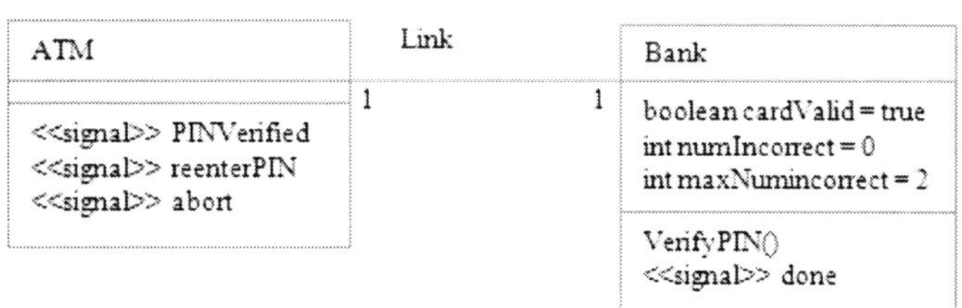

signals that may be invoked on instances by call or receive actions.

The UML class diagrams show a static view of the model. We can associate a UML state machine for each class to define model-objects behaviors. The UML state machine is a variant of classical Harel Statecharts (Dong, 2001). It extends the finite automata by adding hierarchy, concurrent and communication aspects to the automaton. UML state machine depicts the behavior and internal states of an object during its life cycle. As it plays a crucial role in software analysis and modeling.

Syntactically, a state machine is a set of states and transitions. States include simple, composite and pseudo-state. The And-State is the concurrent type of the composite state, while the Or-State is the non-concurrent type, and both of them include more sub-states realizing in this way both hierarchy and concurrency. There are entry, activity and exit actions in a state. Pseudo states include initial, final, history, synchronous, join, fork, junction and choice states.

A transition may be simple or compound. It includes source state, trigger event, guard (a Boolean condition), action and target state. Simple transition rely two states while a compound transition is a set of simple transitions connected with pseudo-state such join, fork or choice state.

For the ATM/Bank example, Figure 2 and Figure 3 show respectively the state machine diagrams which express the behaviors of both the ATM and the Bank classes. The interaction of an ATM with a single hypothetical user and a bank computer, focusing on card and Pin validation, is simulated by the model as it's described in (Knapp, 2002). Once the user enters his bank card, a Request is triggered by the ATM to enter the PIN code. The ATM after that consult the Bank to verify the entered PIN code in a passive mode until it the answer is sent back. If both the Card and the PIN code are valid, the ATM may then precede dispensing money. If in the other case the PIN is invalid, another request is triggered for the user to enter the correct PIN code. If the card is invalid the ATM aborts the transaction and the card is polled out.

As shown in Figure 3, the bank computer validates the Card and the PIN code concurrently. If the card is not valid, the operation is exited immediately and the ATM aborts the transaction. Throughout the two join transitions, the results of the concurrent validations are evaluated. If the card is valid and an incorrect PIN code has been entered, the counter of the invalid PIN entries is incremented. In the case that the counter has exceeded a maximum value, the card is invalidated and the transition is aborted. In contrast, the counter is reset to zero if a correct PIN code is entered.

A state machine represents only the behavior of an object while a UML collaboration diagram shows an interaction between several objects. The elements of such diagram are objects and

Figure 2. State machine diagram of the ATM class

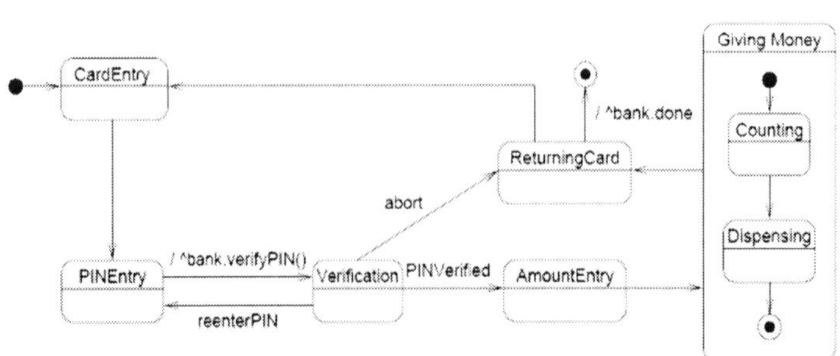

Figure 3. State machine diagram of the Bank class

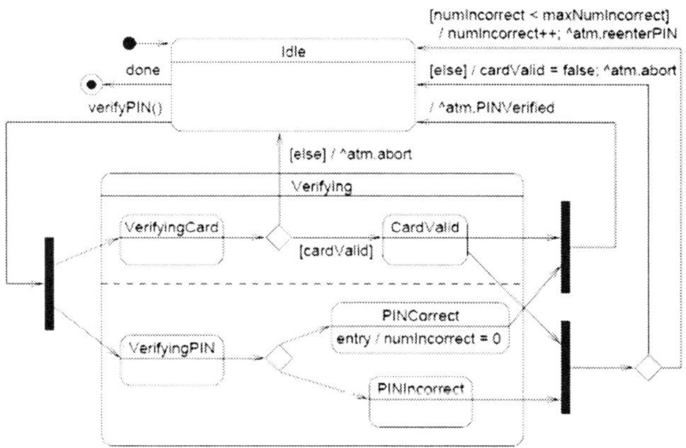

links between them. An object is an instance of class, and a link is an instance of an association between classes. Objects in the diagram interact by exchanging messages. Figure 4 and Figure 5 show collaboration diagrams four the ATM/BANK example.

A collaboration diagram can depict one or several expected behaviors like the collaboration of Figure 4, but it does not exclude other erroneous collaboration as it's shown in Figure 5. In Figure 4, the first message from the ATM (a) asks the bank (b) to verify a PIN by sending a call event VerifyPIN. The bank (b) replies with signal reenterPIN, which require the ATM to ask the user for another PIN entry. The third message of type VerifyPIN is finally acknowledged by the bank via the signal PINVerified. The Figure 5 specifies an undesirable behavior which is when the card has been invalidated by the bank, as acknowledged by sending abort, no PIN entry should be valid.

In the next section, we present an approach that describes how to translate UML model to a rewriting logic specification expressed within the Maude language, In order to perform a formal verification of collaborations against the system behavior represented by the state machines

REWRITING LOGIC AND MAUDE LANGUAGE

Rewriting logic (Meseguer, 1992) is proposed by Meseguer as a unified logical framework in which other logics can be represented, and as a semantic framework for the specification of languages and systems.

In a rewriting logic, the logic formulas are called rules. This latter have the following form,

R:[*T*] -> [*T*] If C.

Figure 4. Expected collaboration

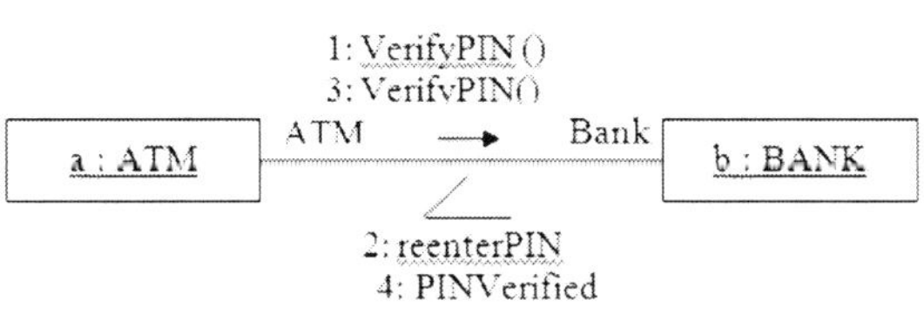

Figure 5. Erroneous collaboration

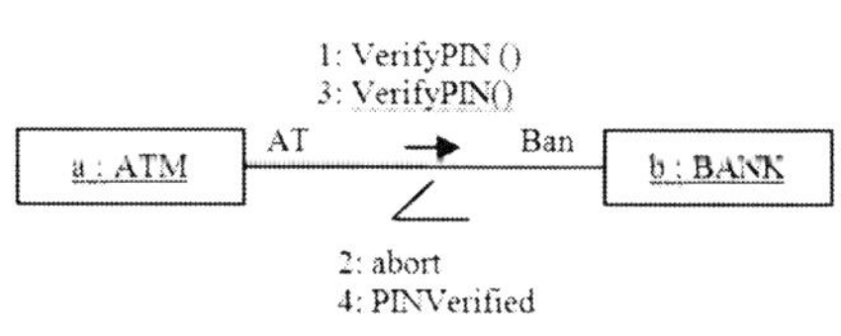

The R rule indicates that a term T becomes T' if the condition C is verified. The rules of rewriting logic are set to reason on a possible change in a concurrent system. They allow us to draw conclusions about the evolution of the system from certain basic type changes.

The Maude language (Clavel, 2002) is a formal specification and programming language based on rewriting logic. It's a state-of-the-art formal tool in the field of algebraic specification.

In Maude there are three kinds of modules;

- Functional modules, introduced by the keyword fmod.
- System modules, introduced by the keyword mod.
- Oriented-Object modules, introduced by the keyword omod. Maude's functional and system modules are respectively of the form:

  fmod ε endfm, and mod $\mathcal{R}$ endm.

For ε an equational theory, and $\mathcal{R}$ a rewrite theory. Functional modules allow defining data types (called sorts), and their functions through equations theory. Equations are declared with the keyword eq or ceq (for conditional equations). Rules can only appear in the system or the oriented-object modules and are declared with the keyword rl or crl (for conditional rules).

The version of rewrite logic used in Maude is order-sorted (Marti-Oliet, 1996). This means that rewrite theories are typed (or sorted), and can have subtypes (subsorts) and that function can be overloaded.

In Maude language, two types of specification are defined; the first deals with system specification, whereas the second related to the specification of properties. The system specification level is mainly expressed by system modules. Those modules can define the behavior of a system based on rewriting rules which offers a high level degree of concurrency. The properties specification level concerns properties to be checked for a given system. In the following section, we present the principal ideas on how to model-check UML collaboration and state machines using Maude.

MAUDE VERIFICATION OF UML MODELS

In UML, each class optionally has a state machine that describes the internal behavior of its instances (Objetcs). The state machine interacts with the environment by sending events to other objects and executing the internal methods as reaction to incoming events.

To verify the behavior of a set of interacting objects represented in a collaboration diagram, we propose to translate the model (classes/objects, state machines, collaborations) to a rewriting logic specification within Maude, where:

- In the system specification level, each class and its associated state machine are translated to Maude oriented object model. The basic idea of the translation process is that transitions between states of a give state-machine can be naturally represented by rewriting logic rules. Maude offers though the appropriate underlying definitions that support oriented object specification (class, Message, Configurations ...etc). Taking the above example, the behavior of the ATM and the BANK classes are defined as object-oriented modules as it is shown in Figure 6 and Figure 7.
- In properties specification level, the collaboration structure between objects and the sequence that we want to check are specified within a Maude oriented object module. This latter includes the other object-oriented modules which depict state machines behaviors. The initial state is a configuration that holds a set of objects and a list of events which represent the collaboration. The behavior of the objects, as we

mentioned above, is described by the included object oriented modules. In our example, the initial state is an instance of the ATM and the Bank Classes.

- Maude search command analyzes all behaviors from a given initial state (configuration of objects and links between them and the sequence of message).

In the following section, we explain details on the way we translate the UML model to the Maude specification language.

FEATURES OF UML MODEL ELEMENTS AND TRANSLATION

Elements of a UML model are expressed as:

Class & Attributes

Classes in UML model correspond to the Maude classes which are declared with respect to the following syntax

```
Class classename | Att1: S1, …, Attn : Sn.
```

Where, Att1 … Attn are attributes and **S1** … **Sn** are sorts (types).

In the Maude specification, to the class attributes the following elements are added.

- An attribute '**STATUS**' of sort '**STATE**' to indicate the state of the object (the class instance).

Figure 6. Maude specification for the ATM class and its associated state machine

```
load full-maude
(omod SMATM is
protecting INT . protecting NAT . protecting STRING . protecting BOOL .
*** Objects names are Strings.
subsort String < Oid .
*** defination of the sort state simple state and composed state
sorts SIMSTATE COMSTATE STATE .                                          *** [1]
subsort SIMSTATE < COMSTATE .                                                      *** [2]
subsort COMSTATE < STATE .                                                         *** [3]
op none : -> COMSTATE [ctor] .                                                     *** [4]
op _||_ : COMSTATE COMSTATE -> COMSTATE [ctor assoc comm id: none] .      *** [5]
*** Specification of collaboration structure
sort seq col .                                                                     *** [6]
subsort Msg < seq .
                *** [7]
op null : -> seq [ctor] .                                                          *** [8]
op _._ : seq seq -> seq [ctor assoc id: null ] .                         *** [9]
op collaboration : seq -> col .
subsort col < Configuration .                                            *** [10]

ops CardEntry PINEntry Verification AmountEntry ReturningCard Counting Dispensing InitialState FinalState : -> SIMSTATE .
                                                                      *** [11]
op GivingMoney : COMSTATE -> STATE .                                            *** [12]
*** defination of the ATM class
class ATM | STATUS : STATE , BLOCKED : Bool , Link : Oid .             *** [13]
*** defination of events
msgs verifyPIN reenterPIN PINverified abort done
 ACKverifyPIN : Oid Oid -> Msg .                                         *** [14]
*** Some variables declaration
vars AT L : String . var X : STATE . vars N N' : Nat . var b : Bool . var s : seq .
var CF : Configuration .

*** transitions of the State machine are represented by Rewriting Logic rules
*** in order to draw a way to execute the system in respect to the given collaboration, the op Collaboration is added to the rules
rl [t1] : < AT : ATM | STATUS : InitialState > => < AT : ATM | STATUS : CardEntry > .      *** [15]
rl [t2] : < AT : ATM | STATUS : CardEntry > => < AT : ATM | STATUS : PINEntry > .
rl [t3] : < AT : ATM | STATUS : PINEntry , BLOCKED : false , Link : L > collaboration(verifyPIN(AT , L) . s) => < AT : ATM | STATUS : Verification , BLOCKED :
true , Link : L > verifyPIN(AT , L) collaboration(s) .
rl [t3ack] : ACKverifyPIN(L , AT) < AT : ATM | STATUS : Verification , BLOCKED : true , Link : L > => < AT : ATM | STATUS : Verification , BLOCKED : false ,
Link : L > .
rl [t4] : reenterPIN(L , AT) < AT : ATM | STATUS : Verification , BLOCKED : false , Link : L > => < AT : ATM | STATUS : PINEntry , BLOCKED : false , Link : L > .
rl [t5] : PINverified(L , AT) < AT : ATM | STATUS : Verification , BLOCKED : false , Link : L > => < AT : ATM | STATUS : AmountEntry , BLOCKED : false , Link :
L > .
rl [t6] : abort(L , AT) < AT : ATM | STATUS : Verification , BLOCKED : false , Link : L > => < AT : ATM | STATUS : ReturningCard , BLOCKED : false , Link : L > .
rl [t7] : < AT : ATM | STATUS : AmountEntry , BLOCKED : false , Link : L > => < AT : ATM | STATUS : GivingMoney(InitialState) , BLOCKED : false , Link : L > .
rl [t8] : < AT : ATM | STATUS : GivingMoney(InitialState) , BLOCKED : false , Link : L > => < AT : ATM | STATUS : GivingMoney(Counting) , BLOCKED : false ,
Link : L > .
rl [t9] : < AT : ATM | STATUS : GivingMoney(Counting) , BLOCKED : false , Link : L > => < AT : ATM | STATUS : GivingMoney(Dispensing) , BLOCKED : false ,
Link : L > .
rl [t10] : < AT : ATM | STATUS : GivingMoney(Dispensing) , BLOCKED : false , Link : L > => < AT : ATM | STATUS : GivingMoney(FinalState) , BLOCKED : false ,
Link : L > .
rl [t11] : < AT : ATM | STATUS : GivingMoney(FinalState) , BLOCKED : false , Link : L > => < AT : ATM | STATUS : ReturningCard , BLOCKED : false , Link : L > .

rl [t12] : < AT : ATM | STATUS : ReturningCard , BLOCKED : false , Link : L > collaboration( done(AT , L) . s) => < AT : ATM | STATUS : FinalState , BLOCKED :
false , Link : L > done(AT , L ) collaboration(s) .
rl [t13] : < AT : ATM | STATUS : FinalState , BLOCKED : false , Link : L > CF => < AT : ATM | STATUS : FinalState , BLOCKED : false , Link : L > CF .
endom )
```

Figure 7. Maude specification for the Bank class and its associated state machine

```
load full-maude
( omod SMBank is
protecting INT . protecting NAT . protecting STRING . protecting BOOL .

ops Idle VerifyingCard VerifyingPIN CardValid PINCorrect PINIncorrect InitialState FinalState : -> SIMSTATE .
*** [11]
op Verifying : COMSTATE -> STATE .
*** [12]
*** definition of the class Bank
class BANK | STATUS : STATE , BLOCKED : Bool , cardValid : Bool , numIncorrect : Nat , MaxNumIncorrect :
Nat , Link : Oid .
*** [13]
*** definition of events
msgs verifyPIN reenterPIN PINverified abort done
 ACKverifyPIN : Oid Oid -> Msg .
*** [14]
*** Some variables declaration
vars BQ L : String . var X : STATE . vars N N' : Nat . var b : Bool .
var s : seq . var CF : Configuration .
*** transitions of the State machine are represented by Rewriting Logic rules
*** in order to draw a way to execute the system in respect to the given collaboration. the op Collaboration is
added to the rules
*** to get rules that represent only the transition remove collaboration.
*** [15]
rl [t1] : < BQ : BANK | STATUS : InitialState , BLOCKED : false > => < BQ : BANK | STATUS : Idle ,
BLOCKED : false > .
rl [t2] : verifyPIN(L , BQ) < BQ : BANK | STATUS : Idle , BLOCKED : false , Link : L > => < BQ : BANK |
STATUS : Verifying( VerifyingCard || VerifyingPIN ) , BLOCKED : false , Link : L > ACKverifyPIN(BQ , L) .
crl [t3a] : < BQ : BANK | STATUS : Verifying( VerifyingCard || X ) , cardValid : b > => < BQ : BANK |
STATUS : Verifying( CardValid || X ) , cardValid : b > if b = true .
crl [t3b] : < BQ : BANK | STATUS : Verifying( VerifyingCard || X ) , cardValid : b , Link : L > collaboration(
abort(BQ , L) - s) => < BQ : BANK | STATUS : Idle , cardValid : b > abort(BQ , L) collaboration(s) if b = false .
rl [t4a] : < BQ : BANK | STATUS : Verifying( X || VerifyingPIN ) > => < BQ : BANK | STATUS : Verifying( X
|| PINIncorrect ) > .
rl [t4a] : < BQ : BANK | STATUS : Verifying( X || VerifyingPIN ) , numIncorrect : N > => < BQ : BANK |
STATUS : Verifying( X || PINCorrect ) , numIncorrect : 0 > .
rl [t5] : < BQ : BANK | STATUS : Verifying( CardValid || PINCorrect ) , Link : L > collaboration(PINverified(BQ
, L ) - s) => < BQ : BANK | STATUS : Idle , Link : L > PINverified(BQ , L ) collaboration(s) .
crl [t6] : < BQ : BANK | STATUS : Verifying( CardValid || PINIncorrect ) , cardValid : true , numIncorrect : N ,
MaxNumIncorrect : N' , Link : L > collaboration(abort(BQ , L ) - s) => < BQ : BANK | STATUS : Idle , cardValid
: false , numIncorrect : N , MaxNumIncorrect : N' , Link : L > abort(BQ , L ) collaboration(s) if N >= N' .
crl [t6] : < BQ : BANK | STATUS : Verifying( CardValid || PINIncorrect ) , cardValid : b , numIncorrect : N ,
MaxNumIncorrect : N' , Link : L > collaboration(reenterPIN(BQ , L ) - s) => < BQ : BANK | STATUS : Idle ,
cardValid : b , numIncorrect : N + 1 , MaxNumIncorrect : N' , Link : L > reenterPIN(BQ , L ) collaboration(s) if N
< N' .
rl [t8] : done(L , BQ ) < BQ : BANK | STATUS : Idle , BLOCKED : false , Link : L > => < BQ : BANK |
STATUS : FinalState , BLOCKED : false , Link : L > .
endom)
```

- An attribute '**BLOCKED**' of sort '**BOOL**' to indicate whether the object is blocked or not.An
- attribute for each link, of sort '**Oid**', to hold the name of the linked object.
- An optional attribute '**Stereotype**' of sort '**String**' to indicate if the current status of the object is an error, normal, or success state.

Line (13) in Figure 6 and Figure 7 respectively represent declaration of ATM and Bank classes.

Maude supports Strings, Naturals, Integers and Booleans sorts. To use other sorts of attributes, we should specify these sorts plus the operations among them.

States

for each state in the state-machine diagram, we define an operation that takes the same name. These operations are sorted as SIMSTATE or COMSTATE (for simple state and composed state).

Lines (1) to (5) in Figure 6 represent the algebraic specification which underlies the definition of states. SIMSTATE, COMSTATE are subsorts of STATE. The COMSTATE can hold simple or composed substates as defined by line (2, 4 and 5) in the same figure.

All possible state declarations are;

- op statename: -> SIMSTATE. *** for simple state declaration
- op statename: SIMSTATE -> STATE. *** for Or-state declaration
- op statename: COMSTATE -> STATE. *** for And-state declaration

The declaration of possible states for the ATM and Bank objects is described in line (11-12) in the Figure 6 and Figure 7 respectively.

Events

Signals, call events, and deferred events are represented by messages. Messages are a part of a configuration and can be exchanged between objects. A message declaration follows the syntax:

```
msg EventName: Oid Oid P1 ….. Pn ->
Msg.
```

Where, msg is the keyword to declare a message of sort Msg. The first Oid (Object Identifier) identify the caller object. The second Oid identify the receiver object and P1…. Pn are sorts (types) of the events parameters.

Call events are synchronous; the caller object is blocked until the receiver object respond for it. To specify this kind of interactions we propose for each call event two messages: a request message (*EventName*) taking the event name and an acknowledgment message (*AckEventName*). The First message is sent from the caller object to the receiver object as a request, after that the caller is blocked, when the receiver got the message, it notifies the caller by an acknowledgment message to unblock it and also to indicate that its message is been consumed properly.

Line (14) in Figure 6 and Figure 7 is the declaration of the events for our example.

Transitions

We specify a transition by a rewriting logic rule which changes the state of an object by modifying the attribute **status** from a value (state) to another.

A transition can be a conditional rewriting rule with the form;

```
crl [transitionName]: T => T' if C.
```

Or only a simple rewriting rule in the case of transitions without guards.

```
rl [transitionName]: T => T' if C.
```

Where, T is the configuration that holds triggering messages, the object in state S1 and the rest of the configuration (objects and messages). T' represents the new configuration where the state of the object is changed to S2 and the actions are performed either by the introduction of a new messages in the configuration, or by changing the object attributes values. And, *C* is a condition that represents the transition guard.

Completion transition, transition across composite states and transition across orthogonal states using join and fork vertices is supported also by our approach.

In Figure 6 and Figure 7, section from line (15) to the end, holds the transitions specification that correspond to the state machines transitions showed in Figure 2 and Figure 3.

Guards

Guards are Boolean expressions enabling transitions. By including the module BOOL we can specify any guard in the Maude specification.

Collaboration

We define a list which holds the sequence of events exchanged between objects during collaboration. This list has an influence in the execution of the transition which generates events: so only transition which generates the top element of the list can be executed. Once the event is generated it's removed from the list. The empty list in the end means that the collaboration specified is verified against the behavior specified by the state machine diagrams. Lines (6-10) in Figure 6 represent the specification of the list, named collaboration, which holds the exchanged events.

In a separate module, we define the initial state of the global system. This state is a configuration which takes the objects and the list which contains the sequence of exchanged events during the collaboration in order to be verified. The behavior of objects is specified in the included oriented object modules that we described previously its construction.

VERIFICATION OF THE SPECIFICATION

Maude provides different ways to execute a given specification, such as (Clavel M. D.-O., 2007):

- The Maude commands rew (or rewrite) and frew (frewrite for 'fair rewrite') Execute (or simulate) one out of the many possible behaviors from a given initial state, by applying rewrite rules to the initial state.
- Maude provides a search command for searching through all possible behaviors from a given initial state. This is done by asking Maude to search for terms which can be reached from initial state and which satisfy a given condition.
- Maude is equipped with a temporal logic model checker for checking whether all behaviors from a certain initial state satisfy a given temporal logic property.

The collaboration is verified if we get an empty list after executing the specification. In contrast, if the list *collaboration* is nonempty, it means that the collaboration is erroneous and could not be done with the given specification.

For the ATM/Bank example, we give tow initial states initState-coll1 and initState-coll2. The first (line 1 in Figure 8,) holds an instance of ATM class with an instance of Bank and the list collaboration which represent the collaboration of Figure4*(collaboration(verifyPIN("a", "b") - reenterPIN("b", "a") - verifyPIN("a", "b") - PINverified("b", "a")).*

The second (line 2 in Figure 8,) holds an instance of both classes ATM and Bank, with the collaboration list which represent the collaboration

Figure 8. Maude correspondent specification of the UML model to be verified

```
load full-maude
( omod MCHECK is
including SMBank .      including SMAtm .
op initState-coll1 : -> Configuration .
*** [1]
eq initState-coll1 = < "a" : ATM | STATUS : InitialState , BLOCKED : false , Link : "b" > < "b" : BANK |
STATUS : InitialState , BLOCKED : false , cardValid : true , numIncorrect : 0 , MaxNumIncorrect : 5 , Link :
"a" >  collaboration(verifyPIN("a" , "b") - reenterPIN("b" , "a") - verifyPIN("a" , "b") - PINverified("b" , "a") ) .
op initState-coll2 : -> Configuration .
*** [2]
eq initState-coll2 = < "a" : ATM | STATUS : InitialState , BLOCKED : false , Link : "b" > < "b" : BANK |
STATUS : InitialState , BLOCKED : false , cardValid : true , numIncorrect : 0 , MaxNumIncorrect : 5 , Link : "a"
>  collaboration(verifyPIN("a" , "b") - reenterPIN("b" , "a") - abort("a" , "b") - PINverified("b" , "a") ) .
endom)
***  we use two commands to verify the collaboration

*** commands to verify the first collaboration
(rew initState-coll1 .)
 (search [1] initState-coll1 =>! ( C:Configuration  collaboration(null) ) . )

*** commands to verify the second collaboration
(rew initState-coll2 .)
 (search [1] initState-coll2 =>! ( C:Configuration  collaboration(null) ) . )
endom)
```

Figure 9. Results of the verification

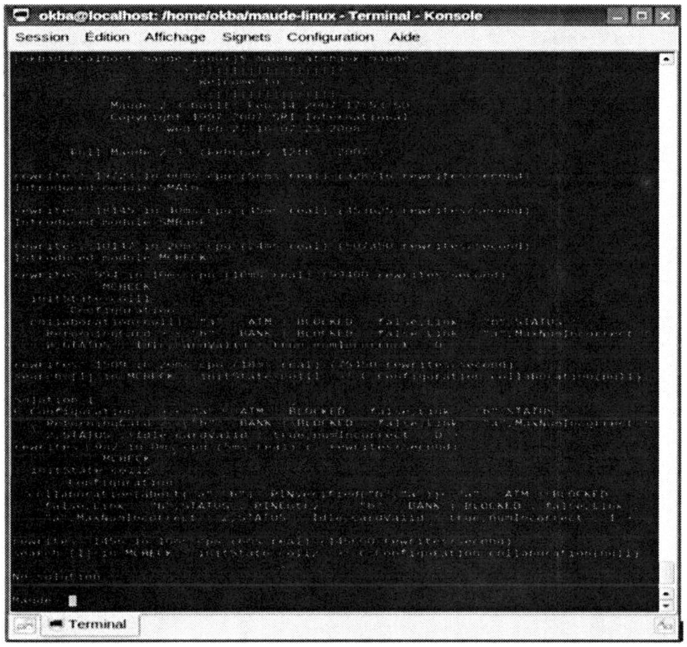

diagram of Figure 5 *(collaboration(verifyPIN("a", "b") - reenterPIN("b", "a") - abort("a", "b") - PINverified("b", "a")))*.

By executing the specification above (Figure 8) we get;

- The first collaboration is verified and the list collaboration is empty as it is shown in Figure 9. The second command is a search from the initial state to a state where the collaboration is empty. The execution of Figure 9 confirms that there is a solution, which means that the collaboration can be executed with respect to the specified behavior.
- The second collaboration is erroneous and it's not verified with respect to the given specification. As it's shown in Figure 9, the collaboration list isn't empty *collaboration (abort("a", "b") - PINverified("b", "a"))*, which explain the fact that the collaboration describes an undesired behavior: when the bank aborts a transaction, the card should have been invalidated, and no subsequent PIN entry should be valid.

CONCLUSION

We presented an approach that deals with the verification of a subset of UML diagrams (state machine and collaborations). The work lie on the translating of some UML diagrams into rewriting logic specification. We gave necessary guidelines on how to translate UML model elements by the Maude language. The verification of the collaboration against the system specification is performed by the Maude write and search commands. The result indicates whether the collaboration is correct or it's erroneous with respect to the behavior represented by the state machines. In our paper, the model verification is a considered a formal logic specification, In contrast with other approaches which use model-checking languages like Promela/SPIN and SMV which are not truly formal languages. As an extension to this work, our attempt is build a prototype tool which performs the automatic translation from UML diagrams to Maude specification language using graph grammars.

REFERENCES

Clarke, E., Grumberg, O., & Peled, D. A. (1999). *Model Checking*. Cambridge, MA: MIT Press.

Clavel, M., Durán, F., Eker, S., Lincoln, P., Marti-Oliet, N., Meseguer, J., & Quesada, J. F. (2002, August). MAUDE: specification and programming in rewriting logic. *Theoretical Computer Science, 285*(2), 178–243. doi:10.1016/S0304-3975(01)00359-0

Clavel, M., Durán, F., Eker, S., Lincoln, P., Martí-Oliet, N., Meseguer, J., & Talcott, C. (2007). *Maude Manual (Version 2.3).* Retrieved fromhttp://maude.cs.uiuc.edu

Compton, K., Huggins, J. K., & Shen, W. (2000). A semantic model for the state machine in the Unified Modeling Language. *In Proceeding of Dynamic Behavior in UML Models: Semantic Questions, UML 2000 workshop*Crane, M. D. (2005). *On the Semantics of UML State Machines: Categorization and Comparison.* Ontario,Canada: School of Computing, Queen's University.

Dong, W., Wang, J., Qi, X., & Qi, Z. (2001). Model Checking UML Statecharts. In *Proceedings of the Eighth Asia-Pacific Software Engineering Conference (APSEC.01).*

France, R., Evans, A., Lano, K., & Rumpe, B. (1998). The UML as a formal modeling notation. *Computer Standards & Interfaces, 19*, 325–334. doi:10.1016/S0920-5489(98)00020-8

Knapp, A., & Merz, S. (2002). Model checking and code generation for UML state machines and collaborations. In *Proceeding of the 5th Workshop on Tools for System Design and Verification.*

Latella, D, Majzik, I., & Massink, M. (1999). Automatic verification of UML statechart diagrams using the SPIN model-checker. *Formal Aspects of Computing, 11*(6), 637/664.

Lilius, J., & Paltor, I. P. (1999). vUML: A tool for verifying UML models. In *Proceedings of the 14th IEEE International Conference on Automated Software Engineering (ASE'99)*, pp. 255-258.

Marti-Oliet, N., & Meseguer, J. (1996). Rewriting logic as a Logical and Semantic framework. In *1st International Workshop on Rewriting Logic and its Application (WRLA'96), Electronic Notes in Theoretical Computer science vol4.*

Meseguer, J. (1992). Conditional Rewriting logic as unified model of concurrency. *Theoretical Computer Science, 96*, 73–155. doi:10.1016/0304-3975(92)90182-F

Meseguer, J. (2002). *Software specification and verification in rewriting logic.* Lectures at the Marktoberdorf Summer School.

Rumbaugh, J., Jacobson, I., & Booch, G. (1999). *The Unified Modeling Language Reference Manual.* Reading, MA: Addison-Wesley.

Shen, W., Compton, K., & Huggins, J. K. (2002). A toolset for supporting UML static and dynamic model checking. In *Proceedings of the 26th International Computer Software and Applications Conference COMPSAC 2002*, pp. 147-152.

Chapter 3
Voice-Based E-Learning Approach for E-Government

A. A. Azeta
Covenant University, Nigeria

Charles K. Ayo
Covenant University, Nigeria

Aderemi Aaron Anthony Atayero
Covenant University, Nigeria

Nicholas Ikhu-Omoregbe
Covenant University, Nigeria

ABSTRACT

Government establishments are most times highly involved in different reorganization programs. The processes in e-Government are diversified and complex, hence the need for an appropriate training and learning strategy for governmental employees. Changing business processes and organizational structures always mean that the personnel have to be familiar with the changed procedures. Consequently, the employees need to be trained to develop capacity for new responsibilities. Existing methods of learning and training do not make provision for certain category of employees such as the visually impaired. They do not provide an alternative learning platform for government of employees that are not physically challenged. Many studies have demonstrated the value of several learning platforms, including mobile learning (m-Learning) but with the problems of access barriers and streamlined participation of most learners. The purpose of this chapter is to propose a voice-based e-Learning system, also known as voice-learning (v-Learning) as a variant of the m-Learning with particular relevance for the visually and mobility impaired learners. V-Learning makes possible ubiquitous learning in e-Government and provides additional capacity and speed of response to help facilitate change. Cost reduction is also achieved and there is no shortage of teachers.

DOI: 10.4018/978-1-61520-789-3.ch003

INTRODUCTION

At the end of this chapter, readers will understand the:

- meaning of e-Government and voice-based e-Learning
- concept of voice-based e-Learning approach for the visually impaired
- technologies for voice-based e-Learning in e-Government
- benefits of voice-based e-Learning systems in e-Government
- challenges in voice-based learning in e-Government
- recommendations for the implementation of voice-based e-Learning in e-Government

BACKGROUND

E-Government is the use of Information and Communication Technologies (ICT) to support government operations and service delivery in a responsive and cost-effective manner (eGovt, 2005). It facilitates administrative and managerial functions, providing citizens and stakeholders with convenient access to government information, facilitating interaction and transactions with stakeholders, and providing better opportunities to participate in democratic institutions and processes (Anttiroiko, 2008).

The use of ICT in government activities has become a common phenomenon in recent years. In the late 1990s, a unique concept known as electronic government (e-Government) was introduced in the field of public administration (Hasan, 2003). ICT has been identified as a tool that provides the services of governance in the areas of e-Administration, e-Voting, e-Democracy, e-Health, to mention but a few. To date, various technologies have been applied to support the unique characteristics of e-Government, including interactive voice response (IVR), voice mail, email, web service delivery, virtual reality, augmented reality, etc.

The web and other technologies have shown great potentials for effective and efficient tools that collect, store, collate and manage voluminous information. The most current information can be uploaded and downloaded on the Internet in a real-time. Government can also transfer funds electronically to governmental agencies or provide information to public employees through the Intranet or Internet. Additionally, governments can perform many routine functions more easily and quickly. Web technologies also facilitate government links with the citizenry for services, political activities, other governmental agencies and businesses.

E-learning is a method of facilitating and enhancing learning based on the use of computer and communications technology. The term is commonly used to refer to learning or training that is delivered over an Intranet or the Internet ("e-Learning Glossary", 2008). There are different categories of e-Learning environment. The first category is the traditional formal education. Here, teacher and students have to be physically present in a classroom. The major communication means between the teachers and students is face to face. Distance education is the second category; with the development of communication network technologies in the industrial age, teachers and students are separated by space and time. Communication between teachers and students is achieved by using traditional mail, phone, radio and television.

The electronic revolution and the invention of Internet gave rise to e-Learning that has become the third category. Since then different types of media like text, audio, video, hypertext simulations and two-way communication have been used commonly in education. The m-Learning that constitutes the fourth category involves the use of mobile communication tools like mobile phone, pocket PC, etc. M-Learning can take place anytime, anywhere with the help of a mobile device.

Voice-based e-Learning, also known as voice-learning (or v-Learning) is proposed in this chapter as a variant of the fourth category (m-Learning) with particular relevance for specific groups in the populace. It means the use of land or mobile phone to access learning content on the Intranet or Internet depending on network coverage availability. It uses technologies such as speech recognition and text to speech (TTS) conversion to create a user interface that enables users to navigate through a dialogue system using telephone and voice commands. Voice-based applications have been developed in several areas such as e-Learning (Azeta *et al.*, 2008a; Gallivan *et al.*, 2002), banking transactions (Azeta *et al.*, 2008b) and a lot more.

Voice-based e-Learning in e-Government is defined as the use of speech technologies to deliver learning and knowledge management content to government employees. For instance, as a staff of a government establishment at any level, whether local, state or federal, one may be scheduled to attend training at the federal government headquarters in the capital city. Lectures are provided through voice interface. To participate, employees are required to dial a telephone number to access the learning materials in a central server using a mobile or land telephone that will connect the caller to a government learning content information management system (GLCIMS).

The processes in e-Government are dynamic hence the need for an appropriate training and learning strategy for employees of government. Techniques exist for learning but they do not cater for employees that are visually impaired nor provide alternative learning platform for employees that are not physically challenged. The purpose of this chapter is to propose a voice-based e-Learning system to serve as an alternative learning platform for normal employees of government, and in particular to suit the physically challenged learners such as the visually or mobility impaired government employees, i.e. employees with partial or no sight, or inability to move from one place to another.

VOICE-BASED E-LEARNING APPROACH FOR THE VISUALLY IMPAIRED

There is no gainsaying the fact that technology is changing fast. It is changing the way we do things and the pace at which we do them. Internet connected Personal Computers (PCs) have become commonplace in our educational institutions and workplaces. Indeed, many people, students, government employees and citizens carry laptops about for their uses which afford them the opportunity to learn and show their computer skills daily.

Those individuals, who, for various reasons, cannot make use of modern computer systems efficiently, will be increasingly left behind in terms of educational opportunities, job skills and employability. Those with physical disability (particularly the visually impaired) are not considered in the context of usability of these technologies.

Voice-based learning is also known as assistive technology. The World Wide Web Consortium (W3C) defines assistive technology as software or hardware that has been specifically designed to assist people with disabilities in carrying out daily activities (Adaptive, 2005). These technologies aid the learning process for learners with disabilities.

Every democratic government should consider the possibility of providing education to her citizens, particularly the physically challenged, and ensuring that people with visual disability in particular can access government information and services with ease. More so, government employees that are visually impaired should be able to benefit from online training using voice technologies.

TECHNOLOGIES FOR VOICE-BASED E-LEARNING IN E-GOVERNMENT

This section examines a number of key technologies used for voice-based e-Learning in e-Government.

VoiceXML also known as voice extensible markup language, is one of the tools recognized by the W3C for building speech applications that can serve educational purposes and provide better accessibility to users (Chin *et al.,* 2006). An e-Learning system that can be provided using speech technology is one that delivers basic teaching by simply listening. For example, students can check their scores or listen to lecture notes by calling a particular telephone number through IVR. Some learners have used speech recognition systems successfully for their studies and for exams, and the use of this technology has helped them to overcome their physical disabilities and go on to higher education (Paul, 2003).

The software architecture of voice-based e-Learning allows users to access the learning content through mobile and land phone. Figure 1 contains software architecture of voice-based e-Learning system. Access to the system is performed through the presentation tier using the registration information of learners. Security management also guarantees that the administrator authenticates all registered learners by issuing a pin for login. The business logic tier provides an interface between the presentation and database tier. It contains the voice gateway and the various modules of the application. The database tier stores and provides data access to information in the voice-enabled e-Learning system.

Similarly the hardware architecture for voice-enabled e-Learning system consists of client devices, servers and database (see Figure 2).

Client Devices

The client devices include mobile devices such as mobile phones and personal digital assistants, land telephones, etc. The mobile device carry out two main functions. First, the mobile device is used to access information and services provided by the web server through the voice gateway. Second, the mobile device is used to connect to e-Learning by dialing a telephone number. The land telephone can also be used to connect to the application.

Figure 1. Software architecture of voice-based e-learning for e-government

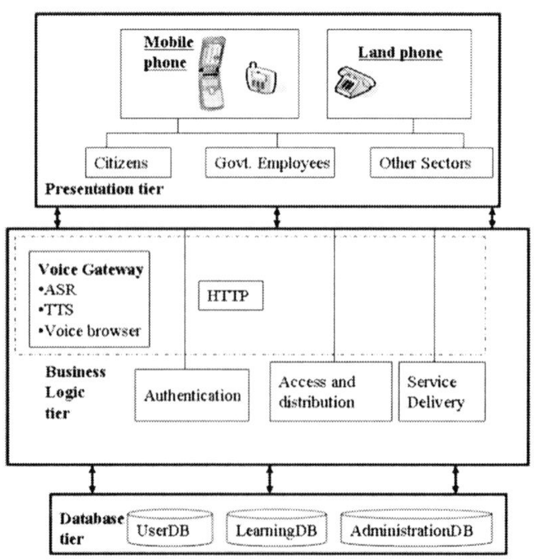

Figure 2. Hardware architecture of voice-based e-learning for e-government

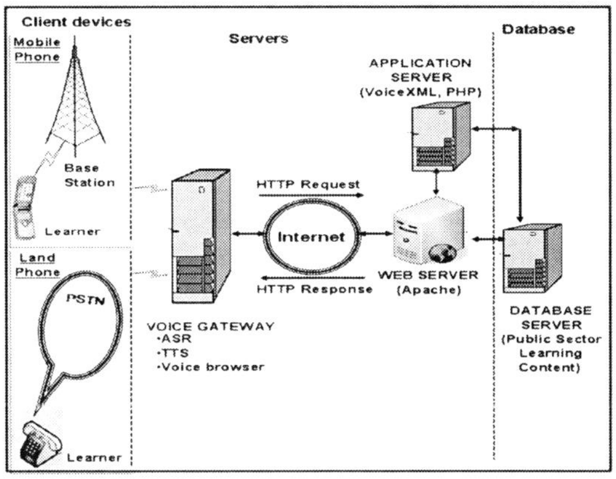

Servers

There are three components of the servers: the voice gateway, application server and web server. The voice gateway is responsible for communicating with the user over the telephone and performing telephony tasks. The voice browser in the VoiceXML gateway collects speech input from the user over the telephone and presents it to the inner components of the VoiceXML gateway for processing. The voice browser also presents the output to the user in the form of spoken words over the telephone. In some cases, voice server and application servers can co-exist in one server in order to reduce dependency on the Internet link between the two servers (Qureshi, 2007).

Voice Browser: A voice browser is the human machine interfacing component of any speech driven voice application. A voice browser provides an interface between the caller and the different components of the voice server.

Automatic Speech Recognition (ASR): ASR is also called speech recognition engine and plays a major role in the development of today's computer telephony applications. Its main purpose is to convert human speech into text form that the application can understand. Speech recognition is the other end of the spectrum that provides assistance to learners with disabilities. This technology has become so advanced that it has found its way into mainstream automotive systems, aiding in the hands free operation of in-car navigation systems. This software has to understand a multitude of voices in a variety of pitches and languages. Indeed a single voice can vary significantly from day to day, whether due to mood, or the effect of a head cold.

Text to Speech (TTS): TTS also known as speech synthesis are the most recognized form of adaptive technology. They provide exactly the reverse of the speech recognition process: that is converting text to speech. A TTS system announces text provided by the application to the caller in the form of spoken words. They are a necessity for the blind or vision-impaired learners to successfully navigate an e-Learning environment (Adaptive, 2005).

Web Server: The web server stores the actual middle-ware application (i.e. Apache) that connect the front-end and back-end interfaces.

Application Server: The application server stores the actual value-added information and content that subscribers wish to access. In this chapter, VoiceXML and PHP have been used for the development of the e-Learning application that is hosted in the application server.

Database

The database contains the MySQL database server which houses the data for the public sector learning content management.

BENEFITS OF VOICE-BASED E-LEARNING SYSTEMS IN E-GOVERNMENT

Voice-based e-Learning systems have the following benefits (Ally, 2008):

- Learners can learn from anywhere.
- Learners can learn at anytime.
- Learners are in more control of their learning.
- Course materials are easy to update.

The other benefits of voice-based e-Learning systems include (Aio, 2008):

Capacity Development

Voice-based learning has the potential to transform learning in government for normal employees and those with visual impairment. Revolutionary change in the sector is creating ever-changing knowledge and skills requirements, and traditional approaches to training and learning are struggling to keep up.

There is the need to increase training and development capacity for members and officers of government. It is unlikely that classroom-based delivery alone can provide sufficient capacity to respond within budget and schedule. V-learning can provide additional capacity and speed of response to help facilitate change.

Change

In a climate of change, new initiatives and information can be picked up quickly and consistently across an organization. How quickly people can get up to speed and contribute effectively can either accelerate or suppress change.

This speed to competency may be difficult to achieve with large, geographically dispersed organizations such as local, state or federal government offices nation wide. The challenge of time, cost and logistics of bringing people together can be prohibitive, particularly with government's due process policy which makes it difficult to pull employees away from their jobs to off site training sessions. This usually results in delays and an inconsistency in the message delivered.

With voice-based online technologies, voice learning can be realized faster and more efficiently than existing learning methods. Voice-learning can achieve just-in-time learning with greater reach irrespective of location (whether on the move, at home or work), speed of response and consistency of message.

Cost Reduction

Data from the Chartered Institute of Public Finance and Accountancy (CIPFA) (Aio, 2008) suggest that government employees across England, Scotland and Wales spend £296 million on training per year, averaging around £150 per employee. With learning requirements growing, and more people needing to be trained in more areas, this is simply not enough to keep pace with change.

While claims that voice-learning is a cheaper form of training delivery can be misleading due to initial development costs, voice-learning can reduce training related expenses such as travel, accommodation and facilities. It can also provide economies of scale at higher learner volumes, as the cost of each additional learner is negligible once the materials have been developed and hosted in a central server.

Assume that 20,000 staff in government requires health and safety training each year. The cost of delivering training to these staff using conventional classroom training is estimated at

£86 per user for a one-day course. This equates to £1.72 million for 20,000 staff. An equivalent online voice learning course could be developed for £100,000 (Aio, 2008). However, this course can be hosted in a web server at virtually little cost to government. The course is also available online at any time a person needs it; and can be updated centrally so that staff always has access to the most up to date materials. These financial benefits accrue to the whole of government establishments engaged in the training that would no longer have to incur the costs of delivering this training through the classroom or other forms of learning.

Even if only five per cent of government employees training is considered and access provided through voice online, the savings to government could be in excess of £30 million per annum. This represents a return on investment of over 600 per cent and also enables a far greater number of staff to be trained with the same or less resources.

Stop Gap for Staff Shortage

The existing learning methods, particularly the face to face, etc, have some support from training schools and teachers. There are growing staff shortages in schools while the demands for teachers will continue to increase. Digital literacy is critical for future generations if poverty eradication is considered a key factor of government agenda, and this places added pressure on government in a democratic society.

Voice-learning as a component of e-Learning is being deployed as a means of fuelling the expansion in training institutes/schools within resource constraints. Deployed effectively, voice-learning could offset the lack of alternative resources for normal learners, while providing the visually impaired learners with a more participatory educational experience. Voice-based learning methods therefore serves as an assisted technology for the disadvantaged learner particularly the visually and mobility impaired learner.

CHALLENGES OF VOICE-BASED LEARNING IN E-GOVERNMENT

Illiteracy and Lack of Awareness

In many democracies, government's targets for capacity building and e-service delivery have major implications for staff development, literacy of officers, members and the community at large. To deliver and access e-enabled voice-based learning materials will require a new level of competence and awareness with ICT on a huge scale.

To use voice-based system, users will need basic competencies and awareness in mobile and land phone usage. Government employees will need the skills to access the e-training services effectively, and voice-learning can also provides a performance support function. Many organizations for example have begun to provide e-learning on their websites to educate customers on their services. There are the complexities of some users having to develop the basic ICT skills to even begin to use voice-learning, and while there are products and programs relating to "learning to learn on a voice-enabled mobile phone", this may require a blended model with face-to-face sessions to prepare people for voice-learning.

High Costs of Voice-Learning Development

While voice-learning can appear to be the best option for specific learning requirements, costs of development can be prohibitive if provided through a service provider. One hour of bespoke voice-learning content from an external supplier can cost an average of £15,000, an amount that most government authorities can scarcely afford. A cost-effective alternative would be to develop materials and content internally and employ the services of an ICT administrator to manage the learning content that will be accessed through voice. This will serve as a remedy since most government authorities do not possess the required skills and knowledge to make it work effectively.

Resistance from Government Employees

There can also be resistance from government employees (the learners) as they are used to attending classroom sessions outside of their office station, which bring about some financial benefits. Such cultural expectations will need to change over time. Another level of resistance may arise from the perception of restrictions of mobile devices in terms of output and input capabilities. Mobile devices often have limited screen display sizes and limited capacity to support audio and video data, and also impose restriction on user input. Some learners may prefer to see the teacher face to face or view graphical information of what is taught. A lot of effort towards enabling mobile devices to access the web has been made (Alimadhi, 2002).

Since very society has different needs and priorities, a one size fit all model does not exist for e-Government and universal standard for e-Government readiness does not exist. Each society and government's readiness for e-Government will depend upon which objectives and specific sectors it chooses as priorities, as well as the resources available at a given point in time, which might depend on budgetary constraints, policies, etc. The necessary pre-conditions for e-Government depend upon a society's most important needs. For example, the level of infrastructure, legal framework and human capital needed for e-Government vary with the objectives being pursued.

Just like any government reform effort, political will is required to implement every e-Government project. Without the active political leadership, financial resources, inter-agency coordination, policy changes and human effort required to plan and implement e-Government will not be sustained (e-Gov, 2002). Political will exists when senior decision-makers have the resolve to exercise leadership in the face of opposition and setbacks.

Civil servants may resist e-Government projects, and may refuse to adopt new procedures. This problem may be more severe in developing countries where human resources may be less robust, the economy less stable and other job opportunities less plentiful.

SUMMARY AND RECOMMENDATION

In this chapter, we have proposes a voice-based e-Learning system as a variant of the m-Learning with particular relevance to the visually impaired learners. If citizens are deprived of expressing their viewpoints and have them represented in government, then individuals won't be able to exercise political powers that would help shape their community and country. Democratic government should provide an electoral law to support voice learning for persons who are physically challenged and are not able to participate in learning for reasons of inability to move from one place to another as a result of some forms of disability.

REFERENCES

Adaptive (2005). Adaptive and assistive technologies in e-learning. Retrieved February 20, 2009, from http://www.adcet.edu.au/StoredFile.aspx?id=1353&fn=adptve_assstv_techn_elearning.pdf

Aio (2008). *e-Learning in Local government: A briefing paper*. Retrieved February 10, 2009, from http://www.idea.gov.uk/idk/aio/1702668

Alimadhi, F. (2002, September). *Mobile Internet: Wireless access to Web-based interfaces of legacy simulations, Master of Science Thesis*. Amsterdam: University of Amsterdam, Faculty of Science, Informatic Institute, Section Computational Science

Ally, M. (2008). *e-Learning Solutions and Innovations*, Workshop Presented at the E-Learning Excellence in the Middle East 2008, Learning Excellence.

Anttiroiko, A. (2008). *An Effective E-Governance Framework: The Key to Enhanced E-Government Services*. Retrieved February 18, 2009, from http://www.uta.fi/laitokset/yhdt/artikkelit/um_ict4dev_anttiroiko_2008-5.doc

Azeta, A. A., Ayo, C. K., Atayero, A. A., & Ikhu-Omoregbe, N. A. (2008a November 18-20). Development of a Telephone-based e-Learning Portal, *1st International Conference on Mobile Computing, Wireless Communication, e-Health, M-Health and TeleMedicine* (FICMWiComTelHealth '08), Ladoke Akintola University of Technology, Ogbomosho, Nigeria.

Azeta, A. A., Ikhu-Omoregbe, N. A., Ayo, C. K., & Atayero, A. A. (2008b, June). "Development and Deployment of VoiceXML-Based Banking Applications," *Journal of Computer Science & Its Application*. [NCS]. *An International Journal of the Nigeria Computer Society*, *15*(1), 59–72.

Chin, C. C., Hock, G. T., & Veerappan, C. M. (2006). VoiceXML as Solution for Improving Web accessibility and Manipulation for e-Education. *School of Computing and IT, INTI College Malasia*. Retrieved July 2008, from, http://intisj.edu.my/INTISJ/InfoFor/StaffResearch/10.pdf

e-Gov (2002). Roadmap for E-Government in the Developing World", *10 Questions E-Government Leaders Should Ask Themselves,* The Working Group on E-Government (2002, April). *Government in the Developing World*. Retrieved February 20, 2009, fromhttp://www.pacificcouncil.org/pdfs/e-gov.paper.f.pdf

E-Learning Glossary, meaning of e-Learning (2008). *Cipherion Translation*. Retrieved February 25, 2009, from http://www.cipherion.com/glossaryelearn.php

eGovt (2005). *An Effective E-Governance Framework: The Key to Enhanced E-Government Services*. Retrieved 20th February 2009 fromhttp://www.cito.gov.jm/files/E-Gov%20Framework%20-%20JCS%20BizTech%20Forum%202005%20paper.pdf

Gallivan, P., Hong, Q., Jordan, L., Li, E., Mathew, G., Mulyani, Y., et al. (2002). VoiceXML Absentee System. In*Proceedings of MASPLAS'02*. The Mid-Atlantic Student Workshop on Programming Languages and Systems Pace University, USA.

Hasan, S. (2003). Introducing E-Government in Bangladesh: Problems and Prospects. *International Social Science Review*, 78.

Paul, D. (2003). Speech recognition for students with disabilities. *Nisbet, CALL Centre, University of Edinburgh* pp. 1 - 6. Retrieved January 18,2009, from http://callcentre.education.ed.ac.uk/downloads/speech_recognition/hitmesse2003.pdf

Qureshi, R. (2007). *Building a Telephony Web Application*. Retrieved August 15, 2008, from http://www.hunzatechnologies.com/telephony-web-tutorial/

Chapter 4
An Approach to Formal Specification of Component-Based Software

Tarek Zernadji
University of Batna, Algeria

Raida Elmansouri
University Mentouri Constantine, Algeria

Allaoua Chaoui
University Mentouri Constantine, Algeria

ABSTRACT

Current research on software reuse in Component Based Software Engineering (CBSE) covers a variety of fields, including component design, component specification, component composition, component-based framework. CBSE is quickly becoming a mainstream approach to software development and most researchers are hoping that it will be solutions to all the problems that led to software crisis. The software engineering techniques specific to this discipline, in phases such as modeling, verification or validation of component based software systems still insufficient and need more research efforts. ECATNets (Extended Concurrent Algebraic Term Nets) are frameworks for specification, modeling and validation of concurrent and distributed systems. They are characterized by their semantics defined in terms of rewriting logic. The objective of this article is to propose a formal specification of software components by using ECATNets formalism. The expected benefits of this work are: Offer a formal notation for describing the different features of concurrent and distributed software components; Defining a formal unambiguous semantic to describe behavior of the composed system.

INTRODUCTION

Component Based Development (CBD) is a new promising approach for building software applications. The central idea of this emerging approach is based on reuse of software building blocks to make entirely new systems by assembly (composition), and thus has the advantage of providing software systems in a shorter time with better quality.

DOI: 10.4018/978-1-61520-789-3.ch004

Building an application is thus seen, not as an integral and complete development (from scratch), but like an assembly of reusable pieces. In this field, technologies supporting the construction and assembly of components has reached a first level of maturity, in particular with the emergence of technological components standards such as EJB (Enterprise JavaBeans), CCM (Corba Component Model), or (D)COM ((Distributed) Component Object Model). The goal of component-based software engineering (CBSE) is to increase productivity, quality, and time-to-market in software development. The software engineering techniques specific to this field (CBSE), in phases such as modeling, verification or validation of components based applications still insufficient and need more research efforts. The heart of CBD is components. A software component is a contractually specified building block for software which can be readily deployed by third parties without understanding its internal structure. A component is a black box which is described by its interfaces throw which it can interact with other components in the system. The ultimate goal of Component-based Software Development (CBD) is third-party assembly. To achieve this, it is necessary to be able to specify components in such a way that we can reason about their construction and composition (Lau, A., Ornaghi, M., 2001). The specifications of components used in practical software development today are limited primarily to what we'll call syntactic specifications. This form of specification includes the specifications used with technologies such as COM, the Object Management Group's Common Object Request Broker Architecture (CORBA), and Sun's JavaBeans (Crnkovic, I., Larsson, M., 2002). The two first ones use IDLs while the third uses the Java programming language. However, syntactic specification does not provide information on the semantic of operations that define the component interfaces, which can help to better understand their behavior. Formal specification methods are good candidate to specify component software.

The objective of our work is to propose a formal approach for component based software modeling using ECATNets (Extended Concurrent Algebraic Term Nets). ECATNets are a kind of High-Level Algebraic Nets. They are proposed as a way for specification, modeling and validation of applications from the area of communication networks, computer designs and other complex systems (Bettaz, 1996). They are built around a combination of three formalisms. The two first formalisms constitute a net/data model, and are used for defining the syntax of the system, in other terms to capture its structure. The net model, which is a kind of advanced Petri net, is used to describe the process architecture of the system; the data model, which is an algebraic formalism, is used for specifying the data structures of the system. The third formalism, which is a rewriting logic, is used for defining the semantics of the system, or in other words to describe its behavior.

In this chapter we will try to explain how to produce a model of a component based software system using our notation based on ECATNets formalism. The model denotes the interconnection of behavioral specifications of connected software components. The elements, composing the whole system, can be for instance a travel agency system with its components: 'a coordinator component', 'book hotel', 'Book flight'. This example will serve to illustrate in this paper our modeling approach. The expected benefits of this work are: Offer a formal notation for describing the different features of concurrent and distributed software components; Defining a formal unambiguous semantic to describe behavior of the composed system; Allowing formal verification of some properties of the modeled systems helping to avoid composition mistakes leading to unexpected and often bizarre behavior.

The chapter is organized as follows. In Section 2, we review some basic concepts about ECATNets. In section 3, we present the notation proposed to specify formally a software component using ECATNets and how connections are made between the components. Section 4 shows an example illustrating our approach. Finally, conclusions and perspectives are presented.

ECATNETS

Petri nets are a graphical and mathematical modeling tool applicable to many systems. They are promising tool for describing and studying information processing systems that are characterized as being concurrent, asynchronous, distributed, parallel, nondeterministic, and/ or stochastic (TADO, 1989). As mentioned above, ECATNets (Bettaz, M., & Maouche, M., 1993), are a category of algebraic nets based on a safe combination of algebraic abstract types and high level Petri nets.

An ECATNets (Zeghib, N., Barkaoui, K., & Bettaz, M., 2006) is a pair ε = (Spec, N) where Spec= (Σ, E) is an algebraic specification of an abstract data types, and N is a Petri net in which places markings are multi-sets of Σ-terms. The graphical representation of generic net N is illustrated in Figure 1.

Places are marked with multi-sets of algebraic terms. Input arcs of each transition t, i.e. (p, t), are labelled by two inscriptions IC(p, t) (Input Conditions) and D(p, t) (Destroyed Tokens), output arcs of each transition t, i.e. (t, q), are labelled by CT(t, q) (Created Tokens), and finally each transition t is labelled by TC(t) (Transition Conditions). IC(p, t) specifies the enabling condition of the transition t, DT(p, t) specifies the tokens (a multi-set) which have to be removed from p when t is fired, CT(t, q) specifies the tokens which have to be added to q when t is fired. Finally, TC(t) represents a Boolean term which specifies an additional enabling condition for the transition t.

Figure 1. A generic ECATNet

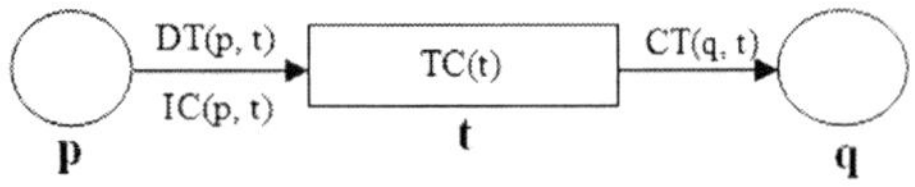

Transition firing and its conditions are formally expressed by rewrite rules. A rewrite rule is a structure of the form "'t: u → v if boolexp"'; where u and v are respectively the left and the right-hand sides of the rule, t is the transition associated with this rule and boolexp is a Boolean term. Precisely u and v are multi-sets of pairs of the form (p, [m]⊕), where p is a place of the net, [m]⊕ a multi-set of algebraic terms, and the multi-set union on these terms, when the terms are considered as singletons. The multi-set union on the pairs (p, [m]⊕) will be denoted by ⊗. $[x]_{\otimes}$ denotes the equivalence class of x (Boudiaf, N., & Chaoui, A., 2006).

The specifications of components used in practical software development today are limited primarily to what we will call syntactic specifications. This form of specification includes the specifications used with technologies such as COM, the Object Management Group's Common Object Request Broker Architecture (CORBA), and Sun's JavaBeans (Crnkovic, I., & Larsson, M., 2002).

MODELING WITH ECATNETS

An interface of a component can be defined as a specification of its access point. The clients access the services provided by the component using these points. If a component has multiple access points, where each one represents a different service offered by the component, then the component is expected to have multiple interfaces (Crnkovic, I., & Larsson, M., 2002). Most components are built on common concepts and have similar characteristics; Ignoring differences in technical details such as implementation language, component implementation restrictions, parameterization mechanisms, interface definition methodologies and self-documentation capabilities, we see that these technologies have essentially similar architectures and functionality (Cox, P. T., & Song, B., 2001). Each technology

Figure 2. Software component specification

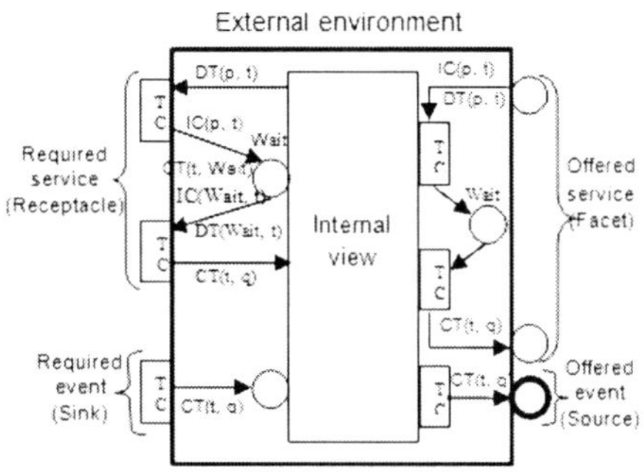

defines a component as a self-contained "black box"; it offers to and requires features from its interacting external world.

Formal Specification of Software Components Interfaces

In this section we present the formal specification of each feature in the software component, by using the net/data formalisms of ECATNets. Offered features (Facets) are considered as services needed by other components, those required (Receptacles) are essential services for the component to fulfill its functions and that are provided by other components. Interaction is represented by event-based communication and method invocations. Each component may send (events source) to and receive (events sink) from its external environment events.

Our conventional graphical notations describing the cited features are illustrated in the Figure 2 using ECATNets formalism. An essential characteristic of a component is explicit separation between the external and internal aspects of the entity being encapsulated to represent a component. In other words, a component has hidden interior and exposed interfaces (tojanović, 2005). In the following section we will explain each interface specification.

Figure 3. Required service specification

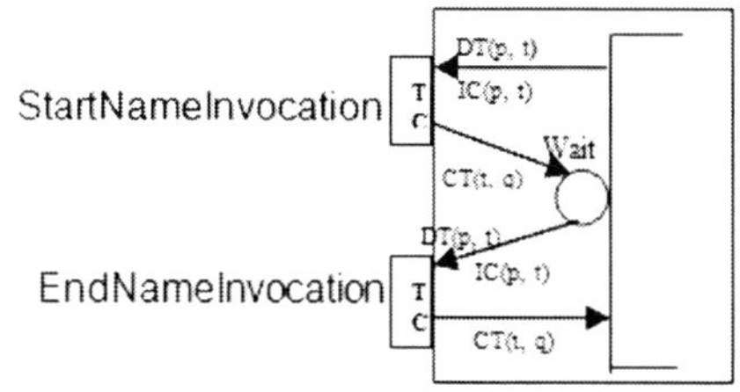

Required Service (Receptacle)

A required service models a synchronous unicast invocation method and is specified by two transitions (StartInvocation, EndInvocation) and a place (Wait) (Figure 3).

The transition StartNameInvocation (SNameInv) specifies the beginning of the invocation. The input arc models the contract representing preconditions that must be met by the internal component behavior to request the method. The name of the method is explicitly given in the name of the transition (example: StartExtractInvocation, Extract is the method name).

The output arc is connected to the "Wait" place, this later models the fact that the component is in blocked state and waiting for a response. That arc is labelled by CT (Created Token) multi-set term that indicates the state the component will reach.

The transition EndNameInvocation (ENameInv) specifies the ending of the invocation. Its input arc coming from the "Wait" place, models the contract representing conditions that would change the component state towards none blocked state. The output arc represents post-conditions that will be valid for the internal component behavior after the execution of the action modelled by the transition.

Offered Service (Facet)

An offered service is modelled by three places (NameRequest, NameResult, and Wait) and two transitions 'SName' and 'EName' (Name: is the

Figure 4. Offered service specification

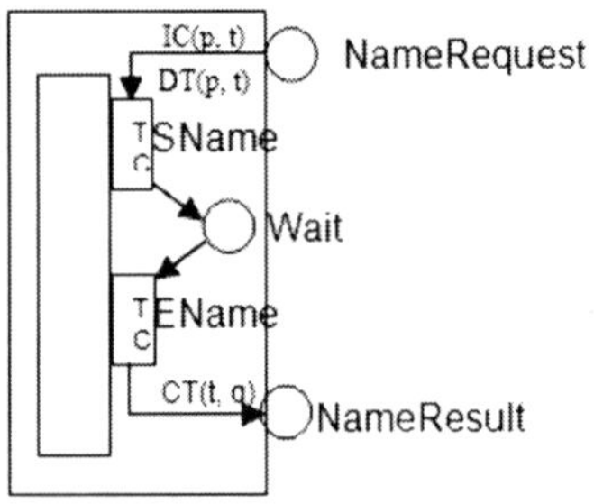

name given to the action associated to the transition) (Figure 4).

The "NameRequest" place models received invocations from surrounding components, thus, a provided service may be requested by multiple components simultaneously. The firing of the transition 'SName' that depends on Input Condition (IC) and Transition Condition (TC) represents the execution of the associated method. The "NameResult" place models the returned service as a result of the fired transition. With the place "Wait" we give a general form to the facet in such a way it models subsequent invocations in a hierarchical composition. That means, where the invoked component makes a call for another service in other component to return the result by firing of 'EName' transition to the one requesting the service. We can omit the use of the place 'Wait' in the model since it is not always necessary.

Offered Event

An offered event describes an event that may be emitted by a component. This event can be of interest to many other components, then, it can be forwarded to a set of receivers.

We modelled offered event by a transition (NameSource) and a place that we call "signal place", to distinguish between method invocation and event-based communication, and give a significant way to represent the sending event (Figure 5).

Figure 5. Offered event

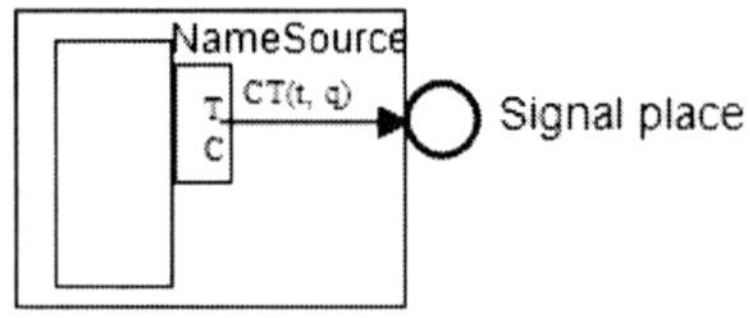

The firing of the NameSource transition will result in CT (Created Token) deposited in 'signal place', to be consumed by the related sink transition.

Required Event

A required event is an event that the component is willing to receive. We have conserved in required event the same graphical notation used to model an event source (Figure 6).

The transition is interfaced to receive the incoming event source. The fact that a transition is fired, models a received event.

Connections Specification

A composition can be obtained between components by connecting each specified feature to another, the offered services with required services and offered events with those required, so we have at the end an assembly of components.

Event Source /Sink Connection Specification

Events source may be connected to any number of events sink, thus modeling the multicast, events sink can also be connected by the same way.

Figure 6. Required event

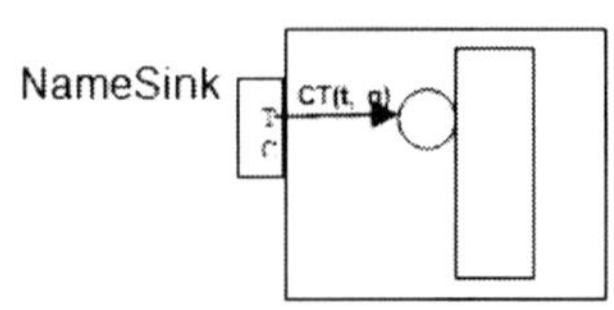

The connection is realized simply by joining the place of the component "A" with "NameSink" transition of the component "B" respecting ECATNets formalism.

The firing of "NameSink" transition depends on the presence of a token CT in the output place of "NameSource" transition. We call this place a "Signal place", to illustrate the event-based communication.

Offered/Requested Services Connection Specification

The connection specification between offered and requested services that model the unicast invocation methods is given by reuse of the client /server pattern defined in (Ramamoorthy, C. V., Ho, G. S., 1980).

The connection is realized by to arcs:

- The first is an output arc from the "SNameInv" transition of component "B" to "NameRequest" place of component "A".
- The second is an output arc from the "NameResult" place of component "A" to "ENameInv" transition of component "B".

The "SNameInv" transition of component "B" is connected to the "NameRequest" place of component "A" by an output arc. Its firing represents the invocation of the requested service and adds CT to the "NameRequest" place, which enabled the "Name" transition in component "A". In other hand, "SNameInv" transition of component "B" deposit a second CT in the "Wait" place which changes the component state. After firing of "Name" transition, tokens are created in the "NameResult" place and thus the result of the service is ready to be received. "ENameInv" transition is now enabled; its firing delivers the result to the component and changes it from waiting state to none blocked state.

EXAMPLE

To illustrate our approach for modeling formally component-based software, we present a known example from the field of Business Process (Havey, M., 2005) that illustrates a distributed application. The process for this application is the following: (1) Get the customer's itinerary. (2) Book a flight with the airline, a room with the hotel, and a car with the car rental agency. These bookings can be made in parallel. We have omitted booking a car in our model for simplicity. (3) If all the bookings succeed, get payment from the customer and send the customer a confirmation. (4) If at least one booking fails, cancel the successful bookings and report the problem to the customer. We have identified three components in this application, as illustrated in (Figure 7) that communicate within the Web. The client submits its request via the travel agency's Web application that will invoke the Coordinator component. This later invokes tow services in parallel from the 'BookHotel' and 'BookFlight' components of the airline and book hotel agency. The interfaces that expose each component should be identified from, for example an IDL specification, Java language specification, or even in a natural language or UML components diagram.

Our approach allows formal verification of behavior of the composed system thanks to rewriting logic Framework. Rewrite rules of ECATNet theory permits describing the states changes of the system and capturing its dynamic. We give the rewrite rules describing the behavior of the system that could be integrated in a Maude language system module specification for verification.

```
Tc1: If (head(Id, IdHot) =
head(Id,AckH))
Tc2: If (Id = head(Id, AckH))
Tc3: If (head(Id, IdVol) =
head(Id,AckV))
Tc4: If (Id = head(Id, AckV))
```

Figure 7. Formal behavioural specification of components assembly

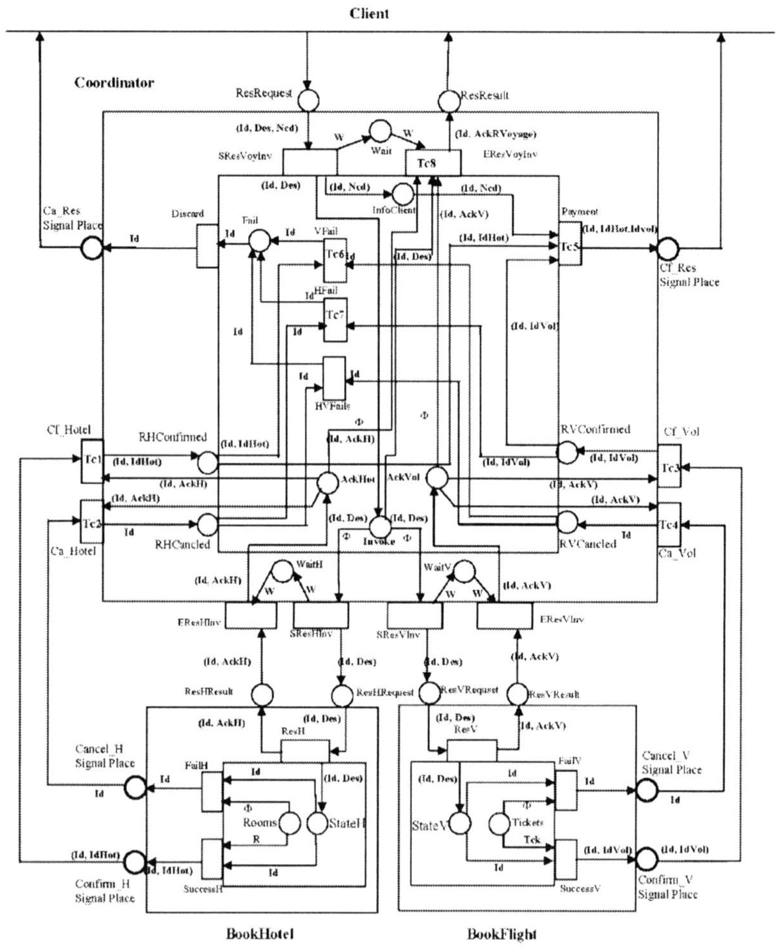

Tc5: If (head(Id, IdHot) = head(Id, IdVol) and head (Id, IdHot) = head(Id, Ncd))
Tc6: If (Id= head(Id, IdHot))
Tc7: If (Id= head(Id, IdVol))
Tc8: If (head(Id, AckV) = head(Id, AckHl) and head (Id, AckV) = head(Id, Des))
head (param1,param2): a function that return the first parameter.
Rewrite rules:
[SResVoyInv]:(ResRequest,<Id,Des ,Ncd>)→ (InfoClient,<Id, Ncd>) ⊗ (Invoke,<Id, Des>)
[EResVoyInv]:(AckHot,<Id,AckH>)⊗(AckVol,<Id,AckV>)⊗(Invoke,<Id,Des>)→ (ResResult,<Id,AckRVoyage>)⊗ (AckHot,<Id, AckH>) ⊗ (AckVol,<Id, AckV>) if [(head(Id, AckV) = head(Id, AckHl) and head (Id, AckV) = head(Id, Des))] → true.
[Discard]: (Fail, Id)→ (Ca_Res, Id)
[Payement]:(InfoClient,<Id,Ncd>)⊗(RVConfirmed,<Id,IdVol>) ⊗(RHConfirmed,<Id,IdHot>) → (Cf_Res,<Id, IdHot, IdVol>) if [(head(Id, IdHot) = head(Id, IdVol) and head (Id, IdHot) = head(Id, Ncd))] → true.
[VFail]:(RHConfirmed,<Id, IdHot>)

```
⊗(RVCanceled, Id) →
 (Fail, Id) if [(Id= head(Id, Id-
Hot))] → true.
[HFail]:(RVConfirmed,<Id,IdVol>)
⊗(RHCanceled, Id) → (Fail, Id) if
[(Id= head(Id, IdVol))] → true.
[HVFail]:(RVCanceled,Id)
⊗(RHCanceled,Id) → (Fail, Id)
[Cf_Hotel]:(AckHot,<Id,AckH>)
⊗(Confirm_H,<Id, IdHot>) →
(RHConfirmed,<Id,IdHot>)
if [(head(Id, IdHot) = head(Id,
AckH))] → true.
[Ca_Hotel]:(AckHot,<Id,AckH>)
⊗(Cancel_H, Id) → (RHCancled, Id)
if [(Id = head(Id, AckH))] → true.
[Cf_Vol]: (AckVol,<Id, AckV>)
⊗(Confirm_V,<Id, IdVol>) →
(RVConfirmed,<Id, IdVol>)
if [(head(Id, IdVol) =
head(Id,AckV))]
[Ca_Vol]: (AckVol,<Id, AckV>)
⊗(Confirm_V,<Id, IdVol>) → (RVCan-
celed, Id)
 if (Id = head(Id, AckV))
[SResVInv]:(Invoke,Φ)→ (WaitV,W)⊗
(ResVRequest,<Id, Des>)
[SResHInv]:(Invoke,Φ)→ (WaitH,W)⊗
(ResHRequest,<Id, Des>)
[EResVInv]:(WaitV,W)⊗
(ResVResult,<Id, AckV>) →
(AckVol,<Id, AckV>)
[EResHInv]:(WaitV,W)⊗
(ResHResult,<Id, AckH>) →
(AckHot,<Id, AckH>)
[ResV]:(ResVRequest,<Id,Des>)→
(ResVResult,<Id, AckV>) ⊗
(StateV,<Id, Des>)
[FailV]:(StateV, Id)⊗ (Tickets, ϕ) →
(Cancel_V, Id)
[SuccessV]:(StateV,Id)⊗(Tickets,Tck)
→ (Confirm_V, <Id, IdVol>)
[ResH]:(ResHRequest,<Id,Des>)→
(ResHResult,<Id, AckH>) ⊗
(StateH,<Id, Des>)
[FailH]: (StateH, Id)⊗ (Rooms, ϕ) →
(Cancel_H, Id)
[SuccessH]:(StateH,Id)⊗(Rooms, R) →
(Confirm_H, <Id, IdHotl>)
```

CONCLUSION

In this paper we proposed a way for modeling component based software, which is realized in terms of a formal specification of individual component features and their connections. We use for this end, ECATNets formalism that consists of a powerful combination of high level Petri nets and rewriting logic. This logic gives a clean formal semantic and allows describing clearly the behavior of the whole system, and makes it subject to meaningful formal analysis for verification. For future work, we plan to build a software graphical tool for modeling component based software with ECATNets using the proposed notation. The generated models will be exported to an existing tool that generates rewrite rules in Maude language for formal verification of the components assembly

REFERENCES

Bettaz, M., & Maouche, M. (1993). How to specify non determinism and true concurrency with algebraic term nets. *Lecture Notes in Computer Science*, *655*, 164–180.

Bettaz, M. D. (1996). Performance comparison of high level algebraic nets distributed simulation protocols. *Winter Simulation Conference*.

Cox, P. T., & Song, B. (2001). A Formal Model for Component-Based Software. *IEEE 2001 Symposium on Human Centric Computing Languages and Environments (HCC'01)*.

Crnkovic, I., & Larsson, M. (2002). *Building Reliable Component-based Software Systems*. London: Artech House.

Havey, M. (2005). *Essential Business Process Modeling*. Newton, NJ: O'Reilly.

Lau, A., & Ornaghi, M. (2001). *A Formal Approach to Software Component Specification*. Montreal, Canada: OOPSLA Workshop.

Ramamoorthy, C. V., & Ho, G. S. (1980). Performance Evaluation of Asynchronous Concurrent systems Using Petri Nets. *IEEE Transactions on Software Engineering*, 440–449. doi:10.1109/TSE.1980.230492

TADO. M. (1989). Petri Nets: Proprieties, analysis and applications. In *Proceedings of the IEEE, 77*(4).

Tojanović, Z. (2005). *A Method for Component-Based and Service-Oriented Software Systems Engineering", Doctoral Dissertation, Delft University of Technology, The Netherlands 2005.* The Netherlands: Doctoral Dissertation, Delft University of Technology.

Zeghib, N., Barkaoui, K., & Bettaz, M. (2006). Contextual ECATNets Semantics. *IEEE*, 36-943.

Chapter 5
A Methodology for the Development of Computer Ontologies Based Extractor Information

Hacene Belhadef
Mentouri University of Constantine, Algeria

Naouel Ouafek
Mentouri University of Constantine, Algeria

Kholladi Mohamed-Khireddine
Mentouri University of Constantine, Algeria

ABSTRACT

In this chapter we propose a new methodology for ontology building, which is based on a set of mapping rules from a conceptual schema (Entity-Relationship) and its corresponding logical model (relational model) toward a conceptual ontology. The proposed methodology consists of three big steps, which are, the Transformation (mapping), the Formalization and the Codification. The crucial step in the building process of this methodology, is the transformation, this last is based on an automatic extraction of information for a conceptual model ER (such as entities, relationship, properties and cardinalities). The data stored in the database (the schema extension) are extracted and used to create instances of the ontology. At the end of this stage we will have a complete conceptual ontology can be used in different applications. The objective behind this work has several aims, which can be exploited in many fields, among others, search and retrieval of relevant terms in a domain of discourse, our methodology minimizes the manual work and gives a good result in an optimal time, the second is to facilitate the migration of an information system based on a classical approach (entity-relationships and relational model) towards another solution based on an ontological approach, while retaining the principle of operation of the first system.

DOI: 10.4018/978-1-61520-789-3.ch005

INTRODUCTION

Most methodologies of ontology construction are based on two phases, the ontologization and the operationalization. Ontologization is to build a conceptual ontology, this last will provide a detailed description of real perceived, that is free or as free as possible, in this case the designer must take into consideration the different sources of knowledge (glossaries of terms, other ontologies, texts, interviews with experts …). The operationalization is to encode the conceptual ontology obtained using an operational language of representation of knowledge (with a mechanism inference).

Currently, most work are based on the acquisition of knowledge from one or several corpus of text, they are based on a linguistic analysis (lexical and syntax) on specific tools as the tool SYNTEXUPERY created by Didier. (Bourigault D., 2002) or FASTR (Jacquemin C., 1997) and tools to extract the grammatical relations as Shallow parser RASP[1] (Briscoe T., 2002). These methods minimize manual work for the extraction of terms and relationships, but in reality, there are several sources of data, not only texts collected to build a corpus, but as in the geographical domain, there are images, spatial data, plans, maps etc. For this reason, it is necessary to develop methods and techniques that reduce the effort needed for the process of acquiring knowledge; this is the objective of the ontology learning. Maedche and Staab (Maedche A., 2001) distinguish different ontology learning which focus on the type of input used for learning, ie, ontology learning from text, dictionary, basic knowledge, schema of semi-structured schema and from database schema (Xu Z., 2004).

Almost 99.9% of businesses using databases, where it comes our ideas, which are based on the reuse of these databases for the creation of ontology, meaning we will replace the database of the company by ontology which gives us a unifying framework and provides metadata or annotations to improve communication between humans and also between organizations. In additionally, the ontology provides:

- A basic conceptual structure from which it is possible to develop knowledge-based systems those are shareable and reusable.
- Interoperability between sources of information and knowledge.
- A clear distinction between "ontology" and "knowledge base" should be done from their roles; ontology provides a system of concepts that are used to build a knowledge base and therefore ontology can be considered as a Meta system in a traditional knowledge base.

METHODOLOGIES FOR THE CONSTRUCTION OF ONTOLOGIES: STATE OF THE ART

Until 1996, the first ontologies have been developed without following methods or methodologies approved. In recent years, many methods have been created for the development of ontologies; in this paragraph we are going to cite some of them without going into details of each one.

The Method "TOVE"

This method is based on the experience obtained by the development of ontology for the project TOVE (TOrento Virtual Enterprise), the ontology is built manually from the business scenarios for which it will be used. The various steps of this method remains without detailed descriptions, moreover it is dedicated to the specification of ontologies for enterprise (Gruninger M., 1995).

Methontology

Developed by the team LAI of the Polytechnic University of Madrid. This methodology includes the construction of ontologies in a process of project management including the steps:

- **Specifications:** determining the future use of the ontology;
- **Conceptualization:** to obtain a model of field in the level of knowledge;
- **Formalisation:** transformation of the conceptual model to a formal model;
- **Implementation:** constructing a operational model used by a computer;
- **Maintenance:** updating the ontology if necessary.

And support activities (integration, evaluation, documentation).

Methontology allows the characterization of ontologies in the level of knowledge and emphasizes the need to work from intermediate structures of knowledge during the conceptualization. All these structures, designed to obtain abundant informal descriptions of the objects to represent them in the KBS, are supposed to identify the closest conceptualization covered by the ontology. Rest we still do not know precisely how to get the contents of these structures, in particular taxonomies of concepts (Fernandez M., 1997; Isaac A., 2005).

KACTUS (MODELING KNOWLEDGE ABOUT TECHNICAL COMPLEX SYSTEMS FOR MULTIPLE USE)

Schreiber and al. her principle is the reuse of existing ontologies and propose mechanisms to permit this reuse[14].

ARCHONTE (ARCHitecture for ONTological Elaborating) proposed by B. Bachimont to build ontologies based on the semantic differential. The construction of an ontology by ARCHONTE, is composed in three steps:

1. Choose the relevant terms of the domain and normalize their senses and then justify the place of each concept in the ontological hierarchy; specifying the relationship of similarities and differences that each concept has with his brothers and his father concept; the principles differentials:
   - The principle of community with the father;
   - The principle of difference with the father;
   - The principle of difference with the brothers;
   - The principle of community with the brothers.
2. Formalize knowledge, which means, for example, to add properties to concepts, axioms, coerce the domain of a relationship.
3. The operationalization in a representation language of knowledge. (Baneyx A., 2007)

OntoSpec: Developed by the team IC of LARIA of Amiens based on the concept of axis semantic grouping sub concepts in a concept according to the characteristics involved in defining their differentiation. (Kassel G., 2002)

TERMINAE[2]: This methodology was developed in the laboratory; it is a component of the platform RFIEC[3]. It is based on the use of tools of automatic processing of natural language analyzing the terms of texts and lexical relationships of a corpus of reference. (Aussenac-Gilles N., 2000)

2.7 KAON[4]: KArlsruhe ONtology is a software platform includes a set of modules: the creation, storage, refining, exploitation, maintenance. The module textToOnto can extract the terms of statistically and extraction of relations is based on lexical syntactic patterns, or a calculation of proximity (depending on the user). (Bozsak E. et al., 2002)

Our Methodology

As we have explained above, and as shown in Figure 1, our methodology consists of three main steps, it distinguishes itself compared with the other by the crucial step in the construction process, which is the transformation, c That is our contribution to create this new methodology, which will undoubtedly help people to work on conventional systems designed by models least semantically rich and implemented by classical models to migrate towards other solutions that are more powerful and rich, expressed by the notion of ontology, without need to know the ontological model and this is done by ensuring transparency between the user and the ontological system, while giving the impression that the user is working on its original system without it being capable, or connoisseur of this new system. The majority of methodologies of ontologies construction are based on a manual retrieval of terms (constitution of a body of text), unlike our case, extraction is done automatically by the extraction module.

Extraction Module

It is based on a tool for automatic extraction of terms and concepts for the construction of a future conceptual ontology. The extractor receives as input the conceptual model ER, its relational database schemata and all tables which constitute the database and produces as output: a set of concepts, a set of relations, a hierarchy of concepts and a set of instances (see Figure 1). The automatic extractor is based on a set of mapping rules; we proposed three types of rules, depending on the type of list to be generating, the first one to generate the list of concepts, the second to generate the list of relations, and the last one to generate the list of instances.

Our extractor can play three roles, depending on the context in which is used, the first role is to make a complete migration of the database to an application ontology, in this case, the extractor generates a list of instances, to be represented in the same file resulting from the phase of formalization. Usually we find this case, where there is a tendency to migrate to a semantic web application, which requires an implementation based on an ontology.

The second role appears in the case where the BD belongs to a corpus, the transformative tool enables the user of the ontology to obtain automatically information from the DB, which minimizes the manual work of extraction of relevant terms of domain.

The third role is used, if one wants to make an annotation on the database "deep annotation" (Volz R., 2006), in this case, it is not interested in data, but much more by the structure of the DB(relational schema) and entities of the correspondent E-A Model.in this case, the extractor generates only a list of concepts, the list of relations, and the hierarchy of concepts, this is called ontology conceptual (Belhadef H., 2008).

The table below, shows an example on the mapping rules, and for more details the remainder of this chapter is referred to our previous paper (Belhadef H., 2008) and are seen as the core of our methodology.

Figure 1. Different phases of the proposed methodology

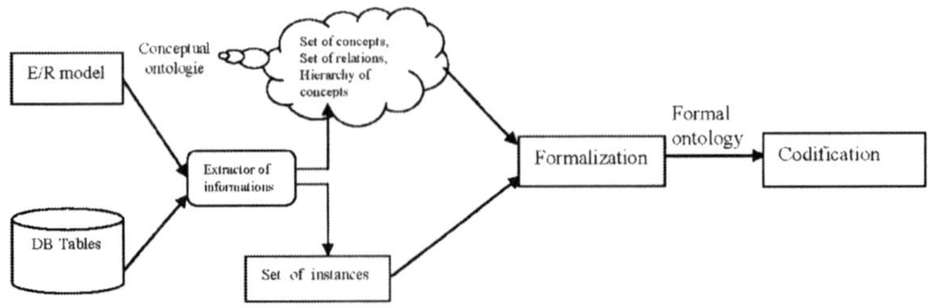

Table 1. Mapping rules

Conceptual model ER	Au niveau de l'ontologie conceptuel Conceptual ontology
Pour toute entité E Î EsFor each entity E ∈ Es	- E sera un conceptE will be a concept - Ajouter une ligne dans la liste avec l'identifiant E comme nouveau conceptAdd a line in the list with the ID (identifier) of E as a new concept
Pour tout attribut A Î As / atts(E) = [..., A:D,...] For each attribute: A ∈As / atts(E) = [..., A: D...]	- A sera une propriété du concept EA will be a property of the concept E - Mettre à jour la colonne d'attribut du concept qui porte comme nom l'identifiant E par la propriété EA avec D le domaine du AUpdate the column "list-of-attributes" of the concept that carries the ID of E as a name, by property E-A with D is the Domain of A NB On rajoute l'identifiant E au nom de propriété puisque au niveau de l'ontologie une propriété ne peut pas être utilisé par deux conceptsNB: add the ID of E into as a prefix in the name of property, because in the ontology, a property cannot be used by two concepts.
Pour tout couple E1, E2 Î Es / E1 isas E2For each couple: E1, E2 ∈ Es / E1 isas E2	- Le concept E1 sera un sous-concept du concept E2The concept E1 will be a sub-concept of the concept E2 - Mettre à jour la colonne sous-concept du concept qui porte comme nom l'identifiant E2 par l'identifiant E1Update the column "sub-concept" of concept that carries as name the ID of E2 by the ID of E1 NB Cette colonne nous sert par la suite à créer la représentation hiérarchique de l'ontologie NB: This column is used thereafter to create a hierarchical representation of ontology
Pour toute E1, E2, ..., Ei Î Es / Ei isas E2For each entity: E1, E2,..., Ei ∈ Es / Ei isas E2	- Ajouter pour toute entité Ei une ligne dans la liste et dans la colonne liste d'attributs ajouter tous les attributs du E avec bien sur le nom Ei - Aj avec AjÎ As / atts(E) = [..., Aj:D,...]Add to each Ei a line in the list - and in the column "list-of-attributes", add all the attributes of E with the name Ei-Aj where Aj∈ As / atts(E) = [..., Aj:D,...]

Formalization and Codification

Steps of formalization and codification are quasi-automatic compared the first step, which is bluntly automatic, using "Protégé"[5] as the ontologies editor most used, which was developed at the department of medicine at the Stanford University, which has tools ready to be used for the formalization and codification. The formalisation allows the introduction of logical axioms that define the behaviour of individuals who are extensions of concepts (Baneyx A., 2007). We used the description logic which gives a formal representation of ontology. Which consists of two parts the first one is the terminology language (TBOX) dedicated to the description of concepts and relationships, and assertionnal language (ABOX) dedicated to the description of instances. The step of codification allows a representation of the ontology in a formal language such as language OWL capable to use inferences mechanisms. The advantage of Protégé that it allows us to codify the ontology in a large set of formal language as RDF, OWL-Lite, OWL-DL, OWL- Full according to the needs of future users of the ontology (human agent, or software agent).

Protégé also allows us to invoke a reasoner as Racer (a plugin used by protege) to automatically calculate the ranking of the hierarchy of concepts, and also to verify the logical consistency of ontology. The inferred hierarchy produces a novel set of relation between concepts which enriches the semantic of the ontology.

Sample Application

The equip research "Vision and computer graphics" of LIRE Laboratory, Computer sciences department of the university Mentouri of Constantine, Algeria had launched a project to develop a GIS for the management of the electricity network of SENALGAZ company.

The Figure 2 shows an extract of the ER model designed for the proposed application, we have applied our method on this excerpt, to show how our tool, then the validation of results.

Figure 2. Extract from standard ER

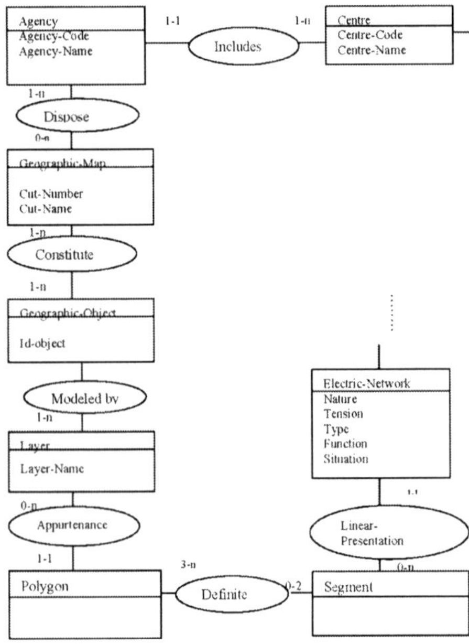

Our extractor tool receives as an input the, ER model and all tables that constitutes the correspondent DB and will generate the different list of concepts (see Figure 3), of relationships, and of instance if necessary.

In addition to information displayed on the ER model of Figure 2, these are the roles of associations which are defined as:

Figure 3.

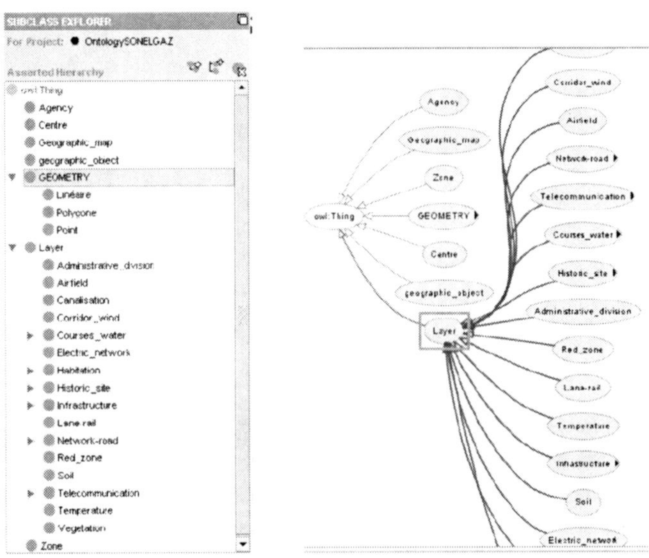

(a) (b)

Table 2. List of concepts

Concepts	Properties	Sub-concept
Zone	Zone-Code, Zone-Name	/
Centre	Centre-Code, Centre-Name	/
Agency	Agency-Code, Agency-Name	/
Geographic-Map	Cut-Number, Cut-Name	/
Geographic-Object	Id-object	/
Layer	Layer-Name	/
Polygon		/
Segment		/
Electric network	Nature, Tension, Type, Function	/
…	………………..	

- **Regroup** (includes: Zone, is-included-in: Centre)
- **Includes** (includes: Centre, compose: Agency)
- **Dispose** (dispose: Agency, component-in: Geographic-Map)
- **Constitute** (constituted-by: Geographic-Map, constitute: Geographic-Object)
- **Modeled-by** (modeled-by: Geographic-Object Models: Layer)
- **Appurtenance** (belongs-in: Layer, contains: Polygon)

These roles will be used to express the relationship and the inverse relationship in the ontology. The extractor applies different rules defined in (Belhadef H., 2008) to receive as results a conceptual ontology defined in the form of a set of tables presented below.

A system developed with this ontology is semantically rich because in the ontological level we reused associations defined in the ER model to link the relevant concepts, by against in the old systems based on Databases, these associations will be lost at the phase of transforming from the MCD to MDP.

In this chapter, we focused on the migration module which differs our methodology by providing the other; it is the subject of our contribution to design a new methodology for construction of ontology. As we have said previously that our methodology is based on the step of transformation, the other two steps of formalization and codification are performed using the software Protégé2000, the concepts are formalized in Description Logic and codification of the ontology is expressed through OWL.

CONCLUSION

In this chapter, we have proposed a new methodology for building an ontology from a conceptual schema and its logical schema, this methodology is based on a set of mapping rules that apply on these two schemas for to produce a conceptual ontology. The conceptual schema of entry (idem logical schema) is expressed by the conceptual model Entity-Relationship (respectively, the relational model).

Table 3. List of relations

Relation	Concept predecessor	Concept successor	Cardinality-relation	Relation inverse	Cardinality- inverse-relation
includes	Zone	Centre	1-n	Is-included-in	1-1
comport	Centre	Agency	1-n	compose	1-1
dispose	Agency	Geographic-Map	1-n	component-in	0-n
modeled-by	Geographic-Object	Layer	1-1	Models	1-n
belongs-in	Layer	Polygon	0-n	contains	1-1

The proposed methodology consists of three main steps, which are the transformation (mapping), the formalization and codification. The critical step in the process of this methodology is the transformation which has, as goal the automatic extraction of information (such as entities, relations, properties, cardinalities,..) contained in the conceptual schema (E-R) and the corresponding relational schema, data stored in the database from the relational model can also be used to create instances of the ontology.

The idea of the transformation proposed in this chapter, may have several objectives and can be exploited in many fields, among others, minimizing manual work for the extraction of terms from a domain of discourse, the second is to facilitate the migration of a domain (application), based on a traditional approach as the conceptual model (Entity-Relationship) to another solution based on an ontological approach, while retaining the characteristics of the first domain and taking advantage of the benefits of the new approach.

The real goal of this work is not limited to developing a simple methodology for the construction of ontology, but to extend it to other models semantically rich, as the MADS model, representing the spatio-temporal data multi-scale (MADS is a model Entity-Relationship extended to spatio-temporal data), the second objective of this work is to exploit the ontology produced by the mapping process, by using mechanisms of deduction and intrrogation, while creating graphical user interfaces to facilitate the posting of results on the web.

REFERENCES

Aussenac-Gilles, N., Biébow, B., & Szulman, S. (2000). *Modélisation du domaine par une méthode fondée sur l'analyse de corpus.* Actes de la conférence IC'2000, Journées Francophones d'Ingénieurie des connaissances, pp. 93-103.

Bachimont, B. (2000). Engagement sémantique et engagement ontologique: conception et réalisation d'ontologies en ingénierie des connaissances. In R. Teulier, J. Charlet & P. Tchounikine (eds.), *Coordinateurs, Ingénierie des connaissances*, chapitre 19. Paris: L'Harmattan.

Baneyx, A. (2007). *Construire une ontologie de pneumologie*. Thèse de doctorat, Université Paris6 page 61; 85. Février.

Belhadef, H., Ouafek, N., & Kholladi, M. K. (2008). *A Set of Mapping Rules E/R and Relational Schema Database towards an Ontology*. First IEEE International Conference on the Applications of Digital Information and Web Technologies (ICADIWT 2008). Retrieved from http://ieeexplore.ieee.org/xpl/freeabs_all.jsp?arnumber=4664361

Bourigault, D. (2002). *Upery: un outil d'analyse distributionnelle étendue pour la construction d'ontologies à partir de corpus. Actes de la 9ème conférence annuelle sur le Traitement Automatique des Langues* (pp. 75–84). TALN.

Bozsak, E., et al. (2002)KAON - Towards a large scale Semantic Web. In Proceedings *of the ThirdInternational Conference on E-Commerce and Web Technologies (ECWeb)*, Springer-Verlag LNCS, pages 304–313.2002.

Briscoe, T., & Carroll, J. (2002). *Robust accurate statistical annotation of general tex*. In LREC.

Fernandez, M., Gómez-Pérez, A, & Juristo, N. (1997). *Methontology: from ontological art towards ontological engineering*, Actes de AAAI, 1997.

Gruninger, M., & Fox, M. (1995). The logic of enterprise modelling . In Brown, J., & O'Sullivan, D. (Eds.), *Reengineering the Enterprise* (pp. 83–98). Chapman and Hall.

Isaac, A. (2005, December). *Conception et utilisation d'ontologies pour l'indexation de documents audiovisuels*. Thèse de doctorat, l'université paris iv – Sorbonne, page 131.

Jacquemin, C., Klavans, J. L., & Tzoukermann, E. (1997). *ACL-EACL'97*. Expansion of Multi-Word Terms for Indexing and Retrieval Using Morphology and Syntax.

Kassel, G. (2002)Ontospec: une méthode de spécification semi-formelle d'ontologies. In *13e journées francophones d'Ingénierie des Connaissances (IC)*, Rouen, France. pp. 75–87.

Maedche, A., & Staab, S. (2001). Ontology Learning for the Semantic Web. *IEEE Intelligent Systems*, *2001*, 1–16.

Schreiber, G., Wielinga, B., & Jansweijer, W. (1995). The kactus view of the 'o' word. *IJCAI'1995, Workshop on Basic Ontological Issues in Knowledge*.

Volz, R., Handschuh, S., Staab, S., Stojanovic, L., & Stojanovic, N. (2003). *Unveiling the hidden bride: deep annotation for mapping and migrating legacy data to the Semantic Web* (pp. 187–206). Elsevier BV.

Xu, Z., Cao, X., Dong, Y., & Su, W. (2004). Formal Approach and Automated Tool for Translating ER Schemata into OWL Ontologies . In *Advances in Knowledge Discovery and Data Mining* (pp. 464–475). Berlin, Heidelberg: Springer-Verlag.

Chapter 6
An Intelligent Framework for Usable Speech-Enabled E-Health System

Oyelami Olufemi Moses
Covenant University, Nigeria

Uwadia Charles Onuwa
University of Lagos, Nigeria

Akinwale Adio Taofeek
University of Lagos, Nigeria

ABSTRACT

People search websites for health information for self-care, but the information provided by these e-health portals are delivered in text form and this does not cater for the needs of the visually impaired, the blind, the low-literate and those that are not computer literate. Also, existing speech-based disease screening initiatives lack reasoning capability to make them attain the level of an expert system. This work presents an intelligent framework for usable speech-enabled e-health system that provides speech-based health information to cater for the needs of those not catered for in graphical user interface. It also introduces rule-based reasoning technique into speech-based disease screening systems. A prototype application was developed to provide health information on malaria fever, yellow fever, typhoid fever and lassa fever, and also allows the caller to diagnose his kind of fever. This will enable the visually impaired, the blind, the low-literate and the computer illiterate access to the same health information available through the graphical user interface and offer a reasoning-induced speech-based disease diagnosis.

INTRODUCTION

World Health Organization (WHO) 2000 report defines a health system to include *all the activities whose primary purpose is to promote, restore or maintain health. It* embraces all the goods and services designed to promote health, including preventive, curative and palliative interventions, whether directed to individuals or to population (WHO, 2000).

According to the WHO report 2007, Africa has the highest verified events of potential in-

DOI: 10.4018/978-1-61520-789-3.ch006

ternational public health concern (WHO, 2007). Imagine four African countries without any living soul-Botswana, Namibia, Lesotho and Swaziland-all because of deaths to preventable, treatable and manageable diseases. Today, the public health security of all countries depends on the capacity of each to act effectively and contribute to the security of all. The world is rapidly changing and nothing today moves faster than information. This makes the sharing of essential health information one of the most feasible routes to global public health security (Masimba, 2007).

Currently, the doctor per patient ratio in Africa is appalling. For example, the Democratic Republic of Congo (DRC), with a population of 57 million (roughly equivalent to the populations of the United Kingdom, France and Italy), has only 5,827 doctors compared with France's 203,000, Italy's 241,000 and the UK's 160,000. Cuba with a population of about 11 million, has roughly the same population as Malawi, Zambia or Zimbabwe. But Cuba has 66,567 doctors compared with Malawi's 266, Zambia's 1,264 and Zimbabwe's 2,086. Not surprisingly, Cuba has roughly the same life expectancy (77 years) as developed countries while the average life expectancy for these African countries is 37 to 40 years (WHO, 2007). Nigeria has an estimated population of 140 million and the ratio of doctors to the population is about 1 to 3,333 (Florence et al., 2007). In Nigeria, people die of minor illnesses that could have been prevented with simple medications and healthy lifestyles (Acho, 2005). The situation is not peculiar to Nigeria but typical of developing nations.

However, in the advanced societies and to a certain level in the developed countries, life expectancy has been increasing. But the increase according to research is noticed more in the better-educated groups (Baker et al., 2007). The level of illiteracy in the developing nations and particularly in Africa is terribly high to the extent that Sub-Saharan Africa accounted for about one in five of the world's 774 million illiterates in 1995-2004 ("EFA Global", 2008) and not being able to read does not just make it harder to navigate each day. Low literacy impairs people's ability to obtain critical information about their health and can dramatically shorten their lives ("Low Literacy", 2008).

The use of Information and Communication Technology (ICT) is however, steadily growing in Africa and other developing countries of the world and more and more people are taking advantage of the benefits it brings. The number of mobile phone users in Africa continues to rise steeply, making the continent an alluring target for both network operators and handset manufacturers, as well as bringing positive knock-on effects for economic development ("Euromonitor International", 2007). In Nigeria alone, the number of mobile phone subscribers as at June, 2008 stood at 53.3 million ("Afrique en ligne", 2008). "Telephones are much more than computers on the planet. That assertion can explain why vocal technologies and interfaces are an important part of Human-Computer Interaction area. Using natural language within interaction is supposed to facilitate exchanges between humans and machines. That's why simple and efficient vocal interactions are awaited in many domains such as E-health, E-learning, E-trade, M-trade and E-administration" (Jose, 2007).

In building voice applications that enable vocal interactions with computers, VoiceXML can be used. VoiceXML is a programming language, designed for Human-Computer audio dialogs that feature synthesized speech, digitized audio, recognition of spoken, DTMF (Dual Tone Multi Frequency) key input, recording of spoken input, telephony and mixed initiative conversations and it is becoming the standard language used for developing interactive voice response (IVR) and voice-enabled applications. A voice application is a collection of one or more VoiceXML documents and a VoiceXML document is composed of one or more dialogs while a single VoiceXML document serves as the application entry point.

Although there are existing e-health portals that provide health information resources and healthcare services, however, the resources provided by these sites are not within the reach of the low-literates, the blind, the visually impaired and those that are not computer literate. Also, although there are existing speech-based disease screening initiatives in e-Health, these implementations lack adequate reasoning capability to find acceptable relevance in the health domain.

This work exploits the increase in the usage of mobile phones in Africa and other developing nations and presents an intelligent framework for usable speech-enabled e-health system that enables access to speech-based health information such as diseases and their prevention, treatment of diseases, specialist doctors, alternative therapy, fruits therapy and hospitals that can be consulted within a proximity. It also allows the caller to diagnose his ailment using rule-based reasoning technique which existing disease voice-based screening systems lack. This will enable those not catered for in the use of graphical user interface to have access to the same information and services through phone for self-care. A prototype application that leverages the architecture and provides information about malaria fever, typhoid fever, yellow fever and lassa fever was implemented. The prototype application also allows the caller to diagnose his kind of fever.

E-HEALTH

eHealth refers to the use of Information and Communication Technology (ICT) in healthcare (Shariq et al., 2007). It is "consumer-centered model of healthcare where stakeholders collaborate using ICTs including Internet technologies to manage health, arrange, deliver and account for care and manage healthcare system" (Hans et al., 2005). Others associated eHealth with activities such as managing, educating, arranging, connecting, obtaining, providing, redefining, supporting, using, assisting obtaining, providing, redefining, supporting, using, assisting and accessing (Hans et al., 2005).

VoiceXML

Description of VoiceXML

VoiceXML is a programming language, designed for Human-Computer audio dialogs that feature synthesized speech, digitized audio, recognition of spoken, DTMF (Dual Tone Multi Frequency) key input, recording of spoken input, telephony and mixed initiative conversations (Jose, 2007). VoiceXML is a specific kind of XML designed to describe voice applications ("VoiceXML 2.x", 2005). VoiceXML describes grammars, prompts, event handlers and other data structures useful in describing voice interaction between a human and a computer. VoiceXML is an extensible markup language for the creation of automated speech recognition (ASR) and Interactive Voice Response (IVR) applications (Grisedale et al., 1997).

History of VoiceXML

The origin of VoiceXML began in 1995 as an XML-based dialog design language intended to simplify the speech recognition application development process within an AT & T project called Phone Markup Language (PML). As AT & T reorganized, teams at AT & T, Lucent and Motorola continued working on their own PML-like languages. In 1998, WBC hosted a conference on voice browsers. By this time, AT & T and Lucent had different variants of their original PML, while Motorola had developed VoXML and IBM was developing its own speechML. Many other attendees at the conference were also developing similar languages for dialog design; for example, HP's TalkML and PipeBeach's VoiceHTML.

The VoiceXML Forum was then formed by AT & T, IBM, Lucent and Motorola to pool their efforts. The mission of the VoiceXML Forum was to define a standard dialog design language that developers could use to build conversational applications. They chose XML as the basis for this effort because it was clear to them this was the direction technology was going. In 2000, the VoiceXML Forum released VoiceXML 1.0 to the public. Shortly thereafter, VoiceXML 1.0 was submitted to the W3C as the basis for the creation of a new international standard. VoiceXML 2.0 is the result of this work based on input from WBC Member companies, other World Wide Web Consortium (W3C) Working Groups and the public (Shariq et al., 2007).

Goals of VoiceXML

The main goal of VoiceXML is to bring the full power of Web development and content delivery to voice response applications and to free the authors of such applications from low-level programming and resource management. It enables integration of voice services with both data services using the familiar client-server paradigm (Voice Extensible Markup" 2004).

VoiceXML Platform Architecture

A VoiceXML platform is the foundation for developing and operating voice automation applications. During the Human-Computer interaction, it executes the commands and logic specified by applications written in VoiceXML. It also provides the speech processing capabilities (speech recognition, speech synthesis, voice authentication, etc). VoiceXML platform architecture is based on HTTP protocol and uses both phone and Internet networks. The Web server is often connected to a database which the user can question and update.

A zoom on the VoiceXML gateway in Figure 1 shows that this computer is equipped with a telephone card, able to manage incoming and outgoing calls, a connection with Internet network and a VoiceXML interpreter charged to carry out all the orders programmed in this language. Just as a Web browser renders HTML document visually, a VoiceXML interpreter renders VoiceXML documents audibly. You can think of the VoiceXML Interpreter as a telephone-based voice browser. Automatic Speech Recognition (ASR) engine, recording of audio files and Dual Tone Multi Frequency (DTMF) telephone keyboard are the

Figure 1. VoiceXML platform architecture Source: (Jose, 2007)

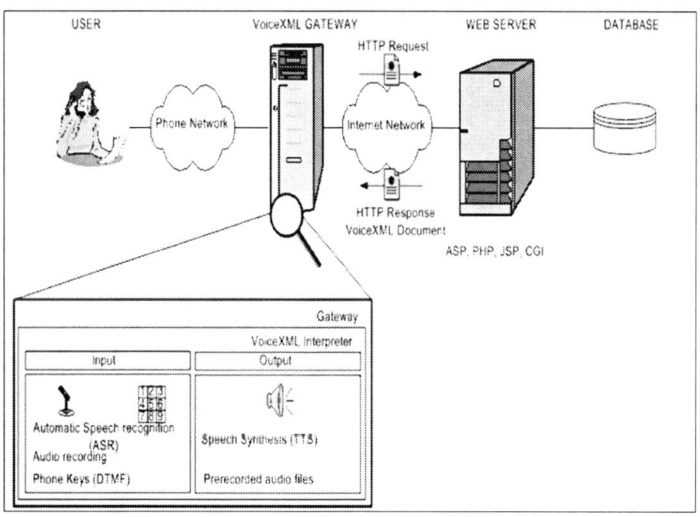

inputs users interact with. Text To Speech (TTS) voice synthesis and restitution of pre-recorded audio files are the outputs the machine can use (Jose, 2007).

VOICE APPLICATION

A voice application is a collection of one or more VoiceXML documents. A VoiceXML document is composed of one or more dialogs. A single VoiceXML document serves as the application entry point ("Building VoiceXML application", 2005).

How a Voice Application Works

Just as HTML is used to create visual application, VoiceXML is a markup language used to create voice application. With a traditional webpage, a Web browser will make a request to a Web server which in turn will send an HTML document to the browser to be displayed visually to the user. With a voice application, it is the VoiceXML Interpreter that sends the request to the Web server, which will return a VoiceXML document to be presented as a voice application via a telephone ("Getting Started").

REVIEW OF RELATED WORK

Evidence gathered from literature revealed that research efforts in the area of e-Health systems can be broadly categorized into GUI-based initiatives and VUI-based initiatives. Notable approaches of GUI-based initiatives include the following: In (Mu-Jung & Mu-Yen, 2007), a framework for an integrated design of intelligent web-based Chinese Medical Diagnostic System (CMDS) for digestive health using ontology was proposed. Medical ontology was integrated into the system development and the methodologies of its implementation for digestive health. CMDS uses Web interface and expert system technology to act as human expertise and diagnose a number of digestive system diseases. Besides, to efficiently elicit the knowledge of digestive system from domain experts and construct the medical ontology, a hybrid knowledge acquisition strategy was proposed. CMDS provides a truly precise analysis for digestive system disease and the prototype system could diagnose up to 50 types of diseases amongst 10 species of primary digestive system. In (Grisedale et al., 1997), the description of a PDA-based interface designed for rural community health workers in India for community health workers to input health information about rural dwellers was made. In (Vishwanath et al., 2002), a description was made of a system for data entry as well as access to decision support by community health workers in India. This was to assist community health workers in their work. Other initiatives include: (Nsuangani & Perez, 2006), where the result of a study conducted on college students' online activities at health websites was presented and it was found out that those who searched the sites were looking for health-related information, products, and services for self-help. The information provided were however in text form which does not cater for the needs of the blind, the visually impaired and those that are not computer literate. In (Medical Library Association, 2008), some websites that people access for self-care were listed and they can also only be accessed through GUI. Since all the initiatives mentioned above are all GUI-based they are not usable by the visually impaired, the blind and those who are not computer literate.

The initiatives that are VUI-based include the following: In (Sherwani et al., 2007), a report of speech-based access to health information by low-literate community health workers to assist them in their job was presented. The information provided was in Urdu language of Pakistan and it was found out that speech technology could help the low-literate. In (James et al., 2001), a report of IVR developed for screening for early Dementia was presented. A Clinical Dementia Rating Scale was used to assess 156 subjects aged 56 to 93 years. These subjects performed a battery tests administered by an interactive voice response system using standard touch-tone telephones. It was discovered that computer-automated telephone screening using either informant or direct assessment is feasible and that such systems could provide wide-scale, cost-effective screening, education and referral services to patients and care givers. In (Mundt et al., 2005), the work presented in (James et al., 2001) was extended to include educating the callers on dementia disease and making referral services. After its development and pilot testing, the system was made available to the public via a toll-free number and advertised in targeted, rural areas in the state of Wisconsin. After 1 year of availability, the data gathered by the system suggested that the majority of the callers remained in the system long enough to, at minimum, listen to educational information. The system received calls from both those concerned about themselves and those concerned about another person. The screening portions of the system received significant use, and most individuals receiving positive screens continued to explore the interactive voice response system, suggesting they sought additional information. In (Kim et al., 2007), a test was carried out to know the feasibility of using IVR to screen for depression among low-income, urban pregnant patients and to solicit their preferences for treatment. Consenting subjects used a phone in a private clinic room to complete an IVR version of the Edinburgh Postnatal Depression Scale (EPDS). The pilot study suggested the practicability of using an automated phone interview to screen for depression in low-income, urban pregnant women. In (Corkey et al., 2005), a pilot interactive voice response cervical cancer screening brief advice interface was described. The subjects used completed computer-assisted telephone interview (CATI) and the results obtained suggested that an IVR reminder might be useful to increase cervical screening rates. In (Rudnickey et al., 1999), Carnegie Mellon University's Communicator provided speech-based travel information. In (Zue, et al., 2000), MIT's Jupiter weather information system was presented while in (Plauche et al., 2006), the Berkeley's TIER group's Tamil Market project designed, developed and tested a spoken language system with low-literate users but the information provided was on crops.

A critical look at the VUI-based initiatives discussed above shows that existing e-health portals that provide health information resources and healthcare services provide them in text form which does not cater for the needs of the low-literates, the blind, the visually impaired and those that are not computer literate. Also, existing disease screening speech-based systems lack reasoning capability to make them attain the level of an expert system in order to have an acceptable level of relevance in the health domain.

This work therefore, introduces the use of rule-based reasoning technique in speech-enabled e-Health system to diagnose diseases and caters for the needs of people in places where healthcare is inadequate to assist them for self-care and aid their efforts in seeking medical care.

SPEECH-ENABLED E-HEALTH SYSTEM ARCHITECTURE

The Speech-Enabled e-Health System architecture is based on a client-server model and is divided into the client layer, middle layer and the data layer (Figure 2). The client layer consists of fixed phones and mobile phones with which the user calls the voice application. The middle layer consists of the following:

1. VoiceXML Gateway
2. Web Server
3. The following modules:
    a. **Service Manager:** This provides access to the other modules.

Figure 2. The architecture for the speech enabled e-health system

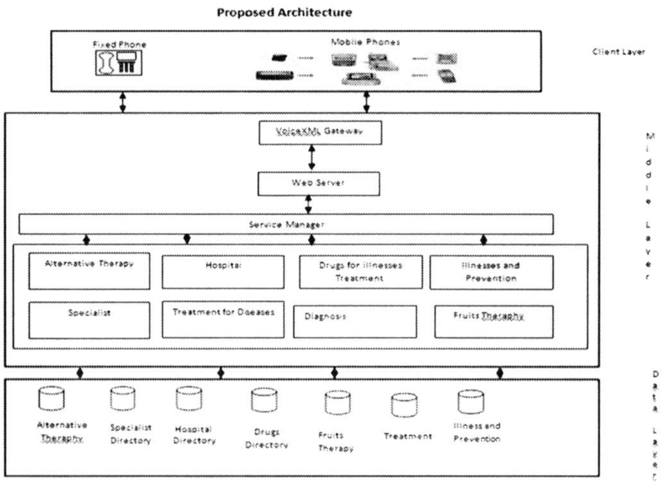

b. **Alternative Therapy:** This provides the user alternative therapy for a particular ailment.
c. **Specialist:** This provides for the caller, information about specialists in a particular branch of medicine so as for him to consult if need be.
d. **Hospital:** This provides information about the hospitals a caller can visit in his proximity.
e. **Drugs for Illnesses Treatment:** With this module, the user is provided information about drugs for the treatment of a particular ailment.
f. **Diagnosis:** This module allows a user of the system to diagnose his ailment. This is done by calling Jess as a Web service to provide the reasoning capability.
g. **Treatment for Diseases:** This provides access to treatment for different ailments
h. **Illnesses and Prevention:** This provides information about illnesses and their prevention.
i. **Fruits Therapy:** This provides information about the various fruits that can be used for curing a patient's ailment.

The data layer contains the following databases:

1. **Alternative Therapy:** This contains various alternative therapies for illnesses.
2. **Specialist Directory:** This contains the names and addresses of specialist doctors so that those that need care from specialists will be able to get one in their proximities.
3. **Hospital Directory:** This contains the names and locations of hospitals in a particular area so as for the user to locate the one nearest to him for visitation.
4. **Drugs:** This contains information about drugs for treating illnesses.
5. **Treatment:** This contains treatment for the patient's ailment.
6. **Illnesses and Prevention Database:** This contains the various illnesses and their prevention.
7. **Fruits Therapy**: This contains information about fruits and their therapies.

The architecture for the system is shown in Figure 2.

DESIGN AND IMPLEMENTATION

In designing the architecture, an attempt was made to study a number of existing web-based health information websites consumers visit for their health concerns and some of the services provided were adapted into the architecture.

For the implementation of the features provided by the architecture, VoiceObjects Desktop for Eclipse was used as the development tool. Applications built with it are generated in VoiceXML. Voxeo Prophecy was used as the media platform while Jess (Java expert system shell) was used as the rule engine and X-Lite soft phone was used

Figure 3. Dialog flow for the application

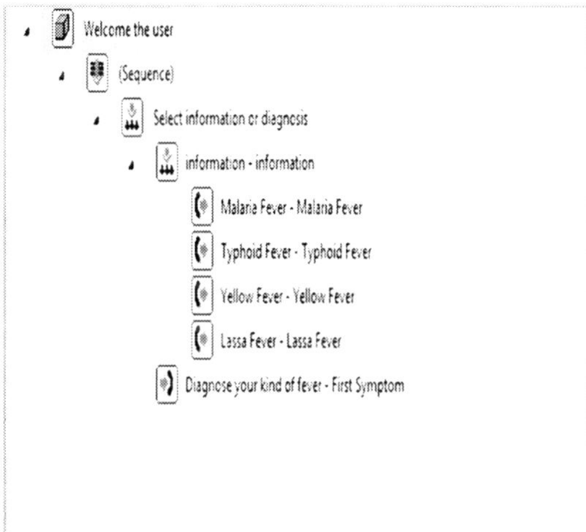

Figure 4. Calling the application using X Lite Softphone

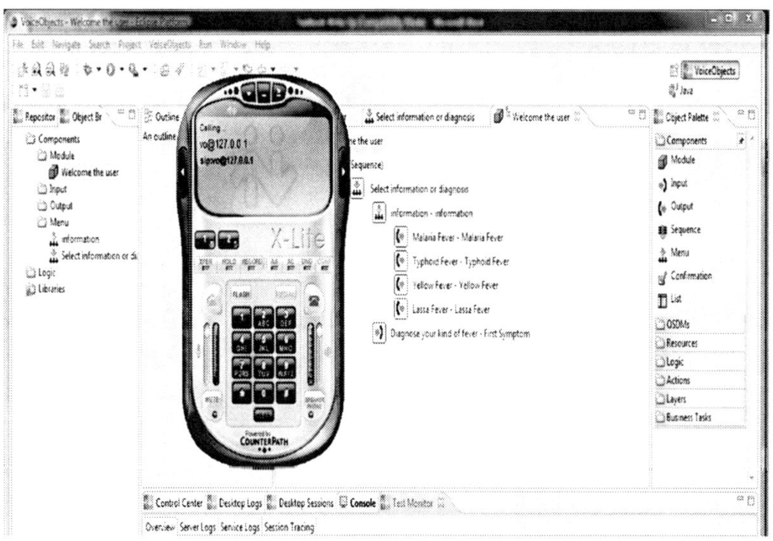

to call the application. A prototype application that provides information about malaria fever, typhoid fever, yellow fever and lassa fever was implemented. The prototype application also allows the caller to diagnose his kind of fever. Shown in Figure 3, is the dialog flow of the application using VoiceObjects Desktop for Eclipse and Figure 4 shows the application being called using X-Lite soft phone.

CONCLUSION

This work has presented an intelligent framework for usable speech-enabled e-health system and a prototype application that leverages the proposed architecture was developed to provide health information and services for malaria fever, yellow fever, typhoid fever and lassa fever. The application made use of rule-based reasoning technique to diagnose any of the four types of fever. This will offer the blind, the visually impaired, the low literate and those that are not computer literate access to the same information available through the graphical user interface and enable them to access reasoning-induced disease diagnosis. This initiative will go a long way in solving the problem of inadequacy of healthcare services in countries where the ratio of doctors to the population is brazenly too small by enabling the populace to embark on self-care.

REFERENCES

Afrique en ligne (2008). *Afrique en ligne*. Retrieved September 10, 2008, from http://www.afriquenligne.fr/nigeria's-gsm-operator,-globacom,-hits-20m-subscribe-base-2008082911686.html

Anantraman, V., Mikkelsen, T., Khilnani, R., Kumar, V. S., Machiraju, R., Pentland, A., & Ohno-Machado, L. (2002). Handheld computers for rural healthcare, experiences in a large scale implementation. In*Proceedings of the 2nd Development by Design Workshop (DYD02).*

Baker, D. W., Wolf, M. S., Feinglass, J., Thompson, J. A., Gazmararian, J. A., & Huang, J. (2007). Health literacy and mortality among elderly persons. *Archives of Internal Medicine*, *167*(14), 1503–1509. doi:10.1001/archinte.167.14.1503

Biriwasha, M. (2007). *15% Now! Campaign: Africa Must Invest in Public Health*. Retreived April 29, 2008, from http://www.rhrealitycheck.org/node/4363/print

Building VoiceXML applications (2005). *Building VoiceXML applications*. Retrieved May 20, 2008, from https://studio.tellme.com/vxml2/ovw/applications.html.

Euromonitor International. (2007). No end in sight for Africa's mobile telephone boom. Retrieved April 23, 2008, from http://www.euromonitor.com/No_end_in_sight_for_Africas_mobile_telephone_boom

Getting Started with VoiceXML. (n.d.). Retrieved May 20, 2008 fromhttp://developer.voicegenie.com/tutorials _VoiceGenie.php

EFA Global Monitoring Report (2008). *Educational, Scientific and Cultural Organization. Regional Overview: Sub-Saharan Africa.*

Grisedale, S., Graves, M., & Grunsteidl, A. (1997). *Designing a Graphical User Interface for Healthcare Workers in Rural India*. ACM CHI.

Huang, M. J., & Chen, M. Y. (2007). Integrated design of the intelligent web-based Chinese Medical Diagnostic System (CMDS) – Systematic development for digestive health. *Expert Systems with Applications*, *32*, 658–673. doi:10.1016/j.eswa.2006.01.037

Khoja, S., Scott, R., Ishaq, A. F. M., & Mohshin, M. (2007). Testing Relibility of eHealth readiness Assessment Tools for Developing Countries. *eHealth. International Journal (Toronto, Ont.)*, *3*(1), 31–37.

Kim, H., & Bracha, Y., & Tipnis. (2007). Automated Depression Screening in Disadvantaged Pregnant Women in an Urban Obstetric Clinic. *Archives of Women's Mental Health*, *10*(4), 163–169. doi:10.1007/s00737-007-0189-5

Low Literacy Equals Early Death Sentence. (2008). *Low Literacy Equals Early Death Sentence*. Retrieved June 24, 2008 from http://www.northwestern.edu/newscenter/stories/2007/07/health.html

Medical Library Association. (2008). *A User's Guide to Finding and Evaluating Health Information on the Web*. Retrieved May 25, from http://www.mlanet.org/resources/userguide.html

Mundt, J. C., Ferber, K. L., Rizzo, M., & Greist, J. H. (2001). Automated Dementia Screening Using a Touch-Tone Telephone. *Archives of Internal Medicine*, 161.

Mundt, J. C., Moore, H. K., & Greist, J. H. (2005). A Novel Interactive Voice Response (IVR) System for Dementia Screening, Education and Referral:One-Year Summary. *Alzheimer Disease and Associated Disorders*, *19*(3), 143–147. doi:10.1097/01.wad.0000174992.68332.0d

Nsuangani, N. M., & Pérez, M. A. (2006). Accessing Web-Based Health Related Information by College Students: An Exploratory Study. *Californian Journal of Health Promotion*, *4*(1), 64–74.

Oh, H., Rizo, C., Enkin, M., & Jadad, A. (2005). What is eHealth? (3): A Systematic Review of Published Definitions. *Journal of Medical Internet Research*, *7*(1). doi:10.2196/jmir.7.1.e1

Oh, H., Rizo, C., Enkin, M., & Jadad, A. (2005). What is ehealth? A systematic review of published definitions. *World Hospitals and Health Services*, *4*(1), 32–40.

Olu Ogunrin, F., Ogunrin, O., & Akerele, A. (2007). Motivating Nigerian Doctors for Improved Healthcare Delivery. *International Journal of Health Care Quality Assurance*, *20*(4), 290–306. doi:10.1108/09526860710754361

Orabuchi, A. (2005). *Poor Healthcare System: Nigeria's moral difference*. Retrieved April 28, 2008 from http://www.kwenu.com/publications/orabuchi/poor_healthcare.htm

Plauche, M., Nallasamy, U., Pal, J., Wooters, C., & Ramachandran, D. (2006). Speech Recognition for Illiterate Access to Information and Technology. In *Proceeding of International Conference on Information and Communications Technologies and Development*.

Ross, C., Parkinson, L., Bates, L., Green, S., & Aye Thida, H. (2005). Pilot of a Novel Cervical Screening Intervention: Interactive Voice Response. *Australian and New Zealand Journal of Public Health*, *29*(3), 261–264. doi:10.1111/j.1467-842X.2005.tb00765.x

Roullard, J. (2007). Web services and speech-based application around VoiceXML. *Journal of networks, 2*(1).

Rudnicky, A., Thayer, E., Constantinides, P., Tchou, C., Stern, R., Lenzo, K., et al. (1999). Creating natural dialogs in the Carnegie Mellon Communicator System. In*Proceedings of Eurospeech,* 1531-1534.

Sherwani, J., Ali, N., Mirza, S., Fatma, A., Memon, Y., Karim, M., et al. (2007). HealthLine: Speech-based Access to Health Information by Low-literate Users. In *Proceedings of IEEE/ACM Int'l Conference on Information and Communication Technologies and Development*, Bangalore, India.

Voice, E. M. L. (VoiceXML) Version 2.0 (2004). *VoiceXML*. Retrieved May 24, 2008 from http://www.w3.org/TR/2004/REC-voicexml20-20040316/

Voice, X. M. L. Forum. (2004). *VoiceXML Forum*. Retrieved May 26, 2008, from http://www.voicexml.org/tutorials/tutorial1_1.html

Voice, X. M. L. 2.x Essentials (2005). *VoiceXML 2.x Essentials*. Retrieved May 20, 2008, from https://studio.tellme.com/vxml2/ovw/essentials-p.html

Zue, V., Seneff, G. J., Polifront, J., & Pao, C., HAZEN, T. J., & Hetherington, I. (2000). JUPITER: A Telephone-Based Conversqtional Interface for Weather Information. *IEEE Transactions on Speech and Audio Processing*, *8*(1). doi:10.1109/89.817460

Chapter 7
An Overview of Internet Developments and their Impact on E-Government in South Africa

Goonasagree Naidoo
University of South Africa, South Africa

S. Singh
University of South Africa, South Africa

Niall Levine
University of South Africa, South Africa

ABSTRACT

The usage of the internet has grown over recent years in South Africa but at a very slow rate. This is the result of several challenges facing the growth of the Internet in South Africa. These challenges are mostly related to the lack of infrastructure for the Internet, high cost of computer technology and service provider challenges. The paper provides an overview of the Internet usage and its impact on E-Government in South Africa. It examines regulatory issues pertaining to the Internet. It also examines Internet growth in the business and government sectors. In the government sector, the Cape Online Strategy, is an initiative by the provincial government of the Western Cape in SA, is an example of a global trend towards greater levels of interactivity between government and citizens. This initiative is an excellent example of how Web-based solutions can be used to deliver certain services to citizens. Another excellent example is an E-justice initiative undertaken by the Department of Justice. The initiative aims at promoting a more efficient system of Justice in SA. The paper also provides an overview of the challenges to Internet adoption in South Africa.

DOI: 10.4018/978-1-61520-789-3.ch007

INTRODUCTION

Many countries worldwide are constantly creating exciting ways in which to use the Internet. South Africa (SA) is no exception. The SA government has launched an e-government policy which is aimed at creating a government that works better, costs less and is results-driven. It is clear that the reinvention of the SA government is tied to the proliferation of the Internet. The Internet is perceived as an instrument to enhance service delivery performance in the South African public service. The internet is also perceived as an essential tool to 'catch-up' to the information age of the developed world and to close the digital gap in SA.

The purpose of this paper is to provide an overview of internet usage in South Africa. It also considers development arising from the internet usage in SA. This paper does not attempt to provide a synoptic overview of all internet initiatives in SA. Instead it mainly provides a snapshot of recent key internet initiatives in SA. Against this background, a qualitative analysis is used.

Internet Usage in South Africa

From a communication perspective, South Africa has 4.729 million landline telephones in use and there are 33.96 million mobile cellular phones. The South African telephone system can be described as the best-developed and most modern network in Africa. The South African telecommunication network consists of carrier-equipped open-wire lines, coaxial cables, microwave radio relay links, fibre-optic cable, radiotelephone communication stations, and wireless local loops (Central Intelligence Agency, 2007).

The Internet user base in South Africa is growing year by year – but at a very slow rate. Figure 1 shows the Internet usage and population statistics for South Africa. From the year 2000 to the year 2006 we see, proportionately, that the usage of the Internet by the population of South Africa is very low. From this slow growth in the Internet user base we can conclude that there are several challenges facing the growth of the Internet in South Africa. Some of these challenges are related to infrastructure for the Internet, cost of computer technology, and service provider challenges.

Figure 1. Internet usage in South Africa (internetworldstats.com, 2007)

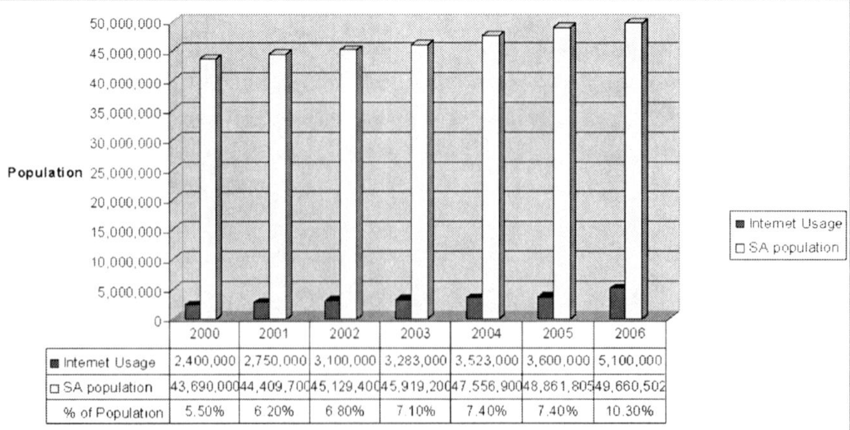

	2000	2001	2002	2003	2004	2005	2006
■ Internet Usage	2,400,000	2,750,000	3,100,000	3,283,000	3,523,000	3,600,000	5,100,000
□ SA population	43,690,000	44,409,700	45,129,400	45,919,200	47,556,900	48,861,805	49,660,502
% of Population	5.50%	6.20%	6.80%	7.10%	7.40%	7.40%	10.30%

Year

Goldstuck (2002) has, over the years, reported on Internet Access in South Africa. He has predicted a very slow-paced growth rate in the usage of the Internet in South Africa. Below is a brief summary of the Goldstuck Report on Internet Access in South Africa for 2002, 2004, 2005 and 2007:

In 2002 the state of Internet access was:

- One out of every 15 South Africans had access to the Internet at the end of 2001. This compares with at least one in two people in countries such as the USA, Canada, South Korea, Singapore and Hong Kong.
- The total number of South Africans with access to the Internet at the end of 2001 was 2.89 million.
- This number was expected to grow by less than 10% to 3.1 million by the end of 2002.
- There is a strong demand by corporate South Africa for broadband Internet access.
- Only a small handful of ISPs are profitable. An increasing number of ISPs are profitable on an EBITDA basis (Earnings Before Interest, Tax, Depreciation and Amortisation). In short, it is no longer uncommon for ISPs to be operating profitably, but they still have a legacy of debt.
- The number of ISPs has grown dramatically, largely due to the rollout of a Virtual ISP service by Internet Solution.
- Business strategies in the ISP industry are maturing to the extent that it has become possible to create a model that explains not only how ISPs evolve, but also how they meet their clients' needs as those needs evolve.
- A tiny proportion of ISPs in South Africa have gone out of business through bankruptcy.
- Mobile access to the Internet has been minimal, with only a tiny proportion of those people who have appropriate devices actually using the devices to connect to the Internet.
- The arrival of GPRS, the so-called 2.5 generation of mobile network technology, may alter the mobile access picture during 2003, but only if appropriate handsets become available.
- Community centres, resource centres and digital villages in townships will continue to underachieve in their goals of bringing Internet access to a sizeable proportion of residents in disadvantaged areas.

In 2004 the state of Internet access was:

- One in every 13 South Africans will have access to the Internet.
- There was a 6% growth, with 3.28 million South Africans expected to have Internet access by 2003.
- The market remains healthy because companies are reinvesting, improving reliability of the networks, and building backup systems.
- ISPs are now focusing on existing customers.
- Factors expected to boost Internet growth in 2004 were: a proposed Second Network Operator (SNO), the launch of high-speed or broadband wireless access by Sentech the para-statal telecoms infrastructure provider, and the favourable rand-dollar exchange rate which makes the cost of technology cheaper.
- School connectivity was seen as a priority.

In 2005 the state of Internet access was:

- One in every 12 South Africans expected to have access to the Internet.
- 3.6 million South Africans were expected to have access to the Internet.
- There has been significant growth in corporate usage of the Internet.

- Growth of Internet access had slowed down, with the dial-up market experiencing no growth in subscribers.
- A competitive Second Network Operator failed to materialise, which impacted on the growth of the Internet.
- ISPs were evolving to provide specialist services.
- School connectivity was experiencing delays of up to three years.

In 2007 the state of Internet access was:

- One in every 12 South Africans expected to have access to the Internet.
- The study showed that there will be more than 800 000 broadband subscriber accounts active in South Africa.
- The dial-up user base has fallen dramatically, dropping by 122 000 users, and falling below the one million mark for the first time since 2001.

One of the reasons that the growth of the Internet in South African has been very slow, is due to the lack of competition in the telecommunications industry – this is discussed more later. To summarise, in 2002 one out of every 15 South Africans had access to the Internet, in 2007 there was only a marginal change to one in every 12 South Africans. The growth rate of the adoption of the Internet has been very slow. The access to appropriate technology and infrastructure has impeded the growth of the Internet in South Africa.

SA is undergoing transformation in the face of global pressures exerted by Internet technologies (Mcniven & Marche, 2003). Goldstuck (2006) suggested that the following factors will drive the future growth of the Internet in South Africa:

- Continued strong economic growth.
- The emergence of the African middle class.
- Improved education levels, including computer literacy.
- Improved affordability of personal computers, both as a result of cheaper products and new financing options.
- Convergence of voice and data.
- Technology improvements.
- Demand for more server/storage capability to meet higher levels of corporate governance requirements.

But although the predictions have been ambitious, the reality has been somewhat less successful. This raises the question – 'when other nations have been so successful, what has impeded South Africa?' The following analyses the regulatory and legislative developments in this arena which in part explain the country's slow communications growth rate.

REGULATORY ISSUES

South Africa has been quite active in the e-revolution. The South African government has developed the following policy documents and regulations, the South African Green Paper (Central Government, 2000) and the Electronic Commerce and Transaction Bill ("Electronic Communication and Transaction Bill," 2002).

The South African Green Paper

The South African Green Paper on electronic commerce (Central Government, 2000) is divided into four categories. Each category contains key issues or areas of concern that need serious consideration in electronic commerce policy formulation:

- The need for confidence in the security and privacy of transactions performed electronically.
- The need to enhance the information infrastructure for electronic commerce.
- The need to establish rules that will govern electronic commerce.

- The need to extend the opportunities of electronic commerce to the entire population.

Electronic Communications and Transactions Bill

The Electronic Communications and Transactions Law, effective from 31 July 2002, governs all companies that conduct electronic commerce in South Africa. The law was designed to facilitate electronic commerce, but may instead increase the regulatory burden and introduce an unacceptable level of uncertainty for some businesses. The law requires:

- Accreditation for certain electronic signatures.
- Takes government control of the ".za" domain name.
- A long list of disclosures for websites that sell via the Internet.

The Electronic Communication and Transaction Bill ("Electronic Communication and Transaction Bill," 2002) has the following regulatory objects for electronic communications and transactions:

- To provide for the development of a national e-strategy for the Republic.
- To promote universal access to electronic communications and transactions and the use of electronic transactions by Small, Medium and Micro Enterprises (SMMEs).
- To provide for human resource development in electronic transactions.
- To prevent abuse of information systems.
- To encourage the use of e-government services.

Some of the objects of the Act are to enable and facilitate electronic communications and transactions in the public interest, and for that purpose to:

- Recognise the importance of the information economy for the economic and social prosperity of the Republic.
- Promote universal access primarily in under-serviced areas.
- Promote the understanding and acceptance of and growth in the number of electronic transactions in the Republic.
- Remove and prevent barriers to electronic communications and transactions in the Republic.
- Promote legal certainty and confidence in respect of electronic communications and transactions.
- Promote technology neutrality in the application of legislation to electronic communications and transactions.
- Promote e-government services and electronic communications and transactions with public and private bodies, institutions and citizens.
- Ensure that electronic transactions in the Republic conform to the highest international standards.
- Encourage investment and innovation in respect of electronic transactions in the Republic.
- Develop a safe, secure and effective environment for the consumer, business and the Government to conduct and use electronic transactions.
- Promote the development of electronic transactions services which are responsive to the needs of users and consumers.
- Ensure that, in relation to the provision of electronic transactions services, the special needs of particular communities and areas, and the disabled, are duly taken into account.
- Ensure compliance with accepted international technical standards in the provision and development of electronic communications and transactions.

- Promote the stability of electronic transactions in the Republic.
- Promote the development of human resources in the electronic transactions environment.
- Promote SMMEs within the electronic transactions environment.
- Ensure efficient use and management of the.za domain name space.
- Ensure that the national interest of the Republic is not compromised through the use of electronic communications.

Though these objectives are utopian, they are the first steps in developing a manageable framework for the sustainable development of the electronic community in South Africa. It is only by actions like this that South Africans can become active role players involved in the development of a strategy for the electronic community in South Africa (Singh, 2002).

The South African Law Reform Commission submitted draft legislation and discussion documents on privacy and data protection for public comment in 2006. The South African Law Reform Commission held a series of workshops on the legislation in February 2006. Numerous public submissions were received, and the Commission made recommendations on the draft legislation. For example, restrictive legislation may negatively impact the ability of South African and foreign companies to receive and send trans-border flows of personally identifiable data (Office of the United States Trade Representative, 2007)

Telecommunications

Until recently (2008) South Africa's main telecommunication provider, Telkom, has maintained a monopoly on telecommunications provision and services, of controlling the underlying network into which other companies wished to inter-connect. Many businesses have complained about high telecommunications prices – even resulting in the emergence of an anti-Telkom website for consumer to vent their frustrations. In 2004 Telkom was cited by the South African Competition Commission for anti-competitive conduct with respect to Value Added Network Services (VANS). A complaint was filed by the South African Internet Service Provider Association alleging further abusive practices by Telkom. In addition to such practices, one U.S. company has pursued extensive legal remedies against Telkom to honour the results of binding arbitration regarding a multimillion dollar contract. Instead of honouring the arbitrator's findings, Telkom took steps to block the arbitral award and appealed the award to a local trial court. In 2005 the Department of Communications sponsored two colloquiums to discuss measures to lower telecommunications prices. At the conclusion of the second colloquium the Department of Communications promised to release an action plan in early 2006. In November 2006 the South African Supreme Court of Appeal found in favour of the U.S. company.

In 2003 the Department of Communications released a draft Convergence Bill with the aim of simplifying the existing legislative framework, empowering the regulator and opening the telecommunications industry to greater competition. Comments received during a public comment period were highly critical of the draft bill and, as a result, the Department of Communications revised the bill. In 2005 the Department of Communications released for comment its modified version, the Electronic Telecommunications Bill. In December 2005 the bill was sent to the South African president for signature. He refused to sign it, citing that the bill gave too much control to the Department of Communications at the expense of ICASA. The president requested a constitutional review of the bill and its companion legislation, the ICASA Amendment.

The Electronic Telecommunications Bill (plus amendment) was passed in June 2006 in a compromise that allows ICASA to maintain some independence. The Department of Communications, however, maintains a strong grip on ICASA, as it approves ICASA funding (Office of the United States Trade Representative, 2007). Although partly privatised, the government retained a 'golden share' in Telkom and thus had a vested interest *not* to liberalise the telecoms market too fast. Government was anxious to protect the high number of state employees and boost treasury funds through lucrative telecoms revenues.

Some of the problems facing value added network services and Internet service providers may be addressed by new telecommunications policies and regulations. On 1 February 2005 the Minister of Communications announced sweeping liberalisation in the telecommunications sector, but later back-tracked on key aspects. Under the proposed liberalisation, mobile operators were to be allowed to use any fixed lines in the provision of their service, value added network services could be offered through infrastructure other than that which is owned by Telkom, and value added network services providers could employ Voice-Over Internet Protocols (VOIP). In addition, private telecommunications network operators would be allowed to sell spare capacity. Little of this actually came to fruition however. As Horwitz and Currie note (2007) "The nearly congenital distrust the ANC-led Government displayed toward independent agencies weakened regulation and hence intensified the incumbent's power. An additional factor in an incumbent's power arises where the Ministry responsible for safeguarding the government's residual financial interest in the incumbent is also the Ministry making policy for the sector. The South African experience shows that the incumbent will tend to have the Ministry's ear, and—perhaps because—the Ministry is keenly attentive to the company's share price in the event of future public offerings." (See further Horwitz & Currie, 2007).

Thus South Africa committed to license a second national operator (SNO) to compete in long distance, data, telex, fax and privately leased circuit services, by 1 January 2004. The Minister of Communications conditionally approved a license for the SNO in September 2004, but disagreements among SNO stakeholders – in which the South African Government was itself a major player in the liberalisation process – over operational control and allocation of equity stakes, delayed the launch until 2006. The result is that Telkom has continued to enjoy monopoly privileges. The SNO was finally licensed by ICASA (Independent Communications Authority of South Africa) in December 2005. It began operations on 30 August 2006 under the name 'Neotel'. Neotel has also entered the business-to-business market and planned to enter the residential market in April 2007.

E-GOVERNMENT INITIATIVES

A number of initiatives have also been undertaken by the South African government such as the government's Batho Pele National Gateway Project, the South African Revenue Service's (SARS) e-filing initiative, the Department of Transports' e-Natis initiative, the Department of Justice, e-Justice initiative and the Cape Provincial Gateway project (Naidoo, 2008). The initiatives undertaken by almost all the departments point to steady progress, with the exception for the Department of Transport (eNatis, 2007). However, the focus of the South African government is predominantly on efficiency improvement through information dissemination, rather than adopting a more comprehensive view, such as incorporating issues such as e-democracy and citizen engagement. Initiatives undertaken by the Department of Justice, e-government initiatives for the World cup 2010, and e-filing initiatives by the South African Revenue Services are discussed to provide a snapshot of e-government initiatives in SA.

Department of Justice

The need to transform the criminal justice system (CJS) in SA necessitated that the justice system of a country be re-evaluated (e-Gov News Jan/Feb 2008:1). This was as a result of the CJS facing extreme criticism, for its failure to keep South Africans safe and to bring perpetrators to justice. Within the department a number of challenges were prevalent such as high rate of absenteeism, lack of motivation, lack of commitment to the organization, poor quality of services, antiquated manual information systems, deterioration of internal relations and incompetent management.

The Department of Justice therefore embarked on a process of transformation and restructuring (Naidoo, 2008). An e-Justice programme was launched in 2000, to re-engineer the court process by utilising appropriate technology, including e-Commerce and Knowledge Management. The programme aimed to improve the effectiveness and efficiency of the justice system. It also aims at playing a meaningful role in combating crime and upholding the Constitution. The e-Justice system seeks to transform the justice administration system from a manual to an automated system. The programme therefore supports the fundamental reforms necessary to establish a more fair, accessible and efficient system of Justice in SA. The purpose of the programme is to reform and modernize the administration and delivery of Justice through re-engineering work processes, use of enabling technologies, strengthening strategic planning and management capacity, organizational development and human resource interventions. E-Justice is one of the ways in which the Department of Justice hopes to alleviate some of the case backlogs and missing case dockets in the department (e-Gov News Oct/Nov 2006:2). Currently, the courts in SA have huge backlogs and prisons in general are overcrowded with a large number of trial-awaiting prisoners.

The eJustice programme comprises of three specialized projects namely (Jiyane 2005):

- Court Process Project (CPP) which incorporates the flow of processes that affect the Departments in the Integrated Justice System, that is the Departments of Safety and Security, of Correctional Services, of Social Development, of Justice and Constitutional Development as well the National Prosecuting Authority;
- the Digital Nervous System (DNS) which aims to deploy information technology infrastructure and related services such as office applications, email connectivity and training to the broader Department of Justice Community. In addition to basic technology provision and support, the DNS has expanded to include business solutions and support, business process management and information management services;
- the Financial Administration System (FAS) is tasked with automating and administering the trust accounts in the Magistrates' Courts, the State Attorneys' offices, and the Guardians Fund in the Masters' offices. Amongst the benefits of the project, will be the provision of timely and relevant information to all stakeholders, reduced time spent in queues by members of the public, reduced human error in calculations, reduced risk of files getting lost, as well as greater citizen convenience.

An example of a multi-million rand e-Justice project termed 'IJS Court centre project' on the court process was initiated in 2000, with a long term implementation framework (Matthews, 2002). It was implemented in different magistrates' courts throughout SA. An automated court case and case management system known as e-Scheduler, has also been implemented at a number of courts where case backlogs are particularly high. The aim of the project is to improve court and case management at the magistrates' court level. The project is not only just about technology, a significant proportion of the programme focused on capacitating people to use the technology efficiently.

An investigation of this project however suggests that the software used by the Court Centre Project is not compatible with the larger eJustice software which has led to some controversy. At present, the system is being used at 471 courts which means, that 90% of courts have it, but 10% are still waiting for it (The Star, 29 August 2008).

A current analysis of the project suggests that a great amount of transparency has been achieved in terms of the length of time for cases to be prepared and adjudicated, and the average time that awaiting trial detainees are detained is reduced. It lists all new cases, stipulates any cases that have been postponed or closed, and carries a list of all children on an outstanding court roll. The project benefits the Department of Justice by reducing the number of people at the magistrate's courts at any given time as well as by reducing the security risk in the court environment. The SA Police Services benefits due to reduction of transport, reduction of prison wardens, and the Department of Correctional Services benefits due to the reduction of administration, transport costs and the number of internal security officials employed in prisons.

It is also evident that there are also benefits regarding inter-departmental coordination, between the Departments' of Justice, Correctional Services and South African Police Services. However, such benefits are only evident at the national sphere of government, with a lack of vertical integration (intergovernmental relations) between and amongst the three spheres (national, provincial and local) of government in SA. Furthermore, there are conflicting priorities between the different levels of government.

Another recent study by the Open Foundation of SA found that the eJustice system has major potential but also faces various challenges. Researchers found, the system is severely limited due to shortcomings centered largely on how data is entered into the systems. These include a confusing mixture of two prominent South African languages (Afrikaans and English) entries; cases involving multiple accused and multiple offences being given a single case number making it difficult to track the progress of a charge for first appearance finalization; inconsistency in declaring cases open or closed where the accused has absconded; and inconsistent classification of offences and outcomes. The initiative also faces severe human capacity shortages to effectively drive the eJustice initiative. Although the system had the potential to revolutionise court case management, reduce trial delays and thwart docket theft and corruption cases, it is evident that what is needed is better commitment to, and integration of, each linked stage in the CJS, from policing through to prosecution and trial, to sentencing and correctional services.

E-Government and World Cup 2010

Another significant e-Government initiative relates to the FIFA Confederations Cup and the FIFA World Cup, being hosted by South Africa in 2010. A huge volume of voice and data traffic will move over the FIFA event network. This requires a reliable partner to develop the fixed-line components of the necessary telecommunications infrastructure. This encompasses the provisioning of fixed-line telecommunications related products and services and, where applicable, the services of qualified personnel necessary for the planning, management, delivery, installation (and de-installation), operation, maintenance and satisfactory functioning of these products and services. In essence, the project will enable the interconnection of important event venues, including the ten FIFA World Cup stadiums, broadcast compounds, media centres, the International Broadcast Centre and FIFA headquarter locations. Likewise the general public - soccer fans – around the world will be able to book for tickets, follow and even see the World Cup wherever they live around the world: a truly global e-government initiative.

The South African Revenue Service E-Filing Initiatives

One of the early achievements has been the e-enablement of the South African Revenue Services (SARS). SARS introduced its electronic filing (e-filing) initiative in 2001, in accordance with the government's broader eGovernment strategy in the public service (South African Revenue Service, 2007). E-filing of tax is a co-ordinated effort between SARS and private business (e-Gov News, Oct/Nov 2001:1). The main aim of an e-filing system is to facilitate the electronic submission of tax returns and payments by taxpayers and tax practitioners. Taxpayers may however still submit their returns in the traditional way. However, e-filing is aimed at improving operational efficiencies in order to deliver a better and quicker service. Those who wish to make use of the e-filing system are required to register at the particular service provider, conclude an agreement and receive a private access code and password to access the available services that are offered by SARS (e-Gov News, Oct/Nov 2002:1). E-filing now enables corporate entities to submit and pay certain tax returns online. For individuals, the electronic submission is still limited to provisional tax returns, while annual individual returns are not yet available for e-filing. It is also envisaged that, in the near future, customers will also be able to pay airport tax and customs duties online.

In August 2005, SARS launched e-filing kiosks at many of its branches and is currently working closely with the four major commercial banks on a payment channel project. SARS has also implemented a single view of the customer by deploying the 'Siebel Public Sector Single View of the Taxpayer' solution. Prior to deploying the new system, SARS faced considerable business integration challenges, with fragmented taxpayer information residing in disparate systems. The result was duplicated effort, taxpayer frustrations and inevitably lost revenue (The e-Business Handbook, 2005).

There are a number of internal and external factors that have contributed to the success of SARS (South African Revenue Services, 2007). Externally, it enjoys the strong political support from government, as well as working governance practices. In this regard, there is a zero tolerance approach to corruption within the department. The e-filing initiative has been effectively implemented. As a result there has been an increase in SARS revenue by over a R100 billion since the inception of its e-Government initiatives in 2000 and 2001 respectively. Furthermore, in 2007 SARS has simplified the tax return forms, thus making the whole process easier. It has also helped to keep up-to-date records on taxpayers, which are easily accessible. It has also helped SARS to understand the risk profiles of customers and industry segments. SARS currently receives between 65 000 and 75 000 electronic payments from taxpayers and traders every month. The electronic service is backed up by a number of useful services such as same-day processing of all transactions. This addresses the problem previously created by backlogs in the system. The electronic service is also used for extensions on Value Added Tax (VAT) from the 25th of the month to the last day of month.

SARS also has a step-by-step guide on its website to educate and guide customers on tax and its related issues. For example, customers are guided on how to correctly go about filing tax returns electronically and manually. The benefits of the e-Government initiative by SARS are enormous. E-filing has eliminated the need for tax payers to manually pay their taxes. All customers should do is register online, and payments can be made electronically. This is an ongoing service, available seven days a week, twenty-four hours per day, and 365 days a year. The new system has integrated the SARS 'silos', bringing with it comprehensive, real-time taxpayer information, lower operational costs, and better citizen service through improved response times in handling tax interactions. SARS estimates that the project paid for itself in less than two months. Ultimately, the SARS revenue take has increased considerably in the last decade, benefitting the state treasury and ultimately its citizens – a testament to the benefits conferred by effective roll-out and implementation of E-Government initiatives

Challenges to Internet Adoption in South Africa

Internet adoption will only be encouraged if the infrastructure supports the technology. A 'digital divide' may arise, for example, in the business world, where the larger, well-established companies effectively use the technology, forcing small and medium companies to adapt or die. Small firms are at times intimidated by the technology, are frequently concerned about the ability of outsiders to tap into the workings of a small firm via computers, and often lack the time or resources to develop an understanding of how information systems can help them. Wang (1999) reports that medium and small business concerns often do not fully understand the concept of information systems and how to effectively use internet resources.

Guomundsdottir (2005) suggests that there are several factors that challenge the growth of the Internet in South Africa. Before these challenges are tackled, however, he aptly suggests that fulfilling the basic needs of the greater population has to become a prerequisite to bridging the digital divide in South Africa. In Table 1 Guomundsdottir (2005) models the South African digital divide as follows.

Other challenges include providing education and training on the usage of the electronic model, addressing the lack of preparedness by government institutions, poor infrastructure, and the lack of resources and unequal access to technology (Naidoo 2008). Also, Internet penetration at home is showing low levels of growth. Only one out of ten South Africans are using the Internet and a very small percentage of South African schools are equipped with computers (Naidoo 2008). While South Africa has a over 42.3m mobile customers, and a penetration of over 100%, (African Mobile Factbook, 2007), it has only recently (2008) surpassed the 1 Million broadband subscriber mark, made up mainly of ADSL and HSDPA subscribers.

The fixed line incumbent Telkom currently has in the region of 415,000 ADSL subscribers, while Mobile Operator Vodacom has 360,000 3G/HSDPA data card users and MTN recently announced that they now have 120,000 3G/HSDPA data card users on their South African network. Thus, there is still plenty of room for growth in the market as the broadband penetration rate is currently only 2%, compared to the OECD average of 18.8%. For most of Africa, Internet access and use is even lower, often well below 5 percent, with over 60 percent of Africa's population living in unconnected rural areas (Commonwealth African Rural Connectivity Initiative, 2009).

Table 1. Different types of digital divides

	Types of Needs	The Type of Divide	Comments
1	Basic needs	The real divide	This includes access to clean water, electricity, justice etc.
2	Hardware – software	Material divide	Poor access or costly technology
3	Mentality – content	Mentality/opportunity divide	How will the Internet really help me?
4	Skills – knowledge – support	Utilisation divide	Lack of basic computer skills and user support
5	Culture – language / social diversity	Suitability divide	The alienness of the Internet; it is modelled more on a Western cultural background

What is the cause of such low connectivity and hence low penetration rates? There is a need for continued incremental and more methodical process of liberalisation and privatisation of the telecommunications sectors in many African countries and a variety of regulatory safeguards need to be put in place to foster competition and promote a conducive environment to assist in connectivity. For example, in South Africa, until 2008, fixed line provision was via the 'parastatal' Telkom monopoly, and prices were deemed extremely uncompetitive, providing a disincentive for consumers to go 'on-line' and hence access e-government facilities. Only in 2009 has a rival, Neotel, come on stream, and this mainly in the commercial urban conurbations rather than the rural areas.

In an effort to improve intra-governmental e-government, South Africa recently announced R378 million to provide "backbone transmission services." The Next Generation Network (NGN) will replace government's current single wide-area network and provide improved stability, capacity and additional services, such as advanced data, voice and video with the intention of making "the single public service a reality" through interoperability and seamless service delivery. Public service delivery would be improved through e-education, telemedicine through e-health projects, connectivity to multipurpose community centres, and strengthening collaboration between the three tiers of government (national, provincial and local).

The project will be implemented by the State Information Technology Agency (Sita), and by using Neotel, twice the amount of bandwidth will be available. The company's "bandwidth on demand" was much cheaper than the next closest offer. In utilising Neotel, Sita is ensuring that cheaper telecommunications for government than was previously available. Currently, a small proportion of Internet users in SA have access to government websites. However, the Batho Pele Portal and the associated call centre provide an opportunity for the public to provide feedback and comment on government or any matter of interest to the citizen.

CONCLUSION

The problems typical of a developing country, such as poor infrastructure, skewed accessibility, corruption, weak educational systems and a history of oral tradition in rural areas (Naidoo, 2008) have been highlighted. SA has experienced increased pressure to deliver an integrated and effective service in the face of public pressure for government services from society. Bureaucratic culture and systematic administrative and political obstacles inherent in government departments pose enormous obstacles to the ability of the SA government to meet these growing challenges.

The continued roll-out of the 'information phase' has characterized the bulk of e-government rollout, with limited online transactability, or mechanisms that allow citizens access to frequently demanded services as close to the customer's home as possible (such as walk-in or call-centres). While it is increasingly common for government departments in SA to have their own Web sites offering a range of white papers, green papers, legislation, policies, speeches and annual reports for download, these are purely informational. There are delays in progressing beyond information-rich Web sites to real e-transactability. With the exception of SARS, discussed above, there is little evidence of transactional Web sites in SA. The portal approach has taken shape with the National government Web site and the introduction of a central services portal, www. Services.gov.za, sitting alongside the National and Cape Gateways (http://www.gov.za/structure/pubserv). Unfortunately, the trend in SA is very much towards provision of information alone, with little in the way of full-on transaction with the government. On a positive note, the National services portal bodes well for South Africa's e-government progress and future development. While there is some evidence of the portal approach, offering a single point of entry to services (National Gateway and Cape Gateway), these are very much geared toward providing basic information, rather than allowing the public to transact with government online.

When considering policy intent, it would appear as though the South Africa's e-government strategy intends to reach all the tiers of government (provincial and local) primarily responsible for service delivery (Naidoo & Kuye, 2003). However, with the case of the e-Justice of the Department of Justice and Constitutional Development and Administration and e-Natis initiative of the Department of Transport, it appears as though this has not happened in practice (e-Gov, News Oct/Nov 2007) and (Mail and Guardian 2007). A real and considerable challenge that remains in the implementation of e-government amongst the lower tiers of government lies in the access, cost and availability of the internet (including telecommunications infrastructure and computer resources) in order to ensure that local governments, and their constituencies, are the final recipients of such as e-government strategy. Once the implementation of the e-government strategy has taken place at the lower tiers of government, reaching the people at grassroots, then only can South Africa's e-government strategy be regarded as successful and truly customer focused.

In South Africa, a great number of challenges arise from the increasing need of the Internet, particularly in the private sector; as well as increasing demands placed on government by citizens for developments in keeping with the private sector and the international community. Questions ultimately arise as to the ability of the South African organisations to meet these challenges in the face of the inherent bureaucratic culture and the structural administrative and political hierarchy of government. In order for internet initiatives to be successful in SA, adequate time and sustained collaboration with all levels of society are critical.

REFERENCES

Agarwal, A., & Ramana, V. V. (Eds.). (2008). Foundations of E-Government. Naidoo, G. (ed.), *An overview of eGovernment policy initiatives in the South African government*. New Delhi. India.

Asgarkhani, M. (2002, December 5-7). *E-governance in Asia Pacific*. International Conference on Governance in Asia. Retrieved from Http://www.cityu.edu.hk/garc/conference/Asgarkhani,Mehdi.doc

Cape Gateway Portal. (2008). *Cape Gateway Portal*. Retrieved June 10, 2008, from http: www.capegateway.gov.za

Central Government. (2000). *Green Paper on Electronic Commerce*. Retrieved from http://www.polity.org.za/govdocs/green_papers/greenpaper/index.html

Central Intelligence Agency. (2007, June 14). *The World Factbook2007*. Retrieved June, 19, 2007, from https://www.cia.gov/library/publications/the-world-factbook/geos/sf.html

Executive Training Programme, C. E. S. P. A. M. (2003, February 26-28). Implementing *e-government in Public Sector Organisations*. Cape Town, South Africa e-Gov News (2006). e-government In *South Africa*, (Oct/Nov) e-Gov News (2007). e-government In *South Africa*, (Oct/Nov) e-Gov News (2008). e-government In *South Africa*, (Oct/Nov) eNatis (2007). eNatis to have a major impact on traffic law enforcement. Retrieved June 14, 2008. From http://www/enatis.com/content/view/85/2

Fraser-Moleketi, G. (2003, August 4). *Post-Cabinet Lekgotla briefing on Governance and Administration*. Issued by the Department of Public Service and Administration.

Goldstuck, A. (2002). *The Goldstuck Report: Internet Access in South Africa*. Pinegowrie, South Africa: World Wide Worx.

Goldstuck, A. (2006). *PC user base in South Africa reaches 5 million*. Pinegowrie, South Africa: World Wide Worx.

Goldstuck, A., Whitford, S., & Super, R. (2006). *The Goldstuck Report: Online Retail in South Africa*. Pinegowrie, South Africa: World Wide Worx.

Guomundsdottir, G. B. (2005, December 5-7). *Approaching the Digital Divide in South Africa*. Paper presented at the NETREED Conference, Beitostolen, Norway.

Gupta, M. P. (2004a). Towards E-governance Management Challenges. InNaidoo, G. (ed.), *Introduction ofE-governance and its implications for developing countries*. New York: McGraw Hill Publishing Company.

Gupta, M. P. (2004b). Towards E-governance Management Challenges. In Naidoo G. & Van Jaarsveldt (eds.),*Electronic government: Strategies and Implementations: E-governance in South Africa: A perspective on initiatives, readiness and development issues*.New York: McGraw Hill.

Horwitz, B., & Currie, W. (2007, September-October). Another instance where privatization trumped liberalization: The politics of telecommunications reform in South Africa —A ten-year retrospective. *Telecommunications Policy*, *31*(8-9), 445–462. doi:10.1016/j.telpol.2007.05.008

Huang, W., Siau, K., & Woi, K. K. (2004). Electronic government Strategies and Implementation. InNaidoo, G. & Singh S. (eds.), *Towards an E-governance Solution-A South African perspective*. Ohio. USA.

Internetworldstats.com. (2007). *Internet Usage and Marketing Report*. Retrieved June 11, 2007, from http://www.internetworldstats.com/af/za.htm

Kyama, G. W. (2005, June 28-29). *e-Government: A view from South Africa*. East African e-government consultative workshop. Grand Regency Hotel. Nairobi, Kenya.

Leitner, K. (2003, July 7-8). *eGovernment in Europe: The State of Affairs. European Institute of Public Administration*, Presented at the eGovernment 2003 Conference Como, Itlay.

Mail and Guardian. (2007). *Traffic-system chaos: Minister was warned*. Retrieved from Http://www.mg.co.za/article.aspx?articleid=308615&area=/breaking_news/breaking_news_national

Matthews, I. (2002). *Feasibility study for criminal justice strengthening project*. A feasibility study. Retrieved May 15, 2008, from http://www.ipt.co.za/cjs%20study.pdf

McNiven, J. D., & Marche, S. (2003). E-government and e-governance: The future isn't what it used to be. *The Canadian Journal of Administrative Sciences*. Retrieved May 21, 2008, from http://findarticles.com/p/articles/mi_qa3981/is_200303/ai_n9178064

SARS. (2002). *File PAYE and Skills Development Levies Online! File Vat and Diesel Refunds Online!* Retrieved November 1, 2002, from http://www.sars.gov.za/commerce

Singh, S. (2002). *Unravelling the Chaos in E-Commerce Land: A Preliminary Framework for Auditors for Systemactically Dealing with Processing of Electronic Transactions*. Paper presented at the International Economic and Management Science Conference: Transformation on South Africa: Management Improvements and Best Practicesin Accountability. Productivity and Customer Service Quality, Vanderbijlpark, South Africa.

South Africa Yearbook 2007/08 (2008). *Integrated Justice System (IJS)*. Retrieved June 20, 2008, from http://www.info.gov.za/aboutgov/justice/system.htm#transform

South African Government Gateway Portal. (2003). *South African Government Gateway Portal*. Retrieved October 17, 2003,http://www.gov.za/structure/pubserv.html

South African Revenue Services. (2008). Retrieved June 20, 2008, from http://www.sars.gov.za

The e-Business Handbook (2005). The 2005 review of innovation at work in South African business. An ITweb informatica Publication. Creda Communication (Pty) Ltd

Van der Merwe, C. (2008). *Fundamental shifts on the cards for SA e-government strategy*. Engeneering news.

Wang, Y. (1999). *A General Analysis of the Impact of Electronic Commerce on Small Businesses and Entrepreneurships in the U.S.* Retrieved March, 10, 2002, from http://www.cs.wits.ac.za/~philip/saicsit/saicsit-99/electronic/exp/Wang.pdf

Chapter 8
Enhancing Democratic Participation:
The Emerging Role of Web 2.0 and Social Media

Jenny Backhouse
University of New South Wales at the Australian Defence Force Academy, Australia

ABSTRACT

The Internet and Information and Communications Technologies (ICTs) have long been seen as potentially contributing to a solution to the problem of voter disaffection and disengagement that has occurred in many western liberal democracies over the past couple of decades. The success of Barack Obama in the 2008 presidential campaign in the United States has highlighted the role that ICTs, in the form of Web 2.0 technologies and social media, can play in enhancing citizens' democratic participation and involvement in political campaigning. This paper examines the nature of Web 2.0 technologies and social media and analyses their role in political campaigning, particularly in the context of the 2007/8 presidential primaries in America and the 2007 federal election in Australia. While broadcast television is still a dominant political player, the empirical evidence suggests that a viable campaign needs to integrate diverse communication strategies tailored to citizens' interests and the political environment. The interactive and participatory technologies of the online world are increasingly key components of such integrated campaign strategies.

INTRODUCTION

During the last decade, and even earlier, e-government researchers have investigated and analysed the role that Information and Communication Technologies (ICTs) might play, or are playing, in numerous aspects of governmental and political processes, including democratic participation. One catalyst for this investigation has been the decline experienced by many liberal democracies in the participation of citizens in the civic and political spheres, particularly as indicated by factors such as diminishing membership in political parties and falling voter turnout at elections (Breindl & Francq 2008; Millard 2009).

DOI: 10.4018/978-1-61520-789-3.ch008

An effective election campaign is a key element in any political system that is based on the representative model of democracy since an election is the phase where voters are able to directly influence the political process. Consequently, if this trend of disengagement of voters from the political process continues, it threatens to undermine the very legitimacy of representative governments. People are the sovereign that gives legitimacy to the institutions of democracy (Dahrendorf cited in Fraunholz & Unnithan 2008, p55). However, to date, implementations of ICTs in support of democratic goals, such as enhanced participation, have generally failed to live up to expectations (Lusoli & Ward 2005; Breindl & Francq 2008).The reality of online deliberation . is far removed from the ideals set out in the mid-1990s (Chadwick 2009, p3).

The rise to prominence of social media sites such as MySpace and Facebook, along with related Web 2.0 technologies, has revived hopes that ICTs will encourage greater citizen participation in all aspects of the democratic process. The stunning success of the online features of the Obama presidential campaign in the Unites States of America during 2007/08 has highlighted the manner in which an innovative online strategy can contribute to citizen engagement and effective campaigning. As Millard observes Obama's intelligent use of ICT in political fundraising and campaigning has opened a new chapter in eParticipation (Millard, 2009).

The popularity of social media, even in the political arena, provides a counterpoint to the numerous well-intentioned efforts over several years to encourage citizen participation in e-government - projects which generally had limited results. Against the slow growth of eGovernment usage it is somewhat ironic that a new wave of applications, which now go under the name of web 2.0, were launched with very little investment and encountered dramatic success in terms of take-up (Osimo, 2008b). This paper considers the nature of Web 2.0 and social media and provides a preliminary examination of their emerging role in enhancing participation in political campaigning.

WEB 2.0

The label Web 2.0 is not, as the name might imply, a newer version of underlying Web technology. It is rather a label that has been applied to recent developments in the manner in which online users interact with the Internet and related technologies. The term was popularized by O'Reilly Media (O'Reilly, 2005). Tim O'Reilly identifies several characteristics which, although not definitive, he considers distinguish Web 2.0 from the manner of earlier uses of the Web, such uses now being labelled Web 1.0. One such characteristic is the use of the Web as a platform for running applications and storing data, rather than simply delivering web pages. O'Reilly acknowledges that some earlier applications, such as Doubleclick, the advertising online placement firm, were already using the web as an application platform. Every banner ad is served as a seamless cooperation between two web sites, delivering an integrated page to a reader on yet another computer (O'Reilly, 2005). Later a raft of popular applications such as the Google search engine and Ebay, built on this idea of the Web as a platform and thereby acted as .an enabler or middleman between the user and his or her online experience (O'Reilly, 2005). Over time, these web-based applications developed more sophisticated user interfaces with many becoming equivalent to the interfaces supplied with personal computing applications, thereby simplifying the user's interaction with the web site. . Web-based applications can now be made to work much more like desktop ones (Graham, 2005).

The emphasis for Web 2.0 was moving from publishing to participation, building the network of users and thus having their collaborative activity improve the site and its utility (O'Reilly, 2005). However, this also was not a completely new phenomenon, since Amazon had always encouraged users to participate by rating books and writing reviews, thereby contributing to the overall value of the site. Wikipedia is another particular example of the power of social networks, participation and collaboration to deliver content. As the actor Stephen Fry says, for Web 2.0 in general ..[there is] genuine interactivitypeople can upload as well as download (cited in Wikipedia, 2007). Similarly the user plays a more significant role in sites such as Flickr, a photo sharing web site. As well as providing the photos, users themselves define the categorisation system, via the tags they create, rather than having a formal system imposed upon them. Interestingly, such sites have typically grown in popularity without formal advertising. Instead, site users themselves spread the word voluntarily to other potential users, a technique known as viral marketing (O'Reilly, 2005).

In a critical vein, Madden (2006) observes that detractors query whether the label Web 2.0 has any real meaning at all and considers that, even if it does, this meaning has morphed over time. Nevertheless, she acknowledges one of the most telling examples of what Web 2.0 applications do [is]: They replace the authoritative heft of traditional institutions with the surging wisdom of crowds (Madden & Fox 2006, p2). Madden sees the rapid growth of Web 2.0 sites, that emphasize social grouping and integration, as evidence that there is a real phenomenon occurring. Her examples, from 2006, include growth comparisons between the spectacularly successful and collaborative encyclopaedia Wikipedia later MySpace with its metaphor of a person (Madden & Fox 2006, p6).

Boutin (2006) suggests a much simpler explanation for the success of some web sites compared to others which equally invite participation. They're easy to use, and they don't tell you what to do (Boutin, 2006). There is some support for this theory. For example, in the early days of the video site YouTube, the site's developers resisted advice to force users to watch ads before they could access their selected video, thus helping the site to maintain a mythological community-driven status (Cloud, 2006). The social networking site Friendster, which exercised tighter control of participants' networking links, has declined in popularity compared to its later, less restrictive, rival MySpace. Thus, the free-spirited MySpace, which allowed anyone to look at anyone else's profile took off (Chafkin, 2007). Free access is also a plus. Wikipedia might have its critics but it's good enough. And it's free (Graham, 2005).

Thus the concept of Web 2.0 is quite loose. It has been used to encompass several disparate technologies and implementations. In fact, Web 2.0 ... defies a widely agreed upon concise definition (Murugesan, 2007, p35). Nevertheless, the term is generally understood to include the range of technologies that facilitate social media: blogs, wikis, RSS feeds, mashups, sites that permit sharing and labelling of content (comments, photos, videos) and sites that enable social networking. Well-known Web 2.0 sites include Wikipedia (sharing content), YouTube (video sharing), Facebook (social networking), Flickr (photo sharing), del.icou.us (labelling content) and Twitter (micro-blogging).

SOCIAL MEDIA BECOMES MAINSTREAM

Irrespective of the validity or otherwise of the term Web 2.0, several interactive sites relying on largely user-generated content and social connection, have achieved remarkable prominence in a short period of time. Big business reacted to this growth with the headline purchases, in 2006, of MySpace by News Corp and YouTube by Google (Wyld, 2007). Time Magazine recognized the role of user-generated online content with its 2006 nomination of You (the online user) as person of the year. Time found It's a story about community and collaboration on a scale never seen before. Web 2.0 is a massive social experiment (Grossman, 2005). As Anderson (cited in Boutin, 2006) points out a real network effect has kicked in.

While the nature and quality of content in social media varies immensely, it is apparent that amateurs can surpass professionals, when they have the right kind of system to channel their efforts (Graham, 2005).

What exactly is social media? While the terms social media and social networking are often used interchangeably, Delaney (2006, p10) considers social media the broader term which encompasses the more specific social networking. Under this categorization, social media emphasizes user-generated content. It includes blogs which permit user comments, along with sites such as YouTube and Wikipedia, which rely on users for substantial content generation. In contrast, social networking emphasizes people and their connections. It works on a 'circle of friends' model whereby people set up personal profile pages which, in turn, link to the profile pages of others (Delaney, 2006, p7). Wyld (2007, p75) defines a social networking site along similar lines as A website that provides a forum for individuals to exchange opinions, create personal profiles, and receive and/or initiate direct interaction with peers. Social networking sites have made it much easier for the general user to create web pages, to communicate with and link to other site members, including friends of friends, using a variety of media (Boutin, 2006). A 2006/2007 survey by Booz Allen found that, in the US, social media sites were visited once a week by 71% of Internet users with 41% similarly doing so in the UK (Zappen, Harrison et al., 2008). Interestingly, this survey found that these users were actively creating, or commenting on, content and were not merely passive onlookers.

As Osimo notes (2008b, p7), Web 2.0 is affecting a variety of e-government domains, however the most visible impact is certainly in the field of political participation. Social networking sites can be particularly attractive to political actors (not to mention marketers), assisting them to hone their message for specific groups. Within these sites, user profiles and interactions inevitably reveal a lot of detail about the people themselves, along with their interests and preferences. In the realm of political campaigns, .social networking sites thus offer many advantages to political actors (Chadwick, 2009, p14).

The growth of Web 2.0 technologies and social media is stimulating e-government researchers to re-contextualise their approach to evaluating e-government and service delivery. As Pascu (cited in Osimo, 2008a, p3) points out, referring to the traditional view that transactional services represent the peak of e-government ICT development: Instead of this transaction focus, recent Internet trends, namely Web 2.0, provide a new and different emphasis on the importance of the 'information' and 'communication' dimension of ICT. This is particularly relevant in the area of eParticipation. Social media allows a two-way communication and the Obama presidential campaign was particularly adept at tapping into that communication. As the political strategist Rick Ridder highlighted: The Obama campaign's use of the Internet epitomizes the personalization of politics (Ridder, 2008). This personalization, in turn, allowed the campaign to raise large sums of money principally via those social networks.

DEMOCRACY AND THE INTERNET

The introduction of the Internet and its spread during the 1990s inspired e-democracy enthusiasts to hope it could fulfil a democratic role which would compensate, to some extent, for the deficiencies which they saw in the offline political realm. [It] ...fostered hopes for a new type of politics based on abundant information, rational deliberation, and active participation (Van Os, Hagermann et al., 2007, p25). In most cases, as noted by Coleman (2001), the reality failed to live up to the early hype. Nevertheless, as more users gained online access, the Internet, with its ability to provide news and information in an easily accessible and inexpensive form, emerged as an expedient resource for interested voters (Shannon, 2007).

Given the rising popularity of the web, political websites seemed an obvious election campaign tool. Websites were relatively inexpensive to set up and could allow political parties to sidestep the gatekeepers of traditional media and communicate directly with voters. Parties had a new opportunity to bypass an increasingly cynical media and address the public directly (Stanyer, 2005, p1050). Over several years, election campaigns in many countries have used the Internet to provide web sites for individual candidates, parties and even for specific campaigns. However, such party and candidate web sites have tended to attract either the party faithful on the one hand or satirists and agitators on the other (Moses, 2007a). Thus they have proved to be an ineffective tool for enthusing uncommitted voters, the voters that an election campaign particularly wishes to target.

In the United States, the blogging phenomenon crossed over into the political realm with prominent blogs, such as Instapundit, Daily Kos and the Drudge Report, gaining some political influence (Scott, 2005). A role in political campaigning followed. In 2004, the Howard Dean campaign in the US presidential primaries introduced the first blog devoted to an American presidential candidate. His Blog for America became immensely popular establishing a network of volunteers and raising significant amounts of money (Healy, 2007). Although Dean ultimately failed to win the Democratic nomination, his campaign demonstrated that online resources and social media, in the form of blogs, could be used effectively to generate enthusiasm and feed campaign coffers by attracting donations from large numbers of individual supporters. On the day of the election in 2004, the Drudge Report had more visitors than the New York Times online (Gueorguieva, 2007). These successes led some to argue that the Internet as a tool for political campaigning had come of age (Trippi cited in Stanyer, 2005, p1050). However, it seems clear such success can depend on a specific set of circumstances, not easily replicated. Dean's online donations far outstripped those of his opponents in the presidential primaries (Janack, 2006). Additionally, election campaigns elsewhere were not able to generate anything like the supporter enthusiasm or level of donations that Dean achieved, as Stanyer (2005) notes referring to the UK environment. It was not until the 2008 presidential primaries in the US, that Barack Obama was able to repeat, and in fact outdo, the fund raising successes of the Dean campaign with massive numbers of small donations via the Internet (Luo, 2008).

CAMPAIGN PARTICIPATION AND SOCIAL MEDIA

By the time of the 2006 Congressional midterm election in the US, web sites for candidates were .. a fixture of the electoral landscape (Gulati & Williams, 2007, p443), although, as noted earlier, they catered mainly to the committed voter. Other innovations such as blogs and mobile technologies have not lived up to expectations for their election role (Gulati & Williams, 2007, p461). In the financial arena, online fundraising had become more significant and the online advertising spend had risen, although both were still dwarfed overall by the traditional outlets especially mainstream television (Gulati & Williams, 2007). The rise to prominence of social media and associated websites, particularly over 2006-7, provided another dimension of possibilities for participative democracy online and specifically for election campaigns.

The 2006 midterm elections demonstrated the first involvement of social networking in campaigning. A drive to increase the registration of voters was launched on MySpace (Gueorguieva, 2007). Facebook, another social networking site, provided profile pages where candidates could provide policy information, allow supporters to post comments and encourage site users to recruit their friends as supporters (Gulati & Williams, 2007). The power of video clips started to become apparent. A clip of Senator George Allen using racist language was posted on YouTube and quickly went viral, possibly contributing to the Senator's subsequent election loss (Gueorguieva, 2007). As Panagopoulos (2007, p424) noted, the Internet was becoming a formidable medium that has inspired tremendous and influential innovations in campaign communications. Social media is one aspect of that innovation.

For the 2007 presidential elections in France, the Socialist party candidate, Ségolène Royal emphasized user involvement via 'participatory democracy'. She preferred direct relations with party members and more importantly with voters (Sauger, 2007, p1169). She used debates and extensive use of her comprehensive website Desires d'avenir to underscore this participatory aspect of her campaign; to draw the electorate into policy discussions and to affirm closeness, understanding and trust of 'rank-and-file' citizens (Sauger, 2007, p1168). Where previously the Internet and blogs had largely been ignored by candidates and French mainstream media, for this election, the media picked up on blog postings and the Internet incontestably formed part of the media landscape of this election campaign (Lusoli, 2007). An extra buzz was added to the campaign by animations such as Disco Sarko on Nicolas Sarkozy' s web site and by the headquarters sites that were established by all four candidates in the virtual reality game Second Life (Moore, 2007).

By 2007, the prevailing online environment meant that blogs and a web presence were not the only online campaign requirements. As Bieber notes, election campaigns now had to recognize numerous voices in the blogoshpere and online communities such as Flickr, MySpace, YouTube or Second Life (Bieber, 2007).

The US presidential primary campaigns commencing in 2007 highlighted the new possibilities. Several presidential candidates, including Senators Clinton and Obama announced their candidacies via videos on the Internet (Panagopoulos, 2007). The TV channel CNN hosted debates between the potential presidential candidates where the questions were provided, not by selected journalists as previously, but by people submitting videos to YouTube (Moses 2007a). Social media sites, such as YouTube and MySpace, set up specific channels or portals for presidential candidates and campaign-related issues (Gueorguieva, 2007). YouTube's YouChoose 08 channel, for example, hosted videos of candidate profiles and candidate statements on key issues as well as user videos and comments. MySpace's The Impact Channel hosted candidate profiles, issued videos, and friends' pages and enabled associated political activities such as voter registration and recruitment of volunteers.

THE FEDERAL ELECTION IN AUSTRALIA

Online political developments in America during 2007 attracted the attention of Australian political enthusiasts and campaign strategists, particularly since Australia was, at the time, gearing up for a federal election eventually held in November of that year. The Australian social media experience mirrored American developments. There was a rush of online enthusiasm with a plethora of dedicated election sites created by Web portals and news media (Sinclair, 2007). Google created a special election2007 channel, claimed to be a world first (Moses, 2007b). It provided a variety of tools including the ability to overlay electorate boundaries over Google Maps, chart trends, access electorate and candidate information, link to YouTube political video channels and search the parliamentary record for statements made by current parliamentarians (Bajkowski, 2007).

Social networking sites set up election 'channels' and invited selected candidates to join. MySpace, for example, provided the Impact forum devised .. to promote political awareness and interaction in their largely young members [approx 50% under 25] (Martin 2007). The politicians that joined had control of the profile and image they presented. This went some way to counteracting the plethora of spoof pages that had already been created on MySpace and elsewhere. The initiative provided politicians with the opportunity to communicate directly with MySpace members, a demographic often difficult to reach, without the intermediary of more conventional media. Large numbers of MySpace members quickly friended particular politicians, although some site members resented the perceived invasion of the communities they had popularized by politicians with seemingly ulterior motives (Martin, 2007; Lawley, 2007).

In Australia, YouTube had been used to host video clips for politicians in a state election earlier in 2007 but videos became a much more prominent feature in the federal election campaign (Moses, 2007b). YouTube was used by both sides to post a series of quick response, tit-for-tat videos. The incumbent Liberal Party Prime Minister, John Howard, launched his first YouTube video clip with a policy statement on climate change, a topic he had previously disparaged. This video and his subsequent videos proceeded to inspire a proliferation of parodies, animations and other send-ups (Glaister, 2007). He was particularly seen as an older politician with a very formal style which did not translate well to the YouTube environment whereas the Labor opposition's response video used humour to show John Howard ...snoring in bed, asleep on global warming (Ricketson, 2007). Nevertheless, the Liberal Party's strategy of posting video clips on YouTube at 5am and then notifying media outlets of their existence usually succeeded in having the videos shown later by TV news and current affairs programs.

In all, over 600 official candidate or party videos were posted on YouTube (Bajkowski, 2007). The Liberal Party's 40 videos on YouTube had 140,000 views while the opposition Labor Party's 64 videos had 460,000 views on YouTube but claimed 1.5 million views across all channels including social media sites. But the real winners came from the thousands of comedic and satirical videos. As Parker notes (2007), opposition leader Kevin Rudd's New Leadership video attracted only 1% of the viewings that were received by an earlier clip of him picking his ear whilst sitting in parliament. This popularity of spoof videos was similar to the American experience and raises questions about the substantive contribution of video clips to campaign goals.

The general consensus was that the Labor opposition made better use of the Internet as a campaign tool. The opposition leader Kevin Rudd excited more interest acquiring record numbers of friends with his official pages on MySpace and Facebook. The Labor opposition's web presence presented a more integrated online strategy with cross-linking between the social networking pages, videos and the dedicated campaign website. In contrast, the Liberal Party did not have a dedicated campaign site and lacked any cross-linking from the Prime Minister's official site to social networking sites (Ricketson, 2007).

ANALYSING PARTICIPATION IN ONLINE CAMPAIGNING

The Real Contribution

In The US, the Internet has proven to be a valuable resource for providing campaign news, raising funds and helping to engage voters. A recent ABC News/Facebook survey found that, although television was still the predominant campaign medium in the US, 40% of Americans used the Internet specifically for campaign news for the 2008 presidential primaries (Langer 2008). This compares to 18% during the 2004 presidential campaign (Gueorguieva, 2007). For young people (aged 18-29), who keep up-to-date with campaign issues via the Internet, PEW Research found that ... the role of social networking sites such as MySpace and Facebook is a notable part of the story (PEW 2008). The Barack Obama campaign raised significant funds online but the campaign also used ...Web 2.0 tools to further engage its participants in campaign work and to better understand the issues that [were] important to voters (Ives, 2008).

In Australia, there was much media hype about the 2007 federal election being the first Internet election but, in truth, the Internet was largely serving a niche, though growing audience. Television and radio still deliver the mass audience to Australian political players and politicians themselves perceive this to be the case (Ricketson, 2007). The advertising spend for the election campaign also reflected this with estimates that online advertising accounted for only 10% of the campaign advertising budget (Bajkowski, 2007). A key issue in the campaign was the labour deregulation styled WorkChoices. The Australian Council of Trade Unions ran a concerted campaign against this controversial legislation. Their campaign, entitled Your Rights at Work, included an award-winning web site but, crucially, also included a $20 million traditional advertising campaign (Williams, 2008).

For minor parties with restricted funding the Web has been presented as an opportunity to economically deliver their message to a wider audience. Minor parties in Australia certainly took up this opportunity, establishing websites and making use of MySpace and Facebook. Following the pattern of candidates in the US, the Australian Democrats launched their 2007 campaign on YouTube (Lawley, 2007). In fact, over half of the 600 official videos posted on YouTube were from minor parties, although the viewing numbers for these videos were miniscule (Bajkowski, 2007). The election results indicate that these tactics were not sufficient to counteract the difficulties faced by minor parties in the Australian electoral system. Included in those who lost their seats was Senator Andrew Bartlett, the Australian parliament's most prolific blogger.

One area where the Internet did play a more noteworthy role was with the online activist group Getup. This group claimed to be a new force on the political landscape and to have contributed to the resulting downfall of the Howard government. While it is difficult to definitively estimate their impact, the group did raise $1.9 million largely through online contributions and mobilised 900 volunteers to work at polling booths in a couple of key electorates (Metherell, 2007). This is significant in the Australian political context and may be a forerunner of what is to come.

REAL ENGAGEMENT

But does this online campaigning promote real democratic participation and engagement? Wilhelm (cited in Janack 2006 p286) has voiced the fear that without real deliberation ...digital democracy may follow the lead of 'mature' media and fail to meet [democratic] expectations. PEW's research (2008) indicates that for most Internet users (52%) in the US, accessing campaign information is typically incidental to their other online activities. This is particularly the case for younger users: 59% of the under 30's come across campaign news online compared to 43% of the over 50's. Friending politicians doesn't mean engagement with issues; it may simply be an artefact of the celebrity culture. Short video clips cannot elucidate sophisticated policy positions. The most popular clips often seem to be the amusing or embarrassing ones rather than more sober expositions of policy platforms e.g. Hillary Clinton singing the 'The Star Spangled' banner off-key was far more popular than Clinton outlining her Iraq strategy (Glaister, 2007).

Leadbeater (2007, p5) notes that, with the rise of modern media and a more individualistic culture, Politics has become less ideological and more personality driven. Even though Australia does not have a presidential system, the emphasis of campaigning is increasingly on the party leaders. The social networking phenomenon seems to accentuate this trend by highlighting the party leaders. While social media might be criticised for blurring the distinction between entertainment and serious politics, Popkin (2007) maintains that this soft news should not be dismissed. Soft news doesn't bring people to politics by enlightening them; it does so by connecting their world to the human interest and drama in politics (Popkin, 2007 p81). Social media might equally serve a political participative role by enhancing that connection.

THE CANDIDATE'S DILEMMA

Not surprisingly, politicians are struggling to cope with the variety and speed of communications which the Internet and mobile technologies now allow (Ricketson, 2007). Internet users have become a financial as well as organizational juggernaut (Kranish, 2007) for political campaigns. As Kranish perceptively notes (2007), the Internet and politics are an uneasy fit. While the Internet enables easier distribution of formal political messages it also provides ease of access for both supporters, perhaps well-meaning but sometimes misguided, and detractors. On the one hand, candidates want to take advantage of the fund-raising and relationship building features of online campaigning but, on the other hand, they want to retain control of their campaign's message and direction. Increasingly, politicians cannot ignore the overall contribution to campaign momentum online social media can generate. The web is about buzz as much as it is a tool (Schatz, 2007).

In the western world, campaign strategies have become increasingly sophisticated. A party or candidate is particular about their message and the precise way it is phrased. Consequently material available online should fit with other campaign material, even to the extent that the words and phraseology matches that of the key advertisements. For example, the US presidential campaign of Mitt Romney purchased key terms such as American family values and budget spending so that popular search engines would then drive the user to Romney's message (Kranish, 2007). Such fine tuning is more difficult to control now that campaign strategists have also to consider participation media, a whole new world (Kosinski cited in Kranish, 2007).

While it has always been possible for rival candidates, disgruntled or enthusiastic voters to publish contradictory campaign material, the expense of mass paper-based publication generally deterred all but the well off or very dedicated. In contrast, the Internet makes it possible for an individual, perhaps a blogger, to achieve sufficient prominence to influence a campaign. For several months before Barrack Obama had formally declared himself a candidate for the Democratic nomination for the US presidential elections of 2008, a fan had posted and maintained an increasingly popular Obama page on Facebook. Once the campaign was underway, the Obama strategists felt the need to formally take over this site to ensure the message conveyed fitted with the campaign strategy (Kranish, 2007).

The ubiquitous digital cameras and camera-enabled mobile phones have made the production of short video clips easy and cheap and the consequent role of citizen reporters more influential. Once posted to YouTube, these videos can have an impact either in terms of number of views on the site itself or by being picked up by TV programs. Spoofs and satires are rife. The slightest misstep, verbal or visual, current or historical, makes candidates vulnerable. US presidential candidates Hillary Clinton and Mitt Romney have both been embarrassed by videos of themselves from several years ago, which do not portray the image or policies they now espouse (Healy, 2007). In a similar vein, it was the Huffington Post via its citizen reporters who published Barack Obama's comments, made in a private assembly, disparaging voters who cling to guns or religion (Carr & Stelter 2008). The remarks which would otherwise have gone largely unnoticed now turned inevitably into a significant misstep for the Obama campaign.

SYSTEMIC AND CULTURAL ISSUES

Any efforts at online campaigning are inevitably embedded in the culture, political system and the wider political and online environment of the country concerned. It's not simply a matter of Internet diffusion. Several countries, including the United Kingdom have relatively high levels of Internet penetration and yet the Internet played a minor role in their pre-2008 election campaigns. It seems perverse, therefore, to suggest that once Internet penetration reaches some kind of critical mass. A decisive impact somehow becomes inevitable (Anstead & Chadwick 2008).

In Japan, the Internet is widely available but restrictive legislation bans the use of electronic media in the couple of weeks immediately prior to an election (Hogg 2007). Video sites such as YouTube are seen as too frivolous for the serious matter of politics and the degree of respect with which politicians should be treated (Hogg, 2007). However, Japan's governing party, the Liberal Democratic Party, has recently set up an official channel on YouTube and the Prime Minister has commenced weekly video addresses (Tabuchi, 2008). This may serve to change the attitude with which online videos are viewed.

It seems that even online campaigning cannot enliven an otherwise boring election. The 2002 presidential elections in Korea generated a lot of enthusiasm with large numbers of contributions to online debates. The Internet played a decisive role (Won-sup, 2007). The same enthusiasm was not forthcoming for the 2007 presidential elections, despite popular Korean portals setting up web sites with one portal even offering prizes for user-generated content. Less than 1% of Internet users of major portals visit the section devoted to the presidential race (Won-sup, 2007).

Political campaigns, both online and offline aim to recruit volunteers, raise funds and encourage citizens to vote. In the US political system, these are particularly significant resource constraints for presidential candidates in the primary campaigns. As Lusoli notes (Lusoli & Ward, 2005), these candidates need to quickly develop their supporter base across a national arena. Online campaigning is especially useful for this challenging task. This is not such an issue in some other political systems. In fact, American parties are unusual political organizations, and quite dissimilar to those found in other, notably European, liberal democracies (Anstead & Chadwick, 2008, p57). In Australia voting is compulsory and this casts a different complexion on election campaigns. Volunteers are not required for tasks such as phoning citizens and persuading them to vote. Fundraising is required but, except for independents, Australian political candidates can generally rely on party support at the local level (and the national level if they are in a marginal seat). Most fund-raising is done at the party level and major party leaders typically already have a national profile. Consequently, the drive for online status and participation is not as urgent.

German politicians similarly campaign in a political and social environment which is very different from the American system. Brauckmann (2009) highlights the distinguishing features which mean that Obama ...would not have succeeded in Germany. According to Brauckmann, German politicians cannot show the same policy responsiveness as Obama. They are tied more tightly to party systems and would need to consult widely with other party members before any changes could be made. Candidates are motivated to control the message and voters are still considered recipients of information rather than participants. Political websites reflect this focus. Additionally, the culture of interactivity on the Internet is not as widely established with only 17% of online users utilizing social networks, compared to 35% of American online users.

Nevertheless, the evidence from the 2007 French elections would suggest that there is not a simple relationship between the political system and the applicability of online campaigning technologies. Whereas the Koreans lost interest in online participation in their 2007 election compared with their 2002 election, for the French the exact opposite seemed to apply. Fraunholz and Unnithan (2008) detail the French experience. In 2002, Internet penetration was low and the established media did not consider online technologies enhanced citizen participation. In contrast, by the time of the 2007 election the number of broadband connections had risen significantly and more citizens were Internet savvy; 69% of UMP party members used e-voting to elect Nicolas Sarkozy as their presidential candidate; citizens and candidates created websites, blogs and videos and participated in Second Life; the traditional press picked up on items from the blogosphere, with some bloggers receiving a high media profile. Rosnay claimed the citizens are inventing a new democracy, based on the media of the masses, as opposite [opposed] to the mass media cited in (Fraunholz & Unnithan, 2008, p64).

PRIVACY AND ETHICAL ISSUES

Political players seeking to leverage social media for campaign participation need to be aware of the wider privacy and ethical issues. Since many of the online sites used to encourage political participation are commercial in nature, or becoming so, there is a potential for problems to arise. While Web 2.0 technologies themselves are open-source and available to all, the applications and sites built upon them are not necessarily so. Many successful social networking sites have been bought out by big business, e.g. News Corporation's purchase of MySpace (Wyld, 2007), who naturally seek to profit commercially from their purchase. Sites that are still in the hands of their original developer typically aspire to similarly monetize the asset that has been developed, usually by targeted advertising. Facebook's Beacon technology aroused the ire of the site's users because of the perceived potential for privacy to be infringed with user's personal data being made available to third party applications (McCarthy, 2007). Problems also arose when a recent change to Facebook's end-user agreement, seemed to assert Facebook's greater rights of ownership of the site's content which had, of course, been generated by end users (Wyld, 2007). Peterson (2008) perceptively notes that, while the Internet can serve to promote democracy and participation, the architecture of participation sometimes turns into the architecture of exploitation.

Another ethical issue impacted by the increasing use of online campaigning is the long-standing concern that the use of e-democracy technologies reinforces the digital divide; the idea that these technologies unduly advantage the societal elite and leave the less privileged even more isolated and excluded (Fraunholz & Unnithan, 2008). While access to the Internet is steadily increasing in most liberal democracies, political players still need to devise strategies that ensure that all citizens can participate fairly and freely in democratic processes.

CONCLUSION

Since the mid 1990's, commentators and researchers have envisaged the influence that the Internet might have on election campaigns, both for the candidates themselves and in terms of citizen participation. Till recently, the successes have been relatively limited and sporadic (Anstead and Chadwick 2008). The triumph of the Obama presidential campaign in the US has clearly demonstrated that, given skilled operators, the right environment and a well-integrated campaign, Web 2.0 and social media can play a significant role in increasing citizen involvement and participation in a particular aspect of the political process, i.e. election campaigning.

Many political campaigns will seek to emulate this success. It remains to be seen whether, or to what extent, that success can be duplicated. President Obama now plans to continue that participatory approach by contacting citizens from his emailing list to encourage them to lobby Congress to support his latest rescue package for the global financial crisis (Ives, 2008). It may prove a challenge for citizens to maintain the enthusiasm in the harsh glare and day-to-day realities of government.

Clearly, there is no silver bullet. The participation generate by Web 2.0 and social media is in no way delivering the idealized rich and sustained deliberation on an often-romanticized Athenian or public sphere model (Chadwick, 2009, p4). Nevertheless, without planning or pre-meditated effort, it has generated more participatory enthusiasm than many hard fought e-government projects designed to enable various forms of engagement, participation, consultation or deliberation. Common sense and the empirical evidence suggests that, to gain the most benefit, individual polities will need to tailor these technologies to suit citizen's motivations and interests, along with the political process, culture and environmental factors (such as e-readiness) within their own governmental systems.

REFERENCES

Anstead, N., & Chadwick, A. (2008). Parties, election campaigning, and the Internet: Toward a comparative institutional approach. In Chadwick, A. (Eds.), *The Routledge Handbook of Internet Politics* (pp. 56–73). London: Routledge.

Bajkowski, J. (2007, November 24). Online Face-offs and Spoofs Win Viewers. *MIS Financial Review*

Bieber,, C. (2007, November 21-25). Open Source Campaigning? How Online Innovations Trigger Offline Changes in Political Organizations. *ESF-LiU Conference. Electronic Democracy: Achievements and Challenges*, Vadstena, Sweden.

Boutin, P. (2006, April 26). A Grand Unified Theory of YouTube and MySpace: Point and Click Sites That Don't Tell You What To Do. Retrieved from http://www.slate.com/id/2140635/

Brauckmann, P. (2009). Why Obama would not have succeeded in Germany. *Sound Off*, Mar 2, Politics. Retrieved from http://www.politic-sonline.com/content/main/soundoff/soundoff.asp?id=444

Breindl, Y., & Francq, P. (2008, November 16). Can Web 2.0 applications save e-democracy? A study of how new internet applications may enhance citizen participation in the political process online. *International Journal of Electronic Democracy*, *1*(1), 14–31. doi:10.1504/IJED.2008.021276

Carr, D., & Stelter, B. (2008). Political campaigns in a Web 2.0 world. *The New York Times*, pp. B1, B11.

Chadwick, A. (2009) Web 2.0: new challenges for the study of e-democracy in an era of international exuberance, *I/S: A journal of Law and Policy for the Information Society*, *5*(1), 1-32.

Chafkin, M. (2007, June). How to Kill a Great Idea. *Inc.com*. Retrieved from http://www.inc.com/magazine/20070601/features-how-to-kill-a-great-idea.html

Cloud, J. (2006, December 16). The Gurus of YouTube. *Time*.

Coleman, S. (2001). Online Campaigning. *Parliamentary Affairs*, *54*(4), 679–688. doi:10.1093/parlij/54.4.679

Delaney, C. (2006). Social Media: Promising Tool, Double-Edged Sword. In Germany, J. B. (Ed.), *Person-to-Person-to-Person: Harnessing the Political Power of Online Social Networks and User-Generated Content* (pp. 7–11). Institute for Politics Democracy & the Internet.

Fraunholz, B., & Unnithan, C. (2008, November 16). Anti-apathy approaches in representative democracies: e-governance and web 2.0 – facilitating citizen involvement? *International Journal of Electronic Democracy*, *1*(1), 51–84. doi:10.1504/IJED.2008.021278

Glaister, D. (2007, March 20). US: YouTube a Test Tube for US Politicians. *AsiaMedia*, Los Angelas: UCLA Asia Institute.

Graham, P. (2005). *Web 2.0*. Retrieved from http://www.paulgraham.com/web20.html

Grossman, L. (2005, December 13). Time's Person of the Year: You. *Time*.

Gueorguieva, V. (2007). *Voters, MySpace, and YouTube: The Impact of Alternative Communication Channels on the 2006 Election Cycle and Beyond. Social Science Computer Review Online First*. Thousand Oaks, CA: SAGE Publications.

Gulati, G. J., & Williams, C. B. (2007). Closing the Gap, Raising the Bar: Candidate Web Site Communication in the 2006 Campaigns for Congress. *Social Science Computer Review*, *25*(4), 443–465. doi:10.1177/0894439307305624

Healy, P. (2007, February 2). US: Web Plays Key Role in Elections. *AsiaMedia*, Los Angelas: UCLA Institute.

Hogg, C. (2007, July 12). Japan's Old-fashioned Campaigning. *BBC News (Asia-Pacific)*. Retrieved from http://news.bbc.co.uk/1/hi/world/asia-pacific/6292602.stm

Ives, B. (2008). How Barack Obama is Using the Web to Further Engage Voters. *EContent*, *31*(5), 12–13.

Janack, J. A. (2006). Mediated Citizenship and Digital Discipline: A Rhetoric of Control in a Campaign Blog. *Social Semiotics*, *16*(2), 283–301. doi:10.1080/10350330600664862

Kranish, M. (2007, May 10). *Internet and Politics an Uneasy Fit*. Retrieved from http://www.politicsonline.com/coverage/boston2007/boston.html

Langer, G. (2008). Politics and the Internet Meet in the Rise of the Wired Electorate. *ABC News/Facebook Poll: The Election and The Internet*. Retrieved from http://abcnews.go.com/images/PollingUnit/1055a1TheElectionandtheInternet.pdf

Lawley, B. (2007, November 19). Hey, Pollies, You're in My Space. Get Out! *ONLINE Opinion*. Retrieved from http://onlineopinion.com.au/view.asp?article=6646

Leadbeater, C. (2007, July). Social Software for Social Change. *Discussion Paper for the Office of the Third Sector*.

Luo, M. (2008, February 20). Small Online Contributions Add Up to Huge Fund-Raising Edge for Obama, *New York Times*.

Lusoli, W. (2007, May 18). Internet Winner of the French Presidential Election? Retrieved from http://www.esri.salford.ac.uk/ESRCResearchproject/blog/index.php/2007/05/18/internet-winner-of-the-french-presidential-election/

Lusoli, W., & Ward, S. (2005). Logging On or Switching Off? The Public and the Internet at the 2005 General Election. In Coleman, S. (Eds.), *Spinning the Web: Online Campaigning in the 2005 General Election* (pp. 13–21). London: Hansard Society.

Madden, M., & Fox, S. (2006, October 5). *Riding the Waves of Web 2.0. More than a Buzzword, but Still Not Easily Defined*. PEW Internet & American Life Project.

Martin, L. (2007, July 23). MySpace Impact. *The Age*.

McCarthy, C. (2007, December 5) Facebook's Zuckerberg: 'We simply did a bad job' handling Beacon, *The Social*. Retrieved from http://news.cnet.com/8301-13577_3-9829526-36.html

Metherell, M. (2007, November 28). Internet Activists Claim Role in Howard's End. *The Sydney Morning Herald.*

Millard, J. (2009, March) eParticipation, *European Journal of ePractice, 2009*(7).

Moore, M. (2007, March 30). French Politics in 3-D on Fantasy Web Site. *The Washington Post.*

Moses, A. (2007, September 13). Australia: the Election's New Front is Online. *AsiaMedia*, Los Angeles: UCLA Asia Institute.

Moses, A. (2007, September 14). Pollies Embrace Google for the 'E-Election'. *The Age.*

Murugesan, S. (2007, July-August). Understanding Web 2.0. *IT Professional*, *9*(4), 34–41. Retrieved from http://ieeexplore.ieee.org/stamp/stamp.jsp?arnumber=04287373. doi:10.1109/MITP.2007.78

O'Reilly, T. (2005, September 30). *What is Web 2.0. Design Patterns and Business Models for the Next Generation of Software*, O'Reilly Media. Retrieved from http://www.oreillynet.com/pub/a/oreilly/tim/news/2005/09/30/what-is-web-20.html

Osimo, D. (2008, August) Benchmarking eGovernement in the Web 2.0 era: what to measure, and how, *European Journal of ePractice, 4*, August.

Osimo,, D. (2008, May 14) *Web 2.0 in government: why and how?* Institute for Prospective Technological Studies Report.

Panagopoulos, C. (2007). Technology and the Transformation of Political Communications. *Social Science Computer Review*, *25*(4), 423–424. doi:10.1177/0894439307305622

Parker, M. (2007, November 3). It Takes a Brave New Politician to Step Online. *The Canberra Times.*

Peterson, S., & Michael, M. (2008, March 2). Loser generated content: From participation to exploitation. *First Monday*, *13*(3). Retrieved from http://firstmonday.org/htbin/cgiwrap/bin/ojs/index.php/fm/article/view/2141/1948.

PEW (2008, January 11). *Internet's Broader Role in Campaign 2008: Social Networking and Online Videos Take Off.* PEW Research Center for the People and the Press.

Popkin, S. L. (2007, April). Changing Media and Changing Political Organization: Delegation, Representation and News. *Japanese Journal of Political Science*, *8*(1), 71–93. doi:10.1017/S1468109907002484

Ricketson, M. (2007, October 15). Cyberspace Democracy. *The Age.*

Ridder, R. (2008). Transatlantic relations under the Obama Administration. *Centre for European Studies.* Retrieved from http://www.thinkingeurope.eu/content.php?hmID=17&smID=43&ssmID=114

Sauger, N. (2007, November). The French Legislative and Presidential Elections of 2007. *West European Politics*, *30*(5), 1166–1175. doi:10.1080/01402380701617548

Schatz, A. (2007, March 19). In '08 Race, Web Tactics are Even More Integral. Retrieved from http://www.politicsonline.com/coverage/wsj2007/wsj.htm

Scott, D. T. (2005). *Tempests of the Blogosphere: Presidential Campaign Stories that Failed to Ignite Mainstream Media.* IlyaMEDIA. Retrieved from http://ilyagram.org/media/fetch/scott.pdf

Shannon, M. (2007). Shaking hands, kissing babies, and blogging. *Communications of the ACM*, *50*, 21–24. doi:10.1145/1284621.1284639

Sinclair, L. (2007, September 13). Web Gears Up for Election. *Australian IT.*

Stanyer, J. (2005). Political Parties, the Internet and the 2005 General Election: From Web Presence to E-Campaigning? *Journal of Marketing Management*, *21*(9), 1049–1065. doi:10.1362/026725705775194094

Tabuchi, H. (2008, February 4). Japan Prime Minister Debts on YouTube. *ABC News: Technology & Science*. Retrieved from http://abcnews.go.com/Technology/wireStory?id=4073578

Van Os, R., & Hagermann, C. (2007). The Netherlands: Party and Candidate Web Sites during the 2004 European Parliament Election Campaign. In Kluver, R. (Eds.), *The Internet and National Elections: A Comparative Study of Web Campaigning* (pp. 23–59). London: Taylor and Francis.

Wikipedia (2007). Web 2.0. *Wikipedia, the Free Encyclopedia*. Retrieved from http://en.wikipedia.org/wiki/Web_2.0

Williams, P. D. (2008). The 2007 Australian Federal Election: the Story of Labor's Return from the Wilderness. *The Australian Journal of Politics and History*, *54*(1), 104–125. doi:10.1111/j.1467-8497.2008.00487.x

Won-sup, Y. (2007, November 21). Unlike in 2002, Campaigners Fail to Attract Netizens. *Korea Times*.

Wyld, D. C. (2007). *The Blogging Revolution: Government in the Age of Web 2.0*. IBM Center for the Business of Government. Retrieved from http://www.businessofgovernment.org/pdfs/WyldReportBlog.pdf

Zappen, J. P., Harrison, T. M., et al. (2008). A new paradigm for designing e-government: web 2.0 and experience design. In *Proceedings of the 2008 international conference on Digital government research*, Montreal, Canada.

Chapter 9
The Nigerian e-Government Strategies (NeGST):
A Strategic Approach to Poverty Eradication in Nigeria

Charles K. Ayo
Covenant University, Nigeria

I.T. Fatudimu
Covenant University, Nigeria

ABSTRACT

Nigeria has made frantic efforts towards achieving the millennium development goals (MDGs) as spelt out in the United Nations' Agenda for the world. A critical assessment of the e-Government strategies in Nigeria is important being responsible for 20% of the population of the entire African continent. This paper presents a review of the e-Government strategies in Nigeria; the human capital development initiatives; the information and communications technology (ICT) diffusion and e-Inclusion. The global and continental ranking of the country is presented as well as recommendations to accelerate developments towards achieving the MDGs. Findings revealed that there are ongoing efforts in Nigeria to address the issue of poverty. The various initiatives of government include: the National/State Economic Empowerment Strategies (NEEDS/SEEDS), the Vision 2020, the National e-Government Strategy (NeGST) and a well-formulated National IT policy to mention a few. The little hindrance encountered in the research is that the available data was only up to the year 2005 and 2006 in some cases. However, based on the human capital development indices such as: economic empowerment and poverty reduction, education, health, employment generation, etc, it was observed that the adult literacy level of 64.2% is satisfactory and better results are expected before 2015. The life expectancy level is constant (54 years) from 2002 to 2007, which is the one of the lowest in Africa. On school enrolment, the major problem is access and poverty. It was observed that only 25% of primary school leavers made it to the secondary school level, while about 14% of the students at this level made it to the tertiary level. Similarly, the average percentage of female enrolment in schools is 45%. The health facilities are under-funded and are grossly inadequate both in quality and quantity. There is an average of 1,700 persons per hospital bed and the ratio of physicians to the populace is about 1:6000. This calls for a state of emergency in this sector.

DOI: 10.4018/978-1-61520-789-3.ch009

One major sector of the economy that is experiencing a boost is the ICT and Telecoms. The sector had brought about a teledensity growth of 0.73 to 37.05 from 2001 to 2007. Consequently, Nigeria has been named the fastest growing Telecoms nation in Africa and the third in the world, with a number of direct and indirect jobs created. Similarly, the rate of Internet diffusion is encouraging bearing in mind that the level was almost nonexistent in 1999. It is obvious that Nigeria would be able to bridge the divide by 2015. Generally, there are some meaningful developments in the country arising from the various poverty eradication schemes but the resultant effect has not imparted positively on unemployment. This is the opinion of the populace and hence the need for government to restrategize, otherwise, fulfilling MDGs by 2015 may not be realistic.

INTRODUCTION

The world representatives assembled in Geneva from 10 – 12 of December 2003, for a maiden summit tagged: *Building the information society: a global challenge in the millennium*. The summit declared a common desire and commitment to build a people-oriented and development-poised information society that is aimed at enabling everyone to create, access, utilize, share information and knowledge (WSIS, 2003). The initiative was to enable individuals, communities and peoples achieve their full potentials by promoting sustainable development and improving quality of life premised on the principles of the United Nations. Arising from the summit is the recognition of ICT as a panacea for sustainable development, hence the evolvement of the concept of e-Government, e-Democracy, e-Policing, e-Health, e-Learning, etc. as contained in the eight (8) developmental goals called the millennium development goals (MDGs), with the overall objective of reducing poverty by 50% by the year 2015 (UNDP, 2000).

Information Technology for Development (IT4D) is defined as the implementation, use and management of IT infrastructures to stimulate social and economic development (Qureshi, 2007). IT offers access to information and expertise; it enhances competitiveness and access to markets; it enhances administrative efficiency; it enhances labour productivity and learning; and it is a veritable tool for poverty eradication.

e-Government refers to the use of information and communications technology in public administration combined with organizational change and new skills to improve public services and democratic processes and to strengthen support for public policies (Vassilios, 2004). ICT has been adopted in Europe, particularly at all levels of administration as a veritable tool for modernising public services, re-engineering administrative processes and empowering the citizens.

Agunloye (2004) presented e-Government as an interaction between citizens, businesses and organizations, government ministries and all the tiers of government. Thus, as against traditional governance in the developing world, that is characterized by hunger, war, poverty, sickness, ethnicity and oppression as well as unemployment, using ICT powered government would lead to transparency, accountability and efficiency in governance in order to deliver better services and wealth for the general well-being of the citizens. e-Government is seen as a route to better governance as it is open and transparent, and an enabler for participatory democracy; it is service-oriented, and it provides personalised and inclusive services to every citizen; and it is a panacea for enhanced productivity and better utilization of the taxpayers' money.

Achieving the MDGs is a herculean task for most nations, particularly, the developing ones. For some years now, Africa has remained at the bottom of the table of the annual UN global e-Government readiness report (UN, 2005).

Governance in Nigeria and Africa in general is characterized by corruption, debt overhanging, unemployment, low productivity, unfocussed policies, insensitivity and bad leadership (Gowon, 2006 & Nwabueze, 2003). All these have grave consequences on developmental issues like education, health, employment, electricity generation, transportation and other major sectors of the economy (Ezigbo, 2006).

Cookey (2005) identified corruption as a *sine qua non* for making progress on growth and human capital development in Nigeria. The high level of corruption has been identified to be responsible for the high degree of misrule, insecurity, hunger, poverty and politically motivated massacre in Africa (Iyayi, 2004).

Nigeria is the most populous black nation in the world and is responsible for 20% of the African population. It is the 6th largest oil producing country in the world but the accrued revenues have not translated to the well-being of the populace on account of corruption by government officials. Consequently, the country has not been able to provide the basic necessities of life for her citizenry; and meeting the MDGs may be an upheaval task. This practice is prominent among many African nations (Tell, 2006).

OBJECTIVES OF THE CHAPTER

The primary objectives of this paper include:

i. to review the e-Government assessment in Nigeria;
ii. to review the MDGs initiatives in Nigeria;
iii. to review the human capital development and poverty level in Nigeria;
iv. to review the level of ICT diffusion in Nigeria;
v. to assess the e-Readiness status of Nigeria.

NIGERIAN E-GOVERNMENT ASSESSMENT

The Global e-Government Report

Africa was the lowest in 2005 ranking among the other continents of the world. However, within Africa, the Giant of Africa, Nigeria, was ranked 22 among the 45 nations in Africa (UN, 2005). Mauritius ranked first with an index of 0.5317 and world ranking of 52, followed by South Africa with an index of 0.5075 and world ranking of 58, while Nigeria occupies the 22nd position in Africa, having an index of 0.2758 and world ranking of 139. The country trails behind Namibia, Lesotho, Cape Verde, Zimbabwe, Kenya, Uganda and Congo among others. This report on Nigeria is disheartening being the 6th largest oil producing nation in the world.

The world best ten countries according to that report: the US (.9062) came first, followed by Denmark (.9058), Sweden (.8983), UK(.8777), Republic of Korea (.8727), Australia (.8679), Singapore (.8503), Canada (.8425), Finland (.8231) and Norway (.8228). Within the next ten countries are: Germany, Japan, Netherlands, Austria, Belgium, Ireland, etc.

However, in the 2008 global ranking, Sweden came first (0.9157) followed by Denmark (0.9134) and US came forth (0.8644). This is an indication of improved services and concerted commitment by these countries to infrastructural provisions (UN, 2008). The story is slightly different in Africa. With the exception of some few countries that improved on the 2005 ranking a number of others performed worse. Nigeria moved from 139 to 136, Eqypt moved from 99 to 79 and a few others but countries like Ghana, Togo, Cote D'ivore, Morocco, Tunisia etc slid backward.

The DFID report of 2006 presented Nigeria with a population of 130 million, where about 75 million people lived with abject poverty; about 2 million AIDS orphans; about 12 million children were out of school; one in every 5 children died before age 5; and a per capital income of $0.30 per person per day (DFID Nigeria, 2006).

Nigerian government is constantly making efforts at achieving the millennium development goals but lack of probity, accountability and transparency as well as lack of the basic infrastructure is a major hindrance. Thus, the global and continental ranking of Nigeria is abysmally low that smaller countries are high up on the ladder. It is thus obvious that the size of the country and her wealth had not translated to the well-being of the citizenry. However, the current efforts of government as contained in vision 2020 is a clear indication of her further commitment not only to eradicate poverty by 2020 but to have the nation listed among the top 20 economies of the world.

The Economic Indices of some Selected African Countries

The Financial Standard Newspaper presents a daily/weekly report of the performance of the economies of some selected countries in Africa. The various criteria used include: inflation rate, interest rate, life expectancy, Internet penetration among others. The excerpts from the papers for over two years are presented in Table 1.

Life Expectance Ratio

From Table 1, the life expectance ratios of some selected African countries are presented in Figure 1. Life expectancy is higher in some African countries like Morocco, Egypt, and Eritrea and fair in some East, South and West African countries. If the dividend of democracy is to improve the well-being of the citizenry, then Nigeria has not fared well, considering its life expectancy rate that is about the lowest in Africa. It is the lowest among the selected countries. The situation in Nigeria can be improved upon through an improved healthcare system, job creation, provision of water and education, and improved economic situation. DFID (2007) reports described the health system in Nigeria as off track because government spending on health is below 5% of the total budget. The same is true of education, which is between 5% and 9%, far below the 26% recommended by UNESCO.

Internet Penetration

Figure 2 is constructed based on Table 1. The Internet has become a major platform for business transaction all over the world. Therefore, access to this medium is very crucial to meeting the

Table 1. Economic indices for some African countries

	Nigeria	Morocco	Niger	Eritrea	Benin	Uganda	Cameroon	South Africa	Ghana	Egypt
GDP Growth	5.5	1.8	0.2	2	3.5	4	4.1	4.9	5.4	NA
Inflation Rate	11.6	2.1	8.1	15	3.5	8.1	4.2	0.2	14.8	NA
Interest Rate	30.5	13.4	NA	16.8	NA	NA	10.8	12	15.5	NA
Life Exp (Male)	46.5	68.5	51.63	57.4	51.9	51.63	63.5	43.8	55	68.77
Life Exp (Female)	47.7	73.4	53.69	60.7	54.22	53.69	47.7	43.7	57	73.93
Internet Users(m)	5	0.5	NA	NA	0.425	0.5	NA	5.1	NA	5
Population (m)	133.58	31.15	13.957	4.401	8.439	29.7	16.322	47.432	22.75	74.033

(Source: Excerpts from Financial Standard Newspaper; and Wikipedia http://en.wikipedia.org/wiki/List_of_countries_by_population_in_2005)

Figure 1. Life expectancy ratios of some selected African countries

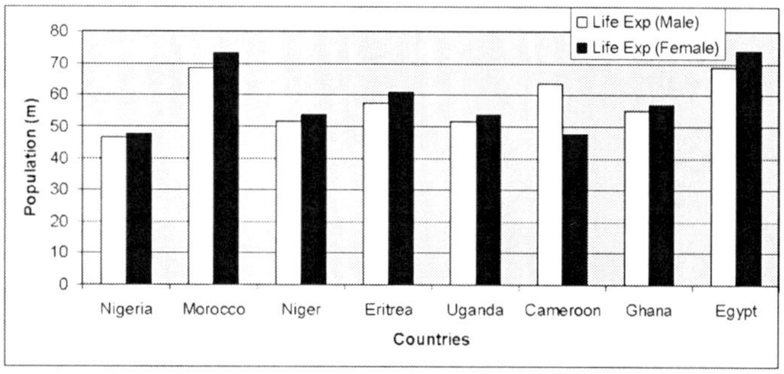

MDGs, particularly poverty eradication through the introduction of e-Commerce, e-Learning and e-Health to mention a few. South Africa has the highest figure (5.1 million). In Nigeria it is 5 million and when compared to the population, it becomes insignificant. Therefore, Nigerian through its recently formulated ICT policy and rural telephony strategy would be able to deploy such services to the rural areas. Although cost and poverty level are a major concern.

THE MDGS INITIATIVES IN NIGERIA

The National Economic and Empowerment Strategies (NEEDS)

After the several years of misrule by the military, the civilian government of Nigeria instituted a dynamic reform team to launch its poverty eradication strategies. NEEDS was a medium-term plan from 2004 – 2007 by the Nigerian government for economic recovery, growth and development (IMF Report, 2007). According to (Olubamise et al., 2007), the strategies include:

i. Reforming government institutions
   - Restructuring and strengthening government institutions
ii. Growing the private sector
   - Reducing government influence in the economy
   - Accelerating privatization
   - Deregulating and liberalizing the economy
iii. Implementing a social charter

Figure 2. Internet penetration rates of some selected African countries

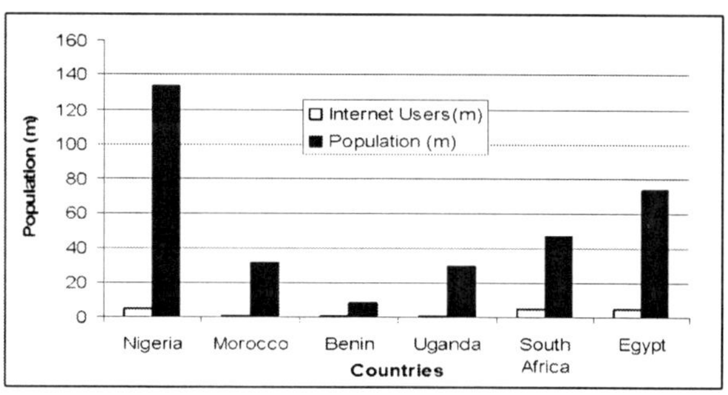

Figure 3. Distribution of internet usage in Nigeria

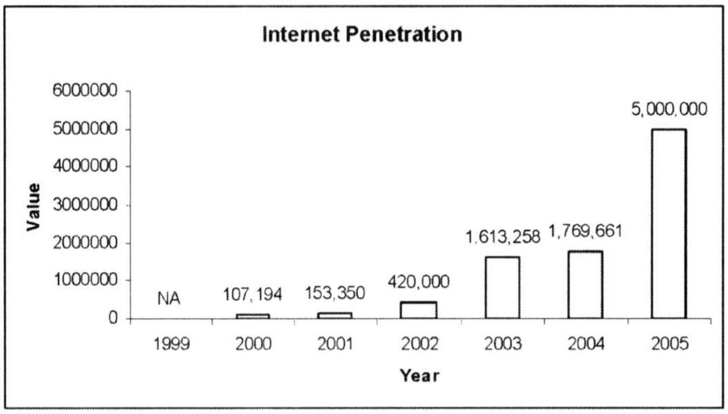

- Improve peoples access to health, education, welfare, employment, security and participation

iv. Adding value-orientation
- Anti-corruption campaign
- Freedom of information
- Enhancing the role of the civil society

For effective results from the reform, the State Economic and Empowerment Strategies (SEEDS) was formed. SEEDS is a local equivalent of NEEDS instituted to drive government reforms to the grass root. It is to make government accountable at all levels and to institute people-oriented policies that would stem down the tide of poverty in the country. At the end of the year 2007, NEEDS-2 was inaugurated to advance the goals of NEEDS from 2008 to 2011. Simultaneously, Vision 2020 was instituted and was aimed at eradicating poverty and transforming the economy of Nigeria in general.

The overall performance of NEEDS is remarkable. The process is still on course; it surpasses the expected targets in many respects, particularly on privatization and liberalization; banking consolidation and civil service reforms; but it is weak in some areas; and still below expectation in the areas of poverty reduction, employment generation and power supply (NEEDS, 2004).

The social charter under NEEDS include: economic empowerment and poverty reduction, education, health, employment generation, gender equality and water sanitation. The projected target for 2007 was to create 7 million jobs, increase immunization to 60%; increase access to safe drinking water by 70%; increase school enrollment rates for girls and increase adult literacy rate to at least 65%. The actual performance revealed that 7 million jobs were not created; unemployment rate declined from 17% in 2004 to 10% in 2006; growth in the education sector is making slow but steady progress; immunization coverage increased from 38% in 2005 to 77% in 2006 (IMF Report, 2007).

The Small and Medium Enterprises (SMEs) Initiatives

SMEs are defined as businesses with less than N100 million (about $1 million) turnover and/or less than 300 employees (Oyelaran, 2007). Similarly, in the International Finance Committee Report 2007, 96% of Nigerian businesses are classifies as SMEs as against 53% and 65% in the US and Europe respectively.

The SMEs are managed under the small and medium enterprises development agency of Nigeria (SMEDAN). It was set up in the year 2003, while similar bodies had been in existence for over 50 years in the developed world (Japan since 1941 and USA since 1953), with a lot of results to show. In the 70's and 80's in Britain, between 500 and 900 new firms were created on a weekly basis and about one million self employed people (Abugu, 2007).

The British model was focused on loan guarantee scheme, tax incentives, linkage of SMEs with appropriate technologies and educational institutions and developing venture capital industry. Nigeria has a lot to learn from this model in order to correct the failed attempts of the past at reducing poverty.

The Vision 2020 Initiative

According to the governor of the Central Bank of Nigeria, Charles Soludo (2007), the Vision 2020 otherwise known as the Financial System Strategy (FSS 2020), was predicated on Goldman Sachs' prediction that the economies of Brazil, Russia, India and China (BRIC) would surpass the G6 based on extrapolation growth rate, capital accumulation, exchange rate among others. The organization further predicted the next eleven (N 11) countries that have the potentials to overtake Italy in GDP and Nigeria and Egypt were the only two African countries included.

Consequent upon this, the FSS 2020 was formulated to place the Nigerian economy among the 20 largest economies in the world by the year 2020 code named vision 20 20202. Thus, the thrust of FSS 2020 is to:

1. Increase commitment to education.
2. Enforce economic, structural and political reforms.
3. Enhance greater integration into the world trade and finance.
4. Improve power supply, transportation and telecoms infrastructure.
5. Reduce overall dependence on primary commodities and improve industrial economy and business environment.

The Nigerian National IT Policy

The Nigerian National IT policy was formulated in the year 2000. It is responsible for the monumental developments in the ICT sector. The vision is to make Nigeria an IT capable country in Africa and a key player in the information society. Its primary mission is to Use IT for: education; creation of wealth; poverty eradication; job creation; governance; health; agriculture; etc. (Ajayi, 2005).

Some On-Going ICT Projects in Nigeria

i. Mobile Internet Units (MIUs)

These are buses equipped with ICT facilities such as PCs, peripheral devices and very small aperture terminals (VSATs) which are used to carry ICT education to rural areas. Currently, there are six MIU buses, but the expectation is to extend the services to all the 774 local government areas of Nigeria (Angaye, 2007).

ii. Wire Nigeria (WiN) Project

This project is tagged Wire Nigeria. It is intended to provide broadband transmission to all the nooks and crannies of the country. The project is expected to facilitate the interconnection of various equipment, facilities and subsystems in order to provide end-to-end transfer of information (Bello, 2007). The project was divided into 3 phases: phase 1 is to connect all State capitals to the fibre network; phase 2 is to connect all Local Government headquarters; and phase 3 is to provide all Nigerians with fibre Network within a maximum of 50 km from where they live. The project is presently at phase 2. Upon completion, the project is expected to reduce rural-urban migration; enhance rural urbanization; improve the quality of live of all; improve standard of education; and improve employment generation.

iii. E-Government Project

This is part of the civil service reforms which was designed to make the Nigerian civil service proactive and to respond quickly to the needs of the general populace. The project was a joint initiative between the public and private sector operators under the aegis of National e-Government Strategies (NeGST) and the National Information Technology Development Agency (NITDA). At the international conference for e-Government organized by the UN in China in 2007, the Nigerian e-Government model was endorsed as a viable option for implementation across the world, particularly, the public private partnership model (Nkanga, 2007).

The project was designed to reduce the bureaucracy that attends to government businesses in the country through the introduction of e-Tax, e-Learning, e-Traffic, e-Procurement, e-Pricing, e-Mail, e-Tourism, e-Payment, e-Revenue, e-Legislation, e-Policing, e-Judiciary, e-Health, e-Agriculture, e-Services, e-Kiosk, e-Buka (e-Cafeteria) etc (Isoun, 2004).

Presently the NeGST has online presence at (http://www.negst.com). Similarly, all the Federal ministries are online, and the country has commenced online payment for services in such areas as tax, company registration, online booking, e-Banking etc.

REVIEW OF THE NIGERIAN HUMAN DEVELOPMENT INDEX (HDI)

People are the real wealth of nations. Therefore, every effort that is geared towards poverty reduction must be centered on human development. Thus, in the UN report of 2006, HDI represents a composite measure of three dimensions of human development which include: living a long and healthy life (measured by life expectancy); level of education (measured by adult literacy and level of enrolment at the primary, secondary and tertiary levels); and standard of living measured by purchasing power parity, PPP, income) (UN report, 2006). From the report, Nigeria is ranked among the countries with low human development and has a position of 159 out of the 177 nations considered.

Therefore, presented in the tables below are the rates of development on some selected macroeconomic and social indicators, enrolment in schools, female enrolment in schools, health development and ICT diffusion.

Table 2 shows the rate of developments of some selected macroeconomic and social indicators. The inflation rate increased from 12.2% in 2002 to 14% and 15% in 2003 and 2004 respectively, and decreased to 11.6%, 8.5% and 6.6% in 2005, 2006 and 2007 respectively because of the reforms instituted in the banking sector of the economy. The downward trend witnessed from 2005 to 2007 is expected to be sustained.

Table 2. Some selected macroeconomic & social indicators

	Year					
Variable	**2002**	**2003**	**2004**	**2005**	**2006**	**2007**
Inflation Rate (%)	12.2	14	15	11.6	8.5	6.6
Growth in Agriculture Sector %)	4.22	6.64	6.5	7.06	7.17	7.42
External Reserve ($ Billions)	7.68	7.46	17.26	28.61	43	51.33
Adult Literacy Rate	57	57	62	62	64.2	64.2
Life Expectancy at Birth (Years)	54	54	54	54	54	54

(Source: CBN Report, 2006 & 2007)

The life expectancy rate is constant (54 years) from 2002 to 2007. The index is a function of a number of factors such as health, employment, education, water supply etc, on these factors, the country is not doing well presently. The adult literacy rate increased marginally from 57% in 2002 to 64.2% in 2006 and 2007. The rate is above average and better result is expected because of the current reforms in the education sector, particularly the universal basic education (UBE). The agricultural sector has equally witnessed a marginal growth from 4.22% in 2002 to 7.42% in 2007. The country had neglected this sector in the past because of the massive revenue from oil and gas. Presently, the oil and gas is responsible for over 80% of the nation's revenue.

One good thing that has happened to the nation is the monumental growth in foreign reserves from the period under consideration, particularly the growth from $17.26 billion in 2004 to $51.33 billion in 2007. This development is attributed to the reforms in the banking and the Telecoms sectors, which has not only sanitized the sectors but has made them a global player.

Unemployment Level

Poverty eradication or reduction is largely a function of unemployment both at the formal and the informal sectors. Table 3 only gives the statistics as far as the formal sector is concerned. At the national level the level of unemployment is 70%. However, going by the figures in the table, there were marginal improvements in employment from 2003 to 2005 but the level of unemployment seems to have deteriorated from 2006 to 2007. The worry generally now is that the various programmes of government have not yielded the expected benefits.

School Enrolment

The total school enrolment figures for the country from 2002 to 2005 are presented in Table 4.

Table 3. Unemployment statistics

	2003	2004	2005	2006	2007
Total Population	129,900,168	134,131,224	138,468,013	140,003,542	144,483,655.34
Total Labour Force	54,929,577	55,538,881	56,170,672	58,933,891	61,249,485
Total Employment	46,800,000	48,124,440	49,486,362	50,886,826	52,326,923
Total Unemployment	8,129,577	7,414,441	6,684,310	8,047,065	8,922,562
Unemployment Rate (%)	14.8	13.4	11.9	13.7	14.6

(Source: CBN Report, 2006 & 2007)

Table 4. School enrolment

	Year			
No of Enrolment at School	2002	2003	2004	2005
1. Primary	19,353,000	24,768,000	25,464,000	26,160,000
2. Secondary	4,866,000	6,152,000	6,343,000	6,534,000
3. T ertiary	746,000	846,000	888,000	930,000
Total	24,965,000	31,766,000	32,695,000	33,624,000

(Source: CBN Report, 2006)

The enrolment in schools is an important factor of human development. However, considering the years under review, 2002 to 2005, the statistics show a marginal improvement across the various tiers of learning. Education at the primary level is the largest because it is largely free and compulsory across the country. From the figures, only about 25% of the primary school leavers proceed to secondary level, while about 14% of secondary school leavers proceed to the tertiary level. The nation has less than 50% of the required infrastructure to meet the yearning needs of the populace, which is due to poor funding of the sector as well as poverty. Most pupils hardly make it to the secondary level before they start to support their parents in one trade or the order. However, arising from the education reform of 2006, particularly the UBE makes education free and compulsory up to the 15th year. Better improvement is expected after some years of implementation.

Female Enrolment

From Table 5, about 50% of the female population in Nigeria attended primary school. The number of the females in the secondary school decreased from 48% in 2002 to 42% in 2003 but gained an increment of 1% each in 2004 and 2005. The percentage of female students in tertiary institutions was 45% in 2003 and decreased to 43% in 2003 through 2005.

Table 5. Percentage of female enrolment in schools

Percentage of Females in Educational Institutions	2002	2003	2004	2005
1. Primary	51	53	53	53
2. Secondary	48	42	43	44
3. T ertiary	45	43	43	43

(Source: CBN Report, 2006)

Health Services

The level of health facilities is low, thus requiring urgent attention. The number of persons per hospital bed was 1,685.50 in 2002, which has increased marginally to 1,722.70 in 2003 and 1,764.40 and 1,806 in 2004 and 2005 respectively. Similarly, the number of persons per physician was 3,190.30 in 2002, which reduced to 3,141.30 in 2003 and further down to 3,100 and 3,059 in 2004 and 2005 respectively. According to a special report on the health situation in Nigeria, a ratio of 1: over 6,000 was reported (Yusuf, 2008). This abysmal situation arose because only 20,000 out of the 60,000 medical doctors ply their trade locally while the remaining ones are abroad in search of greener pastures. The situations of health problems are multi-dimensional. They range from education, water supply, environment, and poverty to funding among others. It has been observed that developments in these sectors is poor, particularly, the provision of safe water.

Ekiwhire (2008) reported that diarrhea, killed 1.9 million people every year with over 4 billion reported cases in recent years. In Africa, diarrhea is 4 times more common than HIV virus.

MAJOR ICT DEVELOPMENTS IN NIGERIA

Telephone Usage in Nigeria

The deregulation of the telecoms industry in the year 2001 is responsible for the growth of telephone subscribers. It shows an improvement in teledensity from 0.73 in 2001 to 37.05 by 2007. The GSM is a major contributor to the growth.

The transformation in this sector of the economy is monumental as the number of GSM subscribers by early 2008 had risen to over 50 million. The sector had created thousands of direct and indirect jobs. If the platform is well harnessed, it could mark the beginning of m-Government,

Table 6. Distribution of some health services

Health Services	2002	2003	2004	2005
1. Population in Nigeria (Census 1991)	122,364,720	126,152,844	129,927,425	133,702,006
2. Population per Physician (No)	3,190.30	3,141.30	3,100.00	3,059.00
3. Population per Nursing Staff (No.)	951.80	922.50	818.00	714.00
4. Population per Hospital Bed (No.)	1,685.50	1,722.70	1,764.40	1,806.00
5. Life Expectancy at Birth (Years)	54	54	54	54

(Source: CBN Report, 2006)

m-Democracy, m-Payment and m-Procurement, that is, the deployment of government, democracy, payment and procurement services on mobile devices respectively, which would improve the e-Inclusion or e-Participation in the polity and the economy.

Internet Usage in Nigeria

Coming from a level that was non-existent in 1999, to a total population of 5 million in 2005 is very commendable. This is the second largest in Africa after South Africa with a value of 5.1 million. However, the value is expected to be higher now and perhaps the highest in Africa because of the commitment of government to the National IT policy, which is expected to extend ICT facilities to the nooks and crannies of the country. Thus, the level of Internet penetration is encouraging as there is phenomenal growth, though, much is still expected from a nation with a population of 140 million.

CONCLUSION

The Nigerian e-Government strategies are aimed at improving the well-being of the citizenry, particularly meeting the MDGs and they have started yielding dividends but very gradually. The MDGs initiatives of the country have brought about major reforms in the economy through the institutionalization of NEEDS, SEEDS, Vision 2020, NeGST, as well as the provision of improved ICT services such as telecommunications and the Internet.

The ranking of the country on e-Government readiness may not be encouraging, but the level of access to ICT is worthy of praise. The position is low because of the population of the country. Mauritius was ranked first but its population is not up to a local government area out of the existing 774 local government areas in Nigeria. However, the ranking of South Africa, Egypt, Algeria whose population is about one-third or half of the Nigerian population is worthy on note.

Table 7. Distribution of telephone usage in Nigeria

OPERATOR	2001	2002	2003	2004	2005	2006	Oct-07
Mobile (GSM)	266,461	1,569,050	3,149,472	9,174,209	18,587,000	32,322,202	49,057,883
Mobile (CDMA)	N/A	N/A	N/A	N/A	N/A	N/A	424,579
Fixed Wired/ Wireless	600,321	702,000	872,473	1,027,519	1,223,258	1,687,972	2,391,442
Total	866,782	2,271,050	4,021,945	10,201,728	19,810,258	34,010,174	51,873,904
Teledensity	0.73	1.89	3.35	8.50	15.72	24.29	37.05

(Source: http://www.ncc.gov.ng/subscriberdata.htm)

Therefore, based on the analysis of the social charter that imparts directly on human development and poverty, it was observed that the adult literacy level of 64.2% is satisfactory and better results are expected before 2015. The life expectancy level is constant (54 years) from 2002 to 2007, and is the one of the lowest in Africa. On school enrolment, the major problem is access and poverty. It was observed that only 25% of primary school leavers made it to the secondary school level, while about 14% of the students at this level made it to the tertiary level. This trend is not encouraging if we must eradicate poverty. Similarly, the average percentage of female enrolment in schools is 45%. This is fair as the 50% benchmark by 2015 is realizable. The health facilities are under-funded and are grossly inadequate both in quality and quantity. There is an average of 1,700 persons per hospital bed and the ratio of physicians to the populace is 1: over 6,000, which is twice the WHO recommendation, a state of emergency should be declared in this sector.

One major sector of the economy that is experiencing a boost is the ICT and Telecoms. The sector had brought about a teledensity growth of 0.73 to 37.05 from 2001 to 2007. Consequently, Nigeria has been named the fastest growing Telecoms nation in Africa and the third in the world, with a number of direct and indirect jobs created. Similarly, the rate of Internet diffusion is encouraging bearing in mind that the level was almost non existent in 1999. It is obvious that Nigeria would be able to bridge the divide by 2015 with the attendant benefits to other areas such as e-Learning, e-Health, e-Commerce, e-Democracy and e-Government to mention a few.

The current NeGST drive of the country is encouraging, particularly the provision of rural telephony would address the issue of access-divide and offer the rural dwellers equal opportunities for economic and social empowerment as well as enhanced participation in the polity (e-Inclusion or e-Participation).

REFERENCES

Abugu, I. (2007, June): *SME: Issues, Challenges and Prospects*, An invited presentation at the International Conference on Financial System Strategy (FSS) 2020 Organized by the Central Bank of Nigeria. Retrieved February 2007, from http://www.cenbank.org/fss/wed/sme_issues,%20challenges%20and%20prospects_ike%20abugu.pdf

Agunloye, O. (2004): *e-Government strategies for west Africa: public-private-partnership*. Retrieved from www.enigeria.org

Ajayi, G. O. (2005). *e-Government in Nigeria's e-strategy*. Retrieved from http://www.nitda.gov.ng/papers

Angaye, C. (2007, November 26). NeGST has no monopoly on e-Government. *Financial Standard*, pp. 46.

Bello, S. (2003): *The Impact of the Wire Nigeria (WiN) Project on Universal Service Provision*. Retrieved February 2007, from http://www.ncc.gov/Workshop%20Papers/Consultative%20Workshop-August%202003/bello's%20presentation%20at%20presentation%20at%20consultative%20forum2.pdf

Cookey, P.(2005, September): Corruption Stall Nigeria Development – World Bank. *Financial Standard*, pp. 9

Ekpiwhire, G. (2008, March 3). Meeting MDGs Safe Water Target, *Financial Standard, 9*(96), 12.

Ezigbo, O.(2007, February).Nigeria Image still not Good, says World Bank. *This Day*.

Gowon, Y. (2006, July 27). *Issues of Government for Nations State of African: Pathways for Leadership Development*, Presented at the first Convocation Lecture of Covenant University, Ota.

ISoun. T. (2004): *Nigeria: Government/Private Sector Partner to deliver e-government*. Retrieved from http://www.e-lo-go.de/html/

Iyayi, F. (2004). *The Conduct of Elections and electoral practices in Nigeria*. Retrieved from http://nigerianbar.com/papers3.htm

National Bureau of Statistics. (2005). *The Nigerian Fact Sheets on Economic & Social Development*. Nigeria: National Bureau of Statistics.

NEEDS. (2004). *Nigeria- National Economic Empowerment Development Strategy*. Retrieved February 2007, from http://www.cenbank.org/out/publications/communique/guidelines/rd/2004/needs.pdf

Nigeria, D. F. I. D. (2006): *Country Profile: Africa*. Retrieved Ocotber 2006, from http://www.dfid.gov.uk/countries/africa/nigeria.asp

Nigeria, D. F. I. D. (2007): *Country Profile: Africa*. Retrieved August 2007 from, http://www.dfid.gov.uk/countries/africa/nigeria.asp

Nkanga, N. (2007). *Nigeria: UN Endorses Nigeria's E-Government Model*. Retrieved from http://www.egovnews.org/?p=2965

Nwabueze, B. (2003). *Constitutional Democracy in Africa*. Nigeria: Spectrum Books

Olubamise, B., & Awe, J. (2007). *NIGERIA: ICT4D Annual Review 2007*. Retrieved September 21, 2007, from http://www.jidaw.com/itsolutions/ict4dreview2007.html

Oyelaran-Oyeyinka, B. (2007, June). *SME: Issues, Challenges and Prospects*, An invited presentation at the International Conference on Financial System Strategy (FSS) 2020 Organized by the Central Bank of Nigeria. Retrieved February 2007, from http://www.cenbank.org/fss/wed/sme_issues,%20challenges%20and%20prospects_oyeyinka%20banji.pdf

Qureshi, S. (2007). *Information Technology for Development*. Retrieved February 2007, from http://www.wmin.ac.uk/wbs/pdf.ITD-Presentation_for_WBS_June_20_2007.pdf

Report, I. M. F. (2007). *Nigeria- Poverty Strategy Paper- Progress Report*. Retrieved February 2007, from http://siteresources.worldbank.org/INTPRS1/Resources/Nigeria-PRSP-PR(August2007).pdf

Soludo, C. C. (2007). *Nigeria's Financial System Strategy 2020 Plan OUR DREAM*, A paper presented at the International Conference on Financial System Strategy (FSS) 2020 Organized by the Central Bank of Nigeria. Retrieved February 2007, from http://www.cenbank.org/fss/mon/FSS2020---Presentation%20at%20International%20Conference.ppt

Tell Editorial. (2006). *Standing Up Against Corruption* (pp. 18–19). Tell Magazine.

UN. (2005). *UN Global E-government Readiness Report 2005: From E-government to E-inclusion*. Retrieved from http://unpan1.un.org/intradoc/groups/public/documents/un/unpan021888.pdf

UN. (2008). *E-Government Survey 2008, From E-Government to Connected Governance*. http://unpan1.un.org/intradoc/groups/public/documents/UN/UNPAN028607.pdf

UNDP. (2000). *Millennium Development Goals*. Retrieved from http://www.undp.org/mdg/basics.shtml

Vassilios, L. (2004). *Information Society Policy link initiative*. Retrieved from http://europa.eu.int/information_society/activities/policy_link/index_en.htm

WSIS. (2003): *World Summit on the Information Society Declaration of principles*. Retrieved from www.itu.int/dms_pub/itu_s/md/03/wsis/

Yusuf, A. (2008, March 17). Nigerian Hospitals-Corridors of Death. *Tell Magazine*, pp 18-23.

Chapter 10
An Exploratory Analysis of the On-Line Dispute Resolution Mechanism

Panagiota-Aikaterina Sidiropoulou
Middlesex University, UK

Evangelos Moustakas
Middlesex University, UK

ABSTRACT

The 21st century is being characterized as the century of evolution for information technology, communication technology and electronic communications. Contemporary society does business using the internet; the forthcoming 'dispute resolution space' (Katsh and Rifkin 2001), where people buy and sell regularly and even a large number of corporations have existence via an internet address. This excitement for further improvement of dispute techniques, in relation to the exploitation of those technologies used for the management of online virtual communication led to the appearance of the Online Dispute Resolution (ODR) mechanism. The choice for settlement of disputes through the modern mechanism provides an easement for interested parties to tackle their disputes from any place and at any time through e-mails, video conferencing or chatrooms, instead of being in courtrooms. The fact that the business's transactions are conducted on the internet causes uncertainty, regarding the security of personal data and business secrets in combination with the lack of a framework that could have supported such scheme. For that reason, the role of Government is taken into consideration in the accreditation of service providers, as well as in the settlement of e-administrative disputes and the securing of e-transactions in general. The necessity for self-regulation, equality of digital divide and government's recommendation for ODR tools is discussed. The current chapter will identify and explore considerable notions, concepts and debates for moving towards the development of an international dispute resolution framework on-line and trustful mechanism internationally.

DOI: 10.4018/978-1-61520-789-3.ch010

WHAT IS ONLINE-DISPUTE RESOLUTION (ODR)?

In late 1960s, the legal world was experiencing a new trend, known as 'Alternative Dispute Resolution' or else with its universal acronym ADR that gradually became one of the most important tools for an immediate and competent settlement of (international) disputes. Basically, ADR refers to any out-of-court proceedings or alternatives to the judicial process. It has been characterized as 'the principal vehicle' (Katsh and Wing, 2006) that exists for over thirty years and deals with offline disputes, because of its flexible, quick and cost-effective approach.

ODR is the 'offspring' of the traditional ADR and not its supplement. None statutory definition can be found or any generally accepted definition of the term. Julia Hornle (2002) characterizes ODR as the Information Technology and Telecommunication via the internet- together referred to as 'online technology'- that applies to ADR (p.1). Similarly, Colin Rule correlates ODR with the utilization of an advanced level of technology. Ethan Katsh suggests that ODR is a network application that illustrates how, as data is generated by interactions between humans and machines, boundaries between dispute prevention and dispute resolution, or between dispute resolution and standard setting, may become less clear (2007 p.105). Alternatively, he acknowledges that ODR is part of the movement to build civic institutions online that are needed to encourage online activity and growth (Katsh 2001 p.19). Kaufmann and Schultz are of the same opinion that ODR is a movement and not a passing trend or some legal or business fad (2004 p.67). They simply define it as a system that deals with dispute settlement methods that exist online. From consumer associations' perspective, the notion of on-line dispute resolution is approached differently. For instance, after a relative international survey entitled as 'Disputes in Cyberspace: ODR for Consumers in Cross-Border Disputes' (2000), they reported and defined ODR as the term they use for ADR services offered entirely by electronic means, without the need of the disputing parties to leave their home/offices. The above approach was regarded by several ODR practitioners as very stringent.

Overall, ODR is a branch of dispute resolution assisted by Information Technology and telecommunications to facilitate the resolution of disputes conducted on net (online), such as consumer disputes, cyberspace and e-commerce disputes, domain name and intellectual property disputes and disputes that arise from issues not involving the internet (offline), like family and employment ones. The On-line Dispute Resolution mechanism can otherwise be called as Virtual ADR, Internet Dispute Resolution (iDR), Electronic Dispute Resolution (eDR), Electronic ADR (e-ADR) or Online ADR (oADR).

THE RATIONALE OF ODR

Gabrielle Kaufmann-Kohler and Thomas Schultz (2004 p.5) wrote that the common reasoning in this field is to reconstruct an architecture online that resembles offline negotiation and mediation. While Katsh and Rifkin (2001) argued that the most valuable challenges are not to use the internet to duplicate the offline dispute resolution or face-to-face environment, but to expand thinking and look for ways that dispute resolution expertise can be of value online (Brannigan 2003). In addition, Online ADR should focus on using the network in ways that maximize the power of technology, power that that may be missing in face-to-face encounters (Katsh 2000 p.6). In 2003, the United Nations Economic Commission for Europe (UNECE) Forum on ODR explained that the rationale behind the early ODR programs was to leverage the cost-efficiency, accessibility, detemporalization and depersonalization of online interaction while preserving all of the procedural advantages presumed to be perfected in existing forms of face-to-face dispute resolution (Choi 2003 p.1). Namely, these services were focused on the settlement of e-commerce disputes, by 'mimicking' face-to-face dispute resolution processes in cyberspace. Later on, disputes that were impossible to be settled within courtrooms, such as those relating to data protection, privacy matters, defamation came into sight as 'excellent candidates' (Choi, 2003) for ODR.

The final stage of ODR development relates to the rapid growth of digital technology, something that was proven with the EU project of the Joint Research Commissions on the specifications for XML (eXtensible Mark-up Language) based ODR tools (OASIS, 2009). The emergence of that movement was a great opportunity to combine the evolution in the cyberspace world, the technological outburst, the fondness of the internet as useful and valuable medium for business 'virtual' activities and the exchange of information, with the flexibility of the traditional extrajudicial processes, in order to create a similar mechanism that can satisfactorily resolve online as well as offline disputes, regardless of geographical location, culture and stereotypes. It was expressed that ODR occurred as a reaction to the constraints of the offline world, not strictly to courts (Kaufmann and Schultz 2004 p.6-7). The main idea is that there are online versions of almost all offline dispute resolution processes (Kaufmann and Schultz 2004 p.6-7).

THE HISTORY OF ODR

Prior 1995, the World Wide Web was an unthinkable world. Only when the internet was founded in 1969 till the beginning of 1990s with the appearance of the first e-mail accounts, online disputes were brought into attention. The Internet Service Providers were absent and only online services such as the AOL, Compuserve, LEXIS and DIALOG were solving disputes through 'informal' mechanisms. Nothing was promising that one day there will be dispute resolution providers. In the United States, the internet was increasingly used by students, academics and administration, while having their own accounts, being registered with the institution. These were the sole users of the internet together with the military until 1992. The National Science Foundation was responsible for the management of the Net. During that time, it prohibits the commercial activity, based on one of its rules set in the Acceptable Use Policy. The 'listservs' were the first forums where subscribers could exchange e-mail messages or participate in several online discussions. 'Netiquette' was like a code of an acceptable conduct. When somebody had inappropriate behaviour, then he was in the state of 'flaming'. In addition, Usenet, MUDs (Multi-User Dungeons) and MOOs (MUD-Object-Oriented) were the most popular virtual worlds where disputes were occurring too. For Howard Rheingold, virtual communities are social aggregations that emerge from the Net when enough people carry on those public discussions long enough, with sufficient human feeling, to form webs of personal relationships in cyberspace (Gillen 2007 p.212). As soon as the ban was lifted, e-commerce gradually began to grow and a number of e-commercial disputes emerged. At the same time, between 1995 and 1998, eBay, Amazon, Microsoft and Google came into sight. In 1994, the first spam case occurred and the Federal Trade Commission (FTC) filled its first internet-related fraud case.

The original concept of ODR scheme officially derived from the presentation of three American pilot projects in 1998, due to problems that had surfaced considering the Internet Service Providers' (ISPs) rights and responsibilities. The 'Virtual Magistrate' was the first project supported by the Chicago-Kent Law School that offered free service online arbitration system, and aimed at sorting out problems that online users faced at any place of the world, concerning libellous messages, postings and corrupt data files (Clark, 2002). It was operated by the Cyberspace Law Institute (CLI) [which directs policy], the AAA [which administers cases], the Centre for Information Law and Policy [which operates the service] and the National Center for Automated Information Research (Clark 2002 p.1710). Its purpose was to examine how to resolve disputes between users and network operators.

A second attempt was made by the University of Massachusetts that established the 'Center for Information Technology and Dispute Resolution' and the 'Online Ombudsman Office', according to which parties could be informed whenever having disputes arising out of their online activities. The online ombudsperson was a confidential and informal information resource, communications channel, and complaint-handler and dispute resolver (Katsh 1996 p.9). This project was aiming at using technological tools for better settlements. Further examples were that of the University of Maryland, with its online mediation project, which was seeking to settle family disputes that were falling under the Maryland law. And the 'Cybertribunal' project prepared under the auspices of the University of Montreal's Centre de Recherché en Droit Public (CRDP). For the first time, arbitration and mediation services were combined. The National Center for Automated Information Research (NCAIR) was a great contributor, since it propelled the ODR scheme by constantly providing funds for projects, conferences and papers relative to ODR. In 1999-2000, ODR finally becomes a necessity with the accelerated expansion of the Web and it is recognized as one of the most fruitful e-dispute resolution means for those engaged in governmental agencies and corporate activities. The difference is that now, there is greater responsibility towards the disputing parties involved in online environments and a need for the adoption of a more integrated framework, which can competently support the mechanism.

ODR TECHNIQUES

ODR covers many alternative techniques for the settlement of business conflicts. Specifically, Katsh (1995) mentions the 'online settlement', the 'online arbitration', the 'online resolution of consumer complaints' and the 'online mediation.' While in 'online settlement', insurance and financial related claims only are automatically settled by finding the range between double-blind bids and demands, in 'online resolution of consumer complaints', when received online, then they are resolved traditionally via e-mails, telephone or personal contact. In 'online arbitration' or 'cyber-arbitration' or 'cybritration', videoconferencing, chat rooms, e-mails are used for the conflict settlement with the presences of skilled arbitrators and in 'online mediation' of skilled mediators respectively after parties' submission of an online form. Kaufmann and Schultz (2004) refer to few other methods named as 'assisted negotiation' or 'technologically facilitated negotiation', 'automated negotiation' or 'blind-binding' and the 'cybercourts'. 'Assisted negotiation helps parties to achieve an agreement through direct, bilateral communications with the aid of threaded message board systems, storage methods, online meeting management devices, and other information technology tools beyond e-mail (Kaufmann-Kohler and Schultz 2004 p.62), thus without offering actual negotiation service. In addition, 'blind-bidding' involves a 'settlement range' identified by the interested parties, who send 'settlement bids-offers' to a computer through a secure, password-protected, Web-based platform (Kaufmann-Kohler and Schultz 2004).

DISPUTE RESOLUTION AND INFORMATION TECHNOLOGY (THE FOURTH PARTY)

Colin Rule (2003) described ODR as the newfangled tool that mixes the usefulness of traditional alternative methods with internet command. It is obvious that the internet is the most important channel for international commercial transactions. What it is implied by the term 'internet' is the use of higher level of Information Technology or of the 'fourth party' to the dispute as it is otherwise called by Katsh and Rifkin (2001) and of telecommunications via internet. The 'fourth party' metaphor embodies the new facilities that assist in neutral's adjudicator information management and communication activities (Katsh & Wing, 2006). Computer Technology offers many applications such as videoconferencing, audio aids, email, computerized document processing, and enables online communication, case processing, claims documentation and automated decision making. According to Professor Richard Shell the technology is there for widely separated parties to meet in cyberspace, exchange and analyze complex information on preferences and needs, do deals, and execute binding settlements (Katsh, 1996 p.1).

International E-Commerce in Dispute Resolution

The development of this mechanism is consequence of borderless nature of electronic commerce, which was generated not because of the internet, but it is actually the basis of e-commerce. Thus, the massive transactions that take place in digital networks and online commercial communications create frequently enormous e-commerce disputes. Nevertheless, the internet is not the only 'instrument' with electronic form. The World Trade Organization (WTO) adds the telephone, the fax machine, the television, the electronic payment, the money transfer systems and the Electronic Data Interchange (EDI) as well. Expertise dispute resolution providers can only manage the eCommerce disputes that arise when e-contracts are violated for instance, regarding the price or time of delivery of the goods.

After the appearance of the dot.com, e-commerce became one of the most attractive areas. Kalakota and Whinston (1997) declare that, the need for eCommerce derived from the request amongst businesses and the governance to increase and ameliorate the use of computers and computer technology, in order to amend consumer interfaces, business procedures as well as the communication of information, inside and athwart companies.

In broad terms, eCommerce is characterized as the practice of interchanging merchandise, either of goods or services, by being remote and by interacting electronically through computer and telecommunication equipment without the need for physical contact. According to Forder and Quirk (2001), it is any commercial activity in which the transaction, or some part of it, is conducted via computers or computer-type devices, usually over the internet (p.5). The e-funds transfer (EFT) was the first e-commerce activity and was offered by the American banks in 1970s.

In the e-commerce market, ODR processes can be offered for the settlement of disputes that are known as disputes between businesses (B2B) and disputes between businesses and consumers (B2C), Business-to-Government (B2G), Customer-to-Customer (C2C) and Consumer-to-Business (C2B) (Bhusry, 2005).

Based on the results of Forrester Research, an independent internet organization, as cited by Korper and Ellis (2001), the apprehension of products and services exchanged among firms through the internet was estimated to represent a respectable percentage of global economy (nearly $317 billion) by 2002. In 1999, the estimation for internet transactions reached $1.3 trillion. During 2001, International Data Corporation forecasted that, U.S. online population would surpass 137 million. It was estimated that 11 million U.S. ménages would have conduct their first online transaction in 2001, making U.S.'s online population to 28.4 million ménages.

ODR and Cyberspace

In 1999, a veteran negotiator Ted Kheel wrote in his book 'Keys to Conflict Resolution' that the traditional dispute resolution has no time or specific place to come about. Online ADR is a cyberspace reality, where internet auctions, state-your-price buying, interactive blind bargaining and bidding, computer-assisted negotiations (Gordon, 2001 p.10) take place, but which will never replace mediator's practice sitting with disputing parties at conference table trying to negotiate their difference, because it still remains the richest communication environment. In 1989, David Gelernter described cyberspace as a 'mirror world', a concept that was not understandable till now, but which provided logical basis later for the concept of online disputes. According to his inspiration, the screen world will mirror 'facets and conflict resolving behaviour of the physical world' (Katsh 1996 p.2) and help in developing ODR processes. The internet developments, like video conferencing and the use of web camera supported cyberspace to become the dominant communications medium world-wide. In 2001, the founder and director of the settlement and trial science firm 'Wilmington Institute Network' in US, Robert Gordon said that it is a safe bet that this existing new medium will one day be use regularly for ADR, due to the internet's near universal adaptability (Gordon, 2001 p.12).

ODR AND THE LAW

Daewon Choi, the Special Assistant to the Executive Secretary and Secretary of the Commission (UNESCAP) (2003) said that the tools of ODR are emerging fast, but without a well considered foundation for how the tools can be utilized, how they should be regulated, and how they should interface with the law, so there is a risk that they will create more chaos then they remedy.

Some initiatives for legal protection and guidance of those involved in online transactions were made by European Union institutions, the WTO, the ICC, the WIPO, OECD or the UN, who tried by drafting documents, regulations, suggesting guidelines, writing reports and projects, organizing conferences to secure traders' interests online and offer them greater protections than those in offline disputes. In 1998, UNCITRAL adopted the Model Law on Electronic Commerce, which now plays an important role in enhancing the use of paperless communication. The European Commission with the EC Recommendations on 'the Principles Applicable to the Bodies Responsible for Out-of-Court Settlement of Consumer Disputes' for binding processes (98/257/EC) and 'the Out-of-court bodies involved in the consensual resolution of consumer disputes' for non-binding ones (2001/310/EC) established principles, according to which out-of-court dispute mechanisms have to comply with. These are the principles of independence, transparency, adversariness, effectiveness, legality, fairness, impartiality, liberty and representation. Another attempt was 'the Council Resolution of 25.5.2000 on a network at Community level of national bodies responsible for the out-of-court settlement of consumer disputes.' This network facilitates the lodging of consumer complaintacts and acts as a contact for consumers who wish to settle their disputes out of court in another Member State. (Piers, M., 2005 p.81) Furthermore, the OECD published the 'Guidelines for Consumer Protection in the Context of Electronic Commerce' (2000/C 155/01) in 1999 for persuading consumer representatives, governments and companies to team up, in order to equip consumers with meaningful access to fair and timely alternative dispute resolution and redress, without undue cost and burden. (Katsh, 1995 p.3) At the same time, the Directive in E-commerce (2000/31/EC) seeks to contribute to the proper functioning of the internal market by ensuring the free movement of information society services between Member States, according to art.

1 (1). In 2003, the International Chamber of Commerce (ICC) in consultation with the ICC Court of Arbitration produced the 'ICC Best Practices for ODR in online B2C and C2C Transactions' in order to offer guidelines for companies engaged in online transactions and for online dispute resolution service providers, but also, to improve the level of confidence while doing business online. Other efforts that contribute to the regulation of ODR were the papers titled 'The Europe's Way to the Information Society', 'a European Initiative in Electronic Commerce', 'eEurope-An Information Society for All' and the Hague Conference on 'Building Trust in the Online Environment: Business-to-Consumer Dispute Resolution'.

IS GOVERNMENT'S INTERVENTION NECESSARY FOR THE EFFECTIVENESS OF ODR MECHANISM?

When referring to ODR it is not possible to avoid examining the role of the government in the mechanism. The Government is an administrative, authoritative and regulatory agency that is also engaged with dispute resolution activities (Katsh, 2008). It can either act as a neutral entity, by providing e-services to the interested parties (citizens, enterprises) or participate in the dispute resolution processes as a disputant. In particular, ODR implies the importance of IT (Internet, World Wide Web, Mobile Computing) in the process by accelerating the bureaucratic procedures, communicating and responding to the needs of the parties, thus leading to the economic development of various countries. E-Government is not only concerned with placing information online, but also placing processes online. Dispute resolution is a process or range of processes that is moving online in a variety of contexts (Katsh, 2008, pp.494-5).

The electronic nature of disputes denotes the developed area of e-Government (eGov) or online Government and at times of electronic governance, which is the favourable place of general public, business communities, politicians, academics and policy makers. In a book entitled e-Government in the Developed Nations, the e-Gov jurisdictional, political approach is distinguished from that of e-Governance, in that it is procedural to cooperative administrative relations. Government's response vision is to use any electronic information from public sector and to communicate it efficiently to the above target groups when transacting (Dawes et al., 2008). Many strategies and mechanisms (Parisopoulos, Tambouris & Tarabanis 2007) have been designed for the implementation of e-Government around the world in European, national, supranational, local and regional level, in order to ensure citizens with eDemocracy, eServices, eJustice and combat corruption. The goals of some of these eGov strategies are the 24/7 access to Government accurate information, equality of digital divide, trust, privacy and security in transactions, economic development, electronic legislation, enhanced transparency and interoperability (Di Maio, 2006). In further extent, the strategic goal of each government is 'to develop electronic knowledge-based economy' (Cellary, 2008) for businesses and the civil society.

In general, the Government should act for the best of its citizens' interests and ensure improvement of their quality of life, offer guidance and training to its workforce, as well as to be flexible and ready to reciprocate to changes. On the other hand, the e-Government is responsible for the processing of administrative transactions (submitting applications, receiving confirmations, receiving decisions) via Information and Communication Technology (ICT), by preserving the citizen-centric character of their official websites. A UN World Public Sector Report (2003) proves that by 2003, over 173 out of the 191 Member States had developed governmental Websites. According to Schiavetta (2005), e-Government relates to the delivery of Government services to benefit citizens, business partners and employees with the aid of instant access to internet by improving internal efficiency and minimizing the costs. A broader term is used by the European Commission, which relates e-Government to the use of ICT in public administrations combined with organizational change and new skills in order to improve public services and democratic processes and strengthen support for public policies (Hill, 2004) and reforms. Additionally, it has described it as agent of transformation in the culture of public sector (Leitner, 2003 p.9) after the alteration of Government's structures and generally is regarded as agent of modernization.

An indicative report (Kelly, 2003) has showed that the Governments of Western Europe will spend US$ 67.8 billion on e-government and information technology in 2003. Moreover, in an assessment of the progress of the UN Member States (UN-PAN and ASPA 2002), the global trends in 2001 revealed the first ten E-gov leaders, which are in a descending order USA, Australia, New Zealand, Singapore, Norway, Canada, UK, Netherlands, Denmark and Germany. Kim et al. (2008) add that even countries with unstable security situations or political system are not excluded from the perspective of e-governance, stating that ICT is not regarded as a luxury, but as a prerequisite of stability, progress and development.

The issue of Government's participation in the on-line ADR project is questioned in many international forums and conferences as its role is significant especially when it concentrates on enhancing the prospect of achieving online interaction and securing e-transactions with its citizens and businesses that may entail the settlement of administrative disputes. Accordingly, we meet the Government to Consumer (G2C), Government to Business (G2B) and Government to Government (G2G) interactions. The ombudsman is already a solution for the Governments, as he administers administrative disputes and handles complaints about maladministration in governmental departments and bureaucracy.

In advance, discussions are made as to which is Government's actual role in ODR, regarding to its credibility in the transactions. The obvious reason is Government's importance in the accreditation of service providers and 'trust marks seals' or 'web seals of approval' or 'labels'. Under such trust mark schemes (self-regulatory), supplier's reliability during business is ensured when registered as a member with providers' dispute resolution services and when the requirements of the Code of Conduct (good online practices) are met. URL known as the *http* address is the only identifiable feature that represents supplier's identity, but which can become the less trustful one in trade. 'E-com trust', 'TRUSTe', 'Square Trade', 'Euro-Label', 'TrustUK', 'BBBOnLine (Better Business Bureau Online)', 'Federation of Direct Marketers (FEDMA)' and 'Eurochambres', 'L@belsite', 'SafeShop', 'TrustUK', 'Trusted Shops', 'Asia Trustmark Alliance (ATA)' [where the Japan Chamber of Commerce and Industry, the Japan Direct Marketing Association, the Electronic Commerce Promotion Council of Japan, the Korea, Institute for Electronic Commerce, Singapore's, Commerce Trust and Taiwan's Secure Online Shopping Association are included] are some initiatives which foster consumers' believability and encourage them to trust private information. This is achieved when Websites are checked as to whether they adhere to privacy policies and consumer protection laws and finally by approving their trust mark, their symbol that has to be attached to their business Web page. These may be initiated by the Government, trade and/or consumer associations. Usually theses schemes are confined to the national level.

In European level, in 2003, the Online Confidence (OC) trust mark seal was an attempt of the Eurochambres, the Association of European Chambers of Commerce, but which had disappointing results as European businesses did not trust it. In 2004, the Global Trustmark Alliance (GTA) tried to combine America's (BBB-Online), Asia's (ATA), and Europe's (OC) self-regulatory programs globally. In 2005, the Standing Committee of Officials of Consumer Affairs E-commerce Working Party reported in its findings (2 and 3) that surveys, like Consumer's WebWatch and BBBOnline, revealed that trust mark schemes competence is doubtful, since customers are ignorant of their existence (Consumers Affairs 2005). Another way of securing that consumers have chosen the most suitable ODR provider is through the 'clearinghouses', a form of 'accreditation plus'.

The form of regulation is still ambiguous. The nature of the internet repulses the idea of allowing Government's intervention. In early ages, the Internet Law and Policy Forum was of the opinion that the cyberspace cannot be regulated, since it is constantly changes and it can never keep pace with any proposed legislation. Also, Consumer Associations, such as the Australian one, reported in the Australian Taskforce on Industry Self-Regulation 2000 that self-regulation can achieve better results when a motivated industry, a small number of large players and maturity exists in combination with the Government regulatory backstop. United States holds the same opinion. Furthermore, in July 2004, the International Conflict Resolution Centre of Melbourne presented the results of a study in the UN Forum on ODR, which reported Australian governmental bodies' intention to include some of the ODR methods as 'additional service' to the existing ones. Amongst all, the Organization for Economic Co-operation and Development (OECD) and the European Union with the Government-sponsored ECODIR project showed their interest in examining whether ODR can be used in the future by Governments. Though, in general, governmental actions are confined to the adoption of general principles, such as confidentiality, effectiveness, fairness, transparency, accessibility or impartiality, rather than to actual regulation.

CONCLUSION

There is no doubt that Government is the 'ideal host' (Kaufmann & Schultz, 2004) for dispute resolution and important participant in the process of expansion of digital economy. So far, studies show that leaders easily assume their responsibilities through the e-Gov scheme (ADBI, 2009). The open network communication together with the migration of paper-based to e-documents and the transparency enhances public administration, thus the settlement of disputes through ODR mechanism, which is one of the most important governmental activities. Though Governments should expand and recommend to the public the use of ODR tools, such as blind-binding or assisted negotiation or even the future cybercourts and ODR providers, because it is a way of getting an immediate redress and resolution of the problems. Besides, interested parties will proceed to such methods only because Government is the sole body that raises trust. The present study deals with not such a new concept for the legal world, since online dispute resolution exists for the last twelve years. As an online equivalent of the traditional alternative dispute resolution, it also achieves the general purpose successfully, that is to make justice more accessible, through the 'cure of the suffering parts of justice process.' Nevertheless, whatever efforts are made for its improvement are never enough. As a consequence, a systematic review of the current topic is undertaken. A synthesis of existing concepts and propositions present an insight overview of ODR in relation to government's intervention in the mechanism for citizens' best interest and in extent to its future contribution, through e-government initiatives, in the securing of online public services and the protection of online transactions.

REFERENCES

Affairs, C. (2005, January) *Webseals of Approval/ final Report*. Retrieved June 26, 2008, from http://www.consumer.vic.gov.au/CA256902000FE154/Lookup/CAV_Publications_Computers_Internet_Discussion_Papers/$file/WebSealsFinalReport.pdf

Asian Development Bank Institute (ADBI). (2009). *Legal aspects of e-government*. Retrieved June 14, 2009, from http://www.adbi.org/book/2004/11/05/725.implementing.egovernment.book/1.2.j.legal.aspects.of.egovernment/

Brannigan, C. (2003). Online *Dispute Resolution: Resolving in Cyberspace*. Retrieved February 3, 2008, from http://www.mediate.ca/onlineresolution.html

Bushry, M. (2005). *E-Commerce*. Firewall Media.

Cellary, W. (2008) Strategic impact of e-government on economy and society In *Proceedings of the 2nd International Conference on Theory and Practice of Electronic Governance, 351*, 149-153.

Choi, D. (2003). Online dispute resolution. Issues and Future directions. In. *Proceedings of the UNECE Forum on ODR, 2003*, 1–3.

Clark, B. (2002, November). ODR: the new kid in town. *The New Law Journal*, *152*(7050), 1710–1711.

Dawes, S., Pardo, T. A., & Jiang, Y. (2008) A holistic framework for understanding government information access initiatives. In *Proceedings of the 2nd International Conference on Theory and Practice of Electronic Governance, 351*, 83-89.

Di Maio, A. (2006). *E-government strategies Highlight key focus areas*. Stamford, CT: Gartner Inc.

Forder, J., & Quirk, P. (2001). *Electronic Commerce and the Law*. New York: John Wiley and Sons Australia Ltd.

Gillen, M. (2007, November). Managing Virtual Communities: Time to turn to the Whetstone? *International Review of Law Computers & Technology*, *21*(3), 211–220. doi:10.1080/13600860701701371

Gordon, R. (2001, February-April). The Electronic Personality and Digital Self. *Dispute Resolution Journal*, *56*(1), 9–19.

Hill, H. (2004) Transformation of the Administration by e-government German Journal of Urban Studies, *45*(2). Retreived September 5, 2008, from http://www.difu.de/publikationen/dfk/en/04_2/04_2_hill.shtml

Hornle, J. (2002) *Online Dispute Resolution- The Emperor's New Clothes? Benefits and Pitfalls of Online Dispute Resolution and its Application to Commercial Arbitration*. Retrieved April 1, 2005, from http://www.bileta.ac.uk/02papers/hornle.html

ICC International Court of Arbitration. (2004). *Using Technology to Resolve Business Disputes Special Supplement*. New York: ICC.

International Chamber of Commerce. (2003). *Resolving disputes online: Best practices for online dispute resolution in B2C and C2C transaction*. New York: ICC.

Kalakota, R., & Whinston, B. (1997). *Electronic Commerce, A Manager's Guide*. Reading, MA: Addison Wesley, Pearson Education.

Katsh, E. (1995). *Law in a Digital World*. Oxford, UK: Oxford University Press.

Katsh, E. (1996). Dispute Resolution in Cyberspace-Symposium: Legal Regulation of the Internet. *Connecticut Law Review*, 1–18.

Katsh, E. (2000, Winter) The new frontier: Online ADR becoming a global priority *Dispute Resolution Magazine* pp.6-8.

Katsh, E. (2004). Bringing online dispute resolution to virtual worlds: Creating processes through code. *New York Law School Review*, *49*, 271–291.

Katsh, E. (2007). Online Dispute Resolution: Some Implications for the Emergence of Law in Cyberspace. *International Review of Law Computers & Technology*, *21*(2), 97–107. doi:10.1080/13600860701492096

Katsh, E. (2008) Dispute resolution and e-government In *Proceedings of the 2nd International Conference on Theory and Practice of Electronic Governance*, Vol. 351, pp.494-495.

Katsh, E., & Rifkin, J. (2001). *Online Dispute Resolution: Resolving Conflicts in Cyberspace*. San Francisco: Jossey-Bass Publishers.

Katsh, E., Rifkin, J., & Gaitenby, A. (2000). E-Commerce, E-Disputes and E-dispute Resolution: In the Shadow of eBay law *Ohio State Journal on Dispute Resolution, 15*(3), 705-734.

Katsh, E., & Wing, L. (2006, Fall). Ten years of inline dispute resolution: Looking at the past and constructing the future. *University of Toledo Law Review. University of Toledo. College of Law*, *38*, 19–46.

Kaufmann-Kobler, G., & Schultz, T. (2004). *Online Dispute Resolution, Challenges for Contemporary Justice*. Amsterdam: Kluwer Law International.

Kelly, P. (2003). E-*government must offer value for money: Report*. Retrieved September 3, 2008, from http://www.electricnews.net/story/show/9379230

Kim, Y., Bhattarai, M., & Ayyad, M. (2008). Electronic Governance in Post-Conflict Countries In *Proceedings of the 2nd International Conference on Theory and Practice of Electronic Governance, 351*, 489.

Korper, S., & Ellis, J. (2001). *The E-Commerce Book: Building the E-Empire*. San Francisco: Morgan Kaufmann, Academic Press.

Kuster, M., Dekkers, M., & Moore, G. (2008). Draft final report of the project team of the CEN/ ISSS eGovernment focus group on the *eGovernment standards roadmap*

Leitner, C. (2003), *eGovernment in Europe: The State of Affairs* EIPA (European Institute of PublicAdministration). Retrieved September 5, 2008, from http://www.eipa.eu/files/repository/product/20070214113429_egoveu.pdf

Lodder, A. R. (2006, June). The Third party and Beyond. *Information & Communications Technology Law*, *15*(2), 143–153. doi:10.1080/13600830600676438

Munshi, V. (2008). E-government in Developed Nations*:* An Insight, *ICFAI Press*. OASIS LegalXML *Online Dispute Resolution TC*. Retrieved May 20, 2009, fromhttp://www.oasis-open.org/committees/tc_home.php?wg_abbrev=legalxml-odr

Parisopoulos, K., Tambouris, T., & Tarabanis, K. (2007) Analyzing and Comparing European eGovernment Strategies, In *Proceedings of the 3rd International Conference on e-Government (ICEG)* (pp.179-188).

Piers, M. (2004, November). -January 2005) How EU law affects arbitration and the treatment of consumer disputes: The Belgian example. *Dispute Resolution Journal*, *59*(4), 77–85.

Rule, C. (2002). *ODR is Alive and Kicking*. San Francisco: Jossey-Bass Publishers.

Schiavetta, S. (2005, April) *Online Dispute Resolution, E-Government and Overcoming the DigitalDivide*. Retrieved April 16, 2008, from http://www.bileta.ac.uk/Document%20Library/1/Online%20Dispute%20Resolution,%20EGovernment%20and%20Overcoming%20the%20Digital%20Divide.pdf

Schultz, T. F. (2004, Fall). Does online dispute resolution need governmental intervention? The case for architectures of control and trust *North Carolina. The Journal of Law and Technology*, *6*(1), 71–106.

United Nations Division for Public Economics and Public Administration (UNPAN) and American Society for Public Administration. (ASPA) (2002) *Benchmarking E-government: A Global Perspective - Assessing the UN Member States*. Retrieved September 5, 2008, from http://unpan1.un.org/intradoc/groups/public/documents/UN/UNPAN021547.pdf

Chapter 11
Factors Affecting the Citizens' Trust in E-Government

Hisham M. Alsaghier
Griffith University, Australia

Marilyn Ford
Griffith University, Australia

Anne Nguyen
Griffith University, Australia

Rene Hexel
Griffith University, Australia

ABSTRACT

In e-government context, trust plays a vital role in helping citizens overcome perceived risks. Trust makes citizens comfortable sharing personal information, make online government transaction, and acting on e-Government advices. Thus, trust is a significant notion that should be critically investigated to help both researchers and practitioners to understand citizens' acceptance to e-Government. Prior research in trust has focused mainly on consumer's trust in e-Commerce. Most of existing literatures on trust in e-government focus on technical perspective such as PKI. This paper contributes by proposing a conceptual model of citizens' trust in e-Government. The proposed conceptual model of citizens' trust in e-government is integrated constructs from multiple disciplines: psychology, sociology, e-commerce, and HCI. The research is aimed also to develop items in order to measure the theoretical constructs in the proposed model. The pool of items is generated based on literature review. Q-Methodology has been utilised to validate the generated measurement items. The outcome of two Q-sorting rounds resulted in developing a survey instrument for proposed model with an excellent validity and reliability statistical results.

DOI: 10.4018/978-1-61520-789-3.ch011

INTRODUCTION

Electronic commerce, or in short, e-commerce and its sophisticated technologies have enabled governments and companies to provide their products and services for their citizens and customers through web sites. Online services are cheaper, more convenient, and easy to provide. Electronic Government or e-government has been classified as one instance of e-commence (Schneider, 2003). Many governments around the world have launched their e-government initiatives to provide citizens and organisations with more convenient ways to access government information and services (Turban et al., 2002). Previous research has been carried out to evaluate the quality and quantity of the provided e-government services and the overall adoption of e-government. One factor that plays a vital role in e-commerce adoption, especially e-government, is a mature trust between citizen and the government. Although trust has been recently studied in e-commerce, there is still yet a lack of sufficient research that investigates the trust phenomenon in e-government. Most of the existing online trust literatures focus on e-commerce in particular B2C e-commerce.

The purpose of this paper is twofold. The first purpose is to identify the factors that most likely affect citizens' trust in e-government. This is contextualised by investigation of the elements and components that transact the trust beliefs in electronic services, wether these elements and components are related to technical aspects such as Human Computer Interaction (HCI), or related to business, psychological, sociological, or cultural perspectives. The second purpose is to develop an instrument to measure the theoretical constructs in the proposed model.

LITERATURE REVIEW AND THEORETICAL BACKGROUND

Overview of E-Government

There are a number of e-government definitions in the existing literature. Most definitions of e-government revolve around the concepts of government's employment of technology, in particular web-based application to improve the access and delivery of government services to citizens, business partners, and other government agencies. World Bank defines trust as "the use by government agencies of information technologies (such as Wide Area Networks the Internet, and mobile computing) that have ability to transform relations with citizens, businesses, and other arms of government." (World Bank Group, 2007)

Stages of E-Government Development

There are various stages of e-government development. According to (Howard, 2001; Lau, 2001), there are four major stages of e-government development:

- Information Publishing: this is a basic form of e-government where government posts information on the official government websites. The presented information may include information about available public services, government contract, and government events.
- Two-way Communication: in this stage citizens communicate with the government through the Internet and make simple requests. Usually, the information requested in not processed immediately online but sent to the requestor by mail or email.
- Transaction: this stage is more sophisticated than previous stages where citizens can

conduct all transactions online. Driving licence renewing is one example of these transactions.
- Integration: this is the most sophisticated stage of e-government development. In this stage, all government services provided from different departments and agencies are integrated together and accessed through single website called e-government portal.

E-Government Categories

E-government has been divided into the following four categories according to who participates: Government to Government (G2G) for all operations inside or between government agencies, Government to Business (G2B) for all interested participants in institutions or private companies and the government, Government to Citizen (G2C) which refers to all dealings between citizens and the government, and Citizen to Citizen (C2C) where interactions occur between citizens in order to understand the dealings with most e-government projects (DeBenedictis et al., 2002). In addition, Ndou (2004) further categorises e-government as G2C, G2B, G2G and Government to Employees (G2E), which is to teach government employees to gain knowledge which is shared between them.

Research Model

In the context of Government-to-Citizen category of e-government, there are two major objectives: providing citizens with effective information access and providing citizens with access to full range of e-government services online (National Research Council, 2002). The basic idea behind e-government is to allow citizens to interact with their government through the internet; for example, they ask questions and receive answers, get updated government regulations, obtain government official documents, fill applications, pay tax and bills, receive payments, and forth. The two forms of citizens' engagement in e-government are receiving e-government information and requesting e-government service (Warkentin et al., 2002). The following research model describes how citizens' trust can affect their intention to engage in e-government.

The theoretical research model (see Figure 1) consists of nine constructs that delineate the conceptual model of citizens' trust in e-government. The model attempts to formulate an important number of factors that have been observed to affect citizens' trust in e-government. These factors have been integrated from different models of trust that are existed in the literature. The proposed model applies to Government-to-Citizen (G2C)

Figure 1. Theoretical research model

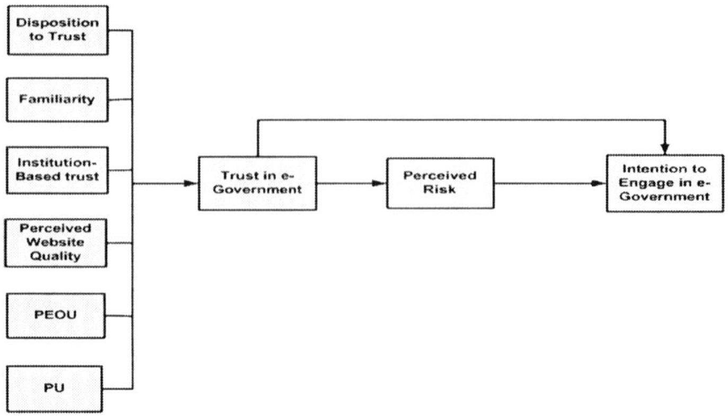

situation and it delineates the roles of significant factors in the process of trust in e-government. Following is the theoretical review in which each construct is derived.

TRUST IN E-GOVERNMENT

In this research, trust is defined as an individual's (trustor, here is citizen) belief or expectation that another party (trustee, here e-government) will perform a particular action important to trustor in the absence of trustor's control over trustee's performance (Mayer et al., 1995). Hence, trust indicates that trustor will rely on trust behaviour (Rotter, 1971b). Trust is occurred in uncertain environment (Schlenker et al., 1973) where the risk is existed (Lewis & Weigert, 1985) and trustor is vulnerable for unfulfilled expectation or harmful outcomes(Zand, 1972). People use trust as mental mechanism to reduce the complexity and uncertainty of living environment (Luhmann, 1979).

Trust has been cited as important and crucial requirement for economic and social interactions (Baier, 1986; Barber, 1983; Dasgupta, 1998; Lewis & Weigert, 1985; Luhmann, 1979; Mayer et al., 1995; McAllister, 1995; Rotter, 1971a). In the context of e-commerce, trust has been also observed as a key value in e-commerce (Gefen, 2000, Gefen & Straub, 2004), and in e-government (Galindo, 2002). Furthermore, trust enables cooperative behaviour (Gambetta, 1988). Hence, Trust beliefs lead for trust behaviour; in this model trust in e-government will lead citizens to engage in e-government (Warkentin et al., 2002).

H1: *Citizen trust in e-government positively influences intensions to engage in e-government.*

Disposition to Trust

Individuals have differences in terms of tendency to trust other party (Rotter, 1971a) wether this party is a person, a group, an organisation, or a business. Disposition to trust "is a propensity or tendency to believe in the positive attributes of others in general" (McKnight et al., 2004 p. 36). Disposition to trust has been identified as a construct for trust in many trust models (McKnight et al., 2002; McKnight & Chervany, 2001; McKnight et al., 2004). McKnight and Chervany (2001) proposed two constructs for disposition to trust *Faith in Humanity* and *Trusting Stance*. Faith in humanity is underline assumptions that others are usually upright, well meaning, and dependable. Trusting stance means that one believes that, regardless of other people reliability, one will obtain better outcomes result from dealing with other people; i.e. trust others until they prove trustor is wrong. Research has shown that disposition to trust has a significant impact on trust in online context (Pavlou & Gefen, 2004; McKnight et al., 2002; McKnight et al., 2004). Trust in the web institution is positively affected by disposition to trust because people who trust other generally will trust institutions involving people (McKnight et al., 2004) such as online vendors. Thus, disposition to trust is positively associated with consumer's trust in e-commerce (Kim & Kim, 2005). In e-government context, disposition to trust has been argued to increase trust in e-government (Warkentin et al., 2002). This leads to the following hypothesis:

H2: *Citizens' disposition to trust is positively associated with trust in e-government.*

Familiarity

Familiarity is stage where people use their previous experience (Luhmann, 1979), interactions, and learning to understand what, where, why, and when people do what they do (Gefen, 2000). It has been argued that familiarity is precondition for trust (Luhmann, 1979) and that trust is occurred in a familiar world, and the familiar features of the world may be changed which in turn may impact the possibility of developing trust in human relations (Luhmann, 1988). The Luhmann's note about the impact of changeability of familiarity on trust is useful in understandability of e-government trust because the e-government environment of providing government services for citizens are different than tradition government environment. Therefore, most of citizens are not familiar with e-government environment especially in the early stage of e-government which will influence citizens' trust in e-government.

H3: *Citizens' familiarity with e-government positively affects trust in e-government.*

Institution-Based Trust

Institution-based trust is the trustor's confidence that the situation structures are existed to facilitate outcome success of trusting behavior (Pavlou et al., 2003) and more impotently to impose sanctions when trust is breached (Humphery & Schmitz, 1998; Lane & Bachmann, 1996). Following McKnight et al. (2002), institution-based trust is defined as "the belief that needed structural conditions are present (e.g., in the Internet) to enhance the probability of achieving a successful outcome in an endeavor like e-commerce" (p. 339). Institution-based trust is generated when trustor believes that safety, guarantee, insurance and other performance structures are presented to secure a situation (Pavlou et al., 2003, Shapiro, 1987). In economic context, Institution-based trust "proved to be the most resilient,..., expanded and elaborated [trust creating mode]" in impersonal economic environment (Zucker, 1986 p. 96). In e-commerce context, institution-based trust has been argued to be best suited for online marketplaces because the secure online transactions (between and buyer and seller) are conducted under the aegis of third party who constitute an *institutional context* (Pavlou & Gefen, 2004).

McKnight et al. (2002) defined two dimensions (sub-constructs) of institution-based trust: *structural assurance* and *situation normality*. Structural assurance is related to structures that existed to promote success such as guarantees, regulation, and legal resources. Situation normality is the belief that success is expected as the environment is normal and in appropriate order. Example of situation normality in internet environment is the expectation that infrastructure of the communication is secure, i.e. security mechanisms and techniques (encryption) are employed to secure the communication channel. Accordingly, the following hypotheses are proposed:

H4a: *Structure assurance trust positively affects citizens' trust in e-government.*

H4b: *Situation normality trust positively affects citizens' trust in e-government.*

PERCEIVED WEBSITE QUALITY

Several research studies have been conducted to identify the design elements that communicate trust in e-commerce web sites. Studio Archetype and Sapient study (1999) is significant research that has investigate trust in e-commerce from HCI perspective. They identified different types of forms that communicate consumers' trust in an e-commerce website. Navigation and Presentation of the websites have been identified in Studio Archetype and Sapient study as very important design elements that facilitate the users' trust in the websites. Based on empirical evidence (Studio Archetype/Sapient and Cheskin Research, 1999), the following hypotheses are proposed:

H5a: *Easiness of navigation of e-government website positively affects citizens' trust in e-government.*

H5b: *E-government website presentation positively affects citizens' trust in e-government.*

TECHNOLOGY ACCEPTANCE MODEL (TAM)

Other important components that are assumed to affect citizens' trust in e-Government are: *Perceived Usefulness (PU)* and *Perceived Ease of Use (PEOU)*. PU and PEUO are two main components in Technology Acceptance Model (TAM) (Davis, 1989; Davis et al., 1989). TAM is an adaptation of the theory of reasoned action (TRA) (Fishbein & Ajzen, 1975). PU is the degree to which the user believes that the using of the system enhances his or her task performance. PEOU is the degree to which the user believes that using the system is easy and free of hard effort. TAM has been applied to the usability of e-commerce websites (Gefen et al., 2003a); also several researchers have hypothesised that PEOU and PU are positively affect trust in e-vendor (Chau et al., 2007; Koufaris et al., 2001; Pavlou, 2003; Tang & Chi, 2005). In e-government context, the following hypotheses are proposed:

H6a: *PEOU of e-government website positively influences citizens' trust in e-government.*

H6b: *PU of e-government website positively influences citizens' trust in e-government,*

PERCEIVED RISK

Risk is closely connected with trust; if there is no risk, there is no need for trust (Luhmann, 1988). Therefore, trust is manifested with present of risk where the possible damage is greater than advantage that is sought (Deutsch, 1960). Trust "derives from the calculus of gains and losses, weighed by perceived risks" (Rousseau et al., 1998). However, "placing trust means suspending, discounting, bracketing the risk, acting as if the risk were not existent" (Sztompka, 2003 p. 31). Therefore, trust effects risk which in turns affects behaviour, i.e. perceived risk moderates the relations between trusting belief and intention to trusting behaviour (Gefen et al., 2003b). Accordingly, the following hypotheses are proposed:

H7a: *Citizens' trust in e-government negatively affects perceived risk.*

H7b: *Perceived risk negatively affects intention to engage in e-government.*

INSTRUMENT DEVELOPMENT

The constructs are theoretically based on a comprehensive review of the literature and grounded in existing theories. Multi-item scales were developed or adapted from the literature in order to measure the constructs. The application of multi-item or summated scales is useful for investigating latent constructs (Borsboom et al., 2003, Colton & Covert, 2007) and, if properly developed, multi-item scales will provide meaningful measurement and the measurements derived from them will be accurate and interpretable (Peterson, 2000). Therefore, the theoretical constructs in this research are composed of three or more items (Cronbach & Meehl, 1955). As delineated in the research model (Figure 1), there are 9 major constructs. We developed the scale to measure *intention to engage in e-government* construct. Items to measure the other constructs were adapted from previous empirical research. The adapted items were considerably modified. Following is the discussion of the literature that supports the items in each construct.

ITEMS GENERATION

The items for *"Trust in E-Government"* construct were adapted from: empirical research on consumer trust in the internet (Jarvenpaa et al., 2000; Corbitta et al., 2003), the empirical research on interdisciplinary typology of trust for e-Commerce (McKnight et al., 2002; McKnight & Chervany, 2001), and the literature of trust building technology in the electronic market (Ba & Pavlou, 2002). The items for *"Disposition of Trust"* were synthesized from an empirical study on the trust measurement in e-Commerce (McKnight et al., 2002), and the literature on the consumer trust relationship in e-Commerce (McKnight & Chervany, 2001). The items for *"Perceived Risk"* construct were drawn from empirical studies on conceptualization of trust, risk and their relationship in e-Commerce (Gefen et al., 2003b; Jarvenpaa et al., 2000), from an empirical work that has investigated the perceived risks as barriers to Internet and e-commerce usage (Liebermann & Stashevsky, 2002), and from an empirical investigation on the effect of perceived risk on purchase intention in the Internet (Kim et al., 2005).The items for *"Familiarity"* construct were primarily based on empirical study on the impact of familiarity on the consumer trust in e-Commerce (Gefen, 2000), and based on the description of the meaning of familiarly in the literature (Luhmann, 1988; Zhang et al., 2007). The items for *"Trust in e-Government"* construct were adapted from an empirical research on the trust measurement in e-Commerce (McKnight et al., 2002), from an empirical study on the role of trust in e-Commerce (Gefen, 2000), and from an empirical investigation of citizens' trust in government and its linkage with their satisfaction with e-Government (Welch et al., 2005). The items for *"Institution-Based Trust"* construct (Situation Normality and Structure Assurance) were drawn from previous empirical research on the institution-based trust and its effect on the trust in the online environment (McKnight et al., 2002), and from a theoretical exploration of institute-based trust (Zucker, 1986). The items for *"Perceived Website Quality"* construct (Navigation and Presentation) were adapted from an empirical study that have identified e-Commerce virtual design elements that effect consumers' trust (Stephens, 2004). The items for *"Perceived Usefulness"* and *"Perceived Ease of Use"* constructs were adapted from an empirical research that have investigated the relation between trust and technology acceptance model in the online environment (Gefen et al., 2003a). Figure 2 shows the number of items in each contrast and sub-construct in the theoreti-

Figure 2. Pool of items entered in the Q-sort analysis

Construct ID	Construct	Subconstruct/ Dimension	Number of Items
1	Disposition to Trust	Benevolence	3
		Integrity	3
		Competence	3
		Trusting Stance	3
2	Familiarity		4
3	Institution-Based Trust	Structure Assurance Trust	4
		Situation Normality	11
4	Website Design	Navigation	4
		Presentation	5
5	Perceived Ease of Use		5
6	Perceived Usefulness		6
7	Trust in e-Government	Competence	6
		Integrity	7
		Benevolence	4
8	Perceived Risk	Security risk	4
		Performance risk	5
		Time Risk	2
9	Intention to engage in e-Government		8
	Total		87

cal research model. These items were used in the Q-sorting, describe next.

SCALE DEVELOPMENT: Q-SORT METHOD

The Q-Sort method is derived from Q-Methodology, a factor analysis technique. Q-Methodology was developed by Stephenson (1953). It has been used by psychology and social sciences to investigate people's subjectivity, i.e. their viewpoints. Unlike R-factor analysis which studies the correlation between variables, Q-methodology examines the correlation between individuals (Brown, 1997). In Q-methodology, the items are the sample in the Q-sort and the people who complete the Q-sort are the experimental condition (Cross, 2004). Therefore, Q-methodology examines the correlations between subjects across a sample of items. One of the main application of the Q-methodology is to assess reliability and construct validity of questionnaire items that are being prepared for survey research (Nahm et al., 2002). Nahm et al. (2002) demonstrated how the Q-sort method can be used to pre-test items after they have being developed or generated based on the literature review and before questionnaire items are the administrated as a survey. The method consists of two stages (Nahm et al., 2002). In the first stage, two independent judges are asked to sort the items of the questionnaire according to different constructs. Based on this stage, the agreement between the two judges (inter-judge agreement) is calculated. In the second stage, items that were classified incorrectly and were found ambiguous in the first stage are reworded or deleted. The two-stage process is repeated continuously until a satisfactory level of agreement is reached.

In this research, items were placed a common pool and were subjected to two sorting rounds by two independent judges in each round. The participants in the Q-sort process (judges) were chosen so they represent the target population of the research and they are experts in the field. Two participants were directors in the e-Government program in Saudi Arabia, one participant was a consultant in the e-Government program in Saudi Arabia, and one participant was a manager of IT departments in a government ministry. Participants were grouped in pairs. Each pair composed two independent judges in each round. The judge were asked to sort a list of items into groups, each group represents one of the 9 constructs. The differences and similarities among sorted items are used as an indicator for the constructs validity.

Q-Sorting Procedures

The research model and its 9 constructs with their definition were presented to the judges. Items, that were generated to measure the constructs, were printed on individual 3 by 5 inch cards. After randomly shuffling the cards (items), each judge was given these cards and asked to sort them into categories. Each category represents one of the 9 constructs. Additional to the nine constructs, a *"Not Applicable"* category was included to make sure the judges will not force any items into a particular category. Each round consisted of different pairs of judges. Judges were allowed to ask any question either related to the sorting procedure or related to the research model and constructs.

Q-Sort Evaluation

In order to evaluate and assess both the validity and reliability of the instrument, three evaluation criteria were used to assess the Q-sort: the inter-judge agreement level, Cohen's Kappa Index (Cohen, 1960), and Moore and Benbasat's "Hit Ratio" (Moore & Benbasat, 1991). The inter-judge agreement level is calculated by counting how many items that both judges agree to place into a particular category. Then, the number of agreed items is divided by the total items number to get the percentage of the inter-judge agreement. The second measure is Cohen's Kappa index which is

Figure 3.

		Judge 1 Acceptable	Judge 1 Rejectable	Totals
Judge 2	Acceptable	X_{11}	X_{12}	X_{1+}
	Rejectable	X_{21}	X_{22}	X_{2+}
	Totals	X_{+1}	X_{+2}	N

"the proportion of joint judgement in which there is agreement after chance is excluded" (Nahm et al., 2002, p. 115). For instance, assume that two judge independently classified a set of N components as either acceptance or rejectable. After the classification was finished, we can construct the following figure (Nahm et al., 2002):

The Cohen's Kappa index can be calculated as following:

$$k = \frac{N_i * X_{ii} - \sum_i (X_{i+} X_{+i})}{N^2 - \sum_i (X_{i+} X_{+i})}$$

where:

N_i: total number of items
x_{ii}: number of items agreed on by two judges
X_{i+}: number of items in the ith row
X_{+i}: number of items in the ith column

Previous research has considered score of Kabb index greater than 0.65 to be acceptable (Jarvenpaa, 1989; Todd & Benbasat, 1993; Landis & Koch, 1977). The third measure is Moore and Benbasat's "Hit Ratio" which measures how many items were correctly placed in the intended category by the judges. The "Hit Ratio" is computed by counting all items that were correctly sorted into intended theoretical construct by each judge, and then divide them by twice the total number of items.

FIRST SORTING ROUND

The first round consisted of 87 items for the nine constructs. The judges in this round were a director in the e-Government program in Saudi Arabia and a manager of IT department in a government ministry. In this round, the inter-judge raw agreement scores averaged 80% (Figure 4) and the initial overall placement ratio of items within the target constructs was 75% (Figure 5) as 131 of 174 items were correctly classified.

The results of the first round indicate some confusion among some constructs. In order to understand this confusion, the off-diagonal items in Figure 5 were examined to look for clusters. On the Institution-Based Trust construct, 11 of the 13 misclassified items are in the Trust in e-Government construct. This is expected since in both constructs there are items that are related to the trust beliefs. A similar effect appears in the Trust in e-Government construct, where 8 of the 10 misclassified items are in the Institution-Based Trust construct. This misplacement of the items confirms the confusion between Trust in e-Government construct and Institution-Based Trust construct, enforcing the need for further clarification between these two constructs in the next round. Another cluster appears in the Perceived Website Quality construct, where 6 misclassified items were placed in the Perceived Ease of Use construct. This is understandable from the fact the ease of the quality of the website promotes and enhances the ease of use. On the Perceived

Figure 4. Inter-Judge Scores: First Sorting Round

Judge 2	Judge 1										
	Construct	1	2	3	4	5	6	7	8	9	NA
	1	10									
	2		4								
	3		1	4				1			
	4				6	3					
	5					3					
	6						4				2
	7			3				11	1		
	8								9		
	9							1		7	
	NA										0
	Total Items: 87	Number of Agreement: 70						Agreement Ratio: 80%			

Figure 5. Items Placement Ratios: First Sorting Round

Theoretical Categories	Actual Categories												
	Construct	1	2	3	4	5	6	7	8	9	NA	Total	%
	1	22									2	24	92%
	2		8									8	100%
	3		2	17				11				30	57%
	4				12	6						18	67%
	5				1	8	1					10	80%
	6						8				4	12	67%
	7			8				24	2			34	71%
	8		2	2					18			22	82%
	9							2		14		16	88%
	Total Items Placement: 174				Number of Hits: 131				Overall Hit Ratio: 75%				

Risk construct, there are two clusters; one on the Familiarity (2 out of 4 misclassified items were placed in this construct) and one on the Institution-Based Trust (2 out of 4 misclassified items were placed in this construct). Similarly, two misclassified items in the Trust in e-Government construct were placed in the Perceived Risk construct. This confusion may be due to the strong link between risk perception and trust, which demands for further clarification of the items that suppose to measure these construct in the next round. On the Intention to Engage in e-Government construct, two misclassified items were placed in the Trust in e-Government construct. Another cluster found in the Institution-Based Trust, where 2 out of 13 misclassified items were placed under the Familiarity construct. On the Perceived Ease of Use construct, there are two clusters; one on the Perceived Website Quality construct (1 out of 2 misclassified items was placed in this construct) and one on the Perceived Usefulness construct (1 out of 2 misclassified items was placed in this construct). Finally, 6 items were classified as not applicable; 2 items from Disposition to Trust construct and 4 from the Perceived Usefulness construct.

Cohen's Kappa for this round was computed as:

$$K = \frac{87 * 70 - 131}{87^2 - 131} = 0.80$$

Following the guidelines of Landis and Koch (1977) for interpreting the Cohen's Kappa, the value of 0.80 indicates an excellent level of agreement beyond chance for the judges in the first round. This value is same as the value of raw agreement (Figure 4). The item placement ratios averaged 75%. The lowest item placement ratio value was 57% for the Institution-Based Trust construct, indicating a low degree of constructs validity. Also, the Perceived Website Quality, Perceived Usefulness, and the Trust in e-Government constructs had a low value of item placement ratio: 67%, 67%, and 71% respectively. On the other hand, several constructs, namely Familiarity, Disposition to Trust, Intention to Engage in e-Government, Perceived Risk, and Perceived Ease of Use obtained 100%, 92%, 88%, 82%, and 80% of item placement ratio respectively, indicating a high degree of constructs validity.

In order to identify the cause of misclassifications in round one, the individual judge classification for each item were examined. An examination of the off-diagonal entries in the placement matrix (Figure 5) was conducted. The ambiguous items that had been fitted in more than one category or fitted in no category were careful analysed. The analysis led to the rewording of ambiguous items including 11 items belonging to Institution-Based Trust, 3 items belonging to Perceived Website Quality construct, 2 items belonging to Perceived Risk construct, one item belonging to Trust in e-Government construct, and one item belonging to Intention to Engage in e-government construct. The analysis led also to deleting the too indeterminate items including 5 items belonging to Trust in e-Government construct, 2 items belonging to Disposition to Trust construct, 2 items belonging to Perceived Usefulness construct, and 2 items belonging to Perceived Ease of Use construct. Overall, 11 items were deleted, and 18 items were reworded. One additional item suggested by two judges was added to the Perceived Ease of Use construct.

SECOND SORTING ROUND

The second round consisted of 77 items for the nine constructs. The judges in this round were a director in the e-Government program in Saudi Arabia and a consultant in the e-Government program in Saudi Arabia. In this round, the inter-judge raw agreement scores averaged 91% (Figure 6), an 11% improvement of the previous round. The overall placement ratio of items within the target constructs was 88% (Figure 7), a 13% improvement from round one, as 131 of 174 items were correctly classified.

Figure 6. Inter-Judge Scores: Second Sorting Round

	Judge 1										
	Construct	1	2	3	4	5	6	7	8	9	NA
Judge 2	1	9									
	2		4								
	3			12				1			
	4				7						
	5				1	4					
	6						4				
	7							9	1	1	
	8								10		
	9									7	
	NA										0
	Total Items: 77	Number of Agreement: 70						Agreement Ratio: 91%			

Figure 7. Items Placement Ratios: Second Sorting Round

	Actual Categories												
	Construct	1	2	3	4	5	6	7	8	9	NA	Total	%
Theoretical Categories	1	18									1	19	95%
	2		8									8	100%
	3			27				6			2	35	77%
	4				15							15	100%
	5				3	8						11	73%
	6						8				2	10	80%
	7							18	2	2		22	82%
	8								20			20	100%
	9									14		14	100%
	Total Items Placement: 154				Number of Hits: 136					Overall Hit Ratio: 88%			

In the second round, the changes done on items in round one had resulted in a very good improvement of the measures. However, a further examination of the off-diagonal entries in the placement matrix (Figure 7) is needed in order to improve potential reliability and construct validity. The analysis of the placement matrix showed that there is a relatively small cluster around the Institution-Based Trust construct. A closer investigation of the items causing this cluster indicates that those items have words such as "confidence" and "rely" which are related to trust, causing a slight confusion between Institution-Based Trust and Trust in e-Government constructs. The analysis led to reword the items so the difference between trust in the Internet in general (Institution-Based Trust) and trust in e-Government in particular is distinguishable. Additionally, 3 misclassified items in the Perceived Website Quality construct were placed in the Perceived Ease of Use construct. A closer look to the items causing the confusion revealed that items that have words like "easier" and "easy" caused a slight confusion between Perceived Website Quality and Perceived Easy of Use constructs. The analysis led to reword two items in Perceived Ease of Use so it is clear to distinguish between ease of searching and requesting e-Government services and the features and characteristics of e-Government websites quality.

Cohen's Kappa for this round was computed as:

$$K = \frac{77 * 70 - 136}{77^2 - 136} = 0.91$$

Following the guidelines of Landis and Koch (1977) for interpreting the Cohen's Kappa, the value of 0.91, a 11% improvement from round one, indicates an excellent level of agreement beyond chance for the judges in the second round. At this point, we decided to stop the Q sorting round two, with Cohen's Kappa of 0.91, the average placement ratio of 88%, and the inter-judge raw agreement of 91%, indicating high level of reliability and construct validity. See Appendix A for the complete items list.

SUMMARY AND CONCLUSION

In this paper a conceptual model of citizens' trust in e-Government is proposed. The model consists of nine theoretical constructs which delineate the concept of citizens' trust in e-Government. An instrument to measure these constructs is developed also in this research. A pool of 87 items was generated. Then Q-methodology was utilized to ensure the constructs validity and reliability. Two Q-sorting rounds were conduced to validate the instrument. After the analysis of the Q-sorting, 77 items remained and are reported in Appendix A. This instrument can be used to investigate citizens' trust in e-Government. The future direction for this research is to administer a large scale survey for user of e-Government.

REFERENCES

Ba, S., & Pavlou, P. A. (2002). Evidence of the Effect of Trust Building Technology in Electronic Markets: Price Premiums And Buyer Behavior. *Management Information Systems Quarterly*, *26*, 243–268. doi:10.2307/4132332

Baier, A. (1986). Trust And Antitrust. *Ethics*, *96*, 231–260. doi:10.1086/292745

Barber, B. (1983). *Logic And Limits Of Trust*. East Rutherford, NJ: Rutgers University.

Borsboom, D., Mellenbergh, G. J., & Heerden, J. V. (2003). The Theoretical Status of Latent Variables. *Psychological Review*, *110*, 203–219. doi:10.1037/0033-295X.110.2.203

Brown, S. R. (1997). *The History And Principles Of Q Methodology In Psychology And The Social Sciences*. Kent, Ohio.

Chau, P. Y. K., Hu, P. J.-H., Lee, B. L. P., & Au, A. K. K. (in press). Examining Customers' Trust in Online Vendors And Dropouts: An Empirical Study. *Electronic Commerce Research and Applications*.

Cohen, J. (1960). A Coefficient of Agreement For Nominal Scales. *Educational and Psychological Measurement*, *20*, 37–46. doi:10.1177/001316446002000104

Colton, D., & Covert, R. W. (2007). *Designing And Constructing Instruments For Social Research And Evaluation*. San Francisco: Jossey-Bass.

Corbitta, B. J., Thanasankit, T., & Yi, H. (2003). Trust and E-Commerce: A Study Of Consumer Perceptions. *Electronic Commerce Research and Applications*, *2*, 203–225. doi:10.1016/S1567-4223(03)00024-3

Cronbach, L. J., & Meehl, P. E. (1955). Construct Validity In Psychological Tests. *Psychological Bulletin*, *52*, 281–302. doi:10.1037/h0040957

Cross, R. M. (2004). Exploring Attitudes: The Case For Q Methodology. *Health Education Research*, *20*, 206–213. doi:10.1093/her/cyg121

Dasgupta, P. (1998). Trust as a Commodity . In Gambetta, D. (Ed.), *Trust: Making And Breaking Cooperative Relations. Electronic Edition*. London: Basil Blackwell Ltd.

Davis, F. D. (1989). Perceived Usefulness, Perceived Ease Of Use, And User Acceptance of Information Technology. *Management Information Systems Quarterly*, *13*, 319–340. doi:10.2307/249008

Davis, F. D., Bagozzi, R. P., & Warshaw, P. R. (1989). User Acceptance of Computer Technology: A Comparison Of Two Theoretical Models. *Management Science*, *35*, 982–1003. doi:10.1287/mnsc.35.8.982

Deutsch, M. (1960). The Effect Of Motivational Orientation Upon Trust And Suspicion. *Human Relations*, *13*, 123–139. doi:10.1177/001872676001300202

Fishbein, M., & Ajzen, I. (1975). *Belief, Attitude, Intention, and Behavior: An Introduction To Theory And Research*. Reading, MA: Addison-Wesley.

Galindo, F. (2002). E-Government Trust Providers . In Gronlund, A. (Ed.), *Electronic Government: Design, Applications And Management*. Hershey, PA: Idea Group Publishing.

Gambetta, D. (1988). Can We Trust Trust? In Gambetta, D. (Ed.), *Trust: Making And Breaking Cooperative Relations*. London: Basil Blackwell Ltd.

Gefen, D. (2000). E-Commerce: The Role of Familiarity and Trust. *The International Journal of Management Science*, *28*, 725–737.

Gefen, D., Karahanna, E., & Straub, D. (2003a). Trust and Tam in Online Shopping: An Integrated Model. *Management Information Systems Quarterly*, *27*, 51–90.

Gefen, D., Rao, V. S., & Tractinsky, N. (2003b). The Conceptualization Of Trust, Risk And Their Relationship In Electronic Commerce: The Need For Clarifications. *Proceedings of The 36th Hawaii International Conference On System Sciences*. Hawaii, Usa.

Gefen, D., & Straub, D. W. (2004). Consumer Trust in B2c E-Commerce and the Importance of Social Presence: Experiments in E-Products and E-Services. *The International Journal of Management Science*, *32*, 407–424.

Humphery, J., & Schmitz, H. (1998). Trust and Inter Firm Relations in Developing and Transition Economies. *The Journal of Development Studies*, *34*, 32–61. doi:10.1080/00220389808422528

Jarvenpaa, S. L. (1989). The Effect Of Task Demands And Graphical Format On Information Processing Strategies. *Management Science*, *35*, 285–303. doi:10.1287/mnsc.35.3.285

Jarvenpaa, S. L., Tractinsky, N., & Vitale, M. (2000). Consumer Trust In An Internet Store. *Information Technology Management*, *1*, 45–71. doi:10.1023/A:1019104520776

Kim, L. H., Kim, D. J., & Leong, J. K. (2005). The Effect Of Perceived Risk On Purchase Intention In Purchasing Airline Tickets Online. *Journal of Hospitality & Leisure Marketing*, *13*, 33–53. doi:10.1300/J150v13n02_04

Kim, Y. H., & Kim, D. J. (2005). A Study Of Online Transaction Self-Efficacy, Consumer Trust, And Uncertainty Reduction In Electronic Commerce Transaction. In *Proceedings Of The 38th Hawaii International Conference On System Sciences.*

Koufaris, M., Kambil, A., & Labarbera, P. A. (2001). Consumer Behavior In Web-Based Commerce: An Empirical Study. *International Journal of Electronic Commerce*, *6*, 115–138.

Landis, R., & Koch, G. G. (1977). The Measurement Of Observer Agreement For Categorical Data. *Biometrics*, *33*, 159–174. doi:10.2307/2529310

Lane, C., & Bachmann, R. (1996). The Social Constitution Of Trust: Supplier Relations In Britain And Germany. *Organization Studies*, *17*, 365–395. doi:10.1177/017084069601700302

Lewis, J. D., & Weigert, A. J. (1985). Trust as A Social Reality. *Social Forces*, *63*, 967–985. doi:10.2307/2578601

Liebermann, Y., & Stashevsky, S. (2002). Perceived Risks as Barriers to Internet and E-Commerce Usage. *Qualitative Market Research: An International Journal*, *5*, 291–300. doi:10.1108/13522750210443245

Luhmann, N. (1979). *Trust and Power*. New York: John Wiley & Sons Ltd.

Luhmann, N. (1988). Familiarity, Confidence, Trust: Problems And Alternatives . In Gambetta, D. (Ed.), *Trust: Making and Breaking Cooperative Relations*. London: Basil Blackwell Ltd.

Mayer, R. C., Davis, J. H., & Schoorman, F. D. (1995). An Integrative Model Of Organizational Trust. *Academy of Management Review*, *20*, 709–734. doi:10.2307/258792

Mcallister, D. J. (1995). Affect- And Cognition-Based Trust as Foundations For Interpersonal Cooperation. *Academy of Management Journal*, *38*, 24–59. doi:10.2307/256727

Mcknight, D., Choudhury, V., & Kacmar, C. (2002). Developing And Validating Trust Measures For E-Commerce: An Integrative Typology. *Information Systems Research*, *13*, 334–359. doi:10.1287/isre.13.3.334.81

Mcknight, D. H., & Chervany, N. L. (2001). Conceptualizing Trust: A Typology and E-Commerce Customer Relationships Model. *34th Hawaii International Conference on System Sciences.*

Mcknight, D. H., Kacmar, C. J., & Choudhury, V. (2004). Dispositional Trust And Distrust Distinctions In Predicting High- And Low-Risk Internet Expert Advice Site Perceptions. *E-Service Journal*, *3*, 35–55. doi:10.2979/ESJ.2004.3.2.35

Moore, G. C., & Benbasat, I. (1991). Development of An Instrument To Measure The Perceptions Of Adopting An Information Technology Innovation. *Information Systems Research*, *2*, 192–222. doi:10.1287/isre.2.3.192

Nahm, A. Y., Solis-Galvan, L. E., Rao, S. S., & Ragu-Nathan, T. S. (2002). The Q-Sort Method: Assessing Reliability And Construct Validity Of Questionnaire Items At A Pre-Testing Stage. *Journal of Modern Applied Statistical Methods; JMASM*, *1*, 114–125.

National Research Council. (2002). *Information Technology Research, Innovation, and E-Government*. Washington, DC: National Academy Press.

Pavlou, P. A. (2003). Consumer Acceptance of Electronic Commerce—Integrating Trust and Risk with The Technology Acceptance Model. *International Journal of Electronic Commerce, 73*, 69–103.

Pavlou, P. A., & Gefen, D. (2004). Building Effective Online Marketplaces With Institution-Based Trust. *Information Systems Research, 15*, 37–59. doi:10.1287/isre.1040.0015

Pavlou, P. A., Tan, Y.-H., & Gefen, D. (2003) The Transitional Role Of Institutional Trust In Online Interorganizational Relationships. In *Proceedings of The 36th Hawaii International Conference On System Sciences (Hicss '03).*

Peterson, R. A. (2000). *Constructing Effective Questionnaires*. Thousand Oaks, CA: Sage Publications.

Rotter, J. B. (1971a). Generalized Expectancies For Interpersonal Trust. *The American Psychologist, 26*, 443–452. doi:10.1037/h0031464

Rotter, J. B. (1971b). Generalized Expectancies For Interpersonal Trust. *The American Psychologist*, 26.

Rousseau, D. M., Sitkin, S. B., Burt, R. S., & Camerer, C. (1998). Not So Different After All: A Cross-Discipline View Of Trust. *Academy of Management Review, 23*, 393–404.

Schlenker, B. R., Helm, B., & Tedeschi, J. T. (1973). The Effects Of Personality And Situational Variables On Behavioral Trust. *Journal of Personality and Social Psychology, 25*, 419–427. doi:10.1037/h0034088

Schneider, G. P. (2003). *Electronic Commerce*. Boston, MA: Thomson Learning Inc.

Shapiro, S. P. (1987). The Social Control of Impersonal Trust. *American Journal of Sociology, 93*, 623–658. doi:10.1086/228791

Stephens, R. T. (2004). *A Framework For The Identification Of Electronic Commerce Visual Design Elements That Enable Trust Within The Small Hotel Industry. School Of Computer and Information Sciences*. Fort Lauderdale, FL: Nova Southeastern University.

Stephenson, W. (1953). *The Study Of Behaviour: Q-Technique And Its Methodology*. Chicago: University Of Chicago Press.

Studio Archetype/Sapient & Cheskin Research (1999) Ecommerce Trust Study.

Sztompka, P. (2003). *Trust: A Sociological Theory*. Cambridge: Cambridge University Press.

Tang, T. W., & Chi, W. H. (2005). The Role of Trust In Customer Online Shopping Behavior: Perspective Of Technology Acceptance Model. In *Proceedings of Naacsos Conference 2005*. Indiana, USA.

Todd, P., & Benbasat, I. (1993). An Experimental Investigation of The Relationship Between Decision Makers, Decision Aids And Decision Making Effort. *Information Systems Research, 31*, 80–100.

Turban, E., King, D., Lee, L., Warkentin, M., & H, M. C. (2002). *Electronic Commerce: A Managerial Perspective,* Upper Saddle River, NJ: Prentice Hall.

Warkentin, M., Gefen, D., Pavlou, P. A., & Rose, G. M. (2002). Encouraging Citizen Adoption of E-Government By Building Trust. *Electronic Markets, 12*, 157–162. doi:10.1080/101967802320245929

Welch, E. W., Hinnant, C. C., & Moon, M. J. (2005). Linking Citizen Satisfaction With E-Government and Trust In Government. *Journal of Public Administration: Research and Theory, 15*, 371–391. doi:10.1093/jopart/mui021

Zand, D. E. (1972). Trust and Managerial Problem Solving. *Administrative Science Quarterly*, *17*, 229–239. doi:10.2307/2393957

Zhang, J., Ghorbani, A. A., & Cohen, R. (2007). A Familiarity-Based Trust Model For Effective Selection of Sellers In Multiagent E-Commerce Systems. *International Journal of Information Security*, *6*, 333–344. doi:10.1007/s10207-007-0025-y

Zucker, L. G. (1986). Production of Trust: Institutional Sources Of Economic Structure . In Staw, B. M., & Cummings, L. L. (Eds.), *Research In Organizational Behavior*. London: Jai Press Inc.

APPENDIX A. MEASURES

Disposition to Trust

1. In general, people really do care about the well-being of others.
2. The typical person is sincerely concerned about the problems of others.
3. Most of the time, people care enough to try to be helpful, rather than just looking out for themselves
4. In general, most folks keep their promises.
5. I think people generally try to back up their words with their actions.
6. Most people are honest in their dealings with others.
7. A large majority of professional people are competent in their area of expertise.
8. I usually trust people until they give me a reason not to trust them.
9. I generally give people the benefit of the doubt when I first meet them.
10. My typical approach is to trust new acquaintances until they prove I should not trust them.

Familiarity

1. I am familiar with looking for government services on the Internet.
2. I am familiar with conducting online translation with government on the Internet.
3. I am familiar with the e-Government web sites.
4. I am familiar with communicating with government agencies and departments through their official web sites.

Institution-Based Trust

1. I feel good about how things go when I do purchasing or other activities on the Internet.
2. I am comfortable making purchases on the Internet.
3. I feel that most Internet vendors would act in a customers' best interest.
4. If a customer required help, most internet vendors would do their best to help.
5. Most Internet vendors are interest in customer well-being, not just their own well-being.
6. I am comfortable relying on Internet vendors to meet their obligations.
7. I feel fine doing business on the Internet since Internet vendors generally fulfil their agreements.
8. I always feel confident that I can rely on Internet vendors to do their part when I interact with them.
9. In general, most Internet vendors are competent at serving their customers.
10. Most Internet vendors do a capable job at meeting customer needs.
11. I feel that most Internet vendors are competent at serving their customers.
12. I feel that most Internet vendors are good at what they do.
13. The Internet has enough safeguards to make me feel comfortable using it to transact personal business.
14. I feel assured that legal and technological structures adequately protect me from problems on the Internet.
15. I feel confident that encryption and other technological advances on the Internet make it safe for me to do business there.
16. In general, the Internet is now a robust and safe environment in which to transact business.

Website-Quality

1. Most of the e-Government web sites are easy to navigate.
2. Most of the e-Government web sites' contents are easily accessible.
3. Most of the e-Government web sites are intuitive.
4. Most of e-Government web sites provide sufficient information to search for the relevant government services.
5. Most of the e-Governmetn web sites are easy to read.
6. Most of e-Government web sites are visually pleasing.
7. Most of e-Government web sites are consistent throughout the site.
8. Most of e-Government web sites are professionally designed.
9. Most of the e-Government web sites show how users can contact and communicate with them.

PEOU

1. Most of the e-Government web sites are easy to use.
2. It is easy to learn how to interact with e-Government web sites.
3. Most of e-Government web sites are flexible to interact with.
4. Communication with the state government is easier through its official websites.

PU

1. I perceived that using the e-Government web sites enables citizens to search for government services and conduct government transactions faster.
2. I perceived that using the e-Government web sites can enhance the effectiveness of citizens' transactions with government.
3. Most of e-Government web sites are useful for searching government services.
4. Most of e-Government web sites are useful for conduction government transactions.

Trust in e-Government

1. I believe that e-Government web sites are competent and effective in providing government services.
2. Citizens can always predict performance of most e-Government web sites from their past experience with teh web sites.
3. Most e-Government web sites exhibit care, concern, honestly and goodwill to their citizens, thus providing a basis to advance the citizens relationship.
4. I believe most e-Government web sites will perform to the outmost of the citizens' benefit.
5. I believe that most e-Government web sites are truthful in their dealings with the citizens.
6. I would characterize e-Government as honest.
7. I believe that most e-Government web sites would keep their commitments.
8. I believe that e-Government web sites are sincere and genuine.
9. I believe that e-Government web sites are trustworthy.
10. I believe that most e-Government web sites would act in the citizens' best interest.

11. If the citizens required help, e-Government web sites would do their best to help them.
12. I believe that e-Government web sites are interested in the citizens well-being, not just their own.

Perceived Risk

1. Using e-Government web sites to transact with government departments and agencies I perceive that it is not secure to send sensitive information.
2. When using credit card to pay for government services through e-Government web sites I feel that credit card details are likely to be stolen.
3. I would fe insecure sending sensitive information over e-Government web sites.
4. Overall, it is not safe to transmit sensitive information over e-Government web sites.
5. As I consider transacting with government departments and agencies via e-Government web sites, I worry about whether they will perform as they are supposed to.
6. If I were to transact with government departments and agencies via e-Government web sites, I would be concerned that they would not provide the level of benefits that I would be expecting.
7. I am not confident about the abililty of e-Government web sites to perform as expected.
8. Considering the possible problesm associated with e-Government web sites performance, a lot of risk would be involved with searching and requesting government services via e-Government web sites.
9. It would be too risky to rely on the information provided in e-Government web sites.
10. Using e-Government web sites to search and request government services will take too much time or be a waste of time.

Intention to Engage in e-Government

1. How likely is it that you would request government services via e-Government web sites?
2. How likely is it that you would continue visiting e-Government web sites?
3. I would be willing to provide credit card information to pay for government services via e-Government web sites.
4. I can always rely on information provided in e-Government web sites.
5. I would be willing to provide my government identification number to e-Government web sites.
6. I would be willing to provide information like my name, address, and phone number to e-Government web sites.
7. I would be willing to pay to access information on e-Government web sites.
8. I will follow the procedures and advices provided in e-Government web sites.

Chapter 12
An SMS-Based e-Government Model: What Public Services can be Delivered through SMS?

Tony Dwi Susanto
Flinders University, Australia

Robert Goodwin
Flinders University, Australia

ABSTRACT

Delivering public services through SMS (SMS-based e-government) is becoming popular in developed and developing countries as a strategy to engage more citizens in using e-government services. Current advances in SMS-based e-government applications by local authorities in developed and developing countries are investigated to determine what extent SMS-based e-government could deliver existing Internet-based e-government services and whether these services can fulfil the actual needs of e-government services users. The currently available SMS-based e-government services are presented as a model with six levels: Listen, Notification, Pull-based Information, Communication, Transaction, and Integration levels. The model classifies the SMS-based e-government services into levels based on the direction of communication, the complexity of the services and the benefits received by citizens; the higher the level the more complex the services and the more benefits received by citizens. The SMS-based e-government model is compared to Internet-based e-government models and typical e-government use to show SMS-based e-government can deliver almost all of the service offerings of Internet-based e-government and meet the requirements of e-government users except for downloading forms. The outcome justifies the development of SMS-based e-government services.

INTRODUCTION

Despite the high number of e-government initiatives in the world, one of the current critical issues in e-government is its low adoption rate particularly in developing countries. Research by Dalziel (2004) across 31 countries found that the use of e-government in developing countries is still low: just 14% compared to developed countries where

DOI: 10.4018/978-1-61520-789-3.ch012

the use is 40% on average. It is a critical issue since one of the main goals of e-government is to improve citizen access to government information and services as well as to ensure citizen participation in and satisfaction with government processes (E-Government Act of 2002). An e-government system is useful to the extent to which citizens actually use the services (Accenture, 2003). Until the gap between what is offered and what is used can be bridged, e-government is far from reaching its maximum potential and government can not justify large investments in e-government and get all of the value possible out of these investments (Al-Adawi, Yousafzai et al., 2005).

In developing countries, Susanto and Goodwin (2006) argue that SMS-based e-government is more likely to increase e-government usage than the current Internet-based e-government. SMS-based e-government may be defined as a strategy and its implementation involves the utilization of Short Message Service (SMS) technology, services and applications for improving benefits to the parties involved in e-government including citizens, business, and government institutions. It may address the existing design-reality gap between the commonly proposed channel (the Internet) and the real ICT situation in developing countries which is high Internet illiteracy, lack of Internet infrastructure, high Internet cost, and low affordability (Susanto & Goodwin, 2006; Basu & Norris in Dada 2006). In developing countries people are more familiar with SMS than the Internet, the number of SMS users is much higher, the SMS infrastructure is more extensive, SMS costs are lower than Internet costs and mobile phones are much more affordable than PCs. For these reasons SMS could be the more appropriate channel to deliver e-government services in developing countries (Susanto & Goodwin, 2006). An empirical experiment in the Philippines showed that people prefer to contact their government using the SMS-based channel (87%) rather than the Internet (11%) (Lallana, 2004, p.30). According to technology acceptance theories, the cheaper service/technology might have a higher speed in adoption (Innovations Diffusion Theory by Rogers 1995), and the facilitation conditions (the available resources and knowledge) have a direct influence on the usage (Unified Theory of Acceptance and Use of Technology by Venkatesh et al 2003). Since e-government services are for every citizen, a leading-edge technology should not be adopted unless most citizens are ready to use it (Lee & Hong, 2002), governments should provide services via the channels people have the technology and skills to access (Dalziel, 2004).

Additionally, SMS-based e-government has proven benefits. Providing public services through the SMS channel significantly reduces time and cost; introduces a cheaper, easier and faster information-accessing channel; improves transparency, accountability, communication, and the relationship between government and citizens; makes the services and procedures easier for the citizens to use; improves the political image of the district, engages more people and increases citizens participation, and promotes e-Democracy (Lallana, 2004; Rannu & Semevsky, 2005; Bremer & Prado, 2006).

As a result, SMS-based e-government is becoming popular in developed and developing countries. For example, by 2008 50 government organizations in the Philippines had provided SMS-based channel for public services. Since 2006, by sending an SMS message to a single number, Singapore's citizens have been able to access 150 public services. In Indonesia most local authorities and majors have provided SMS services for listening to their people. In Australia, SMS has been used as a communications channel for bushfire alerts in Victoria and notification of public transport time-tables in Adelaide. As of January 2009, there have been 700 reports of SMS applications for public services in European countries (eGovernment Research Center 2009, Plans Review and Monitoring Office 2008).

In this paper currently available SMS-based e-government services will be classified and then compared to Internet-based e-government services. The research question for this paper is to what extent can SMS-based e-government services deliver current Internet-based services and meet the users' needs? In Section 2 currently available SMS-based e-government services are investigated and presented as a six-level model of SMS-based e-government. In Section 3, the SMS-based e-government model is compared to Internet-based e-government models in order to analyse whether SMS-based e-government systems can provide all services that can be provided by Internet-based e-government systems.

Also, currently available services in the SMS-based e-government model will be analysed to determine if they provide the currently used features of Internet based e-government and how to deal with the limitations of the SMS channel. Finally, the conclusion will be presented in Section 4.

AVAILABLE SMS-BASED E-GOVERNMENT SERVICES

A common method to categorize e-government systems is based on their service offerings. The service offering refers to the operational service flow between the actors involved in the e-government service in order to achieve the service's objectives and to realize the proposed value (Lee and Hong, 2002). Typically, the existing Internet-based e-government systems are classified into development-stage models which categorise services into presence/catalogue, interactive (two-way communication), transactional, and integration/transformation stages (Laynee & Lee, Baum & Di Maio, Ronaghan, Hiller & Belanger in Coursey and Norris 2008). These models classify e-government systems into stages and predict the linear development of e-government from the lowest step to the highest step, each successive stage is better than previous one and the government has to proceed through each step in sequence.

Available SMS-based e-government services can be classified into six levels based on the service offerings: These levels are Listen, Notification, Pull-based Information, Communication, Transaction, and Integration (see Figure 1). However, this SMS-based e-government model is not a development-stage model. Instead of *stage* or *step*, the proposed model uses the term *level* since it represents the available service offering and not the direction of the systems' evolution, each level is independent of the others and can be complementary to each other (levels can be added to a service in any sequence). It ranks the levels according to the complexity of the system and benefits received by citizens.

SMS-based e-government is a subset of mobile-government. Mobile-government or m-government is the use of mobile and wireless technologies to improve the services of public sector

Figure 1. A six-level model of SMS-based e-government services

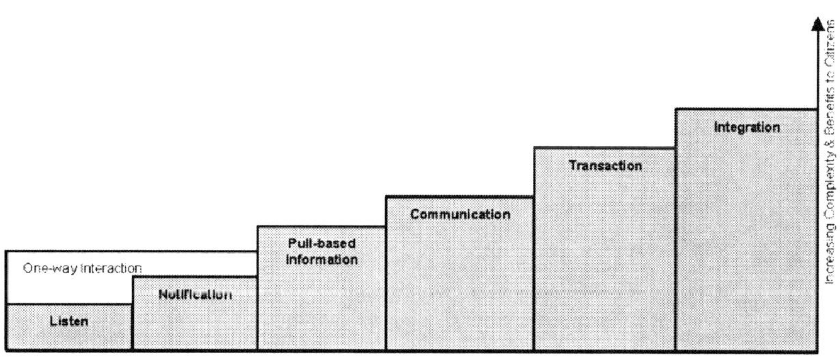

organisations. These technologies include mobile phones, PDAs and laptop computers that are connected to wireless Local Area Networks (LANs).

The benefits delivered by mobile government to citizens are presented in Table 1 (U.K. Cabinet Office 2000b in Lee & Hong 2002, El-Kiki & Lawrence 2006). The higher the level, the more complex the system and the more benefits received by citizens. A major benefit of m-government is that public information and government services are available to citizens and officials anytime, anywhere.

The direction of communication between citizens and government the complexity of the system and the benefits offered by the SMS-based services have been used to define the levels of SMS-based e-government in the model.

Listen Level

The first level contains current SMS applications that are for listening to citizens' opinions, reports, and complaints. Most of these systems enable citizens to send messages directly to mayors, councillors, the council, and the local authority. However, these systems are not designed to reply to the input-messages or to inform the sender of the subsequent actions. This one-way communication mode from citizens to government is categorized as the Listen level.

Examples of SMS-based e-government applications at this level include TXTGMA and text 117 in the Philippines, 9949 channel in Indonesia, and DMH ESCUCHA in Mexico City. The TXTGMA and 9949 channels are the SMS channels to reach the president. The DMH ESCUCHA channel is the SMS channel for the district mayor. Citizens can bring their concerns directly to the president or mayor by sending messages such as complaints about government services, projects, or officials, opinions about new policy, enquiries regarding new programs or reporting corruption. All of the input-messages are classified and forwarded to the right departments or officials to take action.

Table 1. Benefits offered by mobile-government

Benefits	Description
Value for Money	The content and services provide better value for the costs involved.
Quality of Service	Citizens (users) are aware that the services exist, know what services are provided, how they are relevant to them, and how to access them. (Awareness)
	All citizens have access to the services. (Accessibility)
	The services work any time any where. (Availability)
	The services are dependable, up to date and consistent. (Reliability)
	The services are accurate, errors have been minimised. (Accuracy)
	The services have fast response times. (Responsiveness)
	The services are provided in a respectful, considerate, friendly, helpful, polite, and efficient manner. (Courtesy and helpfulness)
Efficient Transactions	The services are easier and more convenient to use. (Usability)
	The services are delivered on time and play an important role in G2C relationships. (Timeliness)
	The services can be trusted. (Trust)
	The services protect users' privacy. (Privacy)
	The services are secure. (Security)
Strategic Data	Through the services, citizens can confidentially inform the government of issues and ask who did what and when. The government replies respect the citizens privacy and security. (Accountability)
	Governments use the services to make any decisions and actions available to citizens. (Transparency)

However, most of the systems do not acknowledge receipt or inform the senders about the subsequent actions.

The main benefit contributed by this level is accessibility. Citizens have a channel to share or broadcast their views on important issues directly to their government. It contributes to the citizens' empowerment. However, the lack of responsiveness and transparency, as well as protection for the senders' privacy and security prevent the public from actively participating in using these services (Signo, 2006).

Notification Level

The second level of the model is for current SMS applications which enable one-way communication from government to citizens. The government is able to notify citizens about their personal information and to broadcast important public information. It is called the Notification level.

Services in this level use a Push-based mechanism, which sends the messages to citizens activated by data on the server, not by a user's request. Technically, the services can be *Push – Event SMS*, *Push – Scheduled SMS*, *Push – Personal Profile SMS*, *Push – Location SMS*, or *SMS broadcasting*.

In the Push-Event SMS, messages are sent to citizens when activated by an event. Examples for these applications are the *e-Broadcasting* system (the Philippines) and M-library in Tartu (Estonia). The *e-Broadcasting* system, which belongs to the Bureau of Internal Revenue in the Philippines, is an SMS-based application that sends a confirmation message to taxpayers including the amount paid when their tax payment is received (Lallana, 2004). The M-library sends out a notification message to citizens registered in the system when a book, movie, or audiotape becomes available for loan (Rannu & Semevsky, 2005).

The Push – Scheduled SMS sends the messages to people when activated by a time based application, such as the DMH CITA system in Mexico City. The DMH CITA sends a reminder or confirmation message of an appointment 24 hours before the appointment. It is triggered by recording a request for the message in the database.

Messages in the Push – Personal Profile are sent to citizens activated by an application recording the profile and preferences of the user. An example of these SMS applications is the *Job Hunt* system (the Philippines) which sends a notification message to the job seeker whenever a matching job is available (Smith, 2005).

The Push-Location SMS system will send a particular message when the user approaches certain locations. An SMS-based tourist guide system is an example of a Push-Location application. The SMS services send to tourists at a location information about the location such as what to see, the artist, or the history of the place (Decker M., 2006).

Finally, the SMS broadcasting system broadcasts messages to all citizens in a particular area (using the Cell-Broadcast Service) or certain people registered in the database (using the point-to-point SMS service) (Susanto & Goodwin, 2006). One example is DMH PROTÉGÉ (Mexico City). It sends alert messages to citizens in the district regarding meteorological and high rain risks, low temperatures, potential disasters, and emergency locations as well as contact numbers (Bremer & Prado, 2006).

Delivering notification services to the public in this level makes citizens customers of the government (the courtesy and helpfulness benefit). The systems enable citizens to get the information easily, conveniently, on time, cheaply or often free (the benefits of usability, timeliness and value for money). Citizens are informed about and more involved in the activities of government (the transparency benefit) that makes the government more accountable to its citizens.

However, privacy is a common issue in this level: should all mobile phone users be included in the services automatically or only with their permission. A mismatch of information services and citizens' needs and difficult registration methods are other common issues of this level.

Pull-Based Information Level

There are SMS applications for public services which enable citizens to access public or personal information by sending request-messages. The services use the pull method: citizens send a 'request SMS' to the service and the requested information is sent back to the sender's handset via SMS. The information options provided by services in this level are limited and the request-text must be in a certain format. These two-way communication services belong to the Pull-based Information level.

Examples of current e-government applications in this level are the NHS Direct service (UK) and the SMS-based vehicle detail system (East Java, Indonesia). The NHS Direct service allows citizens to locate the nearest health services by sending a text message with the name of the service required (such as doctor or pharmacy) and their post code to the NHS Direct number; the sender will receive an instant reply with the details of the requested service, including address, telephone number and distance from the postcode area (e-Government Research Center, 2008). The SMS-based vehicle detail service enables citizens to inquire about a vehicle (tax, model, and owner) by sending the vehicle registration number (dipendajatim, 2007).

Major benefits delivered by this level are accessibility, availability, responsiveness, and timeliness. Citizens can access their personal or public information anytime anywhere. Some challenges in this level include how to provide cheap or even free notification services (value for money benefit), how to choose the information services which are really needed by citizens (awareness), and how to provide simple, easy to use and remember request-message formats (usability).

Communication Level

There are SMS applications for public services which enable people to inquire, to complain or to report about anything without using a specific text format and to get responses/replies immediately. This model classifies these applications as the Communication level.

The simplest system for this level is an SMS gateway operated by a team of people who have been trained to answer any queries, such as TXTCSC (the Philippines). The TXTCSC of the Civil Service Commission of the Philippines is for Filipinos to complain, suggest, commend, inquire, or report about public services, corruption, and inefficient bureaucracy. The TXTCSC answers the queries and complaints within a day. When the system is unable to respond to queries, it refers the text messages to the agencies concerned and reports back regarding the actions (Lallana, 2004).

Another option for providing services at this level is combining the SMS and email channels like in Stirling (UK). The Stirling council receives citizens' messages through the SMS gateway which converts the messages to emails. The contact centre officers respond immediately the emails if they know the answer to the query or direct it to the relevant service. Responses to customers will automatically be converted back into a text message and sent back to their mobile phones (egovmonitor, 2006).

Since it enables citizens to express their opinions, comments or queries to the government using any sentences (without worrying about the text format) and to get the reply immediately, this level offers more benefits in accessibility, availability, responsiveness, courtesy and helpfulness, usability, timeliness, accountability, and transparency. Potential issues at this level are low protection for privacy and security of the senders, and lack of the assurance of fast and effective response to any input-messages (the responsiveness).

Transaction Level

Some SMS-based e-government systems have enabled transactions. Using these systems citizens can pay bills and update their personal data through SMS.

Current examples of these applications are mobile ticketing (UK) and an SMS voting system (Switzerland). The Mobile ticketing enables people to order tickets for major events (such as football matches, rock concerts) just by sending an SMS (SkiData in Monash 2005). They then receive a return SMS which has an image with a 2-dimensional metric-code containing details such as the ticket number, the mobile phone number and the seat number. The people will be charged for their tickets by the mobile service provider once the 2-D codes on their mobile phones are scanned on entering the stadium. The SMS-voting system enables citizens to cast their votes in elections or votes from home or when travelling (itwire, 2008).

Since citizens can complete transactions (money and data) with government agencies anytime anywhere in a secure channel, this level offers more benefits in accessibility, availability, accuracy, responsiveness, courtesy and helpfulness, timeliness, trust, privacy, and security. However, trust and security are still the dominant issues.

Integration Level

The ultimate level of this model is when all the SMS-based systems are integrated and organized in a single portal so people can send messages to a single service number for all services. This level predicts the integrated-SMS systems will be also integrated with the Internet/web-based e-government systems so citizens have options whether accessing the services by sending SMS to one number or through the Internet at one web address. At this level SMS messaging and the Internet may complement each other in a service, for example: a citizen may send a form or pay for a public service electronically by the Internet and get notification via SMS, or pay for the services through SMS and get the receipt by email.

An example of SMS-based e-government which has achieved this level is SGOVT (Singapore). It is a single SMS portal for 150 government services across government agencies. Since July 2006, citizens have been able to access all services just by sending messages to the short code 74688 or SGOVT (idasingapore, 2006).

As the ultimate level, this level should provide all of the benefits of e-government including value for money, high quality of service, efficient transaction, and strategic data benefits. Interoperability among the SMS-based systems, databases, and the Internet-based systems will be a potential issue in this level.

CAN SMS DELIVER ALL INTERNET-BASED E-GOVERNMENT SERVICES?

The currently available SMS-based e-government systems have been able to deliver a wide-range public services from the simplest level for Listening, to the Notification, Pull-based information, Communication, Transaction, and Integration levels. Whether these available SMS-based services have been able to deliver all common Internet-based e-government services or not will now be examined. Current service offerings and typical e-government uses will be the parameters for the comparison.

Internet-based e-government services are commonly classified into stages. While there are several e-government models, generally there are four main stages: Web presence or Catalogue, Interaction, Transaction, and Integration or Transformation. The models assume that the development process is linear and step-wise (Laynee & Lee, Baum & Di Maio, Ronaghan, Hiller & Belanger in Coursey and Norris 2008).

When compared to Internet-based e-government models, SMS-based e-government can deliver almost all of the Internet based e-government service offerings. The Web Presence stage which presents one-way information from government to citizens may be transferred into Pull-based Information level in the SMS-based e-government model. The Interaction stage which offers two-ways communication between government and citizens may be delivered using the Listen, Notification, and Communication levels in the SMS-based e-government model. The Transaction stage may be implemented in the Transaction level of the SMS-based government model. The service offerings in the Integration level of both models are similar.

Taylor Nelson Sofres Plc, one of the world's leading market research and information groups, found that the most common use of e-government services is for information seeking, following by downloading government forms which were then sent back by post or fax (such as tax forms and forms to claim government rebates), providing personal/household information to the government, transactions such as paying for government services or products by credit card or by direct debit to a bank account number (such as driving licenses, traffic fines, government taxes). E-government services for consulting with government are used the least. (Dalziel, 2004 p.6).

Most of these typical Internet e-government applications can be provided by SMS-based e-government applications. Information requests can be delivered by using SMS applications in Notification and Pull-based information levels. Providing personal information to and completing transactions with government may be conducted via SMS-based applications in the Transaction level. Consulting with government could be via applications in the Communication level. However, downloading government forms cannot be done through SMS. It may not be an issue for advanced governments who have started a paperless culture. Forms could be completed by receiving and replying to questions sent via SMS without needing to download the form.

Even if in terms of service offerings and typical e-government applications SMS-based e-government can deliver Internet-based e-government services, it does not mean that SMS-based e-government should replace the Internet-based e-government. The limited bandwidth of the SMS channel which delivers only 160 characters of text without sounds and images for each transmission cannot deliver the complex services possible on the Internet such as long documents, multimedia, or provide the same level of security. However, its simplicity, low cost and pervasiveness are advantages of SMS when providing public services. Governments should provide services appropriate for the SMS channel and utilize the main advantages of SMS as a services channel. For example, when notifying citizens of due dates for tax payments or warning about potential disasters it may be better to use SMS rather than email since citizens are more likely to be alerted and read the message immediately.

In countries with widespread Internet infrastructure rather than replacing Internet services, SMS services can complement Internet services and play a role in encouraging more people to use e-government services. In countries with limited Internet access but widespread mobile phone coverage using SMS e-government is an appropriate way of providing comprehensive government services and encouraging people to become involved.

CONCLUSION

SMS applications for public services are becoming popular in developed and developing countries. Currently available SMS-based applications cover virtually all of the service offerings in Internet-based e-government models, including presenting information, interaction, transaction, and integration.

This paper classified SMS-based e-government applications into six levels: Listen, Notification,

Pull-based Information, Communication, Transaction, and Integration. The higher the level the more complex the system and the more benefits available to citizens.

SMS-based e-government is able to fulfil most of the typical Internet e-government applications: information seeking, providing information to government, completing transactions and consulting, but not downloading forms. SMS-based e-government does not replace Internet-based e-government; it complements it and can be used as a starting point for engaging more people in e-government.

In developing countries with little Internet infrastructure, SMS based e-government provides a means by which most of the population can participate in e-government.

REFERENCES

Accenture (2003) eGovernment Leadership: Engaging the Customer, *The Government Executive Series*. Retrieved from http://www.accenture.com/xdoc/en/industries/government/gove_capa_epa_leadership.pdf

Al-Adawi, Z., Yousafzai, S., et al. (2005). *Conceptual Model of Citizen Adoption E-Government*, the Second International Conference on Innovations in Information Technology, Dubai, U. Retrieved from http://citeseerx.ist.psu.edu/viewdoc/download?doi=10.1.1.92.2165&rep=rep1&type=pdf

Bremer, A. A., & Prado, L. A. L. (2006). Municipal m-Services using SMS,Euro mGov 2006.

Coursey, D., & Norris, D. F. (2008, May-June). Models of E-Government: Are They Correct? An Empirical Assessment. [PAR]. *Public Administration Review*, *68*(3), 523–536. doi:10.1111/j.1540-6210.2008.00888.x

Dada, D. (2006). *The Failure of E-Government in Developing Countries* (pp. 39–43). The Electronic Journal on Information Systems in Developing Countries.

Dalziel, D. (2004) Government Online-A multi-country Study of e-government usage, *The World Association of Research Professionals*. Retrieved from http://www.tns-global.com/corporate/Doc/0/MJHPECQDDJ94195OMMQKECDBC0/GovernmentOnline-ESOMAR_Paper2004.pdf

Decker, M. (2006) Generalized Notification Services: A Simple but Versatile Paradigm for the Implementation of Mobile Data Services, *Euro mGov 2006*. Retrieved from http://www.mgovernment.org/resources/euromgvo2006/PDF/10_Decker.pdf

E-government Act of 2002 (2002). *US-Public Law 107–347, 107th Congress, 116 STAT. 2899*. Retrieved from http://frwebgate.access.gpo.gov/cgi-bin/getdoc.cgi?dbname=107_cong_public_laws&docid=f:publ347.107.pdf

eGovernment Research Center (2008). UK: SMS to help track nearest health services. Retrieved from http://www.epractice.eu/document/4405

El-Kiki, T., & Lawrence, E. (2006). Mobile User Satisfaction and Usage Analysis Model of mGovernment Services, *Euro mGov 2006*. Retrieved from http://www.mgovernment.org/resources/euromgvo2006/PDF/11_El-Kiki.pdf

epractice.eu. (2008). Retrieved August 11,2008, from http://www.epractice.eu/home

Haas, J. (2001). Mobile Security: SMS (& a little WAP), ITSX. Retrieved from http://72.14.205.104/search?q=cache:kJbYby7zyp8J:www.itsx.com/hal2001/hal2001-itsx.ppt+SMS+security&hl=en&ct=clnk&cd=1&gl=auIDASingapore (2006). *Innovative Projects Showcased At the Building Our Singapore - The*

ITU. (2007). Retrieved from http://www.itu.int/ITU-D/ict/statistics/ict/

itwire (2008). *SMS Voting*. Retrieved from http://www.itwire.com/content/view/15481/1105/1/2/

Lallana, E. (2008). *eGovDev4Dev cases on mGovernment*. e. f. Development. Manchester, UK: University of Manchester's Institute for Development Policy and Management.

Lallana, E. L. (2004). SMS, business and Government in the Philippines, ICT4D.ph (a project of the Department of Science and Technology and IDRC). Retrieved from http://unpan1.un.org/intradoc/groups/public/documents/Other/UNPAN024834.pdf

Lallana, E. L. (2007). mGovernment and eDemocracy. *eDevelopment*. Retrieved from http://web.worldbank.org/wbsite/external/topics/extinformationandcommunicationandtechnologies/extedevelopment/0,contentMDK:21534706~pagePK:210058~piPK:210062~theSitePK:559460,00.html

Lee, K. J., & Hong, J. H. (2002). Development of An E-government Service Model: A Business Model Approach, *International Review of Public Administration* 2002, *7*(2).

Plans Review and Monitoring Office. (2008). *Report on National Government Agencies (NGAs) with Short Messaging Service (SMS) Facility*, National Computer Center-Commission on Information and Communications Technology. Retrieved from http://www.ncc.gov.ph/files/sms_report1208.pdf

Public Service in Action Exhibition. Retrieved from http://www.ida.gov.sg/InSG/Dec06/egov.html

Rannu, R., & Semevsky, M. (2005, December). *Mobile Services in Tartu*, Mobi Solutions Ltd, Tartu, Estonia. Retrieved from http://www.mobisolutions.com

Robert, E. M. (1995). *Diffusion of Innovations*. New York: The Free Press.

Satriyantono, T. (2002). *Tantangan Aplikasi Mobile Generasi 3 (3G)*, Seminar MTI-ITB. Retrieved from http://satriyantono.net/blogs2.php?id=1&parameter=1

Signo, S. M. (2006). Pnp Text 2920 Service: A Communication Perspective on M-Government In Philippine Context. *Asian Culture Forum 2006*. Retrieved from http://64.62.231.21:8080/dspace/bitstream/123456789/233/1/cprs2_CS_P.pdf.

Sillanpaa, A. (2001) Mobile Asset Security and How to Make Money on It. *Seminar on Network Security, Publications on Telecommunications Software and Multimedia*. Helsinki University of Technology. Retrieved from http:// www. tml.hut.fi/Studies/T-110.501/2001/papers/index.html

Smith, J. (April 2005). Cutting the wires: why Asian governments are going mobile, *Public Sector Technology & Management*.

Susanto, T. D., & Goodwin, R. (2006 June). Opportunity and Overview of SMS-based eGovernment in Developing Countries. *The Internet Society II: Advances in Education, Commerce & Governance*. The New Forest, UK, WIT Press.

Susanto, T. D., & Goodwin, R. (2006, December) Implementing SMS-based eGovernment Model, 8th *International Conference on Information Integration and Web-based Applications & Services (iiWAS2006)*, Yogyakarta, Indonesia.

Susanto, T. D., & Goodwin, R. (2007 June). Content Presentation and SMS-based e-Government, *International Conference on Electrical Engineering and Informatics (ICEEI)*, Bandung, Indonesia.

Venkatesh, V., & Morris, M. G. (2003). User Acceptance of Information Technology: Toward a Unified View. *Management Information Systems Quarterly*, *27*(3), 425–478.

Chapter 13
E-Government Projects Risk Management:
Taking Stakeholders in Perspective

Fatma Bouaziz
University of Sfax, Tunisia

ABSTRACT

Stakeholders are proactive in the development of e-government initiatives; public organizations should be proactive in identifying all relevant collaborators, working with them and undertaking measures to systematically engage their stakeholders. Building coalitions with both internal and external stakeholders (Pardo & Scholl, 2002) of an e-government project may help in recognizing the critical stakeholders that deserve project managers' attention. Henceforth, e-government has to rely on a broad consensus, commitment and ownership at all levels among government officials as well as the citizens. The diversity of stakeholder interests poses a considerable challenge to project managers. Stakeholder analysis may be applied to e-government projects to assist managers in identifying potential conflicts between project stakeholders at early project stages. Insights on potential stakeholder conflicts can then be used for devising and implementing communication strategies to prevent contradictory stakeholder interests and to avoid conflicts. Empirical evidence is needed in order to validate the suggested approach. Government to government and inter agency cooperation projects may be especially well suited, as complexity rises and multiple public sector organizations seeks to align their objectives to reach common goals.

INTRODUCTION

Almost all countries members of the United Nations (UN) are implementing e-government projects. At 2008, the UN argued that 188 countries among 192 adopted some features of e-government. Tight budgets, looking for increase of internal efficiency and customer value are among motivations for adopting e-government (Flak and Dertz, 2007; UN, 2008). In fact, benefits of e-government include more transparency, better authorities' coordination at different levels of government, fast and efficient operations by

DOI: 10.4018/978-1-61520-789-3.ch013

streamlining processes and lowering costs and growing civic participation (UN, 2005; UN, 2008).

Unfortunately, studies indicate that many of these goals are not obtained and/or lower benefits than expected are achieved (Moon, 2002; De, 2005; Flak et al., 2008). E-government services lack maturity (Moon, 2002) and many of these initiatives remain unsuccessful (Heeks, 2003; UN, 2003; De, 2005). Moreover, whereas almost all states are on line, they stand at different stages of e-government evolution. As it follows from UN report (2008), a high percentage of the countries remain at the first stages of e-government evolution. UN (2008) advanced that some of the developed countries are beginning to migrate to connected government. However, others are in the transactional stage of e-government or they are still at the initial stages of information and enhanced presence.

Several issues may explain the relatively slow process of implementing e-government and its failure. First, evolving to the integration stage seems to be more difficult since social, cultural and organisational barriers may limit the success chances at this level (Murray & al., 2004; Ebrahim & Irani, 2005; UN, 2008). Murray and al. (2004) highlighted that public sector organisations have unique challenges to the implementation process and implementation strategies often require particular attention to the social and political elements inherent in organisational changes. Second, the public sector is characterized by complexity due to a variety of stakeholders with different and often conflicting objectives (Flak & Nordheim, 2006; Flak & et al., 2008). E-government implies integration of government entities and re-organization of work processes (UN, 2008). Thus, various stakeholders may affect or be affected by such initiatives. However, it seems that not all stakeholders perceive e-government projects enthusiastically since their organizational and social status may be impacted (Scholl, 2005). Stakeholders can have different attitudes towards an e-government project. Some of them may have a threatening position. Others may be more collaborative and support the project. Conflicts and self interests may emerge as a challenge to e-government projects implementation. That's why several authors (Murray and al., 2004; Scholl, 2005; Tan and al., 2007) argued that the success of e-government initiatives depends on the identification of the stakeholders, their interests and their expectations since the conception phase of the project.

Consequently, addressing the various stakeholders in an appropriate manner will be necessary. In this sense, Murray and et al. (2004) affirmed that implementation strategies should support the process of managing stakeholder relations in order to reduce the risk of stakeholder conflict and ensure the success of e-government initiative.

Although stakeholders and their different interests have to be identified, studies dealing with stakeholder influence on the development of e-government are sparse (De, 2005; Flak & Nordheim, 2006). Building on stakeholder theory highlighting the evidence of the connection between stakeholder management and corporate performance (Donaldson & Preston, 1995), we argue that the management of the interests of the prime stakeholders may reduce the risk of failure of an e-government project and that stakeholder management must be given attention as an essential component in e-government risk management procedure.

This chapter is organized as follow: definitions of e-government and risk management process are presented in section one. Then, in section two, a discussion on the fit between e-government context and stakeholder theory is engaged. Section three seeks to identify stakeholders of e-government projects. Finally, section four proposes an analysis of the impact of each stakeholder on the success of an e-government initiative.

E-GOVERNMENT: DEFINITION AND RISK MANAGEMENT

UN (2005, p.14) has defined e-government as the use of Information and communication technology (ICT) and its application by the government for the provision of information and public services to the people. Moon (2002) proposed that e-government can be narrowly defined as the use of ICT between government organizations, employee, enterprises, and citizens to simplify and improve information diffusion, communication and public services delivery (Heeks, 2003; Evangelidis, 2004; Ebrahim & Irani, 2005). E-government can also be broadly defined to include all ICT platforms and applications in use by the public sector for a continuous optimization of public services delivery and information dissemination, citizens' participation in political processes, and a transformation of the internal and external relationships and processes by the technology, the Internet and the new Medias (Moon, 2002).

UN (2008) argued that governments are more and more focusing on e-government-as-a-whole concept. In this case, the provision of services at the front office is supported by integration, consolidation and innovation in back office processes and systems (UN, 2008). This effort of integration leads several authors (Lim et al., 2007; Tan et al., 2007) to discuss e-governance issues. UN (2008) highlighted the passage from e-government to connected governance to stimulate reflexion on e-government as a change lever of public sector. Connected governance lies on integration of intergovernmental processes vertically between various government agencies and/or horizontally between agencies at the same level and/or with the inclusion of private sector and other stakeholders (UN, 2008).

Although numerous studies are interested to e-government and e-governance phenomena, it seems that a definition of 'e-government projects' is missing. Turner and Muller (2003) defined projects as a temporary organization to which resources are assigned to undertake a unique, novel and transient endeavour managing the inherent uncertainty and need for integration in order to deliver beneficial objectives of change. So following these authors, e-government projects may be considered as a temporary organization conceived and set up to answer specific objectives of change. They require the mobilization of resources, means and competences, and they are driven under constraints of schedule, costs and quality. Like in all other types of projects, uncertainties threaten their development and expose them to the risk of failure (Bouaziz, 2006).

In fact, Heeks (2003) classified e-government initiatives into three main results:

- *Total failure*: the initiative was never implemented or was implemented but immediately abandoned.
- *Partial failure*: major goals for the initiative were not attained and/or there were significant undesirable outcomes. Major goals are the main objectives a group wanted to achieve with the initiative, while undesirable outcomes are unexpected outcomes that a group did not want to happen but which did happen.
- *Success*: most stakeholder groups attained their major goals and did not experience significant undesirable outcomes.

But evaluating success or failure of an information technology project is in part subjective since it depends on the perception of implied stakeholders who may rank the importance of the various criteria differently (Wateridge, 1998). For example, information technology project managers highlight the importance of respecting schedule and budget, whereas users search for satisfaction and project sponsors look for the benefits' achievement of the implemented system (Wateridge, 1998). Since government operates under constraints of budget, to be within budget and schedule may be of priority. However, focussing on these criteria may occult the importance of others such as users' satisfaction and use of delivered systems extensively recognized as key measures of information systems success (DeLone and McLean, 2003).

Giving that rates of failure of information technology projects are high and to ensure more success chances to these projects, authors (Schmidt et al., 2001; Smith et al., 2001; Bernard et al., 2004; Bouaziz, 2006) highlighted the importance of the risk management of these projects. They presented risk management as a process composed of three steps: (1) the identification of the risk factors (inventory of factors that may threaten the success of a project), (2) the assessment of risk exposure (determination of the probability of the undesirable outcomes and the importance of losses associated to them) and (3) the treatment of the risk (adoption of countermeasures in order to treat the risk factors).

Bouaziz (2006) observed that authors have identified risk factors with reference to socio-technical (Evangelidis, 2004) and organizational theories (Willcocks & Margetts, 1994). According to socio-technical systems theory, risk factors emerge respectively from social and technical sub-systems constituting an organization. Examples of these factors include lack of users' commitment and project complexity. Based on this theory, Evangelidis (2004) proposed a risk assessment framework for public e-services (FRAMES). The author affirmed that an e-service transaction project may be seen as a socio-technical system that comprises three subsystems, and that inter-connects four modules of the transaction service project. These four modules are the customers, the e-service, the organizational level, and the intra-organizational service. Evangelidis (2004) identified risk factors by reference to e-commerce literature and experience. According to the author, risk factors are situated in the level of the four modules comprised in an e-service project.

In organizational change theories, risk factors result from the internal and the external contexts, and from the content of change. They may include lack of top management commitment, lack of competences, project size and complexity and so on (Willcocks & Margetts, 1994). Based on socio-technical and organizational theories, project risk management literature and e-government literature, Bouaziz (2006) identified the most cited risk factors by 23 studies. Among these factors, it seems that user's commitment, top management commitment, competences of information technology managers and users are the most cited. Those actors are among other stakeholders whose willing, competences and commitment may condition an e-government project success. Managing multiple relationships with stakeholders and failure to identify all stakeholders constitute risk factors leading to projects' failure (Schmidt et al., 2001).

THE FIT BETWEEN E-GOVERNMENT AND STAKEHOLDER THEORY

The Role of Stakeholders in E-Government Success

The stakeholder concept can be traced back to the 1930s (Flak & Nordheim, 2006; Flak et al., 2008). This concept has appeared in the management literature in an internal memorandum at the Stanford Research Institute, in 1963 (Freeman, 1984, p.31). Although Scholl (2001) asserts that the concept is not uniformly accepted, it seems that Freeman's (1984) definition of stakeholders is the most used by authors (Scholl, 2001; Flak & Dertz; Gomes, 2006; Lim et al., 2007; Tan et al., 2007a): the concept of stakeholder refers to any group or individual who can affect or is affected by the achievement of the organization's objectives (Freeman, 1984, p.46). Without the support of these groups or individuals, the organization would cease to exist (Mitchell et al., 1997; Tan et al., 2007a).

The definition of stakeholders in the field of information systems aligns with Freeman's definition. De (2005) argued that stakeholder includes all parties who can affect a system, whether their traditional roles and responsibilities are enhanced by the system or depreciated.

However, this definition may not account for those actors who contribute to the implementation of information systems without being directly influenced by it such as information technology managers, systems developers, decision makers, systems vendors, subcontractors.

Nilsson (2008) gave a complementary definition. By the term stakeholder, he referred to any actor whom are in any way involved in, or has a relation to the enterprise, and thus may influence it directly or indirectly. Examples of stakeholders are a steering committee for a project or future users of an IT system in production (Nilsson, 2008).

E-government projects lie on the participation and collaboration of various stakeholders. They require cooperation of stakeholders within government agencies and between heterogeneous government agencies (OCDE, 2003; Ebrahim & Irani, 2005), e-government agencies and citizens and private sector (OCDE, 2003). Authors argued that e-government involves particularly complex settings, consisting of a variety of stakeholders promoting different and often conflicting objectives (Flak & Nordheim, 2006; Flak et al., 2008). Also, e-government lies on the experiences and expertise of different stakeholders and the development of shared understanding and collaborative partnerships between business and information technology actors (Pardo & Scholl, 2002). Moreover, it seems that success in the implementation depends on the ability of the system to meet the expectations and needs of several stakeholders (Lim et al., 2007; Tan et al., 2007a).

So, expectations and needs of diverse stakeholders must to be addressed to assure more chances of success to e-government projects. Pardo and Scholl (2002) proposed that e-government requires a holistic view of the organization, its culture, systems, processes, and stakeholders and that the success of e-government depends on the participation and cooperation of primary stakeholders. Stakeholders may manifest attitudes in favour of an e-government project or they may have personal interests and competing goals that risk hindering it.

Hence, there is a great need for understanding the role of stakeholder involvement, interests, relationships and responsibilities to implement e-government projects with success. Lim and al. (2007) emphasized the need to realign e-government objectives with stakeholder determinants. They added that the success of e-government initiatives lies on the capacity of government agencies to effectively leverage information technology in managing stakeholder expectations. Similar conclusions are advanced by other authors like Pardo and Scholl (2002), Scholl (2005), Tan and al. (2007). Stakeholder theory gives insights in to the management of stakeholders.

Stakeholder Theory

Freeman (1984) was the first to develop stakeholder theory as supported by Flak and Nordheim (2006), Gomes (2006) and Flak and al. (2008). This author argued that, in a context characterized by increased competitiveness, globalization, and complexity of business operations, firms' profitability and sustainability depend on stakeholder's relationship management (Flak & Nordheim, 2006; Flak et al., 2008). In fact, stakeholder theory conceived the organization as a system of stakeholders (Tan et al., 2007) who create together economic value. If Freeman et al. (2004) thought that these stakeholders voluntarily come together and cooperate to improve everyone's circumstance, their purposes are not always congruent; according to stakeholder theory, the organization is rather described as a constellation of cooperative and competitive interests (Donaldson & Preston, 1995).

So, stakeholder theory assumes that an organization's effectiveness has to be measured by its ability to satisfy those agents who have a stake in the organization (De, 2005; Gomes, 2006) and managers should account for groups and individuals who can affect or can be affected by an organizational objective achievement (Donaldson & Preston, 1995; Mitchell et al., 1997; Freeman and al., 2004). Thus, creating value for stakeholders especially for those who are considered as primary stakeholders is important and can affect survival and success of an organization (Mitchell et al., 1997; Scholl, 2005).

Three aspects of stakeholder theory emerge from the use of this theory (Donaldson and Preston, 1995): normative, descriptive and instrumental. The normative aspect means that the theory is used to interpret the function of the corporation, including the identification of moral or philosophical guidelines for the operation and management of corporations (p.71). The descriptive aspect means that the theory is used to describe and sometimes to explain, specific corporate characteristics and behaviours (p.70). The instrumental aspect means that the theory is used to identify connections, or lack of connections, between stakeholder management and the achievement of traditional corporate objectives (p.71). Scholl (2001) contended that in its instrumental interpretation stakeholder theory maintains that those firms that are managed for optimal stakeholder satisfaction thrive better than those firms that only maximize shareholder (that is, profit) interests.

Figure 1. The input-output model (Donaldson & Preston, 1995)

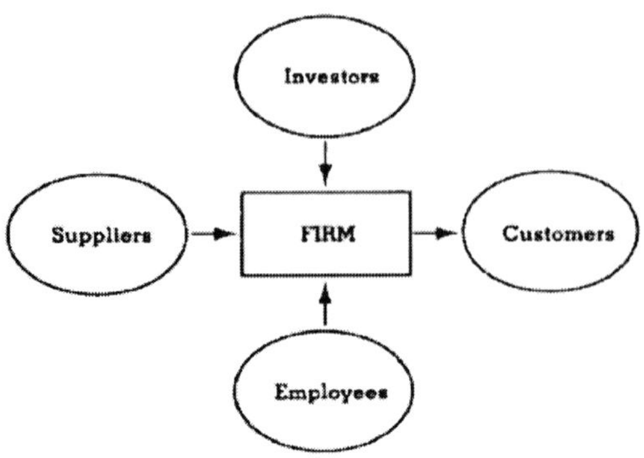

Donaldson and Preston (1995) opposed two models (Figures 1 and 2) to illustrate stakeholder theory ideas. According to these authors, stakeholder conception of organizations implies that all actors are involved with an organization to obtain benefits; whereas in the input-output model, actors provide input which the firm converts to benefits for its customers.

The Applicability of Stakeholder Theory to E-Government

Stakeholder theory is primarily developed to deal with concerns in the private sector. Donaldson and Preston (1995) declared that stakeholder issues involve considerations and conceptual issues (e.g. the meaning of property rights) unique to corporate setting. So applicability of the stakeholder theory to e-government projects may be doubtful. Doubts increase because of the differences between public management information systems and management information systems in the private sector. In fact, greater interdependencies that at least partly lead to increased accountability, procedural delays and red tape characterize the environment of public management information systems (Flak & Dertz, 2007). In addition, it is suggested that management information system practices are not automatically adopted in public sector environments, but rather adjusted and adapted to fit the public context.

Figure 2.

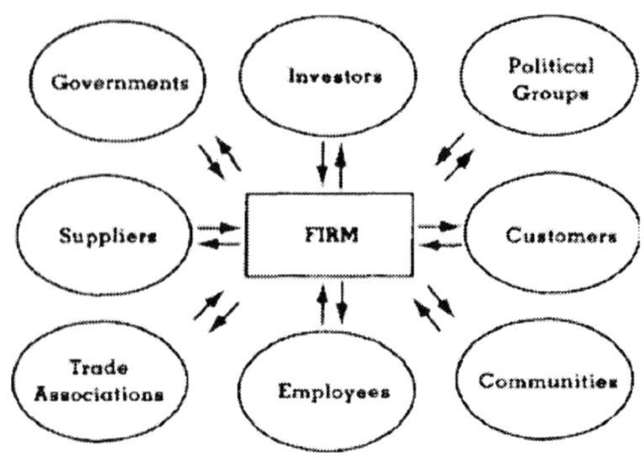

However, Flak and Dertz (2007) and Flak et al. (2008) quoted that stakeholder theory has been applied in various settings to support strategy development and implementation and can be appropriate in different contexts like information systems and health care management. Specifically, Flak and Dertz (2007) argued that no significant evidence have been found that categorically prevents the transfer of functioning ideas, techniques and theories from the private sector to the public sector. Furthermore, for Gomes (2006), the application of the stakeholder theory in the public sector seems to be in accordance with the wave of New Public Management. This body of theory aims to introduce business-based ideas to the public sector. Consequently, this author deduced that the stakeholder theory can be seen as an approach by which public decision-makers scan their environments in search of opportunities and threats. Scholl (2001) and Flak et al. (2008) concluded that no serious conceptual mismatch has been identified between stakeholder theory and a government's objective of providing policy and services for citizens and organizations – society's stakeholders.

In addition, Scholl (2001) found that the insights from stakeholder theory can be applied in parts to managerial decisions about major e-government initiatives. He justified this conclusion by the fact that public management responsibilities begin to resemble private sector management tasks not only formally but also regarding the emerging network nature of organizations in both spheres. Thus, the importance of stakeholder theory as a useful theory in the case of public sector and in particular e-government is extensively highlighted (Scholl, 2001; Murray et al., 2004; Lim et al., 2007; Tan et al., 2007a; Flak et al., 2008).

In fact, public sector is characterized as a complex setting with many stakeholders who often have multiple, vague and diverging goals (Flak & Nordheim, 2006; Flak et al., 2008; Sæbo et al., 2008). Stakeholder's issues must be addressed through implementation strategies which support the process of managing stakeholder relations to reduce the risk of conflict and ensure the success of e-government initiatives (Murray et al., 2004). De (2005) advanced that e-government managers have to deal with the questions of resistance, conflict and complex stakeholder relations. To do so, stakeholder theory can be useful since it allows identification of entities and relationships between them. This will enable better translation of requirements for design and guidelines for development and implementation of an e-government initiative (Sæbo et al., 2008). Thus, stakeholder theory may offer a structured approach well suited for stakeholder analysis in e-government context (Sæbo et al., 2008) and a logical first step for a viable theoretical alternative for the study of e-government (Tan et al., 2007a; Lim et al., 2007).

THE STAKEHOLDER MANAGEMENT

The Steps of Stakeholder Management

Stakeholder theory is primarily a management instrument (Flak & Dertz, 2007). It describes existing situations, predicts cause-effect relationships, and recommends attitudes, structures and practices that, taken together, constitute stakeholder management (Donaldson & Preston, 1995).

Stakeholder management in private sector is based on three steps (Lim et al., 2007): identification of salient stakeholders, categorization of salient stakeholders and management of salient stakeholders. Salience refers to the question why some stakeholder claims are attended to while others are not. To identify salient stakeholders, Mitchell and al. (1997, p.854) proposed a model based on three dimensions: (1) the stakeholder's power to influence the firm, (2) the legitimacy of the stakeholder's relationship with the firm, and (3) the urgency of the stakeholder's claim on the firm. According to Mitchell and al. (1997), stakeholders possessing all three attributes are more salient towards managers than stakeholders who only possess one or two of the attributes and are thus termed definitive stakeholders.

Depending on the configuration of attributes possessed by a particular stakeholder, appropriate managerial actions are necessary. The stakeholders requiring attention are only those who are perceived to be highly salient by the managers (Mitchell et al., 1997). Conversely, if stakeholders do not have the capability to exert sufficient influence to hinder organizational functions, there is no necessity to allocate resources to accommodate their requirements (Donaldson & Preston, 1995; Mitchell et al. 1997). Thus, managers should prioritize the most influential stakeholders as they have the capacity to determine a firm's survival capability and to concentrate corporate resources on critical stakeholders (Donaldson & Preston, 1995). Then, they must devise business strategies that align with their interests (Lim et al., 2007; Tan t al., 2007a).

However, stakeholders might assume different stances towards an organizational outcome over time (Mitchell et al., 1997; Scholl, 2005). So, the three dimensions of their salience need to be reassessed over the project life cycle. Consequently, the identification of salient stakeholders has to be a dynamic process (Mitchell et al., 1997; Scholl, 2005; Tan et al. 2007a).

Unfortunately, given the socio-political distinctions between public and private organizations (lower degree of market exposure, centralization of power, wider range of constituents), Lim and al. (2007) contended that the guidelines in stakeholder management are not entirely transferable to the public domain. For this reason, Lim and al. (2007) and Tan and al. (2007a) proposed refinements to the principles of stakeholder management to be relevant in e-government case. They adopted three steps of stakeholder management: (1) identification of key stakeholder groups within an organization; (2) recognition of differing interests among groups of stakeholders; and (3) definition of an IT-enabled governance system that caters to and furthers the interests of the stakeholders. To identify e-government stakeholders, these authors are based on two aspects. On one hand, stakeholder commitment considered as a decisive virtue of e-government initiatives as it defines the psychological attachment or desire among various factions of the stakeholder community to voluntarily contribute to the best of their abilities in shaping public e-services (Lim et al., 2007). On the other hand, acceptance perceived to be tantamount to the alignment of stakeholders anticipations with the inherent attributes of its (system) corresponding functional manifestation. And often, such psychological receptivity towards delivered technological features, serve to perpetuate stakeholders' behaviour in fulfilling pre-assigned roles and duties within the e-government arrangement (Lim et al., 2007). As signalled by these authors, the revised principles are:

1. Stakeholders can no longer be left out of the development of e-government initiatives and public organizations should be proactive in identifying all relevant parties. Depending on the level of commitment versus acceptance for involved parties, governments must pursue more cooperative ventures to engage their stakeholders;
2. In acknowledging stakeholders' expectations, e-government practitioners should not simply give in entirely to stakeholders' demands. Rather, they should distinguish among probable stakeholder categories and assess the technological restrictions underlying the information technology transformed public service so as to map out the boundary for devising and implementing control and collaboration mechanisms in the system. The choice of technological improvements should be weighed against the larger social cost brought on by their implementations.
3. Instead of relying on futile attempts to integrate the expectations of every stakeholder, government agencies should develop cor-

responding strategies to align the interests of different stakeholder categories.

The Stakeholders Categories in E-Government

Stakeholder theory acknowledges that any organization or project is surrounded by a variety of stakeholders that can affect (or be affected by) the organization or project. It's also recognised that only critical stakeholders deserve managers' attention. So, categorization of stakeholders is helpful to understand the interests of key stakeholders and to create consensus among critical project partners and reduce zones of conflicts.

Many classifications of stakeholders are proposed by authors. One classification distinguishes between primary and secondary stakeholders (Scholl, 2005; Gomes, 2006; Tan et al., 2007a). Primary stakeholders are those who have formal and economic relationships with the organization (Gomes, 2006). They are those playing a vital role in the survival of the organization; without the continuing participation of these stakeholders, the organization may suffer serious consequences or even cease to function (Mitchell et al., 1997; Tan et al., 2007a). As the involvement of the primary stakeholders in the outcome is direct, a detailed analysis of their particular needs remains essential. Conversely, secondary stakeholders are those agents not directly related to the organization despite being able to influence and be influenced by its operation and outcomes (Gomes, 2006). They are who affect (or are affected by) the corporation, but they are not engaged in transactions with the corporation and are not essential for its survival (Tan et al., 2007a).

De (2005) grouped stakeholders into demand side and supply side stakeholders. The demand-side stakeholders use the services of the e-government system and, on occasion, provide the revenues that sustain the systems. They influence the eventual success of the system through use or non-use and are directly impacted by the service efficiencies achieved. The supply-side stakeholders funds, designs, implements and maintains the system. They dominate the implementation process and are mostly informed by their own ideological commitments or by the technological imperatives of their commercial partners. They have control over all the resources and deploy them according to their understanding of demand-side needs. De (2005) highlighted that individuals, groups and organizations belong to supply side or demand side stakeholder groups according to their relationship to the system. Also, there could be individuals or groups who belong to both categories. He added that this categorization enables a richer understanding of the e-government implementation process. Conflicts arise in the expectations of demand-side and supply-side stakeholders. These conflicts may be viewed as goals, formally stated or informally understood, that stakeholder groups had of the system during its design or implementation. However, this stakeholder's classification doesn't give an idea about the critical stakeholders. If stakeholders may belong to both categories, it would be difficult to deal with them and to manage their interests and conflicts. Then, it will be appropriate two exclude interferences between stakeholders when defining categories.

Lim et al. (2007) based their categorisation of e-government stakeholders on commitment and acceptance. They considered these constructs as distinct since the commitment of stakeholders towards an e-government initiative does not guarantee an automatic acceptance of its actual manifestation. Commitment denotes stakeholders' willingness to go beyond symbolic participation, and stakeholders who display high levels of commitment manifest more collaboration. Conversely, acceptance concerns stakeholders' affirmative assessment of the functional properties of the system such that they assure a certain degree of control in system utilization. So, Lim et al. (2007) distinguished between four main categories of stakeholders. They associate to each category implications on stakeholder relationship management (Table 1).

THE STAKEHOLDERS OF AN E-GOVERNMENT PROJECT

Mapping E-Government Stakeholders

Multiple stakeholders have to intervene in an e-government project. Involvement, mutual understanding, conflict resolution, and collaboration facilitate meeting of the objectives and expectations of the crucial stakeholders to the success of the initiative (Pardo & Scholl, 2002; Lim et al., 2007). In fact, taking into account stakeholders minimizes conflict, problems, self interest search and negative behaviours and consequently avoids the risk of failure. Therefore, communication with stakeholders to gain their commitment and to inform them about the project's goals, risks, and visions is important.

E-government implies interactions between the government and the citizens (Government to Citizens), the government and the business (Government to Business), and the government agencies (Government to Government). These dimensions of e-government give a first idea, yet simplifying, on some of the stakeholders that may be concerned by an e-government project. Government and citizens are identified as the primarily entities of e-government stakeholders (Scholl, 2001; Flak & Nordheim, 2006; Tan et al., 2007a; Sæbo et al., 2008). But, they lack precision since they are vaguely defined (Sæbo et al., 2008). Sæbo et al. (2008) proposed sub categories of these two entities: (1) Government: Politician, Administrator, Service provider. (2) Citizen: Consumer, Activitist, Direct decision makers.

Heeks (2003) proposed the following stakeholder checklist:

- Project manager/team: those who will analyse, design and build the e-government system;
- Supplier(s): those who will supply the technology and other resources required by the e-government system;
- Operators: those who will be carrying out the activities/processes that make the e-government system work;
- Clients: primary clients are on the immediate receiving end of what the e-government

Table 1. E-government stakeholders' categories and implications on stakeholder relationship management (adapted from Lim and al., 2007).

Types of Stakeholders	Description	Implications for Stakeholder Management in E-Governments
Engineers	Stakeholders who are both receptive towards the technical propositions of the e-government initiative and committed towards its strategization.	Establishment of a levelled platform to facilitate symmetrical communications and dialogic relations
Dissidents	Stakeholders who are committed towards the strategization of the e-government initiative even though they may not be receptive towards its technical propositions.	Cultivation of an open and receptive culture to accommodate and consider dissenting opinions
Seasoners	Stakeholders who are receptive towards the technical propositions of the e-government initiative even though they may not be committed towards its strategization.	Promotion of a transparent and approachable organizational structure to dismiss socially exclusive behavior
Skeptics	Stakeholders who are neither receptive towards the technical propositions of the e-government initiative nor committed towards its strategization.	Induction of strategic value networks to provide mediating relational elements or incentives to induce psychological conversions

system does or outputs; there may also be secondary clients (possibly outside the organisation) who will be affected indirectly by the system since they are served by the primary clients;
- Champion(s): the person (or group) who drives the project on and seeks to justify its implementation;
- Sponsor(s): the person (or group) who pays for the expense and effort required to develop the new e-government system;
- Owner: the manager of the organisation or department that will own and use the system, who is ultimately responsible for the system;
- Other stakeholders: who have a significant influence on the project or on whom the project will have a significant influence.

The classical way of modelling stakeholders is by presenting a focal organization or project at the centre of a nexus of stakeholders (Flak & Nordheim, 2006). This emphasizes the relationships between the focal organization and its' stakeholders. Building on stakeholder theory, we argue that the management of the interests of the prime stakeholders may reduce the risk of failure of an e-government project. We have identified some of these stakeholders and their relationships with e-government projects (Figure 3).

An Analysis of the Stakeholders Impact on an E-Government Project

E-government has to rely on a broad consensus among government officials as well as the citizens. Commitment and ownership at all levels facilitate e-government implementation (Pardo & Scholl, 2002). In this paragraph, an analysis of the impact of each of the stakeholders on an e-government project and eventual measure to be adopted by project managers to deal with them is proposed.

Politicians are publicly elected decision and policy makers (e.g. mayor, councillor, parliament member) (Sæbo et al., 2008). On one hand, as elected officials they may have an interest in the development of e-government projects that they propose as a solution for reform, efficiency and transparency. Heeks (2003) didn't exclude that politicians motivate e-government projects implementation for personal interests.

On the other hand, political leadership and will is indispensable to support e-government projects. According to (OCDE, 2003), political leadership has an important role in shaping and backing e-government initiatives. Political leaders contribute to the establishment of the e-government vision,

Figure 3. A map of the stakeholders intervening in an e-government project

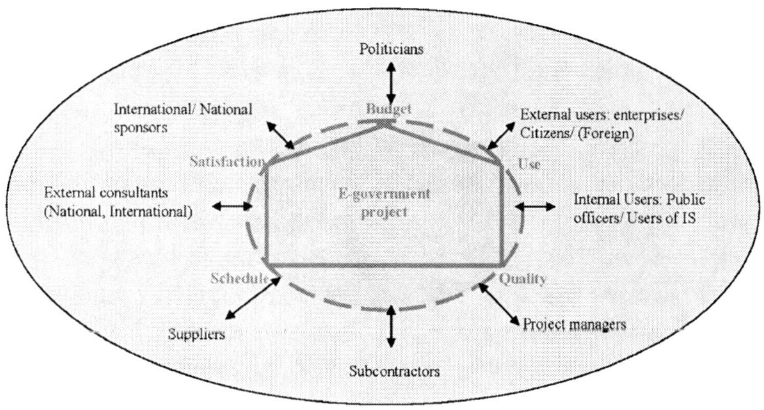

define priorities, filter citizens' needs, make the decisions and provide will to carry them out.

Also, strong political leadership can increase management motivation and sense of responsibility (OCDE, 2003, p.93). In certain cases, political will and leadership is crucial to impose to government agencies to afford the requisite human, technical and financial resources and participate in common projects, to surmount difficulties and resolve adversarial situations. Lim and al. (2007) find that politicians may be included as a key stakeholder group because the project group considered any project with the potential to increase efficiency and possible future staff reduction or re-location as politically controversial.

Administrators are middle and higher level salaried career employees executing politicians' policies (e.g. city manager, health department head) (Sæbo et al., 2008). Senior management involvement is extensively recognized as a critical factor to the success of an e-government initiative (Pardo & Scholl, 2002; Heeks, 2003; OCDE, 2003). Continued, personal and active involvement of senior management is critical in making decisions, providing resources, overcoming resistance to change, soliciting interdepartmental and interagency cooperation, improving cross-organizational collaboration and cooperation.

But, senior management may lack competencies, expertise and information in the domain of ICT. This may have negative consequences on the e-government projects since poor decisions may be taken. To gain senior management involvement, organizations can install a Chief Information Officer (CIO) whose primary role is to build and manage the organization's ICT infrastructure, the skill base, and the relations between ICT related organizational stakeholders (Pardo & Scholl, 2002).

Service providers are lower level salaried career employees carrying out day to day government jobs directly or indirectly interacting with citizens (e.g., case officers in school department, advisors and information providers in taxation office) (Sæbo et al., 2008). They are the users of the delivered systems. Users may resist to change and reject a system for poor system design, the structuring of tasks, personal relationships with designers and developers of new systems (Pardo & Scholl, 2002), lack of involvement, lack of formation and information. The participation of the users to e-government systems is usually representative. According to Lim et al. (2007), the recruitment of internal 'experts' into the system development team acted as a precautionary measure to preserve localized knowledge resources that have been acquired through specialization in existing work processes. A cross-functional project committee of 'power-users' reflects the range of business requirements that corresponds to the spectrum of processing functions in the public agency. This in turn reduced the probability of incompatibilities or even outright rejection by core staff members since their requirements are accounted for in developed systems. However, in certain cases, formation and assistance to users are provided only once the new systems are implemented. Sometimes, they don't have to manifest negative attitudes toward systems that they must to use in respect of instructions and orders.

Corporate and information technology executives and business and information technology managers are those who assume the tasks of project management. Selected stakeholders from corporate and information technology groups must to cooperate together. Lack of commitment on the side of the business management creates misunderstandings and conflicts between business and information technology managers; whereas commitment and ownership at all levels are necessary to implement e-government related business process changes (Pardo & Scholl, 2002). Adversely, to confide an e-government project to information technology managers may privilege technical aspects. That is way a close cooperation between them is indispensable. On their side, information technology managers should detain a mix of technical, human and organisational competences to correctly manoeuvre the project. Lack of competences of these actors may constrain the deployment of the e-government project.

Consumers use the services offered by the government (Sæbo et al., 2008). They are customers of governmental transactions (Lim et al., 2007) (business, civil society). To encourage acceptance of an e-government initiative, a public agency has to look for relevant stakeholders and strive for their consensual support for the system during its development. Also, it must provide e-government services that respond to the real need of the consumers. Unfortunately, De (2005) advanced that supply side stakeholders usually provide e-government systems according to their understanding of the demand-side needs. Consumers are rarely included in the design or implementation of e-government systems. That is way they may lack motivations for supporting e-government systems. On another side, to be able to use e-government services, consumer must detain the requisite skills and access to infrastructure facilities. Information, communication and marketing efforts for the e-government initiatives may be also indispensable to enhance their use by consumers.

Furthermore, to enhance the appeal of the system among consumer, the design and implementation schematics may be defined through regular focus group where interactions help to reinforce bidirectional appreciation of systemic components (Lim et al., 2007). According to these authors, with extensive involvement of stakeholders in defining the techno-structure of the system, the embedded functionalities may be welcomed by its various recipients as a fresh change from its conventional administrative practices.

Direct Decision makers are citizens who are responsible for the decisions being made in a direct democracy system (Sæbo et al., 2008). One objective of e-government is to amplify citizens' voice in the process of governance through easily accessible virtual communication channels (Lim et al., 2007). The integration of IT into public services empowers proactive citizens through the diffusion of information (Tan et al., 2007a). According to Scholl (2001), the citizens assume a crucial role in e-government and e-democracy settings. Consequently, e-government has to rely on a broad consensus among government officials as well as the citizens (Pardo & Scholl, 2002).

De (2005) suggested that there are instances where demand-side stakeholders such as citizens' groups and civil society groups may be included in the implementation processes of e-government. But they are rarely included in the design or implementation of e-government systems that is way it becomes hard to get their motivations for supporting e-government systems.

International sponsors are international organisations that encourage government reforms, contribute to the financing of the projects, but may impose the following of long procedures.

International consultants give support to the internal equip of the government agency by providing assistance and competences. But they can propose 'prêts-à-porter' solutions without considering context particularities.

Subcontractors (National / International) are business partners of governmental agencies (Lim and al., 2007). OCDE (2003) highlighted the importance of public – private partnerships to deploy e-government initiatives. But public-private partnerships may pose conflicts due to opportunism and lack of competences of the business partners. They don't usually deliver the requisite systems within schedule and specified characteristics. Acquiring competences in relationship management of public private partnerships and adopting a risk management of information technology outsourcing procedure may be helpful in this regard.

Providers / suppliers of information technology solutions (National/ International): System vendors refer to organizations that supply the government with information systems and technological solutions.

Identification of stakeholders and management of relationships with them induce projects failure (Shmidt et al., 2001). So underestimate the influential role of stakeholders may lead the project to a problematic situation. But it seems to be more appropriate to identify interrelationships between stakeholders to understand stakeholders' shared/ unshared objectives and common/ uncommon beliefs towards the project. Stakeholders having shared motivations and interests may form coalitions and act jointly in favour or against a project. Lim et al. (2007) and Tan et al. (2007a) supported that government agencies should develop corresponding strategies to align the interests of different stakeholder categories instead of relying on futile attempts to integrate the expectations of every stakeholder. Nevertheless diversity and multiplicity of stakeholders are unexplored areas in project risk management (Schmidt and al., 2001). Moreover, relationships between various stakeholders have received less attention (Flak & Nordheim, 2006).

A correspondence between risk management process and the management of stakeholders may be made. Adopting a dynamic process of stakeholders' management over the project life cycle enables to take account potential changes in their salience.

CONCLUSION

Since stakeholders can no longer be left out in the development of e-government initiatives, public organizations should be proactive in identifying all relevant collaborators, working with them and undertaking measures to systematically engage their stakeholders (Tan and al., 2007a; Sæbo, et al., 2008). Building coalitions with both internal and external stakeholders (Pardo & Scholl, 2002) of an e-government project may help to recognize the critical stakeholders that deserve project managers' attention. Henceforth, e-government has to rely on a broad consensus, commitment and ownership at all levels among government officials as well as the citizens (Pardo & Scholl, 2002).

In fact, according to Murray et al. (2004), to support the implementation of e-government, the process of identifying and managing a broad range of stakeholders must be considered to ensure that the implementation process encompasses all levels of government. To steer the project's stakeholders a strategy has to be developed that considers the relevancy of the stakeholders to the project. The objectives of these stakeholders need to be attended to. This does not mean that all stakeholders' needs should be met; but it must be an agreement between stakeholders regarding the e-government project which align with overall goals and strategies. Also, stakeholder theory does not imply that all stakeholders, however they may be identified, should be equally involved in all processes and decisions (Donaldson & Preston, 1995).

Flak et al. (2008) demonstrated the usefulness of stakeholder theory to surface conflicts between different stakeholder groups. Contradictory stakeholder objectives can represent an important barrier for realizing potential benefits from e-

Table 2. Correspondence between the risk management and the management of stakeholders processes

Risk management steps	Stakeholders management steps
- The identification of the risk factors - The assessment of risk exposure - The treatment of the risk factors	- Inventory of stakeholders surrounding a project. - Assessment of stakeholders' salience (with reference to commitment and acceptance constructs as suggested by Lim and al. (2007)). - Identification of salient stakeholders (at this level the perspective of project managers might be vital since managers decide which stakeholders are salient and require management attention (Mitchell and al., 1997). - Identification of potential coalitions and interrelationships between stakeholders. - Proposition of solution to manage stakeholders' interests and conflicts.

government initiatives. Thus, stakeholder theory provides a powerful method for investigating and analyzing the impact of stakeholder diversity in e-government settings. Moreover, stakeholder management must be considered as an integral part in e-government projects' risk management procedure.

The diversity of stakeholder interests poses considerable challenges to project managers. Stakeholder analysis may be applied to e-government projects to assist managers in identifying potential conflicts between project stakeholders at early project stages. Insights on potential stakeholder conflicts can then be used for devising and implementing communication strategies to prevent contradictory stakeholder interests and to avoid conflicts.

However, a review of the e-government literature reveals that viewpoints emphasizing stakeholder theory usefulness are only based on descriptive case studies. Empirical evidence is needed in order to validate the suggested approach. Government to government and inter agency cooperation projects may be especially well suited, as complexity rises as multiple public sector organizations seeks to align their objectives to reach common goals.

REFERENCES

Bernard, J. G., Rivard, S., & Aubert, B. A. (2004). L'exposition au risque d'implantation d'ERP: éléments de mesure et d'atténuation. *Systèmes d'Information et Management*, *9*(2), 25–50.

Bouaziz, (2006, December 14-16), Managing e-government projects failure and risks, *Internet & Information Systems in the Digital Age: Challenges & Solutions, 7th International Business Information Management (IBIMA) Conference*. Brescia Italy.

De, R. (2005). E-Government Systems in Developing Countries: Stakeholders and Conflict. In Wimmer, M. A. (Eds.), *EGOV 2005, LNCS 3591* (pp. 26–37).

DeLone, W. H., & McLean, E. R. (2003). The DeLone and McLean Model of Information Systems Success: A ten-Year Update. *Journal of Management Information Systems*, *19*(4), 9–30.

Department of Economic and Social Affairs - Division for Public Administration and Development Management United Nations. (2008). *e-Government Survey 2008 From e-Government to Connected Governance*. Retrieved Novermber 4, 2008, from http://unpan1.un.org/intradoc/groups/public/documents/UN/UNPAN028607.pdf

Donaldson, T., & Preston, L. (1995). The stakeholder theory of the corporation - Concepts, evidence, and implications. *Academy of Management Review*, *20*(1), 65–91. doi:10.2307/258887

Ebrahim, Z., & Irani, Z. (2005). e-Government adoption: architecture and barriers. *Business Process Management Journal*, *11*(5), 589–611. doi:10.1108/14637150510619902

Evangelidis, A. (2004). FRAMES-A Risk Assessment Framework for e-Services, *Electronic. Journal of E-Government*, *2*(1), 21–30.

Flak, L. S., & Dertz, W. (2007). Stakeholder Theory and Balanced Scorecard to Improve IS Strategy Development in Public Sector, In *Balanced Scorecard - Multi Sector Perspectives*. Hyderabad, India: Icfai University Press. Retrieved Janurary 22, 2009, from wwwold.hia.no/iris28/Docs/IRIS2028-1109.pdf

Flak, L. S., & Nordheim, S. (2006). Stakeholders, Contradictions and Salience: An Empirical Study of a Norwegian G2G effort. In *Proceedings of the 39th Hawaii International Conference on System Sciences*.

Flak, L. S., Nordheim, S., & Munkvold, B. E. (2008). Analyzing Stakeholder Diversity in G2G Efforts: Combining Descriptive Stakeholder Theory and Dialectic Process Theory. *e-Service Journal, 6*(2), 3-23.

Freeman, R. E., Wicks, A. C., & Parmar, B. (2004, May-June). Stakeholder Theory and The Corporate Objective Revisited. *Organization Science, 15*(3), 364–369. doi:10.1287/orsc.1040.0066

Gomes, R. C. (2006). Stakeholder Management in the Local Government Decision-Making Area: Evidences from a Triangulation Study with the English Local Government. *Brazilian Administration Review, 3*(1), 46–63.

Heeks, R. (2003). eGovernment for Development. eGovernment Success/Failure: Assessing Your Own Project. University of Manchester, UK: IDPM, Retrieved March 10, 2004, from, 2003, http://www.egov4dev.org/

Heeks, R. (2003) eGovernment for Development: eGovernment Success/Failure: Definitions. University of Manchester, UK: IDPM. Retrieved from http://www.egov4dev.org/.

Lim, E., Tan, C. W., & Pan, S. L. (2007). E-Government Implementation: Balancing Collaboration and Control in Stakeholder Management. *International Journal of Electronic Government Research, 3*(2), 1–28.

March, J. G., & Shapira, Z.Managerial perspectives on risk and risk taking. *Management Science, 33*(11), 1404–1418. doi:10.1287/mnsc.33.11.1404

Mitchell, R. K., Agle, B. R., & Wood, D. J. (1997). Toward a theory of stakeholder identification and salience: Defining the principle of who and what really count. *Academy of Management Review, 22*(4), 853–886. doi:10.2307/259247

Moon, M. J. (2002). The evolution of e-Government among municipalities: Rhetoric or reality? *Public Administration Review, 62*(4), 424–443. doi:10.1111/0033-3352.00196

Murray, S., William, G., & Huges, M. (2004). *Implementation strategies for e-government: a stakeholder analysis approach.* Retrieved November 4, 2008, from http://is2.lse.ac.uk/asp/aspecis/20040151.pdf

Nilsson, A. (2008). Management ofTechnochange in an Interorganizational e-Government Project. In *Proceedings of the 41st Hawaii International Conference on System Sciences.*

OCDE. (2003). *The e-Government imperative.* Retrieved from www1.worlbank.org/publicsector/egov/e-GovernmentImperative.pdf

Pardo, T., & Scholl, H. J. (2002). Walking Atop the Cliffs: Avoiding Failure and Reducing Risk in Large Scale E-Government Projects. In *Proceedings of the 35th Hawaii International Conference on System Sciences.*

Sæbø, O., Sein, M. K., & Flak, L. S. (2008). *The need for a Cumulative Tradition in eGovernment Research: Conceptualizing the fundamental entities*, Retrieved from www.electronicgovernment.se/SIGeGOV/7_Sabo.pdf

Schmidt, R., Lyytinen, K., Keil, M., & Cule, P. (2001). Identifying software project risks: An international Delphi study. *Journal of Management Information Systems, 17*(4), 5–36.

Scholl, H. J. (2001). *Applying Stakeholder Theory to E-Government: Benefits and Limits.* Retrieved from http://projects.ischool.washington.edu/jscholl/Papers/Scholl_IFIP_2001.pdf

Scholl, H. J. (2005). Interoperability in e-Government: More than Just Smart Middleware, In *Proceedings of the 38th Hawaii International Conference on System Sciences.*

Smith, H. A., McKeen, J. D., & Staples, D. S. (2001). Risk Management in Information Systems: Problems and Potentials. *Communications of AIS, 7*(13), 1–29.

Tan, C. W., Pan, S. L., & Lim, E. (2007). Managing Stakeholder Interests in E-Government Implementation: Lessons Learned from a Singapore E-Government Project. *International Journal of Electronic Government Research*, *3*(1), 61–84.

Turner, J. R., & Muller, R. (2003). On the nature of the project as a temporary organization. *International Journal of Project Management*, *21*, 1–8. doi:10.1016/S0263-7863(02)00020-0

UN, (2005) *From e-Government to E-inclusion*, UN Global e-Government Readiness Report. Retrieved September 21, 2007, from unpan1.un.org/intradoc/groups/public/documents/un/unpan021888.pdf

UN, (2008). United Nations e-Government Survey 2008: From e-Government to Connected Governance. Retrieved February 2008, from unpan1.un.org/intradoc/groups/public/documents/UN/UNPAN028607.pdf, access: 02-2008

Wateridge, J. (1998). How can IS/IT projects be measured for success? *International Journal of Project Management*, *16*(1), 59–63. doi:10.1016/S0263-7863(97)00022-7

Willcocks, L., & Margetts, H. (1994). Risk assessment and information systems. *European Journal of Information Systems*, *3*(2). doi:10.1057/ejis.1994.13

Chapter 14
An ICT-Based Network of Competence Centres for Developing Intellectual Capital in the Mediterranean Area

Marco De Maggio
University of Salento, Italy

Pasquale Del Vecchio
University of Salento, Italy

Gianluca Elia
University of Salento, Italy

Francesca Grippa
University of Salento, Italy

Giustina Secundo
University of Salento, Italy

ABSTRACT

The rising of the knowledge economy, enhanced by the fast diffusion of ICTs, drives a wider perspective on the divide among Countries, interpreting it more and more as the result of an asymmetry in the access to knowledge and in the readiness to apply it in order to renew the basics of their development dynamics. Looking at the Mediterranean Area, the positive correlation between the Networked Readiness Index and the Global Competitive Index developed at Global Economic Forum – INSEAD, shows that the opposite sides of the Mediterranean Sea are performing a development path at two different paces. In the effort to face the challenge of supporting the creation of Intellectual Capital able to apply, diffuse and benefit from e-business, in 2005 the e-Business Management Section (eBMS) of Scuola Superiore ISUFI – University of Salento launched the "Mediterranean School of e-Business Management". The present work aims to offer a presentation of its genesis, its most distinctive features, operational model and action plan. The preliminary results of its activities show the role and the main challenges of the School in addressing the needs of the Mediterranean Countries towards a logic of partnership for the development of their intellectual assets.

DOI: 10.4018/978-1-61520-789-3.ch014

INTRODUCTION

The beginning of the 21st Century's was marked by a pervasive change in the geo-political scenario, characterized by a new international division of work and distribution of production. The fast diffusion of the Information and Communication Technologies accelerated the rising of a novel technological cycle. At macro-economic level, this brought to a natural mechanism of "*casting out*" of some economic realities from the global competitive landscape. This bi-polarization trend differentiates the economies involved in the global market from those excluded from the new production systems proper of the "knowledge economy", based on the access to information and technology [Castells, M. (2000)].

The interpretation of these phenomena brought to the conceptualization of the "*Digital Divide*", a multidimensional phenomenon reshaping the map of the world [Sachs, J., (2000)], encompassing a *global* dimension, referring to the divergence in Internet Access between industrialized and developing Countries; the *social* dimension, referred to the richness of information in each nation; and a *democratic* dimension, referred to the adoption of digital resources for the participation in public life [Norris, P. (2001)].

The phenomenon, that started to be investigated only under the views of the diffusion of ICT physical infrastructure and of ICT access, becomes more and more the expression of an asymmetry in the access to knowledge and in the capability to use it in order to radically renew models, processes, and development dynamics.

On the one hand the development and diffusion of the ICT at a global scale supported an exponential growth of the capability to compute, manage, share and broadcast information. On the other one it caused the rise of the level of knowledge and competencies required to employ the new technologies and to create new appropriate applicative solutions.

The wished leapfrog in the age of digital networks, knowledge and globalization [Negroponte, N., (1998)] can be achieved only if a competitive ascending spiral is activated starting from growing investments in technological infrastructures, human resources, and innovation, focusing on a productivity increase in traditional sectors and development in sectors with a higher employment of technologies and knowledge. To face the challenge of reducing the "*Digital and Knowledge Divide*" and speed up the leapfrog of the emerging economies, it becomes necessary the investments in all the components of the Intellectual Capital [Bontis, N. (1998)]. This requires:

- a radical change in training and education;
- the development of new learning strategies;
- the introduction of new technologies to support the organizational processes;
- the enhancement of interactions among markets, universities and a wide community of actors that present a concrete context of application;
- the promotion of networks of organization and local communities for the innovation advancement;
- the support of national and international co-operation for Intellectual Capital creation.

In the effort to face these challenges, in 2005, the e-Business Management Section of Scuola Superiore ISUFI – University of Salento, launched the *Mediterranean School of e-Business Management*, a program funded by the Italian Ministry of Education, University and Research.

The initiative was aimed at proposing a systemic approach to the *"Digital and Knowledge Divide"* in the Mediterranean Area, through the creation of a network of Competence Centres for developing Human, Structural and Social Capital, focusing on the exchange and integration of practices in Business and ICT management, to leverage the capability of Mediterranean Countries to leapfrog the global economy.

Next paragraphs describe the competitiveness scenario within the Mediterranean Area, highlighting the correlation between the delay in the ICT penetration and the country's competitiveness; then the relationship between Human and Technological Capitals is investigated, and the emerging needs at organizational level of introducing the suitable competences to grasp the opportunities coming from ICT adoption. Within this framework the *Mediterranean School of e-Business Management* is presented and described.

LITERATURE REVIEW AND EMPIRICAL ANALYSIS

The analysis of nature and context of Digital and Knowledge Divide within the Mediterranean Area countries relies on two main research fields, that provided the background for this study:

a. the research on conditions enabling or hindering the successful adoption of ICT in organizations at both public and private ground, and
b. the collection of real data related to the readiness of these countries to introduce and boost the potential of ICT, the state of adoption of e-business models, and to the state of the conditions enabling these processes at country level within Mediterranean countries.

Previous research has emphasized the influence of contextual and industry impediments in ICT diffusion and e-business adoption processes (Molla, A., Licker, P.S., 2005): beside macro issues, organizational attitude, commitment and readiness to change have been also investigated (Humphreys, 2005, Bernerth, J., 2004). Accordinlgy, more productive and innovative ICT adopters are characterized by the set of organizational "practices" that are in place, mainly related to the strong strategic focus and heavy investments in human capital (Brynjolfsson, 2002). More than an application-building effort, the take-up of e-business seems thus to be a capacity development venture addressed to enhance "soft" or human capital factors as critical triggers of successful technology adoption (Taylor, 2004). A basic assumption is that firms managed by informed and qualified entrepreneurs are more likely to adopt advanced e-business applications (Lal, K., 2005), also through technological collaboration with external organizations.

Intra and inter-organizational collaboration, enhanced by Internet and other digital networks, may be the real driver of long-term success in e-business adoption. In fact, the benefits from investing in channel relationships and coordination may prove to be more sustainable than many investments that firm make in technology or process innovations (Clark, 2001). Managers base their competitive advantage no more on internal and existing resources but rather on the ability to create and combine resources in new ways, leveraging on distributed networks of dynamic capabilities (Daniel, E.M., 2003). Among processes which are critical in e-business adoption, the importance of organizational learning as well as knowledge acquisition, application, and sharing has been also studied (Hsiu-Fen, 2005). A common thread through many knowledge management initiatives is the challenge of developing and supporting new network-based communities, through which companies can improve internal collaboration and work more closely with partners and customers (Mentzas, 2006). Co-creative communities are revolutionizing economy and the diffused way of thinking (Tapscott, D., 2006), and virtual communities proliferate at an unprecedented rate, addressing critical organizational and Information System (IS) issues.

Moving the focus from a micro to a macro-level, the integrated development of human and relational capital from one side, and technology enablers from the other can help overcome the forms of isolation or digital divide, based on different technology and knowledge development, among economic realities which are "in" and those which are "out" (Castells, M., 2000). In this sense, the World Bank mentions the need of a *leapfrog* strategy to sustain a quantum leap in the development of countries and their economic and institutional framework. Governments, universities and researchers are challenged to understand how Internet and digital networks can be used to facilitate knowledge sharing and collaborative work, and which public and private efforts should be enacted to streamline digital and organizational change.

The observation of the geographical context was relevant for this study.

Under the view of the drivers of the new economy, the Mediterranean Area shows at a glance a clear divergence between the northern and the southern sides.

A survey undertaken in Mediterranean countries in the frame of MEDA Program (European Union MEDA Programme, 2002) reports an average of 27% of employees working in SMEs located in Algeria, Cyprus, Jordan, Lebanon, Morocco, Syria, Tunisia and Turkey which use ICT mainly for e-mail messaging and information search. A second relevant data reveals that the 87.5% of firms surveyed are not "networked" with providers and the 93% are not networked with customers. More, the perspective of being part of a network, not necessarily Internet-based, is not even envisaged by the 93.6% of firms. The situation is similar in Europe where the "dimensional" gap in e-business adoption is particularly evident among SMEs and large firms. The European e-Business Market Watch 2006 reports that only the 8% of SMEs surveyed use ICT to connect with suppliers, and 11% to connect with customers. The MEDA report highlights that the 18.9% of companies express a lack of interest towards ICT solutions and the 49.5% do not consider the development of related skills as a necessity.

At a first glance, reasons for the situation here described might stay in organizational constraints related to company size, investments and capabilities required. A closer look would be interesting to understand at what extent the reluctance is linked to a lack of awareness of potential benefits, an amplified perception of costs needed to develop infrastructure and know how, and a competitive rather than cooperative attitude.

The analysis of the trend of the current economic scenario requires the application of indicators able to express the consistency of the "*Digital and Knowledge Divide*", and to correlate it to the perspectives of the medium-long term development dynamics. Among them the "Networked Readiness Index" (NRI) is a complex measure, able to weight the different components of the "*Digital and Knowledge Divide*". It was developed at INSEAD (France) in collaboration with "World Bank" and "World Economic Forum", and allows for a better understanding of a nation's strength and weaknesses with respect to ICT (INSEAD, 2008). It is based upon the following premises:

1. *Readiness*: there are three important stakeholder's categories to consider in the development and use of ICT: individuals, businesses, and governments;
2. *Environment*: there is a general macroeconomic and regulatory environment for ICT in which the stakeholders play out their respective roles;
3. *Usage*: the usage rate and the impact of ICT on the three stakeholder's categories are related to their capability to use and benefit from ICT.

The "Global Competitiveness Index" has been developed at World Economic Forum and is based on 12 pillars grouped in three categories: "basic requirements", containing the pillars of institutions, infrastructure, macro-economic stability, health and primary education; "efficiency enhancers", containing the pillars of higher education and training, goods market efficiency, labour market efficiency, financial market sophistication, technological readiness, market size; "innovation and sophistication factors, containing the pillars of business sophistication, and innovation. This index, that captures the stages of economic development of a Country, results positively correlated with the NRI (Clark, 2001) for the year 2007, showing that if the actors of an economy are not networked ready, it will be hard for the economy to transition to the innovation driven stage of development.

The NRI 2007 – 2008 for the Mediterranean Area gives evidence of the cited divergence. The average value at the world level of 3.93 marks the approximate ridge of the "in" and "out" countries, and draws the separation of European side countries, with an average value of 4.50, and the African side, with an average value of 3.87.

If we consider the preparedness of a country or region towards the Knowledge Economy, the divergence becomes clearer. The Knowledge Economy Index (KEI) is an aggregate index, developed by the World Bank's Knowledge Assessment Methodology (KAM) (Daniel, E.M., 2003), as the simple average of 4 sub-indexes, which represent the pillars of the knowledge economy: Economic Incentive and Institutional Regime (EIR), Education and Training, Innovation and Technological Adoption, Information and Communications Technologies (ICT) Infrastructure. The KEI average value at the world level of 6.33 shows again a different situation in the Mediterranean regions, in North side ones, with an average value of 8.16; and South side ones, with an average value of 4.07, showing the lowest ranks in Economic Incentive and Education components.

Jordan is showing a positive trend toward the inclusion in the new global economy. The NRI index showed an improvement of 10 positions from the 2006-2007 to the 2007-2008 ranking, switching from the 57 to the 47, achieving the value of 4.08, one of the highest in the South Mediterranean coast. As well, the Global Competitiveness Index developed by the World Economic Forum saw the improvement from the position 49 to the 52, during the same period.

To reduce these differences and overcome the state of isolation of "out" countries, it seems important not only to invest in ICT, but also to improve the Human Capital, and to set consistent actions devoted to create the more conducive environment for the exploitation of the Knowledge Economy opportunities.

There are three key considerations which can be extracted form the theory and empirical analysis made [4]: (a) the relevance of human capital competencies and awareness as fundamental triggers in technology implementation; (b) the importance of integrating knowledge and processes in an inter-organizational perspective; (c) and the role of collaboration to leverage the potential of individuals and organizations. Moving from these insights, next two sections describe the organizational model and the technology platform designed and developed for the *Mediterranean School* in the attempt to enact the networking of knowledge, people and processes as facilitators of successful e-business implementation.

THE MEDITERRANEAN SCHOOL OF EBUSINESS MANAGEMENT

The Mediterranean School of e-Business Management is an initiative of e-Business Management Section of the Scuola Superiore ISUFI, launched in 2005 and funded by the Italian Ministry of Education, University and Research.

Geographically positioned at the heart of the Mediterranean Area, the Scuola Superiore ISUFI of University of Salento was born in 1999 and is characterized by a clear vocation for the cooperation across the Southern Mediterranean Countries.

During the launch phase of ISUFI it was decided that at least the 30% of participants in each higher education program, PhD and Master Courses, had to be selected in South Mediterranean, not European Countries. At the end of a

5 years period of experimentation, a dense community of young talents trained at eBMS-ISUFI was already involved in the activity of Institutions, Universities and Companies distributed mainly in the South Mediterranean Area.

The awareness of the value of this growing community and the opportunity to expand the Mediterranean Network of the ISUFI partnerships to other Universities and Institutions, created the perspective of developing a Mediterranean School, with the mission to activate a virtual cycle of education, research and entrepreneurial actions to create a network of excellence centres, and streamline a synergic development of Intellectual Capital through ICT-based business innovation. The initiative leverages on key capabilities such as a constant focus on leadership processes, the relevance of international partnerships, the centrality of innovative learning and knowledge management approaches to support change, and the integration of business and technology aspects.

The institutional start of the Mediterranean School of e-Business Management was framed in the Italian-Moroccan Intergovernmental Agreement, signed during the Second Catania Pattern to the Creation of Euro-Mediterranean Space of Higher Education and Research in 2005.

The Agreement led to the first step in the process of creation of the Mediterranean School through the first partnership between eBMS-ISUFI and Al Akhawayn University of Ifrane (Morocco).

Afterwards, other agreements for collaboration and partnership were signed between eBMS-ISUFI and the University of Jordan, the Technopole Elgazala (Tunisia) and the "Confédération Générale des Entreprises du Maroc" (CGEM), to widen the network of Competence Centres that build the structure of the Mediterranean School.

The role of the central node of the network created across the Mediterranean coasts is the Italian node of the Network, the Euro-Mediterranean Incubator, created in Lecce within the eBMS ISUFI, and acting as the propeller hub and the headquarter of the whole Mediterranean School.

Consistently with its mission, and the social and economic contexts of each one of the partner Countries, the Mediterranean School of e-Business Management aims to achieve the following objectives:

- demonstrate the benefits of Digital Innovation and Organizational Change through pilot projects in agri-food, tourism, cultural heritage, aeronautics, automotive, electronics and public administration;
- create, reinforce and consolidate competencies and professional qualification in e-Business Management to diffuse a productive and innovative use of ICT;
- ensure the diffusion of new managerial theories and practices based on the integration of Business Management and ICT Management;
- support the launch of pilot projects for changing relevant industries of Mediterranean economies;
- contribute to mobility of students in the Euro-Mediterranean space;
- support SMEs creation, collaboration, and networking among Italian, Jordanian, Tunisian and Moroccan businesses.

The Distinctive Features and the Operational Model

The distinctive features of the Mediterranean School of e-Business Management derive from its main objectives that are:

- fostering the transition of the Mediterranean Area toward the Digital and Knowledge Economy;
- integrating the available knowledge at the global scale in an interdisciplinary way, to support the development of competencies in Business and Technology Management;

- investing in human capital to enhance the capability of young talented people to absorb and apply knowledge;
- activating horizontal links among whichever level of actors and Countries to prevent the bi-polarization of development between the opposite sides of the Mediterranean area.

The presented goals shape the distinctive features of the Mediterranean School as follows:

1. Network. The logic of "integration" and "partnership" has been the most characterizing element of the Mediterranean School of e-Business Management since its beginning. It points the creation of a wide Mediterranean "network" supported by the raising of centres of excellence, aimed at building consistently with the local national policies, the intellectual capital necessary to accelerate the leapfrog to the development of the overall region, preventing the casting out of the countries on the score of the global competitive dynamics. At the moment, the network is constituted by 4 main nodes: the Euro-Mediterranean Incubator created by eBMS-ISUFI in Lecce (Italy) and the three Competence Centres developed in Morocco, Jordan and Tunisia in collaboration with its Mediterranean partners (the Al Akhawayn University in Morocco, The University of Jordan, the Technopole Elgazala in Tunisia, the "Confédération Générale des Entreprises du Maroc").

To reduce the differences among Mediterranean Countries in the preparedness towards the Knowledge Economy, and overcome the state of isolation of "out" countries, it appears necessary not only the investment in ICT, but also the creation of a conducive environment for exploiting the emerging development opportunities. The ICT enabled network is able to support the common learning, knowledge sharing and entrepreneurial behaviours to enhance benefits coming from ICT.

Network is seen as the suitable dimension for developing and disseminating strategic know-how, and to enhance relationships among different actors, Companies, Universities, Institutions, in sectors such as agri-food, tourism, cultural heritage, aeronautics, automotive, electronics and public administration.

2. Interdisciplinarity/Knowledge Integration. The Mediterranean School of e-Business Management program is based on an integrated system of Research, Higher Education, ICT diffusion accompaniment actions, to blend business models and traditional processes of production with the ICT technological innovations, to contribute to the creation of a new generation of "leaders" able to drive the change and modernization of Mediterranean Countries.

The Interdisciplinary approach, already experimented at eBMS-ISUFI, is a core characteristic of the Mediterranean School. It allows to break down the separation among the traditional branches of Business and Technology Management, to build "just in time" the competency toolkit to manage the emerging challenges of the current scenario. It is conceived to enable the processes of cross-fertilization among crucial sectors of the traditional economy and the dynamics of the new one, to provide suitable applicative solutions to face the needs of the Mediterranean regions.

3. Young Talents: the levers of growth. The strategic asset of the Mediterranean School of e-Business Management is represented by its human capital. The perspective of creating a multi-cultural leading class able to manage ICT driven change, disseminate innovative practices, and develop the competencies necessary to sustain the modernization of Mediterranean Economies, focuses on the young talented people as the main actors and beneficiaries of the human capital creation initiatives of the School. They are selected in the Mediterranean Countries, from the Academy as well as from the Corporate context. Once trained in the Mediterranean School they act as innovators and disseminators of knowledge and experiences in different regional contexts.

4. A New sense of Partnership: the Multilateral cooperation. The promotion and the extension of the network to the overall Mediterranean area is oriented to a growing democratization of the cooperation, to activate horizontal links among whichever level of actors and Countries. The vision of a further step beyond the bilateral cooperation will drive the fulfilment of a dense multilateral network, able to prevent the bi-polarization in the development of the opposite sides of the sea, that risks to be strengthened by the creation of different trade areas, like the Great Arab Free Trade Area (GAFTA) started with the Agadir process, and the Euro-Mediterranean free trade area, planned for the 2010 by the Barcelona Agreement.

The promotion of the economic development of each region is intended as a path of co-creation of the conducive conditions, with a deep and operative involvement of local actors, representatives of Institutional, Entrepreneurial, Business and Academic Entities. The sensitiveness to the needs of the local players and the sharing of the country related issues allow a new way of cooperating that goes beyond the knowledge and technology transfer from the North to the South, to emphasize the mutual commitment to build together solutions and new opportunities for the development of the whole Mediterranean Area.

Operational strategy and activities of the Mediterranean School of eBusiness Management follows the model of the Euro-Mediterranean Incubator in Lecce, by which all the Competence Centres created in the Mediterranean Area inherited their logical structure and functionalities. It is represented in Figure 1.

It is organized in four main core programs (Higher Education initiatives, Research initiatives, Executive Education initiatives, Continuous Learning initiatives). The programs are designed in partnerships with market and institutional stakeholders, and they are focused on traditional industries (tourism, agrifood), hi-tech sectors (aerospace, software), education and public administration. These programs aim to develop individual and organizational change management capabilities; they share a common learning strategy based on a competency development approach through which participants think, work and reflect together through action learning projects, case studies discussion, complex problem analysis. A virtual global learning environment supports the four core programs, through the offering of on line multimedia materials and interactive learning services.

According to the vision that "In the advancing Digital Economy, Intellectual Capital will be increasingly the most important driver of competitive advantage, development and innova-

Figure 1.

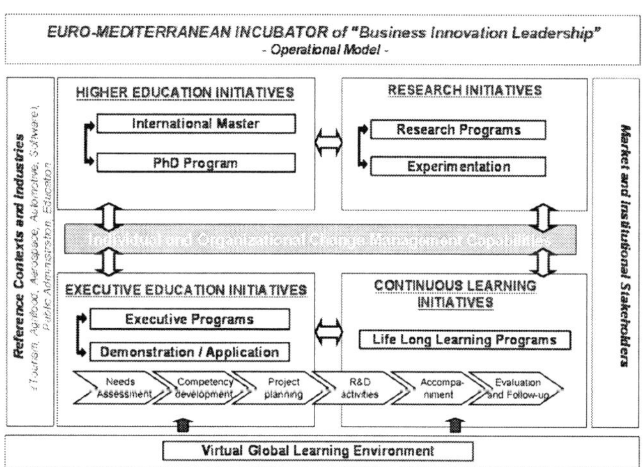

tion of countries and organizations", the Euro-Mediterranean Incubator aims at accelerating the leapfrog of Southern Mediterranean regions towards the digital economy in two ways:

- enhancing the knowledge in business innovation through market-oriented, basic and applied research projects and learning programs; and
- creating Business Engineers and Change Managers able to integrate organizational and digital innovation to implement new business models and accelerate business transformations.

Research activities, innovation projects and advanced education programs are designed in partnerships with market and institutional stakeholders. The results are applied to traditional industries (tourism, agrifood), hi-tech sectors (aerospace, software) and public administration. The Incubator's core programs are constituted by 4 complementary actions:

Action 1: International Master and PhD Programs in e-Business Management

This action aims to the creation of experts and researchers in e-Business field, ensuring a higher mobility between the Countries and firms partners of the initiatives. The action is characterized by the integration between content and competencies about Business and ICT Management; a "learning in action" approach oriented to the application of integrated solutions for managerial practices; strong linkage between research and entrepreneurship, at local and international dimension. The action is addressed to young talents with technical and managerial background.

Action 2: e-Business Readiness Program for SMEs

This action aims at providing integrated projects for training, capacity building and the diffusion of a major feeling of awareness within SMEs about the digital innovation issues. The program foresees two different actions according to the professionalization of "tutors" and "managers" targets: they have to develop at different level the capability to activate and manage the promotion of e-Business practices in SMEs, and to train other tutors and managers, enabling a virtuous cycle of dissemination of the digital innovation.

Action 3: Digital Innovation in Industries and in Public Administration

The action aims to create and promote the development of a hub of scientific, technological and entrepreneurial competences within SMEs and the public administrations.

The implementation of pilot projects is aimed at demonstrating the benefits of digitalization in the following sectors:

- *agri-food* sector, developing systems for the supply chain integration, the creation of e-marketplace for the aggregation of offer and demand, and traceability of the food value chain;
- *tourism*, developing systems for destination and incoming management;
- *aeronautic and automotive,* to set up new methodologies and techniques enabling collaborative working environment for new product development (NPD);
- *public* sectors, for the implementation of intelligent systems of territorial management and the creation of knowledge hub to allow the development of effective decision making processes.

Action 4: Lifelong Learning Program

This action is transversal to the previous ones, and consists of making available a set of web-learning modules and resources. An interactive and multimedia system enables the development of a cyber space where effective innovative learning approaches are implemented like case based and problem based learning. The Virtual Global Learning Environment is conceived as a network of experiential laboratories operating through platforms and new generations ICTs infrastructures for the creation of the sets of competences and capabilities necessary to activate and manage the process of transition and change required by the new technologies.

The set of methodological tools and technological platforms made available by the Incubator, supports the network of the Mediterranean School in the implementation of its strategic programs.

They constitue the ICT Platform of the Mediterranean School, that is described in the following paragraph.

The ICT Platform

The integration of information and knowledge management with the overall strategy, as well as the centrality of business and industry-related issues, represent two aspects which have been strongly addressed in the design of the technology infrastructure of the *Mediterranean School*.

Contemporary business systems are indeed characterized by a growing interdependence between organizational strategy, procedures and Information Systems (ISs) (Sachs, J., 2000), and management ISs address the application of people, technologies, and procedures to solve business problems.

The technological platform of the *Mediterranean School* is composed by two integrated subsystems:

- a *general purpose subsystem*, including knowledge management, web learning, project management, multimedia, social network analysis, business process engineering, and e-business components and applications;
- an *industry-specific subsystem*, including components and applications for tourism, agrifood and aerospace sectors;

A shared *technical facility* represents the backbone of the two subsystems and it is constituted by an integrated environment of hardware, software, network and security components. The hardware infrastructure is based on blade server technologies and a shared storage area network (SAN). The wide usage of open source operating systems (mainly Linux), the integration of wired and wireless networks through Virtual Local Area Network (LAN) management policies, and a two-level security infrastructure for accessing to resources represent the most important features of the system. Next chart (Figure 2) represents the whole ICT architecture and its main components:

In the next sections, a detailed description is provided of the general purpose and industry-specific subsystems, and their related components and applications.

Figure 2.

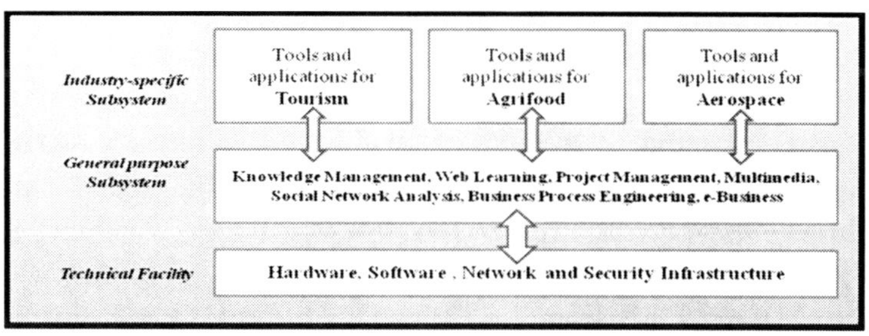

A. General Purpose Subsystem. The general **purpose subsystem includes 7 categories of** components: knowledge management, web learning, project management, multimedia, social network analysis, business process engineering, and e-business. The system is supported by an innovative platform which was awarded in 2006 in Denver (Colorado, USA) with the International *"Brandon Hall Research"* prize in the category "*Learning Technology*". All the components and applications are described hereafter.

1. **Knowledge Management** components aim at creating collaborative and distributed processes of knowledge creation, sharing, search and application. The following services are provided:
   - *Community*, to facilitate the development of learning communities/ communities of practice aimed to exchange experience, project knowledge, and ideas. Individual and group chat, thematic forums, areas for sharing knowledge and exchanging documents, spaces for collaborative work and virtual meeting represent the main applications.
   - *Content Management*, to manage information, news, bookmarks and posts on electronic blackboards.
   - *Document Management*, to manage the whole lifecycle of project documents (or other), including the aspects of workflow to support process automation.
   - *e-Library*, to manage physical and digital library resources such as e-books, CDs, DVDs, other videos sources.
   - *Recommendation Engine*, to suggest news, documents and references to domain experts useful to deepen a topic, to solve a problem, or to execute a specific task.
   - *Search and Retrieval*, to retrieve resources stored in the knowledge base of the system. Different types of search are available which leverage on both the syntactic and semantic features of a text: search based on tags added in the cataloguing phase (*metadata search*), search of keywords contained in the text (*text-based search*), search based on the navigation of domain taxonomies (*taxonomy-oriented search*), and search based on graphical navigation of conceptual maps (*knowledge map*).
   - *Web Mining*, to retrieve useful resources (news, papers, etc.) from many different possible web sources. This "new" knowledge is periodically tagged and catalogued, in order to be available for a successive search.
2. The **Web Learning** component aims to support unstructured and just-in-time learning processes designed to develop specific business and technology management competencies. An innovative learning strategy is implemented which is problem-driven, project-based and strongly integrated with knowledge management. The following services are provided:
   - *Recommendation Engine*, to suggest learning patterns and resources in line with a given competency profile/level to achieve, as well as with the personal interest and preferences.
   - *Skill Gap Analysis and Competence Profile Management*, to identify possible competency gaps and manage the different profiles existing within a project team or learning community.
   - *Structured Learning Program Management*, for realizing structured on-line learning paths and curricula.
   - *Tracking and Reporting*, to monitoring the "performance" of a given

learner and/or a specific learning path.

- *Unstructured Learning Program Management*, to allow the creation of non-predefined learning paths and curricula, in the perspective of *just-in-time* learning.

These services operate on different categories of content. The *Competence Taxonomy* is a key component structured in three levels: *"Knowledge Domains", "Competencies"* and *"Learning Objectives"*. A second class of content is represented by *Competence Profiles* managed by the system through a punctual monitoring of levels achieved and gaps to fill. Third, the system also contains *SCORM objects*, i.e. the traditional learning modules realized according to SCORM standards, and the *Multimedia Knowledge Objects* (MKO), which aggregate different file types (ex. pdf, word, power point, excel) coming from the Knowledge Management subsystem. Finally, learning paths created according to a *problem based* strategy are implemented in the *Multimedia Learning Modules* (MLM). Figure 3 synthesizes the main architecture of the web learning system in terms of services/processes, content and components:

3. **Project Management** components provide a set of functionalities useful for a flexible and integrated management of projects. Among the distinguishing features, two aspects are particularly innovative: first, a native integration with document management services (to optimize retrieval and reuse of project documents and deliverables while enriching the knowledge base); second, the integration with Web Learning applications (to optimize resources/competencies allocation on project tasks, and to develop competency development plans founded on a *project-based* learning strategy). The following services are provided:
   - *Phases/Activities Management*, to structure a project in terms of phases and activities. Each activity is then associated to a responsible for the preparation and submission of final deliverables.

Figure 3.

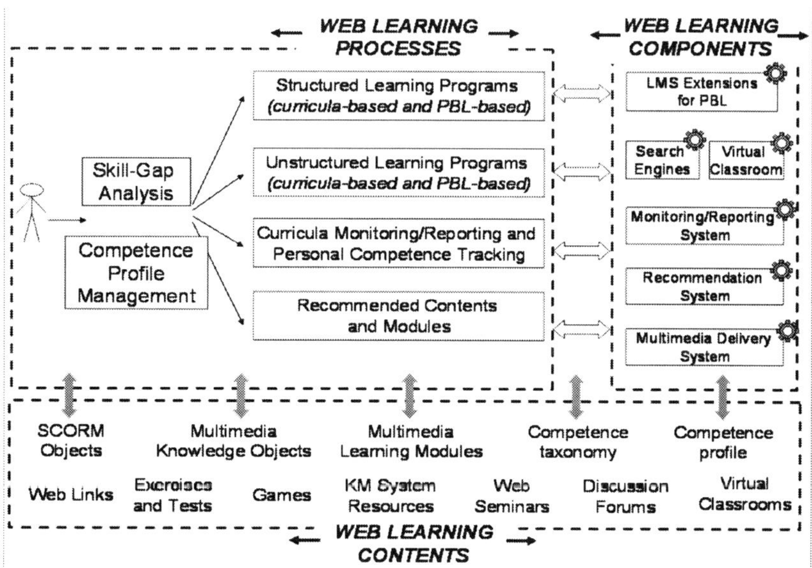

- *Recommendation Engine*, to suggest *just-in-time* those learning paths which can help an actor to execute a specific project task, in the case he/she does not possess the competency profile/level required.
- *Reporting*, to provide project managers with integrated snapshots, both synthetic and analytic, about the advancement state of a project (use of traffic light icons), possible delays, milestones and deliverables, and the responsibilities of people in single phases and activities.
- *Workflow Definition*, to manage and automatically orchestrate the workflow of project documents, including their review and final approval.

4. Web Learning, Knowledge Management and Project Management components are supported by a **Multimedia Lab** for the acquisition, processing, storage and delivery of multimedia content. The main characteristics and components of the Multimedia Lab are:
   - high resolution fixed and mobile acquisition systems;
   - automatic acquisition system based on sensors;
   - a 4-terabyte storage system, a post-production system;
   - a streaming system to broadcast content;
   - a documents scanning system;
   - tools for the semi-automatic translation of content in other languages (included Arabic).
5. **Social Network Analysis** components are aimed to provide a diagnostic methodology and a set of tools to track the evolution of interdependent organizations and communities, in terms of knowledge creation and exchange processes, learning performance, social capital development and competency growth. The following services are provided:
   - dashboard and analysis of individual metrics such as actor's "centrality degree", "betweeness" centrality and "contribution index";
   - dashboard and analysis of group metrics such as group's "centrality degree", "betweeness centrality", "network density" and "core/periphery" structure;
   - software tools for the analysis and representation of social networks dynamics.
6. **Business Process Engineering** components are aimed to support the design of alternative process configurations leveraging on shared process knowledge, also based on best practices of different industries and organizations. The following services are provided:
   - web-based process repository, developed in collaboration with the MIT Center for Digital Business, of more than 5000 process descriptions related to different industries and a set of tools for viewing/editing process descriptions;
   - process modeling and re-engineering methods and tools;
   - process benchmarking methods and tools;
   - metrics-based process analysis and redesign;
   - query language capability for keyword-based and attribute-based search.
7. **e-Business** components are aimed to provide an experimental setting for the simulated use of e-business applications, through illustrative industry-based examples and customized tools. The following services are provided as modules of a whole e-business suite available:
   - ERP – Enterprise Resource Planning;

- CRM – Customer Relationship Management;
- SRM – Supplier Relationship Management
- SCM - Supply Chain Management;
- BI - Business Intelligence.
- Marketplace services such as Web-store and B2B exchange facilities

B. Industry-Specific Subsystems. They aim to contextualize the design and experimentation of market-oriented pilot projects, ICT development and application in three specific sectors: tourism, agrifood and aerospace.

1. The **tourism platform's** services are organized in three main categories, for three different types of users: tourists, firms and institutions.

Services to *tourists* include "search" services (ex. of information about destinations, attractions and services by geographical area, theme/interest or category, with the possibility to store, organize, access, modify and reuse the information collected); "interactive" services (ex. asynchronous and synchronous communication with local tourism enterprises and institutions, tourists and residents); and "transactional" services (ex. booking directly on the Internet).

Services to *firms* (mainly primary suppliers but also intermediaries and carriers) include "publication" services (ex. offerings on the Internet), "e-marketing" services (management of products/services promotion and pricing, relationships with suppliers and customers, according to the level of *e-readiness* and the managerial capabilities of the enterprise), "e-booking" and "e-payment" services on the Internet, "collaboration" services (ex. exchange of documents, invoices and information as well as project management functionalities), and "management" services (ex. accounting, employees payroll, business intelligence).

Services to *institutions* (mainly local and regional tourism authorities, but also national or higher level organizations) are mainly related to tourism planning and development and the integration of information, with a particular focus on managing and monitoring the offer of tourism destinations. Examples are represented by tourism marketing planning, dashboards, management of tourists' and suppliers' accounts, management of ICT platforms and destinations' web sites, as well as the communication of data to external institutions.

2. The ICT platform for **agrifood** has been designed with the objective to create a digital marketplace and information systems based on the idea of the "virtual enterprise", and the improvement of vertical and horizontal relationships within the agrifood supply chain.

The *agrifood platform's* services are organized in three main categories:

- B2B – Business-to-Business: Tendering, e-Catalogue, Auctions, Traceability and Logistics, Contract Management, Offering aggregation, Financial Service, Insurance Service, Order Management, Ratings
- EAI – Enterprise Application Integration with internal: Enterprise Resource Planning (ERP); Customer Relationship Management (CRM); Supplier Relationship Management (SRM); Supply Chain Management (SCM); Business Intelligence (BI).
- Support Services for Interactions with B2B operators: Information Services, e-Consulting, Collaborative Service, Market Intelligence, e-Learning, Knowledge Management.

3. The ICT platform for **aerospace** has been designed with the objective to provide an integrated environment to optimize important new product development processes such as Multidisciplinary Integrated Modelling (MIM), Multidisciplinary Design and Optimization (MDO), Product Lifecycle Data Management (PDM), and technology assessment. The main applications developed and available are:

- applications for *collaborative working*, including knowledge management systems, collaborative working environment, and enterprise portals;
- applications for *Product Life Cycle Data Management*, including technologies and systems for multidisciplinary analysis, requirements management (QFD Method), configuration management, business process modelling and IT management;
- applications for *Product Design*, including CAD/CAE (Computer Aided Design/Engineering), design for Six Sigma, Knowledge Based Engineering (CAx customization, automation and Integration), multidisciplinary design optimization and robust design, virtual prototyping (digital mock-up and digital pre-assembly).

In the following section, the model "in action" is showed, with the main output in terms of human, structural and social capital development, and some implications for public and private managers concerned with ICT development and e-business adoption in southern Mediterranean countries.

THE FIRST YEARS OF THE MEDITERRANEAN SCHOOL: PRELIMINARY RESULTS

Since the beginning, the Mediterranean School of e-Business Management had the opportunity to launch and experiment several actions and pilot projects in collaboration with Mediterranean public and private stakeholders. These initiatives have been realized both in the main node of the Mediterranean School (located in Lecce, Italy, at the e-Business Management Section of Scuola Superiore ISUFI), and in the local nodes in Jordan, Morocco and Tunisia.

Specifically, all these initiatives contributed to develop and consolidate the Intellectual Capital of the Mediterranean School, that is described and classified in terms of Human capital, Structural capital and Social capital as follows.

A. As for the *Human Capital* dimension, the education programs of the Mediterranean School helped many talented people to develop competencies and skills for effective design and development of business innovations based on web technologies. In more detail
   - a young Scientific Community of people has been created, engaged in interdisciplinary research and education activities, for a total of 66 units (27% coming from the Southern Mediterranean Countries) with an average age of 30 years (89% Graduates and 11 Undergraduates).
   - 38 young talents have been involved in PhD program, 16 of them (42%) coming from southern Mediterranean countries.
   - 160 young talents have been involved in 9 editions of the International Master's Program, 67 of them (42%) coming from southern Mediterranean countries and of 10 young Moroccan managers involved in e-Business awareness programs.

B. Referring to the *Structural Capital* component, the main results realized and obtained in the framework of the Mediterranean School are constituted by the three nodes created in Jordan, Morocco and Tunisia. Each node is configured as a *Competence Centre* who conveys and attracts local interests of public institutions, private companies, universities and research centres, and promotes with them some innovation projects focused on experimenting the benefits coming from the adoption of ICT in traditional industries and processes. In each Competence Centre, a set of facilities, technological equipments, access to technological infrastructures, methodologies and platforms available in the main node in Italy, guarantee and ensure an effective implementation of the innovation pilot projects.

At international level three cross-disciplinary edge research fields have been developed and consolidated:

(i) Open Networked Business Management; (ii) Learning, Innovation and Value Network; (iii) Collaborative Product Design Management. A portfolio of 24 research projects related to the introduced fields have been acquired competitively at the Italian and European Community levels, with the participation of leading academic institutions as well as national and multinational companies.

The scientific production amounted to 126 scientific works, 38 of them published in international journals and monographs, 11 in national journals and monographs, and 77 published in referee-based proceedings of international conferences.

In October 2006 the School received an international award in Denver, Colorado (USA), by the "Brandon Hall Research" in the category "Learning Technology", related to the creation of an innovative web learning platform which embeds a problem-based learning approach.

C. Under the *Social Capital* perspective, the Mediterranean School of e-Business Management built a network of international relationships among the Italian, Moroccan, Jordanian, and Tunisian nodes, and supported the relationships between each node and the referring local national context of entrepreneurial and academic communities. Today it is consolidated a huge network of collaboration of national and international partners, and stakeholders representing relevant industries, with a major focus on aerospace, agro-industry, education, public government, software, and tourism. The faculty benefits from the contribution of more than 50 professors and executives representing 10 nationalities.

CONCLUSION AND FUTURE DEVELOPMENTS

The competitiveness of the new economies is the result of the integration at national and international level of both human and structural capital. The existence of a Digital and Knowledge Divide between the opposite sides of the Mediterranean Sea claims a combined effort both at national and international level. At national side, the local actors are called to support the development of capabilities to link technologies and business management in order to face the merging organizational needs. The international actors are called to orient public resources towards investments required to allow the leapfrog of the Southern Countries in the development process of the knowledge economy. The networking dimension is, at both levels, the most suitable one to activate virtuous cycles of mutual empowerment, internally and externally, involving academies, universities, companies and institutions without boundaries distinctions. Under this perspective, the Competence Centres of the Mediterranean School of e-Business Management were generated following a model based on the capability of:

- creating environments for a more effective learning process;
- enhancing the level of commitment for realizing training programs focused on concrete issues related to the e-Business;
- promoting relationships with the national economic actors, and strategic alliances to increase on the field the value of the research conducted.

The relevant results achieved by the Mediterranean School in consolidating and developing the Intellectual Capital of the Mediterranean network, according to the Human, Social and Structural dimensions, confirm the rightness of its vision as well as the effectiveness of the strategy persecuted. They also establish the ground for future steps that will see the School engaged in the improvement of the partnership just established, and a closer collaboration between public and private nodes. The widening of the network to the overall Mediterranean area is oriented to a growing democratization of the cooperation, to activate horizontal links among whichever level of actors and Countries. The vision of a further step beyond the bilateral cooperation will drive the fulfilment of a dense multilateral network, able to prevent the bi-polarization in the development of the opposite sides of the sea.

REFERENCES

Bernerth, J. (2004). Expanding our understanding of the change message. *Human Resource Development Review*, *3*(1), 36–52. doi:10.1177/1534484303261230

Bontis, N. (1998). Intellectual Capital: An exploratory Study that Develops Measures and Models. *Management Decision*, *36*(2), 63–76. doi:10.1108/00251749810204142

Brynjolfsson, E., & Hitt, L. (2002). *Digital organization: preliminary results from an MIT study of Internet organization, culture and productivity*, MIT Working Paper.

Cardoso, J., Bostrom, R. P., & Sheth, A. (2004). Workflow management systems and ERP systems: differences, commonalities, and applications. *Information Technology Management*, *5*, 319–338. doi:10.1023/B:ITEM.0000031584.14039.99

Castells, M. (2000). *The Rise of the Network Society*. London: Blackwell Publishing Ltd.

Clark, T. H., Croson, D. C., & Schiano, W. T. (2001). A hierarchical model of supply-chain integration: information sharing and operational interdependence in the US grocery channel. *Information Technology Management*, *2*, 261–288. doi:10.1023/A:1011497025090

Daniel, E. M. (2003). The role of dynamic capabilities in e-business transformation. *European Journal of Information Systems*, *12*(4), 282–296. doi:10.1057/palgrave.ejis.3000478

European e-Business Market Watch, (2005). *Overview of International e-Business Developments*.

European Union MEDA Programme, (2002). *ICT Solutions for Mediterranean SMEs*.

Hsiu-Fen, L., & Gwo-Guang, L. (2005). Impact of organizational learning and knowledge management factors on e-business adoption. *Management Decision*, *43*(2), 171–188. doi:10.1108/00251740510581902

Humphreys, P., Mcadam, R., & Leckey, J. (2005). Longitudinal evaluation of innovation implementation in SMEs. *European Journal of Innovation Management*, *8*(3), 283–304. doi:10.1108/14601060510610162

INSEAD. (2008). *Global Technology Information Report 2007 – 2008*. Retrieved from http://www.insead.edu/v1/gitr/wef/main/explore/framework.cfm

Lal, K. (2005). Determinants of the adoption of e-business technologies. *Telematics and Informatics*, *22*(3), 181–199. doi:10.1016/j.tele.2004.07.001

Mentzas, G., Apostolou, D., Kafentzis, K., & Georgolios, P. (2006). Inter-organizational networks for knowledge sharing and trading. *Information Technology Management*, *7*, 259–276. doi:10.1007/s10799-006-0276-8

Molla, A., & Licker, P. S. (2005). e-Commerce adoption in developing countries: a model and instrument. *Information & Management*, *42*(6), 877–899. doi:10.1016/j.im.2004.09.002

Negroponte, N. (1998, January). The Third Shall be First: The Net Leverages Latecomers in the Developing World, *Wired Magazine*.

Norris, P. (2001). *Digital Divide: Civic Engagement, Information Poverty, and the Internet worldwide*. Cambridge, UK: Cambridge University Press.

Sachs, J. (2000, June). A New Map of the World, *The Economist*.

Tapscott, D., & Williams, A. D. (2006). *Wikinomics: How Mass Collaboration Changes Everything*. New York: Portfolio.

Taylor, M., & Murphy, A. (2004). SMEs and e-business. *Journal of Small Business and Enterprise Development*, *11*(3), 280–289. doi:10.1108/14626000410551546

www.worldbank.org/kam

Chapter 15
Last Online Deposits Spatial Data in the Web

Mohamed-Khireddine Kholladi
University Mentouri of Constantine, Algeria

ABSTRACT

The posting of interactive mapping is essential for the dissemination of information to the general public and in all areas. All the elements constituting a spatial object are represented by agreements with symbols. Each element is represented at the level of reality. The posting of maps on the Internet can take many forms. It can be static maps, as a picture. Interactions with the user can be included on the maps produced. These are movements and functions of the zoom presentation (display information, change of scale, global view). At this level, it is also possible to examine, by selection of the objects represented on the map (common facilities). This level is commonly known as Web mapping. The dynamic mapping is used when information is to be renewed or if the geographical extent of the area is large. In this case, a server handles in real-time updated database to provide users answers to their complaints. The functions proposed in this case are close to those of GIS software (acquisition, manipulation, management and processing of geographical data). In this chapter we will explore the possibility of integrating a dynamic mapping on the Web.

INTRODUCTION

For over thirty years, the cards are offered as a faithful reproduction of a geographical space object. All its components are represented by agreements with symbols. Each is represented on the scale of reality. The maps posting on the Internet can take many forms. It can be fixed cards, as a picture. As a result, the site or any part thereof is not connected to a database. The pages are already built and are displayed (e.g. PDF) on the user as they were originally created. Interactions with potential users can be included on the maps produced. These are movements, and zoom functions as the display presentation of information, the change of scale, the global view, and so on.

DOI: 10.4018/978-1-61520-789-3.ch015

It is also possible to examine, by selection of geographical space on the card, such as municipalities, schools, etc. This level is commonly known as Web-mapping. The dynamic mapping is applied when the information is to be constantly updated or if the coverage of the area is great. In this case, allows a server to query real-time database updates to give users answers to their complaints (De Blomac F, 2009), (Dupasque X, 2005), (Dupont G, 2004) and (Mauvière E, 1999). The functions proposed in this case approximate those of a geographical information system (GIS) for the acquisition, handling, management and processing of geographic data. The publication of the geographical information as numeric cards takes more and more interest because of the progress reached in the domain of the new technologies of information and the communication and the arrival to maturity of the software of spatial representation of the data or geographical information system (GIS) [De Blomac F, 2001].

In this chapter, we will focus on the possibility of integrating a dynamic mapping on the Web. Our aim is to provide an overview of the potential of the Internet for GIS and to give what he wishes to put their GIS dynamic web to choose between different opportunities (AFIGEO, 1998).

STATE OF CARTOGRAPHY ART

The mapping allows the use of techniques for achieving the cards. It is used to better understand and define the space, territories and landscapes. It is also used in related sciences, demography and economy in order to propose a reading of the geo-phenomena. How can we be a part of the irregular shape of the spherical earth on a globe? To be able to give a reliable description of a territory and to locate objects in space, it is essential to know the exact shape of the earth. That is the purpose of surveying and mapping work. The ellipsoid is the reference surface to represent the best shape of the earth. It is useful to perform the necessary calculations, if you want to perform the topographic location of objects by using measures. The physical figure which best represents the shape of the earth called geoids. This is the form of the mean sea level. After the location of each point in space measurements of angles and distances, calculations of the projections means from the three-dimensional reality to the representation plane (Dupont G, 2004).

ONE POINT ON THE TERRESTRIAL SURFACE LOCALIZATION

The altimetry permits to determine the height of one point that is expressed by the difference between the point and a surface of reference as the sea level. The geoids are the surface of reference for the observations of altimeter. The measure of the heights called levelling makes itself by lines, whose intermediate points are marked with the help of ankles implanted in the facades of the buildings. The set of these reference marks constitutes the network of levelling of the studied geographical zone. All information on these reference marks is listed by the direction of the land-registry of the wilaya.

The plane coordinates of one point are calculated near to the centimetre with the help of triangles, where we measured the angles and the distances with tachometers. To orient their observations, the geometers determined the coordinates of the mosques minarets or the water castles that represent very visible reference marks from afar. The administration of the land-registry and the topography manages the geodesic basis network composed of score thousand points. The system of positioning by GPS satellites (Global Positioning System) permits the precise determination of the coordinates of one point quickly on earth. To be able to produce a card or a plan from the measured data, we conduct calculations of a mathematical projection. Several geodesic systems exist. An important system is the WGS4 that is the basis of the GPS system (Laurini R. & Thompson D, 1992).

THE CURVES OF LEVEL

The level curve is a polyline that passes by all points of the land situated to the same altitude. The earth relief is represented on a plane card by level curves and points sides. If one represents a mountain cut in horizontal plates of equal thickness, the contours of these plates, seen from top, draw the curves of level that follow the relief shape. The disposition of the level curves on the card informs on the shape of the relief (stiff slope or soft slope). The value of the heights curve is registered on the level curve. The orientation informs of slope direction. The numbers are always orienting upstream (Kholladi M. K, 1999b).

PRODUCTION OF A CARD

The photogrammetry is a cartographic technique that permits to measure all visible elements from aerial photos of the territory. From a plane equipped with a special camera, some aerial photos are taken to very short intervals, so that two successive photos cover themselves to about 60% in direction of the skimming. Thanks to the principle of the stereoscopy, we can measure and reconstitute all elements situated inside the 60% of cover from a couple of aerial photos. The height of the skimming depends on the scale of the card that we want to produce. Today the planes of photogrammetry are equipped with the GPS system.

A relation between the earth and the aerial photo is established by the signalling of the points knew on the land. These points can be detected on the photo, what permits to situate all points of the photo in the system of coordinates wanted. To re-establish the three-dimensional relief from the aerial photos, the cartographer uses a grant natural of the man: the faculty to see in three measurements. At the time of the restitution photogrammetric, the aerial photos are installed by couples in a device named restitutor, which permits to re-establish a model of the relief and to seize all visible elements numerically to stock them in a data base. The restitution represents an important phase in the chain of production of a card.

Our main challenges are the seizure of all sought-after elements, the seized interpretation correct of the objects and the guarantee of the geometric precision required. The result of the restitution must be controlled therefore and must be completed by information of descriptive, nominative and administrative nature, where the nature of a building (of dwelling, agricultural, commercial or industrial), its attributes (school, town hall, reservoir, etc.), the names of the streets and the toponyms (localities, inhabited places) and the administrative and other limits. The scale of a card expresses the report of reduction between the reality and the representation on the card. A big scale of card permits to represent a lot of details, when a card has a small scale. It gives us a better general preview on a whole region. Different applications require some cards to different scales (Kholladi M. K, 1999a; [Kholladi M. K, 1999b; and 9Laurini R. & Thompson D, 1992).

The topographic card is a faithful representation of the reality. To arrive there, the cartographer restores the information in a legible and comprehensible cartographic picture. Its instruments are the symbols, the signatures, the colours and the texts. The graphic elements used in the card are regrouped and are explained in the legend of the card. The choice of the symbols and colours is guided by the principle to bring closer for example to best the graphic representation to the reality, the use of the bruise for the rivers, of the green for vegetation and symbols for the camping, the sports, etc. An analysis of the different editions of a card permits to retrace so much in detail the evolution of the regional development spatial such economic and social. The information on the date and the shape of the update of the edition are indicated in the legend of the card, what denotes the actuality of the card. Available until now as cards and plans, the geographical information presents itself henceforth as computer data base, which permits exchanges of more efficient data, as well as exploitation and a lot more rational update (AFIGEO, 1998).

GEOGRAPHICAL INFORMATION SYSTEM "GIS"

A Geographical information system is a computer tool permitting to represent and to analyze all geographical objects as well as all events that produce themselves of it [Demegre J, 2005]. The GIS offer all possibilities of the data bases (as requests and statistical analyses) and that, through a unique visualization and geographical analysis clean to the cards.

Many other domains as research and the development of new markets, the survey of a construction impact, the regional development, the management of the networks of water, electricity, gas or transportation, the follow-up in real time of vehicles, the civil protection, the follow-up of the evolution of the pollution of a territory, the follow-up of the desertification, etc. are concerned as directly by the power of the GIS to create some cards, to integrate all type of information, to visualize the different scripts better, to present the ideas better and to measure the impact of the possible solutions better.

A GIS permits the storage of the information concerning the world under the shape of bound thematic layers the some to the other by geography (as on the Figure 1) (Kholladi M. K, 2004a; Kholladi M. K, 2004b; Laurini R. & Thompson D, 1992 and Laurini R. & Millert-Raffort F, 1993).

The Systems of Geographical information exploit two different types of geographical models: the vector model and the model raster as on the Figure 2. If one has a GIS and data, one can ask simple questions as (Kholladi M. K, 2004a) and (Laurini R. & Thompson D, 1992):

- To whom does this parcel of land belong?
- Which of these two zones is the most distant?
- Where are the exploitable lands for a given economic activity?

Figure 1. Example of thematic layers

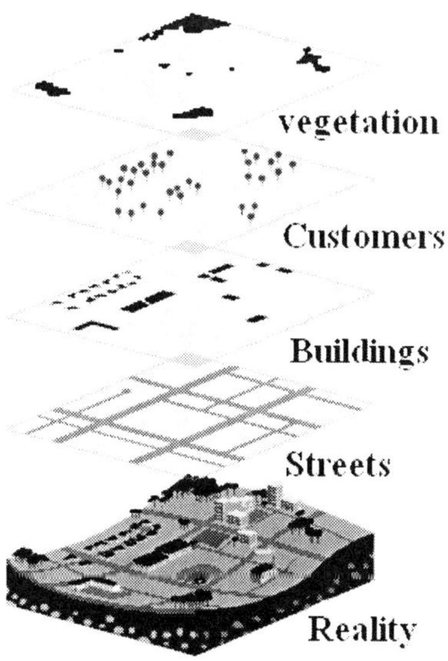

Figure 2. The two models of the reality representation: vector and raster

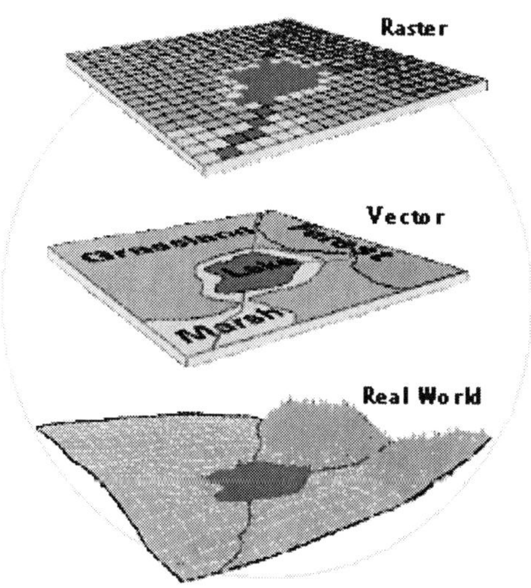

Figure 3. A road neighbourhood request

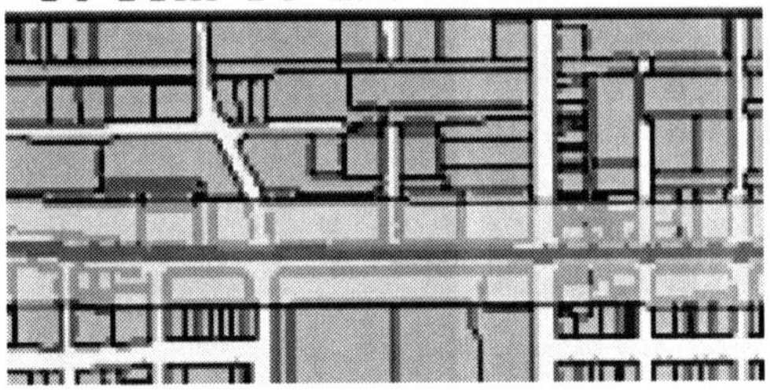

Some of the questions integrating an analysis, as for example:

- What are the virgin lands to construct new houses?
- What are soils adapted to the plantation of a type of tree?
- If I construct a freeway here, what will be the density of the traffic of it?

The GIS arranges many and powerful tools of analysis, but two among them appear as particularly essential: the proximity analysis and the spatial analysis.

PROXIMITY ANALYSIS

How much does existing houses in a zone of 80 meters on both sides of a road to big circulation? (See Figure 3). What is the total number of customer in a ray of 5Km around a big surface?

To answer these questions, the GIS has calculations algorithms named "buffering" in order to determine the relations of proximity between the objects.

SPATIAL ANALYSIS

The integration of data by different information layers permits to do a spatial analysis. This analysis by crossing of information, if it can take place visually (to the tracings identical superimposed the some to the other) requires the crossing often with alphanumeric information. The crossing of the soil nature, of its declivity, of the present vegetation with the owners and the taxes paid is an example of sophisticated analysis that permits the GIS use (as on the Figure 4) (Kholladi M. K, 2004a) and (Laurini R. & Milleret-Raffort F, 1993).

The card is a much better tool of synthesis and presentation of information. The cards created with a GIS can integrate the reports, the three-dimensional views, the photographic pictures and all sorts of elements multimedia henceforth easily. The capacity of the GIS concerning the data research and the geographical requests execution allowed numerous enterprises or administrations to save the hundreds of millions of Algerian Dinars. A realtor can use a GIS to find houses of a certain

Figure 4. The thematic layers superposition

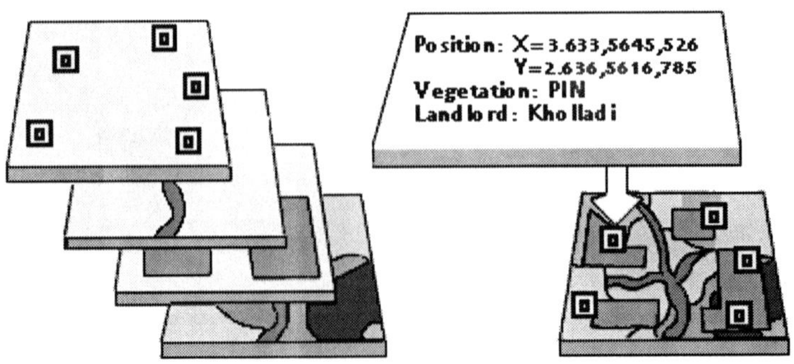

surface, with three rooms and including a garage. It gets a list of the houses answering these criteria as well as their geographical localization thus simultaneously as on the Figure 5.

This request can be refined thereafter with the help of two new criteria: a renting lower to 5000 DA per month and situated unless about hundred meters of a school. The result of this new request will be displayed in the same conditions as on the Figure 6 (Kholladi M. K, 1999a]) and (Sohm J, 2003).

WEB MAPPING

The needs to communicate some information in the domains of management of the risks, of the regional development, or more environment, the publication of cartographic data on Internet is means of indispensable communication (De Blomac F, 2001), (De Blomac F, 2005) and (Soussain G, 2003). The Web Mapping or the diffusion of the cards via the Internet network is a domain in full expansion thanks to the development of the solutions Open Source. Following the GNU philosophy that allows the copy, the diffusion of the software and the modification of the code source, these generally free programs and of emergent free use at a rhythm sustained.

The concept of the Web cartography consists in three components: geography, information and the Web. The approach of the Web Mapping is adapted to a large public no specialist: simple interface, oriented "cartographic atlas" and on line GIS, consultation by connection to weak debit,

Figure 5. Request of a house research with criteria

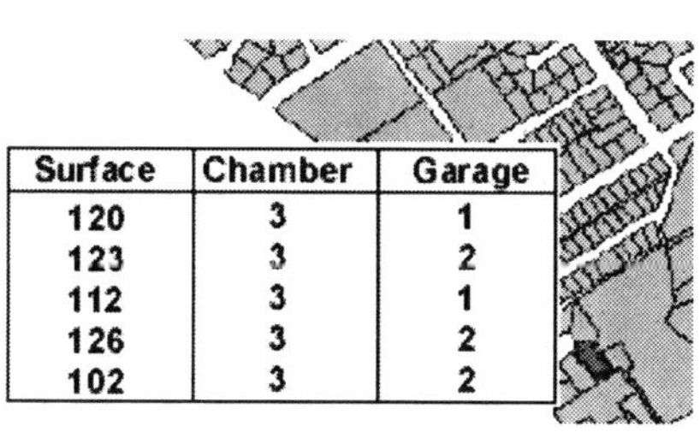

Surface	Chamber	Garage
120	3	1
123	3	2
112	3	1
126	3	2
102	3	2

fast and independent solution of the navigators, without Plug in (De Blomac F, 2009) and (Soussain G, 2001). It permits a complete integration in an existing site and the possibilities of interactions: the dual brightness of the entities, the complementary information, the display of the themes, etc. The cartographic functionalities are:

- **Navigation:** inside a same document
- **Global view:** seen permitting to localize the zone of visualization on a general preview of the document.
- **Zoom:** the user has the possibility to zoom in the size of the visualization zone.
- **Icons:** presence of interactive symbols in the visualization.
- **Zones of click:** interactive zones in the visualization triggering some events (pop up, info bubbles, etc.).
- **Management of layers:** possibility to visualize several layers (tracings)
- **Requests user:** Semantics and/or geometric, thematic, predefined or no.
- **Update:** interface of update of the spatial data and/or attributes without programming.

GENERAL PRINCIPLE OF A CARTOGRAPHIC WORKING SERVER

The cartographic server is the automatic ticket window where we make a call to display some

Figure 6. Composed spatial requests

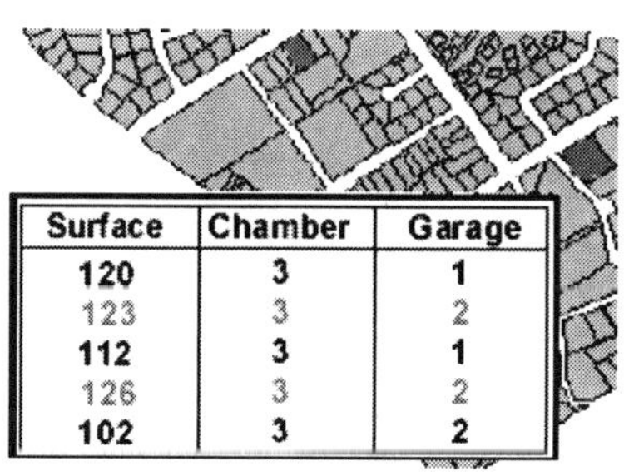

Surface	Chamber	Garage
120	3	1
123	3	2
112	3	1
126	3	2
102	3	2

cards on its station of work. The architecture is of type client-server. The user, from his terminal, spear of the requests to ask for a particular card display. The cartographic server the interprets and send back the card under the shape of a matrix picture (png, jpg, etc.) or vectorial (svg, swf, etc.). The cartographic motor can be controlled by languages of script as PHP, java script, Python or Perl that allow him to generate a card dynamically in answer to the user's request (Thomazeau J., 1997) and (Soussain G., 2003).

The cartographic server can look for the information necessary to the realization of the card in its own resources, but also on servers of distant data. The diffusion of the on line data requires an installation side server with software as Apache (project Open Source) or IIS (Internet Information Services, of Microsoft) that turn in task of bottom and give access to the cards servers to the intranet and to the Internet. These servers often see their functions spread by interpreters of scripts as PHP or ASP. The cartographic server leans on these elements to receive some requests and to send back the pictures and data. Client side, a navigator Web is sufficient, accompanied by a viewer, to display the card (cf. Figure 7) (Durand H, 2003) and (Pewe B, 1997).

The data can be managed by specific software, the SGBDR, such PostgreSQLs, MySQL, Oracle, among others, that can be installed directly on the server containing the cartographic server or on another server, distant. PostgreSQL and its extension spatial PostGIS is the management system of relational data bases the more succeeded in the domain of the free software. PostGIS is included henceforth in the official distribution of PostGreSQL. It offers functionalities deepened to stock and to treat geographical reference of the spatial objects.

The different software bricks have been tested with the systems of exploitations Windows XP and Linux Mandrake 10 to value their interoperability. To simulate the situation of exchange of data via Internet, MapServer 4.4, PHP/MapScript, the SGBDR extended PostgreSQL 7.5 of PostGIS 0.9.1 with its interface graphic phpPgAdmin has been compiled on a dedicated server Linux. The user will have permissions of reading and writing in the arborescence of the indexes of the machine server, for the storage of the solutions side server while the solutions client side will be placed on the local machine in a Windows XP pro environment (De Blomac F, 2001).

SOLUTIONS CLIENT SIDE

The software tested client Open Source, QGIS, UDIG, THUBAN and JUMP, are software GIS in full evolution having functionalities advanced from afar for the consultation and the geographical data edition (see Figure 8).

In practice, these applications are not always located entirely side server because they can require the downloading of a light plug-in by the customer (for example the Rosa applet). Of basis, the solutions side server Open Source brings the possibility from a classic navigator Internet to visualize the generated dynamically geographical layers. Currently, new more advanced function-

Figure 7. The cartographic server

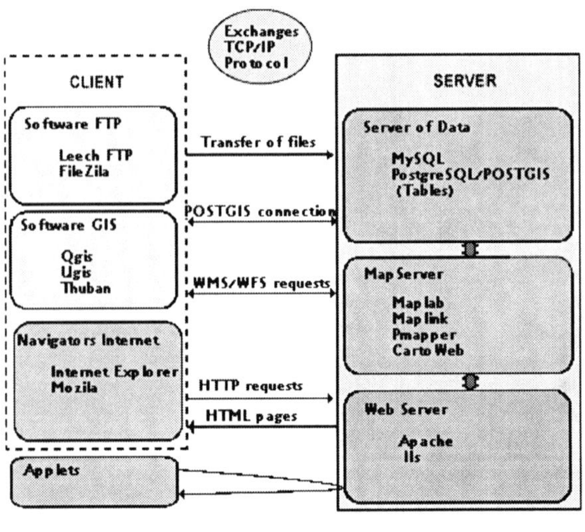

Figure 8. Solutions server side

Nom	Description	Remarques
JUMP www.projet-sigle.org www.jump-project.org	Traitements complexes sur données Géographiques Connexion WMS, PostGIS	Nombreux plugin nécessaires Accessibles aux moins expérimentés
Quantum GIS www.qgis.sourceforge.net	Visualisation, manipulation de données vectorielles et raster Connexion WMS, PostGIS	Installation facile Interface en français et conviviale Simple d'utilisation Pas toujours fiable
UDIG www.udig.refractions.net	Edition de la géométrie des couches Connexion WMS, WFS, PostGIS	Très fort sur les connexions distantes Nécessite une plateforme Java JRE JDK
THUBAN	Traitements complexes sur données Géographiques Connexion WMS, WFS, PostGIS	Nécessite une plateforme Python

alities appear as the possibility to add or to modify on line information.

THE DM SOLUTIONS PRODUCTS

These are MAPLAB, CHAMELEON, KA-MAPS and CARTOWEB3. Figure 9 summarizes the features of each of them.

Other Solutions

On the Web, we can find a big number of other available solutions in downloading. They are counted on the sites of FreeGIS and Maptools, and are of easiness of access and use variables. In general the simple and easily adaptable solutions for its own geographical data are viewers as Veremap or Pmapper. This last proposes a set of tools for example interesting Java scripts as the zoom by cursor, the legend in hierarchical tree and the impression in pdf. Then comes the more complex solutions and evolved like Mapbender or MapLink. On-line, it is possible to select a polygon and to modify its geometry (see on the Figure 9) (Marshall J, 2001) and (Mauvière E, 1999).

Actually the solutions client-server can be completely complementary, one (server) permitting to do some treatments clean to the problematic of the GIS (crossings of layers, requests, analysis

Figure 9. Web mapping solutions

Nom	Description	Remarques
MAPLAB+CHAMELEON www.maptools.org	Interface graphique pour construire le mapfile Connexion WMS Personalisation de l'interface	Accessibles aux moins expérimentés Outils pas toujours fiables
CARTOWEB3 www.cartoweb.org	Visualisation, manipulation de données vectorielles et raster Impression pdf, interface multilingue, fonctionalités Web Connexion PosigGIS, WMS	Installation complexe Nécessite une configuration particulière
MAPLINK www.maplink.sourceforge.net	Possibilité d'édition en ligne de la géométrie des couches Requêtes WMS, WFS	Installation ardue, ...

thematic), the other (customer) through the intermediary of the mapfile displaying the card in an accessible interface on Internet. Otherwise, we see the modules Open Source that transplants them on the big commercial GIS as Amein maintained by Territories for ArCGIS 8 and Wortomap developed by usable Tydac with MapInfo 7.8 that allows him to export the mapfile of the GIS to display the same card in an interface Map Server.

Web Carto as Solution of Web Dynamic GIS

The Web Carto product is an interactive Web-GIS, based on the motor cartographic Open Mapserver source. It permits the presentation, but also the acquirement of geographical data through the Internet. It is a tool permitting to generate some cards from various spatial data, according to the instructions contained in what we call some Mapfile, of the files ".map", regrouping the parameters describing the way whose cards must be presented. We can beside use a model html (commonly named a template), that will manage the layout of the display of the data generated.

The most often, it is used on a server Internet to generate some pictures in Web pages, and so to permit the display but also the questioning, the modification, of cartographic pictures on an Internet site. We can also use MapServer in local, on its computer, to generate the cards, to do the requests and analyses. The diagram of the present Figure 10 how MapServer integrates in a system server Internet (Gifford F, 1999).

The main libraries used by MapServer are:

- GDAL and OGR: Interpretation and conversion of the spatial data.
- Proj.4: Reproduction, transfers and distortion of the spatial data.
- GD: Generation and modification of pictures to the formats bitmap of the Web (Herself will possibly have need of the JPEG libraries and PNG).
- FreeType: Management of the fonts.

We can also mention the libraries that are going to allow the generation of cards particular formats:

- MING for the format flash.
- PDFlib for the PDF format.

MapServer accepts a big number of formats data raster, there again thanks to the library of GDAL functions. Without this library only some formats geographical reference rasters is supported: GeoTIF, hair *, gif *, png *, jpeg *, and Erdas Lan. The possibilities raster of your installation of MapServer goes therefore essentially to depend on the capacities of GDAL that have been

Figure 10. MapServer in a server Internet

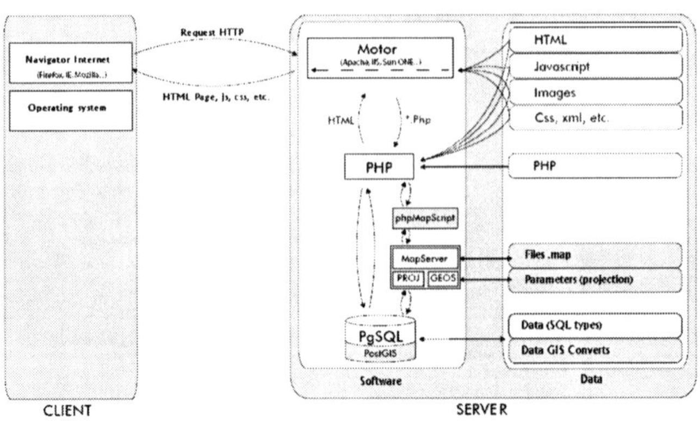

specified at the time of its compilation. To add a layer raster in a Mapfile, here is the syntax of the LAYER block:

```
LAYER
  NAME Scan
  DATES Constantine.tif
  RASTER TYPE
  STATUS ONE
END
```

SERVERS TO THE NORM WEB MAP SERVICE (WMS) OF THE OGC

The use of a WMS source requires the presence of a block PROJECTION in the MAP block, as well as the use of a METADATA block that is going to specify the request made to the server. We have for example:

```
CONNECTION http://www2.dmsolutions.
ca/cgi-bin/mswms_gmap?
CONNECTIONTYPE WMS
METADATA
wms_srs  EPSG:42304 EPSG:42101
EPSG:4269 EPSG:4326 EPSG:42304
wms_name
prov_bound
wms_server_version  1.1.0
wms_formatlist  image/gif,image/
png,image/jpeg,image/wbmp
wms_format  image/gif
END
```

THE CARTOWE3 PRESENTATION

Most solutions of interactive cartography proposed on the market are descended of the world of the GIS and don't often answer fully the needs of the dynamic Internet sites. Camptocamp its developed CartoWeb thus, a Web application of Geographical information System (GIS) interactive, while especially respecting the specific needs of the web. It is also conceived especially to integrate easily in nearly all types of sites dynamic internet. It permits to put easily in evidence the spatial aspects of the data presented notably, even though these are not part of a GIS (Jongler D. & Lestrat I., 2001), (Jongler D. & Lestrat I., 2002) and (Kholladi M. K., 2008).

The proposed solution is especially interesting since it permits the visualization (diffusion) and the seizure (collection) of the geographical objects (lines, points, surfaces) through different Web sites. It permits to benefit from a solution of web-GIS to very attractive costs, since this solution doesn't require the purchase of licenses commercial GIS. However, CartoWeb integrates without any problem in an environment existing GIS, since the formats supported by this system are compatible with most formats of the GIS applications of the market.

SPECIFICATIONS

The Web Carto product is an interactive Web-GIS, not only permitting the presentation, but also the acquirement and the geographical data management through the Internet and more especially the Web. The Web Carto has been developed while respecting the specific needs of the Web in the GIS domain, to know (De Blomac F, 2005):

- Spatial visualization of the data in the Web sites (Webmapping).
- Edition and seizure of data through the Web (interactive Web-GIS).
- Integration of the interactive Web-GIS in a site web, existing or in creation, simplified to the maximum.
- Interaction facilitated of the geographical functionalities with the relational data bases (out GIS) of the site web.

- Possibility to insert the cartography directly in any page of a site in the content (harmony between the site and the GIS tools).
- Possibility to share and/or to rent geographical information (cartographic funds).
- Weak cost of acquirement and implementation.
- Compatibility with the applications GIS standards of the market.
- Compatibility with the GPS and the PDA.
- Respect of the norms and standards (OGC WMS, OGC SFS, GML, XML, XHTML, and SOAP).

ADVANTAGES OF USE

We will mention in some points the advantages of the CartoWeb system:

- Enhancement of the spatial information in a Web site.
- Easy setting up, little programming.
- Weak cost of implementation (not of expensive license - federation of the costs of acquirement of the cartographic data).
- Possibility to seize and to modify geographical information via Internet.
- Compatibility and integration with the GIS customer server of the market.
- Possibility to rent the access to functionalities (ASP fashion).

CartoWeb will be used in particular for [De Blomac F, 2009]:

- To distribute the cards or plans on the Web with specific thematic information and all functionalities of navigation (zoom, displacement, etc.).
- To bind spatial information to the informational content of the data bases.
- To seize and to modify the on line geographical information, by the edition of objects of type points, lines or surfaces.

ARCHITECTURE OF WEB CARTO

The Web Carto is an efficient solution to the needs concerning treatment and diffusion by Internet of managed data or produced by a GIS classic client-server. A strong point of Web Carto is the easiness of interaction between present data in external data bases and the geographical data. It permits the presentation, but also the acquirement of geographical data through internet.

It has been developed while having to the mind the specific needs of the Web in the domain of the GIS. It is generally used as application standalone. However Web Carto is constructed on an architecture multi third that permit, if in the need be, to establish it as Web Service. It is then possible for several Web sites to use the same geographical server. It possesses two fashions of working in direct or in SOAP (sees Figures 11 and 12).

Functionalities of the CartoClient are activated on simple passage of parameters (see Figure 13). The development of CartoWeb respects the main condition for a perennial computer application, to know an efficient separation between the data, the treatment, the presentation and the language. There is not a code HTML mixed to the code of PHP treatment. The texts of the interface also separated. It permits to put a multilingual site in place therefore easily. It assures the application

Figure 11. Direct Mode

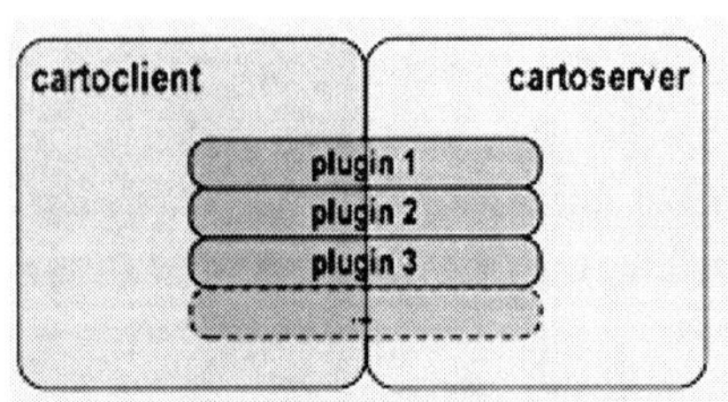

Figure 12. SOAP Mode

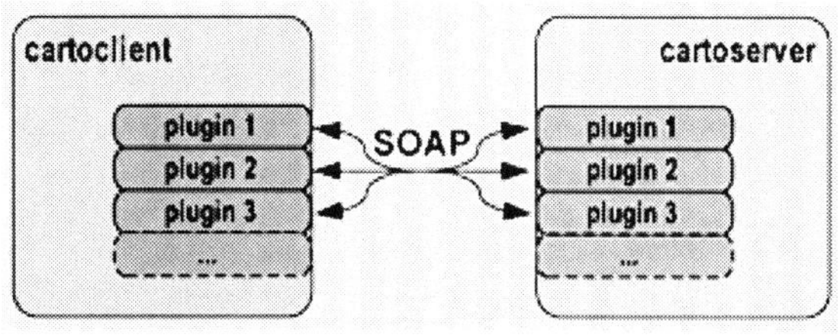

evolutivity, since the central functionalities are not touched at the time of a change of graphic charter or the addition of a peripheral functionality.

CREATION OF A PROJECT OF WEB MAPPING

The Gait Describes the Project Configuration.

Project Installation

In a line of order the message of solicitation (DOS, shell), to throw the manuscript of installation of cw3setup.php.

```
<PHP-INTERPRETER>cw3setup.php to in-
stall
--base-URL http://localhost/car-
toweb3/htdocs /
--development of profile
--<nameOfProject> of project
```

So no mistake occurred we must be able to reach the project by http://localhost/ cartoweb3/ htdocs/client.php of typing for the navigator and to choose the project from the slim drop-down of the projects.

DATA OF LOADING

As we can see it, the project that we created is empty. Thereafter, we will load the spatial data of the project. To add the next one in the Mapfile (project_name.map): To PUT THE TYPE THE COLOR NAMED 240 of region of NAME of MODEL of class region of ttt of CALIBER of reg_algerie of POLYGON DATA 240 240 OUTLINECOLOR 255 EXTREMITY of extremity of CODE id_attribute_string of 165 96 of MÉTA-GIVE extremity of END

Figure 13. The architecture Composition

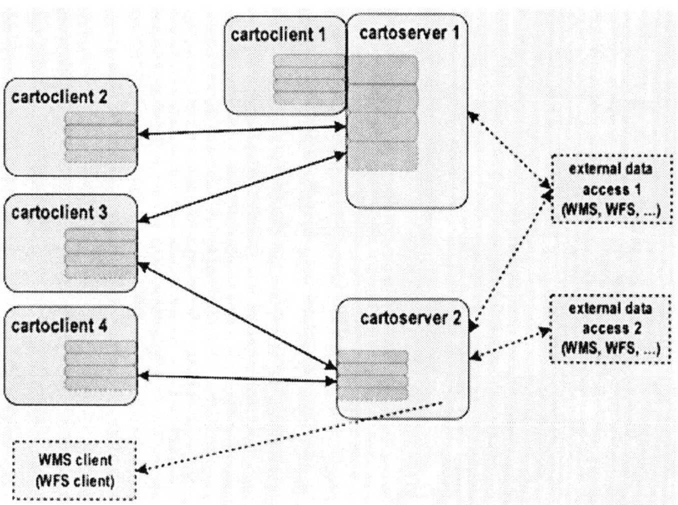

And in the file of layers.ini (server_conf/ project_name /) to add what follows:

- layers.region.className = layers.region. label layer = Regions
- layers.region.msLayer = region
- And to add the new identification of layer in the list of children of layer of the root:
- layers.root.children = region
- To publish besides the file of project_name. ini in a publisher of text in order to place some initial mapstates by default as chosen layers.
- To add what follows:
    - mapInfo.initialMapStates.default. layers.region.selected = rectify
    - In your navigator, the click on the button of reset_session and one must see the regions of Algeria that one wants to display.
- To add our data, one must simply proceed from the following manner:
    - to get our available data, by default in the shirt of data
    - to modify the Mapfile size,
    - to modify the size defined in the initial Mapstateses (project_name.ini),
    - to add the definitions of layers in the mapfile (project_name.map),
    - to add the definitions of layers in the layers.ini.
    - to hand to zero the session in the navigator, and to get our data to display.

CONCLUSION

The realization of dynamic cards on Internet is essential when we want to distribute geographical information. Often used in the localization of the places by their addresses, in the calculation of itineraries or for the geographical marketing, its uses are increasing and enlarge toward new sectors. Descended of the data processing applied to geography, this tool stands to the crossing of techniques allying the relational data management, the representation and the spatial analysis, the programming in script language (Kholladi M. K., 1999a).

Actually, we find either of the reusable components (Chameleon), of the interfaces web (CartoWeb, Ka-Map), either of the more complete solutions of help to the management and to the realization of Web applications (MapLab). As bending on the construction of a card on line, only QGIS in customer and MapLab thanks to its MapEdit tool side server permits to publish graphically and dynamically a mapfile. In this domain many progress remain last one has to be done because this last is not flexible enough in its syntax and in its adaptability to the different environments (Jongler D. & Lestrat I., 2001).

REFERENCES

AFIGEO, (1998, May). *L'information géographique française dans la société de l'information: état des lieux et propositions d'action*, p. 35.

De Blomac, F. (2001). *L'open source, véritable alternative pour les SIG?* p. 4.

De Blomac F, (2005). *Les systèmes d'information géographique territoriaux-La mise en ligne des données géographiques: principes et expériences*, Cybergeo: European Journal of Geography, n°318, p. 123.

De Blomac F, (2009, June 01). *Publier des cartes sur Internet: ces solutions qui nous viennent du graphique*. SIG La Lettre, n°108, p. 3.

Demegre, J., & Salge, F. (2004). *Que sais-je? Les SIGs,* p. 84.

Dupasque X, (2004, April). *Etats des lieux des solutions Internet de diffusions des données géographiques*, Géo événement.

Dupont G, (2004, January 23). *L'IGN cartographie la France en numérique*, Journal: Le Monde, p. 2.

Durand H, (2003, April). *Du SIG à la donnée sur internet: Quel mode de diffusion pour quel public*. Journée professionnelle SIG-LR.

Gifford, F. (1999). *Internet GIS Architecture - Which Side Is Right for You?* p. 11.

Jongler D. & Lestrat L, (2001, February). *Dossier technique: les SIG et Internet*, Signature n°20, CERTU, p. 11.

Jongler, D., & Lestrat, L. (2002). *Cartographie sur Internet*, Fiche technique du CNIG (Aide à la Maîtrise d'Ouvrage) n°64, p. 8.

Kholladi M. K, (1999a, November 15-17). *Mécanismes de raisonnement spatiaux sur des objets géographiques*, Séminaire International sur les SIGs, " AL-SIG'99 » organisé par le Conseil National de l'Information Géographique "CNIG", Alger, p. 9.

Kholladi M. K, (1999b, November 15 17). *Modèle Numérique de Terrain par la Méthode de Triangulation de Delaunay avec Contraintes*, Séminaire International sur les SIGs, "AL-SIG'99 » organisé par le Conseil National de l'Information Géographique " CNIG », Alger, p. 21.

Kholladi M. K, (2004a, September). *Raisonnement et Manipulation Spatial sur des Objets Urbains "RMSOU"*, CISC'2004: Conférence Internationale des Systèmes Complexes, Jijel, p. 13.

Kholladi, M. K. (2004b, December). *Geographical Information System for Urban Spatial Analysis*, ACIT'2004: The International Arab Conference on Information Technology, Mentouri University of Constantine, Algeria, pp. 188-193, ISSN: 1812-0857.

Kholladi, M. K. (2008, October 15-16). *Carto Web Solution for the Web Mapping*, IACET: International Arab Conference of e-Technology, Arab Open University, Amman, Jordan, pp. 105-113.

Laurini, R., & Milleret-Raffort, F. (1993). *Les bases de données en géomatique*. Paris, France: Editions Hermès.

Laurini, R., & Thompson, D. (1992). *Fundamentals of Spatial Information Systems, the APIC*. Series Academic Press.

Marshall, J. (2001). *Developing Internet-Based GIS Applications*, p. 11.

Mauvière, E. (1999). *La cartographie sur le web*. p. 40.

Pewe, B. (1997). *GIS online*, p. 125.

Pottier, P. (2000). *La sémiologie et communication cartographique*, Fiche technique du CNIG n°40, p. 6.

Sohm, J. C. (2003). *Image et graphique pour le web*, p. 5.

Soussain, G. (2001). *Publier des cartes sur internet: Les repères*. p. 64.

Soussain, G. (2003). *Cartographie sur Internet: synthèse à l'usage d'une maîtrise d'œuvre*. p. 7.

Thomazeau, J. *(1997)*. Le Web support d'applications client/serveur, une voie suivie par la DSI pour le système d'information de gestion du CNRS, *p. 12.*

WEB SITES TO VIEW

http://www.camptocamp.com/

http://www.cartoweb.org/

http://www.commentcamarche.net

http://www.esrifrance.fr/

http://www.geoscopies.net

http://www.ieti.fr/Panorama_SIG_WEB.pdf

http://www.mysql.com

http://www.opensource.org

http://www.ors-idf.org/etudes/pdf/carto-web.pdf

http://www.portailsig.org

http://www.sitewww.ch/dossier_solution_cartographie.php

http://www.webrankinfo.com/actualites/tags/cartographie-sur-internet.htm

Chapter 16
Ontology Based Business Rules and Services Integration Environment

Aqueo Kamada
CTI – Information Technology Center Renato Archer, Brazil & State University of Campinas, Brazil

Adriana Figueiredo
CTI – Information Technology Center Renato Archer, Brazil

Marcos Rodrigues
CTI – Information Technology Center Renato Archer, Brazil

ABSTRACT

Nowadays, the relationships among people, governments and organizations are subject to fast changes. The increasing demand for new services conducts to the need to create services from scratch and by integrating disparate and heterogeneous legacy systems. The problem is that the monolithic form as most of the systems were implemented turns the change excessively slow and expensive. Considering that some business logic portions are quite volatile and susceptible to changes and other portions are quite stable and less susceptible to changes, this paper proposes ontology based integrated development environment (IDE) that can capture business changes and quickly implement them into computational systems. The volatile portions are externalized as business rules and the stable portions as SOA based services. Business rules' facts and conditions are linked to services, which are discovered in the business rules development or maintenance time. The IDE aggregates a set of tools to automate the modeling of business rules in the business people's terminology and to automate the integration of services. It is based on a set of ontologies to deal with metadata related to services, vocabularies and business rules. Business rules are modeled according to OMG's Semantics of Business Vocabularies and Business Rules Metamodel.

DOI: 10.4018/978-1-61520-789-3.ch016

INTRODUCTION

A computational system should reflect the knowledge of the business domain in which the system is used. Due to the business high competition, communication speed and degree of the customers' information, the organizations have to make changes in their computational systems in a much more accelerated rhythm than in past decades. Consequently, the computational solutions for the business problems cannot accompany the speed in which the change necessities appear. In this context, governments and companies need to incorporate new technologies to implement solutions integrating business processes and services already existent with new processes to generate other services. In this way, all the time, processes and services need to be reviewed so that the organization can act according to the changes that happen in the business scenario. For most of the organizations the adaptation capacity to the new realities in a fast and efficient way is a crucial challenge to maintain their competitiveness or their survival in the business.

Commonly, documents containing procedures, contracts, regulations and laws define the strategies, policies and relationships among organizations and consolidate that knowledge. From those documents arise the rules that define the behavior of the business processes in the organizations (Hildreth, 2005). Thus, a set of such rules, known as business rules, that contain important information for the realization of the business represent the business essence and define how an organization must behave to deal with its daily situations.

Business processes can be described by a variety of means, such as, objects, actions and events. Hence, business processes can be described by splitting them up to patterns, which can be represented by business rules through event-condition-action schemes. Therefore, a business rule describes the actions that have to be executed if an event happens and a condition is met. In this way, business rules can provide some modularization capabilities for business processes and offer advantages in terms of flexibility and reusability. Thus, business process changes can be easily implemented by changing the business rules and the reuse of individual business rules can be easily done across different business processes (Schmidt, 2001).

In this context, many services have to interoperate seamlessly, such as ordering, billing and calculation services to perform actions related to a specific business process. In addition, the set of services is not fixed, because business process changes and extensions require the integration of additional services. The services are dispersed across different organizations and implemented using different platforms, programming languages, and due to the fact that there is no centralized organization, the services are changing independently. Therefore, the execution of business processes means not only the distributed execution of business processes, but also the integration of a changing set of heterogeneous services (Schmidt, 2001).

The difficulties and inflexibility to quickly reflect the business' changes into the computational systems motivated this research. The identified reasons for those difficulties are as follows: (1) in most of the computational systems the business rules are dispersed in the documentation and in the executable code and this turns the maintenance slow and expensive (Halle, 2001) and (2) the orthogonality between the perspectives of the process composition mechanisms and the business rules mechanisms make the integration of these mechanisms difficult in terms of collaboration in treating the business logic (Charfi & Mezini, 2004) and (Orriens & Yang, 2006).

In the government and business applications there are portions of the business logic that are dynamic and sensitive to the business changes and other portions that are quite stable. However, the monolithic form in that most of the applications were implemented with the dynamic portions built-in in the computational code make difficult the implementation of the changes. These portions, dynamics and stable, need to be appropriately structured and maintained separate so that they can be updated independently. Then, these dynamic and stable portions need to be integrated to perform new services in the context of the fast changes that the business demands.

This situation justifies the need for an approach that can capture the business changes and quickly convert them into the computational systems. In this context, this work proposes an Integrated Development Environment (IDE) to formalize services and business rules ontologies, in the business people's terminology, so that this ontological information can be used to generate equivalent computational code for rules and services.

The next section provides a background overview of business rules and discusses some aspects related to business rules and Web Services and the convergence movement between them. Section 3 provides a general idea of the service and business rule development and execution framework. Section 4 presents an overview of the e-Government scenario used to exercise the proposed ideas and then presents some aspects related to the services and business rules integrated development environment. Section 5 discusses some related works and the final section provides a conclusion and future researches.

FOUNDATIONS ON BUSINESS RULES

This section presents the concept of business rule in the context of this work, some specific business rules examples related to specific communities and it discusses some aspects related to the Object Management Group's SBVR metamodel (OMG, 2008).

Definition of Business Rule

Although there are a lot of discussion around the definition of what business rule means (OMG, 2008), (IBM, 2004), in the context of this work, a business rule is a rule that can be interpreted by computers, that defines or restricts some aspects of a business, introducing obligations or needs, according to the organization policies..

Business Rules Examples

Following are some examples of business rules that permeate the business organizations. It should be explained that the great majority of such business rules is not properly exposed and, therefore, is not under the control of business rules mechanisms. The lack of efficient mechanisms for business rules management is the root of the inflexibility problems when implementing the changes in the computational systems.

Some business rules in the context of car rental:

- A car must have a registration number.
- A car should not be released to the customer if the credit card was not presented as the payment guarantee.
- A driver of a rental car must be a qualified driver.

Some business rules in the context of air ticket reservation:

- The price of an air ticket from São Paulo to Rio de Janeiro is $ 300.00 if the flight departure and arrival happen in the middle of the week. And R$ 150.00 if the flight departure or flight arrival happen in the weekend.
- Every air ticket reservation will be lost if it is not paid until 48 hours before the flight time.

Some business rules in the context of civil identification:

- A citizen that lost the identity card needs to register a notification notifying the loss.
- An identity card should be canceled if a notification was registered by loss.
- The identity card should not be canceled if the data supplied in the notification are not the same of the identity card.

SBVR METAMODEL: SEMANTICS OF BUSINESS VOCABULARY AND BUSINESS RULES

Due to the lack of consensus to define rules in the terminology of businesses, OMG published the SBVR (Semantics of Business Vocabulary and Business Rules) metamodel (OMG 2008). The main objective of the SBVR metamodel is to allow business people to define the policies and the rules that drive the organizations in the business people's own language, in terms of the artifacts with which they perform the businesses. Besides, the other objective is to capture those rules in a clear way, without ambiguity, and quickly transformable in other representations, as the representations for business people, for software engineers, and for business rules execution tools. The SBVR metamodel specify (1) a metamodel for the specification of business rules by business people, with a MOF (Meta Object Facilities) representation; (2) a metamodel for the capture of vocabularies and definitions of the terms used in business rules; and (3) an XML representation of business rules and vocabularies based on XMI to allow the interoperability of rules and vocabularies among software tools that manipulate business rules, according to the MOF 2.0/XMI Mapping Specification (OMG, 2005). The resulting SBVR metamodel is not intended for the business people, instead it is intended for software engineers that build tools for business people, because it is located in the CIM (Computation Independent Model) level of the MDA (Model Driven Architecture) (OMG, 2003), as suggested by OMG.

The foundation of business rules in SBVR has its origins in the idea presented in the Business Rules Manifesto (BRG, 2003), where Rules are based in facts, and facts are based on concepts that are expressed by terms. Terms express business concepts; facts make assertions on these concepts; rules restrict and support these facts. That basic idea, which appeared in 1995 in the context of Business Rules Group (BRG, 2009), has been called of mantra of business rules. For convenience, that mantra is, frequently, abbreviated to Rules are based in facts, and facts are based on terms. Figure 1, extracted from SBVR (OMG, 2008) shows how the specification supports the idea of that mantra.

Business Vocabulary

An important aspect of business rules is that they can and they should be presented to business people in their own terminology. In other words, the business rules should be intelligible for business people that have the responsibility for the business activities for which the rules are applied, and for the people that understand how the rules link to the objectives of the business. The syntax of the rules can be textual or graphic, but the vocabulary should be a business vocabulary, significant to the people that do and perform the business rules, as specified in SBVR metamodel (OMG, 2008).

Business Rules and Web Services Convergence

Recently, the researches and technologies related with business rules faced a new pulse due to their potential to capture and to facilitate the implementation of the changes that happen in the organizations' daily activities. Many business rules mechanisms (Fair Isaac, 2007b), (ILOG, 2007), (Friedman-Hill, 2003), the called business rules

Figure 1. SBVR support for the business rules "Mantra"

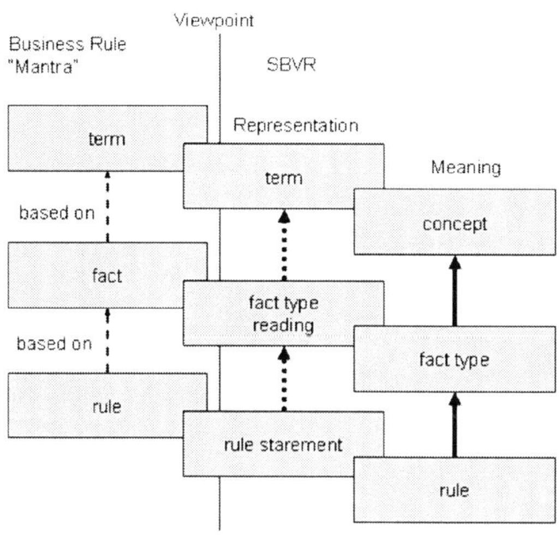

engines and Business Rules Management Systems (BRMS), which are well established, already demonstrate the effectiveness of their use in some sectors of the business, especially in the finance and insurance sectors. The business rules mechanisms guarantee flexibility by making possible that potentially all the decision points of process flows can be edited and stored in a managed rules repository. Thus, they make it possible that the applications can access the rules mechanism and the proper rules can be updated quickly by the business analysts. The most common problems in all of the rules mechanisms refer to the difficulty in the rules formalization in natural language associated with the respective execution support and to the difficulty in the combination of the business rules with other aspects of business processes.

On the other hand, the researches and the technologies related with the Service Oriented Architecture (SOA) (Barry, 2003), (He, 2003) also faced a strong pulse with the Web services popularization (W3C 2004) due to their potential in the integration and interoperation of distributed services, independently of location, development platform, execution environment and of programming language (Mahmoud, 2005). Also in this area the rules mechanisms can have an important role (Fair Isaac, 2007). The legacy applications present strong reasons for the organizations to experiment rules mechanisms and SOA technology. When the organizations have many built-in rules in a legacy application migrating them to rules mechanism and maintaining the stable processes as Web Services allow the users to make changes without having to rewrite code constantly (Cuecent, 2008). Again, the most common problems refer to the difficulty in the combination of business rules with Web services.

In the last few years the initiatives including business rules mechanisms in the context of the service composition machines, such as BPEL (Business Process Execution Language), have been contributing to facilitate the services composition process, although they do not have the ability to appropriately treat the business rules in a collaborative way with the execution of services (Nagl, Rosenberg & Dustdar, 2006), (Geminiuc, 2006). The Business Process Management System (BPMS) community is paying attention to business rules mechanisms, leading to partnerships between BPMS suppliers and business rules mechanisms suppliers (Hildreth, 2005).

The Business Rules and Services Framework

This section presents the Service Development and Execution Framework based on business rules that allow implementing quickly in the computational systems the changes demanded in the daily businesses of the organizations. Although an overview of the framework is provided, as an evolution of (Kamada, 2006) and (Kamada & Mendes, 2007), the main focus will be on the IDE for business rules and services ontologies. Figure 2 presents the Service Development and Execution Framework.

The **Client** is a Web software module responsible for treating the citizen's request based on

Figure 2. Business rule and service development and execution framework

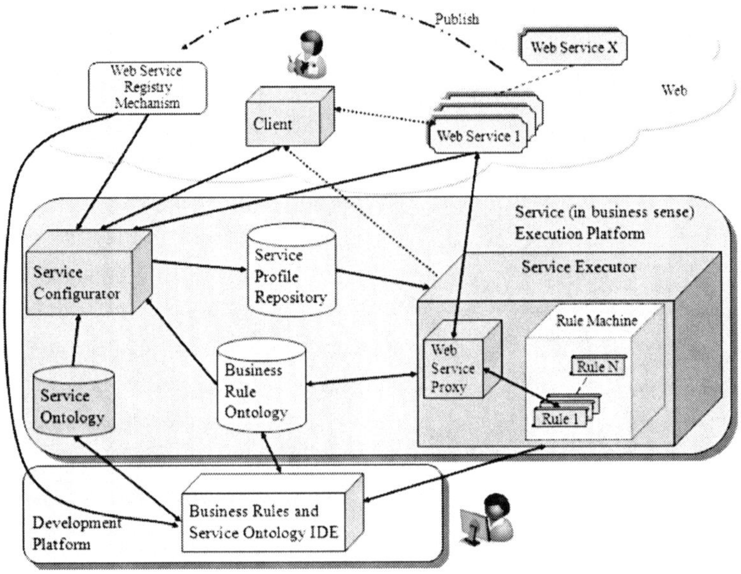

human life events. It starts with orientations, such as *Please, enter a short sentence indicating what happened to you or what do you want to do.* The answer to *what happened to you* represents the citizen's life event and *what do you want to do* represents the citizen's request. In fact, the Client module interacts with the *Service Configurator* to discover a citizen's need that, in practice, leads to the realization of a Service (in a business wide sense).

The Service Configurator is responsible for generating a set of metadata elements by interacting with the user through the Client module to delimit the service scope based on the user's life events and request. The Service Configurator obtains the elements related with the user's description from the *Business Rules Ontology* and *Service Ontology* and, if it is the case, it interacts again with Client module to determine the user´s need. These elements are consolidated in an entity nominated as *Service Profile*, which maintain metadata needed for the service realization, such as, service name, service identification, service URL (Universal Resource Locator), service general parameters and a set of service components with respective specific data. Each service component can be a Web service or a service in the business sense and maintain their own metadata, such as, service name, service identification, service URL and service general parameters. The Service Profile will be stored in the *Service Profile Repository* that will be accessed by the *Service Executor*. The Service Profile Repository is just a storage space as an auxiliary resource to implement a producer-consumer like mechanism in order to guarantee the necessary asynchronism between Service Configurator and Service Executor.

The Service Executor, based on Service Profile information, is responsible for recovering in the Business Rules Ontology the pertinent business rules, instantiating a rules machine, translating the business rules, recovering the locators (URL) of the *Web services* in the *Registry mechanism*, generating *proxies* for the Web services, executing the business rules and returning the result to the Client Web module. The elements of the repositories are created and managed by the IDE. Many proposals of business rules execution architectures consider the use of basic modules, such as rule engine that interacts with a Business Rule repository (Chisholm 2004). What is not well resolved in the most popular business rule engines is the combined execution of business rules and Web services, originated, for example, in the context of citizen's life events. In this proposal, the Service Executor encapsulates a *Rule Engine* and interacts with Business Rule Ontology. The Business Rule Ontology stores terms, facts and business rules of specific application domains or that makes sense for a user's community.

Business Rule and Service Ontology Integrated Development Environment

This section provides some details of the Business Rule and Service Ontology Integrated Development Environment. To facilitate this task, first it is introduced an e-Government scenario used to extract the requirements for the service modeling IDE and to clarify some concepts in the rest of this paper.

E-Government Scenario

This subsection presents an overview of the e-Government scenario used in the proof of concept for the proposed service development and execution model. This scenario is inserted in the context of a Brazilian e-Government applications environment, in the São Paulo State (eGOIA 2006), (Cardoso et. al 2004) and (Hoepner et. al 2005). To simplify it is considered only some services related to the civil identification community and the specific life event of a citizen that had his/her identification card (IdCard) lost or stolen.

When a citizen has his/her IdCard stolen or lost he/she will go to a government Web portal to access a Service named BO Registration to registry the incident. Actually, the citizen fill in an official form called BO (Bulletin of Occurrence) provided by a government back office system called BO System. Then, the IdCard Cancellation Service provided by another back office system called Civil Identification System is accomplished to avoid the improper use of the IdCard. After that, the IdCard Replacement Request Service provided by these two legacy systems plus a set of five complimentary legacy systems can be accomplished by the citizen to request for a new issue of the IdCard. The request for a new IdCard Replacement issue can also be done any time and almost for any reason, such as, for example, when people are getting older or when people may not be recognized because of the old document's photograph, or even due to name change by marriage or even signature change.

Although the IdCard Replacement Request Service is already offered to the population, it is not performed in an integrated and automated way as suggested in this work. The service was chosen because it presents a great variability of context data. This great variability of context data is due to the fact that the legacy systems that manipulate these data were built by different government's units, in different times and using different platforms and development languages (eGOIA 2006). For all these aspects, those legacy systems make available applications quite stabilized in terms of changes and, therefore, they are ideal to be wrapped as Web services.

IDE Requirements

The chosen scenario seems to be very rich to extract the necessary requirements for the proposed IDE. Thus, from that scenario can be derived the application domain, which is, in this case, the civil identification community application domain.

As in any community, the users of the civil identification community use a common terminology, sharing the same understanding about the words, procedures and activities that are part of their daily business routine.

Figure 3 gives an idea of how could be the external interface of the IDE. It should provide functionalities to define terms, facts, business rules and services using that community terminology. In this way, citizen, IdCard and BO are terms designating a concept, which ultimately represent object types; citizen lost IdCard and BO is registered are facts; It is obligatory that the IdCard is cancelled if citizen lost IdCard is a business rule; and IdCard Replacement Request is a Service name. All these elements are meaningful to that community and should be defined using the IDE.

When the business analyst defines terms, verbs, facts and rules they will be stored in the Business Rule Ontology according to the model represented in the Figure 5. When any rule is included in the Business Rule Ontology it is related to a rule set, which will be associated to a Service model stored in the Service Ontology. Details on the IDE requirements can be seen in (Kamada 2006).

THE IDE

The elements, terms, verbs, facts, rules and services should be precisely defined and structured in the repositories, so that the access is easy and consistent. Thus, the IDE is based on the use of ontologies to structure the services, considering the business rules contained in the Business Rules Ontology and the Web services published in the Registry mechanism.

The IDE provides an Editor to define and maintain the elements that compose the vocabularies, business rules and services. The associations between the process Editor class and the several classes that deal with the elements are displayed in Figure 4. The Editor includes the basic operations recommended by some design patterns to get, set, insert and remove the elements under its control.

The proposed editor bases on the use of templates associated to the different types of existent rules. The SBVR metamodel defines some types of rules, such as those that treat obligations, prohibitions and needs. The definition of a service includes the definition of several business rules. Taking advantage of Ross's ideas (Ross 2003) that propose the use of templates to facilitate the specification of business rules, this Editor provides a set of templates associated to the rule types defined in SBVR, as can be seen in the Template

Figure 3. Interface prototype for the business rule and service ontology editor

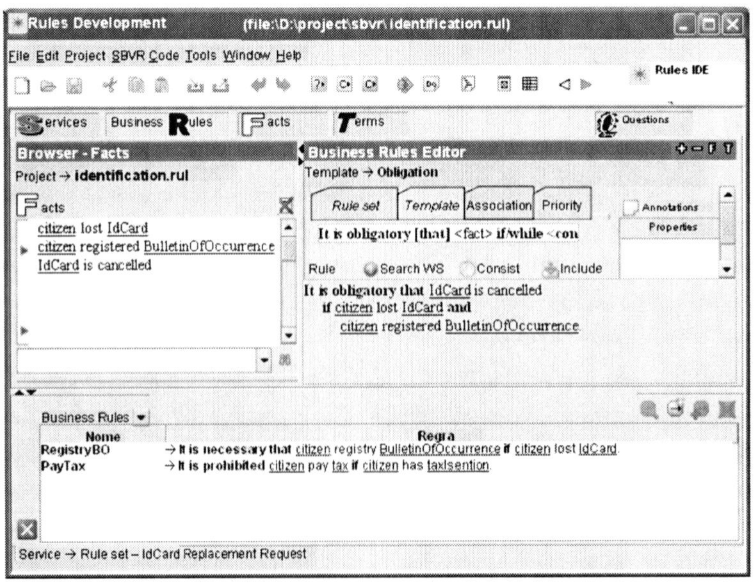

Figure 4. Business rule and service ontology editor classes diagram

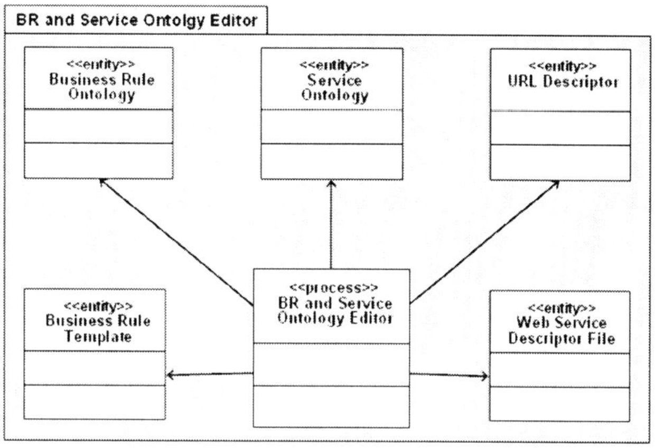

tab in Figure 3. In this way, for the modal type is obligatory that that treats of obligations the template has the following syntax: It is obligatory [that] <fact> [if/while <condition>]. Therefore, the IDE also includes an internal structure to store the templates and a set of operations for the template maintenance.

Although not always of immediate perception, some facts that define the type of the rule in fact represent actions, whose realizations are associated to the execution of part of the service. Thus, some <fact>s that compose the modal type It is obligatory that are translated in actions, that, once performed, they will have as result the assertion that the facts are true. This kind of action, in general, represents segments of the business logic quite stabilized, in the sense of little vulnerability to changes, so that the encapsulation of these ac-

Figure 5. Class diagram for business rule ontology

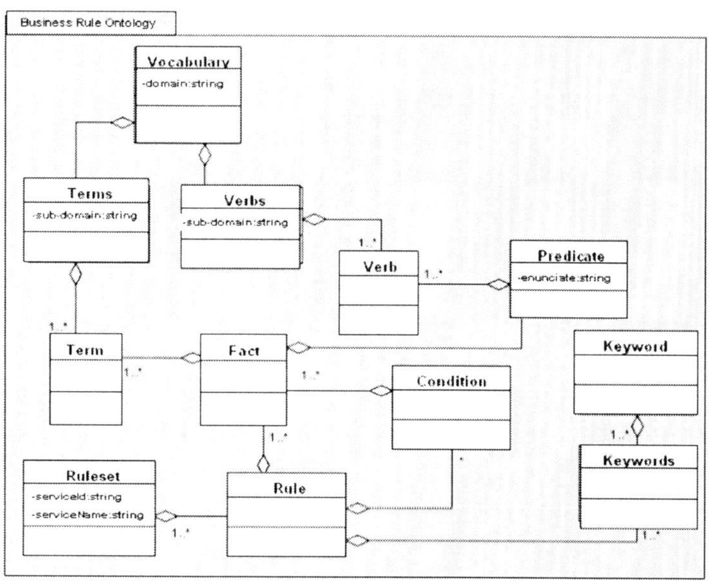

tions as Web services becomes quite interesting. In this sense, the actions itself or the names of the rules give indications of the need or not of a Web service to perform such action. Therefore, in the creation or edition time of a business rule the Editor searches the Registry for such a Web service and makes an early binding between the business rule and the Web service associated to the actions. The early binding is quite providential because it avoids the risk of, in the execution time, not to meet a certain Web service that would perform part of the service. In this instant, the Editor joins information of this early binding connection in the structure nominated Service Ontology, associated to the service. This Ontology is stored in the Ontology Repository so that, in the execution time the Executor, using the descriptions of the Web services, prepare the invocations.

The interaction between a civil identification business analyst and the Editor to define a rule could be as following.

- The business analyst selects in the IDE the community's vocabulary (File→Open - identification.rul) and the set of rules from which the rule will be part (Rule Set tab).
- The Editor gets the rule set from the Business Rule Ontology and the eventual rules already defined will appear in the inferior panel.
- The business analyst selects the wanted template.
- The Editor gets the template and presents it in a window of the Editor.
- When the business analyst points to a field of the template the Editor gets the list associated to the field. For instance, in the template It is obligatory [that] <fact> [if/while <condition>], pointing to <fact> or <condition> the list of facts related to the selected vocabulary is obtained from the Business Rule Ontology. Once the fact is chosen and pointing to one of their fields the list of terms that make sense in that context is obtained in the Business Rule Ontology.
- Some <facts> and <conditions> in order to become true assume that some actions have to be executed, which can be performed by a Web service. The business analyst selects Search WS and, with the words contained in a <fact> or <condition> the Editor searches for URL Descriptor in the Registry mechanism to discover if there is some Web service that performs the action.
- For each valid URL the Editor looks for the respective WSDL file.
- The Editor opens each WSDL file and obtains the key-elements, such as, the Web service URL and the operation names. These elements are inserted in the Service Ontology to which the rule in definition should be associated.
- When the business analyst selects Insert the Editor links the rule to the rule set that is being treated and insert it in the Business Rule Ontology.

The eventual terms and facts still not defined when creating a business rule will be included in the vocabulary, in the Business Rules Ontology.

Business Rule Ontology

The Business Rule Ontology instantiates a structure similar to Business Vocabulary+Rules, defined in SBVR (OMG 2008). Thus, it organizes the business terms, concepts and rules specified in the business terminology that make sense for a user community. It also organizes the relationships and the existing associations among these elements. To provide the ability in the definition of connections among concepts that are of the organization interest the repository maintains a semantic structure in the business terminology. Figure 5 displays the classes diagram for the Business Rules and Vocabulary Repository.

A vocabulary is composed of two fundamental groups of elements: terms and verbs. A term represents a concept about an object and, according to SBVR metamodel, also represents an instance, which for extension is a fact, that it is also a thing. Thus, terms are used to represent anything, any concept, or any significant fact for a business community. The verb is the fundamental element of a predicate and it is the base for the representation of facts.

On the other hand, a Rule set is a collection of business rules grouped together for some purpose, as defined in SBVR metamodel (OMG 2008). As the purpose could be the accomplishment of a service, then the rule set could be associated to a service, which would be represented in the Service Ontology. The business rules are composed by keywords, facts and conditions. The keywords are very useful in the model creation to formalize rules without ambiguities. A fact is a simple period and it is composed of one or more terms that can be associated to a predicate. Facts can be grouped in conditions. All these elements need to be properly organized in the repository so that the business rules are formalized referencing these elements consistently.

Considering the e-Government scenario and the IdCard Replacement Request Service the associated rule set contained in the Business Rules Ontology could be formalized as shown in Table 1. The rules definition is adherent to the SBVR metamodel.

Figure 6 presents an instance, included in the Business Rule Ontology, for the IdCard Cancellation rule model.

Service Ontology

The Service Ontology formalizes the relationships among names and terms and their respective meanings associated to the Web services. This formalization is explicit and specifics terms used to name the concepts, properties, and relationships, whose understandings are accepted and shared in the context of specific community's jargon. For instance, the services ontology for the finance community should formalize the names of the Web services as terms, and also the relationships among these names. Therefore, besides the terms as loan, interest rate, customer and credit history, there are also the names of the Web services that perform actions, such as, loan application, credit history verification and to customer registration that are fundamental to structure the Web services ontology for the finance domain. The class diagram for the Service Ontology formalizes these relationships as can be seen in Figure 7.

The Service Ontology structure takes into account that the realization of a Service demands the execution of a series of activities that are performed by different areas of an organization. These activities were automated in computational applications in different times and in different platforms and programming languages. With the current available technologies the encapsulation of these applications as Web services became an alternative with high demand in a lot of organizations. That tendency reinforces the need of new mechanisms to integrate these Web services to create new services according to new requirements. Considering this, the Service Ontology holds a set of properties of the ontology itself,

Table 1. Rule set to IdCard replacement request

Rule set 1 - Rules to IdCard Replacement Request
Rule 1.1 – **It is possible that the** citizen requests **an** IdCard replacement issue **if at least one of the following facts is true:**
• **the** citizen lost **his/her** IdCard **and the** citizen registered **a** BO **and the** IdCard is cancelled
• **the** citizen wants to change **his/her** photograph
• **the** citizen wants to change **his/her** name
• **the** citizen wants to change **his/her** signature
Rule 1.2 – **It is obligatory that the** IdCard is cancelled **if all these facts are true:**
• **the** citizen lost **the** IdCard **and**
• **the** citizen registered **a** BO
Rule 1.3 – **It is obligatory that the** citizen registers **a** BO **if at least one of the following facts is true:**
• **the** citizen lost **his/her** IdCard
• **the** citizen has **his/her** IdCard stolen

Figure 6. Model for IdCard cancellation rule

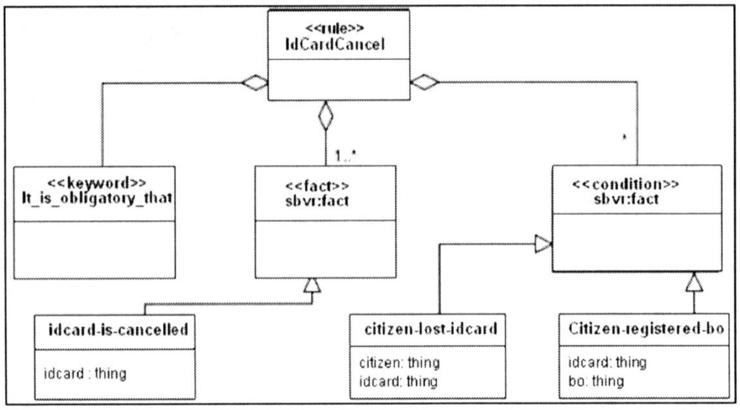

Service and Web services. Each Web service, for its turn, holds a set of operations with their respective parameters. Those relationships are fundamental elements in the Service Ontology because they represent the relationships among the terms that are, in this case, the names of the Web services. The instance of the Service Ontology for a specific Service is generated by the IDE.

The instances of these relationships representations for specific service ontology are generated through the IDE, in the services and business rules development time. Table 2 shows an OWL Service Ontology sample for the relationship between IdCard Replacement Request Service with its related Web services for BO Registration and IdCard Cancellation.

RELATED WORKS

This section discusses some works related to the business rules execution. All these works mention the absence of an appropriate treatment so that the Web services composition mechanisms work in a collaborative and integrated way with the business rules mechanisms. Hence, all of them confirm that, the technologies and existing standards for business computational systems development

Figure 7. Class diagram for service ontology

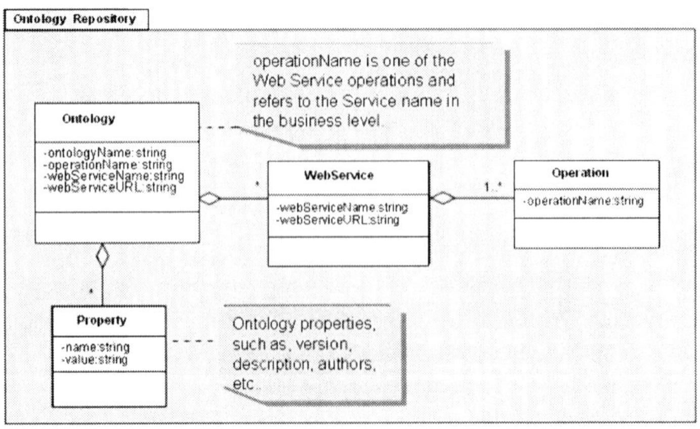

can not satisfy the demands to perform agile and dynamic businesses.

Charfi and Mezini propose the hybrid composition approach using business rules extracted from Web Services composition specifications described, for instance in BPEL. They discuss two technological alternatives to implement business rules in modularized units: one using Aspect Oriented Programming (AOP) concepts (Elrad et al., 2004) and the other using rules engines. The weakness of this alternative is that it presents a great open issue. This issue falls exactly in the most important aspect of the proposal: the integration of rules and processes. The authors alert to the fact that the simplicity of the user's point of view is accompanied by a larger complexity in the underlying orchestration engine.

Orriens and Yang proposed a framework, called BCDF (Business Collaboration Development Framework) that increases the flexibility and adaptability of computational systems, where business rules are used to drive and to restrict collaborations among business processes. This proposal, although it still doesn't have a complete implementation, it presents a sophisticated development model. An aspect that deserves improvements is the one that refers to its low usability in the definition of rules, which should be described in RuleML (RuleML, 2006), which is very far from the terminology used by the business analysts. It means that, in this proposal, the reduction or elimination of the semantic gap among the business people and software engineers' languages was not taken into account.

Table 2. Sample of service ontology in OWL

```
<owl:Class rdf:ID=IdCardReplacementRequest>
          <rdfs:comment>IdCard replacement request</rdfs:comment>
          <rdfs:subClassOf rdf:resource=#service/>
</owl:Class>
<owl:DatatypeProperty rdf:ID=ServiceId>
<owl:equivalentProperty rdf:resource=#WebServiceId/>
<rdfs:domain rdf:resource=#service/>
<rdfs:range rdf:resource=http://www.w3.org/2001/XMLSchema#string/>
</owl:DatatypeProperty>
<owl:Class rdf:ID=BORegistration>
          <rdfs:comment> Web Service to registry BO (Bulletin of Occurrence) in case of
citizen has IdCard stolen or lost.</rdfs:comment>
          <rdfs:subClassOf rdf:resource=#service/>
          <rdfs:subClassOf>
                    <owl:Restriction>
                              <owl:onProperty rdf:resource=#isPartOf/>
                              <ow:allValuesFrom rdf:resource=#IdCardReplacementRequest/>
                    </owl:Restriction>
          </rdfs:subClassOf>
          </owl:Class>
<owl:Class rdf
<owl:Class rdf:ID=IdCardCancellation>
          <rdfs:comment> Web Service to cancel IdCard in case of citizen has IdCard stolen
or lost.</rdfs:comment>
          <rdfs:subClassOf rdf:resource=#service/>
          <rdfs:subClassOf>
                    <owl:Restriction>
                              <owl:onProperty rdf:resource=#isPartOf/>
                              <ow:allValuesFrom rdf:resource=# IdCardReplacementRequest/>
                    </owl:Restriction>
          </rdfs:subClassOf>
          </owl:Class>
<owl:Class rdf
...
```

Recently two big players in commercial BPMS and Application Servers acquired other companies and third party products to extend their BPMS offering with full blown BRMS capabilities. Now IBM owns ILOG JRules (ILOG, 2009) and Oracle owns Oracle WebLogic Server (Oracle, 2009) and Haley. As ILOG JRules 6 is considered one of the most complete BRMS (Bloor Research, 2006) some of its characteristics are analyzed. JRules 6 allows the use of the complete object model and XML Schemas. Thus, Java objects and XML are combined in the Business Object Model (BOM). Based on BOM models, the objects and their methods are translated into fragments of natural language. In this way, for instance, the Customer object can be associated to the fragment customer and the method *getAge* can be associated to the fragment the age of. Considering this abstraction level, the following rule can be built using these elements in natural language: If <u>the age of customer</u> is greater than *18* AND... Then..., where, text in bold is used to show key elements of JRules 6 builder, <u>underlined text</u> is used to show the translation of BOM objects, and *text in italic* is used to show the user's input for JRules 6 builder. The advantages of this product are that it is already in a well stabilized version, it is based on the JSR 94 standard (Java Community Process, 2006), and it accepts rules described in natural language. The drawback is that, although the rules are described in natural language and the methods associated to the fragments can be operations of Web services, the associations need to be performed by software engineers. This happens because the business analysts don't have enough knowledge to perform the associations of terms and predicates with the respective objects and methods. Therefore, also in that product, the reduction or elimination of the semantic gap among business people and software engineers' languages is not possible.

CONCLUSION AND FUTURE RESEARCHES

The increasing demand for new services conducts to the need to create services from scratch and by integrating disparate and heterogeneous legacy systems. The problem is that the form as most of the systems were implemented makes the change excessively slow and expensive. This work proposes an IDE for modeling of business rules and service integration that can quickly implement the changes demanded in the organizations in the computational systems.

The premise of the work is that the use of the business rules technology combined with the emerging technologies derived from multiple research areas provides an alternative solution much more flexible and promising than the traditional approaches for application development and execution. By externalizing the knowledge of the business that are spread out in the business documents and procedures, the business rules supply a solution possibility for the development of applications that need to be modified quickly. However, the existent rule mechanisms still cannot capture the rules in the business terminology and transform them in executable code without the software engineers' help.

The paper proposes an IDE consisted of a set of tools to automate the modeling of business rules in the business people's terminology and integration of services. The IDE is based on a set of ontologies to manage metadata of services, vocabularies and business rules, guaranteeing the necessary support in terms of semantics, persistence and integrity for the manipulated artifacts.

The proposed services and business rules IDE makes innovative contributions compared to other initiatives in business rules. The IDE (1) helps business analysts in the definition of rules, using a language familiar to them, in other words, using the terms with which they accomplish their businesses; (2) can capture the rules, using templates, and express them in computation independent models (CIM); (3) helps business analysts in the definition of terms and typical predicates that compose the community's vocabulary, where the terms and predicates will be the base for the facts definition; (4) renders the individualization and externalization of dynamic portions of the application logic as business rules; (5) makes possible to link the business rules with related Web services, in the instant of creation of the rule, excluding the need of the software engineer's intervention to do the connection.

The results indicate that the concepts, ideas and proposed platforms for the business rules development model are promising. Besides business rules technologies, services (SOA), repositories and ontologies, it seems that the complete solution for the mentioned problems includes the research to integrate other technologies, such as, model transformation, automatic program generation and compilation. Following are the list of topics that deserve future researches:

- Inclusion of a mechanism in the IDE to contemplate process composition modeling using, for instance, languages such as BPMN and that could make transformation to executable languages like WS-BPEL.
- Inclusion of a mechanism in the IDE to facilitate the process of identification and formalization of business contracts related to business services.
- Proposition of a mechanism to help the business analyst to link business rule actions to Web services. May be considered Web 2.0 application facilities, such as recommendation system linked to trust, preference and rated content to create highly trusted environment for business analyst to decide which Web service is the most adequate in a specific rule action.
- Development of a proof of concept implementing the IDE, including the repository instances for Service Ontology and Business Rule Ontology, adherent to the MOF metamodel, with standardized query and manipulation language.

REFERENCES

W3C (2004) *Web Services Architecture*, Working Group Note 11. Retrieved April 2009, from http://www.w3.org/TR/ws-arch/

Barry, D. K. (2003). *Web Services and Service-Oriented Architectures: The Savvy Manager's Guide*. San Francisco: Morgan Kaufmann.

Bloor Research. (2006). *ILOG Jrules 6.0, Analysts Rave About JRules6! White Paper.* Retrieved April 2009, from http://www.ilog.com/products/jrules/whitepapers/index.cfm

BRG. (2003). *The Business Rules Manifesto*. Retrieved April 2009, from http://www.business-rulesgroup.org/brmanifesto.htm

BRG. (2009). *Business Rules Group*. Retrieved April 2009, from http://www.businessrulesgroup.org/home-brg.shtml

Cardoso, J., Mendes, M., Figueiredo, A., Kamada, A., Monte, R., Hoepner, P., & Bolliger, S. (2004) *Implementing Electronic Government: The eGOIA Project*. In: 3o. EU-LAT Workshop on e-Government and e-Democracy, Santiago do Chile, Chile.

Charfi, A., & Mezini, M. (2004). *Hybrid Web Service Composition: Business Processes Meet Business Rules*. New York: ICSOC'04.

Chisholm, M. (2004). *How to Build a Business Rules Engine - Extending Application Functionality through Metadata Engineering*. New York: Elsevier Inc.

Cuecent. (2008). *Standard based Framework*, Cuecent BPMS. Retrieved April 2000, from http://www.bahwancybertek.com/cuecentBpms.html

Dhillon, G., & Hackney, R. (2000) IS/IT and dynamic business change. In *Proceedings of the 33rdAnnual* HICSS, Maui, Hawaii. eGOIA (2006) Electronic Government Innovation and Access. Retrieved April 2000, from http://www.egoia.sp.gov.br/portugues/project.htm

Elrad, T., Aksit, M., Clarke, S., & Filman, R. E. (2004). *Introduction to Aspect-Oriented Software Development*. Reading, MA: Addison Wesley Professional.

Fair Isaac. (2007b). Enterprise Software for Business Rules Management, Fair Isaac Corp. Retrieved March 2007, from http://www.fairisaac.com/fic/en/product-service/product-index/blaze-advisor/blaze-advisor.htm

Fair Isaac Corp. (2007). *Achieving Decision Consistency Across the SOA-based Enterprise: Using Business Rules Management Systems in an SOA*, White Paper. Retrieved April 2009, from http://researchlibrary.theserverside.net/detail/RES/1129644089_373.html

Friedman-Hill, E. (2003). *Jess in Action*. Greenwich, CT: Manning Publication Co.

Geminiuc, K. (2006). *A Services-Oriented Approach to Business Rules Development, SOA Best Practices: The BPEL Cookbook*. Oracle Technology Network.

Halle, B. V. (2001). *Business Rules Applied* (1st ed.). New York: Wiley.

He. H. (2003) What is Service-Oriented Architecture?. *O'Reilly WebServices.XML.com.*

Hildreth, S. (2005). *Rounding Up Business Rules*. ComputerWorld Software. IDG.

Hoepner, P., Agune, R., & Mendes, M. (2005). (eGOIA)), A joint Latin American and European Project. In *IV Fórum Global de Combate à Corrupção (IV FG)*. Brasília, Brazil: Electronic Government Innovation and Access.

ILOG. (2007). *Deploying Rule Applications with ILOG Jrules*, White Paper. Retrieved April 2009, from http://www.ilog.com/products/jrules/whitepapers/index.cfm?filename=WP-JRules-6Deployment.pdf

ILOG. (2009). *ILOG Business Rule Management Systems*. Retrieved April 2009, from http://www.ilog.com/products/businessrules/

Java community Process (2006). *JSR-94 Java Rule Engine API*. Retrieved April 2009, from http://jcp.org/en/jsr/detail?id=94

Kamada, A. (2006) *Service Execution based on Business Rules*, PhD Thesis in Computing Engineering, Unicamp, Campinas, Brazil.

Kamada, A., & Mendes, M. (2007). *Web Services Composition based on Business Rules*. Cambridge, MA: IASTED/SEA Software Engineering and Applications.

Mahmoud, Q. H. (2005, April) Service-Oriented Architecture (SOA) and Web Services: The Road to Enterprise Application Integration (EAI), SDN - Sun Developer Network. Retrieved from http://java.sun.com/developer/technicalArticles/WebServices/soa/

Nagl, C., Rosenberg, F., & Dustdar, S. (2006) ViDRE–A Distributed Service-Oriented Business Rule Engine based on RuleML. In*Proceedings of the 10th IEEE International Enterprise Distributed Object Computing Conference*. Hong Kong.

OMG. (2003) *MDA Guide Version 1.0.1*. Retrieved April 2009 from http://www.omg.org/docs/omg/03-06-01.pdf

OMG. (2005) *MOF 2.0/XMI Mapping Specification, v2.1.1*. Retrieved April 2009, from http://www.omg.org/docs/formal/05-09-01.pdf

OMG. (2008) Semantics of Business Vocabulary and Business Rules (SBVR), v1.0 *OMG Available Specification*. Retreived April 2009, from http://www.omg.org/docs/formal/08-01-02.pdf

Oracle (2009) *Oracle WebLogic Server*. Retrieved April 2009, from http://www.oracle.com/technology/products/weblogic/index.html

Orriens, B., & Yang, J. (2006). *Specification and Management of Policies in Service Oriented Business Collaboration*. The Netherlands: Tilburg University

Ross, R. G. (2003). *Principles of Business Rule Approach*. Reading, MA: Addison-Wesley.

Rule, M. L. (2006) *The Rule Markup Initiative*. Retrieved April 2009, from http://www.ruleml.org/

Schmidt, R. (2002). *Web Services Based Execution of Business Rules*, RuleML 2002 - International Workshop on Rule Markup Languages for Business Rules on the Semantic Web. Sardinia, Italy.

Wu, L., Meng, X., & Liu, S. (2007). *Service-oriented encapsulation of manufacturing resources*, IEEE International Conference on Services Computing (SCC 2007).

Chapter 17
Electronic Commerce in the Arab World

Robert Jeyakumar Nathan
Multimedia University, Malaysia

Mohammed Saeed Ahmed
Multimedia University, Malaysia

ABSTRACT

This chapter presents a literature discussion and empirical research that examines the factors that affect Electronic Commerce (EC) adoption in the Arab countries. The five countries that are represented in this research include Saudi Arabia, Qatar, Kuwait, United Arab Emirates and Yemen. The purpose of this research is analyzing the crucial factors affecting EC adoption among the Arab consumers. The chapter presents the effect of risk perception, trust and consumer knowledge on their EC adoption. It also highlights consumer's knowledge mediation in affecting their perception of risk and trust towards EC adoption. Upon filtration, three hundred samples were selected for data analysis. Descriptive and inferential statistical analyses including statistical mediation technique were carried out to analyse the data. Results reveal knowledge as the most important factor that contributes to EC adoption and it mediates consumers' perception of risk and trust in contributing to their EC adoption. The preliminary findings of this research was presented in the International Arab Conference of E-Technology held in Amman, Jordan from 14th to 16th October 2008 and subsequently published in the first issue of the International Arab Journal of E-Technology. This chapter presents the complete research with further data analysis, extended reports and discussions on issues relating to EC adoption.

INTRODUCTION

The advancement and convergence of telecommunications and computer technology has created the possibility of conducting businesses over the Internet, known as the Electronic Commerce (EC). In the recent years, Internet usage has grown tremendously in countries around the world including in the Arab Countries [Amin, H. (2000)] [ElShenawi, N. (2001)][Gray, V. (2001)]. The Internet popularity has grown at a phenomenal rate

DOI: 10.4018/978-1-61520-789-3.ch017

as it changed from its initial purpose as a defense tool, now to commercial applications.

The Arab countries represent a large part of the geographical world and capture a major share in the global economic pie. These countries tend to be economically more inclined towards service-based industries. There is much that the Arab countries could achieve if they could tap into the business possibilities of using the Internet. In reality, they are yet to experience the optimum benefit of adopting the Internet technologies.

The recent Arab Council for Judicial and Legal Studies (ACJLS) was held in Manama, Bahrain, on September 11-12, 2007. The workshop examined current trends and best practices in EC and the Challenges with Technology & the Law, EC and the Methods of Contracting and Transactions Online, Electronic Contracting, and a conclusive discussion on the regional perspectives and challenges in adoption EC. Over seventy senior legal professionals including from Ministry of Justice officials, judges and other judicial leaders, attorneys and academics from 11 countries in the Middle East and North Africa attended the workshop. Additionally, the Arab Advisors Group conducted a research analysis during the second half of 2007. The research focused on EC expenditure in Kuwait, Saudi Arabia, the UAE, and Lebanon. As a result, the research observed that total number of EC users in these four countries has exceeded 5.1 million people in 2007. The council also highlighted that the Arab countries are in general still lagging behind due to the lack of national information infrastructure, national information networks and advanced computer technology. Internet penetration in the Middle East stands at 17.4% while the rest of the world is 20.1% [Devlin, J.] [Internet World Statistics (2008)].

Various factors contribute to the lag of Internet and EC adoption in the Arab countries; one of it is the late introduction of the Internet in this region. When the Internet phenomenon was spreading like wild fire across the globe, the initial reaction of the Arab countries in adopting it was rather skeptical. Computer technologies crept in slowly into the Arab countries and Internet penetration happened at a much slower pace during the introduction years in these countries as compared to the developed countries of the West.

In countries such as Yemen and Iraq, there are still restrictions on hard currency transfers and consumers will find it difficult to make an online transaction and make payments online. One research conducted in the UAE suggests that the slow acceptance of EC is due to consumers' lack of knowledge about the advantages of using the Internet and their view of it as a Western product propagating Western values and cultures [Shaheen Al-hosni, 2000]. The Arab nationals, particular the respondents who participated in the said research viewed Internet and computer technologies as a western propaganda and are against the tenets of the Arab culture.

Internet usage in the Arab countries was considered important only in the mid 1980s. Most consumers do not surf Internet from home, instead they go to Internet cafes. As a result, they do not spend much time online. Most users use the Internet connections to make cheap long-distance phone calls as well as chatting. The majority of the Internet users here are concentrated in the Gulf countries (UAE, Saudi Arabia, Oman, Bahrain, Kuwait and Qatar), countries whose population does not exceed 11 percent of the whole region's total population. In addition, consumers in the Gulf region enjoy the possibility of completing transactions directly by using credit cards or other methods of payment. In other countries such as Yemen and Iraq, there are still restrictions on hard currency transfers, and consumers will find it difficult to complete transactions and effectuate payments online without these services.

Most studies on EC have often focused predominantly on Western countries although the Internet and EC it is perceived as global phenomenon. EC also impacts developing countries and the Internet penetration in these countries are on a steep curve. Studies indicate that EC adoption depends heavily on how it is used by the adopters and this in turn is influenced by the fit between the technology and the adopters [Unhelkar, B., 2003]. Most developing country markets have not always been successful in adopting technologies, hence studies that will unveil the reasons for the lack of acceptance and adoption in much needed. Researchers and practitioners also agree that there are still uncertainties in the significance of EC among consumers in developing countries hence its benefits for these countries are not fully realized [Mahmoud M., 2007]. There are more studies needed to examine consumer perception and EC adoption in the Arab countries as it seems to be neglected in the mainstream studies of EC adoption across the world.

Researchers and practitioners should not be caught off guard not examining and taking advantage of the Internet and EC phenomenon happening in the Arab countries. Consumers in the Arab countries are now jumping onto the wagon of Internet and EC. More and more people are now subscribing to the Internet and are becoming computer and Internet savvy. In complement, the latest statistics show a huge growth of the Internet usage in Arab countries. As of March 2008, there are an estimated 42 million Internet users in the Arab countries. These countries are experiencing a phenomenal growth of Internet usage in the last 8 years with 1176.8% growth compared to the world average growth of 281.8% for the last 8 years [Internet World Statistics, 2008]. The increase in the number of local Internet Service Providers (ISP) has increased consumer demands and the usage of Internet services. More and more users are now starting to surf the web from home instead of having to visit Internet cafes. In addition, the development and production of Arabic language-based Web browsers and software are further boosting the Internet penetration in the region. Hence it is strongly believed that the consumers in this region are highly promising and will play an important and significant role in the use and development of the EC in the years to come.

ELECTRONIC COMMERCE ADOPTION FACTORS

The Arab countries find various similarities including religion, customs and values, history, and language. However, they differ mainly in terms of wealth and size. Among the Arab countries, Tunisia was the first to introduce the Internet in the country in 1991. Four years later, in August 1995, the UAE went online as well as some other countries such as Bahrain, Oman and Qatar. The UAE is doing exceptionally well in adopting the online technologies as a whole. With phones available to almost every person in the country and an estimated number of Internet users per 1,000 people that exceeds the same metric in the UK; United Arab Emirates has the potential to be among the leaders in the world on Internet preparedness. Latest technological initiatives and conventions often take place in UAE, and especially Dubai, the playground of the first Arab Internet city and electronic government. This is partly due to:

- Leadership with a clear modernization of vision;
- Sufficient financial resources; and
- Attractive place to work for highly skilled expatriates from South Asia, Western Europe, and the USA.

Though UAE is leading in its Internet preparedness, it is not the case with the rest of its neighbouring countries. It has been opined that the slow acceptance of the Arab people to the EC was due to the lack of knowledge about the relative advantage of Internet and their view of it as a Western product propagating Western Values and cultures. Knowledge about EC is important since it helps in using it strategically. The lack of knowledge in the use of computers, Internet and

EC, are major problems hindering the use of IT among the Arab country consumers. Through the years, people in these countries have preferred face-to-face interactions over other modalities of doing business, purchasing products and communicating with each other. Familiarity with English language is also found to be essential for using the Internet as most websites are constructed in the English medium. This language barrier for most consumers coupled with shortage of Arabic software further contributes to the reluctance of consumers to use the Internet and surf websites.

Prior experience of using the Internet is an important factor that affects users' decision making in using EC for Online purchasing, as it can shape individuals' beliefs on the perceived usefulness and the ease of use of EC [Salam, A., 2005]. Consumers' knowledge of EC helps them in conducting information search through the Internet [Shim, S., 2001][Song, C-S. & Shin, J-C., 1999]. Studies also have found that knowledge and skills gained through experience of using the Internet and computer helps to reduce consumers' perceived risk in Online shopping [Salam, A., 2005][Shaheen Al-hosni, 2000]. An author contended that the higher a consumer's Internet usage skill, information search performance, and search proficiency is, the higher will be his or her inclination to using the Internet to conduct Online transactions [Han, S-R., 1996].

On the other hand, the Arabic culture is high on group and family collectivism and power distance, and low on future orientation. It is a high-context culture where personal relationships and the context of the communication process are more important than the content of the communicated message. Oral communication is preferred over written communication. Thus, face-to-face communication, or even a telephone call is valued more than e-mail or fax-based communication.

Trust in the Arab culture is established through an elaborate social process [Odedra Straub, M., 2003]. For Business-to-Business or Business-to-Consumer to work, trust must be established not only between the parties, but also among the parties and the technologies used. As the Internet continues to grow in popularity as a place for business transactions, the issues of trust and credibility are brought to the forefront [Corbitt, B.J., 2003][Tan, S. J., 1999]. As the Internet continues to grow in popularity as a place to transact business, the issues of trust and credibility are brought to the forefront. Consumers want to know that they are receiving the exact item they have purchased. They also want the security of knowing that their credit card numbers and other personal information are safe and will not be used by unauthorized people.

Risk refers to a lack of predictability about the outcome of a problem, or to a lack of predictability about the consequences of a decision [Hertz, D, 1984]. Since users are concerned about the risk of using the Internet to purchase a particular product, they prefer to visit the stores and pay cash as the payment method of choice rather than using the Internet to complete the transaction. Concerns over risk, security and fear of technology exacerbate the situation.

EC carries a strong business and socioeconomic implications for the Arab countries and its firms, while opening many new opportunities to access the global markets. Most Arab countries have already started to overcome their computer shortages through computer education programs in universities, schools and other institutions of learning in order to encourage Internet and web-based education.

RESEARCH OBJECTIVE

The objective of this research chapter is to examine factors that influence EC adoption among consumers in the Arab countries. Based on the literature review scrutiny, three factors were determined for further research in relation to the Arab countries consumers i.e. Knowledge, Risk Perception and Trust. The objective of the research is divided into four specific objectives as below; from section 3.1 through 3.4. Hypothesis is formulated for each research objective and included at the end of every objective listed below.

To Investigate the Association Between Arab Consumers' EC Knowledge and Their EC Adoption

Consumer's knowledge refers to the level of knowledge the consumer have in terms of the Internet and EC. It is believed that consumers with different levels of knowledge in Internet and EC will have varying acceptance and adoption rate of the EC. The unique nature of Internet environment is relevant to the acceptance of EC and the intention of consumers to purchase [Ratchford, B. T., 2001]. Studies show that prior purchasing experiences are positively related to purchase intentions in EC [So, W.C.M., 2005][Sohn, Y-S., 1999]. Knowledge is defined in this research as consumers' aggregate skills and understanding of the Internet and EC system. EC Adoption is defined in this research as the willingness of consumers to use or participate in EC transactions. To this extent, a hypothesis is formed as below to test consumer's knowledge and their EC adoption.

H1: There is a significant relationship between consumer's Knowledge and EC adoption

To Investigate the Association Between Arab Consumers' Risk Perception and Their EC Adoption

Perceived risk can be defined as the uncertainty in the purchase environment where consumers may consider the purchase outcomes and the importance or serious results associated with making a wrong or unsuitable decision [Hunter, 2004]. EC, unlike traditional commerce involves various risks (product performance, delivery, credit card information, etc.) that consumers perceive as risky for an Online transaction [Salisbury, W., 2001][Tan, S. J.,1999)][Vijayasarathy, L.R., 2000]. Perceived risk has been found associated with the frequency of EC use [Forsythe, S., 2003] [Liebermann, Y., 2002]. Perceived Risk is defined in this research as users' risk estimate of the Internet and Online transactions. The hypothesis to test this relationship is formulated as below.

H2: There is a significant relationship between consumer's Risk Perception and EC Adoption.

To Investigate the Association Between Arab Consumers' Trust and Their EC Adoption

Trust is an important element affecting consumer behavior. Review of literatures stress that consumer trust is a very important element in a successful Web-based business. Lack of trust is likely to discourage online consumers from participating in EC [Lee, H.Y.,2006]. Furthermore, it is realized that among the important elements of consumer EC trust is institutional trust which refers to the consumers' perceptions about the Internet environment; such as safety and security, legal and technical protection and trustworthiness of third party service providers which includes credit card payment facilities, banks, etc. [Cheung,2006]. Several empirical studies have theorized consumer trust in EC leading to their intention to participate in EC [Lee, M.K.O. & Turban, E. 2001][McKnight, H.D,2002][Tan, F.B. & Sutherland, P.,2004][Tan, Y.-H.,2001]. Trust in this research is defined as consumers' level of security and safety confidence in the Internet and in using an EC system. To this extent, a hypothesis is formed as below to test the relationship of trust towards consumer's EC adoption.

H3: There is a significant relationship between consumer's Trust and their EC Adoption.

To Analyze The Mediation of Knowledge In Mediating Consumers' Risk Perception and Trust In Affecting EC Adoption

Mediation occurs when the effect of one variable on another variable occurs via a third intervening (mediating) variable. According to Kenny and colleagues [Baron, R., & Kenny, D.,1986] [Judd, C.,1981], mediation effects occur if the three conditions below are met:

i) The independent variable significantly predicts the dependent variable;
ii) The independent variable significantly predicts the intervening variable (mediator); and
iii) When the dependent variable is regressed on both the intervening (mediator) and the independent variable, the intervening variable (mediator) significantly predicts the dependent variable, while the predictive utility of the independent variable is reduced.

The conditions above can be summarized as below:

1. If the mediator is not significant in this regression, then there is no mediation effect.
2. If the mediator and the independent variable are significant in this regression, then there is partial mediation.
3. If the mediator is significant but the independent variable is not significant in this regression, then there is full mediation.

According to Kenny et al. only Condition 2 and Condition 3 are essential for demonstrating mediation effects [Kenny, D,1998]. This research hence would like to find out if there is any mediating effect of Knowledge in EC Adoption. If there is a mediation effect, the research would seek to discover if it is a full or partial mediation effect.

H4: Consumers' Knowledge mediates their Risk Perception and Trust in affecting EC Adoption.

METHODOLOGY

Research Variables and Conceptual Framework

The dependent variable in this research is EC Adoption; the intervening variable (mediator) is Knowledge; while the independent variables are Risk Perception and Trust; as reflected in Figure 1.

Research Instrument

A questionnaire was designed, tested and deployed to collect the data for this research. The questionnaire consists of 2 sections.

Section 1 contains the demographic information of the respondents. The information required covered age, gender, nationality, income level and levels of education attained.

Section 2 measures the independent and dependent variables in the research. This includes Knowledge, Risk Perception, Trust and EC Adoption. A five-point Likert scale (strongly disagree to strongly agree) was used to measure several items measuring each of the variables.

Sampling and Filtering

Due to the difficulty in data collection in the Arab countries, purposive sampling method, i.e. Snowball Sampling was used to aid data collection. The authors circulated the questionnaire among known respondents in the Arab countries including Saudi

Figure 1. Research conceptual framework

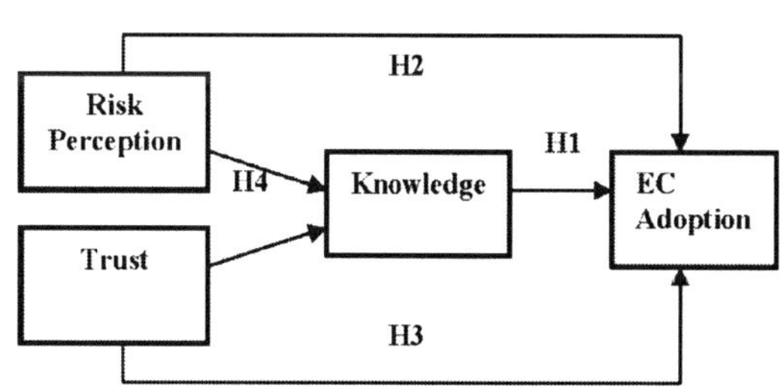

Arabia, Kuwait, United Arab Emirates, Qatar, Yemen and others. The contacted respondents then recommended their friends and relatives to participate in the research by forwarding a soft-copy of the questionnaire to their friends. The cycle went on until more than 300 samples were collected. All the collected samples were then transcribed into the Statistical Package for Social Sciences (SPSS) Version 12 for data analysis. The final collected data is further filtered to achieve a high quality and consistent data. Respondents who did not complete the survey were removed from the final data.

RESULT AND DISCUSSION

Descriptive Statistics

Table 1 shows that male respondents represent 63.7% (191 respondents) while female respondents represent 36.3% (109 respondents) in this research. There is an obvious difficulty in reaching to female respondents to participate in studies such as this in the Arab countries. This difficulty is attributed to the cultural and religious barriers, whereby a person (stranger) is not supposed to casually approach or speak with women. The authors faced this difficulty during data collection especially in Saudi Arabia and Yemen, it was however less apparent in Oman and Qatar. To facilitate the data collection, most female respondents in this research have been selected from schools, universities, organizations and government agencies through the help of friends and relatives. Using the snowball sampling, respondents were introducing other respondents to the research upon participating in the survey.

From Table 1, 24.7 percent of the total respondent is from Yemen, followed by 24 percent are from Saudi Arabia. This is justified as these two countries have the largest population in the region compared with the other countries in this research. However, respondents from Kuwait, Qatar, and

Table 1. Respondents' gender and nationality

		Gender		
		Male	Female	Total
Nationality	Kuwait	26	21	47
	Saudi Arabia	48	24	72
	Qatar	31	16	47
	Yemen	54	20	74
	UAE	25	21	46
	Others	7	7	14
Total		191 (63.7%)	109 (36.3)	300 (100%)

the UAE were quite similarly represented with percentages that range between 15 to 16 percent. Other respondents (4.7 percent) who participated in this survey are from other Arab countries in the region including Oman, Egypt and etc. Figure 2 depicts the diagrammatic distribution of respondents (male and female) from various Arab countries who participated in this research.

Table 2 shows that 53.7 percent of the respondents participated in the survey use the Internet on a daily basis. Most of these users come from the Arab Gulf area. This can be attributed to the high living standards in these countries that have enabled the citizens to take advantage of technological progress and the digital revolution at low prices.

The cross-tabulation above between gender and highest level of education achieved (Table 3) shows that male and female respondents are somewhat equally represented in this research. Also, a Chi-Square test for the above yield a Chi-Statistics of 1.657 with a p-value 0.798 (not significant at 5% significance level). The analysis reveals that male and female respondents have no statistical difference in their education levels obtained.

Further to the findings in Table 3 above, this analysis in Table 4 also shows a somewhat equal distribution between male and female in relation to their online purchasing habits. Both genders

Figure 2. Nationality of respondents participated in the research

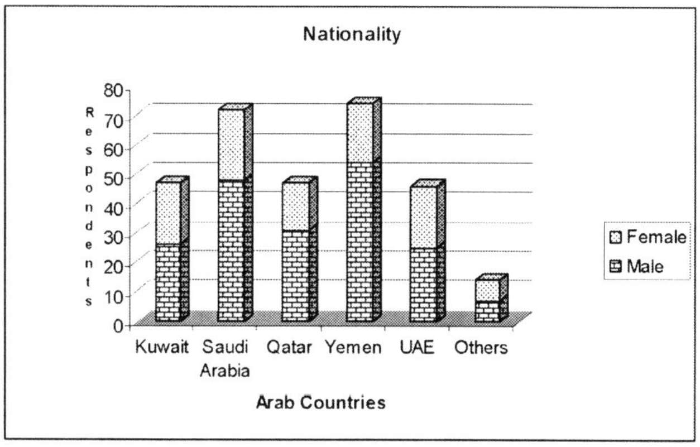

Table 2. Internet usage rate

	Frequency	%	Cumulative %
Daily	161	53.7	53.7
Several times a week	96	32.0	85.7
Weekly	26	8.7	94.3
Bi-weekly	2	.7	95.0
Monthly	12	4.0	99.0
Hardly at all	3	1.0	100.0
Total	300	100.0	

Table 3. Cross-tabulation between gender and highest education achieved

		Gender		
		Male	Female	Total
Highest education	College	31	15	46
	Bachelor	96	58	154
	Masters	50	28	78
	PHD	12	8	20
	Others	2	0	2
Total		191	109	300

Table 4. Cross-tabulation between gender and online purchase behaviour

		Do you purchase Online?		
		YES	NO	Total
Gender	Male	51 (26.6%)	140 (77.3%)	191 (100%)
	Female	37 (33.9%)	72 (66.1%)	109 (100%)
Total		88	212	300

seem to be not far apart in their online purchasing habits. A Chi-Square test yields a Chi-Statistics of 1.756 with a p-value = 0.185 (not significant at 5% significance level). This shows that the respondents' gender do have any significant effect on their online purchase behaviour.

The cross-tabulation result above (Table 5) between hours spent online and users' intention to purchase online shows an apparent trend. It seems to indicate a positive association between hours spent online per day and likelihood to make an online purchase. A Chi-Square analysis for this data yield a Chi-Statistics of 35.230 with a p-value that is less than 0.001 (significant at 5% significant level). This analysis proves the association between hours spent online per day and user's intention to make online purchases. Users who have spent more hours online per day have a higher tendency to make purchases online.

Further analysis was done to see if there's any gender effect on time spent online. Figure 3 displays a diagrammatic representation of the re-

Table 5. Cross-tabulation between hours spent online and intention to purchase online

		Hours Spent Online Per Day				Total
		Less than 1 hour	1-4 hours	5-8 hours	More than 8 hours	
Intention to Purchase	Least Likely	16	15	3	6	40
Online	Not Likely	29	48	25	10	112
	Neutral	14	26	22	5	67
	Likely	3	33	27	11	74
	Most Likely	1	1	4	1	7
Total		63	123	81	33	300

spondents participated in this research and the hours they spend online.

The cross-tabulation result above (Table 6) between gender of respondents and hours spent online shows a somewhat equal distributed of the genders in the hours spent category. To confirm if there's a gender effect on hours spent online, a Chi-Square analysis was carried out. The result yield a Chi-Statistics of 5.773 with a p-value of 0.123 (not significant at 5% significant level). Arab consumers' gender to not seem to affect the time they spend online in using the Internet.

Reliability Analysis

The reliability analysis was carried out for each independent and dependent variable in the research.

Consumer Knowledge

Consumer knowledge and its contribution to EC was measured through 5 questions as found in Table 7. Reliability analysis conducted to the variables shows high Cronbach's Alpha reliability score. A Cronbach's alpha score of 0.70 or higher is satisfactory to ensure reliability of tested items [Stewart, K. A.,2002].

Risk Perception

Consumer risk perception and its contribution to EC was measured through 5 questions as found in Table 8. The result show that the variable (Risk Perception) measured in this research is reliable for data analysis.

Figure 3. Gender of respondents and hours spent online

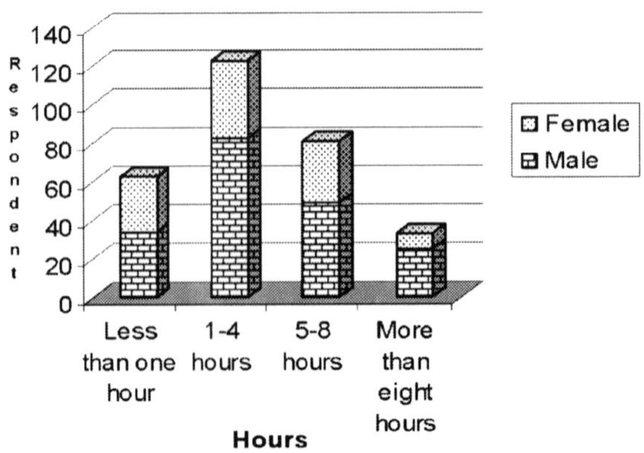

Table 6. Cross-tabulation between respondents' gender and hours spent online

		Gender		
		Male	Female	Total
Hours Spent Online Per Day	Less than one hour	34	29	63
	1-4 hours	83	40	123
	5-8 hours	49	32	81
	More than eight hours	25	8	33
Total		191	109	300

Table 8. Reliability analysis for consumer risk perception

	Mean	Std. Deviation
I am concerned about my information privacy over the Internet.	4.67	1.13029
I am concerned the products do not perform as intended	4.59	1.01228
Pre-purchase information helps to lower risk of buying online	4.42	1.14926
I am comfortable to make online payments using credit card	3.72	1.44055
Perception of risk influences my decision when buying products online	4.57	1.20710
Risk (GRAND MEAN)	4.39	1.187896
Cronbach's Alpha 0.721 for N (5)		

Consumer Trust

Consumer trust and its contribution to EC was measured through 5 questions as found in Table 9. The result show that the variable (Consumer Trust) measured in this research is reliable for data analysis.

Consumer Electronic Commerce Adoption

Consumer EC adoption was measured through 4 questions as found in Table 10. The result show that the variable (EC Adoption) measured in this research is reliable for data analysis.

Table 7. Reliability analysis for consumer knowledge

	Mean	Std. Deviation
I have sufficient knowledge about computer and Internet	4.62	1.22
I have adequate English language knowledge in using the Internet	2.80	1.40
I use the Internet for online chat and discussion	4.31	1.34
My interaction with EC websites is clear and understandable	3.42	1.54
I have sufficient skills to make online transactions	3.20	1.79
Consumer's Knowledge (GRAND MEAN)	3.75	1.458
Cronbach's Alpha 0.731 for N (5)		

Table 9. Reliability analysis for consumer trust

	Mean	Std. Deviation
I trust the information presented on EC websites	3.91	1.49309
Developing trust with online businesses requires seeing and talking to them	4.15	1.44341
Matters of security influence my online shopping decisions	4.27	1.21739
I trust the quality of the products sold through Internet	3.93	1.37909
I trust online delivery system	4.04	1.41128
Trust (GRAND MEAN)	4.06	0.38885
Cronbach's Alpha 0.70 for N (5)		

HYPOTHESIS TESTING

Table 11 shows the result of Multiple Linear Regression (MLR) between 1) Knowledge, 2) Risk Perception and 3) Trust (Independent Variables) with EC Adoption (Dependent Variable).

Table 10. Reliability analysis for e-commerce adoption

	Mean	Std. Deviation
I will purchase products online	2.65	1.06314
I intend to use EC to communicate with global companies	2.91	1.13236
To what extent would you adopt e-commerce?	3.11	1.32960
I intend to use EC to save time and effort	2.97	1.16497
E-Commerce Adoption (GRAND MEAN)	2.91	1.17252
Cronbach's Alpha 0.910 for N(4)		

Table 11. MLR between independent and dependent variable in the research

	USC		SC	t	Sig.
	B	Std. E			
(Constant)	.325	.261		1.243	.215
Knowl-edge	.418	.044	.509	9.573	.000*
Risk	.039	.051	.038	.754	.451
Trust	.066	.048	.074	1.367	.173

* = Significant at 0.05 significant level
USC = Unstandardized Coefficients
SC = Standardized Coefficients

The result of Multiple Linear Regression (MLR) yield the R Square value of 0.31, which reveals that approximately 31% of the variation in EC adoption is explained by the three variables in this research, i.e. Knowledge, Risk Perception and Trust. A regression formula is formulated for EC adoption based on the findings in Table 11:

EC Adoption = 0.33 + 0.42 Knowledge + 0.04 Risk Perception + 0.07 Trust

However at 5% significant level, only one out of the expected 3 predictors contributes to the dependent variable. Only Knowledge is found to significantly affect EC adoption. Hence, H1 is substantiated while H2 and H3 are not substantiated.

Further analysis is carried out to investigate the mediating effect of Knowledge. Table 12 shows the result of MLR analysis between Risk Perception and Trust towards Knowledge.

The MLR test yield R Square value of 0.20, which reveals that approximately 20% of variation in Consumer Knowledge is contributed by Risk Perception and Trust. Knowledge is found significantly regressed with both variables, i.e. Risk Perception and Trust.

From the previous analysis (Table 11) where the research failed to substantiate H2 and H3, coupled with this finding (Table 12), the research gathers enough evidence to conclude that Knowledge has a full mediation effect on mediating the effect of Risk Perception and Trust towards EC adoption. H4 is hence substantiated.

All the hypotheses tests reveal Knowledge, Risk Perception and Trust as important factors that affect users' EC adoption in the Arab countries. Knowledge is found to be the most important factor among these three factors. Although Risk Perception and Trust are found not to directly contribute towards EC adoption (Table 11), both factors are found significant in contributing to the variation in Knowledge as found in Table12.

CONCLUSION

The research sought to empirically test factors that affect EC adoption among Arab consumers. Due to the difficulty of obtaining respondents to participate in the research using probability sampling technique, a purposive sampling method i.e. snowball sampling was employed. Upon filtering the total collected data, 300 samples were finalized for data analysis.

The respondents who participated in this research are well represented from both genders. Statistical analysis shows that there is no significant gender effect towards Internet usage or online purchase among the Arab consumers. Both genders

Table 12.MLR between risk perception and trust towards knowledge

	USC		SC	t	Sig.
	B	Std. E			
(Constant)	1.574	.334		4.708	.000
Risk	.115	.068	.093	1.701	.090**
Trust	.409	.060	.377	6.864	.000*

* = Significant at 0.05 significant level
** = Significant at 0.1 significant level
USC = Unstandardized Coefficients
SC = Standardized Coefficients

represented in this research also did not differ in terms of their educational levels obtained. This is indeed an encouraging finding that leads to a conclusion that ladies are not lagging behind men when it comes to Internet usage and EC adoption.

The research also finds that longer Internet usage hours among respondents lead to higher inclination towards online purchases. This is understandable and concurs with the rest of the findings in this research. Users who spend more time using the Internet would tend to acquire greater knowledge and understanding of the online systems. This agrees with other studies in this area that have associated consumers' knowledge and experience to EC participation [9][24][27]. Users who are knowledgeable about the Internet and EC are more likely to use the Internet and adopt EC solutions. The inexperienced Internet users and users with less knowledge of Internet and EC assume greater risk and lacks trust in the online systems.

Knowledgeable consumers can use EC more adequately in order to reap more benefits through it. Also, studies have shown that consumers' knowledge affects the entire company in their planning to adopt EC solutions [Sohn, Y-S.,1999]. Consumers' Internet knowledge such as the Internet usage skills, using search functions, and search proficiency makes them more confident and in control in engaging in Online transactions [Han, S-R.,1996][Shim, S.,2001].

This research empirically finds that Perceived Risk and Trust are mediated by consumers' Knowledge. Further analysis has revealed a full mediation effect of Knowledge. This is a unique finding observed in this research as most studies in this field have not tested Knowledge mediation of Risk and Trust [Cheung, C.M.K.,2006][Corbitt, B.J.,2003][Forsythe,,2003][Lee, H.Y.,,2006][Pavlou, P.A., 2003][Senecal, S., 2000]. The Arab consumers are found unique in their EC adoption behaviour in this sense. Their Risk Perception leads to their better understanding of the EC system. Their Trust of the system also contributes to their aggregate Knowledge of the Internet and the EC. Together, the consumers' total Knowledge of the Internet and the online system leads to EC Adoption.

The research evidently concludes that EC adoption can be significantly improved in the Arab countries if consumers are given adequate Knowledge on Internet and the EC. Consumers' Risk Perception and Trust should be treated as components within Consumer Knowledge of EC. Giving consumers clarifications of online risk and trust issues will contribute to their overall understanding and aggregate Knowledge of EC. Government initiatives which include computer laboratory installations in schools are highly commendable. As this research has shown, one way of increasing EC adoption is by increasing the hours potential consumers spend online per day. This can be achieved with more computers and Internet facilities made available for the community. A society that has gathered higher knowledge and clearer understanding of the online system will certainly play an active role in online participation. This research concludes through empirical evidence that the Arab countries are well prepared in facing the EC revolution; and given more knowledge of the Internet, they will certainly be on par with other leading countries in EC adoption.

LIMITATION AND FUTURE STUDIES

A non-probability sampling method i.e. Snowball Sampling was employed due to the difficulty of getting respondents using probability sampling method. In a strict statistical sense, the findings lack statistical inference to generalize the findings to the overall population. However, there is no strong evidence to disregard this sample as representative of the overall population as there was no known bias in the present sample selection process. Also, upon filtration, the research only used 300 finalized samples for data analysis. Nevertheless, a bigger sample representing each Arab country consumers would have made the findings of this research more exemplary.

Despite sampling limitation, the research has made significant contributions in highlighting the important factors to be considered in encouraging EC adoption among Arab consumers.

Future research could work towards overcoming the limitations of this research. Further studies can be carried out to specifically examine the Risk Perception of Arab consumers and its effect towards their aggregate Knowledge of EC.

There are other areas as well that could be studied such as usability factors and their effect to EC adoption among Arab consumers. Web usability has been found to be a vital issue that affects EC usage [20]. Moreover, the Arab countries' various market segments could also be research to discover underlying issues within each market segments and their online participation.

REFERENCES

Amin, H. (2000), *Internet in the Arab African World*. Retrieved from www.highwayafrica.org.za/archive/2000/pages/monamin.doc

Baron, R., & Kenny, D. (1986). The moderator-mediator variable distinction in social psychological research: Conceptual, strategic, and statistical considerations. *Journal of Personality and Social Psychology*, *51*, 1173–1182. doi:10.1037/0022-3514.51.6.1173

Cheung, C. M. K., & Lee, M. K. O. (2006). Understanding consumer trust in Internet shopping: a multidisciplinary approach. *Journal of the American Society for Information Science and Technology*, *57*(4), 479–492. doi:10.1002/asi.20312

Corbitt, B. J., Thanasankit, T., & Yi, H. (2003). Trust and e-commerce: a research of consumer perceptions. *Electronic Commerce Research and Applications*, *2*(3), 203–215. doi:10.1016/S1567-4223(03)00024-3

Devlin, J., Guerrieri, P., & Page, J. (n.d.). *MENA and the WTO: a post Seattle agenda*. Retrieved from www.worldbank.org/mdf/mdf3/papers/global/Devlin.pdf

ElShenawi, N. (2001). *E-commerce in Egypt*. International Telecommunication Union Regional Seminar on E-commerce for the Arab Region IDSC, Egypt.

Forsythe, S., & Shi, B. (2003). Consumer patronage and risk perceptions in Internet shopping. *Journal of Business Research*, *56*, 867–875. doi:10.1016/S0148-2963(01)00273-9

Gray, V. (2001). *Barriers to Internet penetration in the Arab World*. Muscat, Oman: Arab Region Internet and Telecom Summit.

Han, S.-R. (1996). Present and future of non-store retailing. In *Proceedings of Korea Marketing Association Spring Conference* (pp.49–59).

Hertz, D., & Thomas, H. (1984). *Practical Risk Analysis: An Approach through Case Histories*. Chichester, UK: Wiley.

Hunter, L. M., Kasouf, C. J., Celuch, K. A., & Curry, K. A. (2004). A classification of business-to-business buying decisions: risk importance and probability as a framework for e-business benefits. *Industrial Marketing Management, 33*, 145–154. doi:10.1016/S0019-8501(03)00058-0

Internet World Statistics. (2008). *Internet World Statistics*. Retrieved from http://www.Internetworldstats.com/stats5.htm

Judd, C., & Kenny, D. (1981). Process analysis: Estimating mediation in treatment evaluations. *Evaluation Review, 5*, 602–619. doi:10.1177/0193841X8100500502

Kenny, D., Kashy, D., & Bolger, N. (1998). Data analysis in social psychology. In Gilbert, D., Fiske, S., & Lindzey, G. (Eds.), *The Handbook of Social Psychology, 1* (pp. 233–265). New York: McGraw-Hill.

Lee, H. Y., Ahn, H., & Han, I. (2006). Analysis of trust in the e-commerce adoption. In *Proceedings of the 39th Hawaii International Conference on System Sciences*, Big Island, HI.

Lee, M. K. O., & Turban, E. (2001). A trust model for consumer Internet shopping. *International Journal of Electronic Commerce, 6*(1), 75–91.

Liebermann, Y., & Stashevsky, S. (2002). Perceived risks as barriers to Internet and e-commerce usage. *Qualitative Market Research, 5*(4), 291–300. doi:10.1108/13522750210443245

Mahmoud, M., & Ugur, Y. (2007). An analysis of E-business practices in the Arab culture. *Cross Cultural Management, 14*(1), 68–73. doi:10.1108/13527600710718840

McKnight, H. D., Choudhury, V., & Kacmar, C. (2002). Developing and validating trust measures for e-commerce: an integrative typology. *Information Systems Research, 13*(3), 334–359. doi:10.1287/isre.13.3.334.81

Nathan, R. J., Yeow, P. H. P., & Murugesan, S. (2008). Key Usability Factors of Service-Oriented Websites for Students: An Empirical Research. *Online Information Review, 32*(3). doi:10.1108/14684520810889646

Odedra-Straub, M. (2003). E-commerce and Development: Whose Development? *Electronic Journal on Information Systems in Developing Countries, 11*(2), 1–5.

Pavlou, P. A. (2003). Consumer acceptance of electronic commerce: integrating trust and risk with the technology acceptance model. *International Journal of Electronic Commerce, 7*(3), 101–134.

Ratchford, B. T., Talukdar, D., & Lee, M. (2001). A model of consumer choice of the Internet as an information source. *International Journal of Electronic Commerce, 5*(3), 7–21.

Salam, A., Iyer, L., Palvia, P., & Singh, R. (2005). Trust in e-commerce. *Communications of the ACM, 48*(2), 72–77. doi:10.1145/1042091.1042093

Salisbury, W., David, R. A., Pearson, A., Pearson, W., & Miller, D. W. (2001). Perceived security and World Wide Web purchase intention. *Industrial Management & Data Systems, 101*(4), 165–176. doi:10.1108/02635570110390071

Senecal, S. (2000). Stopping variables in Online buying processes: An innovation diffusion approach, Proceedings of the 6th Americas Conference on Information Systems, pp. 1380-1385.

Shaheen, A.-H. (2000, June 19). *The Utilization of the World Wide Web for Decision-Making in the United Arab Emirates (U.A.E) Business Settings: The Case of Dubai*. Tallahassee, FL: Graduate School of Information Studies, Florida State University.

Shim, S., Eastlick, M. A., Lotz, S. L., & Warrington, P. (2001). An Online prepurchase intentions model: the role of intention to search. *Journal of Retailing, 77*, 397–416. doi:10.1016/S0022-4359(01)00051-3

So, W. C. M., Wong, T. N. D., & Sculli, D. (2005). Factors affecting intentions to purchase via the Internet. *Industrial Management & Data Systems, 105*(9), 1225–1244. doi:10.1108/02635570510633275

Sohn, Y.-S., & Ahn, K. H. (1999). Theoretical and empirical research on the impacts of consumer knowledge on adoption of e-commerce market. *Korean Marketing Review, 14*(1), 75–91.

Song, C-S., & Shin, J-C. (1999). Adoption of Internet shopping In *Proceedings of Korean Academy of Commodity Science and Technology*, 27–53.

Stewart, K. A., & Segars, A. H. (2002). An empirical examination of the concern for information privacy instrument. *Information Systems Research, 13*(1), 36–49. doi:10.1287/isre.13.1.36.97

Tan, F. B., & Sutherland, P. (2004). Online consumer trust: a multi-dimensional model. *Journal of Electronic Commerce in Organizations, 2*(3), 40–58.

Tan, S. J. (1999). Strategies for reducing consumers? risk aversion in Internet shopping. *Journal of Consumer Marketing, 16*(2), 163–180. doi:10.1108/07363769910260515

Tan, Y.-H., & Thoen, W. (2001). Toward a generic model of trust for electronic commerce. *International Journal of Electronic Commerce, 5*(2), 61–74.

Unhelkar, B. (2003, November 24-25). *Understanding the Impact of Cultural Issues in Global e-Business Alliances*, 4th International We-B Conference, Perth, Western Australia.

Vijayasarathy, L. R., & Jones, J. M. (2000). Print and Internet catalogue shopping: assessing attitudes and intentions. *Internet Research: Electronic Networking Applications and Policy, 10*(3), 191–202. doi:10.1108/10662240010331948

Chapter 18
Efficient Implementation of E-Government Interoperability in Labour Market Information Systems Based on Service Oriented Architecture: A Case of Thailand

Apitep Saekow
Thammasat University - Rangsit Campus, Thailand

Choompol Boonmee
Thammasat University - Rangsit Campus, Thailand

ABSTRACT

In many countries, governments have been developing electronic information systems to support in labour market in form of on-line services, web-based application as well as one-stop service. One of the biggest challenges is to facilitate the seamless exchange of labour market information (LMI) across governmental departments. This chapter introduces an efficient implementation of Thailand's e-government interoperability project in LMI systems using service oriented architecture (SOA) based on XML web service technology. In Thailand, the Ministry of Labour (MOL) has developed a Ministry of Labour Operation Center (MLOC) as the center for gathering, analyzing and monitoring LMI to assist the policy makers. The MOL consists of four departments: department of employment, department of labour protection and welfare, department of skill development, and social security office. Thsse departments utilize electronic systems to manage LMI such as employment, labour protection and welfare, skill development and social security. Provincially, MOL has 75 branches called "labour provincial offices" located at 75 provinces in Thailand. Each office has developed a "Provincial Labour Operation Center or PLOC" as the operating center in the province where the information system called "PLOC" system has been developed to analyze and monitor the localized labour information for the provincial policy-makers. Since these systems differ, it requires the process of data harmonization, modeling and standardizations using UN/CEFACT CCTS and XML NDR for achieving the common XML schema

DOI: 10.4018/978-1-61520-789-3.ch018

standard, with the implementation of SOA to integrate efficiently all those systems. We apply TH e-GIF guidelines for interoperable data exchanges and the XML schema standardization. In Thailand, the first Thailand e-Government Interoperability Framework – the TH e-GIF - came into being in November 2006. This chapter illustrates main concepts of TH e-GIF, the project background and methodology as well as key leverage factors for the project.

INTRODUCTION

Ministry of labour (MOL) in many countries has introduced major reforms to make the labour market more flexible, transparent and efficient (Alessandro, 2005). As an effect MOL has developed electronic government for making available on-line services, web-based application as well as one-stop service for labour sector. In 2002, the Japanese Ministry of Health, Labour and Welfare developed a web portal named 'Hellowork' for their online job information service (Genda, 2006). This lists jobs registered across Japan. The service has been continuously improved since its launch in 1999 with a comprehensive array of options available to job seekers. As well as providing a complete service for job seekers and employers, the Interactive Employment Service (IES) in Hong Kong attempts to bridge the digital divide by providing kiosks in job vacancy centers to make the more than 10,000 vacancies per month posted on IES instantly available at the point of need (Grance & Malcolm, 2002). A similar service is offered by 'Job centre Plus' in the United Kingdom, which is installing touch-screen Job point kiosks in Job centers in Britain to replace outdated vacancy display boards, allowing free access to every vacancy held by the Job centre network in Britain as well as vacancies from European employment service agencies and other third-party agencies (Coleman, 2004). Furthermore, the Job Clearing System (JCS) is one of the applications offered by the Electronic Labour Exchange (ELX) in Malaysia. Employers can use the JCS system to seek out future employees and to publish job vacancies. Vacancies can be posted on the site immediately by completing an online form, and the ELX provides support for users who encounter problems in using the services, including a telephone and e-mail helpdesk (Vijayakumari, 2001). Under co-ordination of the Crossroads Bank for Social Security (CBSS) it disposes of a data warehouse with integrated information about the labour market and social protection. The data warehouse allows establishing statistics that one single institution is not capable to calculate. The management of the data warehouse has been entrusted to the CBSS (Stephen & Vivienne, 2003). Another helpful research for improving labour market is an Semantic Interoperability Infrastructure for e-government services in the employment sector (SEEMP) (Della & Cerizza, 2007). SEEMP aims at enhancing the already provided e-Employment services by developing a highly advanced, ontology-based, peer-to-peer (P2P) based interoperability infrastructure. Based on a Service-Oriented Architecture, it offers access to semantically-enriched employment services. SEEMP will allow interoperability between the existing National/Local job market places (PES systems) at pan-European.

In Thailand, Ministry of Labour (MOL) has tried to develop electronic government to support labour market. In 2005, MOL has developed Ministry of Labour Operation Center (MLOC) as the center for gathering, analyzing and monitoring labour statistic information to assist the policy makers. MOL consists of four departments: department of employment, department of labour protection and welfare, department of skill development, and social security office. Those departments create labour information: employment, labour protection and welfare, skill development, and social security. Electronic links between four departments and MLOC are required. The MLOC retrieves and analyzes labour information from the departments. Also MOL has 75 sub-branches called "labour provincial office" located at 75 provinces in Thailand. The provincial officers need to perform the localized labour information to support their policy and decision making. In the project, another information system called "Provincial Labour Operation Center or PLOC" has been developed. The accumulated information of MLOC is localized and is transferred electronically to the PLOC system. The PLOC system has been developed for all provinces. Regarding interoperable data transfer among the systems, XML schema standards have been developed. We apply TH e-GIF guidelines (Thailand MICT, 2006) for interoperable data exchanges and XML schema standardization. In Thailand, the first Thailand e-Government Interoperability Framework – the *TH e-GIF* - came into being in November 2006. Without those XML schema standards the inter-system electronic interoperability would not be possible. This chapter introduces the efficient implementation of Thailand e-Government interoperability in LMI systems using serviced oriented architecture (SOA) based on XML web service technology. It also introduces concepts of MLOC and PLOC systems, their interoperable architecture, and how the systems are tested and assured.

This chapter is structured as follows: the second section presents background of Thailand e-Government, the project, and LMI for the project. The next section describes project methodology, software design, and network design and system security. The fourth section presents interoperable architecture and XML schema standard. The following chapter outlines the system test and assessment. The final section illustrates key leverages factors for success in the project and conclusions respectively.

BACKGROUND

Thailand e-Government

Since 1994, Thailand e-Government has been developed by the Sub-Committee of Promotion of Promotion of Utilization of Information Technology in Public Organization under the National Information Technology Committee (NITC). Several activities have been arranged to support and promote this initiative such as computer training for mid-level officers, specifying minimum requirements of IT equipments for government agencies, CIO's appointment in public sector, conducting IT Master Plan of ministries, departments & provinces, etc (Boonruang, 2001). In 2000, ASEAN countries endorsed the e-ASEAN initiative to promote potential of information technology in order to strengthen their competitiveness in the world economy. The e-ASEAN initiative focused on five areas: (1) The establishment of the ASEAN information infrastructure, (2) The growth of e-Commerce, (3) The establishment of a free-trade area in products, services, and investments, (4) The development of e-Society, and (5) The establishment of e-Government (Sukasame, 2002). e-Government is one of the five key areas that ASEAN countries have committed to implement. On July 3, 2000, the Economic Cabinet considered the issues raised in e-ASEAN initiative, and envisioned that Thailand must first work on developing of e-Thailand as priority in order for preparing readiness for the country and minimize drawbacks in the development process of IT infrastructure. The e-Thailand initiative resulted from e-ASEAN initiative has driven NITC to appoint a sub-committee for e-Thailand development of which e-Government is one of the key development areas. Consequently, Thailand e-Government project has been set up (Sukasame, 2002). The project important mandate is to coordinate and facilitate public organization in rendering good services through electronic media as Red-tape reduction one stop service, Rapid Response, Rural

Coverage, and Round-the-clock or 24*7 service. E-Thailand key areas are e-Government, e-Society, e-Commerce Facilitation, Information Infrastructure and Liberalization (Sukasame, 2002). However, the major goals of the e-Government Project in two years time (2003) are to coordinate and facilitate the implementation of Pilot Projects on various public services and to set up standards, guidelines, and manuals for interoperability for public agencies and electronic services in implementing the e-Government program. To this direction, the Government had proposed to develop an e-Government Interoperability Framework as a mechanism tool for achieving the interoperability. Furthermore, the National Electronics and Computer Technology Centre (Nectec) is working out a measurement system to rate government agencies' progress toward e-Government. It will be called e-Government Services Measurement System (eGSMS). It is implemented to evaluate the readiness of agencies to provide e-Government and stimulate them to do so by monitoring their websites. Each agency's e-Government development will be evaluated once a year on four categories: (a) frequency of information update, (b) electronic form provision, (c) electronic transaction with security, and (d) digital signature and network integration with other agencies to provide one-stop service (Karnjanatawe, 2002).

e-Government Interoperability in Thailand

In November 2006, Thai Government announced Thailand electronic government interoperability framework (TH e-GIF) as a collection of technical standards, methodologies, guidelines and policies (Thailand, 2006). The main objective of TH e-GIF is also to facilitate government in adapting to the digital era with the introduction of technical policies and specifications for achieving Information and Communication Technology (ICT) systems coherence across the public sector (G2G – Government-to-Government) and between the State and citizens (G2C – Government-to-Citizens) or businesses (G2B – Government-to-Business). It is suitable for high level administrators, executive managers, operating officers, and IT officers of both government and private sectors, concerning data system developments. The contents cover the framework of government electronic data systems integration for interoperability development, policies, success factors, system development procedures, and progress priority of e-government, including detailed explanation and recommendations for executive operators, information officers, system analysts, programmers, and other ICT officers. It also includes procedures and technical standards for Data Simplification, Harmonization and Standardization, Dictionary Entry Name and Data Modeling by UN/CEFACT CCTS Standard, as well as XML data structure, and other technical standards with their management procedures.

TH e-GIF Interoperability Level Classification

TH e-GIF has been designed as guidelines in information system development for interoperability, which government units can use as references for effective information system design and development for interoperability applications as well as to applied TH e-GIF guidelines in variety formats of higher levels of interoperability. There are five levels of interoperability: Level 1: Technical Standard and Specification, Level 2: Services Registry, Level 3: XML Schema registry/ repository, Level 4: Core Component Library and Level 5: Formalized business process using UML/ UMM, depicted in Figure 1.

Through the TH e-GIF adoption, currently the Government units have not been mandated yet. They can utilize the guidelines based on their readiness. In case, the units plan to achieve a comprehensive interoperability that covers a dimension of business process, semantic and technical, the guidelines for every level must be ad-

Figure 1. The-GIF level classification

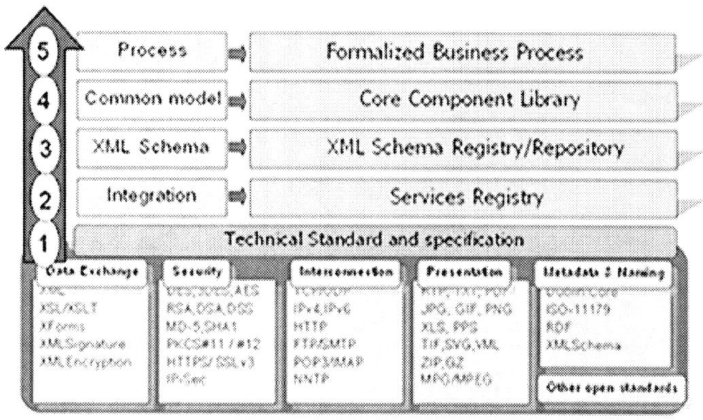

opted from Level 1 to Level 5. If the units need only data delivery and data exchange between different units, Level 1-4 will be applied. Besides, the Level 1-3 are needed for merely standardizing XML schema in data exchange. In order to achieve a fundamental interoperability system, Level 1 will be applied with the use of common technical standards that are divided into five components: Interconnection, Data Transfer, Data Collection and Presentation, Data Security and Other Open standards.

e-Government for LMI

Since Thai government has tried to develop electronic government for citizen services e-Government roadmap has been planned and strategized. The strategies mainly are categorized into four issues: e-government agency establishment, e-government services, and IT infrastructure development and law and policies revision. Accordingly, government infrastructure network (GIN) has been developed to connect all e-government agencies that are located at governmental departments. Moreover, many networks such as Prime Minister Operation Center (PMOL), Minister Operation Center (MOC) and department operation center (DOC) are evolved.

In order to make the labour market in Thailand more flexible, transparent and efficient, in 2005 Ministry of Labour (MOL) of Thailand has developed Ministry of Labour Operation Center (MLOC) as the center for gathering, analyzing and monitoring LMI from 75 provinces. MOL consists of four departments: department of employment, department of labour protection and welfare, department of skill development, and social security office. Those departments procreate labour information: employment, labour protection and welfare, skill development, and social security. MOL also has 75 sub-branches called 'labour provincial office' located at 75 provinces. In order to localize labour information, another information system called 'Provincial Labour Operation Center' (PLOC) has been developed. In 2005, the PLOC project was proposed as a pilot. It was first targeted to cover only 10 provinces. In 2006 and 2007, it was extended to cover 45 and 60 provinces respectively. Recently, the PLOCs were completely developed for all 75 provinces in Thailand.

LMI in the Project

In the project, we consider LMI included Labour Market, Employment Promotion, Skill Develop-

Table 1. Labour information

Labour Market	
Employment Status	*Total population - Worker capacity - Employed persons Unemployed persons - Seasonal unemployed persons – Labour force*
Circumstance	*GDP - Trade balance - Labour productivity - Capacity utilization rate Wage/salary - Company close down - Termination of employment Thai labour standard - Insured person - Temporary legal alien workers - Illegal alien workers registration*
Employment Promotion	
Trend of Labour Demand	*Overall trend of labour demand - Labour demand trends in Northeast, North, South and Central - Job vacancy - Job applicant Job placement – Work at home – Self-employed supported by DSD Unemployment support - Oversea employment*
Skill Development	
Demand	*Above 15 – Employed workers – Seasonal workers – Not in labour force – Unemployed workers*
Training	*Course preparation for work – Skill improvement – Skill Aided Foreigner course - Government agency -*
Assessment	*National skill standard – Individual worker skill – Oversea job seekers – Labour standard certificate*
Labour Benefits	
Law	*Labour protection under social security act - Number of not complying employers – Safety labour inspection – Home worker protection act – Agriculture worker protection act – Submission of demand – Conflict - Dispute -*
Accident	*Occupational injury – Compensation payment – Rehabilitation Social security benefit*
Funding	
Status	*Social security fund – Fund investment – Return investment Estimation*
Reward	*Reward fund status – Investment – Return investment*
Support	*Support employee fund status – Word at home fund status – Loaning – Oversea job seeking – Skill development*

ment, Labour Benefits and Funding. Table 1 outlines labour information concerned in the project.

METHODOLOGY

System and Network Architecture

In the project, we designed the standardized integration architecture based on SOA in order to achieve better flexibility while implementing labour information exchanges across departments and their information systems. The architecture moves away from application-centric development processes to a new methodology that offers advances in software reuse flexibility and connectivity to end users (Don and Evan, 2004). Figure 2 shows the system and network architecture based on SOA for overall system. The overall system is composed of MLOC system, PLOC system and four data exchange servers (DXS). All systems are connected over intranet network of ministry of labour called 'MOL intranet'. Since previous occasion, labour information has been stored in legacy storage system. The system uses different database systems format such as DB2, Oracle, Informix, Microsoft SQL and Text file. In this project, new additional systems include MLOC, PLOC and DXS had been developed. MOL system is a server-based computer with system application software installed. It connected to four data exchange servers (DXS) and PLOC system. PLOC system is also a server-based computer with the application. It is located at 'Provincial Information

Figure 2. Network architecture for overall

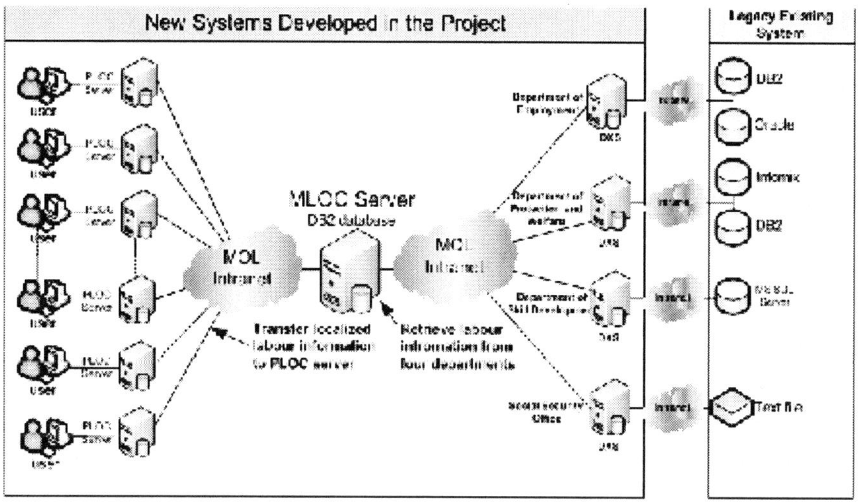

Technology Service Center'. In the project there are 75 PLOC systems for all 75 provinces. All of the systems are directly linked to MOL system. The DXS is a data exchange server. It manages data from the legacy storage system. There are four DXSs. Each DXS is located in department.

Through the network architecture, MLOC automatically retrieves labour information included labour market, employment promotion, skill development, labour benefits and funding from the DXSs. The information will be stored on MLOC server. It will be statistically localized and will be provincially transfer to 75 PLOC systems. In province, users can access the localized information through a web browser on computers that connected to MOL intranet. In case of additional data from other resources needed, MLOC also supports offline data retrieval.

Regards to the network architecture, the systems are designed to be operated over MOL intranet. They communicate over TCP/IP network. It provides an interconnection among the systems in the project. The individual IP address and Domain Name Service (DNS) have been assigned for each system and an IP multicasting was implemented as the internet abstraction of hardware multicasting. This allows transmission of an IP datagram to a set of hosts that form a single multicast group.

System Application Software

In the project, the system application software was designed based on web based technology. It consists of three main components: database server, application server and web server. The database server was implemented using MySQL or DB2 under Operating System Solaris 10. The application server was developed by project programmers using Java 5.0, Jfreechart 1.0.1, Poi2.5.1, XercesImp (XML) and Xalan (XML). Tomcat server 5 was installed for running a web server.

System Security

Over MLOC and PLOC network, secure sockets layer (SSL) has been applied. The SSL secures data packages transferred across networks. Based on SSL, digital certificate was implemented to verify authorization between clients and servers. The system security has been categorized into three main levels: server level, client level and data encoded level. At server level security, a client communicates to a server using SSL. The SSL verifies the right server for the client using digital certificate. Also, when a server communicates to a client, the SSL verifies the right client for the server before transferring data. To secure data transferred, all the data will be encoded using public key infrastructure (PKI) technique.

Interoperability

Service Oriented Architecture

The Service Oriented Architecture is a paradigm that describes how to organize and utilize capabilities of existing IT systems into loosely coupled, platform independent and highly interoperable services (OASIS, 2006). A service in a SOA is a small piece of software that provides uniform access to functions and data of an IT system. The construction and usage of a service are based on international standards (Robert and Nick 2005). These standards enable the construction of business services layer. Through the services, functions and data of the underlying IT systems can be accessed in a platform, programming language and location independent way (Robert and Nick, 2005)

Integrating XML Technologies into SOA

Relevant Standards

- **XML:** The Extensible Markup Language 1.0 standard is a text-based markup language specification from the World Wide Web Consortium (W3C). Unlike HTML, which uses tags for describing presentation and data, XML is strictly for the definition of portable structured data. It can be used as a language for defining data descriptive languages, such as markup grammars or vocabularies and interchange formats and messaging protocols (Joseph, 2006).
- **SOAP:** Simple Object Access Protocol is an XML-based lightweight protocol for the exchange of information in a decentralized, distributed environment. SOAP defines a messaging protocol between requestor and provider objects, such that the requesting objects can perform a remote method invocation on the providing objects in an object-oriented programming fashion. SOAP forms the basis for distributed object communication in most vendor implementations of SOA. Although SOA does not define a messaging protocol, SOAP has been referred to as the Services-Oriented Architecture Protocol due to its common use in SOA implementations (Joseph, 2006).
- **WSDL:** The Web Services Description Language is an XML vocabulary that provides a standard way of describing service IDLs. WSDL is the resulting artifact of a convergence of activity between NASSL (IBM) and SDL (Microsoft). It provides a simple way for service providers to describe the format of requests and response messages for remote method invocations (RMI). WSDL addresses this topic of service IDLs independent of the underlying protocol and encoding requirements. In general, WSDL provides an abstract language for defining the published operations of a service with their respective parameters and data types. The language also addresses the definition of the location and binding details of the service.
- **UDDI:** The Universal Description, Discovery, and Integration specification provides a common set of SOAP APIs that enable the implementation of a service broker. The UDDI specification was outlined by IBM, Microsoft, and Ariba to help facilitate the creation, description, discovery, and integration of Web based services. The motivation behind UDDI.org, a part-

nership and cooperation between more than 70 industry and business leaders, is to define a standard for B2B interoperability. XML's strength is to describe and manipulate complex data. As one successful implementation shows, The JUNOScript API encodes data for both requests and replies in the W3C's Extensible Markup Language (XML). XML's simple encoding allows the representation of arbitrary hierarchies of data using ASCII text in HTML-like tags. The order and structure of the elements can be defined using either

- **UN/CEFACT CCTS:** CCTS provides a way to identify, capture and maximize the re-use of business information to support and enhance information interoperability. The foundational concepts of CCTS are Core Components (CC) and Business Information Entities (BIE). Core Components are building blocks that can be used for all aspects of data, information modeling and information exchange. Core Components are used for creating interoperable business process models and business documents. Core components are conceptual models that are used to define Business Information Entities (BIEs). The BIEs are the logical data model object used for information exchanges. Core Components encompass Aggregate Core Components (ACCs) and Basic Core Components (BCCs), and Association Core Components (ASCCs). Business Information Entities (BIE) encompasses Aggregate Business Information Entities (ABIEs), Basic Business Information Entities (BBIEs), and Association Business Information Entities (ASBIEs) (UN/CEFACT CCTS, 2006).
- **XML Naming and Design Rules:** XML Naming and Design Rules specification defines an architecture and set of rules necessary to define, describe and use XML to consistently express business information exchanges. It is based on the World Wide Web consortium suite of XML specifications and the UN/CEFACT Core Components Technical Specification. This specification will be used by UN/CEFACT to define XML Schema and Schema documents which will be published and UN/CEFACT standards. It will also be used by other Standards Development Organizations who are interested in maximizing inter- and intra-industry interoperability (UN/CEFACT XML, 2006).

Project Architecture Based on SOA

One of the most essential MLOC's goals is to gather labour information from the DXSs. Then the retrieved information will be statistically analyzed and transferred to PLOC systems for provincial policy makers. Among these systems, the interoperable architecture design needs to be given to shape an infrastructure allowing the information exchange. The technology used for the realization ofback-end functionalities involves web-services. The services interfaces description follows therefore WSDL specifications. Since those systems differ, XML standards have been developed for common data exchanges. The interoperability gives the possibility to transfer labour information about employment, labour protection and welfare, skill development, and social security.

XML Web Services Technology in the Project

In the project, we implemented CBIS over the network as services in a SOA. Generally, services are created using XML Web Services (William, 2003). A XML Web Service is a software component that can be built into or on top of an IT system to provide access to its functionality and data (Robert, 2005). To create high interoperability between IT systems, the description of, and access to, Web Services are based on a common languages and protocol to achieve integration based on open and shared standard (David, 2006). A Web Service encapsulates (hides) IT systems, often complex, language specific implementation and provides a new interoperable interface that can be exposed on, and invoked from, a network (David, 2006). This interface describes the service's data model and the aspects of the service that are needed by service consumers to determine whether a given service is appropriate for the service consumer's needs (OASIS, 2006). This interface is described in the Web Services Definition Language (WSDL), which is XML based standard for describing Web Services (James, 2005).

XML Schema Standard

Thai Government has established precise guidelines about the interoperability design and approach in Thailand Electronic Government Interoperability Framework (TH e-GIF). TH e-GIF was first launched in November 2006. It mainly set out the policies, standards, guidelines and technical structures for interoperability purposes. In the project we apply guidelines and techniques in TH e-GIF to build the project's XML schema standard. The TH e-GIF utilizes CCTS technique (United Nations, 2003) for building a national common set of data model and uses UN/CEFACT XML naming and design rules (United Nations, 2006) for developing XML schema standard. Regards to labour information shown in section 2.3, we have generated their XML schema standard for interoperability in data exchanges.

SYSTEM TEST AND ASSURANCE

In order to test and ensure our systems we designed the system testing and assuring focused on two areas: Network Quality Test and Data Transfer Test. Network testing focuses on ensuring networking connectivity and performance. Data transfer test proposes to assure data sending and receiving among the systems.

Network Quality Test

As described, MLOC and PLOC system have been operated over TCP/IP protocol within a large network. They include a MLOC system, four DXS and 75 PLOC systems. Among the systems, XML data has been transferred based on web service technology. Figure 3 shows a concept of data transfer between two computer systems using web services technology. The service requester sends Request Message (M_{req}) to Service Provider. After the service provider received $M_{req,}$ it will return Response Message (M_{data}). To ensure the quality of network among them, we designed and implemented test procedures to calculate bandwidth and time usage.

Figure 3. A concept of data transfer between two systems

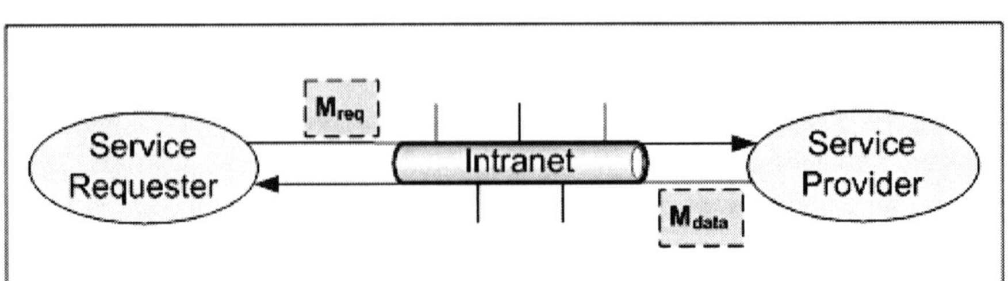

Finding Bandwidth and Time

The service requester sends M_{req} to server provider and waits until the service provider completed returning M_{data}. The total time (t_{Total}) used for all processes will be calculated from the following formula:

$$t_{Total} = (S_{data} / BW) + t_{Delay}$$

where t_{Total} is all time spent from sending data until receiving data.

S_{data} is a size of data packages.
BW is bandwidth
t_{Delay} is delay time of system processing.

According to the above formula, if two different sizes of data are transferred t_{Total1} and t_{Total2} will be resulted as follows:

$$t_{Total1} = (S_{data1} / BW) + t_{Delay}$$

$$t_{Total2} = (S_{data2} / BW) + t_{Delay}$$

Hence,

$$BW = (S_{data1} - S_{data2}) / (t_{Total1} - t_{Total2})$$

Accordingly, we tested the network between MLOC and PLOC system, and between MLOC and four DXSs. We obtained the results. A part of the results is shown in Table 2.

Data Transfer Test

We test data transferability between MLOC and PLOC following steps:

1. Select a PLOC server for test case.
2. Operate MLOC system to send data packages to the PLOC.
3. Check the result of the data received on PLOC system.

Table 2. A part of BW and time delay results

Province/Department	Computer name	IP address	Bandwidth (bps)	Time delay (s)
Department of employment	docxml.tu-rac.com	10.10.10.221	8,717,464	0.002
Department of labour protection and welfare	dolxml.tu-rac.com	172.16.0.20	9,638,803	0.002
Department of skill development	dsdxml.tu-rac.com	10.100.52.5	7,091,698	0.003
Social security office	ssoxml.tu-rac.com	172.16.100.200	178,748	0.000
Chiangmai	chiangmai.ploc.mol.go.th	20.65.112.5	87,775	0.180
Songkhla	songkhla.ploc.mol.go.th	20.65.144.5	14,324	0.101
Roiet	roiet.ploc.mol.go.th	20.65.181.5	20,276	0.135
Ranong	ranong.ploc.mol.go.th	20.65.167.5	3,252	4.770
Khonkaen	khonkaen.ploc.mol.go.th	20.65.176.5	104,209	0.018
Phuket	phuket.ploc.mol.go.th	20.65.166.5	8,923	0.891
Nonthaburi	nonthaburi.ploc.mol.go.th	20.65.38.5	8,421	0.342
Chiangrai	chiangrai.ploc.mol.go.th	20.65.114.5	5,203	0.612
Trang	trang.ploc.mol.go.th	20.65.148.5	8,212	0.648
Ayutthaya	ayutthaya.ploc.mol.go.th	20.65.99.5	8,222	0.252
Pattani	pattani.ploc.mol.go.th	20.65.151.5	5,988	0.275

Figure 4. A screenshot of test result for Phrae province

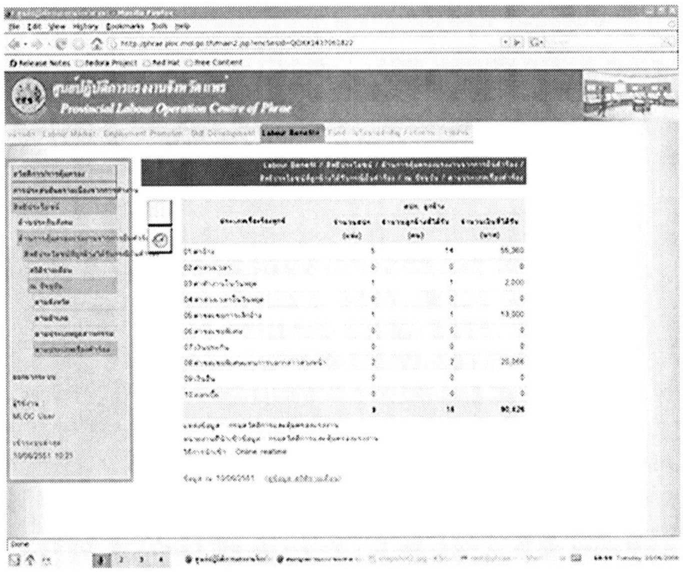

Figure 5. Key leverage factors for success in the project

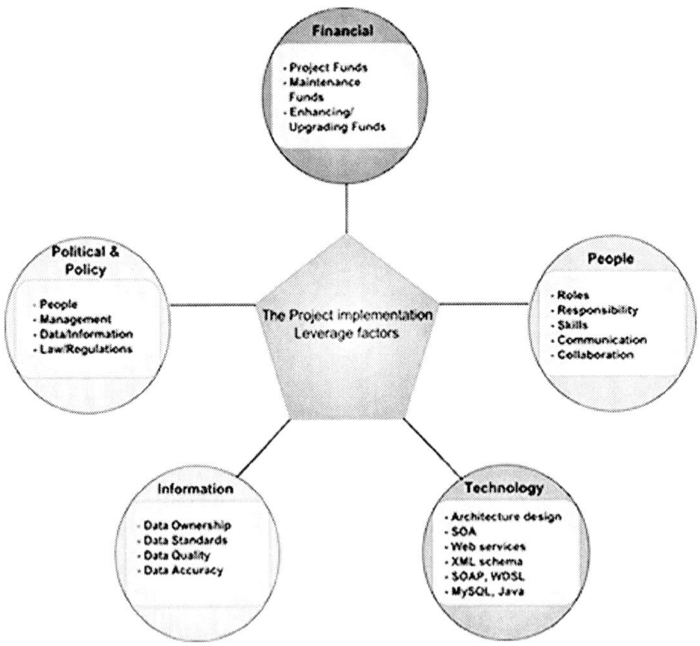

We apply the above steps for all 75 PLOC systems. Figure 4 shows a screenshot of test results for data transfer from MOL system to Phrae's PLOC system.

KEY LEVERAGE FACTORS

In this e-Government project implementation, we found that the key leverages factors for success are financial, political & policy, people, information and technology. Figure 5 shows a model of the key leverage factors for success in the project. The model was designed referenced to the key leverage points for policies (Mohamad & Dan, 2007).

Financial

- Financial for the e-government implementation includes project funds, maintenance funds and enhancing/upgrading funds is one of the key leverage factors. Long-term funding plan needs to be well organized and supported as some of e-government implementation projects would take many years to achieve the target. Lack/inconsistency of funding can cause project failure.

Political and Policy

- A political support across government to push for change and resources is required to take "ownership" of the projects and commit their time on a sustained basis. Without ongoing, active political leadership, the financial resources, inter-agency coordination, policy changes and human effort required to plan and implement e-government will not be sustained.
- The policy to share information with the public and across government agencies/departments needs to be set. At different levels, information sharing strategies are required. Smooth, rapid information-sharing enables government to take a more functional approach to services, as opposed to the usual department-by-department approach. A government's information policies are a key readiness consideration.
- Promulgation of relevant laws and regulations is essential. Establishing protections and legal reforms will be needed to ensure the privacy, security and legal recognition of electronic interactions and electronic signatures in the e-government implementation.

People

- The officers within e-government: Sufficient numbers of skilled, ICT literate personnel (including managers with experience in e-Government, evaluating and implementing ICT solutions) are crucial. Not everything can or should be outsourced to the private sector.
- Establishment of communication strategies to ensure that people understand the vision, the changes that will occur and the tangible benefits for them from e-Government. E-Government budgets must therefore include funds to promote and publicize projects through various media channels.
- Change management issues must also be addressed. The level of resistance to change and level of involvement by officials in setting policies and practices will greatly impact how fast or smooth the implementation of e-government will be.

Information

- Data ownership: in the project, some data exchanges across difference departments need to be performed with data authorized by the ownership.
- Data standards: non-standards can cause the failure of data exchanges in the project. In this project, we standardized exchanged data following TH e-GIF.
- Data quality: Ensuing the data quality is to design/perform data models to fit for their intended uses in operations, decision making and planning
- Data accuracy: the correctness of data is important. During data input/transfer processes, it is essential to design/develop a

testing to ensure the data meet requirements or accuracy.

Technology

- Choosing right technology: each project will need the right and appropriate technology for its implementation. The technology uses should have ability/availability for upgrading.
- Suitable/Well telecommunications infrastructure: The level of telecommunications infrastructure needed will depend on the e-government projects pursued. Significant investment in national ICT infrastructure in a coordinated approach will be needed to realize e-government applications.

Though statistic data of labour is significant for planning and decision, the controls of the above leverage factors are required in order to obtain a high quality and up-to-date data.

CONCLUSION

This chapter describes an efficient implementation ofThailand e-government interoperability project in LMI systems using service oriented architecture (SOA) based on XML web service technology. The project was started in 2005 supported by Ministry of Labour (MOL). In the project, we first developed computer based information systems (CBIS) as LMI systems. The systems are to gathering, analyzing and monitoring LMI for the policy makers. Ministry of Labour Operation Center called 'MLOC' has been developed as the center where the centralized LMI system named "MLOC" system has been installed. Provincially, MOL has 75 Provincial Labour Operation Center (PLOC) located in 75 provinces. Each center has the LMI system called "PLOC" system installed. All PLOC systems are connected to the MLOC system over MOL intranet for LMI exchanges. For the project implementation, we achieved XML schema standards of LMI by adopting the guidelines in TH e-GIF and the standardized integration architecture based on SOA. Without those XML schema standards and the architecture, the inter-system electronic interoperability would not be possible. Finally, our testing significantly indicated that it has been successful in LMI exchanges between MLOC and PLOC systems. The key leverages factors for success are financial, political & policy, people, information and technology.

REFERENCES

Alessandro, M. (2005). Borsa Lavoro Lombardia: e-Gov Interoperability in the labour market. In*Proceedings of e-Gov-Interop'05 conference*, Geneva, Switzerland.

Coleman, N., Rousseau, N., & Carpenter, H. (2004). *Jobcentre Plus Service Delivery Survey* ((IAD Social Research Division Research Report No. 223). London.

Davies, V., Taylor, J., Hartfree, Y., & Kellard, K. (2004). *Delivering the Jobcentre Plus vision: Qualitative research with staff and customers (Phase 3)* (Research Report No. 222). IAD Social Research Division. London.

Don Libes, D. F., Wallace, E., Steves, M., Feeney, A. B., & Barkmeyer, E. (2004). *The challenges of automated methods for integrating systems.* Innsbruck, Austria: Software Engineering.

Dowson, L., House, S., & Sanderson, I. (2004). *Jobcentre Plus Customer Satisfaction 2003: Findings from qualitative research* (DWP Research Report No.191). Leeds, UK.

Genda, Y., & Maganuma., M. (2004). NEET – *Freeter demo naku Shitsugyo-sha demo naku* (NEET – Neither Freeters nor Unemployed). Togen-sha.

Grace, O. M., & Lee, M. W. (2002). Labour-market policies in Shanghai and Hong Kong: A study of "one country, two systems" in Greater China. *International Journal of Manpower*, *23*(6), 505–526. doi:10.1108/01437720210446379

James, P. (2005). *How BPEL and SOA Are Changing Web Services Development. IEEE computer society*. May/June.

Joseph, B. (2006). Service Oriented Architecture (SOA): A New Paradigm to Implment Dynamic E-business Solutions. *ACM-Ubiquity, 7*(30).

Karnjanatawe (2002). ICT Ministry pushes e-Government plans - will help agencies to offer e-Services, *Bangkok Post*.

Karnjanatawe (2003). Gateway to govt sites - single access point to public e-Services, *Bangkok Post*.

Mohamad A., Michael C., Dan, H., Kevin C., & Vishram, P. (2007, May). *SOA Governance Framework and Best Practices, version 1.1*. Redwood Shores, CA: Oracle.

OASIS Group. (2006), *Reference Model for Service Oriented Architecture 1.0, Public Review Draft 1.0*. Retrieved from http://www.oasis-open.org/committees/download.php/16628/wd-soa-rm-pr1.pdf

Robert, J., Van, E., Gerwen, N., & Graave, J. (2005). Art Lighthart, Ron van Rooij, Service Oriented Architecture, ICT-bibliotheek Den Haag.

Stephen, J. R., and Vivienne, J., (2003). eGovernment Leadership: Engaging the Customer, The Government executive series, Accenture Innovation delivered.

Stodder, D. (2006). Loosen Up, *Intelligent Enterprise*. Retrieved from http://intelligent-enterprise.informationweek.com/showArticle.jhtml;jsessionid=phdmli3mgm4fjqe1ghpskhwatmy32jvn?articleid=181503583

Sukasame, N. (2002). *The development of e-service in Thai government*. BU Academic Review.

Thailand, Ministry of Information and Communication Technology (2006) *Thailand e-Government Interoperability Framework Version 1.0*.

UN/CEFACT CCTS. (2006). *Core Component Technical Specification, Part 8 of the ebXML-Framework*. Retrieved from http://www.unece.org/cefact/ebxml/CCTS_V2- 01_Final.pdf

UN/CEFACT XML. (2006). *UN/CEFACT XML Naming and Design Rules Version 2.0*. Retrieved from http://www.unece.org/cefact/XML-Naming-and -Design-Rules-V2.0pdf

Vijayakumari, K. (2001). International migration and labour market adjustments in Malaysia: The Role of Foreign Labour Policies. *Asia-Pacific Migration Journal, 10*(3-4).

William, A. E. (2003, December). An evaluation framework for deploying Web Services in the next generation manufacturing enterprise. *Robotics and Computer-integrated Manufacturing, 19*(6), 509–519. doi:10.1016/S0736-5845(03)00061-9

Chapter 19
E-Services and the Digital Divide:
The Role of Tertiary Education in Improving Public Engagement and Trust in E-Delivery of Services

Neil Gordon
University of Hull, UK

ABSTRACT

This chapter considers aspects relating to the role of tertiary (i.e. higher) education in improving the engagement of the public with government provided E-services. Some of the issues considered include those of tackling the digital divide – which can exist because of technical issues in provision of the actual infrastructure, financial issues limiting access to available provision and educational barriers – as well as how to develop trust in online technologies. The challenges of the networked society include a number that can be best addressed through education. These include: 1) Engagement with new technologies and new paradigms; 2) Trust in a virtual environment; 3) Understanding of processes and engagement with online services;4) Mapping of existing personal paradigms to the virtual world. Education itself faces challenges in the networked world. Tertiary education in particular is potentially vulnerable to the changes that the modern networked world brings; however, it can also gain through some of the new opportunities. Of particular note is the potential to unlock students' research skills and enable true inquiry by students within their studies – skills which should prepare them as active participants in the knowledge rich and information easy society within which they will be developing.

INTRODUCTION

E-government or public e-services offer ways for governments to engage with their citizens and for the citizens to find information and potentially to interact with and even direct government. Globally, governments have recognized the importance of this and numerous projects to develop e-government facilities have been developed; for example, within the U.K. the move to make 100% of public services available online (HMSO, 2002). This chapter considers these issues in the global context - whilst a number of the examples

DOI: 10.4018/978-1-61520-789-3.ch019

are based on the author's knowledge within the U.K. the issues are relevant to other nations.

Similarly, citizens around the world have been appreciating the benefits of being able to access services online, for example to submit tax returns and purchase state based services online. However, the take up of such services are necessarily limited to those who are able and willing to take advantage of them. Whilst the availability of internet access is increasing, there are still large differences in the availability within certain countries, and even within a country variability can exist of the availability across socio-economic groups.

Improving the provision and level of engagement with e-government may be achieved through an acknowledgement of the issues by the policy makers and service providers, as well as by improving the education of the population – in this context, information literacy can be considered a key skill, and is recognized by some education systems as such, where information skills are developed alongside language and numeracy skills (Eisenberg, 2008). However, there can be a tension between developing more traditional skills and subjects – for example, history, literature and science – and finding space in the curriculum in which to teach the new information skills. A further concern amongst some is the unknown affect of exposing developing minds to information technology at too early a stage, with the increasing influence and penetration of such skills into all aspects of a child's life that their development is affected in ways that are potentially detrimental to their longer term well being (Guardian, 2009). With this in mind, tertiary education can be particularly influential – as university level students are at a suitable level to learn the skills needed to engage with modern e-services whilst not being so juvenile as to suffer potential ill effects. Furthermore, these students will provide the future policy makers and technology implementers who can influence future systems.

THE CONTEXT

A well known way to characterize business with consumer interactions is in terms of the Business-to-business (B2B), Business-To-Customer (B2C), customer-to-business (C2B) and customer-to-customer (C2C) models. Similarly, with respect to governments and citizens, we can characterize interactions as G2C and C2G (Carter, 2005). G2C are familiar – in that governments provide information to citizens has long been done using traditional media, such as paper based publishing or public television broadcasts. C2G, whilst available in limited ways – for example by direct lobbying of representatives – has been more of a problem. Traditional approaches – such as taking marketing type samples of the population, or public led mechanisms such as petitions have been harder to organize and run on a mass scale. However, the potential to gather information from the population is now much greater through distributing the work out to the public themselves.

In the context of e-government, another aspect to consider is the global nature of the Internet, and the potential impact this has on an individual. The rights and responsibilities of individuals as members of the Internet community – the netizens - complement and can conflict with those as members of nation states. A key feature for governments to consider when rolling out e-government services is to not exclude their own citizens through dangerous assumptions. One feature which is relevant across the world is the extent to which the population has the basic skills to engage with e-services. For example, taking the latest figures for the U.K. on the education at age 16 (key stage 4), only 47.2% achieved 5 passes including mathematics and English at grade C (see DCSF 2008). This indicates potential problems should services be provided mainly, or in some cases exclusively, online.

The opportunities referred to above can be broadly characterized as those of finding information about public services, and of providing information or requesting things directly. We explore these briefly now before considering the role of tertiary education in facilitating these functions and potential interactions.

PROVIDING DATA: FINDING INFORMATION ON PUBLIC SERVICES

The wealth of information available via the Internet is well known as causing difficulties for many users. Search engines have gained in popularity and usage – to the extent that terms such as Google have become verbs in language – reflecting the desires and needs of people to find data, and to require assistance in this. However, the volume of information available can cause information overload and lead to some people feeling that they need direction on where to start looking. Furthermore, one key difficulty even when a likely site has been found is knowing whether the site is a legitimate and trustworthy one, or a potential phishing site or simply a fake site.

With regards to finding relevant information and the appropriate sites, then the semantic web offers opportunities to provide the kind of data that users need. However, there is still some way to go before reliable and standard information is provided – even on public information sites provided by governments. Even when such information is available, a new generation of search engines will be needed to provide access to the semantic information in a way that is accessible to the general public user (Times, 2008). For now, the key feature for the effective use of the mass of information being provided by governments is the education of the public in effective and efficient ways of finding the information that they need.

One particular difficulty for e-government is providing reliable online information – reliable in both content and in availability. There have been numerous cases of public websites being inundated and ultimately overwhelmed with access requests. This reflects the difficulty in modeling the needs and requirements of the public to access data. One example of this came from the U.K. national archive – when census data was put freely online for people to access, the demand quickly overwhelmed the service which went down as servers were unable to cope. A study in 2003 (Gupta, 2003) found that experience of e-government initiatives was chaotic and unmanageable – and early experiences can prejudice the public in their uptake and engagement with later e-government developments.

GATHERING DATA: ISSUES AROUND SUBMITTING DATA TO PUBLIC SERVICE WEBSITES

The collection of data about their citizens by governments is a necessary feature of managing people. Census data for planning purposes and income data for taxation are two typical and essential features. Similarly, ensuring that electoral records are accurate and up to date is an essential element of democracy and is necessary for the functioning of most societies. The potential efficiency savings in gathering data and processing citizens' requests for services is immense and already being taken up in many countries - for example, in the U.K. this applies to processes such as income tax and paying for road tax. However, such interactions require that the pubic have ready access to the Internet or other systems that can access the relevant government ones, and that they are willing to trust their data to these. This raises questions about equality of access and of education, along with the development of the skills to know how to securely use online systems.

Dataveillance concerns are something that concerns some people about online activity. This is acknowledged with regard to e-commerce (Ashworth, 2006) as well as with national security issues. Concerns about privacy can lead some people to be loathe to use certain online facilities, and to be reluctant to submit information to online sites – whether commercial or pubic bodies. This particular issue has a number of aspects – one being how any data provided will be legitimately used, and another being illegitimate usage. Privacy policies and data protection laws can help with this in terms of reassuring some members of the public, but such policies and legal frameworks are themselves subject to numerous problems – in particular, consistency and application. Poorly implemented systems can cause numerous concerns and real problems with respect to illegitimate usage – examples range from failure to apply security technologies properly, to simply failing to develop robust and secure systems. Technological solutions can be developed to assist with some of these, but many require clear governmental policies, which are adopted by all the sub-bodies, and which are then applied consistently by the systems which implement them.

The crossover between the main two functions that we have just considered is where e-service sites provide data that the pubic submitted – whether that data was itself submitted by an e-government facility or through a more traditional means. This reflects one of the key concerns for many users of systems - what happens to the data they have provided. Privacy policies and clear statements of the intended use of data are the main ways that people would expect to be informed of this intended use. However, where government requires data, then there may be no option but to provide it in spite of potential negative effects. One example of this from the U.K. was the land-registry office. This public body keeps track of land and property ownership. Citizens carrying out transactions such as house buying submitted information via the traditional process – in fact the data in question was passed on by solicitors acting on behalf of their clients – and this data was processed by the land registry and made publically available via a website. There was no particular reason for individuals to be aware of this, but the data that was made available became the focus of criminal fraudulent activity (Sunday Times, 2007). This type of problem illustrates the dilemma for public bodies in making data available, as well as the legitimate concerns that the public have about the use of their data.

In a similar way to the question of whether there is anything new in e-commerce (Gordon, 2006), we can consider whether e-government offers anything new. In response to this question, one of the more exciting aspects of e-government is the potential to support and encourage E-democracy. A common concern for many nations is the lack of engagement with the democratic or at least governing process. E-services can offer ways for the public to vote – at the least for representatives, but ultimately the potential exists to allow for referendums or even to begin to get regular feedback and input from the population on policy decisions. The questions this raises in terms of security, political change and other aspects mean this still has some way to go, but the impact of social networking, the Internet and other Web 2.0 technologies means that this genie may be difficult to keep in the bottle.

ISSUES ON TEACHING THE INTERNET AND WEB TECHNOLOGIES

Key information skills for using the Internet and living the virtual existence it can provide reflect the issues identified above. These include the skills to know how to gather data to provide information and to be able to reflect upon and critically analyze the information found. They also include the skills to know how to produce data, and how to recognize the indicators that a site or system is reliable and trustworthy. A third area is in knowing the rights and responsibilities that the online citizen has.

The following describe how these topics have been taught by the author in a module for university students across a range of ages and stages, from pre-university level through to diploma level university students, and for students from a range of subjects. The experiences recorded are enlightening in terms of the assumptions in students that they challenge and some of the issues that they identify. Further antidotes from experiences with well educated (professorial colleagues) and others within the staff of tertiary education indicate the scale of the problems that governments face in ensuring that they maximize the uptake of e-government by their citizens.

Whilst many students entering tertiary education now are likely to have had a great deal of opportunity and experience with the Internet and more specific computer systems, the skills they have acquired in terms of understanding the distinction between the type of information they have found can be more limited. The following points reflect the experiences of the author with his students.

- Lack of awareness of the distinction between finding and providing information. This is demonstrated when students provide a reference list, which includes search engines in the list, both as a single entry (www.searchengine.com) and as specific search results (www.searchengine.com/search?hl=en&q=e-government). The analogy that can help students see the mistake here is that of referring to a library where they located and read a book, as opposed to recording the source itself.
- Lack of critical analysis of the reliability of the source. Whilst online repositories are extremely useful, and Wiki sites can be an effective way to find information on a subject, they are not reliable in the sense that the actual data can change and may at any point in time be unedited or reviewed and simply wrong. Using such a site to gain some pointers to other sites, and in particular to more reliable references is an appropriate use. However, a growing number of students – even at PhD level – are making use of such repositories as main references.
- Difficulties with interpreting the order of search results: the fact that different search engines may provide different results, and that a result that is near the top of a search may be there for a variety of reasons, related to how well it matches a search term according to the specific algorithm used, as well as commercial influences (where search facilities can be skewed for a price or by design of the information provide), and political ones – where a nation state imposes extra limitations on the range and scope of searching.
- Lack of understanding of the technologies that can assist in providing reassurance and ultimately security. An understanding of the use of online tools such as encryption technologies and the effectiveness and limitation of such tools is important if individuals are to use online facilities. Few students have personal digital signatures, let alone use them in a regular and sustained way. Similarly, they frequently lack an awareness of the open nature of many internet protocols – such as the lack of any encryption of standard emails. The fact that many email systems support digital signing and offer security features is missed by those who could make use of them.
- Naivety regarding online threats. The threats that undermine e-commerce and the internet generally can equally undermine the further progress with e-government initiatives. Even well educated and technologically aware individuals can fall prey to online scams and malware. Whilst technologically sophisticated users are aware not to respond to an email requesting a username and password, such attacks can be successful when users are not on their guard. Similarly, malware is surprisingly

effective, and can be difficult to diagnose and remove. Whilst not a barrier to those who expect and require online access and facilities, they can frighten less technical potential users – to the point where they would refuse to engage with online facilities. For E-commerce this is a loss in potential customers and clients, but for e-government this is a loss in access to a potentially sizeable proportion of the public.

- Data mining and the aggregation of data from numerous sources offers powerful ways for public bodies and commercial entities to collect useful information. However, many students display ignorance of the potential misuse, whilst others fear the misuse and lack the skills to avoid it. One related aspect is the persistence of data – the caching of pages in online archives and within search engine databases, as well as copies on servers themselves – means that students are unaware of the difficulty of removing a digital history once it is established. When combined with the lack of awareness of the legal standing of electronic statements they are opening themselves up to future problems.

The above examples of some of the issues facing online usage, which can impact on engagement with e-government and lead to the question of what is the framework within which the netizen exists and functions. By teaching topics around these areas, topics such as the ethical and technical considerations when using e-services: issues of Privacy and personal data protection, Liability and Security and topics on how to use the e-services effectively- such as the techniques to find and manage information – future citizens can be made ready to make use of e-government facilities.

The global nature of the Internet, the complexity of laws that apply, and the numerous opportunities for data to be aggregated and potentially misused mean that this education needs developing in national citizens, and the natural point at which to develop that is tertiary education as by that point the individuals should be well placed with their knowledge of their rights and responsibilities as citizens, and can begin to become aware of the global dimension. This can reinforce engagement with national issues, and reassure them on their future use of e-government services.

CONCLUSION

Tertiary education can play a key role in underpinning both the development of, and engagement with, e-government. This has links with other strategic changes – such as the growing focus on sustainable development and in this context in developing sustainable ICT systems. Education at pre and at tertiary level needs to provide the skills that future citizens will require. At the University level, this means developing both practical specific skills along with the intellectual skills of critical analysis. The change in the nature of knowledge and of access to information should encourage a move to inquiry based learning (Brayshaw, 2008 and 2009). Wider issues mean ensuring that future policy makers and system designers avoid dangerous assumptions – such as access to e-services, the level of education of the general population and in the suitability of the I.T. systems that are developed.

Regarding access, designing systems and providing widespread access requires large scale investment and planning. Whether this is based on providing e-service set-top boxes - akin to that achieved with the French Minitel system (Cats-Baril, 1994), or perhaps e-service kiosks, via libraries or using mobile phone technologies, access is something that requires investing in. Providing the skills and developing a culture that engages in this would require a long term strategy and approach. Tertiary education can provide that education to the next generation of policy makers and system designers and implementers to prepare the ground for the development of successful e-government systems and support.

REFERENCES

Ashworth, L., & Free, C. (2006). Marketing Dataveillance and Digital Privacy: Using Theories of Justice to Understand Consumers' Online Privacy Concerns. *Journal of Business Ethics*, *67*(2), 107–123. doi:10.1007/s10551-006-9007-7

Brayshaw, M., & Gordon, N. (2008). Inquiry based Learning in Computer Science teaching in Higher Education. *Innovations in Teaching And Learning in Information and Computer Sciences*, *7*(1), 22–33.

Brayshaw, M., & Gordon, N. (2009). Inquiry based learning in computer science: a natural approach to learning. In: P. Levy & P. McKinney (eds), *Proceedings of the 3rd Learning Through Enquiry Alliance Conference*, 25-27 June 2008, Sheffield, UK: Centre for Inquiry-based Learning in the Arts and Social Sciences (CILASS): University of Sheffield, pp 31-39.

Carter, L., & Bélanger, F. (2005). The utilization of e-government services: citizen trust, innovation and acceptance factors. *Information Systems Journal*, *15*(1), 5–25. doi:10.1111/j.1365-2575.2005.00183.x

Cats-Baril, W., & Jelassi, T. (1994). The French Videotex System Minitel: A Successful Implementation of a National Information Technology Infrastructure. *Management Information Systems Quarterly*, *18*(1), 1–20. doi:10.2307/249607

DCSF. (2008). *GCSE and equivalent results in England, 2007/09*, Department for Children, Schools and Families. Retrieved March 2009 from http://www.dcsf.gov.uk/rsgateway/DB/SFR/s000815/index.shtml

Eisenberg, M. (2008). Information Literacy: Essential Skills for the Information Age. *DESIDOC Journal of Library & Information Technology*, *28*(2).

Gordon, N., & Brayshaw, M. (2006). E-commerce And E-business: A New Paradigm Or Old Business In New Clothes? *E-Society*, 178-182.

Guardian (2009). *Facebook and Bebo risk 'infantilising' the human mind*, The Guardian Online. Retrieved March 2009, from http://www.guardian.co.uk/uk/2009/feb/24/social-networking-site-changing-childrens-brains

Gupta, M. P., & Jana, D. (2003). E-government evaluation: a framework and case study. *Government Information Quarterly*, *20*(4), 365–387. doi:10.1016/j.giq.2003.08.002

HMSO, *Better Public Services through e-government*, Report by the Comptroller and Auditor General, HC 704-I Session 2001-2002: 4 April 2002.

Sunday Times. (2007). Mortgage fraudsters have been stealing homeowners' identities by using the internet, *The Sunday Times online*. Retrieved October, 2008, from http://property.timesonline.co.uk/tol/life_and_style/property/article2830910.ece

The Times. (2008). Google could be superseded, says web inventor, *The Times Online*. Retrieved March 2009, from http://technology.timesonline.co.uk/tol/news/tech_and_web/article3532832.ece

Chapter 20
E-Learning and E-Management in Tunisian Universities

Rafik Braham
University of Sousse, Tunisia

Lilia C. Belcadhi
University of Sousse, Tunisia

Narjess T. Chebaane
University of Sousse, Tunisia

Maha Khemaja
University of Kairouan, Tunisia

ABSTRACT

In the year 2000, policy makers in Tunisian higher education decided to explore ways in which e-learning and e-management could be introduced to enhance university administration and teaching. This effort was by no means an isolated one at the international level. Indeed, it comes as a major spin-off of Information and Communication Technologies (ICTs) that led to the emergence of e-learning and web-based education and training, enabling remote access to information and knowledge. Developing countries, such as Tunisia which was the host in 2005 of Phase II of the World Summit on Information Society (WSIS) **(***Baldoni, M., 2005***)**, *have great expectations from the social and economic consequences of the Internet. These countries see the Internet as an opportunity that should not be missed. For this reason, the government has put in place several programs, all of which provide for its citizens e-services, that were, prior to the advent of the Internet, either impossible or real headaches. An important category of these services apply to the sector of higher education. They range from e-learning to student information systems accessible from the web. In this context, the e-learning team in the Higher Institute of Informatics and Communications in Hammam Sousse (ISITC), University of Sousse, has developed and deployed a number of online courses in a blended learning format. Various e-learning projects covering both pedagogical and technical aspects as well as doctoral research works have been under way to support this activity. The deployment of e-learning courses is supervised by the Virtual University of Tunis with technical help from our university. In this chapter, we describe our experiments, the results achieved thus far and some lessons that we have learned. We discuss e-management practices in universities around the world and address issues of concern and human factors at stake especially from the students' point of view.*

DOI: 10.4018/978-1-61520-789-3.ch020

INTRODUCTION

All universities around the world provide today some form of e-learning and e-services to its students and staff. Universities in developed countries rely so much on Internet and no single university that is among the top ranked can afford to disregard Internet. For universities in less developed countries, for example in some African countries, more efforts are needed especially from the infrastructure point of view. Well-aware of this situation, policy and decision makers in Tunisia invested in Internet relatively early with respect to other countries in the region. By the mid 1990's, Internet connections were common, in particular at university colleges. In 1996, the National Internet Agency was created to promote and regulate Internet services. In the few years that followed, the country has witnessed a surge in Internet based services, especially in the media and the public sector.

In this chapter, we focus on one category of these services, namely those applicable in the sector of higher education, ranging from e-learning to student information systems accessible from the web. In addition to this introduction, the chapter includes five sections. In Sections II and III, we describe e-learning programs in Tunisian universities. Sections IV and V are research oriented. They give an account respectively on e-learning assessment via the web and automatic generation of pedagogical scenarios. Finally, Section VI describes e-services in the context of higher education. At the end, we provide a comprehensive discussion.

E-LEARNING PROGRAMS

As mentioned in the introduction, the second half of the 1990's was a busy period for Internet fans in Tunisia. But the year 2000 represents a turning point in the history of our universities, as decision makers in the higher education system took concrete steps to engage in some kind of e-learning activities. But hard questions had to be answered first since this subject was new to everyone, administrators and teachers alike. A major question was then whether to choose a centralized e-learning management system or a decentralized one. The decision was in favor of the former option and at the beginning of 2002, the Virtual University of Tunis ("UVT," 2008) was created by the ministry in charge of higher education.

The other major question was then to determine its main objective. Since that period, a major concern was the sharply rising number of students. This number is expected to grow from 220,000 in 2002 to almost 500,000 ten years later. It was hoped that UVT would help in this regard. Its precise objective was set for it to provide 20% of all university-level courses at distance, i.e. web-based (before 2009). Ministry officials were hoping that e-learning would provide a viable solution to crowded lecture rooms.

This interest in e-learning was not unique of course to Tunisian universities. Just in the Mediterranean region, a number of projects were underway. A network of Mediterranean universities called "Tethys" was created in that period and several Tunisian universities were members. Its purpose was to promote e-learning within the Mediterranean region.

It is precisely in this context that we launched an e-learning program at the Higher Institute of Informatics and Communication Technologies of Hammam Sousse (ISITC), which is a part of the University of Sousse ("UC," 2008). This program included blended learning courses, research projects and symposia organization. All this activity was coordinated with UVT and the services of our university. Although this article will focus on work at ISITC, similar programs may be found in other colleges and universities nation wide.

TEACHING EXPERIMENTS

The e-learning experiments, carried out at ISITC, have gone through various stages involving several aspects. The first action was related to the choice of adequate courses. One choice criterion was to carry out e-learning for courses where the number of students was quite high and simultaneously the number of teachers was insufficient. After discussions with members of the e-learning team, it was decided to start with an Object Oriented Programming course (OOP) and later on a Data Base (DB) course.

The second aspect dealt with course contents. The essential aims by these contents are to improve the training by selected modules through integrating multimedia components, making use of graphics and animated sections. Finally, the authors together with the technical staff at the University of Sousse designed the course according to style of UVT. The result was an online course, organized into chapters and learning sessions. Each session comprises text (definitions, rules...), figures, graphs, examples and animations to illustrate various concepts. Exercises and answers were also provided at the end of each sequence, as well as multiple choice questions and previous course exams.

The third aspect concerned the choice of student groups. Taking into account the fact that this experiment was a pioneering one, some students and teachers were reluctant as expected. The e-learning team tried thus to introduce the idea of this new mode of training in a progressive way paying a particular attention to student needs. It was decided for the first year of the experiment to use two student populations: one population would follow purely traditional face to face courses; and the other population would be submitted to e-learning course format. In the following year, we felt that the experiment was a success and it was decided to switch to full e-learning for the OOP course. The students had weekly hours in a lab, for accessing the course content on the INES LCMS and for doing their exercises under the supervision of a teacher.

The results encountered through this first experiment were encouraging and it was decided to utilize the e-learning format only for all students. More precisely since 2004, this course is offered in hybrid mode, which means that students have access to the course content on the learning management system; tutors have to insure students' follow up and the access control to resources. Students have however to be present in labs to do their programming exercises. At the end of each lab session, they have to deposit their assignments directly on the LCMS, Moodle to be precise ("MOODLE," 2009). Moodle facilitates collaborative work. It is indeed a student-centered environment where learners are able to work independently and reflect on their own work and on the work of their peers.

These experiments showed that students were motivated. They tried hard to respect the deadlines announced for the various assignments on the LCMS, and participated actively in the discussion forums about course content. Learners also found that access to the LCMS helps them prepare for their final exams. There nevertheless some difficulties particularly related to the limited access to labs as well as some technical difficulties, especially at the beginning of the semester such as registration on the LCMS.

As far as the DB course is concerned, it was decided to change teaching and learning techniques. The students were given the possibility to meet their teacher weekly for 1.5 hours, to do exercises, and to discuss eventual difficulties that may have risen during readings. Furthermore, the students had another opportunity to meet in the lab for 1.5 hours bi-weekly to have access to course material online.

They can do their exercises with the teacher's assistance, they can discuss (with the teacher and /or between them) or request further explanations about the course using forums.

Another e-learning experiment has been organized in the ISITC through the teaching of the C2i (IT and Internet Certificate) course. The objective of C2i is to enable students to master the skills that are now required for pursuing higher education programs and to become capable of developing these skills as the technology itself develops. Because the course is new, an objective assessment is not available yet.

RESEARCH I: ASSESSMENT

A. Web-Based Assessment

Assessment in educational environments is a process of drawing reasonable inferences about what learners know (both in theory and practice) on the basis of evidence derived from observation of what they say, do or make in selected situations. Assessment is considered as an important aspect for both distance and face-to-face education. For this reason, assessment is one of our main research interests. We may distinguish three main categories of assessment that can be used in any educational program ("QAA," 2007):

- Diagnostic assessment: provides an indicator of a learner's aptitudes and preparedness to a course.
- Formative assessment: provides feedback to learners on their progress but does not contribute to the overall assessment.
- Summative assessment: provides a measure of achievement or failure made in respect to a learner's performance in relation to the program of study.

Our research focuses on formative assessments, which are part of the learning process and aim to assist the learner by diagnosing their problems of understanding, giving them feedback and guiding them in their efforts. Formative assessment assesses the quality of learning, whereas summative assessment assesses the quantity and retention of learning by the end of the unit of instruction.

Learning in open environments over heterogeneous resources demands effective personalization approaches to provide learner orientation and individualized access support. It also requires advanced approaches for assessment which are capable of dealing with such e-Learning environments. Our approach for personalization of web based assessment has been applied on the OOP course described in Section III above. In this course teachers usually provide three types of assessment:

- **Self assessment:** This assessment is not graded. It is presented in the form of activities integrated into the course, short questions and exercises to be carried out. Emphasis is placed on the most significant points of the lesson. Solutions are generally available online.
- **Graded work:** This work aims to check the knowledge acquisition of learners, often through concrete study cases. It comprises homework and tests at face to face practice sessions.
- **Final exam:** it is taken under normal exam conditions in usual classrooms. This is a comprehensive test covering all course material. It may include questions, programming exercises, code development, case studies, etc

Since we are interested in the automatisation of assessment and its deployment on the Web we chose to focus on "self assessment", which is part of the formative assessment category. We looked at some existing assessment systems and explored the functionalities they offer. We then analyzed these systems comparatively to detect the main problems they imply. We focused on two particular issues: the first is related to the potential for these systems to ensure that the generated tests include a set of questions that are suitable for the learner's level of knowledge. The question is whether to draw for each lesson of the course a dedicated question database and define several pools for these questions. Another possibility consists in using metadata. Indeed, when the system holds some information about the question such as type, topic assessed, keywords, and parts of the course it relates to, it will be able to select the appropriate resources to each individual user according to his preferences.

The second issue in Computer Assisted Assessment is that the developed assessment materials are made less reusable and less distributable by a general lack of provision of standardized or interchangeable formats. Indeed, the adoption of assessment standards such as IMS/QTI ("QTI," 2007) is not the priority of most producers of CAA systems. Developed assessment materials are therefore neither portable nor conducive to sharing between lecturers and products (the question bank concept). Moreover, they significantly reduce the motivation for, and value of, such materials. The reusability and sharing of assessment materials are critical issues that need to be addressed by the CAA systems and facilitate the personalization of these materials.

This research also investigated possibilities to implement Semantic Web technologies to provide dynamic assessment and adaptive course presentation to the learner. Indeed, the Semantic Web could be considered as a suitable platform for the implementation and delivery of e-learning courses because it enables querying and navigation through learning materials according to an ontology-based annotation. It also facilitates the selection of relevant learning parts of a course according to the user's level of knowledge and on the basis of a personalized assessment.

We then observed that there is a large variety of systems that offer assessment and assistance to the learner. Nonetheless, the assessment functionality in most of these systems is described with reference to a specific environment, which means that the functionality is only described in terms of the system that supports it. So long as the assessment functionality is dependent upon the system's characteristics, it is difficult to give a precise comparison of assessment systems. We observed that there is currently no common language that enables the description and analysis of the assessment functionality. Thus, a formal description of personalized assessment which allows a system-independent characterization of the assessment functionality is needed.

B. Formal Description

The large variety of CAA systems and complexity of their components make it difficult to analyze these components in depth. Indeed there is no common language to express the functionality of web-based assessment systems. We infer that there is currently a need to establish formal expressions that enable system developers to describe the functionalities of their systems and compare them with others. In addition, this formalization is helpful in constructing a model of the user, which is a representation of those characteristics according to which assessment personalization will occur. We thus investigated ways of providing a logic-based description for personalized web-based assessment.

We studied the possibilities for knowledge representation and the reasoning from this knowledge, to enable a personalization of learning and assessment in an educational environment. A rather natural approach is the use of logic, which is considered as the foundation of knowledge representation. In the area of artificial intelligence and the World Wide Web, logic plays an important role in knowledge representation. Indeed, knowledge can be expressed in logic in a transparent manner through the highly expressive power of logic. Moreover, logic is considered as a well-understood formal semantics, which assigns an unambiguous meaning to logical statements.

The formal description has been consequently established in First Order Logic (FOL) (Baldoni et.

al., 2005). FOL seemed to be a good compromise. First, it is a powerful, machine-understandable and well-known formalism. All other rules systems are founded on FOL and can be considered in some sense as extensions of FOL: they include all the quantifiers and logical operators of FOL with the same meanings. Second, transcribing rules from natural language to FOL can be very easy and knowledge can be expressed in a transparent way. Indeed this language provides a well-understood formal semantics, which assigns an unambiguous meaning to logical statements. It has also a precise notion of logical consequence, which determines whether a statement follows semantically from a set of other statements (premises).

The aim of this logic-based definition is to describe the main characteristics and functionalities of web-based assessment systems. On the basis of the logic description, inference techniques-including ontology reasoning mechanisms- can be applied. A translation of these FOL rules in a query language for the Semantic Web was therefore necessary to enable reasoning over distributed annotations of resources on the basis of an ontological knowledge.

As an example of the FOL rules that we defined to describe the personalization of assessment on the Semantic Web we give the following rule that states that a learning object is recommended for pre-assessment if at least one of its prerequisite concepts from the knowledge base has not been learnt by the user:

```
∀U; ∀LO ∃
(∃C prerequisite_of_resource(C;LO) ∧
¬p_obs(C; U; Assessed))
→ learning_resource_annotation
(LO;U;Pre_assessment_recommended).
```

Further details concerning the established rules can be found in (Cheniti-Belcadhi et. al., 2005).

It is worth noting that our objective was to build assessment personalization using Semantic Web technologies to enable interoperability and reusability of data. It is therefore necessary to choose a Semantic Web query language, which enable the reasoning and the inference over semantically annotated data. The principle of "inference" is to derive new data from the already known data.

One of the languages that enable inference mechanism over semantic web is TRIPLE. The main purpose of this language is to query Web resources in a declarative way, e.g. for intelligent information retrieval based on background knowledge like ontologies. Given that we describe the data needed for assessment and learning using the semantic Web language RDF, this language seemed to be an appropriate choice. Indeed it is able to support RDF reasoning including resources, namespaces and models, while providing rules with expressive bodies based on FOL syntax. As an example of the produced rules in TRIPLE we give the following rule which asserts that for a learning resource LO a pre assessment is recommended if the learner U has not validated at least one of its prerequisite concepts. Recommendations are personalized according to the ongoing learning progress of the user and with respect to the available set of learning and assessment resources at a given time:

```
FORALL LO, U
assessment_state(LO, U, Preassessmen-
tRecommnended) ←
learning_resource(LO) AND user(U) AND
EXISTS C(prerequisite_of_resource(LO,
C)
AND NOT (concept_assessed(C, U))).
```

C. An Assessment Prototype Features of SWAP

We developed a Semantic Web Assessment Personalization Environment (called SWAP) that enables learners' dynamic assessment and adaptive course presentation. We describe in this section its features and the following section its architecture.

Web based assessment is considered as a value-added service in an e-learning procedure, which aims at evaluating and measuring the outcome of learning experiences. Providing the learners with personalized tests that are appropriate to their needs and prior knowledge would guarantee an efficient learning process. Current research in the Semantic Web could be used to achieve this objective by using the concept of ontology, which plays a role in facilitating the sharing of meaning and semantics. It provides all means for ontology development, ontology-based annotation of assessment material, their composition in tests as well as the delivery of these tests. The Semantic Web architecture is powerful enough to satisfy the computer assisted assessment requirement. Assessment material is semantically annotated and for a new assessment demand it may be easily combined in a new test. According to their level of knowledge, learners can be easily presented with appropriate tests. The process is based on semantic querying and navigation through assessment material, enabled by the ontological background. Languages such as RDF, RDFS and OWL can be used for metadata representation and reasoning.

In the context of this research we designed a modular system architecture of reusable components, which supports the shareability and interoperability of the components as well as the use of others components within an open system. This architecture is established by setting up Web services which use data semantics and offer means for flexible service composition through automatic selection, interoperation of existing services, and verification of service properties and execution of monitoring. Furthermore, the proposed architecture is domain-independent and can be used for a variety of courses. We can reach reasonable automation and dynamic realization of the assessment functionalities through the implementation of Web services tasks. The system embodies personalized Web services that deliver assessment and generate learning resources proportionally to domain ontology, learner's requirements and interaction with the learning environment.

The SWAP environment for online assessment allows the flexible use of assessment techniques, and provides in addition an adaptive selection, embedding and presentation of assessment and learning materials according to the learners' performances. It combines research from two major disciplines: adaptive educational hypermedia (Brusilovsky, 2001) and Semantic Web technologies. Research in adaptive educational hypermedia has ascertained several techniques for adaptation. We provide adaptive, personalized access to materials in order to guide the learner, and develop an assessment service based on the adaptive selection of questions. Indeed, the enhancement of the assessment process with adaptive capabilities enables a dynamic and individualized process, as it is tailored to the learner's performance. It also reduces the number of questions required to estimate the learner's knowledge standard, resulting in a less tedious assessment process.

Some adaptive systems would allow the learner to directly select and browse the learning material needed (Brusilovsky & Paylo, 2003). However, these systems are unable to diagnose the learner's learning goal and prior knowledge based on his browsing. Moreover, in some adaptive tutoring systems the student may have a predefined test allowing the extraction of a model from domain knowledge, but this predefined test can not estimate correctly the exact knowledge of the learner and provide him with the appropriate learning material.

In our work, we combine Semantic Web technologies and learning standards to enhance the interoperability of resources. The Semantic Web based personalized assessment system fosters the implementation of an ontology-based adaptive assessment scenario, thereby enabling the adaptive generation of questions and online courses to acquire a good estimation of learner's level of knowledge.

D. Architecture of SWAP

SWAP is a generic assessment system that was part integrated into the Personal Reader Framework ("Personal Reader", 2007). Its architecture embodies personalized Web services that deliver assessment and generate learning resources within the learning environment.

The SWAP system is composed of services available for the user without centralized control. This architecture is a rigorous approach for applying Semantic Web technologies. Indeed, SWAP is composed of Web services which deliver assessment and generate learning resources with respect to domain ontology, learners' requirements and interaction with the learning environment.

Communication between different Web services is carried out through RDF documents. The RDF descriptions refer to ontologies that allow the search and presentation of information needed. To enable the personalized assessment support, meta-information about the course, the learning and assessment resources and about learners themselves is required. The SWAP system makes use of learning standards LOM ("LOM," 2007) and Dublin Core to support interoperability. It is also designed to be QTI compliant in order to enhance the exchange of assessment resources.

The architecture that we proposed is capable to be adjusted to different application domains. This is achieved through a non monolithic approach, in which several, independent components, each serving a specific purpose, are assembled. This architecture was introduced in (Cheniti-Belcadhi et. al., 2005).

The Web service technology focuses on such requirements. A Web service encapsulates a specific functionality, and communicates with other services or software components via interface components. We consider each (personalized) information provision task as the result of a particular service (which itself might be composed of several services, too). The aim of this approach is to construct a flexible environment in which the user can select and combine various kinds of information according to his needs.

The SWAP system is composed of five services: Login service, Visualization service, Connector service, User profile service and Personalization services.

A visualization service is responsible for the display of the resources requested by the learner, i.e. either the learning resources or the assessment resources. It is the interface between the user and the SWAP system. It is responsible for user administration, reception of user queries and inputs and display of results. In addition, it gathers further necessary input data, e.g. the description of learning resources or the used ontologies, and forwards this information with the user profile to the "Connector service". Having processed the input data, its main task is to then display to the user those output data received from the "Connector service". Information is represented through HTML pages on the basis of "Java Servlets" and "Java Server Pages" (JSP).

A key component of the SWAP architecture is the Connector service. Communications among all services go through the Connector service. Its main task is to convert the different formats of metadata descriptions used by the Assessment service instances and provide a generic interface for the Visualization service instances. In addition, the Connector service has to fetch the learning resources, the assessment resource descriptions and the ontology from the Web. It then aggregates all the documents and forwards them to the Personalization services. Last, the Connector service uses a reasoning program to apply the rules required to process a request to the Connector service.

The User profile service is responsible for the generation of a learner's profile featuring his history and built upon the last interactions he saved and answers he provided to the proposed tests. It is also composed of two other services: the usage monitoring service and the Learner performance service. The learner's interactions with the assessment and learning resources are recorded through the usage monitoring service. The Performance service updates information on the learner on the basis of his results in the pre- and post- tests.

The SWAP system is also composed of the following Personalization services:

- A Navigation service that provides a personalized navigation through the learning and assessment resources on the basis of the information provided in the learner's profile.
- An Assessment service composed of two other services that can be requested independently: the Test generation service and the Question evaluation service. Its role is to provide a personalized assessment to the learner based on the information provided in his profile. The test generation service is responsible for the construction of tests. The question evaluation service is in charge of assessing the learner's answers.

SWAP provides two options for assessment: (1) pre-test, to investigate the learner's prior knowledge of selected learning resource and initialize his profile accordingly and (2) post-test, to stimulate the learner to contemplate and reflect on the subject studied, assess his performance and evaluate the learning outcomes. The construction of pre-tests and post-tests is a dynamic process that depends on the learner's current level of knowledge. The navigational behaviour of the learner through the content is considered in addition. The assessment procedure takes into account the learning resources that the learner visited. This type of information is saved in the learner's profile. In the pre-tests, questions relating to the prerequisite concepts of the selected learning resources are displayed. In post-tests, questions that are relevant to each objective of the current selected resource are presented to the learner. A description of the system functionalities can be found in (Cheniti-Belcadhi et. al., 2008).

The SWAP system allows every learner who uses it to have a personalized interface, which he can access by logging in with his password. The interface is divided into two parts: a left part and a right part. The left part visualizes the results received via the Connector service. Learning resources for which a pre-test can be constructed based on the information in the learner's profile will be marked with a yellow ball. In case a post-test can be created for the selected learning resource a red ball will be displayed. When an assessment resource is selected, it will be displayed in the right part of the window. On the left, an assessment interface which visualizes the results received via the Connector service is displayed. The possible answer choices are contained in the details section. Once a choice is selected by the leaner, it will be recorded in the profile, and the corresponding feedback (whether the response is correct or not) will then be displayed. In case the assessment resource has been answered correctly by the learner, it will be saved as solved in the profile and will not be associated anymore to a pre-test or post-test of a learning resource.

The personalized assessment approach adopted in our system operates as follows:

- **1st step:** The system looks for the initial level of knowledge by requesting the learner's profile from the User profile service.
- **2nd step:** Once the learner has selected a learning resource, metadata of the currently visited learning resource is identified. The Connector service submits to the Assessment service the description of the learning resource, together with the ontology and the learner's profile. The Assessment service then selects the assessment resources that have to be associated to the pre- and post-tests of the selected learning resource. It possesses reasoning rules which makes it able to query for assessment resources and metadata, and

reason over distributed data and metadata descriptions.

- **3rd step:** the results of personalized pre-tests and post-tests generation together with the personalized assessment recommendation for the selected learning resource (red and yellow balls) are displayed to the learner by the Visualization service.
- **4th step:** Once the learner has selected an assessment resource, its metadata are identified. When he works on the assessment resource, the answers are evaluated, forwarded to the user profile service and saved in the profile. Assessment resources that were correctly solved by the learner are no longer considered as candidate assessment resources.

E. System Evaluation

An evaluation of the SWAP system was performed, with a particular focus on usability and effectiveness. We defined two categories of users: beginners and advanced. A panel of ten students with different a priori knowledge of C++ programming was selected. Five of these were enrolled in the second year of a computer science curriculum, and were considered to be part of the beginners' category. The remaining students were in their first year of computer engineering studies at ISITC at the University of Sousse. They were put under the advanced rubric, as they had taken already a course in Object Oriented Programming.

In the evaluation, each student -without undergoing any prior training on how to proceed- used the system during a course session. This gave him the opportunity to navigate through the course content and answer some of the 24 questions on Object Oriented Programming with C++.

Several improvements to the first version of SWAP are currently underway as part of an on-going research project. The main issue in using IMS QTI is that it offers a restricted set of test types: Multiple Choice Question, Fill in the Blanks and Short answers. Our main concern is that we are interested to offer also assessment to programming exercises. One possible solution to have such type of questions in QTI would be to propose to learners programming code including some programming errors, and ask the learner to correct these errors. Another alternative would be to define test data in the specification of the tests and to have the possibility to invoke an external program such as a compiler, so that learner would have the possibility to validate his solution according to the test data.

We have therefore studied in-depth all types of questions offered in QTI and investigated the possibility of adapting existing questions to programming. We are also currently developing an editor that permits the generation of questions with conformance to the QTI specification and the generation of new types of questions.

RESEARCH II: PEDAGOGY WITH LEARNING DESIGN

Distance learning implies pedagogy different from that used in face-to-face context, namely "e-pedagogy". With this type of pedagogy, some difficulties appear. A major challenge is to combine pedagogy and technology so as to communicate knowledge in the most effective and efficient way.

Until now, several pedagogical contents generating tools appeared, especially authoring tools. Although these tools reduce technical constraints, they remain limited in the pedagogical support which takes into account the expertise of teaching. The study presented here is an attempt to explore an expert teacher's model of thinking and teaching during his activities of designing pedagogical contents, i.e. modelling the e-pedagogy through these contents. The goal is to perform on the basis of this model is to assist teachers in the develop-

ment of e-learning contents, as well as in their activities of teaching.

An on-line course must be designed around activities that are most likely to lead students toward the pedagogical goals defined by the curriculum. In fact, some goals can be achieved by attending lectures or reading assigned texts, and others require more active experimentation, practice or discussion. Until now, several pedagogical contents generating tools appeared, especially authoring tools. Although these tools reduce technical constraints, they do not provide a pedagogical support of quality, i.e. contents which take into account the pedagogical aspect and expertise of teaching.

Another important element is student learning styles. The Felder-Silverman's 4-dimensional model (Vasilyeva et al., 2006; Graf & Kinshuk, 2006) is particularly popular in this regard. Some research works are developing methods for the construction of student learning styles, based not only on questionnaires as is generally the case, but also on the behavior of learners as extracted from data gathered by an LMS. In our work, we are developing pedagogical approaches, and at the same time, providing support to the important progress made in recent years in the field of learning technologies (LTs) through the use of relevant standards and corresponding information models such as those for LOM and IMS-LD/QTI.

We describe a teacher-oriented assistant under development that can provide guidance for teaching activities within LD framework, which puts activities in the center of the learning process. The system's goal is to assists teachers in designing their courses by simulating an expert-teacher reasoning. It is composed of models inspired from those used in Intelligent Tutoring Systems (ITS) with some adaptations. Furthermore, we propose to use ontology to define knowledge relative to a specific domain (a Data Base Management System course).

IMS-LD SPECIFICATION

Many organisms and consortiums were interested in the pedagogical aspect while designing instructional environments. The work on Educational Modeling Languages (Koper & Tattersall, 2005), and the subsequent integration into the IMS Learning Design specification (IMS-LD), is the most important initiative to date, in integrating instructional design issues into the eLearning standards' movement. In particular, it aims to represent the learning design of units of learning in a semantic, formal and machine interpretable way.

A learning design is defined as the description of the teaching-learning process within a unit of learning. It represents learning activities and support activities that are performed by different persons having different roles (teachers, learners,…) in the context of a unit of learning using learning objects and services. IMS LD is divided into three levels ("IMS Learning Design," 2009):

Level A contains all the core vocabulary needed to support pedagogical diversity. It lets to define the sequences of a unit of learning. Level B adds Properties and Conditions to level A, which enable personalization and more elaborate sequencing and interactions based on learner portfolios. It can be used to direct the learning activities as well as record outcomes. The separation of Properties and Conditions into a separate Schema also enable it to be used independently of the rest of the Learning Design Specification. Finally Level C adds Notification to level B, which, although a fairly small addition to the specification, adds significantly to the capability, but potentially also to the implementation task where something similar is not already in place.

Experimental Set-Up

As part of our research, a web-content design experiment using one of LD compatible tools, namely the MOT+Learning Design has been conducted. This system uses the MISA Method (Paquette,

Crevier, & Aubin, 1997) for engineering learning systems developed at LICEF Research Center. It is a graphical editing tool enabling users to model different fields of knowledge and build different types of graphical models. First, we have chosen a Data Base Management System (DBMS) course as an example of the domain model.

The MOT+LD gives as a result an XML file (a manifest) compatible with IMS LD specification. Since the MOT+LD tool supports only level A of the IMS LD specification, the manifest file was exported to Reload Learning Design Editor, developed at the University of Bolton, in order to add levels B and C of the specification. Furthermore, learning objects (LOs) related to the course were added at this step to constitute, with the manifest, an entire package (IMS Content package). Finally, this zipped package was exported to Reload LD Player to be checked and executed. Figure 1 shows a screen capture of the outcome. The later package can then be integrated into an LCMS.

Some of this experiment steps were carried out manually due to lack of compatible tools. The experiment shows that it is not clear how to automate and integrate into LD activities and scenarios on the basis of ontologies and corresponding languages. In this direction, we propose a system that automates these tasks. It consists of a support system for teachers to assist them in making decisions while designing online learning contents based on IMS-LD specification by simulating an expert-teacher reasoning. This system is based on an ontologies-driven approach and LD compliant. Furthermore, we attempt in this system to put emphasis on pedagogical strategies. In the following we present the system's architecture.

Methodology and System Architecture

The system is composed of models inspired from those used in Intelligent Tutoring Systems (ITS) with some adaptations. The system architecture is built around several models.

In the following, we will explain the models constituting the system.

- **The online course model:** This model is defined initially by an e-learning expert and specifies the general online course structure. A course is composed of several lessons and each lesson is constituted of activities of different knowledge levels. To specify this structure, an ontology relative to the IMS-LD specification was elabo-

Figure 1. Screen capture of a DBMS course (in French)

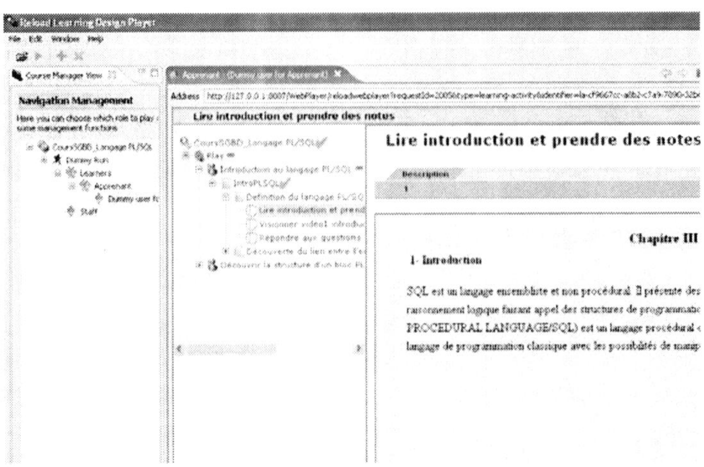

rated (Figure 2). This ontology was modeled using the MOT+OWL tool developed at LICEF. Based on this ontology a set of rules was defined in a rules base and will be inferred by the system in order to provide guidance while designing the IMS-LD scenario.

- **The domain model:** This model represents the useful expert knowledge related to the considered course. It is this component of the system that provides specific domain knowledge, as well as its place within the course. This model is defined by the domain expert and is represented using ontology too.
- **The student model:** This model defines the learner profile, level of understanding (based on assessment), motivation and preferred learning style.
- **The pedagogical engine:** Its role is to simulate the decisional behavior of an expert teacher. The main objective of this module is to answer the following questions: why intervene? When to intervene? How to intervene?

Providing teachers with assistance requires, first of all, identifying and analyzing clearly the main tasks to elaborate. Then we have to determine the structure of a unit of learning and the concept of pedagogical method, by specifying activities that learners and support staff can play using learning objects and services in the learning environment.

Then we establish a task graph representing tasks that must be performed by a designer within an instructional scenario generation process. This graph outlines assistance steps that will be suggested by the system in specifying the appropriate learning scenario, the appropriate support scenario, the appropriate learning activity (or activities) for the learner, the appropriate assistance activity (or activities) and the required resources to the realization of these activities and productions

Figure 2. Course ontology compliant with IMS-LD specification

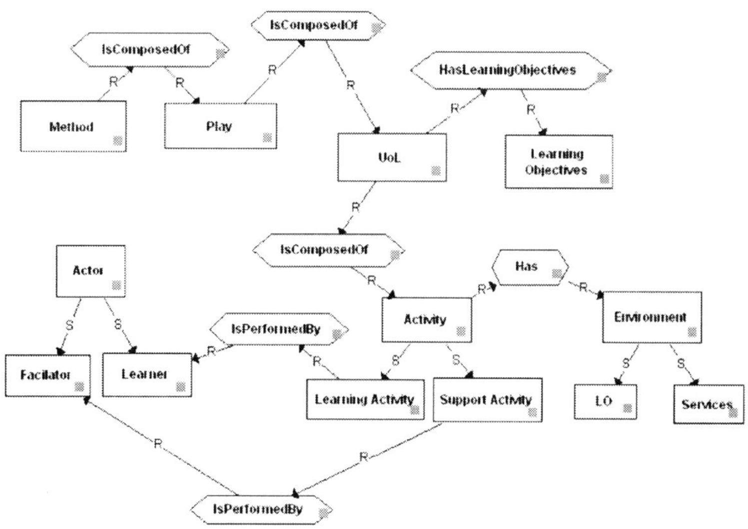

LEGEND:
S: Specialization
P: Precedence
R: Regulated by

resulting from these activities. We distinguish the following principal tasks:

- Choose learning scenario,
- Create learning activities,
- Choose support scenario,
- Create support activities.

Learning can be identified with the process of acquiring new knowledge, behaviors, skills, values, preferences or understanding, and may involve synthesizing different types of information. Consequently, to determine the assistance concerned by each task cited above, we proceed to model these elements within an instructional design process. Thus we consider, as described in MISA (Paquette, Aubin & Crevier, 1999), the following learning scenario types: reception, reception-exercise, case study, guided discovery and construction. Concerning the support scenario, we distinguish the following types: support by presentation, support by tutorials, support by analogy, support by questioning and methodological support.

Furthermore, based on previews researches described in the literature, we distinguish four levels of knowledge: facts, procedures, concepts and principals. In addition, a learning activities classification according to the intellectual behavior taxonomy developed by Bloom (Bloom, 1956) was elaborated.

We also define two important parameters while elaborating a curriculum: actual skill level and target skill level of the target population. Table 1 gives a taxonomy of cognitive skills used to model these two parameters.

We assign to each task of the graph a set of pedagogical rules constituting then the system rules base. These rules provide teachers with assistance with regard to a particular learning context (type of knowledge, learner's learning style, and level of target skill).These rules were implemented with the Semantic Web Rule Language SWRL which is the combination of the OWL DL and OWL Lite with the Datalog RuleML.

Table 2 gives examples of these rules.

Table 1. Skills taxonomy

class	Sub-class
Reception	Pay attention
	Integrate
Reproduction	Instanciate, explain
	Transpose
	Use, simulate
Production	Analyse, classify, diagnostic
	Repair, correct, modify
	Synthesize, plan, model
Auto-control	Evaluate
	Auto-control, auto-manage

Discussion

The work we presented provides two aspects. First, an investigation about LD environments has been carried out. Its purpose was to find out to what extent the LD framework has matured in terms of three dimensions: available tools, supported standards (including programming languages) and compatibility with existing material (i.e. course content). We conclude that fortunately designers do not have to start from scratch but much effort still remains.

The second original aspect of this paper deals with pedagogical strategy. This part is not yet taken in charge by automating tools within the LD framework. For example, we face particular difficulty with ontology integration in this framework. Our current research goal is to keep working within IMS-LD frameworks enhanced with instructional design intelligent paradigms.

Table 2. Examples of rule syntax and corresponding explanations

Rule	Explanation
Innovator(?x) → learning_scenario(construction)	IF learners' learning style is "*innovator*" THEN prefer a "*construction*" learning scenario
Facts(?x) ^ swrlb:greaterThan(facts_proportion, 40) ^ swrlb:lessThan(targ_skill_level, 2) → learning_scenario(reception) ^ assistance_scenario(presentation)	IF the unit of learning contains more than 40% of "facts" and the targeted skill's level is less than 2, THEN prefer a "*reception*" learning scenario and "*presentation*" assistance scenario.
Learning_scenario (reception) → learning_act_type (Type_perception) ^ has_learning_activity_type (reception, perception_type)	IF the chosen learning scenario is "*reception*" THEN prefer activities of "*perception*".
Type_act_app(Type_production) → Modalite_intervention(Reactive) ^ Type_act_support(Type_evaluative)	IF learning activities type is "*reception*" THEN prefer "*reactive*" intervention and "*evaluative*" support activities.

I. E-MANAGEMENT AND E-ADMINISTRATION

Tunisian universities, together with the ministry in charge of higher education, engaged in a number of e-management projects in addition to on-going e-learning programs. This positive development comes in harmony with a nation-wide trend that gained momentum in 2005, date of Phase II of the World Summit on Information Society. But the Internet awareness in the country was actually quite high even before, and the period 1995-2000 was marked by important milestones especially in the public sector. The early services were however more static and later services provided much more interactivity with the user. This is due of course to the evolution of the World Wide Web itself, which evolved from Web 1.0 to Web 2.0 and beyond.

This trend is world-wide as well. For example in Europe, e-government and e-health have become important research subjects and the European Union currently sponsors several projects in their Framework Programs (FP6, FP7, etc.). In the sector of higher education, several student services using Internet as a front-end for student access have been put on-line during the last few years in universities around the world. These services provide orientation for new students, registration and applications for graduate studies.

Three key elements may be considered when designing and offering public e-services: utility, effectiveness and undesirable side-effects (we are only looking at the social side of the subject since we are dealing with the public sector).

1. Utility: when a service is proposed to the public, its goal is to respond to a pressing need, for example to solve a problem or to reach a new public or a public of specific needs (elderly, children, etc.).
2. Effectiveness: the online version of the service could be more cost effective and it would help achieve a better use of public money in terms of citizens' satisfaction.
3. Undesirable side-effects: again, being a public service, drawbacks cannot be ignored or masked by mere financial gains. In this regard, a simple solution would be to employ a combination of a conventional service and an e-service.

As any public services, e-services in higher education must take into account not just the administration perspective but the student/faculty perspective as well. Even from an administrative point of view only, it is not always clear whether there is sufficient coordination between say the central administration and the local/regional offices. This factor is important in systems like the Tunisian higher education system where private universities play a secondary role (in 2007-2008, less than 2% of students are in private colleges).

An e-management project that satisfied the above requirements is currently being implemented at the Higher Institute of Management and Computer Science of Kairouan (ISIGK), Tunisia, in the framework of a programme launched by the ministry to support quality in higher education (known as the "PAQ" project).

The project comes after an in-deep evaluation of job processes and information exchange between concerned actors in ISIGK. Its aim is to develop a portal-based solution that will offer e-services for students, teachers, administrators and other stakeholders, and provide quality management in the institute.

The following services will be provided:

- **Contents and knowledge management services:** with a focus on knowledge and experience sharing.
- **Collaboration:** it aims at bringing teachers, students, administrators and enterprises together and facilitating rich mutual interactions.
- **Processes management:** to improve organizational performance through new managerial and business models linked with a business strategy.

Figure 3 shows the complete information system architecture.

The system's solution adopted for the project provides the following features:

1. It simplifies how actors interact with content, process and business data.
2. It boosts actors' productivity by simplifying everyday activities through careful design of specific process workflows, with emphasis on improving pedagogical teacher activities.
3. It gives access to business data produced by other kind of applications provided by the institution and personalized views and interactions with those applications.
4. It enables administrators to make better-informed decisions by presenting and assembling business critical information from separate sources using Integrated Business Intelligence capabilities such as Web Parts and Key Performance Indicators and business data connectivity technologies.
5. It supports Web services and interoperability standards including XML and SOAP. This feature is especially useful to enhance communications between the portal solution and other applications such as the LMS used for e-learning (namely Moodle), the library

Figure 3. Architecture of the ISIGK e-management portal

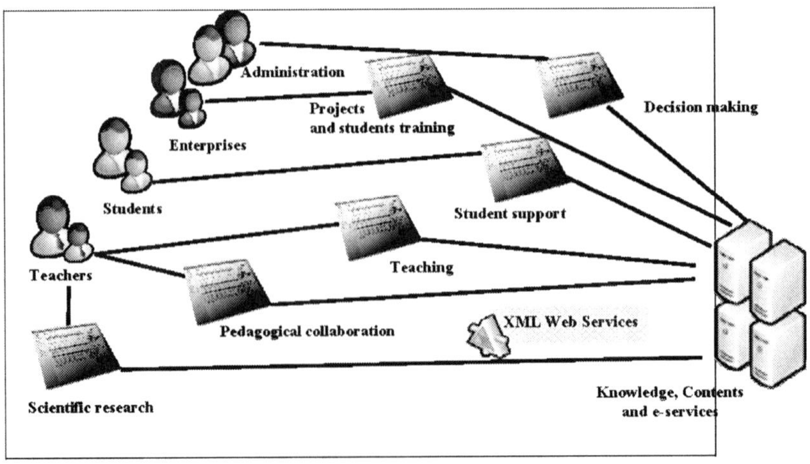

management application, the pedagogical management system, etc.

II. DISCUSSION

A. E-learning

We have presented e-learning teaching experiments and research programs at our college. The first component dealt with the development and the deployment of a number of online courses as part of blended learning. We hope this effort will continue in the future.

It is important to note that some difficulties have been encountered during the blended e-learning experiments. They can be divided into two main categories: technical difficulties and pedagogical difficulties. Technical difficulties include problems of Internet connections and access and long response times of the LMS. These difficulties are expected to subside with the continuous development of networking infrastructures. Pedagogical difficulties are related to student reluctance to use new learning tools, such as the LMS. They often preferred paper and printed course material. Finally, despite the fact of putting in place labs for student access, they are not sufficient because of other use. In addition, not all students have their own computers and Internet connections (such as ADSL), especially that some of them are living in dorms or rental places that are not always connected. We have seen however that the situation has been improving over the years thanks again to public investments in Internet infrastructures. Students have to adjust to e-learning and abandon traditional studying habits. They have to get used to work alone and/or in collaboration work was scheduled.

Furthermore, pedagogical problems concerned teachers as well. The lack of experience of some tutors and teachers has sometimes slowed down the processes of course design and course teaching. In order to avoid such problems, it is necessary to organize more training for the tutors/teachers and provide motivation. These experiments gave the e-learning team the opportunity to get continuous feedback from the learners. Based on that, it was possible to review and continuously adjust our e-learning strategies. As our experience has now matured on both pedagogical and research sides, we hope in the future to orient our efforts towards applying research results in teaching activities. We believe that this strategy is our best means of motivating our students of Generation Y.

B. E-Management and E-Services

The ministry of higher education introduced a number of student services accessible on-line (http://www.mes.tn). Some of these services account for an important amount of electronic payments. The main benefits are less paper work and less travel. The disadvantages affect especially new students who may not fully understand the benefits. But once they try them, they realize their practicality and get used to them. Their advantages overrun the drawbacks, especially in the long term as the system becomes mature.

Because e-Services are new, their engineering aspects are not completely understood. Methodologies, principles and techniques for their design and development are needed so that new theoretical models can be established (Goldkuhl, 2007). There is also a strong appeal for a bigger role for users so that user-centered e-services are sought. This is particularly true now more than before as e-services move from information-oriented portals to transaction-oriented sites.

As e-services become also more complex, out-sourcing and partnerships are becoming essential (Sirkemaa, 2007), especially that e-services "consumers" do not accept low quality anymore. Simultaneously with partnerships, decision makers should be aware of the drawbacks and pitfalls of vendor driven e services.

Since e-services in our universities and even in developed countries can be seen as a relatively new phenomenon, several of their aspects are not well understood. In general they improve transparency and accountability. They require a close coordination between several actors. They also assume a minimum knowledge of technical aspects by the users. In the long run, this requirement may not be a problem as the Internet generation and actually Generation Y is arriving now at universities including those in developing countries.

For all these reasons, e-services are expected to gain a wide spread and public acceptance.

ACKNOWLEDGMENT

The development of E-learning courses was made possible by technical help from the University of Sousse and funding provided by UVT. The research work was carried out at ISITC/Prince which is funded by the Ministry of Higher Education, Scientific Research and Technology.

Our research in the field of assessment and the formalization of personalization using Semantic Web technologies has been developed in collaboration with Pr. Nicola Henze, Head of the Semantic Web research Group at the University of Hanover in Germany.

REFERENCES

Baldoni, M., Baroglio, C., & Henze, N. (2005). Personalization for the Semantic Web. In *Proceedings of the 1st international Summer School. Reasoning Web., Malta,* pp.173-212.

Bloom, B. S. (Ed.). (1956). *Taxonomy of Educational Objectives, the classification of educational goals – Handbook I: Cognitive Domain.* New York: McKay.

Brusilovsky, P. (2001). Adaptive Hypermedia. *User Modeling and User-Adapted Interaction, 11*, 87–110. doi:10.1023/A:1011143116306

Brusilovsky, P., & Paylo, C. (2003). Adaptive and intelligent Web-based educational systems. *International Journal of Artificial Intelligence in Education, 13*, 159–172.

Cheniti-Belcadhi, L., Braham, R., Henze, N., & Nejdl, W. (2005). A Generic Framework for Assessment in Adaptive Educational Hypermedia. *IADIS International Journal on WWW/Internet, 3*, 17-28.

Cheniti-Belcadhi, L., Henze, N., & Braham, R. (2008). Assessment Personalisation on the Semantic Web. *Special issue: Intelligent Systems and Knowledge Management. Journal of Computational Methods in Sciences and Engineering, 8*, 1–20.

Goldkuhl, G. (2007). Towards a Practical Theory Founded in Socio-instrumental Pragmatism. [Retrieved fromhttp://www.ijpis.net]. *International Journal of Public Information Systems, 3*, 135–159.

Graf, S. & Kinshuk (2006). An Approach for Detecting Learning Styles in Learning Management Systems. ICALT 06, 161-163

IMS Learning Design Information Model. (2009). *Version 1.0 Final Specification.* Retrieved March 3, 2009, from http://www.imsproject.org/learning-design/ldv1p0/imsld_infov1p0.html

Koper, R., & Tattersall, C. (2005). *Learning Design: A handbook on Modelling and Delivering Networked Education and Training.* New York: Springer.

LOM. (2007). *LTSC Learning Object metadata standard.* Retrieved March 10, 2007, from http://ltsc.ieee.org.http://ltsc.ieee.org/wg12/index.html

MOODLE. (2009). *Open source community based tools for learning.* Retrieved February 25, 2009, from http://moodle.org

Paquette, G., Aubin, C., & Crevier, F. (1999). MISA, A Knowledge-based Method for the Engineering of Learning Systems. *Journal of Courseware Engineering, 2.*

Paquette, G., Crevier, F., & Aubin, C. (1997). *Méthode d'ingénierie d'un système d'apprentissage (MISA)*, Centre de recherche LICEF, Télé-université. Revue Informations In Cognito, In French, Retrieved from http://www.licef.teluq.uquebec.ca/gp/docs/pub/ingenierie/misa.doc

Personal Reader Framework. (2007). *Personal Reader Framework*. Retrieved January 11, 2007, from http://www.personal-reader.de

QAA. (2007). *Quality Assurance Agency, Code of Practice for the Assurance of Academic Quality and Standards in Higher Education*. Retrieved June 5, 2007, from http://www.qaa.ac.uk/public/cop/codesofpractice.htm

QTI. (2007). *IMS Question & Test Interoperability Specification, V1.2*. Retrieved March 10, 2007, from http://www.imsglobal.org/question/index.cfm

Sirkemaa, S. (2007). The Role of Partnerships in Development of E-Services - Highlighting Public Sector Organizations. *International Journal of Public Information Systems*, *3*, 201–212.

US. (2008). *University of Sousse*. Retrieved from http://www.uc.rnu.tn/ (can also be accessed via http://www.mes.tn)

UVT. (2008). *Virtual University of Tunis*. Retrieved from http://www.uvt.rnu.tn

Vasilyeva, E. (2006). The Challenge of Feedback Personalization to Learning Styles in a Web-Based Learning Systems. *ICALT*, *06*, 1143–1144.

Chapter 21
Effort Estimation Model for Each Phase of Software Development Life Cycle

Sarah Afzal Safavi
COMSATS Institute of Information Technology, Pakistan

Maqbool Uddin Shaikh
COMSATS Institute of Information Technology, Pakistan

ABSTRACT

The assessment of main risks in software development discloses that a major threat of delays are caused by poor effort / cost estimation of the project. Low / poor cost estimation is the second highest priority risk [Basit Shahzad]. This risk can affect four out of a total five phases of the software development life cycle i.e. Analysis, Design, Coding and Testing. Hence targeting this risk alone may reduce the overall risk impact of the project by fifty percent. Architectural designing of the system is a great activity which consumes most of the time in SDLC. Obviously, effort is put forth to produce the design of the system. It is evident that none of the existing estimation models try to calculate the effort put on designing of the system. Although use case estimation model uses the use case points to estimate the cost. But what is the cost of creating use cases? One reason of poor estimates produced by existing models can be negligence of design effort/cost. Therefore it shall be well estimated to prevent any cost overrun of the project. We propose a model to estimate the effort in each of these phases rather than just relying upon the cost estimation of the coding phase only. It will also ease the monitoring of project status and comparison against planned cost and actual cost incurred so far at any point of time.

BACK GROUND AND MOTIVATION

Existing estimation techniques such as Functions point estimation and use case estimation rely upon the artifacts generated in earlier phase. These artifacts (i.e. Use case diagrams, class diagrams, sequence diagrams, activity diagrams, state chart diagrams etc) depict the architectural design of the entire system. These diagrams are not generated out of a blue or are not instantly available without putting any effort.

Standard task set and the percentage of work duration associated with it decomposes the ratio of effort put in each phase.

DOI: 10.4018/978-1-61520-789-3.ch021

It is evident in Table 1 that although major ratio (i.e. 40%) of work effort is put in code and unit test phase. The rest 60 percent effort is put in different areas of the project development life cycle. Hence this signifies the importance of estimating cost for these phases of software development life cycle.

Usually the effort estimation is done after the analyses phase when the project reaches into coding stage. The cost / effort is measured in terms of line of codes for each functionality to be incorporated into the software. Therefore it is very clear to understand that only 40% (i.e. as shown in Table 1) of the total software development effort is estimated. Whereas this estimation is delayed until all the analyses and design has completed. We have adapted a different approach and suggest that effort estimation shall be carried out for each phase of the development process.

We propose this model to avoid the risk of low cost estimation as earliest as possible in the development process.

Current software cost estimation methods first try to know the size of the software to be built. Based upon this size the expected effort to be put is measured. Estimated effort further is utilized to calculate the duration (i.e. Time required) and cost (monetary/human resources) of the project.

Table 1. Standard Task Set & Work Duration % age [4]

Activity	Standard Work Effort%
Definition Phase	
Business Requirements	6%
Functional Specifications	10%
Delivery Phase	
Detailed Design	14%
Code and Unit Test	40%
System Testing	20%
User Acceptance Testing	10%
Total Effort	**100%**

Calculating the size of project is the foremost logical step to be taken in order to estimate the effort. If we do not know the distance to be travelled we can not estimate the cost and duration per mileage. Therefore we also first measure the size of the entire project.

We know that there are mainly three categories of software projects i.e.,

- **Organic Mode:** These are relatively small, simple SW projects (application programs e.g. Thermal analysis program)
- **Embedded Mode:** System programs which are developed within tight HW, SW and operational constraints (flight control SW for aircraft).
- **Semi-Detached Mode**: An intermediate level (size and complexity, utility programs) SW projects with mixed experience, mixed requirements. It can be mixture of organic and embedded software as well.

Therefore these categories of the software project would effect the estimation of each phase. We propose the modular approach to be adapted for the development efforts so that even large scale enterprise information systems can also be decomposed into a mix of several modules of organic, semi detached, and embedded system. Therefore the focus can be put in individual module accordingly.

Following are the sections which individually discuss the methods to estimate the expected effort to be put in each phase of software development life cycle.

MEASURING THE SIZE OF EACH PROJECT

We do not try to measure the size of the project as a whole rather focus on measuring the size of each phase i.e. Analyses, design, coding and testing phases. This can provide us different milestones in the road map of project development.

Our main objective is to suggest the estimation methods for analysis, design and testing phasing. We do not focus much on coding phase, as we would refer to the already done work for this phase. We estimate the size of each phase based on the artifacts and project products which are produced in that particular phase. E.g. the analyses phase produces the detailed user requirements document (use cases etc), design phase produces the class diagram, database Model i.e. E-R diagram, Sequence diagrams, activity diagrams etc. based upon these deliverables in each phase the time and effort to produce these are estimated.

Figure 1 shows the step wise flow chart of entire project planning process. After the identification of project scope/objectives, characteristics and infrastructure, the identification of all the activities is done. This identification of activities at early stage may provide the strong basis to estimate the size of each individual phase of software development process. As this involves the work break down structure to be defined and can identify the product / deliverable of each phase.

Figure 1.

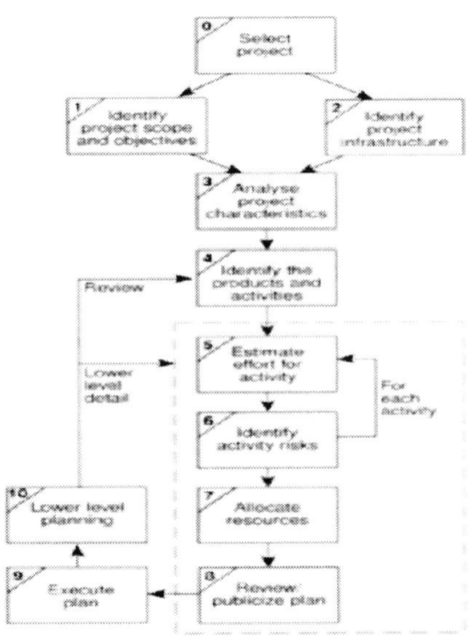

Figure 1 also shows that based on this identification of each activity the cost and risk are estimated for each activity. As this is part of project planning. Therefore we can obtain this information in the most earliest phase of project planning and do not need to wait for longer duration as have to wait in existing cost estimation models to estimate the cost of construction of the software.

Hence early stage activity identification can help us to estimate the cost/effort for each phase i.e. analysis, design, coding and testing.

Moreover the responsibility of the analysis and design of the system goes to the systems analyst. Generally system is viewed in terms of a collection of sub systems therefore each sub system analysis and design is the responsibility of any individual analyst. Hence the human resource need is very clear for analysis and design phase. But when team work is done in coding and testing phases then more stressed has to be put to estimate the required human resources.

Bruegge defines the following work products to be generated in each phase of software development life cycle.

Bruegge describes and decomposes the overall system model and design into three types of design models i.e.

1. Analysis model
2. Object Design model
3. Behavioral model

REQUIREMENT ELICITATION & ANALYSES PHASE SIZE AND EFFORT ESTIMATION

In earlier phase of the development process the scope is defined. This may also provide an intuitive vision of project size to the experienced project managers.

Unified Process for software development defines the work products in different phases. [R.S. Pressman]

During the analyses phase we propose *Inception points* to be identified and estimated. Inception points refer to the points which must be analyzed about in context of the interest of each stakeholder. As use cases represent the points of some business operation or systems functionality, which needs to be clearly understood and modeled therefore we call them inception points. We must know the accurate number of inception points and the effort needed to develop those points. Unified process for software development describes the following main work products in Inception phase.

1. Definition of the problem
2. Identification of all stakeholders
3. Identification of Functional / non functional requirements
4. Validation of requirements [R.S. Pressman]

Therefore all the main inception points can be clearly identified. Inception point will mainly focus around the identification of the users / stakeholders (possible actors & functionality needed) and requirements. The size can be estimated for this phase by estimating the requirements. This can further be utilized to estimate the cost to build the use cases for each requirement.

We suggest that the elicitation of requirements may consume effort / cost relevant to the number of requirements and user present.

Table 2 can signifies the need to enumerate each requirement, moreover each requirement will produce a use case and would also identify all its possible actors. Hence this can produce the effort needed to build those use cases which need to be documented in the software requirement specification document.

Use cases can also be weighted to measure their complexity. So that the size can be determined and the time taken to create those use cases can be determined.

We have categorized the use cases based upon the number of processing points. actors, and the extension use cases which emerge from that particular use case.

We conducted a survey to get the opinion from experienced software engineers and project managers in different software houses. We had distributed the questionnaire which primarily contained the questions to ask about the time needed to develop different types of use case as described in the Table 3. We have processed the survey data and have obtained the average time for each category of the use case.

Hence we can sum up the total number of inception points and can multiply them by the number of hours required for each type of use case. Summing up the time required in hours for each type of use case can then further give us the total number of hours required to build inception points.

Design Phase Size and Effort Estimation

Object design model and behavioral model are produced during the design phase. We can estimate the size of each model alone and can sum the effort to obtain the total design phase effort. We can identify the *Design Points*, therefore we

Table 2. Project size based on no of requirements

No of Requirements	No of Users	Project Size
Less than 25	1-10	Small
25 – 50	11-50	Average
50 – above	50 above	Large

Table 3. Use case types

No of Processing Points	No of Actors	No of <<extend>> Use case	Time taken to develop	No of Person
1-3	1-2	1-2	3 Hours	1
4-5	3-5	3-5	5 Hours	1
5 +	5 +	5 +	7 Hours	1

Figure 2.

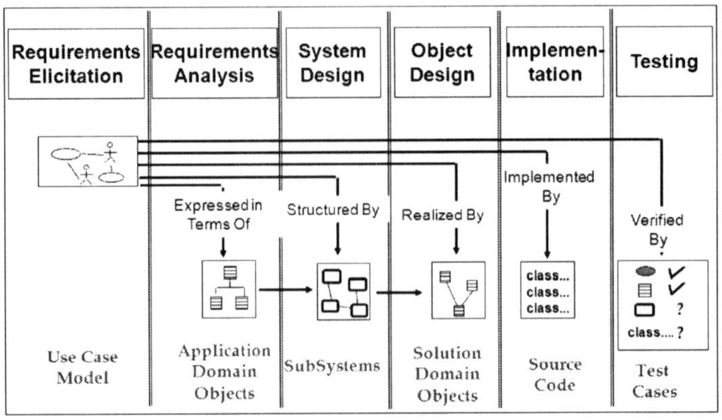

can add the weight associated to each design point and hence can measure the size and effort of that particular design point. This gives the lower level granularity to perceive the effort and size of each possible system feature to be designed. Hence further gives us tighter grip on the project progress.

Following can be the possible design points:

i. Entity classes
ii. Boundary classes
iii. Control classes
iv. System decomposition
v. System integration
vi. Aggregation / composition of objects
vii. Generalization / specialization of objects
viii. Object interaction
ix. Interfaces
x. Application logic

OBJECT DESIGN MODEL SIZE AND EFFORT

The main artifact of the Object model is class diagram.

Class diagram is comprised of several entity, control and boundary classes. If Entity Relationship diagram has already been produced then the effort can be lessened as persistent object are already been identified. Furthermore each type of classes need to be designed very carefully as control classes depict all the processing and interaction responsibilities among the classes. Where as boundary classes are responsible for the interfacing with either other system components, users, or external system for electronic data interchange. We declare each class to be a design point. A class in the system primarily depicts a system's object which interacts with other objects in system's environment. Hence a class does not dangle into a void but have solid connections and interactions with other classes that must be very accurately and rightly designed. Therefore we can categorize the class based on the complexity of their design. A class would be difficult to design if it has many associations, aggregations, generalizations, functionalities, overloading, overriding etc.

Table 4 depicts the parameters to judge the complexity ratio of any class to be designed therefore the effort would be relevant to the complexity ratio.

Our conducted survey tells us that based upon the complexity ratio any class can take 2, 5, or 8 hours for designing. Remember that this time is for design of the class but coding can take extra effort in the coding phase. Therefore if we can obtain the total number of design points and multiply them with the hours required to get the total hours required for the entire class diagram.

Table 4. Class categories for design complexity

Complexity Ratio	No of Associations	No of Interactions	No of Methods	No of Interfaces	Time Required (Hours)
Low	None	None	1-5	1 - 2	2
Medium	Single	Single	5-10	2 – 5	5
High	Multiple	Multiple	10-20	5 – 10	8

BEHAVIORAL MODEL SIZE AND EFFORT

Behavioral model comprises of different diagrams which depicts the state, interaction of different classes with each other and the sequence of activities performed in the system to achieve any objective or perform business function. These diagrams are sequence diagram and state transition diagrams mainly.

We declare each of these diagrams to be the design point as it is very essential to trace the possible states of the system so that a good design can be obtained. Whereas the sequence diagrams is the most sophisticated diagram that shows the complete step by step functionality and participating classes. But if the functionality of the existing system has been well understood then creation of sequence diagrams become easier. Our surveyed data reveals the facts that each of these diagrams can be different in complexity level i.e. low, medium, high. Parameters involved for determining the complexity level are summarized in Table 5.

We perceive each of such diagrams as design point and can sum up the total number of hours required for each to obtain the total size and effort estimate to develop behavioral model.

DATA MODEL SIZE AND EFFORT

Mainly an objective is set to achieve an Entity Relationship diagram to depict the over all database design for the entire software system. E-R diagram itself involves several steps to be carried out. The size of database model itself may relate to the type of software project. Embedded software may not be using any large data base but may work using few files available in the read only memory. Whereas organic and semi detached software projects may require the data to be accessed from large databases. Complexity

Table 5. Complexity parameters for behavioral model diagrams

Complexity Ratio					
State Chart	No of States	No of Transitions / Events	No of Activity of State	No of Actions associated with states	Time Required (Hours)
	1-5	1-5	1-5	1-5	3
	5-10	5-7	5-7	5-7	5
	10-15	7-10	7-10	7-10	8
Sequence Diagram	NO of Classes	No of Actors	No of Events	No of Control, boundary & Entity Objects	Time Required (Hours)
	1-5	1-5	1-5	1-5	3
	5-10	5-7	5-7	5-7	5
	10-15	7-10	7-10	7-10	8

Table 6. Complexity parameters and ratio to develop E-R model

Complexity Ratio	No of Entities	No of Relationships	No of Aggregations	Normalization Degree	Query Joins
Low	10-20	5-10	1-5	1-3	10-15
Medium	20-35	10-20	5-10	1-3	15-25
High	35-50	20-40	10-20	1-5	25-50

further increases when database has to be distributed. For the time being we do not discuss about distributed databases and leave it for our future work. Therefore we aim to estimate the size of conventional database to be built.

The following Table 4 summarizes the parameters that would affect the size of the database.

The larger the number of entities to be designed, larger the database size increases. It is time consuming task to identify the persistent objects (i.e. entities) in the system. Then to design its attribute set. Different types of attributes i.e. composite, derived and multi-valued attributes are difficult to design and to decide that which entity would be the best suitable place for any particular attribute.

Based upon the complexity ratio we had conducted a survey to know that how much time and personnel is required to build the E-R model. We have analyzed the data and got the average time and no of personnel required to develop E-R model.

We have considered the flexibility range in the commencement of the activities as well, therefore have concluded the time and personnel requirement in to range of lower and upper limit.

Table 7. Required Effort for E-R model

Complexity Ratio	Days Required	Personnel Required
Low	7 – 10	1 – 2
Medium	10 – 25	1 – 3
High	25 - 40	1 - 5

CODING PHASE SIZE AND EFFORT ESTIMATE

Much work has been done to focus at the code phase effort and size estimation. Mainly Constructive Cost Model and Use case Point method strive hard to achieve this objective. But still there is room for the refinement. But as our main objective was to talk about the other phases effort and size therefore we would refer to COCOMO for the cost estimation of coding phase. Line of Code is the basic parameter to judge the size of code, which further produces the personnel and months needed to construct the code of the software.

TESTING PHASE SIZE AND EFFORT ESTIMATE

Test points must be identified to know about the total number of test points. This can be eased by reviewing the use cases as usually every use case would have a test case against it. Hence the test points can be known to obtain the size of the test phase.

Usually testing is merged in coding phase and not focused individually, therefore no particular time frame is allotted to testify the system's features. Testing has many dimensions i.e.

1. Component testing
2. Usability Testing
3. Unit Testing
4. Integration Testing
5. System Testing[Bernd Bruegge]

It has been observed that where user is involved for the testing purpose then it takes longer to testify the functionality. There may be different aspect of usability to be tested. Therefore such tests can double the testing duration.

We declare each test case to be a test point. Therefore each test point can be well identified and the number of test cases can be known so that the time taken for each test point can be added to know the total time required for the test case.

CONCLUSION

We have discussed the idea of estimating the size and effort of each software development life cycle phase at the very abstract level. Hence proving the need of estimation in each phase rather than relying only on the coding phase estimation. But there is enough room to further refine the idea. We save the opportunity for future to come up with some concrete mathematical model to estimate the size and effort of each phase at a further fine granularity level. The main objective behind this research is to reduce the likelihood of major risk i.e. low / inaccurate cost estimation. Therefore improving the probability of software project success. More over our model also aims to improve the project planning by focusing at more accurate resource allocation. Accurate resource allocation is tightly coupled with the estimated requirement of the resources. Therefore this work can provide project managers a new horizon to think over the reduction of risk reduction possibilities.

REFERENCES

Baresi, L., Morasca, S., & Paolini, P. *Estimating the Design Effort of Web Applications*. Presented at the Ninth International Software Metrics Symposium (METRICS'03)(p. 62)

Bruegge, B., & Dutoit, A. H. (n.d.). *Object-Oriented Software Engineering: Using UML, Patterns and Java*. Upper Saddle River, NJ: Prentice Hall.fff

Hughes, B., & Cotterell, M. (n.d.). *Software Project Management, 2nd Edition*. New York: McGraw-hill international

Info-Tech. (n.d.). *The project Estimation Workbook*. London, Canada. *Info-Tech Research Group*.

Shahzad, B., Iqbal, J., & Aslam, S. (n.d.). *Phase wise risk estimation through relative Impact technique* Pressman (n.d.). *Software Engineering: A Practitioner's Approach*. Boca Raton, FL: R.S. Pressman & Associates Inc.

Chapter 22
Developing a Secure Integrated E-Voting System

Charles K. Ayo
Covenant University, Nigeria

J.O. Daramola
Covenant University, Nigeria

A. A. Azeta
Covenant University, Nigeria

ABSTRACT

The electoral system is paramount to the survival of democracy all over the world. Current happenings around the world, particularly in the developing world where poor conduct of elections had left a number of countries devastated are of great concern to world leaders. Therefore, efforts are ongoing to introduce a voting system that is transparent, convenient and reliable. This chapter presents an overview of an integrated electronic voting (e-Voting) system comprising: the electronic voting machine (EVM), Internet voting (i-Voting) and mobile voting (m-Voting). Similarly, issues of interoperability of the integrated system are discussed as well as the needed security measures. It is however recommended that emphasis be directed at EVM for use within the country while others are restricted to special cases of remote voting for citizens living abroad or living with certain deformities.

INTRODUCTION

In democratic societies, voting is a prominent tool for collecting and reflecting peoples' opinions. Traditionally, voting is conducted in centralized or distributed places called polling booths (Yang et al., 2006). Before the Election Day, the entire voting population is delineated into reasonable sizes of not more than 500 people per location and polling booths situated in each location across the country. At the booths, votes are cast by each eligible voter under the supervision of electoral officers with party representatives in attendance. At the close of the Election Day, votes are counted manually and the result taken to the collation centres where they are transferred to the state/regional headquarters for announcement. The rapid and extensive developments of Information and Communications Technologies (ICTs) have transformed the contemporary industrialized societies

DOI: 10.4018/978-1-61520-789-3.ch022

into a network of societies called Global village. With the increasing penetration of the society by ICTs, their applications in public administration (e-Government) and in democratic decision making process (e-Democracy) have brought about meaningful developments over the conventional systems (Ayo *et al*, 2007).

The term ICT embraces all electronic devices such as the wired and wireless networks including the Internet. Hence ICT offers various platforms of implementation like the Internet (i-Government, i-Business, i-Voting etc); the wireless or mobile platform (m-Government, m-Business, m-Voting etc); and the wired platform (e-Government, e-Business, e-Voting etc). However it must be noted that all the platforms are electronic in nature but for specificity, they can be so categorized (Pierre *et al*, 2006).

Electronic voting (e-Voting) is one of such areas where the impact of ICT is sought globally, particularly in the developing nations of the world, to help ameliorate some of the problems plaguing the electoral processes. Electronic voting refers to the use of electronic devices to vote in referendums and election. Traditional voting systems were developed to ensure strict compliance with the principles of democratic elections and referendums. These principles include (ACE Encyclopaedia, 2008):

1. Freedom to vote.
2. Secrecy of vote.
3. Non-modification of the votes cast.
4. Lack of intimidation during elections.

Therefore, a basic precondition for e-Election is the feasibility of implementing the voting system without undermining the basic principles as listed above. However, besides the needs for simplicity and ease of use of e-Voting systems, they must demonstrate at least some measure of security offered by the traditional voting systems.

Consequently, the following issues are considered as the minimum requirements for e-Voting systems. Any e-Voting system must ensure that (ACE Encyclopaedia, 2008):

1. Only eligible voters have the right to vote.
2. Every vote cast is counted but once.
3. Every voter is free to make his/her decisions without intimidation or coercion.
4. The secrecy of vote is maintained throughout the voting process.
5. Every eligible voter has access to vote without prejudice to educational level, location and disability.
6. The entire voting process is very transparent.

EVOLUTION OF E-VOTING

The history of the voting techniques is dated back as far as the 19th century. The various systems are arranged as follows.

Paper Ballots

This is the foremost method of voting and it is still in use in virtually all nations of the world. Voters mark boxes next to the names of candidates or next to the party logos, and place them in a ballot box. The ballots are counted manually. Their drawback is that counting is laborious and subject to human errors (Jan, 2001).

Mechanical Lever Machines

This system offers a way of reducing ballot tampering by eliminating document ballots. That became possible with the introduction of the lever voting machine in 1892 (Eric, 2003). Voters cast ballots by pulling down levers that correspond to each candidate. The machines prevent voting for more than one candidate (David, et al, 2003).

Punch Cards

Punch cards offer voters the opportunity to punch holes on computer readable ballot cards to indicate a choice in an election. Some systems use mechanical hole-punching devices for punching the holes while others provide the voter with pins to punch out the holes. The latter has led to incomplete punches, resulting in more errors in reading the cards (California Internet Voting Task Force, 2002).

The Optically Scanned Ballot

This is also called mark-sense or Bubble Ballot Paper. It contains the offices and the names of the candidates with a small circle (radio button) by its side. Voting is done by shading the small circle against the preferred candidate and counting is done via an optical scanner. That is, the papers are all scanned into a machine for automatic counting.

Direct Recording Electronic (DRE)

This is an electronic version of the lever machine. It offers electronic and automated casting, counting and tallying of total votes. The system displays electronic ballot on a screen for a voter to thumbprint against a preferred candidate after which the vote is cast and summaries produced. The issue against this method is lack of audit trial but can be catered for with minimum effort.

There are a variety of e-voting setups:

1. **PollingPlace e-Voting:** This involves casting of votes through an electronic means (voting machines) within a polling booth or station.
2. **Remote e-Voting:** This involves casting votes anywhere outside the polling station through an electronic means and transference of the votes through the Internet or telephone to designated locations.

The DRE equipment is situated at the polling station with which voters cast their votes usually through a touch screen mechanism. However, with the remote e-Voting, the system allows voting at remote locations without a physical presence at the booth. Voting can be done at home and computer kiosk, through the use of PCs and cell phones.

THE MERITS AND DEMERITS OF E-VOTING

The Merits

E-Voting offers:

a. Reduced common mistakes with the use of touch screen monitor.
b. Immediate feed-back on votes cast for urgent error correction.
c. Reduced multiple voting tendencies.
d. Convenience of voting.
e. Reduced ballot paper usage.
f. Enhanced speedy processing of results.
g. Backup of votes for audit trail.
h. Enhanced confidentiality, transparency, security and trust.
i. Reduced chances of bribery and intimidation.
j. Good voting platform for the handicapped, particularly the sight impaired through headphones and Braille keypad.

The Demerits

The demerits to watch out for include:

a. Over-voting/under-voting.
b. Broadcast storm arising from simultaneous transmission of results from polling booths to headquarters.
c. Equipment malfunctions in the course of election.
d. Proprietary source code could be a source of fraud (open source may be adopted).

e. Poorly implemented security measures may result to backdoors for hackers.
f. Most touch-screen systems run Windows CE which may require security upgrades to prevent virus and worms when connected to the Internet.
g. Election rigging through code manipulation by software developer.
h. Wire tapping by hackers during vote transmission.

SOME E-VOTING PROJECTS IN THE WORLD

Various e-Voting projects had been developed in a number of countries in the world. The procedures employed involved seeking legislative backing; contracting the projects; and conducting trials or tests in public areas to the satisfaction of the generality of the populace. In some countries, the project did not go beyond the trial phase because of some negative reports noted. The negative reports notwithstanding, e-Voting has a lot of merits. Table 1 are some of the countries where e-Voting had been experimented, tried and/or adopted.

Some Documented Problems on E-Voting Systems

Below are some problems associated with the adoption of e-Voting systems (Wikipedia, 2008):

1. **Denial of Service (DoS) Attack:** In Fairfax County, Virginia, during the 2003 election, it was observed that about 953 voting machines tried to forward results simultaneously at the same time. This led to traffic jam that delayed posting of results for a day because of the number of systems involved. Therefore, for a successful adoption of e-Voting system, the issue of traffic management must be looked into.
2. **Non-functional Voter Card Encoders:** Some voters were disenfranchised in Alameda and Sandiego in 2004 California

Table 1. List of countries with e-voting projects by type

Country	Type	Date
Australia	Polling Place e-Voting	First in 2001
Austria	Remote e-Voting	First in 2003
Belgium	Polling Place e-Voting	First in 1999
Brazil	Polling Place e-Voting	First in 1996
Canada	Remote e-Voting (Internet/Telephone)	First in 2003
Estonia	Remote e-Voting	First in 2004
France	Polling Place e-Voting & Remote e-Voting	First in 2003
Germany	Remote e-Voting	First tested in 1999
India	Polling Place e-Voting	First in 2003
Portugal	Polling Place e-Voting	First in 2004
Spain	Remote e-Voting	First in 2003
Switzerland	Remote e-Voting	First in 2004
The Netherlands	Polling Place e-Voting &Remote Place e-Voting	First in 2004
UK	Polling Place e-Voting & Remote e-Voting	First in 2002
USA	Polling Place e-Voting & Remote e-Voting	First in 2000

[Source: ACE Encyclopaedia, 2008]

primaries arising from faulty card readers. There was a law suit against the machine developers (Diebold), which was settled by paying about $2.6 million. Therefore, equipment malfunctioning is an issue to be given serious attention.

3. **Improper Calibration of Marksense Scanner:** In Napa County, California in 2004 elections, the system overlooked about 6,692 absentee ballot votes because of improper calibration. Similarly, during the early voting in 2006 and 2008, votes meant for particular candidates were swapped due to calibration errors. Calibration error at design time should be given due consideration.
4. **Possible Eavesdropping:** The Dutch Minister of Home Affairs in 2006 withdrew the license of 10% of the voting machines manufacturers; Sdu NV because it was proven that one could eavesdrop on voting from about 40 meters using Van Eck phreaking.
5. **Systemic Failure:** The New York University Law School released a report with more than 60 examples of e-Voting machines failures in 26 states in 2004 and 2006 elections.

INTEGRATED VOTING SYSTEM

The proposed integrated voting system is composed of three major platforms: an e-Voting machine (EVM); wired Internet; and mobile Internet. The traditional paper-based ballot is not considered. An e-Ballot reduces the chances of multiple voting arising from multiple thumb-printing that may result during folding of the paper or erroneous thumb-printing. With a manual ballot, voters are only entitled to one ballot and once marred, there is no replacement. However, with an e-Ballot, voters have the chances of correcting mistakes before submitting the ballots (Giampiero, 2008).

Electronic Voting Machines (EVMs)

These are basically polling site e-Voting system. Their configurations showed low-end processors: Diebold-400MHz Intel PXA-255; ES&S IVOTRONIC- 25MHz Intel 386; SEQUOIA VS-300 MHz; Urna (BVM)-386 IBM compatible, etc. The machines run on a variety of proprietary operating systems: VirtusOS, Windows CE and Linux. They equally have a variety of other peripheral devices: screens (touch and non-touch), flash memory, backup battery and PCMCIA – smart card removable memory (Boutin, 2004; Jason, 2003; Whitney, 2000).

The advantages of these configurations include the fact that the machines can be networked to interoperate with other ones; they can transmit data from one node to another; and can be designed and customized to meet the local/cultural needs of the various countries.

Internet Voting (I-Voting)

This refers to voting over the Internet through a PC with Internet connection to cast a vote and transmit same to another remote computer/server. Personal Digital Assistants (PDAs), Telephone or mobile phones can be used for this purpose (Kelvin, 2002).

The proponents of i-Voting suggest that it could increase turnout, particularly among younger voters who are familiar with Internet technology. I-voting has a lot of benefits but its security is in doubt because of its public nature, however, there are concerted efforts geared toward securing this medium.

Types of i-Voting

1. **Polling Station i-Voting:** PCs with Internet connections are provided at a location for all to use. There are electoral officers at each location to authenticate voters before voting.
2. **Remote i-Voting:** Voters cast their votes at remote locations through personal computers

using electronic authentication and computer security technologies.

Mobile Voting (M-Voting)

The provision of computing power on wireless devices opens an avenue for mobile transactions, particularly as mobile devices (smart phones, PDAs, cell phones and notebooks) are equipped with browsers (Gonzalez, 2003). Currently, about two-third of the world population has access to mobile devices. Thus, for enhanced participation in elections, it offers a good platform for voting anywhere, anytime, and at one's convenience (Dennis, 2002).

However, there are significant difference between developing applications for the wired Internet and the mobile Internet. The wired Internet applications are based on hypertext transfer protocol (HTTP) and the Internet markup language called hypertext markup language (HTML). Thus, the platform assumes that all devices have similar display sizes, memory and software capabilities, hence they are considered to be relatively static (Duford, 2002).

Mobile applications on the other hand are based on wireless application protocol (WAP) and wireless markup language (WML). This is because of the inherent nature of mobile devices such as: small screen format with limited display and navigation capabilities; low computation capability; limited data-entry capability due to the size of the key-pad; low bandwidth and high cost of data transmission; and network latency and other delays. Thus the HTTP/HTML features will not work well on WAP/WML devices (Duford, 2002).

Therefore, deploying applications to the mobile devices calls for simplicity, usability and user-friendliness, and consideration for end-users.

ARCHITECTURAL FRAMEWORK FOR E-VOTING SYSTEM

The proposed framework is composed of five (5) basic components as shown in Figure 1:

i. The wireless devices and providers
ii. The host organization and environment
iii. The e-Voting kiosk
iv. The e-Voting machine
v. The central electoral office.

The Wireless Devices and Providers

This sector comprises of the wireless devices: WAP cell phones and other mobile devices that are under the control of the Wireless Application

Figure 1. Deployment architecture

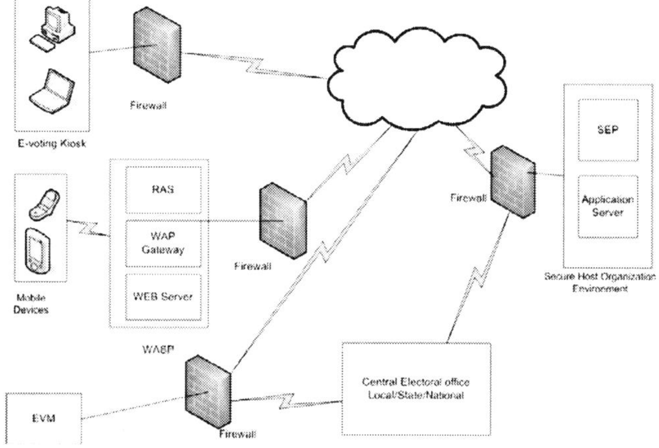

Service Provider (WASP). The WASP environment is composed of:

a. Remote Access Servers (RASs): Servers that establish connections between mobile devices, the wireless providers, and the wired Internet.
b. Web Servers (WSs): Servers that manage the various web applications such as mails, applications etc.
c. WAP Gateway: This is the major link between the WASP and the wired Internet. The function of the gateway among others include: decrypting secure socket layer (SSL) encrypted traffic and re-encrypting it with wireless transport layer security (WTLS) meant for the wireless devices and vice-versa; and basically providing Internet access to its subscribers (Dennis, 2002).

The security features governing transmissions from the mobile devices and WASP is WTLS. The encrypted message is further routed through a firewall for enhanced security. The security measures are further fortified using the public-key cryptography, digital signature and digital certificate (Tallinn, 2005).

The Host Organization and Environment

This environment offers a secured wired environment through a 1024-bit SSL encryption, which is stronger than the WTLS encryption offered by WASP. This environment is composed of:

a. Secure Enterprise Proxy (SEP) that performs the SSL/WTLS translation within the secure environment rather than being done on the WAP gateway within the WASP environment to prevent the "Gap in WAP" situation.
b. Application Server that is the repository of the e-Voting applications.

The "Gap in WAP" syndrome describes a situation where there is security breach during the process of SSL/WTL conversion.

E-Voting Kiosk

This section represents the environment or public locations where e-Voting facilities are made available for public use. The locations are equipped with PCs, EVM, and Internet facilities among others.

E-Voting Machine (EVM)

The machines could be customized e-Voting systems, PCs or a special purpose computing system. The existing configurations include:

i. Premier Election Solutions (Formerly DIEBOLD ACCUVOTE-TS).
ii. Elections Systems and software (ES&S IVOTRONIC).
iii. Sequoia Voting System.
vi. Hart InterCivic.
v. URNA Eletrônica

These systems run on either Windows CE or a proprietary Operating System with compact flash for storage of votes and a backup battery that can last the period of the election (Boutin, 2004). Thus, to prevent multiple voting, the machine should offer Internet access through a micro browser to update voters register. The voters' registers are localized into the area of registration and voting for easy reference.

Central Electoral Office

This is the central, local, state and national electoral office that is responsible for collating and declaring local or regional results to the party agents to ensure transparency. Having declared the result at the polling booth, the flash storage is forwarded to the central office where the results of the e-Voting machines are added to the result on the Application server. The system has provisions for audit trail through the flash disks and the results in the application server.

Interoperability Issues

Interoperability between the wired and wireless Internet can be achieved in two ways (Ayo, West):

i. Using extensible markup language (XML) and extensible style sheet language (XSL) to target multiple devices. That is, rather than creating multiple sites for the various devices, data can be extracted as XML and XSL templates can be used to generate HTML and WML documents for the various devices.
ii. The use of Aether systems' Scoutweb to WAP-enabled devices is a web-based application. It offers interfaces for websites and mobile devices. Scoutweb supports over 30 different devices and helps translate HTML to mobile content on the fly given a set of rules.

PROPOSED SYSTEM IMPLEMENTATION

The overall objective of this chapter is to present a framework for an integrated voting system. That is, an efficient and effective system that satisfies the desires of the electorates by offering several platform of operation as presented in Figure 2. An electorate can vote through any of the three options: EVM; i-Voting; or m-Voting. The EVM is an example of a polling station e-Voting, that displays the e-Ballot and electorates go through the user-friendly procedures to cast their votes. Similarly for i-Voting or m-Voting. Once the medium of voting is ascertained, the appropriate format is displayed on the respective devices. For

Figure 2. Integrated voting system

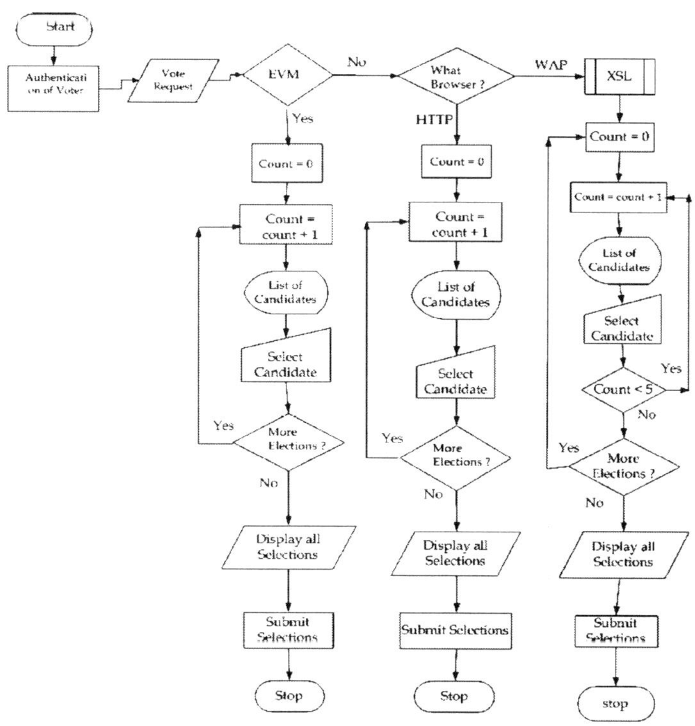

i-Voting, the HTML equivalent of the e-Ballot is displayed for the electorates. However, for mobile devices, the WML format is displayed, which is a function of the size of the screen. In some, it could be the five candidates per screen for Palm devices or a single candidate per display screen depending on the size of display.

The major design considerations of the system include: (i) Provision of Voter Verifiable Audit Trail; (ii) Prevention of Multiple Voting; (iii). Prevention of Over-Voting/Rigging; (iv) Provision of avenue for Disabled Voters; and v. Provision of Adequate Security Measures.

PROPOSALS AND CONCLUDING REMARKS

i. We propose five (5) candidates (parties) for each election. The candidates can be displayed at once on the PC and EVM, but displayed one candidate per screen, or all candidate(s) per screen, depending on the mobile device.
ii. Multiple elections (presidential, gubernatorial, etc) can be conducted a day. After each election, the next elective office and candidates are displayed for selection/voting until all elections for the day are concluded in one stream.
iii. There is much flexibility in the system as voters are availed the opportunity of perusing their selections before they are submitted to the server.
iv. A biometric smart card-based voters cards proposed foe enhanced security and integrity.
v. After each election, the voter's card is blocked to prevent further use on the day of the election, nor can it be used through another medium to vote. Thus over-voting is prevented.

In conclusion, this paper presented the different flavours of e-Voting systems: the polling station e-Voting and remote e-Voting. The integrated and deployment architectural frameworks were presented.

While the various components of the system would function as a separate entity, it is however recommended that i-Voting be reserved for remote voters living abroad and m-Voting for persons living with certain forms of disability. Security issues were discussed through the deployment architecture showing the various devices required to safeguard the integrity of the votes cast.

REFERENCES

Ayo, C. K., Babajide, D. O. (2007). Design and Implementation of a Secure i-Voting System. *Journal of Computer Science and its Applications, 14*(2), 38-51.

Boutin, P. (2004). *Is E-voting Safe*. Retrieved June 2006, from http://www.pcworld.com/resource/

California Internet Voting Task Force. (2000). *A report on the feasibility of Internet Voting*. Retrieved August 2006, from http://www.ss.ca.gov/

Coleman, K. (2002). Internet Voting- Issues and Legislation in CRS Report for Congress. Retrieved November 2008, from http://www.ipmall.info/hosted_resources/crs/RS20639.PDF

Duford, S. (2004). Building a Wireless Web Solutions: Tools and Justifications for Building a Wireless Web Solutions. In Purba, S. (Ed.), *Architecture for E-business System* (pp. 263–286). Oxford, UK: Auerbach.

Encyclopaedia, A. C. E. (2008). *Requirements for e-Voting, Accessed date: Nov. 2008*. Retreived from http://aceproject.org/ace-en/focus/e-voting/e-voting-requirements

Feng, Y., Ng, S.-L., & Schwiderski-Grosche, S. (2006). *An Electronic Voting System Using GSM Mobile Technology*. Retrieved November 2008, fromhttp://www.ma.rhul.ac.uk/static/techrep/2006/RHUL-MA-2006-5.pdf

Fischer, E. A. (2003).*Election reform and electronic voting system (DREs): Analysis of security issues*. CRS report for congress. Retrieved August 2006, from http://www.amcham.co.nz/Newsletters/Elections20041.pdf

Giampiero, E. G. (2008). Secure and Easy Internet Voting. *IEEE Press, February,* 52-56.

Gonzalez, D. (2003). *A roadmap to wireless: The state of the technology, Air2Web*. Retrieved June 2006 from http://www.air2web.com/pdf/roadmap.pdf

Jan, K. T. (2001). *Information Security architecture – An Integrated approach to security in the organization.* Boca Raton, FL: CRC press LLC.

Jason, L. (2003). *The business of E-voting and how it can put wrong candidate in office*. Retrieved June 2006, from http://www.dissidentvoice.org/Articles8/Leopold_E-Voting.htm

Jefferson, D., et al. (2004).A security analysis of the secure electronic registration and voting experiment (SERVE). Retrieved August, 2006 from http:// www.servesecurityreport.org

Pierre, R. (2006). Mobile e-Government Options: Between Technology-driven and User-centric. *Journal of E-Government, 4*(2), 79–89. Retrieved from http://www.ejeg.com.

Steve, M. (2004). *E-Democracy: stealing the Election in 2004*. Retrieved June 2006 from http://www.globalresearch.ca/articles/ MOO407A.html.

Tallinn (2005). *E-Voting System Overview*. Retrieved November 2008 from http://www.vvk.ee/elektr/docs/Yldkirjeldus-eng.pdf

Whitney, Q. (2000). Voting for usability: Background on the issue. Retrieved June 2006 from http://www.wqusability.com/articles/voting-background2000.html

Wikipedia (2008). *Electronic Voting*. Retreieved December 2008, from http://en.wikipedia.org/wiki/Electronic_voting

Chapter 23
An Overview of E-Health Development in Australia

Say Yen Teoh
RMIT University, Australia

Mohini Singh
RMIT University, Australia

Josephine Chong
Auckland University of Technology, New Zealand

ABSTRACT

This chapter is a discussion of e-health development in Australia. The Australian government has been very proactive in e-government and applications of e-government such as e-health in the last five years. E-health is an important application of e-government in Australia for innovation of the public sector, as well as due to its very sparsely populated large rural areas. E-health development in this chapter is analysed using Layne and Lee's (2001) e-government development model due to the similarities in the stages of development of both applications. This chapter illustrates that in Australia e-health development is mostly at the informational stage. It also indicates that e-health developments can be established in four stages of information; transaction; vertical and horizontal integration of services.

INTRODUCTION

E-health is a new application of e-government, widely adopted around the world. Australia, like its international counterparts is also adopting e-health to improve health organisational processes and to deliver relevant services and information quicker to its citizens. The public sector regards IT as a crucial component in reinventing government. The utilization of IT by government has enabled efficient service-state delivery, improved effectiveness and reduced bureaucracy (Sarikas & Weerakkody, 2007).

E-government has been defined as the use of ICTs to improve the efficiency, effectiveness, transparency, and accountability of government (The World Bank, 2006); use of ICTs, particularly the Internet, to provide optimal public administration services to citizens (OECD, 2003); and the use of web-based information systems by governments to enhance the delivery of public services to citizens and businesses (Silcock, 2001).

DOI: 10.4018/978-1-61520-789-3.ch023

E-government is similar to e-business in relation to stages of development (Janssen, Kuk & Wagenaar, 2008). The similarities include establishment of an Internet presence, application of different kinds of models and creating customer value (Layne & Lee, 2001). E-government development is an extension of e-business principles (Janssen, Kuk & Wagenaar, 2008), and e-health, e-tax, e-citizenship, e-democracy and e-voting are major applications of e-government.

In this chapter we discuss e-health development based on e-government and e-business development models. In Australia, Healthcare is 87 billion dollar service industry (Department of Human Services, 2008) for the prevention, management and response to health risks for the nation. This accounts to 9% of Australian GDP. Such a strategy is aimed to provide a safer, high quality, more equitable and sustainable health system for Australians from all regions, including patients from rural and remote areas (Department of Human Services, 2008). Although e-health is a major application of e-government services in Australia, to date there is a lack of any comprehensive evaluation on the development and maturity of e-health services. This chapter aims to provide an insight into the development and maturity of e-health services in Australia.

The remainder of this chapter is structured into four sections. Section 2 is a review of literature on e-government, e-health and the e-government maturity model. Section 3 describes the research method employed in this study. Section 4 analyses the development and maturity of e-health services in Australia. Finally, the last section concludes with the main research findings, an overview of the current state of Australian e-health services.

LITERATURE REVIEW

E-government is the use of information technology in general, and e-commerce in particular, to provide citizens and organizations with more convenient access to government information and services to citizens, business partners and suppliers, and those working in the public sector (Turban, 2002). Other definitions of e-government suggest that it is the transformation of public administration towards modern administration and democracy (Wimmer & Traunmuller, 2001); and the use of technology to simplify and automate transactions between governments, constituents and business (Milford, 2000). The Australian government has been actively exploiting information technology (IT) to enhance efficiency and accessibility in the provision of e-services to citizens. Singh et al. (2008) advocate that in Australia e-government services are deployed by all three levels of administration, the Federal, State and Local. They also advocate that the most popular e-government services in Australia to date are informational, followed by services that are interactive such as health (Medicare) and transactional which include e-tax and vehicle registration. They also confirm that citizens prefer bundled services with access to from a one stop shop. Other e-government services adopted by the government of Australia include e-procurement and e-health (AGIMO, 2006). The focus of this chapter is e-health.

E-health refers to all forms of electronic healthcare delivered over the Internet, ranging from informational, educational and commercial "products" to direct services offered by professionals, non-professionals, businesses or consumers themselves (McLendon, 2000). It also includes a variety of the clinical activities that have been traditionally known as telehealth, delivered via the Internet (Eysenbach, 2001) Simply stated, e-health is making healthcare more efficient, while allowing patients and professionals to do the previously impossible (McLendon, 2000). Medical Business News (2000) referred to e-health as convergence between the Internet and the health care industry to provide consumers with a wide variety of information relating to the health care field, whereas DeLuca (2001) explains e-health to be the electronic exchange of health-related data across organizations.

The benefits of e-health outlined by Eysenbach (2001) include:

- Efficiency, with reduced costs and avoidance of duplicate or unnecessary diagnostics;
- Enhanced quality of care, supporting effective communication between patients and their physicians;
- Evidence based, with rigid and scientifically evaluated efficiency and effectiveness
- Empowerment of patients by providing them with easy access to a knowledge base of medicine and personal electronic records enabling them to control their health status; and
- An extension of the scope of healthcare with e-healthcare networks delivered across space and time.

The applications of e-health according to Min et al. (2007) are categorised into e-hospital, mobile healthcare, telemedicine, and health portals, discussed in the following section.

ELECTRONIC-HOSPITAL

In an e-hospital setting, most of the hospital operations are executed electronically. The deployment of IT can compile the patient's quantified information in an electronic form making it easy to access and retrieve (Mount et al., 2000). One of the most popular and commonly used computerized healthcare systems is the electronic medical record (EMR) system (Sujansky, 1998). It integrates patients' health information with physicians, hospitals, government agencies and pharmacies (Khalil & Jones, 2007; Mukherjee & McGinnis, 2007; Sujansky, 1998). Thus, e-health facilitates health information exchange between users, which lead to improved accessibility. For instance, a patient medical health record and history can be accessed by authorised doctors in different hospitals. Although this can help avoid duplication of diagnostic testing, imaging and history taking, and allow patients to access individual health status from an integrated system, privacy of information and unethical activities are important concerns in this application (Mukherjee & McGinnis, 2007). Some e-hospitals are internally networked in a local area network and linked across limitless geography via wide area networks with remote and secure access to systems via virtual private network interfaces (Curtis, 2007). This networks offer optimal efficiency in hospital management system supporting prescription delivery, patient booking, and diagnosis by applying information technology in intra-hospital activities, hospital-to-hospital, and hospital-to-pharmacy management procedures (Min et al., 2007).

MOBILE HEALTHCARE

Mobile healthcare (m-healthcare) encompasses mobile computing, medical sensor, and communications technologies for healthcare (Istepanian et al., 2004). M-healthcare systems are supported by different mobile devices such as mobile phones, personal digital assistants (PDA), and wireless technologies such as GSM, 3G and wireless LAN. M-healthcare enables users (patients and medical staff) to communicate ubiquitously via wired and wireless networks (Falchuk & Leob, 2007). M-healthcare also supports ambulance services to predict emergency and stroke morbidity and integrates mobile health monitoring services (Istepanian & Local, 2003). It is very useful for ambulances as it enables the transmission of medical information via wireless connections to the hospital. It facilitates paramedics to communicate effectively with the hospital's physicians in preparation for the patient's arrival. Quick response time in the pre-hospital arrangements can drastically reduce mortality (Pavlopoulos, 1998).

Another type of m-healthcare service is mobile health monitoring which utilizes medical sensors for health management (Kyriacou, et al., 2003). The medical sensors facilitate physicians to diagnose, monitor and treat patients by providing them with the flexibility to manage their health status anytime and anywhere. These are useful for helping patients monitor their health and well-being especially those suffering from diabetes, high blood pressure or heart disease. Pulse oximetry and respiratory flow data can be electronically transmitted to the medical officer in charge for advice on diabetic patients and for the correct dosage of insulin. In general, convenience and ease of communication are the key elements of m-healthcare services.

TELEMEDICINE

Telemedicine is the exchange of medical information from one site to another via electronic communications to improve citizens' health status (American Telemedicine Association, 2001). It evolved as societies progressed with the use of technologies more competently (IDS Healthcare, 2009). Telemedicine requires remote connections through integrated services digital networks (ISDN) to deliver health services at a distance (Health Connect, 2005) such as the delivery of healthcare services from urban to rural hospitals via telecommunications. For instance, in 2002, the Department of Health and Ageing in Australia launched the Clinical IT in Aged Care project with the aim to enhance the quality of care for residents in aged care homes through the use of medical sensors (AHIC, 2007). It is also used in Australia to monitor the health status of aged patients (AHIC, 2007).

In order to deliver accessible telemedicine services to Australia's rural population, Broadband for Health Program was initiated to allow general practitioners and the Aboriginal Community Controlled Health Service providers to uptake the business grade broadband services for accessibility to e-health information (HealthConnect, 2005). This connectivity enables the transmission of still images, video and other forms of medical information to be exchanged between rural and urban healthcare providers. With the Internet connectivity, rural citizens can seek online medical consultation from their urban physicians regarding their treatment via electronic mails. Thus, in theory, such service offers rural communities the option to access standard healthcare services, unfortunately, in practice, telemedicine in rural and remote Australia is still underserved, due to the lack of reliable Internet connectivity (Curtis, 2007).

HEALTH PORTALS

Health portals are hailed as entry points to collections of websites in providing reliable health information (Glenton, et al., 2005). This growing popularity of health portals is driven by the evolution of patient-driven health care (Davis et al., 2007; Starfield et al., 2005). Historically, patients played a passive role in which they could only sought medical advice from doctors in their neighbourhood (Eysenbach, 2001). However, with the Internet revolution, patients are better informed on health-related issues and alternative modes of healthcare services. Today, patients are generally attracted by thousands of easy accessible healthcare portals for access to different types of health and medical information. However, the dissemination of healthcare-related information via portals has been overwhelmed in the developed countries and is prone to potential dangers of inaccurate and inappropriate use of information (Mitchell, et al, 2005; Skinner, et al., 2003). Hesse and Schneiderman (2007) contend that due to an array of healthcare information available on the Internet, there is a need for patients to be able to differentiate the quality and reliability of the online healthcare information. However, the current trend shows that patients tend to rely on the online information for self-diagnosis (Eysenbach, 2001). This sparks a rising concern regarding the potential risks associated with information on health portals. Some organisations have been proactive in controlling and maintaining quality of information on health portals, as well as determine the individual rights to participate in decisions regarding their health care (Glenton, et al., 2005). For example, the Australian HealthInsite (Glenton et al., 2005), the English NHS Direct Online, the German Telematic Platform and the Danish Sundhed.dk (Andreassen, et al., 2007) are widely used in these developed countries to ensure patients obtain the right information. In responding to the information quality control, the UK government has introduced a standardised index (www.discern.org.uk) to control the quality of the health information (Boomba, 2005). Such standards are not yet available in Australia.

AN OVERVIEW OF E-HEALTH DEVELOPMENT

E-health is an application of e-government and requires support from governments (WHO, 2004). Currently, the United States is the leader of e-government followed by Singapore and Australia (United Nations, 2005). Thus in the following section e-health developments in the USA, Singapore and Australia are discussed.

E-health in the United States (http://www.usa.gov/index) and Singapore (http:www/ecitizen.gov.sg) provide an array of healthcare services via their e-government portals. They include a list of healthcare providers, healthy lifestyles, health topics, information on health insurance and healthcare services. In addition, Singapore's portal provides online services such as appointment booking, medical queries, pharmacy and request for medical reports. Though the United States is rated as an e-government leader, the implementation of a national EMR in the USA is yet to be achieved (Middleton and Brennan, 2005). Similarly, Singapore is still working towards the implementation of a national EMR. Singapore is also adopting a telemedicine framework which is aimed at encouraging volunteerism among medical specialists to provide free assessments at their convenience to support healthcare for senior citizens at the homes via care-givers (MOH, 2007).

E-HEALTH IN AUSTRALIA

In Australia, the responsibility for the delivery of healthcare services is shared by all three levels of administration, the federal, state and local governments (Department of Health Services, 1997). According to the Australian Bureau of Statistics (ABS, 2003, 2006), healthcare and government portals are the top 20 accessed by citizens. Owing to the growing demand for healthcare information online (Lee, et al., 2007), the federal government has taken the initiative to play a crucial role in health policymaking and financing so as to facilitate and deliver quality healthcare services to the nation. To maintain e-health standards, the state and local governments are responsible for executing and delivering healthcare services in each state.

The Australian government supports e-health by developing HealthConnect which is an integration of electronic health records between various stakeholders operating in this category. It bridges the information gap between the public and private health systems and supports clinical decision making, improving quality and coordination of care for patients (Australian Government Department of Health and Ageing, 2008). During emergencies health professionals can access diagnoses, contacts and a medication list (HealthConnect, 2005). In addition, the Australian Centre for Military and Veterans' Health (CMVH) is also now using e-health with electronic health records, telehealth systems, connectivity and integration of systems, health knowledge networks, clinical decision support systems, health surveillance systems and operational health support systems (ADF Health, 2007) to support military personnel. These initiatives are operating in different states in Australia (HealthConnect, 2005). With these developments awareness of e-health has grown within the Australian health community (ADF Health, 2007).

E-HEALTH DEVELOPMENT ISSUES

E-health development issues can be categorised into two major aspects: organizational and technological. In the organisational context, the e-health stakeholders comprise clinicians and health service providers, consumers, health workforce, health service managers and e-health professionals (AHIC, 2007). To ensure efficient and effective e-health services, it is crucial for a mutual understanding between all stakeholders for effective partnerships (Lasker et al., 2001). Effective partnerships in e-health according to Wickramasinghe et al., (2005, p.322) are:

- meaningful collaboration with healthcare recipients;
- preparation for upcoming technological developments;
- balancing between connectivity and privacy; and
- better understanding of the balance between face-to-face and virtual interaction.

On the other hand, a major technological e-health issue is the reluctance of adoption of IT by some physicians. Although the deployment of IT can improve efficiency and reduce workload for physicians, there still are many medical practitioners who are accustomed to the traditional way of delivering healthcare services. This is because it takes time and effort for them to learn to use new technologies (Anderson, 2007). According to an empirical study by Henderson et al. (2006), although 88.8% of physicians in Australia are deploying IT in the health industry, they are merely using IT to perform administrative tasks such as electronic prescribing (94.7%), ordering tests (82.2%) and keeping patient data in an electronic format (79.5%).

Low technological adoption rates reduce the benefits and strengths of e-health and also the extension of healthcare networks across time and space for patients (Eysenbach, 2001). To realise the benefits of e-health it is important for physicians and all stakeholders in the industry to embrace technologies.

Another technological issue in e-health is patients' electronic medical records. Over the years, the Australian government is robustly undertaking several projects to electronically link each patient's health information, so as to create a single integrated electronic medical record (NEHTA, 2000). However, problems such as interoperable electronic health information systems, weak specification and infrastructure requirements and privacy issues, the progress of electronic medi cal records to date is very slow (LeMay, 2008). Even with the rapid improvement of the wireless security protocols, often it seems not fast enough to keep pace with the ingenuity of hackers and other intruders who wish to gain illegal access to information (Mirza & Norris, 2007). Poor Internet connectivity especially for countries such as Australia that have large sparsely populated rural areas hampers the delivery of telemedicine even further (Curtis, 2007). Death rates of rural citizens tend to be higher, and could gain tremendously from e-health (Australian Institute of Health and Welfare, 2007).

From the above discussion of literature it is clear that e-health developments are progressing in different parts of the world, as part of e-government initiatives. For Australia, a large country with dispersed rural citizens some of who are disadvantaged, e-health is a promise widely needed for their well being. Thus in this chapter we explore e-health developments in Australia.

Since e-health is part of e-government, the maturity model for e-government development is explored in the next section.

E-GOVERNMENT MATURITY MODELS

As suggested by Andersen and Henriksen (2006), maturity models in e-government provide a state of a given level in a continuous process, and not as distinct stages of development. Although there are a number of maturity models that can be used to describe e-government maturity (Shahlook, Saghafi & Abdollahi, 2008), this chapter is based on the four stage model of Layne and Lee (2001).

The four stages of growth proposed by Layne and Lee (2001) is as follows:

Stage 1—Cataloguing: The first stage is cataloguing of government information online. This involves the initial efforts of governments to present information about their activities online. An online presence reduces governments' need to employ many people to service citizens. This online information, which at this stage is non-transactional, is available 24 hours a day, seven days a week.

Stage 2—Transaction Phase: The second stage of e-government entails transaction capability. This allows citizens to transact with online governments (administration) electronically to pay for services. This stage improves efficiency for both citizens and administration and offers citizens greater convenience.

Stage 3: Vertical integration refers to integration between different levels of the same government. This refers to integration of federal, state and local governments for different functions or services of government. It enables citizens to access a service at any level of government through one access point. The benefit of this stage is the elimination of the organization barrier (Irani et al., 2006).

Stage 4—Horizontal integration: An enhanced integration of e-government services for different functions horizontally. It is online integration between different levels and different functions of government. It occurs when businesses are able to pay property taxes to one local government and renew their business license at the same time because both levels of administration provide access to information from one point of access (Reddick, 2004). Ultimately its aim is to provide citizens "one stop shop". Layne and Lee's e-government development model is presented in Figure 1 in the following section.

In Figure 1, the vertical and horizontal dimensions indicate the activity centric applications. The rationale for adopting the Layne and Lee model to predict e-health development is that it depicts the development by building models of its stages (Yildiz, 2007), and as discussed earlier, e-health is an application of e-government.

METHODOLOGY

To explore the development of e-health services at three levels of administration in Australia, the Federal, State and Local, we were guided by the Layne and Lee's (2001) model of e-government development. We identified Australian based health web sites presented in Table One, to establish the stage at which it was developed. We examined the type of information included on the site, capabilities for interactivity, transactions, and for vertical and horizontal interactions amongst other e-government services on these sites. Important e-health sites in Australia from the three levels (federal, state and local) of administration were identified and explored for the above criteria. These include health related web sites from all eight states in Australia presented in Table 1.

Figure 1. Layne and Lee model: Integration of technological organizational complexity (Layne & Lee, 2001)

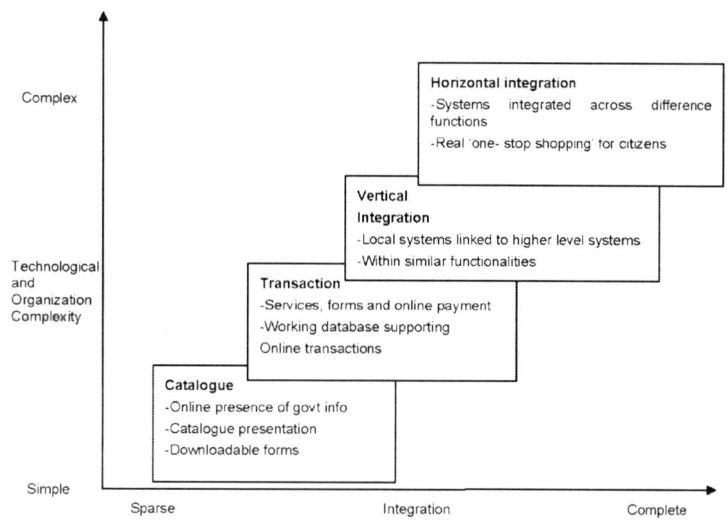

Table 1. Australian e-health sites

Australian E-health Sites Examined for Information, Transaction Capability and Vertical and Horizontal Integration	
State-wide level	http://www.health.gov.au/ http://www.healthinsite.gov.au/ http://www.medicareaustralia.gov.au/
Australian Capital Territory	http://www.health.act.gov.au/
Northern Territory	www.health.nt.gov.au
New South Wales,	http://www.health.nsw.gov.au/ http://www.nsw.gov.au/health.asp http://www.nsw.gov.au/health.asp
Queensland	http://www.qld.gov.au/ http://www.qld.gov.au/about/health-and-communities/
South Australia,	http://www.sa.gov.au/site/page.cfm?
Tasmania	www.tas.gov.au http://www.tas.gov.au/tasmaniaonline/Nav/Topic.asp?Topic=Health
Victoria	http://www.health.vic.gov.au/ http://www.vic.gov.au/health-community.html
Western Australia	http://wa.gov.au http://wa.gov.au/governmentservice

ANALYSIS AND DISCUSSION

An analysis of Australian e-health maturity is discussed in the following section based on Layne and Lee's (2001) e-government development model.

Stage 1: Catalogue (Information) Level

From the e-health web sites listed in Table 1, it is clear that in Australia a wide variety of relevant health related information is provided from e-government portals at the federal and state levels. These include information for citizens as well as professionals. For the citizens many different types of support regarding health are available online. Australia being a country with large rural area information for rural health support is also available on these sites.. Current health issues such as information and actions to take regarding swine flu are also included on these sites. For the health professionals, information on ethics and standards, as well as job opportunities is included.

Although most of the states provide similar types of information, e-health sites for two states

Victoria and New South Wales are more developed than others regarding e-health information. This stage of e-health development is supported by the Broadband for Health Program (http://bfhp.pip.com.au/) which creates a platform for sharing of resources and information between the citizens and the government. In addition, the web site for Medicare, which is an agency of the Australian Government that administers health-related programs are well developed at this cataloguing stage for information, downloadable forms for claims, and connected with cataloguing of other government information online (for example it is connected to disaster assistance site- http://www.disasterassist.gov.au/vic_fires_09/index.htm). In general, our study showed that Australian E-health is well developed at the cataloguing (information) stage. This is illustrated in Table 2 below.

Stage 2: Transaction Level

The transaction level supports two-way communication between citizens and e-health service from all three levels the federal, state and local governments. In other words, it integrates database with online interfaces (Shahkooh, et al, 2008) for medical information to be transmitted from the wireless ambulance to the hospital (Metropolitan

Table 2. E-health sites that represent the Catalogue (information) level (Stage 1)

Level of Government	E-health Site	Types of Information
Federal Government Australia Central Territory	www.australia.gov.au www.act.gov.au	Medicare online, ambulance service, aged health service, aboriginal health services, common health topic, health insurance, health service, rural healthMedicare online, aged health service, aboriginal health services, common health topic, health insurance, health service
Australia Central Territory Victoria	www.act.gov.au www.vic.gov.au	Medicare online, aged health service, aboriginal health services, common health topic, health insurance, health serviceMedicare online, ambulance service, aged health service, aboriginal health services, common health topic, health insurance, health service
Victoria New South Wales	www.vic.gov.au www.nsw.gov.au	Medicare online, ambulance service, aged health service, aboriginal health services, common health topic, health insurance, health serviceMedicare online, ambulance service, aged health service, aboriginal health services, common health topic, health insurance, health service
New South Wales Queensland	www.nsw.gov.au www.qld.gov.au	Medicare online, ambulance service, aged health service, aboriginal health services, common health topic, health insurance, health serviceAmbulance service, common health topic, health service, rural health
Queensland Western Australia	www.qld.gov.au www.wa.gov.au	Ambulance service, common health topic, health service, rural health Medicare online, ambulance service, aged health service, aboriginal health services, common health topic, health insurance
Western Australia South Australia	www.wa.gov.au www.sa.gov.au	Medicare online, ambulance service, aged health service, aboriginal health services, common health topic, health insurance Ambulance service, aged health service, aboriginal health services, common health topic, health insurance, health service, rural health
South Australia Tasmania	www.sa.gov.au www.tas.gov.au	Ambulance service, aged health service, aboriginal health services, common health topic, health insurance, health service, rural healthAmbulance service, aged health service, aboriginal health services, common health topic, health insurance, health service, rural health
Tasmania Northern Territory	www.tas.gov.au www.health.nt.gov.au	Ambulance service, aged health service, aboriginal health services, common health topic, health insurance, health service, rural health Aged health service, aboriginal health services, common health topic, health insurance, health service, rural health
Northern Territory	www.health.nt.gov.au	Aged health service, aboriginal health services, common health topic, health insurance, health service, rural health

Ambulance Service, 2006). For example, an e-hospital's web-based pharmacy allows citizens to transact information when they do electronic prescribing (HealthConnect, 2005). While another example to illustrate the two-way communication service for both government and citizen is by the use of aged care online claiming system

(https://www2.medicareaustralia.gov.au:5443/pcert/AgedCareEBbizWeb/logon.do)

This service was introduced to streamline business processes supporting the payment of Aged Care subsidies by allowing users to transmit forms online and claim payment directly with Medicare Australia (Australian Government-Medicare Australia, 2009). Such e-health transaction services supported by the e-government have improved the efficiency for both the citizen and government as compared to the first stage of cataloguing. Australian e-health web sites supporting transactions are presented in Table 3.

Stage 3: Vertical Integration Level

This stage encompasses the integration of similar e-health services provided by different levels of Australian government. In Australia, the vertical integration of e-health services is supported by HealthConnect and NEHTA (National E-health Transition Authority). HealthConnect (www.healthconnectsa.org.au) is responsible for the development and coordination of e-health activities in Australia (McAlindon, 2007). It also supports states and local governments with the required infrastructure and national standards for collaboration between health service providers in their region for effective information sharing (NEHTA, 2008). To support such service, systems have to be interoperable so that information can be exchanged efficiently (Khim et al., 2004). On the other hand (NEHTA introduced standardised key clinical information to facilitate e-health interoperability and integration between stakeholders in similar industries or the same regions (NEHTA, 2008). It has taken care to ensure that all data in clinical communications across all health IT systems is presented in a standardised format. NEHTA is also supporting the development of IEHR (Individual Electronic Health Record) that is being introduced in Australia to integrate the key health information from a number of different systems together and

Table 3. E-Health sites that represent the transaction level (Stage 2)

Level of Government	E-health Site	Types of Information
Tasmania	https://paypaperbills.postbillpay.com.au/ServiceTasmania/>	Department of Health and Human Services • provides online payment facility for invoices to citizens
Federal	(http://bfhp.pip.com.au/)	Health Program • Integrates online database that facilitated doctors to access the latest medical information online, send patients' Medicare claims to the Health Insurance Commission via HIC Online and conduct online banking. • Provides a platform for sharing of resources and information between the citizens and the government.
Federal	http://www.health.gov.au/internet/main/publishing.nsf/Content/eprescribing	Electronic Prescribing and dispensing of medicines • enables electronic prescribing and dispensing • online supply of medicine • online claiming process
Victoria	http://www.ambulance.vic.gov.au/Main-home/Membership/Join Now.html	Ambulance services • online payment for an ambulance service
New South Wales	http://www.ambulance.nsw.gov.au/fees/paying_an_account.html	Ambulance services • online payment for an ambulance service

make it accessible via a single portal (National E-Health Transition Authority, 2009). It is obvious that such an effort is essential in ensuring the success of the vertical integration stage. Examples of e-health sites that support vertical integration of e-health sites are presented in Table 4 below.

Stage 4: Horizontal Integration

This stage of e-health development will be possible once vertical integration of e-health services is established. For Australia to achieve horizontal integration of e-health sites there is a need to integrate e-health records from various stakeholders including healthcare providers, hospitals, government, pharmacies, and other healthcare groups. This will facilitate communication, interaction and information exchange between healthcare industry groups (Mukherjee, & McGinnis, 2007). For e-health services to be fully-integrated in Australia, the following six issues are to be addressed. They are: (1) legal issues, (2) financial issues and (3) privacy and security, (4) lack of shared knowledge, (5) the diversity and fragmentation of the Australian health care system and (6) lack of national capacity in e-health with shortages of skilled e-health professionals (AHIC, 2007). At this stage none of the e-health sites investigated was fully integrated horizontally.

Maturity of Australia E-Health Services

Although Layne and Lee's model is not the only model that can illustrate the development of e-government applications such as e-health, it was a good guide to establish e-health development in Australia. In view of the above analysis of e-health development in Australia based on the four stages of e-government development by Layne and Lee's (2001) it is obvious that e-health in Australia is evolving. At this stage the only well developed category is the provision of information or cataloguing. The next stage of transactions is minimal, and vertical integration of services is not apparent either. Our research reveals that the current maturity level of Australian e-health services is at the informational stage only. This finding is depicted in Figure 2 with developments indicated in shades of grey indicating dark for developed and light for less developed with clear for undeveloped.

In order for Australia to reach a full maturity level of e-health services the federal, state and local governments have to look at both technological and organizational issues as suggested by Layne and Lee (2001). From this study, it is apparent that the Federal and State level governments have their own health information management systems which are at this stage independent. Other health entities such as ambulance and insur-

Table 4. E-health sites that support vertical integration (Stage 3)

Level of Government	E-health Site	Types of Information
Federal	www.healthconnectsa.org.au	Electronic Medical Records • develops a system of electronic health records to improve the flow of information across the Australian health sector (McAlindon, 2007)
Federal	http://www.health.gov.au/internet/main/publishing.nsf/Content/eprescribing	Electronic Prescribing and dispensing of medicines • enables electronic prescribing and dispensing • online supply of medicine • online claiming process

Figure 2. Stages of e-health development in Australia

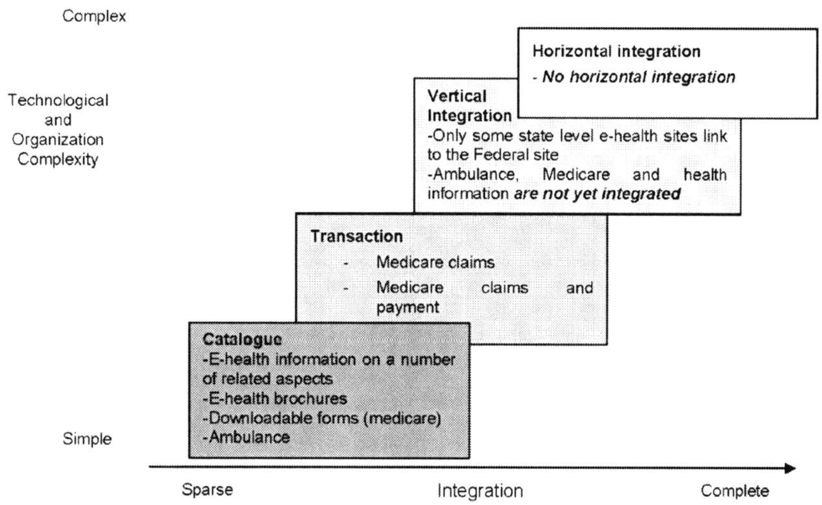

ance services are also independent. The participation of various stakeholders is sometimes a barrier to e-health development (Wickramasinghe et al., 2005). For a fully developed e-health system, mutual understanding of each stakeholder's perspective is important (Eng, 2001). A way to overcome such an issue is to provide the stakeholder engagement plan to outline each stakeholder's role in the facilitation of e-health services by reducing the costs of the conflict (AHIC, 2007). Other suggestions in overcoming such a challenge are still lacking and will be certainly needed in the Australian context.

E-health in Australia at this stage includes information on hospitals, pharmacies, Medicare, insurance, ambulance services, health, ethics, and research and health warnings on new epidemics. One unique e-health application is information on fire victims due to a recent fire in Australia that has left many people homeless, depressed and lonely. Other e-health applications discussed in the review of literature such as telemedicine, e-hospital, m-healthcare, and telemedicine at this stage are ideas only.

CONCLUSION

This chapter has depicted the developments of e-health in Australia based on Layne and Lee's e-government maturity model. E-health is one the e-government's applications, which is imperative to improve health organisational processes and to deliver relevant services and information quicker to its citizens. The four applications of e-health encompass e-hospital, m-healthcare, telemedicine, and health portals (Min et al., 2007; Chong, et al., 2008). For these years, the Australian government has been enthusiastically exploiting ICT to bring better healthcare services to the citizens. In view of all the initiatives invested, apparently, Australian e-government health services are at the present time only at a semi-mature stage. To achieve the a full maturity level of provision of e-health services in Australia, the federal and state governments would have to critically and appropriately address the organizational and technological issues as well as coordinate the information from all stakeholders in this public sector application.

REFERENCES

Accenture (n.d.). *High Performance Government*. Retrieved May 25, 2008, from http://www.accenture.com

Advance Healthcare Group Limited. (2005). *Advance and IBA enter online pharmacy and electronic prescribing collaboration and convertible note Investment*. Retrieved May 25, 2008 from, http://www.ahgl.com.au/files/document/9_Collab.pdf

America Telemedicine Association. (n.d.). *America Telemedicine Association*. Retrieved May 25, 2008, from http://www.atmeda.org

American Telemedicine Association. (n.d.). *American Telemedicine Association*. Retrieved May 25, 2008, from http://www.atmeda.org/news/overview.htm

Anderson, J. G. (2007). Social, ethical and legal barriers to E-health. *International Journal of Medical Informatics*, *76*, 480–483. doi:10.1016/j.ijmedinf.2006.09.016

Andreassen, H. K., Bunjnowska-Fedak, M., Chronaki, C. E., Dumitru, R. C., Pudule, I., & Santana, S. (2007). European citizens use of E-health services: A study of Seven Countries'. *BMC Public Health*, *7*(53), 1–7.

Australian Government. (2006). *Australian Government Department of Health and Ageing*. Retrieved May 25, 2008, from http://www.health.gov.au/internet/budget/publishing.nsf/Content/budget2006-ageingoverview.htm

Australian Government. (2008). *Australian Government - Department of Health and Aging*. Retrieved May 25, 2008, from http://www.health.gov.au/internet/ministers/publishing.nsf/Content/mr-yr08-je-je023.htm

Australian Government. (n.d.). *Australian Government- Medicare Australia*. Retrieved May 8, 2009, from http://www.medicareaustralia.gov.au/provider/aged-care/online-claiming/index.jsp

Australian Government Portal. (n.d.). *Australian Government Portal*. Retrieved May 8, 2009, from http://www.australia.gov.au/States_and_Territories

Australian Institute of Health and Welfare. (n.d.). *Australian Institute of Health and Welfare*. Retrieved May 25, 2008, from http://www.aihw.gov.au/publications/age/oag04/oag04.pdf

Baker, L., Wagner, T. H., Singer, S., & Bundorf, M. K. (2003). Use of the Internet and e-mail for health care information. *Journal of the American Medical Association*, *289*, 2400–2406. doi:10.1001/jama.289.18.2400

Bomba, D. (2005). Evaluating the Quality of Health Web Sites: Developing a Validation Method and Rating Instrument. In*Proceedings of the 38th Hawaii International Conference on System Sciences*.

Chong, J. L. L., Singh, M., & Teoh, S. Y. (2008). *An Exploration of E-Health in the Public Sector: the Australian Perspective*. International Conference on e-Government, Australia, October 23-24.

Curtis, R. (2007). What is e-health and why is it important? *ADF Health*, *8*, 82–83.

Department of Human Services. (1997). *Department of Human Services: Public Health in Australia*. Retrieved May 8, 2009, from http://www.dhs.vic.gov.au/nphp/publications/broch/contents.htm

Department of Human Services. (2008) *National E-health Strategy Summary*, Paper presented to Australian Health Ministers Conference.

Eng, T. R. (2001). *The EHealth Landscape -A Terrain Map of Emerging Information and Communication Technologies in Health and Health Care*. Princeton, NJ: The Robert Wood Johnson Foundation.

Eysenbach, G. (2001). What is e-health? *Journal of Medical Internet Research*, *3*(2), 20. doi:10.2196/jmir.3.2.e20

Falchuk, B., & Leob, S. (2007). Mobile Healthcare: Technologies and Architectures. *Life Science Systems and Applications Workshop, 2007*, 180–183.

Healthcare, I. D. S. (n.d.). *Ehealth History, Real Time Data Transfer, Advised Therapy, Distant Sufferer, Telephony, Videoconferencing*. Retrieved March 24, 2009, from http://www.com/hospital _management/global/UK_EHealth_Association /EHealth_History_Telephony_Videoconferencing/5_0/g_supplier_5.html

HealthConnect – A Health Information network for all Australians (2005a). About HealthConnect', June 2005.

Henderson, J., Britt, H. C., & Miller, G. (2006). Extent and Utilisation of Computerisation in Australian Practice. *The Medical Journal of Australia, 185*(2), 84–87.

Hesse, B. W., & Shneiderman, B. (2007). e-Health Research from the User's Perspective. *American Journal of Preventive Medicine, 32*, 97–103. doi:10.1016/j.amepre.2007.01.019

Holliday, I., & Tam, W. K. (2004). E-health in the East Asian tigers. *International Journal of Medical Informatics, 73*, 759–769. doi:10.1016/j.ijmedinf.2004.08.001

Istepanian, R. S. H., Jovanov, E., & Zhang, Y. T. (2004). M-health: Beyond Seamless Mobility for Global Wirless Healthcare Connectivity – Editorial paper. *IEEE Tans. Information Technology in Biomedicine, 8*(4), 405–412. doi:10.1109/TITB.2004.840019

Istepanian, R. S. H., & Lacal, J. C. (2003). *Emerging mobile communication technologies for health: some imperative notes on m-health*, Paper presented to Engineering in Medicine and Biology Society, 2003. Proceedings of the 25th Annual International Conference of the IEEE.

Janssen, M., & Kuk, G. (2009). *E-Government Business Models: Theory, Challenges and Research issues*. Hershey, PA: IGI Global.

Janssen, M., Kuk, G., & Wagenaar, R. (2008). A Survey of e-Government Business Models in the Netherlands. *Government Information Quarterly, 20*(4), 353–363.

Khalil, M. M. & Jones, R. (2007, November 18). Electronic Services – An Introduction to Theory and Application. *Libyan Journal of Medicine, 2*(4).

Khin, T. W., & Cooper, J. (2004). Information Age. Electronic Health Record and Australia Healthcare. *International Journal of The Computer, the Internet and Management, 12*(3), 14-21.

Kyriacou, E., Pavlopoulos, S., Berler, A., Neophytou, M., Bourka, A., & Georgoulas, A. (2003). Multi-purpose HealthCare Telemedicine Systems with mobile communication link support. *Biomedical Engineering Online*, 2.

Lasker, R. D., Weiss, E. S., & Millers, R. (2001). Partnership Synergy: A Practical Framework for Studying and Strengthening the Collaborative Advantages. *The Milbank Quarterly, 79*(2), 179–205. doi:10.1111/1468-0009.00203

Layne, K., & Lee, J. (2001). Developing Fully Function E-Government: A Four Model. *Government Information Quarterly, 18*, 122–136. doi:10.1016/S0740-624X(01)00066-1

Lee, A., Neilson, J., Tower, G., & Van Der Zahn, J. - L.W., Mitchell. (2007). Is Communicating Intellectual Capital Information Via the Internet Viable: Case of Australian Private and Public Hospitals. *Journal of Human Resource Costing & Accounting, 11*(1), 53–78. doi:10.1108/14013380710746401

LeMay, M. (n.d.). *E-health: Australia's $5bn black hole*. Retrieved March 2009, from http://www.zdnet.com.au/news/software/soa/E-Health-Australia-s-5bn-black-hole/0,130061733,339293816,00.htm

McAlindon, A. (2007). A window on the world of health ICT, HIMSS AsiaPac07. Retrieved April 15, 2009, from http://www.chik.com.au/files/HIMSSAsiaPacDel07.pdf

Metropolitan Ambulance Service. (n.d.). *Metropolitan Ambulance Service*. Retrieved May 25, 2008, from http://www.oracle.com/customers/snapshots/metropolitan-ambulance-service-ebs-casestudy.pdf

Middleton, B., & Brennan, P. F. (2005). Accelerating U.S EHR Adoption: how to get there from here recommendations based on the 2004 ACMI Retreat. *Journal of the American Medical Informatics Association*, *12*(1), 13–19. doi:10.1197/jamia.M1669

Milford, S. (2000). Racing to e-government: using the Internet for citizen service delivery. *Government Finance Review*, *16*(5), 21–22.

Milosevic, Z. (2006). *Addressing interoperability in e-health: an Australian approach*. Paper presented to 10th IEEE International Enterprise Distributed Object Computing Conference Workshops. Paolo Alto, CA.

Min, D. S., Lee, B. W., Yoon, S. W., Lee, Y. B., Kim, J. K., & Park, M. C. (2007). Actual Condition of Korea e-Health: What Do Enterprisers Want for developing e-health Industry? *E-Health Networking, Application and Services*, 9th International Conference 2007, pp 304-307.

Ministry of Health (MOH). (n.d.). *Transforming Healthcare*. Retrieved on May 25, 2008, from http://www.moh.gov.sg/mohcorp/speeches.aspx?id=12394

Mirza, F., & Norris, T. (2007). Opportunities and Barriers for Mobile Health in NewZealand,'. *Medinfo*, *2*(1), 102–106.

Mitchell, K. J., Becker-Blease, K. A., & Finkelhor, D. (2005). Inventory of Problematic Internet Experiences Encountered in Clinical Practice. *Professional Psychology, Research and Practice*, *36*, 498–509. doi:10.1037/0735-7028.36.5.498

Mount, C. D., Lelman, L. R., & Douglas, R. M. (2000). An integrated electronic health record and information system for Australia. *Med J.*, *172*(1), 25–27.

Mukherjee, A., & McGinnis, J. (2007). E-healthcare: an analysis of key themes in research. *International Journal of Pharmaceutical and Healthcare*, *1*(4), 349–363. doi:10.1108/17506120710840170

National, E. -Health Transition Authority (2000). *Connecting Australia*. Retrieved on May 25, 2008, from http://www.nehta.gov.au

National, E. -Health Transition Authority (2008). Retrieved on May 25, 2008, from http://www.nehta.gov.au/nehta-news/473-aust-govt-national-e-health-strategy

National, E. -Health Transition Authority (n.d.). *Clinical Communications*. Retrieved on May 25, 2008, from http://www.nehta.gov.au

OECD. (2000). In Outlook, I. T. (Ed.), *The Economic and Social Impacts of Electronic Commerce: Preliminary Findings and Research Agenda* (pp. 1–50).

Pattichis, C. S., Kyriacou, E. C., Pattichis, M. S., Panayides, A., Mougiakakou, S., Pitsillides, A., & Schizas, C. N. (2007). A brief overview of m-health e-Emergency Systems. *6th International Special Topic Conference on ITAB*, 2007, vol. 44, (pp.143- 153). Tokyo, Japan.

Pavlopoulos, S., Kyriacou, E., Berler, A., Dembeyiotis, S., & Koutsouris, D. (1998). A novel emergency telemedicine system based on wireless communication technology – Ambulance. *IEEE Transactions on Information Technology in Biomedicine*, *2*(4), 261–267. doi:10.1109/4233.737581

Reddick, C. (2004). Empirical Models of E-Government Growth in Local Governments. *E-service Journal*, *3*(2), 59–84. doi:10.2979/ESJ.2004.3.2.59

Sarikas, O. D., & Weerakkody, V. (2007). Realising integrated e-government services: a UK local government perspective. *Transforming Government: People. Process and Policy*, *1*(2), 153–173.

Shahlook, K. A., Saghafi, F., & Abdollahi, A. (2008) Retrieved March 2009, from http://www.ieee.org/portal/site

Sharma, S. K. (2006). Electronic healthcare: issues and challenges. *International Journal Healthcare, 2*(1).

Silcock, R. (2001). What is e-Government? *Parliamentary Affairs*, *54*(1), 88–101. doi:10.1093/pa/54.1.88

Singh, M., Sarkar, P., Dissanayake, D., & Pittayachawan, S. (2008, June). Diffusion of E-Government Services in Australia: Citizens' Perspectives. In *Proceedings of the European Conference on Information Systems (ECIS)* 2008, Galway, Ireland, Skinner, H., Biscope, S., Poland, B., & Golberg, E. (2003). How adolescents use technology for health information: Implications for health professionals for focus group studies. *Journal of Medical Internet Research*, *5*(32).

Stanberry, B. (2001). Legal ethical and risk issues in telemedicine. *Computer Methods and Programs in Biomedicine*, *64*, 225–233. doi:10.1016/S0169-2607(00)00142-5

Starfield, B., Shi, L., & Macinko, J. (2005). Contribution of Primary Care to Health Systems and Health. *The Milbank Quarterly*, *83*(3), 457–502. doi:10.1111/j.1468-0009.2005.00409.x

Sujansky, W. V. (1998). The benefits and challenges of an electronic medical record: much more than a "word-processed" patient chart. *The Western Journal of Medicine*, *169*(3), 176–183.

Turban, E., King, D., McKay, J., Lee, J., & Viehland, D. (2008). *Electronic Commerce A Managerial Perspective* (International Edition). Upper Saddle River, NJ: Prentice Hall.

United Nations Department of economic and Social Affairs (2005). *Global E-government Readiness Report: From E-Government to E-inclusion*. Retrieved on May 8, 2008, from http://unpan1.un.org/intradoc/groups/public/documents/un/unpan021888.pdf

Western Australian Local Government Association. (2009). *Productivity Commission Health Workforce Study*. Retrieved on April 6, 2009, from http://www.pc.gov.au/_data/assets/file/0003/10596/sub086.rtf

Wickramasinghe, N., Fadlalla, A. M. A., Geisler, E., & Schaffer, J. L. (2005). A Framework for accessing e-health preparedness. *International Journal of Electronic Healthcare*, *1*(3), 316–334 doi:10.1504/IJEH.2005.006478

World Bank. (2006). *World Bank*. http://www.worldbank.org/edevelopment

World Health Organization. (n.d.). *Strategy 2004-2007 health for Health-care Delivery*. Retrieved on May 25, 2008, from http://www.who.int/eht/en/eHealth_HCD.pdf

Yildiz, M. (2007). E-government research: Reviewing the literature, limitations, and ways forward. *Journal of Government Information Quarterly*, 646-665.

Chapter 24
Building Security Awareness Culture to Serve E-Government Initiative

Ali Maqousi
Petra University, Jordan

Tatiana Balikhina
Petra University, Jordan

ABSTRACT

Recently, many countries have adopted E-Government initiatives for providing public E-Services to their citizens. These initiatives, together with the existing and emerging private initiatives which offer E-Services, lead to a dramatic increase in the number of Internet users. This will form what is now known as E-Society. All E-Government initiatives consider citizen-centered approach, where user's security and privacy is a major issue. The level of citizen's engagement in these initiatives will depend on the extent of his/her confidence in the security system used by these initiatives. This imposes the need for developing computer security packages. These packages are intended to help users protect their assets such as information, databases, programs, and computer services from any harm or damage. The level of harm or damage that could happen to assets varies from one user to another. This variation depends on: users' awareness of possible threats, their knowledge of the source of threats, and if they are applying security controls or not. This paper aims to analyze current users' level of awareness and to propose possible methods in order to increase the level of users' awareness i.e. education, continues education, and training. This chapter is organized as follows: the first section presents an introduction, where the importance of security awareness to E-Government initiatives is highlighted and also it presents a research idea, the second section introduces the experimental design for a more comprehensive research that we are looking to carry on in later stages and specifies the objective of this stage, the third section presents results and discussions where we provide our own proposal of methods to increase the level of users awareness; finally, a conclusion is presented.

DOI: 10.4018/978-1-61520-789-3.ch024

INTRODUCTION

Importance of User Security Awareness to E-Government Initiatives

One of the most significant threats to information security could come from the system's users, because they are quite familiar with the infrastructure. It is not always dissatisfied workers and corporate spies who are a threat. Often, it is the non malicious, uninformed employee (user) ["Corporate Technology", 2008]. "E-Government" refers to the use by government agencies of information technologies (such as Wide Area Networks, the Internet, and mobile computing) that have the ability to transform relations with citizens, businesses, and other arms of government ["worldbank", 2009]. Ntiro in [Ntiro, 2000] states that E-Government has three main domains to cover: the improving government processes (E-Administration), connecting citizens (E-Citizens and E-Services), and building external interactions (E-Society). In E-Administration domain E-Government initiatives deal particularly with improving the internal workings of the public sector. However, second and third domains the Initiatives deal particularly with the relationship between government and public agencies from one side, and citizens and other institutions on the other side.

To deal with citizens as customers who consume public services means: talking to them to provide details about public service activities, listing to them to increase their input into public sector decisions and actions, and improving the services delivered to them in terms of quality, convenience, and cost. As the end user for the E-Government is a citizen, and to spread the use of public E-Services, the E-Government policy should consider a citizen-centered approach. However many people don't use E-Government for several reasons, such as unfamiliarity with ICT, lack of access, lack of training, and concerns about privacy and security of information. As far as the privacy and security of information is of a concern in this research, there is a need for providing a way of assuring citizens that their personal information will not be compromised. This challenge could be achieved by building a user security awareness culture. In this chapter we present our proposal to build user security awareness. The proposed security policies aim to increase and maintain a certain level of user security awareness and could be implemented along side with E-Government services or/and within specific organizational administration tools.

The Internet is the most powerful means for delivering E-Government [Patricia, 2003]. The Internet represents different things to different people, it provides a powerful new framework for connection, commerce, and communication, forming what is called E-Society. However, it also brings the outside world directly into our homes or working environments. This transformation puts new requirements on our online security and safety. Being aware of these your new surroundings and thereby realizing the potential threats you may be facing is the first step in your security plan [FrontLine, 2008]. Different situations in which people could face e-threats could be classified as: home, business and academic environments.

Home users include several categories of people beginning from children and they have very diverse level of computer knowledge and security awareness. As these users face security threats at homes alone the psychology issues play here main role.

Psychologically, when we leave the safety of our homes and venture into the outside world, we instinctively raise our guard and become more alert to possible dangers. Once we back home, we lower our guard and relax. Those actions are so embedded that we do them without thinking—but staying safe and secure online requires us to keep our guard or awareness up even when inside our homes or other places where we usually feel safe["Microsoft", 2008].

Because we all are part of the e-society as the Internet transforms our computers into a doorway through which the world can enter our homes, staying safe online means using the tools that can help us to control who and what comes in, and exercising our own good judgment about the people we choose to trust. Home users have to protect themselves, for example, by learning about new security tools through online training offered by leading software companies ["Microsoft", 2008].

In business environment an organization has to ensure that the staff acts in appropriate manner to keep sensitive information secure. Nowadays there is a broad increase in reliance on IT systems and information stored electronically. This is coupled with an extraordinary increase in the use of Internet services [ENISA, 2008].

Often huge amounts of money and time are invested by organizations in technical solutions while the human factor receives less attention. Technical solutions are necessary to address vulnerabilities such as viruses, denial of service attacks, etc. However, the involvement of humans in information security is of equal importance and many examples of security issues such as "Phising" and Social Engineering, where humans are involved, exist [Kruger H.A, 2008]. Therefore, information security awareness is major component within industry good practice for security.

In an academic environment security awareness could be comparable to the organization environments, especially for administrative and academic staff. But, as the threat from organized Internet crime is on the rise, awareness tends to play more crucial role in the future and an adoption of a strong security culture is needed to become a goal of an educational process of students. Moreover, academic institutes to fulfill their role in serving the community are required to make the first steps towards building secure e-society.

After we have presented the importance of security awareness and in order to carry on with this research, it would be useful to define what information security awareness is. The Information Security Forum (ISF) one of the world's leading independent authorities on information security defines information security awareness as: "An ongoing process of learning that is meaningful to recipients, and delivers measurable benefits to the organization from lasting behavioral change" [Kruger H.A., 2008].

RESEARCH IDEA

Recently, the growth in using Computers and the Internet imposes the need for developing computer security packages. These packages are intended to help users protect their assets such as information, databases, programs, and computer services from any harm or damage. The level of harm or damage that could happen to assets varies from one user to another. This variation depends on users' awareness of possible harm and damage, their knowledge of the source of threats, and whether they are applying security control or not. This research aims to analyze users' opinions about computer and Internet security and to propose a specific policy(ies) to different groups of users in order to increase the level of users' awareness.

Computer and Internet security is an active research area; therefore, the result so far is a huge amount of security packages in the market that are ready to be used. However, just purchasing these packages, with improper usage, the absence or insufficient training, result in inadequate benefits to different users. A small number of users know the importance of having security packages to protect their assets, but how many of them already has one or more of these security packages? Few users have security packages, but how many of them received proper training on how to use them? After training, do they apply the gained expertise to secure their assets? Do these trained users have specific security procedures to follow? How many users know about the existence of security packages? How many users are concerned about protecting their assets? How many users know that their unprotected machines could have an impact on other users' assets? The answers to all these questions would help build a statistical study of user awareness of computer and internet security. Based on this study's results we aim to build a number of policies - one for each group of users - that could be implemented. The policy would include not only a number of proposed security packages, but also a set of steps to be followed. Of course the study and the proposed policies will consider the culture and the available resources of Jordanian and Middle East users.

EXPERIMENTAL DESIGN

In this research, computer users are divided into three major groups; academic users, business users and home users. Academic users belong to educational institutions, academic staff and students. Business users belong to business institutions, top administration, executive managers and employees. Home users are all other users not specified in the first and second groups. Based on this user categorization, this research will be carried out in three stages correspondingly. The first stage studies users like academic staff and university students. In stage two, users from a number of business institutions will be considered. Stage three will consider home and other users. Dividing the research into three stages aims firstly to gain more confident analysis as the research goes on, and secondly, due to different user requirements the proposed policies should be different. The research starts with academic users as we believe that academic users represent the majority of educated computer and Internet users, and that it is easier to get access to them.

The main objective of the whole research is to develop security policies that would lead to an increase in the level of security awareness by computer and internet users.

To achieve the main objective the following sub-objectives are of concern:

1. Test users' awareness of computer and internet security.
2. Develop a number of security policies, one for each group of users.
3. Develop an application's requirements for a general security package that would be used by all users.

At this stag we decided to start with one case that can be evaluated and then to be generalized, therefore, we selected academic institution to represent the academic environment, this paper presents the first results that helps to test users' awareness level. To survey users we use questionnaire method to gather information and make some statistics about the current level of users. Then we intend to suggest a mechanism that can be used to increase current level and last to measure (test) again users' level. We consider this work as a preliminary investigation towards achieving the overall objective of the research.

The questionnaire includes three major parts: the first one is intended to test users' connectivity, software sharing, data sharing; previous experience of software and hardware failure; and ends with testing the presence of any security package. The second part is concerned with the way users deal with security packages. The third part is focused on one of the well known security controls, and some advanced knowledge and practices of security.

The number of surveyed staff is 82 which comprise 19.9% of all Petra's employees. Results of surveyed students of the academic institution have been eliminated as we need more samples (up to this point we have only 131 samples out of 4500 students).

RESULTS & DISCUSSION

The Need for Raising Users' Awareness

Unsurprisingly, most of surveyed users are connected to the Internet via a LAN. They share the software and data, which emphasizes the nature of our E-Society. However, 10% of them don't know if they are connected to other computers or not, which tells us that there is a need for training users on how to identify their systems. Although sharing data and software inside an academic institute is a normal behavior, there is a need to identify the way of proper sharing such as using passwords in order to protect shared files. Most of the users (83.75%) have experienced loss or damaged data, and 79% of them have experienced hardware or software failure on their systems, moreover, only 16.25% of the users were able to recover the data. These figures show how huge the impact of unsecured systems and knowing that 95% of the users are agreed on the importance of securing their data and systems make it inevitable to raise the awareness of the users. Finally, results show that 91.25% of the users have at least one security package, but we will examine the way they transact with these security packages via analyzing the results of next part of the questions. Figure 1 shows a graphical representation of first part results.

THE WAY USER TRANSACTION WITH SECURITY PACKAGE

Although this study was performed at an academic institute there are only 30% of the users who gain licensed software. As we all know the source of software if not authorized the software may be vulnerable to threats. Results show that only 4% of the users have got proper training on how to use security packages, other users (96%) have learned by them selves, or had no training at all. These untrained users may use security packages unwisely. This has been confirmed by analyzing the question how user practice the security package, the results show that only 34.75%, 33.33% and 43.38%, of the users were regularly run security packages, update security packages, or follow instructions of security packages correspondingly. Having published policies on how to transact with security packages and delivering proper training we believe that the above mentioned figures can be increased. Figure 2 shows a graphical representation of second part results.

THE IMPACT OF USER'S EDUCATION, CONTINUES EDUCATION, AND TRAINING

We believe that learning from previous lessens is a good way to develop future working plan that

Figure 1.

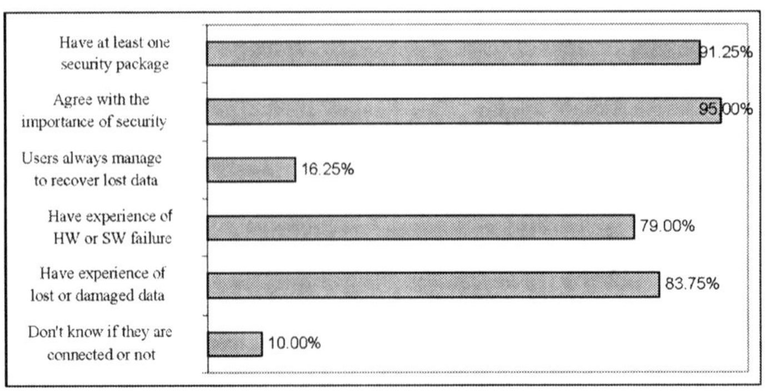

Figure 2.

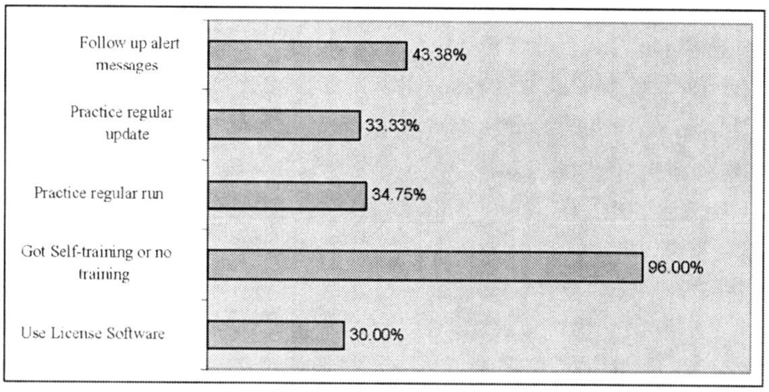

leads to achieve certain goal. Increasing the level of awareness means building security culture, nowadays, using user-name and password is incorporated strongly in our daily working actions. The majority of surveyed users (96%) believe in the importance of user-name and password and 97.5% are using them, this result has been achieved because of: firstly, the academic environment they belong to, and secondly, many years have passed since E-Society encouraged and in some cases enforced to have and use user-name and password. We want to build upon this experience to promote education as a mean of increasing level of users' awareness in academic and none academic environments. Of course, this is just an example of security culture, but it is not enough to say that those users who have user-names and passwords are sufficiently aware, the results of the survey show that only 22.5% change their passwords frequently, only 33.75% protect their passwords very carefully, and 41% use passwords that can be guessed easily. Therefore, users still need to be encouraged, enforced, and also monitored to follow certain security policies. Few respondents (25%) were familiar with general and emerging security terms, almost 70% of them never use encryption. This is again, shows the need for continues education to maintain a certain level of awareness. Quarter respondents prefer to have training on security issues, which means that training as a way of increasing user security awareness is a desirable method. Figure 3 shows a graphical representation of third part results.

Figure 3.

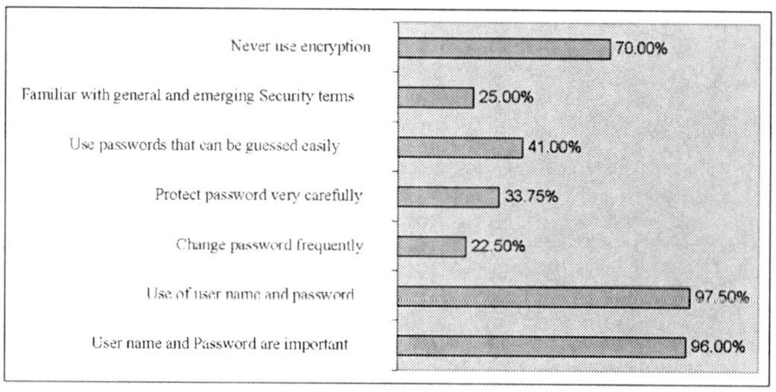

In order to achieve continues education to the users we have developed a web site. The users of the web site are the employees and students of the organization. The web site includes several ways to educate users and to keep them informed with latest news and technologies that might by used to secure users' assets. One of the main services provided by the web site is the possibility to enable users to participate in different periodic surveys. Figure 4 and Figure 5 show snapshots of the main pages presented in the web site.

Figure 4.

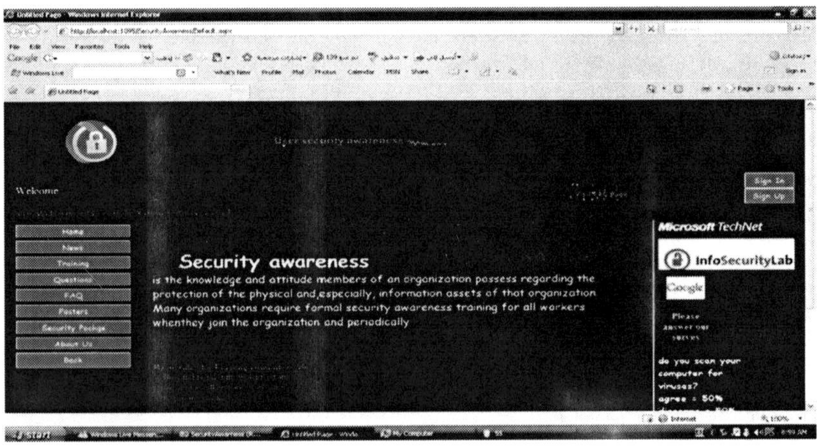

Figure 5.

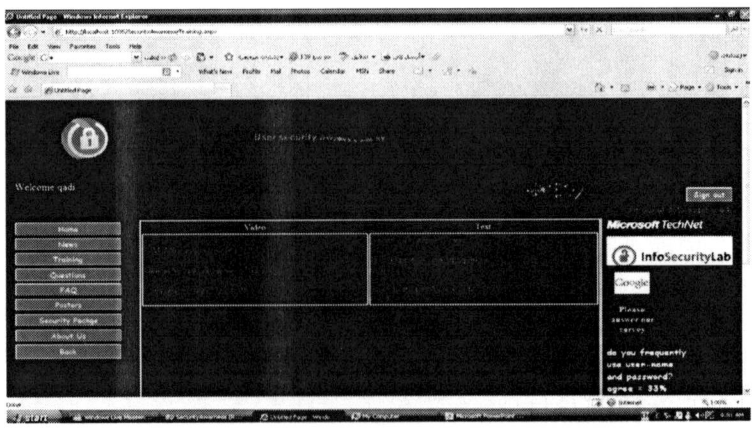

CONCLUSION

We live in an E-society where the Internet and computers become the main tools that help us to participate as users and perform our daily activities. E-Government adds new security challenge since its end users are citizens, businesses and employees. To protect our valuable assets against emerging threats, first of all we need to be aware of possible e-threats. As a part of a more comprehensive research, in this paper we present results of preliminary investigation of how to increase the level of user security awareness. Sample of academic environment users were surveyed in order to build a more general approach. The results show that the current level of awareness needs to be increased, the ways proposed for increasing the level of awareness are: education, continues education, and proper training. Next stage of the research is planed to put details of proposed methods and then making another judgment to see how the results changed.

REFERENCES

Corporate Technology Group. (2008). *The threat within: is your company safe from itself?* Retrieved February 2009, from http://www.ctgyourit.com/newsletter.php

ENISA. http://www.enisa.europa.eu/doc/pdf/deliverables/enisa_measuring_awareness.pdf, May 2008

FrontLine. (n.d.). www.frontlinedefenders.org. Retrieved May 2008, from http://www.frontlinedefenders.org/manual/en/esecman/chapter1_2.html

ISF. (n.d.). *Security Forum*. Retrieved June 2008, from https://www.securityforum.org/index.htm

Kruger, H.A., Drevin, L., & Steyn T. (n.d.). *A framework for evaluating ICT security awareness*. Retrieved May 2008, from http://www.computer.org/portal/site/security/menuitem.6f7b2414551cb84651286b108bcd45f3/index.jsp?&pName=security_level1_article&TheCat=1001&path=security/2006/v4n5&file=bsi.xml&

Microsoft. (n.d.). *Cyber Security Month*. Retrieved May 2008, from http://www.microsoft.com/protect/promotions/us/cybersecuritymonth_us.mspx

Ntiro, S. (2000). *eGovernment in Eastern Africa*. Dar-es-Salaam, Tanzania: KPMG.

Pascual, P. J. (2003, MAY). *"e-Government" e-ASEAN Task Force*. New York: UNDP-APDIP

Chapter 25
Mapping and Data Base Modeling for Public Sector Strategic Enterprise Resource Planning

J.D. Thomson
RMIT University, Australia

ABSTRACT

This Enterprise Resource Planning database model provides a systematic, logical and regular basis for the collection, collation, dissemination and mapping of strategic Enterprise Resource Planning data. Selective access to this accurate and timely data will improve public sector strategic Enterprise Resource Planning performance, accountability and administration. It will assist the public sector to be more effective and efficient in resource allocation and investment outcomes measurement, is transparent, and will encourage the development of trust, networks and social capital amongst public sector employees and their suppliers. The model has been successfully demonstrated through the establishment and analysis of an Enterprise Resource Planning data base with the Australian Department of Defence (ADoD). The Australian ADoD is a Federal Government Department with a FY 2008/9 spend of AU$9.3bn on products (goods and services), their support and maintenance, from almost every industry sector, on a global basis. While the implementation of Enterprise Resource Planning is usually viewed as a means of reducing transaction costs, in practice such implementation often increases transaction costs. Public sector bureaucratic hierarchies and their governance systems contribute to transaction costs. This research provides an Enterprise Resource Planning database model so that the public sector can achieve improved field mapping and strategic Enterprise Resource Planning using existing data and resources at lowest transaction cost.

DOI: 10.4018/978-1-61520-789-3.ch025

INTRODUCTION

Enterprise Resource Planning (ERP) systems are computer based technologies that integrate data across an organization and impose standardized procedures on the data's input use and dissemination (Grant, Hall, Wailes & Wright, 2006). Because of this capacity for integration and standardization, ERP systems are supposed to transform the nature, structure and management of work, thereby delivering significant cost savings regardless of the organizational context or structure (Davenport, 1998; Buckhout, 1999; Laughlin 1999; Trunick, 1999). Grant et al (2006) examined the extent to which a technologically determinist concept advanced by consultants and vendors held true with respect to three case studies – one embraced ERP, one adopted ERP on its own terms, and one rejected it. In the first case, ERP delivered some benefits where there was a good fit between the software and existing practices and processes, but where these had to be changed there was considerable resistance from staff and it was difficult to realise the promised benefits. In the second case, management needed the software to be customised to fit existing practices and turned off some of the functionality, with the outcome being that the ERP was no better than the legacy systems it replaced. In the third case, the perceived inability of the ERP software to suit critical business needs and to build an in house system led to rejection. It was also found that the social construction of particular discourse and the negotiation of meaning was an ongoing recursive process (Grant & Hardy, 2004), with each of the cases highlighting the importance of the social context in shaping the process of technology adoption. Grant et al (2006) found that much of the rhetoric surrounding ERP was technologically deterministic and that ERP customization to suit a client should be avoided because of the cost, and the need for the organization still to fit with the ERP requirements.

BACKGROUND

Literature Review. There is much organizational information associated with the Enterprise Resource Planning function. Each year, Enterprise Resource Planning represents around 50% to 60% of public sector spend. Thus the innovative conversion of Enterprise Resource Planning data to intellectual capital using electronic technology is invaluable for the management of public sector's Enterprise Resource Planning and strategic sourcing activities. For the public sector to use its existing Enterprise Resource Planning information to create knowledge of value, it needs to access with ease and minimum transaction cost, an Enterprise Resource Planning data base. Enterprise Resource Planning data useful for knowledge management is often spread throughout different public sector functions such as accounting, project management and supply logistics. Wittman & Cullen (2000) predicted that such content may become a key value driver. It is a 'core' business of public sector. Because of the ability of e-technology to collect, correlate, track and aggregate e-transactions quickly and easily, this content has the potential to become a valuable source of strategic and operational knowledge. Enterprise Resource Planning enables such masses of information, previously dispersed and fragmented, difficult and expensive to bring together manually in a timely way, to now be brought together and interrogated in seconds. This contributes to improved efficiency and effectiveness, and to a lowering of transactions costs.

Reducing the transaction costs of the public sector involves multi-stakeholder engagement; broader forms of accountability, risk sharing and responsibility; and 'the inevitability of transparency networks forcing organizations to adopt new systems of governance' (Williams, 2000, p90). These transparency drivers include the speed, flexibility and reach of public sector employees driven by the accelerating power and persuasiveness of knowledge management; the growing power of employees, customers and suppliers to find out information about public sector behaviour, inform others and organize; the creation of new public sector regulatory regimes for transparency and a shift to global structures that enhance their accountability in the global economy; the discovery and adoption of new public sector economic measures for social capital that will transform the way growth and value creation is accounted for in the economy and capital markets; and the central role of knowledge, trust and corporate reputation in driving business success in the networked economy (Williamson 2002a). Williamson (2002a) is of the view that transparency is already well on its way to establishing itself as a powerful norm in global policies and a transformative force within the firm and its stakeholder relationships. Public sector management of Enterprise Resource Planning is a demonstrable part of this global governance transformation. Enterprise Resource Planning by its very nature, provides many powerful 'panoptican' surveillance opportunities (Bentham, 1787). This may be useful in public sector in ensuring transparency and reducing negative behaviours such as corrupt practices, so encouraging value creation rather than knowledge hoarding – thus contributing to the lowering of transaction costs.

Research Aim

This research aims to provide an Enterprise Resource Planning database model which will assist in public sector strategic sourcing, planning and mapping; and reduce the transaction costs of procurement activities through building social capital, trust and transparency, and efficient and effective strategic sourcing and reporting arrangements.

The Generic Database Model

The generic model was based on the development of a comprehensive Enterprise Resource Planning data base for the Australian Department of Defence (ADoD). The relational database software used Structured Query Language (SQL) through MS Access, but most SQL database software would be suitable. Selecting the key attributes for such a model is critical. The performance required by its public sector users must be paramount. The performance criteria set for this database were several. Firstly, it had to be reliable, accurate and timely ie kept up to date with new data entry as transactions occurred. Secondly, it had to meet the user's many and varied needs on an established work priority basis but be capable of modification or adjustment should these needs change. Thirdly, it had to be user friendly, easy and intuitive to use, simple to understand in concept and structure, and be perceived and accepted by the users as of value and not as a threat to their jobs. Finally, it needed to be developed, installed and maintained using existing resources and at minimum transaction cost.

To achieve these criteria, the boundaries of the model were based on the existing financial data for each financial year's transactions. This data was already available, but spread throughout the ADoD in various functional areas such as accounting, project management and logistics. Exploratory research found there were around 250,000 electronic procurement transactions per annum, around 200,000 of which were under AU$2,000 in individual value. The data for these commodity purchases was available through bank card statements and so were not seen as being necessary to include in this database. Details of the remaining (approximately) 50,000 procurement transactions, each above the bank card delegation of AU$2,000, were made available and thus formed the basis of the database.

A unique attribute common to every transaction was identified. This unique field, the ADoD's Purchase Order number, provided the means by which transaction data within and across each financial year was identified. This unique attribute thus provided the basis for the individual records of related data to be selected, interrogated, dissected, grouped and extracted in many shapes and forms. A 'flat file' approach made access to all data easy and quick by people with very limited training. The SQL MS Access relational database flat file structure did not overload or make the database complicated or difficult to interrogate. Relational database fields were subsequently added as 'pull down' menus, such as Zip Codes and industry codes. Pull down menus for buyer and seller attributes, such as address, contact person, email addresses, telephone numbers and so on were also added. Procurement reports were structured to meet a variety of needs at the various organizational levels, for example, strategic, tactical, operational or for other specific needs. Future such reports could be designed and developed by users.

The structure of the extended relational database fields with each individual record tied to its unique Purchase Order number was based on the chronology of the longitudinal Enterprise Resource Planning process ie in the order in which the process occurs - from buyer to product/price to seller to delivery to final location. This included fields for the buyer's name, buyer's address and contact details, contract, contract type, account number, purchase order number and date, portfolio, department, division, branch, agency, and postcode, and details of payment arrangements and progress; product description and ANZIC industry code (Australian Bureau of Statistics, 1998), value and industry sector; seller company number, name and address, and contact details. In this format, the data was able to be intuitively understood and interrogated by users of the database, who were able to draw upon accurate and timely procurement records continuously updated with new information at the end of each month. This process was to be automated in due course. So the ADoD's procurement history in electronic format over six financial years was established by three existing employees over twelve months ie no consultants were used to develop or to establish this public sector 'core' business database.

An important issue was the accessibility of the procurement information to general and specialist users, and the ability of these users to easily interrogate the information. Many were familiar with MS Access had few difficulties. Others not so familiar underwent a short training program with an MS Access trining organization at minimum cost. The data was made available to users on a flat file basis, that is, all attributes and individual records were made available to all users all of the time. This meant that up to date Enterprise Resource Planning information was being used so that government Enterprise Resource Planning employees could provide answers to questions, however these were framed, or provide formatted regular reports, or develop specific reports, using the one central database of up to date information i.e., one database, many uses. It was designed and built to be responsive, intuitive and easy to use, and adaptable. For the ADoD, typical or unpredictable questions included Ques-

Table 1. An example of some few of the possible database attributes (columns) and records (rows).

P/O no	Date raised	P/O total amt (AU$K)	Bill to date (AU$K)	A/C description	Buyer Cost Centre	Supplies description	Order Qty	Supplier	Supplier details
446	18Dec	9,103	8,197	Tactical radios	DCPM-A	PINTAIL radios	20	Stanilite Electronic	Surfer's Paradise, QLD
447	25Dec	7,557	6,000	Lep'chaun	DNSDC	Lep'chaun lease	1	Dan Murphy	Donegal, Ireland
448	01Jan	6,320	0	Radar	MM(W5)	Goods	65	Disney Land	Hollywood, USA

tions With/Without Notice from Australian Federal Government Ministers requesting advice on, say, ADoD related industry located in a Ministerial electorate, how much was being spent there, with which company, when, for what and so on; what spend did the ADoD have with a particular company or country; or what was the ADoD's contractual arrangements and their state of completion with certain suppliers. Others included ADoD exposure to certain companies whose financial status was deteriorating.

In being able to access such a database, reports and responses to government or other stakeholder questions could be easily, quickly and accurately formulated by many staff, thus significantly reducing the transaction costs previously associated with these activities, particularly coordination costs.

Demonstrable Applications of Reduced Transaction Costs

With a global generic Enterprise Resource Planning database, the coordination and knowledge management problems associated with incomplete Enterprise Resource Planning transaction information and corporate governance issues are reduced. With accurate scrutiny of historical Enterprise Resource Planning data from several previous financial years, the ADoD is better able to choose the more efficient and effective Enterprise Resource Planning arrangements so reducing its transaction costs. It is also able to better synchronize the motivation of the ADoD and its suppliers by reducing the differences of interest and information between the two, with ever increasing transparency and trust. The Enterprise Resource Planning database is immediately able provide accurate details of each product (good or service) purchased, by whom and from which supplier in which industry, when and where, as well as the current status of an account. This transparency in itself reduces the potential for, or possibility of, corrupt practices.

Enterprise Resource Planning data is able to be used for strategic procurement purposes. For example, e-supplier data can quickly reveal different or in some cases the same suppliers supplying the ADoD with the same 'off the shelf' product at significantly different prices. This knowledge can be used to re-arrange competitive bids by fewer sellers at better prices and so lower overall prices and transaction costs. Alternatively, because the knowledge management of this Enterprise Resource Planning data is so accurate and easy to access, there may be no need to limit the number of suppliers of a particular product but price setting may be to a buyer's advantage. Such technological innovation enables an organization to review, revise and renew its existing buyer-seller relationships.

Governments, for a wide range of reasons, need to know with whom they are doing business, what business, and what financial exposure they have at any particular point of time. They need to know now, not in a month, or a week, or tomorrow, but now. Access to such an electronic procurement database will enable an organization to know the number and value of transactions, and with whom they are doing business. This is demonstrated across two financial years (Table 2). Each of the transactions comprising the data can be individually sourced. The database provides an immediate, accurate, timely summary of information for government. Without the database, it is difficult, slow and costly to obtain such up to date data from the various government functional departments such as accounting, project management or logistics.

Table 3 provides a typical summary extract from two financial years of the database. This extract demonstrates the number of notifications of value greater than the bank card delegation limit of AU$2,000 and the total value of the notifications in this category. This information is useful if the level of delgations is to be reconsidered, particularly as each product (good or service) comprising the data can be identified. This infor-

Table 2. Value and number of buyer transactions

Value Bracket of Procurements	F/Y 1 No of Transactions	F/Y 1 Value of Transactions $m	F/Y 2 No of Transactions	F/Y 2 Value of Transactions $m
$150m and over	4	1404	2	1515
$100m to $150m	nil	nil	nil	nil
$50m to $100m	3	178	4	306
$20m to $50m	7	195	6	187
$10m to $20m	18	241	12	177
$5m to $10m	28	191	28	197
$1m to $5m	193	395	253	549
$100k to $1m	2221	590	2205	583
$30k to $100k	4746	250	4410	231
$2k to $30k	43769	327	42035	309
Less than $2k	~ 200,000	50	~ 200,000	50
Value Bracket of Procurements	F/Y 1 No of Transactions	F/Y 1 Value of Transactions ($m)	F/Y 2 No of Transactions	F/Y 2 Value of Transactions ($m)
Total greater than $2k	50,989	3,768	48,955	4,054

mation can also assist in determining whether a particular purchasing officer is as efficient as another, or if there are significant regional differences.

Major ADoD Enterprise Resource Planning contracts, usually high tech projects, were a focus of the organization's strategic Enterprise Resource Planning management policy because of the potential for local high tech industry development and the national benefits derived therefrom. The Table 4 summary, easily extracted from the Enterprise Resource Planning data base, provides an indication of whether such a strategic sourcing policy was working or not. Detailed investigation of each contract from the database gave technology, performance, and other supplier details over two F/Ys. Governments and government ministers are often interested in knowing how much Defence

Table 3. Electronic purchasing statistics: Global summary

Financial Year	FY1	FY2
Number of Notifications >AU$2,000	50,989	48,995
Value of Notifications >AU$2,000 (in then year $m)	3768.06	4054.03
Value of Notifications (AU$m) at constant prices	3768.06	4159.94

Table 4. Procurement Contracts greater than $5m

F/Y	Total value ($m)	Total number of contracts	Total value to local suppliers ($m)	Total number of contracts awarded to local suppliers
1	2208.7	60	1074.1	52
2	2382.8	52	1528.3	43

is spending in their electorates, and this information is easily extracted using the Post (Zip) Code field.

Governments are usually interested in support of local industry and offshore spend. If there is a calamity (eg tsunami), then it is necessary for a government to quickly be aware of its exposure to affected suppliers ie with whom, for what, when. Table 5 provides an example of aggregated data of country of origin over two financial years, with each item identified.

With this strategic purchasing and supply information, strategic sourcing strategies can be developed or confirmed, based on fact rather than speculation or fiction. The detail of each transaction upon which this summary is based is also immediately available.

Compilation of summary data by each ADoD business centre for each financial year is also easily, accurately and quickly achieved (Table 6). This summary of the procurement activities being undertaken by each ADoD business unit each financial year can be used by management to review the human resources allocated to each centre, and their performance commensurate with the type of procurements being undertaken. Resourcing equity across business centres should be a key issue for management, and should provide the basis for program budgeting of ADoD capability delivery.

The ADoD spends across almost all UN/Australian Bureau of Statistics Industry Sectors, a possible exception being primary industry. Each procurement is placed in an industry sector, which

Table 5. Purchases Greater than $100,000 from non local suppliers

Country of Origin	F/Y1 Number	F/Y1 Value	F/Y2 No	F/Y2 Value
Belgium	5	$2,121,098	3	$593,843
Canada	7	$40,493,060	14	$10,200,698
Denmark	1	$7,271,003		
Fiji	1	$670,000	1	$835,000
France	4	$2,603,403	5	$785,369
Germany	3	$548,256	14	$10,329,825
Greece			1	$288,720
Indonesia	1	$200,000		
Ireland	1	$173,040		
Israel	2	$416,963	2	$324,628
Italy	2	$333,379	2	$1,070,079
Netherlands	2	$375,028	3	$686,914
Norway			1	$4,370,377
NZ	12	$5,196,147	11	$6,376,322
Singapore	1	$152,480		
Spain	1	$127,001		
Sweden	2	$1,466,168	2	$1,488,098
Switzerland	6	$1,207,153	5	$1,763,009
UK	33	$14,770,414	49	26,080,506
USA	126	$1,1444,801,682	174	$958,953,255
Total	210	$1,222,926,275	286	$1,024,146,643

Table 6. Purchasing by business unit

ADoD Program (Business Centre)	Number of Notifications (each > AU$2,000)	Value of Notifications (AU$m)
Forces Executive	1532	40.37
Navy	6734	359.77
Army	11845	342.57
Air Force	14251	452.51
Strategy and Intelligence	211	10.25
Acquisition	2778	1660.40
Budget and Management	7589	731.31
Science and Technology	3308	62.59
London	973	33.25
Washington	1496	72.61
Unstated	272	2.42
Total ADoD	50989	3768.06

industry sectors contributed to each procurement, and to break this spend down into its various industry sector components. In summary, Table 7 provides the top ten principal industry sectors within which the ADoD invested its procurement activities for one F/Y as an example of the use of the data in the database. Every other F/Y was also so analysed. This information is valuable for a multitude of purposes, nationally, for private sector investment purposes, and so on. Again, the details supporting each one of the contributing Enterprise Resource Plannings can be made immediately available.

Table 7. Top Ten ADoD industry sector spend for one F/Y

Industry Code	Industry Sector Title	Notifications	Value (AU$m)	% by value
15	Transport equipment	4457	1380	37
22	Construction and Construction services	4889	729	19
27	Consultancy, Property and Business services	6313	477	13
18	Computer, office Equipment and Electrical equipment not elsewhere classified	7196	422	11
Industry Code	Industry Sector Title	Notifications	Value (AU$m)	% by value
11	Chemicals, Petroleum and Coal Products	2332	146	4
19	Industrial machinery and equipment	2507	108	3
17	Electrical equipment,hardware,household appliances	3846	91	2
16	Photographic, Professional and Scientific equipment	2398	56	1
8	Textiles, clothing and footwear	1366	49	1
25	Communication services	435	47	1
Total		35739	3505	93

A summary of the top ten ADoD suppliers by value each F/Y was also made from the database material. This data is of significance from industrial, national and international perspectives (Table 8).

Mapping of Public Sector Procurements

Strategic purchasing requires a close relationship and integration between manufacturers and major buyers, that is, a tight relationship between seller and buyer and high buyer demand predictability. The products being purchased are industry specific and are sourced from industry specific suppliers and distributors. They usually require specialised logistics and fulfilment mechanisms. They are of strategic importance to the buyer (and often to the seller also), and market efficiency is high. Electronic procurement will do much to reduce the cost of the supply chain through the sharing of inventory and information. To achieve this, the manufacturer or importer shares the inventory and warehousing costs with a major customer. For the buyer, the inventory is on consignment, and is paid for as consumed. Browser based inventory systems give full visibility of inventory over the Internet. Replenishment is by the manufacturer, and issues can be charged to an electronic purchasing card. An Internet based purchasing and inventory management application service provider is required to enable payment via the electronic purchasing card. Contractual arrangements include known prices, cost sharing, agreed minimum stock levels and use of the electronic purchasing card. Purchases are charged by the seller to the buyer on product issue only. Transactional arrangements include full visibility of information over the Internet, and joint stocktakes. Financial arrangements included delegation of financial authority to buyer procurement staffs. The purchasing card is charged on the issue of product only, and the third party banking merchant controls apply to the card, which may be supplier nominated. There is a regular audit of transactions, with a third party cost centre manager approval of charges and reconciliation of card debits to use. Under these conditions of predictable demand, tight collaboration between the buyer and supplier ensures high service levels.

Where there are few buyers but many sellers, a seller will want to develop a tight relationship with a buyer, but the buyers will want to use their

Table 8. Top ten ADoD suppliers by value

No	Supplier	No of procurements	Value (AU$m)	% by value
1	Lockheed Martin	14	916	24
2	Civil and civic	9	239	6
3	NQEA	36	188	5
4	ADI	646	165	4
5	Raytheon	3	156	4
6	DAS	1730	99	3
7	Rockwell	55	91	2
8	CSP	26	77	2
9	Forgacs	4	63	2
10	Shell	490	50	1
	Total top ten suppliers	2987	2046	54
	Other suppliers	48002	1723	46
	Total suppliers	50989	3768	100

buying power to gain the best possible 'deal' from competing sellers.

Where there are many buyers and few sellers, a seller will want a loose relationship with buyers to ensure the seller can achieve the best possible price for its products from a large number of buyers.

Where there are many buyers and many sellers, responses are likely to be opportunistic, and the products are likely to be largely undifferentiated.

These network relationships are shown in the following diagram (Figure 1).

Each quadrant in the e-marketplace model has its own business application, the knowledge of which enables product placement based on selected value drivers. For example, low value high volume products will more likely be in the 'marketplace quadrant', while high value low volume items are more likely to be in the 'longer term relationship' or 'strategic' quadrant. Suppliers through differentiation of their product from other suppliers will try to move towards Quadrant 2 where a monopoly or oligopoly situation can prevail. Similarly, public sector organizations will prefer a monopsonistic situation (Quadrant 3). An

Figure 1. Mapping model for public sector strategic procurements

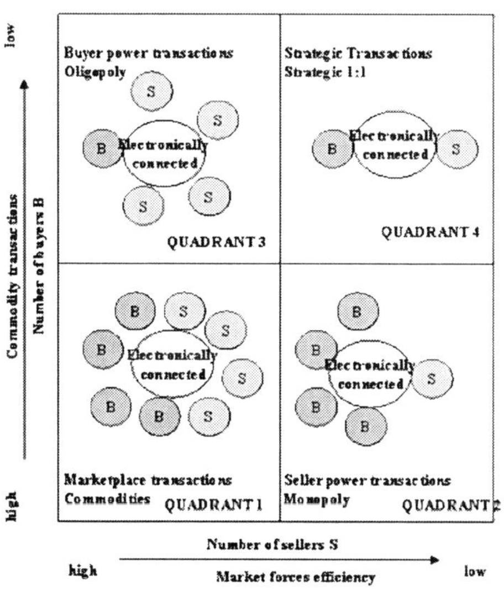

actual application to a business unit's annual procurement is shown in Figure 2.

The four quadrants of the model and their relationship with the electronic supply/value chain and electronic acquisition/technology arrangements are briefly explained in the following sections, using case studies to demonstrate each model.

Buyer Model (Few Buyers, Many Sellers)

The Buyer Model quadrant is appropriate in cases where there are a large number of potential sellers and this may result in multiple or fragmented formats, where the buyer is able to leverage buying power through the use of say, reverse auction tools. A reverse auction is where a supplier's winning bid is the lowest, rather than the highest, so suppliers compete against each other through an auction process to win the auction by making the lowest bid. Buyers can demand supply through these processes, so forcing the many suppliers to comply with the buyer's Enterprise Resource Planning, requirements and processes.

The value proposition for the one or few buyers is that they can demand a common format for all electronic applications, specifications and contracts across all sellers; enforce compliance through workflow and supply chains; achieve internal and external process efficiency; automate and integrate back office systems to achieve seamless purchase and accounting efficiency. In this quadrant, purchasing power and overall control is with the buyer. The use of an e-market may increase the potential buying power of the buyers, and will depend upon the individual purchasing power each buyer has. If an individual buyer considers it has sufficient marketplace buying power without carrying the overheads an electronic market and at least partial if not total loss of purchasing control that follows, then it is unlikely to enter such a relationship. Sellers could end up incurring costs while upgrading systems

Figure 2. Field mapping application of the ERP model

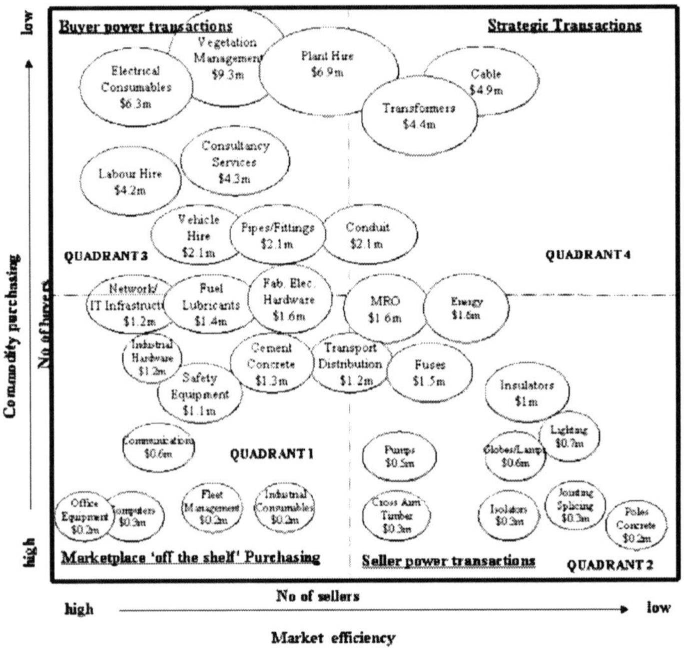

and integrating with buyer backend systems. Implications for the electronic marketplace are that it could be difficult to develop an underpinning value proposition for itself, and there could be a large number of suppliers selling commodity items with high supply costs relative to the value of the items. Under these circumstances, a buyer is likely to gain its best value from a direct relationship with a supplier ie a buyer is likely to avoid the use of an e-market intermediary, as this will simply add more cost.

CONCLUSION

This research has aimed to provide a futuristic Enterprise Resource Planning database model to reduce the transaction costs of Enterprise Resource Planning activities of public sectors through the building of social capital, trust and transparency, and efficient and effective strategic sourcing arrangements. The Enterprise Resource Planning database model was successfully demonstrated through the establishment and analysis of an Enterprise Resource Planning data base with the Australian Department of Defence (ADoD).

Public sectors are implementing the Enterprise Resource Planning of products. Through this research with the ADoD, it has been possible to provide a generic Enterprise Resource Planning model as to how this may be achieved efficiently and effectively at a low transaction cost for public sector. While the implementation of information technology is usually viewed as a means of reducing transaction costs, through this research, this has been proven so in practice. A striking feature of this Enterprise Resource Planning model is its potential to overcome many rent seeking attitudes and knowledge hoarding difficulties to make Enterprise Resource Planning information available to all at a low transaction cost. This can have a significant impact on the behaviour of public sector employees, as it can improve transparency and trust, efficiency and effectiveness, so positively influencing management and governance practices while reducing transaction costs.

This Enterprise Resource Planning database model for public sector provides a systematic, logical and regular basis for the collection, collation and dissemination of strategic Enterprise Resource Planning data. Selective access to this accurate and timely data will measurably improve Enterprise Resource Planning performance, accountability and administration in public sector purchasing. In the future, it will assist public sectors to be more effective and efficient in resource allocation and spend, is transparent, and will encourage the development of trust, networks and social capital amongst employees and with suppliers.

The management of Enterprise Resource Planning information is an all pervading public sector function, and a catalyst and sensor for information into, within, and out of public sector. By using tools and techniques with higher information processing capacity, the management of public sector Enterprise Resource Planning information can become more valuable, informative and efficient. The strategic management of future Enterprise Resource Planning provides the promise of helpful economic coordination across public sector. This database model provides accurate and timely information, which can be accessed by all. It is ubiquitous, secure, robust, protected, routinely used and a trusted source of accurate Enterprise Resource Planning data. Public sector employees can be connected into this network, a transparent network that facilitates the building of social capital and trusted relationships, and which provides access to and transparency of quality information unconstrained by barriers, at a low transaction cost.

The Enterprise Resource Planning model developed for future use by public sectors was built upon existing information already available and necessary for the management of public sector accounts, financial reports, projects and logistics. What the model provides is a means to comprehensively integrate these various disparate data to provide strategic knowledge. This knowledge can be made available to employees and suppliers as appropriate, or on a selective basis. The model database is inexpensive and quick to install, a task which can be undertaken by a few existing appropriately skilled employees. Consultants are unnecessary. It links public sector employees into a knowledge network, and increases Enterprise Resource Planning power and understanding. It provides a common language and central database for the articulation of Enterprise Resource Planning issues, a detailed, regularly updated Enterprise Resource Planning history, and provides a foundation for the further development of Enterprise Resource Planning strategy, frameworks and structures. In this, trust and transparency become valuable management tools. The model supports peer to peer relationships and information exchange that transcend individual systems and organizations. This empowers the public sector 'boundary spanners' and enables and encourages, organizational transformation in public sector.

In conclusion, the management of Enterprise Resource Planning at minimal transaction cost is a government's core business.

Through intelligent improved management of existing procurement information, this information can provide a valuable, informative and transaction cost efficient strategic supply transformation for public sector. This paradigm change does away with single points of contact by providing communication and access across public sector to the same central Enterprise Resource Planning database (one database, many uses), so removing the need for coordination or restricted access. The ever increasing amount of Enterprise Resource Planning information accessible by the many, each for their own unique purposes, means lower coordination costs and hence lower transaction costs.

REFERENCES

ANSI/ISO/IEC. (1999). *International Standard (IS). Database Language SQL—Part 2: Foundation (SQL/Foundation)*. Stockholm: Swedish Trade Council.

Arthur, W. B. (1994). *Increasing returns and path dependence in the economy*. Ann Arbor, MI: University of Michigan Press.Barnard, C. I. (1938). *The Functions of the Executive*. Cambridge, MA: Harvard University Press.

Australian Bureau of Statistics. (1998). *1291.0 - A Guide to Major ABS Classifications*. Canberra: Commonwealth of Australia.

Bentham, J. (1787). *The Panopticon Writings*. London: Verso.

Buckhout, S., Frey, E., & Nemec, J. (1999). Making ERP Succeed: Turning Fear into Promise. *Technology (Elmsford, N.Y.)*, *15*, 60–71.

Chaffey, D. (2002). *Enterprise Resource Planning and E-Commerce Management*. Upper Saddle River, NJ: Prentice Hall.

Chamberlin, D. D., & Boyce, R. F. (1974). Sequel: a structured English Query Language. In *Proceedings of the 1974 ACM SIGFIDET Workshop on Data Description, Access and Control* (pp. 249–264). Association for Computing Machinery.

Coase, R. H. (1937). The Nature of the Firm. *Economica*, *4*(16), 386–405. doi:10.1111/j.1468-0335.1937.tb00002.x

Cordella, A. (2001, June 27-29). *Does Information Technology Always Lead to Lower Transaction Costs?* Presented at The 9th European Conference on Information Systems, Bled, Slovenia.

Cordella, A. (2006). Transaction costs and information systems: does IT add up? *Journal of Information Technology*, *21*, 195–202. doi:10.1057/palgrave.jit.2000066

Cordella, A., & Simon, K. A. (1997, August 9-12). *The Impact of Information Technology on Transaction and Coordination Cost*. Presented at theConference on Information Systems Research in Scandinavia (IRIS 20), Oslo, Norway.

Davenport, T. (1998). Putting Enterprise into the Enterprise System. *Harvard Business Review*, *76*(4), 121–131.

De Geus, A. (1997). *The Living Company*. Cambridge, MA: Harvard Business School Publishing.

Fukuyama, F. (1999). *The Great Disruption*. Bury St Edmunds, UK: St Edmundsbury Press.

Grant, D., Hall, R., Wailes, N., & Wright, C. (2006). *The false promise of technological determinism: the case of enterprise resource planning systems'; New Technology, Work and Employment*. Oxford, UK: Blackwell Publishing Ltd.

Grant, D., & Hardy, C. (2004). Struggles with Organizational Discourse. *Organization Studies*, *25*(1), 5–13. doi:10.1177/0170840604038173

Hagel, J. III, & Armstrong, A. G. (1997). *Net Gain: Expanding Markets Through Virtual Communities*. New York: McKinsey and Co Inc.

Hayek, F. (1945, September). The Use of Knowledge in Society. *The American Economic Review*, *35*, 519–530.

Hill, R. (2003, May 20). *Network Centric Warfare*. Presented at theAddress to the ADF Network Centric Warfare Conference, Australian War Memorial, Australian Government.

Kant, I. (1781). *Critique of Pure Reason*. London: Norman Kemp Smith, MacMillan.

Krueger, A. (1974). The Political Economy of the Rent-Seeking Society. *The American Economic Review*, *64*, 291–303.

Kuhn, H. W., & Nasar, S. (Eds.). (2002). *The Essential John Nash*. Princeton, NJ: Princeton University Press.

Laughlin, S. (1999). An ERP Game Plan. *The Journal of Business Strategy*, *20*(1), 32–37. doi:10.1108/eb039981

Matthewson, J. A. (2001). *Enterprise Resource Planning a jargon-free practical guide*. Boston: Butterworth Heineman.

McGregor, D. (1960). *The Human Side of Enterprise*. New York: McGraw Hill.

Nonaka, I., & Takeuchi, H. (1995). *The Knowledge Creating Company*. New York: Oxford University Press.

O'Neill, O. (2002a). *Trust and Technology. Presented atThe Reith Lectures 2002, BBCi*. The Open University.

O'Neill, O. (2002b). *Trust*. Presented at The Reith Lectures 2002, BBCi, The Open University. Park, N. K., Mezias, J. M., & Song, S. (2004). A Resource-based View of Strategic Alliances and Firm Value in the Electronic In Park, P. (Ed.), People, Knowledge, and Change in Participatory Research. *Management Learning, 30*(2), 141-157.

Porter, M. E. (2001). Strategy and the Internet. *Harvard Business Review*, *79*(3), 62–78.

Rifkin, J. (2000). *The Age of Access*. London: Penguin Books Limited.

Schein, E. H. (1988). *Organisational Culture and Leadership*. San Francisco: Jossey-Bass.

Tarnas, R. (1991). *The passion of the western mind: Understanding the ideas that have shaped our world view*. New York: Harmony Books.

Thomson, J. D. (1996). *Australian Department of Defence Purchasing Statistics Bulletin 1989/90 to 1995/96*. Canberra: Commonwealth of Australia.

Trunick, P. (1999). ERP: Promise or Pipedream. *Transport and Distribution*, *40*(1), 1–39.

Veblen, T. (1899). The Theory of the Leisure Class: An Economic Study of Institutions. *American Journal of Sociology*.

Ventor, D. (2003, March 13). IT at the Heart of Shock and Awe: With US Invasion, Era of Network Centric Warfare has dawned, *Computer World*.

Williams, M. (2000). The World Bank, the World Trade Organization and the Environmental Social Movement. In Higgot, R., Underhill, G., & Bieler, A. (Eds.), *Non-State Actors and Authority in the Global System 2000*. New York: Routledge.

Williamson, O. E. (1991, June). Comparative Economic Organization: The Analysis of Discrete Structural Alternatives. *Administrative Science Quarterly*, *36*, 269–296. doi:10.2307/2393356

Williamson, O. E. (1991). Economic Institutions: Spontaneous and Intentional Governance. *Journal of Law Economics and Organization*, *7*(Special Issue), 159–187.

Williamson, O. E. (1996). *The Mechanisms of Governance*. New York: Oxford University Press.

Williamson, O. E. (2002). Empirical Microeconomics: Another Perspective. In Augier, M., & March, J. (Eds.), *The Economics of Choice, Change and Organization*. Brookfield, VT: Edward Elgar.

Williamson, O. E. (2002a, January). *The Lens of Contract: Private Ordering*. Berkley, CA: University of California.

Williamson, O E. (2002b, January). *The Theory of the Firm as Governance Structure: from Choice to Contract*. Berkley, CA: University of California.

Wittmann, C., & Cullen, M. (2000). *B2B Internet*. Philadelphia: First Union Securities.

Chapter 26
Surviving with SMS

Mohammad Shirali-Shahreza
Sharif University of Technology, Iran

Sajad Shirali-Shahreza
University of Toronto, Canada & Sharif University of Technology, Iran

ABSTRACT

The mobile phone is one of the technologies which are widely used these days. It is available in most countries and all people, even children and elderly people can use it. It seems that in the near future, each person will have at least one mobile phone. So it is a good choice for communication in emergency situations, such as a heart attack or after an earthquake. In this chapter, we will survey a number of systems which are designed for communication in emergency situations and then explain three systems which are developed by the authors. The first one is for locating and rescuing victims after an earthquake. The second system is for calling an emergency team by patients in emergency situations. The third system is for finding lost people with amnesia. In addition, we review some of related works which use mobile phones for communication in emergency.

INTRODUCTION

With the expanding use of mobile phones and the development of mobile telecommunications, many features are added to the mobile phones in order to attract more customers. One of the services that was provided on the mobile phone was the SMS (Short Message Service).

The SMS is the transfer and exchange of short text messages between mobile phones. The SMS is defined based on GSM digital mobile phones. According to the GSM03.40 standard (ETSI, 2000), the length of the exchanged message is 160 characters at most, which are saved in 140 bytes depending to how information is saved according to the standards. These messages may be a combination of digits and letters or be saved in non-text binary form. Using the same binary messages, one can also send pictures as well. The pictures, however, are two-color and have a low quality.

DOI: 10.4018/978-1-61520-789-3.ch026

SMS messages are exchanged indirectly and through a component known as the SMSC (SMS Center). SMS messages have the following advantages:

- Communication is possible when the network is busy;
- We can exchange SMS messages while making telephone calls;
- Sending offline SMS messages;
- Providing various services such as e-commerce.

One can also receive reports on the status of the SMS message or define a validity period for the SMS message (Nokia, 2001).

Nowadays by inventing new technologies, many services are changed. One of these areas which is using new technologies is servicing in Emergency situations. The services in this field are also changed by effect of mobile phones. For example some telemedicine services are designed for doing first aid for patients in their house by doctor from hospital without needing to go to hospital.

In this chapter, we will survey some of systems which are using mobile phones for communication in emergency situation. Then we will explain three systems which are designed by authors and are based on SMS service of mobile phones.

First we describe our system which is designed for rescuing after earthquake disasters. In this system, we use mobile phone to locate and rescue victims after earthquake.

Then we describe our system which is designed for calling emergency team by patients in emergency situations. For example if patients feeling cardiac arrest, by this method he/she can contacts the hospital easily and the proportionate emergency team will be sent to the patient home with necessary devices.

Finally we explain our system which is designed for finding lost person with Amnesia's disease. All of the above systems are using SMS for communication.

Using of other systems such as MMS (Multimedia Message Service) is not recommended because these services are not available in many countries and all phones does not support such advanced services. Also, the costs of using these systems are more than SMS.

Another point is that SMS is enough for our needs and we did not need advanced features of those systems. In addition, using services such as MMS in critical situations can introduce problems in network. Because the numbers of messages which exchange are huge and the load which these services put on network is more than SMS, the network may get problems or down the system completely.

Our methods are using GPS (Global Positioning System) to track down the location of persons. But using GPS system is not necessary, because in spite the high precision and accuracy of GPS, this system does not act well in indoor areas (Bamford et al., 2006). On the other hand, GPS system is not available on most of mobile phones and it needs a separate device which increases the expenses. Therefore, using the network based locating system (such as using Cell ID) is also acceptable, although it has less precision.

The main advantages of our methods are as follows:

1. All mobile phones, even black-and-white models and old-fashioned ones are capable to send and receive SMS. So this method covers a wide range of users.
2. The proposed methods can be used in developing countries due to the usage of cell phones and SMS, which is a public and cheap service on the cell phones, widely available across the globe.
3. The majority of cell phones support Java language. So our program runs on the majority of mobile phones.

4. Nowadays, most people, even the elderly are familiar with mobile phones. Moreover, the proposed method will work even without least of familiarity with mobile phones and just a button-pressing is enough.
5. The problem of busy lines is irrelevant here as SMS can work offline and even simultaneous during a call.
6. In case of traveling abroad, no language barrier exists, because information is put through in English. This helps user to send information in English anywhere abroad.
7. The mobile phone network is reliable and the possibility of it becoming out of order in situations such as earthquake or public riots is less than other networks including the fixed telephone network (Figure 1).
8. There is also no problem for telling the current address as it is possible to automatically track down the present location of the mobile phone by GPS.

Figure 1.

In our methods implementation, the programs has been written by J2ME (Java 2 Micro Edition) programming language. This language is a version of Java specially developed for small devices such as pocket pc computers, PDAs and mobile phones. We mainly tested our methods on Nokia N71 mobile phone. Also the Evermore BT-R700 GPS receiver has been used. This device contacts the cell phone with the use of Bluetooth technology and locates the device for the cell phone.

These methods can be implemented not only for the mobile phone, but also for the other devices such as PDA (Personal Digital Assistant) and Pocket PC.

SMS IN DISASTERS

Earthquake is one of the natural disasters which have a lot of victims each year. If the rescue mission for saving victims be done in first hours after the earthquake, the number of earthquake victims can be lowered.

Currently, there are advanced methods and robots for human search in earthquake disaster (Figure 2) (Takemura et al., 2004).

But most of these methods cannot be used in under developing countries because these equipments are expensive (Shiroma et. al., 2004). So, applicable methods are needed for these countries. So we present a method which can also use in

Figure 2. NAJI rescue robot used in Bam Earthquake (Shahri et al., 2005)

under developing countries (Shirali-Shahreza and Shirali-Shahreza, 2006).

Based on the SMS specifications, this service can be used for communicating with injured people, become aware from their health condition and location and guide rescue team to his location. Therefore we purpose a method to find and survive victims from devastated buildings by using mobile phones. Our method consists of three steps: After the earthquake, the Earthquake Emergency Center sends an SMS message to all subscribers in the earthquake region and asks them about their health condition.

At this point, the designed program which is running on the recipient mobile phone, get the message and examine that. The program can recognize messages from Earthquake Emergency Center by checking the message sender's number. If the message was from Earthquake Emergency Center, the program will ask user about his health condition and does he need help from Earthquake Emergency Center or not.

If the user requests help or if he did not reply in ten minutes because he is injured or unable to answer, the program will send an SMS to Earthquake Emergency Center automatically.

In this message, there is a help request. If the mobile phone supports location-based services, the current location of mobile phone is also sent to Earthquake Emergency Center so the rescue team and rescue robots can go to victims' location and help him.

Also, after this time, the mobile phone starts to play special pattern of beeps in definite periods so rescue team and rescue robots can find the victims location under devastated buildings. Because playing some beeps in periods consume very low power, most mobile phones can continue to work for more than 2 days; which is adequate time for saving victims because the best time to save people after earthquake is the first 24 hours after earthquake.

Continuous beeps or beeps with short distance can disturb people which are in short distance like victims under devastated buildings. In addition, these types of beeps use more power and phone battery will be discharged in shorter time.

The beeps which played are so that rescue robots use them to find victims location. In countries which did not have advanced rescue robots, these beeps are used to inform rescue team persons about victims' location. So by this method we are able to send robots to places which are difficult for human to go.

There are similar works which are done using mobile phone. Here we describe some of them. In continue we will briefly survey some of the systems based on mobile phones which are designed for emergency situation.

Mobile phone locations are used to find people during rescue missions in different countries. For example in USA, in E911 (which is an extended version of 911 – the USA police and emergency telephone), the mobile phone providers are asked to send location of people who called police through mobile phones with 50-100 meters accuracy. Using these system, police and rescue team can find people in situations which victim did not know where he is or cannot speak or call is disconnected.

In Europe, the 112 system (112 is the police and emergency system of European countries) is similar to E911 with the difference that there is not any defined accuracy for people's location. So, European mobile service providers usually use "Cell ID" to find mobile phone location approximately using longitude and latitude. The accuracy of this method depends on cell area and differs from 100 meter to 1000 meter (Warrior et. al., 2003).

In both of these systems, the location of mobile phone is found after call and this is the person who makes call first. But in our method, we use SMS service to avoid problems such as heavy traffic of network or busy lines, because we must contact thousands or millions of users in situation such as earthquake. In addition, in our method, this the Earthquake Emergency Center which first contacts users and if the user request help or if he is injured and cannot reply, his location is found with help of mobile phone and then rescue team are sent to his position. But in those systems, this is the person who initiates call which is impossible if the person is injured.

In addition, as we said in introduction, advanced method and special robots are designed to find and rescue people in natural disasters (Tadokoro, 2005). But because these methods need high technology and are expensive, they are not suitable for use in underdevelopment countries (Takemura et al., 2004) and we must design methods which are applicable in such countries. Our method is applicable in underdevelopment countries because it uses SMS which is a general and cheap service on the mobile phones and is available in many countries. Also this method did not require any additional equipment because the location of victims is sent to Earthquake Emergency Center and the rescue team can find the exact location with help of beeps.

This project tested on popular mobile phones such as Nokia 6600, third generation (3G) mobile phones such as 6680 and mobile phones with advanced location-based services such as Nokia N71. In Figure 3 a screenshot of our program is showed.

Figure 3. A screenshot of our rescue SMS program

SMS FOR EMERGENCY MEDICAL SITUATION

Providing first aids to the patient before arrival at the hospital is one of the important and influential factors in saving the life of patient. Contacting emergency team and offering brief information of the patient can help the emergency team in dispatching specialist medical team as well as equipment proportionate to the patient's conditions. As an example, the time of giving medical care to the patients in cases of heart diseases is critical.

But today, many people including the elderly live alone. Therefore, there is no one to take care of them and inform the emergency service when they need help. If such people need to contact emergency service, they face many problems such as:

- They may lose consciousness before any call to emergency center occurs.
- They may fail to recall phone numbers especially in elderly people due to feeble memory. Similarly, they might have forgotten their residence address.
- The patient may fail to provide correct information to emergency center because of his undesirable conditions or under stressful situation.

Considering the above facts, a system is needed to enable the patient to contact emergency lines in a short period and to send the necessary information including the residential address, medical history and so on automatically.

According to SMS specifications, this service can be used for calling emergency centers. For this purpose, the following method is proposed (Shirali-Shahreza, 2006).

The purpose of this method is to establish communication with the emergency center and provides brief and useful information about patient via SMS. This service automatically sends SMS through mobile phones, even when the patient cannot do it.

In this method the patient first enters his personal information including his name and age into the special program, and then adds his brief medical history such as cardiac diseases, diabetes, blood pressure, blood fat, psychiatric disorders, depression and so on. At the end, he enters the emergency phone number, mobile phone number of his family doctor and one or more of his relatives' mobile phone numbers so that the SMS could be sent to these people in cases of emergency need. This information is saved in a text file on the mobile phone.

This program is activated by pressing a special key on the mobile phone for a few seconds. When feeling sick, the patient presses the defined key on the mobile phone and keeps it pressed for a short time so that the special program is activated.

After running the program, it finds the present location of the mobile phone through GPS system.

Then, according to information received from the patient beforehand, an SMS with the following content is produced:

- The first line of message contains the personal information of the patient, including first name, surname, age and so forth.
- In the following lines the present location of mobile phone which indicates where the patient is located are provided.
- The final lines will provide his medical records such as cardiac diseases, diabetes, blood pressure etc.

Afterwards, the SMS will be sent to emergency center, family doctor and the patient's relatives or friends, whose phone numbers are previously received and recorded in the text file (Figure 4).

Thus, the emergency department guesses the present sickness of the patient based on his medical history and dispatches a specialist along with necessary equipment to the address of the patient in addition to the emergency doctor. If the emergency unit guessed diagnosis is correct, the specialist doctor will also help the emergency doctor in providing necessary medical assistance before reaching the hospital.

The specialist doctor's help increases the chances of the patient for recovery to a considerable degree. Also, the family doctor and the friends or relatives of the patient get informed of his conditions and can come to the patient's place.

So far, different works have been done in the area of medical care through wireless devices and networks (Wu et. al., 2005). But the activities on wireless devices as the PDAs and mobile phones have been less reported due to the limitations of these devices (Pavlovski et. al., 2004) and such devices have been mainly used for wireless communication. Especially, the use of SMS has been very limited due to its special limitations (Hassinen & Laitinen, 2005).

Among the projects reported so far, the method presented by Pavlopoulos et al. (Pavlopoulos et. al., 1998), which is named AMBULANCE, is similar to our method. This method is intended to establish contact between the emergency medical team and the specialist doctors in the hospital during the transfer of the patient to the hospital and for conducting the medical operations needed by the patient until reaching the hospital. For this purpose, some equipment should be placed inside

Figure 4. A screenshot of our emergency SMS program

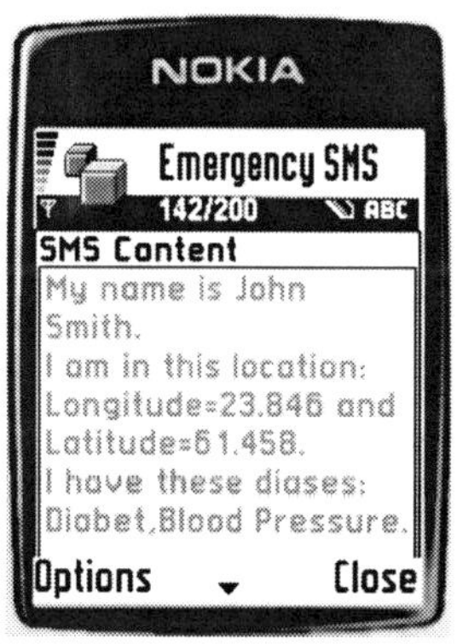

Figure 5. The AMBULANCE system diagram (Pavlopoulos et al., 1998)

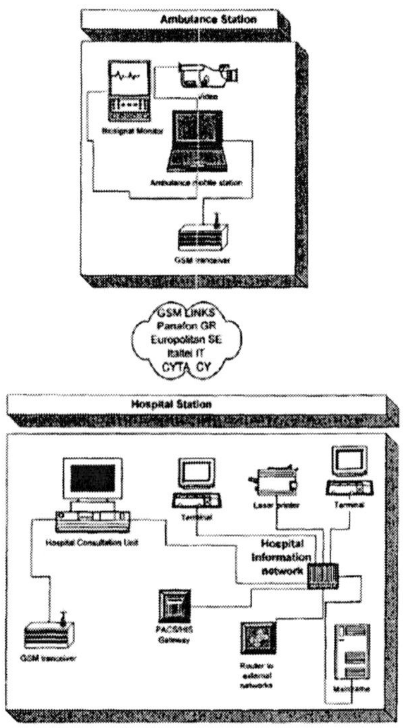

the ambulance and other equipment in the hospital to establish the communication (Figure 5).

In ambulance, a device must be set up to keep records of patient life conditions and a portable PC to communicate with hospital. The portable PC is fitted with a frame grabber card, a camera and a mobile phone with GSM Modem in order to establish contact with hospital and transfer information. A workstation in hospital will process input information from ambulance under supervision of a specialized doctor.

Accordingly, the ambulance dispatches life conditions of patient for hospital moment by moment and similarly the specialized doctor sends back necessary medical orders according to these information and when needed, he may ask the emergency team to provide an image of a specific organ of patient to be provided through the camera connected to the computer and the doctor issues subsequent orders.

Although our proposed method has many differences with the above method, we compare the appropriate features of these methods.

- Establishing of non-stop contact between hospital and ambulance may trigger continuous heavy line traffic, while SMS never bring about any line traffic. They are applicable even at time the network is fully busy, while Pavlopoulos' method needs free phone lines.
- The cost of phone contacts especially with mobile phones and for a long time is far higher than SMS.
- The Pavlopoulos' method needs advanced equipment, while our method only needs a mobile phone and even compatible with ordinary mobile phones.
- This project demands a high investment for installing needed devices like camera, portable PC, workstation and so on while our method needs only a mobile phone.

It is noteworthy that these two methods have major differences in applications and implementation and so no comparison may be a good parameter to evaluate each. In other words, both of them are appropriate in their fields.

SMS FOR FINDING PEOPLE WITH AMNESIA

By rapid growth of technology in recent years, many services are created for people who are suffered from diseases.

Some people are suffered from diseases such as Alzheimer, which is cause the loss of memory (amnesia). Amnesia is a condition in which memory is disturbed. The causes of amnesia are organic or functional. The usual first symptom noticed in these people is short term memory loss which progresses from seemingly simple and often fluctuating forgetfulness (with which the disease should not be confused) to a more pervasive loss of short-term memory, then of familiar and well-known skills or objects or persons. Therefore these patients may be got lost when they are out of house and finding them is not easy.

Here we propose a method for finding the lost people such as a person with Alzheimer's disease by mobile phone using SMS (Shirali-Shahreza and Shirali-Shahreza, 2007).

The purpose of our method is to locate the lost person and send his/her address along with some information about patient to the Police station via SMS, to find him/her by a Police team.

In this method we first enter the patient's personal information including his/her first name, surname and his/her disease into the special program, and then add the addresses of his/her house and workplace to it. At the end, we enter the Police station phone number and mobile phone numbers of one or more patient's relatives, so that the SMS could be sent to these persons in case of the patient is getting lost. This information is saved in a text file on the mobile phone. The mobile phone is given to the patients and he/she always carry the mobile phone with him/her.

The special program is activated by pressing a special key on the mobile phone for a few seconds. When the patient got lost, he/she presses the defined key on the mobile phone and keeps it pressed for a short time so that the special program is activated. After activating the program, it finds the present location of the mobile phone through GPS system.

If the patient press special key for a few seconds, according to information received from the patient beforehand, an SMS with the following content is produced (Figure 6):

- The first line of message contains the personal information of the patient, including first name, surname, and his/her disease.
- In the following lines the patient's home and workplace addresses are provided.
- In the final lines the present location of mobile phone which indicates where the patient is located are provided.

Afterwards, the SMS will be sent to Police Station and the patient's relatives or friends, whose phone numbers are previously received and recorded in the text file. In this manner, the Police get informed about the patient and his/her location, immediately takes the necessary measures to find and survive him/her.

This method also can be used for other diseases such as people with neurosis. The necessary information is put on the patient mobile phone, so the police can identify the lost person by checking his/her mobile phone.

CONCLUSION

In this chapter, after reviewing some of the systems which are using mobile phones for communication in emergency situations, we describe three systems which are developed by authors.

In all of the three systems, the main goal is finding the person and helps him/her. In first system, we want to locate the victims after earthquake and rescuing them. The second system is for call-

Figure 6. SMS sent by the lost person who needs help

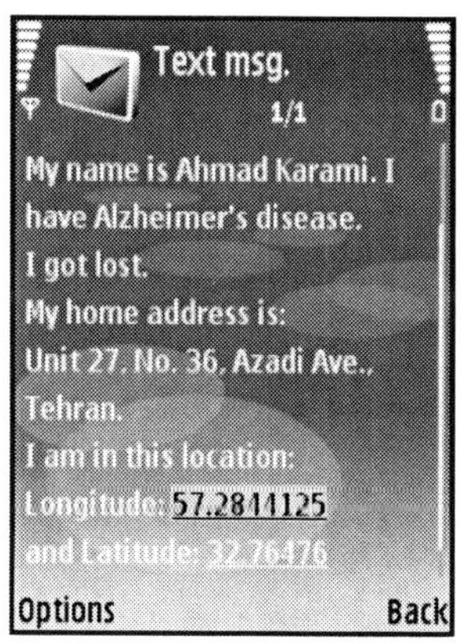

ing emergency team by patient in situation such as heart attack. The third system is for helping families of person with amnesia disease to find them when they are lost. All of these systems use SMS service of mobile phones for communication.

These systems show that mobile phone can be used very well in emergency situation. For example, mobile phones are a good choice for communicating between rescue team or even rescue team and victims after disasters such as earthquake. In addition, patients can use mobile phones to contact their doctors or families in emergency situation, because usually they have access to their mobile phones all time.

REFERENCES

Bamford, W., Coulton, P., & Edwards, R. (2006). Location-based Mobile Blogging. In *Proceedings of the 2nd IEEE International Conference on Information & Communication Technologies: from Theory to Applications (ICTTA'06)*, (vol. 1, pp. 39 – 40). Damascus, Syria.

ETSI. (2000). *GSM 03.40 v7.4.0, Digital cellular telecommunications system (Phase 2+). Technical realization of the Short Message Service (SMS)*. ETSI.

Hassinen, M., & Laitinen, P. (2005). End-to-end Encryption for SMS Messages in the Health Care Domain. *Studies in Health Technology and Informatics*, 316–321.

Nokia (2001). *Sending Content over SMS to Nokia Phones, Version 1.0*. Forum Nokia.

Pavlopoulos, S., Kyriacou, E., Berler, A., & Koutsouris, D. (1998). A mobile system for emergency health care provision via telematics support-'AMBULANCE. In *Proceedings of the IEEE International Conference on Information Technology Applications in Biomedicine 1998 (ITAB 98)* (pp. 150–154).

Pavlovski, C. HeeSam, K., & Wood, D. (2004). Ubiquitous mobility in clinical healthcare. In *Proceedings of the IDEAS Workshop on Medical Information Systems: The Digital Hospital (IDEAS-DH'04)* (pp. 147-153).

Shahri, A. M., Norouzi, M., & Paikan, A. (2005). RoboCupRescue - Robot League Team MRL (IRAN). In *Rescue Robot League Competition, RoboCup 2005*. Osaka, Japan.

Shirali-Shahreza, M. (2006). Emergency SMS. In *Proceedings of the SICE - ICASE International Joint Conference 2006 (SICE - ICCAS 2006)* (pp. 1139-1142). Busan, KOREA.

Shirali-Shahreza, M., & Shirali-Shahreza, S. (2006). Rescue SMS. In *Proceedings of the SICE - ICASE International Joint Conference 2006 (SICE - ICCAS 2006)*, (pp. 1300-1303). Busan, KOREA.

Shirali-Shahreza, M. H., & Shirali-Shahreza, M. (2007). Finding a Person with Amnesia's Disease by Mobile Phone. In *Proceedings of International Conference on Robotics, Vision, Information and Signal Processing 2007 (ROVISP07)* (pp. 681-682). Penang, Malaysia.

Shiroma, N., et al. (2004). Development of rescue robotic systems for both daily and emergency use. In *Proceedings of First IEEE Technical Exhibition Based Conference on Robotics and Automation, (TExCRA '04)* (pp. 85-86).

Tadokoro, S. (2005). Special Project on Development of Advanced Robots for Disaster Response (DDT Project). In *Proceedings of the 2005 IEEE Workshop on Advanced Robotics and its Social Impacts* (pp. 66-72).

Takemura, F., et al. (2004). Proposition of a human body searching strategy using a cable-driven robot at major disaster. In *Proceedings of 2004 IEEE/RSJ International Conference on Intelligent Robots and Systems (IROS 2004)* (pp. 1456 – 1461).

Warrior, J., McHenry, E., & McGee, K. (2003). They know where you are [location detection]. *Spectrum, IEEE,* 40(7), 20 - 25.

Wu, J., Wang, S., & Lin, L. (2005). What Drives Mobile Health Care? An Empirical Evaluation of Technology Acceptance. In *Proceedings of the 38th Annual Hawaii International Conference on System Sciences (HICSS '05),* (pp.150–159)

Chapter 27
Early Worm Detection for Minimizing Damage in E-Service Networks

Tarek S. Sobh
Egyptian Armed Forces, Egypt

Heba Z. El-Fiqi
Zagazig University, Egypt

ABSTRACT

One of the most powerful weapons for attackers is the Internet worm. Specifically, a worm attacks vulnerable computer systems and employs self-propagating methods to flood the Internet rapidly. Since a "Worm" is self-propagated through the connected network, it doesn't need human interaction or file transmission to replicate itself. It spreads in minutes; Slammer worms infect about 75,000 nodes through the internet in about 10 minutes. Since most of antivirus programs detect viruses based on their signature, then this approach can't detect new viruses or worms till being updated with their signature, which can't be known unless some systems had already been infected. This highlights worms are still on the top of malware threats attacking computer systems, although the evolution of worms detection techniques. Early detection of unknown worms is still a problem. This chapter produce a method for detecting unknown worms based on local victim information. The proposed system uses Artificial Neural Network (ANN) for classifying worm/ nonworm traffic and predicting the percentage of infection in the infected network. This prediction can be used to support decision making processes for network administrators to respond quickly to worm propagation in an accurate procedure.

INTRODUCTION

Network attacks such as computer virus and worms that scan computers randomly have caused billions of dollars in damage to enterprises across the Internet [Erbschloe M., 2005]. There are different worm detection techniques. [Guofei, G., 2004] classified them according to the worm characteristic used by detection technique. One approach is using worm signatures, it depends on the identical or similar traffic the worm causes while spreading, but it is only effective if worm signatures are known, so it cannot detect zero-day and polymorphic worms. By using polymorphic

DOI: 10.4018/978-1-61520-789-3.ch027

payloads, instead of static signature, the worm can evade detection [Nazario J., 2004].

There is another approach which depends on the Internet Control Message Protocol (ICMP) packet analysis. Due to random scanning behavior of worms, these scans often reach inactive IP addresses. But this approach focuses on global strategies and requires a large monitored network.

The computer worm, which is a self-propagating malicious code, spread themselves without any human interaction and launches the most destructive attacks against computer networks. Since worm exploits a security vulnerability corresponding to a specific network port number, Vulnerable hosts exhibit infection-like behavior when infected. Researchers use this observation as base for worm detection approaches. Nazario [Nazario J., 2004] produces destination port as one of the basic parameters that is used to describe the signature of the worm. For worms that target Web servers, this would be set to port 80. Other worms that attack other applications would use different ports. [Chen X. & Heidemann J., 2004], [Guofei, G., 2004], and Michael [Michael, L., 2003] uses this idea to build their worm detection models. Previous work uses anomaly method [Guofei, G., 2004] or mathematical model [Chen X. & Heidemann J.,2004] to produce the maximum number of packets received by a port that produces non-worm traffic. Most of previous work could not predict the new value if the behavior of this network is changed and could not detected slow worm.

[Li, P., M. Salour, & X. Su, 2008] describes the worm's life as consisting of many phases: target finding, transferring, activation, and infection. The first two phases cause network activities, worm behaviours in these two phases are critical for developing detection algorithms. A Supervised Artificial Neural Network (ANN) can be trained to take the values that represent the current behavior of the network under non-worm traffic and worm traffic. After sufficient number of iterations, it can be used as a control unit in the proposed system to identify the worm traffic. Then packet filter can be used to stop the worm's spread by filtering Transmission Control Protocol (TCP) port at the border of the network. This chapter produces an artificial intelligence system for worm detection, that can detect worm virus in network with accuracy of %99.96.Also this system can predict the percentage of worm infection in the network with absolute error average from 0% to 4%.

BACKGROUND

Since the Morris worm arose in 1988, Internet worms have been a persistent security threat, for example, the Code Red worm compromised at least 359,000 machines in 24 hours on July 19, 2001 [Chen Z., 2007]. The Slammer worm was unleashed with a 376-byte user datagram protocol (UDP) packet and infected more than 90% of vulnerable hosts in 10 minutes on January 25, 2003 [Chen Z., 2007]. These active worms caused large parts of the Internet to be temporarily inaccessible and cost both public and private sectors millions of dollars. Moreover, the frequency and the virulence of active-worm outbreaks have been increasing dramatically in the last few years, presenting a significant threat to today's Internet. Therefore, it is imperative to characterize the worm attack behaviors, analyze Internet vulnerabilities, and study countermeasures accordingly.

Malware in Network Attacks

Malicious code is a software or firmware that is intentionally placed in a system for an unauthorized purpose. Some of its basic types are *Trojans*, *Viruses*, and *Worms*.

Trojan horses are both problematic and a basic type of malicious code designed primarily to give attackers access to system files [Erbschloe M., 2005]. Trojan horse may be written to steal logon passwords, log user keystrokes, or even allow an attacker full administrative control on the targeted computer. This type of malicious code is contained inside apparently harmless programs or data, thus it is called "Trojan Horse".

Virus is a computer program that initiates an action on a computer without the user's consent. It is replicated by being copied or initiating it's copying to another program, computer boot sector or document. Viruses can be transmitted as attachments to an e-mail note or in a downloaded file, or be presented on a diskette or CD.

Worm is a malicious program that originates on a single computer and searches for other computers connected through a LAN, WAN or Internet connection [Nazario J., 2004]. When a worm finds another computer, it replicates itself onto that computer and continues to look for other connected computers on which to replicate. A worm attempt continuously to replicate itself indefinitely or until a self-timing mechanism halts the process.

Both worms and viruses spread from a computer to other computers. However, viruses typically spread by attaching themselves to files (either data files or executable applications). Their spread requires the transmission of the infected file from one system to another. Worms, in contrast, are capable of autonomous migration from system to system via the network without the assistance of external software.

Closer Look at Worms

Currently the research on Internet worms mainly focuses on the function structure, execution mechanism, scanning strategies, propagation models, countermeasure technology, etc. Moore, Shannon et al [Moore D.,2003] proposed three factors to evaluate the validity of anti-worm prevention system: response time, containment strategy, and deployment scenario.

Many definitions were given to internet worms in last year's, Spafford [Spafford E., 1988] redefined the computer virus as "A piece of code that adds itself to other programs, including operating systems. It cannot run independently it requires that its 'host' program be run to activate it". in 2003, Kienzle and Elder [Kienzle D., 2003] gave the definition of Internet worm based on four aspects, namely, malicious code, network propagation, human intervention, and standalone or file-infecting. The definition of a network worm is "A piece of malicious code that propagates over a network without human assistance and can initiate actively attack independently or depending on file-sharing". Based on the propagation strategies, they grouped the worms into three categories: E-mail worms, windows file-sharing worms, and traditional worms.

Nazario, Anderson et al [Nazario J., 2001] dissected worm systems into their as shown Figure (1). A worm may have any or all of these components, though a minimum set must include the attack component. These components are:

- **Reconnaissance:** this component of the worm is responsible for discovering hosts on the network that are capable of being compromised by the worm's known methods.
- **Specific attack capabilities:** these are used to launch an attack against an identified target system. Attacks can include the traditional buffer or heap overflow, string formatting attacks, Unicode misinterpretations (in the case of Internet Information Services (IIS) attacks), and misconfigurations.
- **Communication components:** they give the worms the interface to send messages between nodes or some other central location.
- **Command components:** they provide the interface to the worm node to issue and act on commands.
- **Intelligence components:** to communicate effectively, the worm network needs to know the location of the nodes as well

Figure 1. Basic worm components

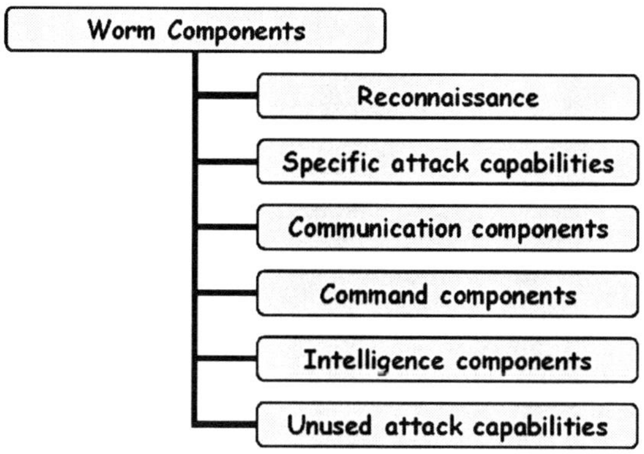

as characteristics about them. The intelligence portion of the worm network provides the information needed to be able to contact other worm nodes, which can be accomplished in a variety of ways.

- **Unused attack capabilities** like "catch all". But in 2004 Nazario [Nazario J., 2004] has redefined these components as five components and he merge both the specific attack capabilities and the unused attack capabilities into one component called attack components.

Not all of these components are required to have an operational worm. Again, only basic reconnaissance and attack components are needed to build an effective worm that can spread over a great distance. However, this minimal worm will be somewhat limited in that it lacks additional capabilities, such as Distributed Denial of Service (DDoS) capabilities or a system level interface to the compromised host.

Classification of Worms

Worms can be classified based on many criteria, such as target discovery, propagation model, propagation carries, activation methods and payloads.

Target Discovery

Previously, most worms that had infected a system would virtually ignore the address space of the local network to which the infected host connected. But today's worms scan not only randomly selected external addresses on the Internet, but also internal address space, virtually ensuring that if there is one infection within a local network there will soon be multiple ones [Nathanael P., 2005]. Additionally, today's worms and viruses have achieved considerable success by doing something that previous generations of these types of malware generally did not do, they deceive users. Most of today's worms and viruses attempt to trick users into opening attachments by using clever subject lines, message content and attachment names. By reading files containing user addresses in infected systems, they also deceive users into thinking that messages generated and sent by these worms and viruses are from someone they know. Users all too readily open attachments containing malicious code, thereby instantly infecting their systems [David W., 2005]. Figure (2) shows classification of worms based on target discovery.

Ideal Worm Strategies

The worm which has the complete IP addresses of all vulnerable hosts in the internet, it is called idealized worm since they are very difficult to be implemented by attackers on the global scale of the internet.

Idealized Worm has two Advantages, it's very high speed to affect all the vulnerable hosts in few seconds, and no worm detection system can detect them. But on the other hand it is difficult to collect IP addresses rather than problems caused by large payload.

- *Perfect worm*

A perfect worm knows the addresses of all vulnerable hosts in the internet, all infected hosts

Figure 2. Classification of worms based on target discovery

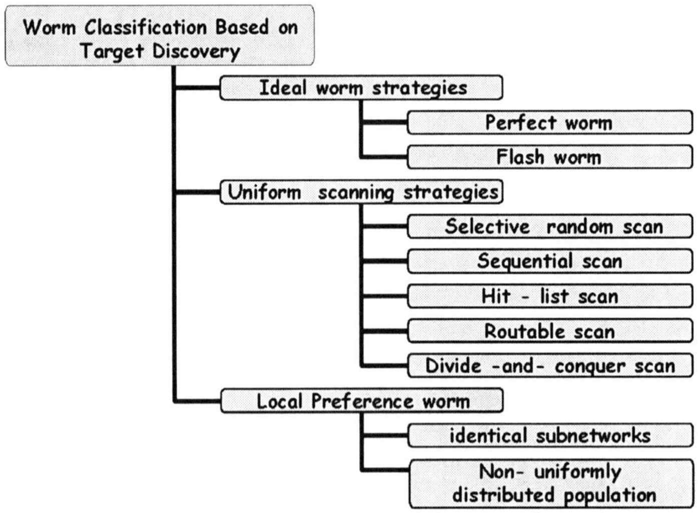

fully co-operate with each other such that they will not try to scan and infect an already infected hosts. Perfect worm propagation [Stoppel, D., 2006] follows:

$$\frac{dI}{dt} = \begin{cases} nI(t), & I(t) < N \\ 0, & I(t) = N \end{cases} \quad (1)$$

Where *I(t)* is the total number of infectious hosts at time *t*, n is the average worm scan rate, and *N* is the total number of hosts under consideration. Since no scans are wasted, each scan cause infection, this type of worm gains the privilege to be the fastest propagation worm.

- *Flash worm*

Flash worm knows the IP addresses of all vulnerable hosts in the internet, and uniformly scans the vulnerable population. Flash worm propagation [Zou C.C., & Towsley D., 2003] follows:

$$\frac{dI(t)}{dt} = \frac{n}{N} I(t)[N - I(t)] \quad (2)$$

Uniform Scanning Strategies

In uniform scanning strategies, worm randomly selects a host in its scanning space as the scanning target [Guofei, G., 2004].

- *Selective random scan*

Selective random scan is a worm that randomly scans the entire IP address space to find targets. CodeRed, Slammer, and Slapper [Qing S., 2005] [Yaneza J.L., 2008] are selective random scan worms. Sapphire - one of the fastest worms in history - used a random scanning [Dantu R., 2007].

When trying to investigate their propagation models, the address space should be considered first. By using IPv4, address space = 2^{32} possible addresses, then this type of worm's category are propagated as follows:

$$\frac{dI(t)}{dt} = \frac{n}{2^{32}} I(t)[N - I(t)] \quad (3)$$

In addition to the advantages of being the simplest strategy to implement, and the ability of spreading rapidly, it can be coupled with other scanning strategies to produce more effective results. This type of worm's category can be detected early as a result of the heavy network load traffic it causes.

- *Sequential scan*

Sequential scan means that a worm scans IP addresses sequentially after checking IP address (X) the worm continues to check IP address (X+1) or (X−1) if the search direction is reversed. The worm propagation follows:

$$\frac{dI(t)}{dt} = \frac{n}{\Omega} I(t)[N - I(t)] \qquad (4)$$

Where Ω = the size of worm's scanning space. Blaster worm 2003 is an example of sequential scan worms [Zou C.C., 2003], it chooses first address of its class C, sub network with a probability 0.4.

Sequential scan like local reference, once it finds networks, density populates with vulnerable systems. If it is used with many susceptible hosts, the propagation will be more effective. But it has big problem since it creates a lot of redundancies.

- *Hit-list scan*

A hit-list worm first scans and infect all vulnerable hosts on the hit-list, then randomly scans the entire internet to infect others. During Hit-list scan phase, it can be modeled like "Flash Worm" on the list of vulnerable hosts.

$$\frac{dI(t)}{dt} = \frac{n}{H} I(t)[N - I(t)] \qquad (5)$$

Where H = Hit-list size. During scanning the entire internet phase

$$\frac{dI(t)}{dt} = \frac{n}{2^{32}} I(t)[N - I(t)] \qquad (6)$$

But I (0) = H = Hit-list size. It is used to accelerate scanning worm but it needs huge effort to create the hit-list itself [38].

- *Routable scan*

In routable scan, worms reduce scan space Ω based on routing information in a network. The worm propagation follows:

$$\frac{dI(t)}{dt} = \frac{n}{\Omega} I(t)[N - I(t)] \qquad (7)$$

Where worm scanning space Ω is the number of routable IP addresses. Routable scan is distinguished by its high infection rate, based on Border Gateway Protocol (BGP) routing prefix is 3.5 times than those using random scan [Qing S., 2005]. Although, during the propagating processes, the worm must take a routing IP address database this instead results in the great big bulk.

- *Divide-and-conquer scan*

When a Divide and Conquer scan worm infects a target, it passes half of its scanning space to the target and then continues to scan remaining half of its original scanning space [Zou C.C., 2003]. The worm propagation follows:

$$\frac{dI(t)}{dt} = \frac{n}{\Omega - I(t)} I(t)[N - I(t)] \qquad (8)$$

Its advantage is represented in that no two infected hosts will waste their infection power on a same target. But if the selected node had turned off or broke down, all addresses send to it will be lost.

Local Preference Worm

Local preference scan is the scanning strategy where an infected host scans IP addresses close to its address with a higher probability than addresses farther away.

- *local preference scan with identical subnetworks:*

It is used where vulnerable hosts are uniformly distributed and there is the same number of infected hosts in each subnetwork

The worm propagation [Zou C.C., 2003] follows:

$$\frac{dI(t)}{dt} = \frac{n}{\Omega} I(t)[N - I(t)] \tag{9}$$

When vulnerable hosts are uniformly distributed in a worm's scanning space, local preference scan does not help a worm in its propagation speed.

- *local preference scan with non-uniformly distributed population:*

Scan strategy is used where computers are not uniformly distributed within the IPv4 address space. The worm propagation follows:

$$\frac{dI(t)}{dt} = \frac{\beta' + (m-1)\beta''}{m} I(t)[N - I(t)] \tag{10}$$

Where β' is the pair wise rate of infection in local scan for a local preference scan worm, β'' is the pair wise rate of infection in remote scan for a local preference scan worm, and *m* is the number of "/n" prefixes that contain vulnerable hosts ($m \leq K$).

The Code Red II worm used local preference on both class A networks and on class B networks [Zou C.C., 2003].

Propagation Model

An accurate internet worm propagation model can have an insight into worm behavior, identify the weakness in the worm spreading chain and provide accurate prediction for the purpose of damage assessment for a new worm threat. Figure (3) shows classification of worms based on propagation model.

- *Simple Epidemic model*

Each host is in one of the two states: susceptible or infectious. The model also assumes that once infected by a virus, the host remains in the infectious state forever [Zou C.C., 2003] [Qing S., 2005].

Figure 3. Classification of worms bases on propagation model

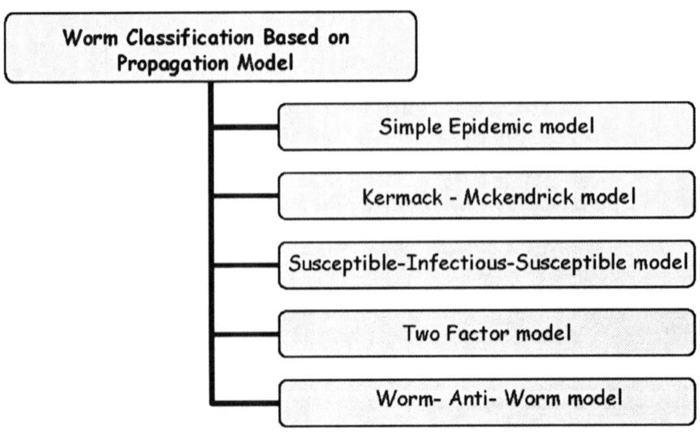

- *Kermack –Mckendrick model*

The host in Kermack-McKendrick model (KM model) maintains one of three states: susceptible, infectious or removed [Zou, C.C., 2002].

- *Susceptible –Infectious - Susceptible model*

The Susceptible–Infectious Susceptible (SIS) model assumes every host has the same possibility of being infected repeatedly (i.e., recovered host has the same possibility of being infected as susceptible host). However, the model doesn't take account of the situation that the infected hosts are patched or updated to be immune from the worms [Yang W., 2003]. The SIS model is not applicable to describe the infection of Internet worms.

- *Two-Factor model*

Two-Factor model considers more external factors and anti-worm measures than the models above [Zou, C.C., 2002][Qing S., 2005]. One factor is the dynamic countermeasures taken by ISPs and users, the other is the slowed down worm infection rate as rampant propagation of worm causes congestion and troubles to some routers.

- *Worm-Anti-Worm model*

This model considers two types of worms: a malicious worm A and an oppositional one B. We divide the propagation process into two stages: when B is absent, the propagation of A is subject to the Two-Factor model, when B is present, there are four potential cases: (1) B detects and cleans A, and patches the hosts infected by A, (2) B only detects and cleans A, (3) B patches all susceptible hosts, and (4) B patches all susceptible hosts, and detects and cleans A. in the first two cases, B only searches the infected hosts, while in the latter two B searches all susceptible hosts. The first situation follows the KM model, where the immunity speed of the susceptible hosts is higher than that when B is absent. The second situation is typically an SIS model. The last two situations supplement the Two-Factor model in the aspects of countermeasures, and principally influence the cleaning speed of worm A in the subsequent propagation stage.

Propagation Carriers and Distribution Mechanisms

The means by which propagation occurs can also affect the speed and stealth of a worm. A worm can either actively spread itself from machine to machine, or it can be carried along as part of normal communication.

- *Self-Carried*

A self-carried worm actively transmits itself as part of the infection process. This mechanism is commonly employed in self-activating scanning or topological worms, as the act of transmitting the worm is part of the infection process. Some passive worms, such as CRClean [Nicholas W., 2003], also use self-carried propagation.

- *Second Channel*

Some worms, such as Blaster [Nicholas W., 2003], require a secondary communication channel to complete the infection. Although the exploit uses RPC, the victim machine connects back to the infecting machine using TFTP to download the worm body, completing the infection process.

- *Embedded*

An embedded worm sends itself along as part of a normal communication channel, either appending to or replacing normal messages. As a result, the propagation does not appear as anomalous when viewed as a pattern of communication. The contagion strategy [Staniford, S., 2002] is an example of a passive worm that uses embedded propagation. An embedded strategy, although relatively stealthy, only makes sense when the target selection strategy is also stealthy. Otherwise, the worm will give itself away by its target selection traffic, and reaps little benefit from the stealth that embedded propagation provides. Thus a scanning worm is unlikely to use an embedded distribution strategy, while passive worms can benefit considerably by ensuring that distribution is as stealthy as target selection. The speed at which embedded worms spread is highly dependent on how the application is used, as is how far from the natural patterns of communication such a worm could deviate in order to hasten its propagation without compromising its stealthness.

Likewise, the distribution of the worm body or related payloads can either be one-to-many, as when a single site provides a worm or module to other sites once they've been initially infected, many-to-many, as when multiple copies propagate the malicious code, or a hybrid approach where the basic worm propagates in a many-to-many manner with updates received through a central site. In general, many-to-many distribution can be considerably faster, if a limiting factor is the time it takes to perform the distribution. Many-to-many distribution also removes the ability for others to block further distribution by removing the source of the malicious code from the Internet.

Activation Methods

The means by which a worm is activated on a host also drastically affects how rapidly a worm can spread, because some worms can arrange to be activated nearly immediately whereas others may wait days or weeks to be activated.

- *Human Activation*

The slowest activation approach requires a worm to convince a local user to execute the local copy of the worm. Since most people do not want to have a worm executing on their system, these worms rely on a variety of social engineering techniques. Some worms such as the Melissa email-worm [CERT, 2008] indicate urgency on the part of someone you know ("Attached is an important message for you"), others, such as the Iloveyou [CERT, 2008] attack, appeal to individuals' vanity ("Open this message to see who loves you"), and others, such as the Benjamin [Symantec, 2008] worm appeal to greed ("Download this file to get copyrighted material for free").

Although Melissa was a word macro virus - a piece of code written in Microsoft Word's built-in scripting language embedded in a Word document - later human initiated worms have usually been executable files which, when run, infect the target machine. Furthermore, while some worms required that a user start running a program, other worms exploited bugs in the software that brought data onto the local system, so that simply viewing the data would start the program running. The continued spread of these worms is disturbing, as they can be effectively used as secondary vectors1 such as in the case of Nimda [CERT, 2008] and/or to install additional malicious software such as programs which allow an attacker to control a machine.

- *Human Activity-Based Activation:*

Similarly, many worms are activated when the user performs some activity not normally related to a worm, such as resetting the machine, logging in and therefore executing login scripts, or opening a remotely infected file. This activation mechanism is commonly seen in open shares windows worms (such as one of Nimda's secondary propagation techniques) which will begin execution on the target machine either when the machine is reset or the user logs in, as these worms write data to the target disk without being able to directly trigger execution.

- *Scheduled Process Activation*

The next fastest worms activate using scheduled system processes. Such programs can propagate through mirror sites (e.g., OpenSSH Trojan), or directly to desktop machines. Many desktop operating systems and applications include autoupdater programs that periodically download, install and run software updates. Early versions of these systems did not employ authentication, so an attacker needed only to serve a file to the desktop system to infect the target. Other systems periodically run backup and other network software that includes vulnerabilities. The skills an attacker requires to exploit these depends on the scheduled process's design and implementation: if the attacked tool does not include authentication, a DNS redirection attack may suffice, but if it does, then the attacker might need to acquire the private keys for both the update server and code signing.

- *Self Activation*

The worms that are fastest activated are able to initiate their own execution by exploiting vulnerabilities in services that are always on and available (e.g., Code Red exploiting IIS Web servers) or in the libraries that the services use. Such worms either attach themselves to running services or execute other commands using the permissions associated with the attacked service. Execution occurs as soon as the worm can locate a copy of the vulnerable service and transmit the exploit code. Currently, preventing these attacks relies on running software that is not vulnerable, although the effect of an attack can be reduced by limiting the access of services that are always on.

Payloads

The payload, the code carried by the worm apart from the propagation routines, is limited only by the goals and imagination of the attacker. Different sorts of attackers will desire different payloads to directly further their ends. Most of the following types of payloads have been seen in the wild. None/nonfunctional: by far the most common is simply a nonexistent or nonfunctional payload. A worm with a bug in the propagation code usually fails to spread, while bugs in the payload still leave the worm able to spread. Such a worm can still have a significant effect, both through traffic and machine load (as seen with both the Morris worm and Slammer [Moore D., 2003]) and by actively advertising vulnerable machines.

- *Internet Remote Control*

Code Red II opened a trivial to use privileged backdoor on victim machines, giving anyone with a web browser the ability to execute arbitrary code. This even gave rise to anti-Code-Red sites[Nicholas W., 2003] which exploited the backdoor to issue the commands to disable IIS and reset the machine.

- *Spam-Relays*

Part of the Sobig worm's associated Trojan [Nicholas W., 2003], creates an open-mail relay for use by spammers. By creating numerous relay machines across the Internet, spammers can avoid blackhole-based mechanisms which block known-spamming IP addresses.

- *HTML-Proxies*

Another aspect of Sobig's Trojan is the distribution of web-proxies by redirecting web requests (through DNS) to randomly selected proxy machines, it becomes significantly more difficult for responders to shut down compromised websites which are used for various illegal activities, including scams which attempt to entice users to input financial data (a technique called phishing).

- *Internet DoS*

Another common payload is a Denial of Service (DoS) attack. Code Red, Yaha, and others have all contained DoS tools, either targeted at specific sites or retargetable under the attacker's control. Distributed DOS (DDoS) tools such as Stacheldraht have included stealthy and encrypted communication channels. We have yet to see an attacker take advantage of Internet scale DoS opportunities. With 100,000 or 1,000,000 controllable "zombies", the attacker could target the DNS system, update sites, and response channels all at the same time.

- *Data Collection*

Computers are increasingly used to store and manipulate sensitive data. A worm could use target these capabilities and some already have. SirCam performed inadvertent espionage, by attaching random files to its mailings, but a worm could just as easily preferentially search for document with various keywords, credit card numbers, or similar information. Criminals are sometimes interested in identity theft, and significant subsets of the blackhat community are involved

Network Attacks and Worm Detection

By studying reports produced by Trend Micro last two years, the worms still one of the most infection malware codes dangerous. Eight of the top twenty threats counts of 2006 are worms [Yaneza, J.L., 2006]. Worm_NYXEM.E is on the top of this list. Also in the top twenty malware report - in Dec 2006 to May 2007 [Yaneza, J.L., 2007]- nine worms made it into the top twenty, reflecting the attractiveness of speedy propagation to malware authors. The first and second place in the top ten detections in Trend Micro 2007 malware trends report [Yaneza, J.L., 2008] are worms. Wang [Wang, J., 2007] produces a system for early detection of worm based on ICMP collecting. It records the number of some type of data packets in detection interval. In detecting abnormal events, the system takes response actions and block susceptible IP and port. A router-based system to identify worm attacks by computing entropy values of selected packet attributes is presented by Hanxun et al. [Hanxun, Z., 2007]. Another model is developed by Weaver [Weaver, N., 2007]. This containment algorithm is suitable for deployment in high-speed, low-cost network hardware, which can stop a scanning host after fewer than 10 scans with a very low false-positive rate. Kim [Kim, J., 2005] produces an algorithm to reduces both sensitivity and false alarm with weighted average queue length that smoothes sudden traffic changes. The algorithm counts the number of connection requests with different destinations, in contrast to simple length of delay queue as in the typical throttling algorithm. The queue length measuring strategy also helps reduce worm detection time and false alarm. Another method is detecting large-scale worm attacks using only end-host detectors.

Predicting Percentage of Infection

Several approaches are produced attempting to estimate the damage and predict the spread of worms; Kephart and White [Kephart, J.O., 1991] developed The Epidemiological model, which is a simple model that explains the spread of computer viruses by employing biological epidemiology. The number of infected hosts depends on vulnerability density and scanning rate. The two-factor worm model by Zou et al [Zou, C.C., 2002], describes the behaviour of worm based on two factors, the dynamic countermeasure by ISPs and users, and a slowed down worm infection rate. This model explains observed data for Code Red and the decrease in scanning attempts during the last several hours before it ceased propagation. The Analytical Active Worm Propagation (AAWP) model by Chen [Chen, Z., L., 2003] extends the model of worms that employ random scanning to cover local subnet scanning worms. Parameters in this model include the number of vulnerable machines, size of hit lists, scanning rate, death rate, and patching rate. AAWP better models the behaviour of Code Red II than previous models. An approach to minimize the damage due to worm infection in enterprise networks is produced by Sanguanpong [Sanguanpong, S., 2007] does not require observing variables during attacks. Therefore, it can be used to predict worm damage before the attack occurs. The result produced by Sanguanpong [Sanguanpong, S., 2007] has accuracy ranged from 83.33% to 90.91%, and False-Positive error rate of 0% to 4.16%

Behavioural Detection vs. Signature-Based Detection

Signature-based detection has been the first technique used to fight malware and still remains at the heart of nowadays antivirus software. Jacob [Jacob, G., H., 2008] describes that these detection techniques search system objects such as files for suspicious byte patterns referenced in a base of signatures. Signatures can precisely identify the threat and name it; signature-based techniques are bound to detect known malware or trivial variants. But signatures are no longer simple byte patterns but complex meta-structures carrying dynamic aspects and a semantic interpretation. On the other hand, behavioural detection is thus more generic and more resilient to modifications than form-based detection.

Local Victim Information

Zou, Gao [Zou, C.C., 2003], and Staniford, [Staniford, S., 2002] tried to explore global strategies techniques but it require a large monitored network (say, 2^{20} nodes) to distinguish worms from other scanning activities. Some of them look to make nation-wide Internet worm control authority, others proposed to deploy sensors around the Internet. Although there is a need to global co-ordination to protect the Internet from worm intrusions, global detection strategies don't produce complete solution. Dagon and Xinzhou [Dagon, D., 2004] discuss the idea of that since global detection strategies require large amounts of sensor data before detecting worm outbreaks, some local networks might be infected before learning about a worm outbreak. In global detection strategies, in order to gain sufficient worm traffic to become detectable, these strategies have to wait a lot of local networks to fall as victim to the worm. Other Researchers like Guofei [Guofei, G., 2004] uses the idea of using distributed system that detects worm probing traffic through local traffic observations. From local networks point of view, it is more useful to know which machines are infected and how the attack is progressed. Thus worm detection techniques for smaller local networks needs more research.

Intelligence Techniques Used in Detecting Network Attacks

A recent survey of intrusion detection [Kabiri, P., 2005] suggests using artificial intelligence (AI) techniques to recognize malicious software (malware) in single computers and in computer networks. It describes the research done in developing these AI techniques, and discusses their advantages and limitations. Moskovitch [Robert Moskovitch, 2008] uses machine learning techniques in classification of a computer behaviour into malicious and benign. He focuses on the feasibility of accurately detecting unknown worm activity in individual computers while minimizing the required set of features collected from the monitored computer. Four feature selection methods were used to reduce the number of features and four learning algorithms were applied on the resulting feature subsets; four commonly used Machine Learning algorithms: Decision Trees, Naive Bayes, Bayesian Networks and Artificial Neural Networks. The evaluation results suggest that by using classification algorithms applied on only 20 features the mean detection accuracy exceeded 90%, and for specific unknown worms accuracy reached above 99%, while maintaining a low level of false positive rate. Andrzej Bielecki [Bielecki, A., 2004] developed a neural approach to worm detection designed as a part of a multi-agent system intended to manage IP networks. The efficiency of virus recognition is about 95%. One of the AI techniques mentioned in that survey [Kabiri, P., 2005][Stoppel, D., 2006] is Artificial Neural Networks (ANN).

Stopel [Stoppel, D., 2006] produces an approach for detection of the presence of computer worms based on Artificial Neural Networks (ANN) using the computer's behavioural measures. In order to evaluate the different techniques, several computers were infected with five different worms and 323 different features of the infected computers were measured. Stopel [Stoppel, D., 2006] uses ANN and two other known classifications techniques, Decision Tree and k-Nearest Neighbours, to test their ability to classify correctly the presence, and the type, of the computer worms even during heavy user activity on the infected computers. When compare the three approaches, the ANN approach have computational advantages when real-time computation is needed, and has the potential to detect previously unknown worms. In addition, ANN may be used to identify the most relevant, measurable, features and thus reduce the feature dimensionality. The model proposed by Stopel [Stoppel, D., 2006] [Stoppel, D., 2006] detect malicious activity of worms by looking at the attributes derived from the computer operation parameters such as memory usage, CPU usage, traffic activity etc. This model drawback appears in misclassifications that still face difficulties related to the detection of the worms in the beginning of their activity.

The Proposed Model

This model is used to identify worm traffic from normal traffic; also it can predict the Infection Percentage in the network, which can be used by the administrator to take the appropriate action. This model depends only on the data collected from the local victim information. As seen in Figure 4, this Model consists of 4 modules: *(1) Traffic Statistical Analyzer Module (TSAM) (2) Port Matching Module (PMM) (3) Artificial Neural Network Module (ANNM) (4) Response Module (RM).* The system works as follow: The incoming and outgoing traffic are monitored, using sniffing tool. This traffic is used by TSAM to calculate some statistics. This monitored traffic is used as input to the PMM, which use the idea of infection-like-behaviour in worm spreading to identify suspected worm traffic. Then Administrators apply the no of hosts online as an input to ANNM, which uses the data collected from other modules to classify the traffic into worm traffic or normal traffic, and to predict the percentage of infection in the network. The administrator can uses ANN outputs to take the appropriate action to protect the network, and to alarm other subsystems, or partners about the spreading of the detected worm virus. Until administrator can apply the solution based on the company policy, The RM can be used to block the traffic on the suspected port/ports used in propagation of the detected worm.This action is used to prevent the propagation of the worm in the network, but it cannot heal the infected nodes.

TSAM

This module is responsible of calculating statistical values based on the analysis of incoming and outgoing traffic. It captures the traffic and calculates the number of packets per time unit, no of packets produced by each source/destination port in time Unit.; also it can produce no of packets per protocol in a time unit. But only: No of packets, No of packets per port that is used as input to the data set for ANN.

PMM

Being fully automated, a worm's behaviours usually repetitious and predictable, making it possible to be detected. Guofei [Guofei, G., 2004] states that "After a vulnerable host is infected by a worm on a port I (i.e., the host is the destination of an early worm attack), the infected host will send out scans to other hosts targeting at the same port I in a short time". This module shown in Figure (5) uses this idea to produce no of packets per port that match the worm infection behaviour. Since there is no way to know if a packet source is victim or slave attacker; so each record is being examined as if it is from the victim or from slave attacker. Then in a selected unified time interval, if a packet is send from a slave to a victim on specific port, followed by a packet is send from this victim IP address to the same destination port, thus is counted as worm-like behaviour on that port. A dynamic table is made to produce no occurrence of this worm like behaviour per each used port.

ANNM

A Supervised ANN can be trained to take the values that represent the current behaviour of the network under non-worm traffic and worm traffic. After sufficient number of iterations, it can be used as a control unit in the proposed system to identify the worm traffic.

First Proposed ANN Model

In this model, shown in Figure (6), the idea was to use one ANN to produce the two desired output.

Second Proposed ANN Model

In this model, two ANN networks are used: First ANN in Figure (7-a) is used to solve the classification problem. This ANN produces two outputs: Worm behaviour class, and normal behaviour class. The ANN result is producing to any class the traffic is belonging. Second ANN, which produced in Figure (7-b), is used to solve prediction problem. Then ANN produces the percentage of infection in the network.

Figure 4. The proposed model used for detecting worm behaviour using ANN

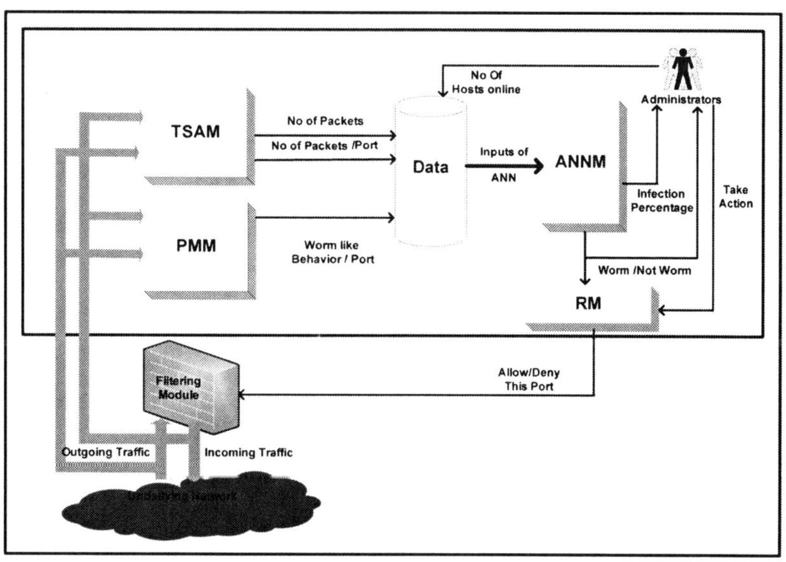

Figure 5. Flowchart of PMM

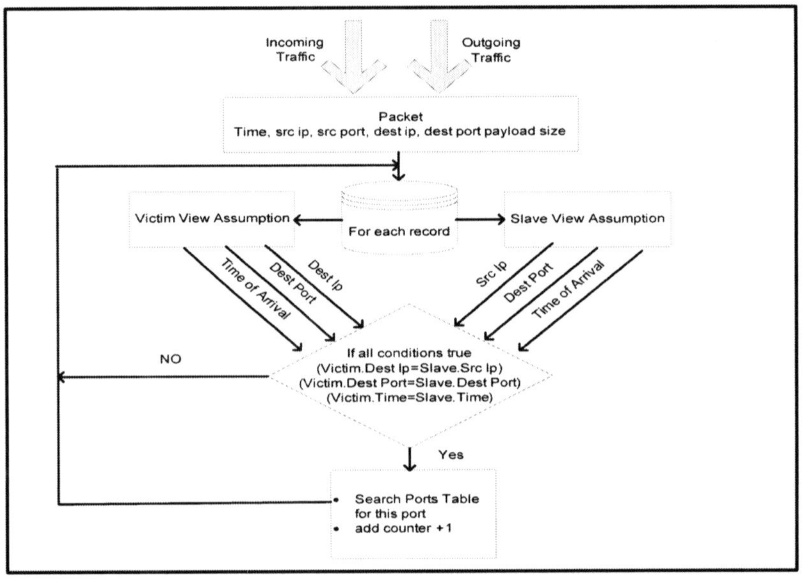

Figure 6. First proposed ANN model

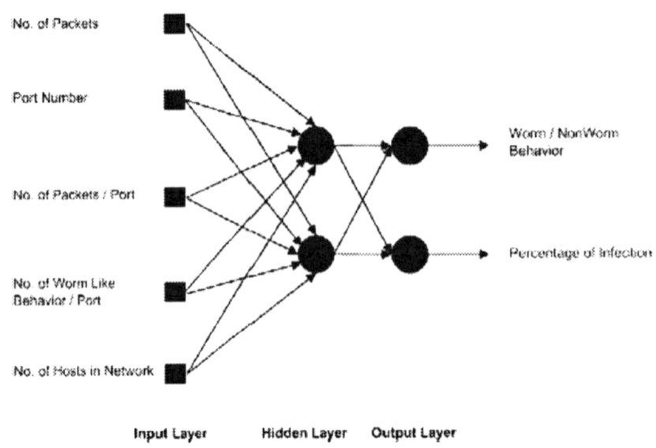

RM

This module is responsible of applying the action recommended by the administrator. It can be designed to take automatic action. Its objective is to reconfigure the packet firewall to block traffic on the suspected port/ ports that is used in worm propagation. Administrator can then take an appropriate action based on the company/ organization security policy. Using this system, administrator knows if the monitored network is infected or not, and in case of infection the percentage of infection.

Implementation

The implementation of this model is done for all the modules, except the response module; which will be implemented in future work.

GTNets Simulator

Network simulations are used to study the worm propagation. Sharif [George, F.R., 2004] built worm models into GTNets [George, F.R., 2003] and was able to simulate networks having hundreds of thousands of hosts and measure the effect of

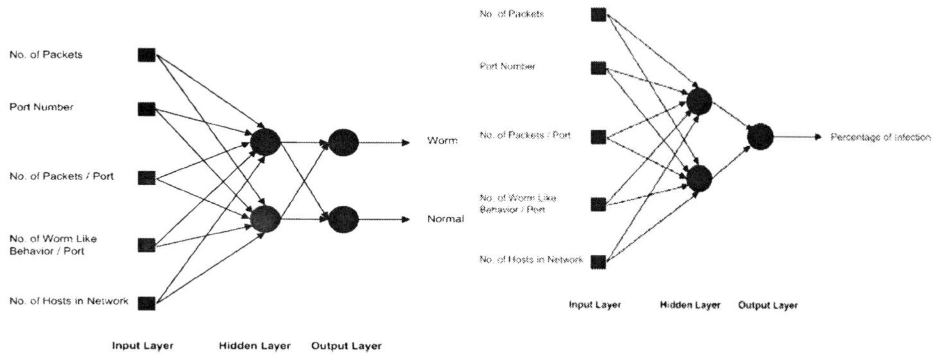

Figure 7. (a) Second proposed ANN model (classification); (b) Second proposed ANN model (predication)

different network parameters on the worm spread rate. Michael et al [Michael, L., 2003] used the SSFNet simulator with packet-level details for a small section of the network and represented the rest of the Internet with an analytic model. In this system the worm models in GTNets is used, which model the behaviour of scanning worms [George, F.R., 2004].

ANNM (A Procedure for Developing ANN Based Application)

Collecting Data

Data are collected using a developed application called (Worm Detection Traffic Analyser). Input Data includes 5 features elected from many features that help in identifying worm behaviour from non-worm network behaviour. All of these inputs are Numerical value. The normalization of value from (0 to 1) is done by the tool used for building the ANN model (NeuroSolution).

Dataset Separation into Training and Test Set

The Dataset consists of 5430 Examplers: 4230 Examplers are used for training (% 78), 1200 Examplers are used for testing (% 22). Collected data are gathered from different experiments, each experiment produces many examplers, and the sequence within the same experiment is matter. Because when this application is used in the real life application, the sequence of traffic is producing information in the network traffic, data are related in this way. But every experiment is completely separated from other experiments. Then experiments orders are randomized to accomplish different conditions randomly, but within the same experiments result, data can't be randomized.

Network Structure / Topology

After testing different topologies, the best result was chosen to produce the model. The Network Training Paradigm is Supervised Learning implemented using Multilayer Perceptron (MLP) which is feed forward neural network that uses Back propagation algorithm. After testing some activation functions, best results are produced by Sigmoid Function. Also Momentum at step size 100 produces the best results as learning rule

Training Process

There are two methods for updating weights that can be used: On-Line, Batch learning. After testing both of them, best results are produced by online updating.

RESULTS

Evaluation Parameters

Confusion Matrix for Classification Problem

In the field of artificial intelligence, a confusion matrix is a visualization tool typically used in supervised learning. Each column of the matrix represents the instances in a predicted class, while each row represents the instances in an actual class. For evaluation purposes, the *True Positive Rate (TPR)*, which is the number of positive instances classified correctly and shown in Equation 1, is measured, and the *False Positive Rate (FPR)*, which is the number of negative instances misclassified and shown in Equation 2, is measured. The *Total Accuracy* measures the number of absolutely correctly classified instances, either positive or negative, divided by the entire number of instances shown in Equation 3. The *absolute error* of Prediction ε can be calculated using Equation 4. *Mean Squared Error (MSE)* is the average of the square of the difference between the desired response and the actual system output (the error), the formula for the mean squared error is shown id Equation 5.

$$TPR = \frac{|TP|}{|TP| + |FN|} \quad (11)$$

$$FPR = \frac{|FP|}{|FP| + |TN|} \quad (12)$$

$$Total\ \ Accuracy = \frac{|TP| + |TN|}{|TP| + |FP| + |TN| + |FN|} \quad (13)$$

$$\mu = | P - P^* | \quad (14)$$

$$MSE = \frac{\sum_{j=0}^{P}\sum_{i=0}^{N}(d_{ij} - y_{ij})^2}{N\ P} \quad (15)$$

Where P= number of output processing elements, N= number of Examplers in the data set, y_{ij}= network output for Examplers I at processing element j, d_{ij}= desired output for Examplers I at processing element j.

First Model Results

Experiment 1

Six tests are done to test percentage of infection; one normal traffic test plus 5 different worms test, Example of some results are shown in Figure 8. In Figure 8-a, the error in prediction in the case of normal traffic not exceeds 5.00E-04. Figures 8-b to 8-d show that the error in the prediction is low and sometimes it turns to zero as in Figure 8-d.

Test Using Simulation Code Red II Worm like for 383 Seconds

The Parameters used in this test are: Network Size is 18000 nodes, Hosts online are 15266, Worm Type is TCP worm, TCP Threads is 6, Vulnerability is 1.0, Payload length is 3818 byte, Infection port is port 80, Worm Target Vector: Local Preference Scan (P = 0.5 for same first byte, P = 0.375 for same first two bytes and P =0.125 for random IP). MSE of test is 5.9E-05. Results are presented in Figure (9).

Experiment 2

Test using 25 different worms are done. These 25 tests are done to find the trend and powerness, and weakness of the system. The test results are used to compare this model to the second proposed model.

Figure 8. (a) Predication of infection percentage in normal traffic; (b) Predication of infection percentage in worm 1 test; (c) Predication of infection percentage in worm 2 test; (d) Predication of infection percentage in worm 3 test.

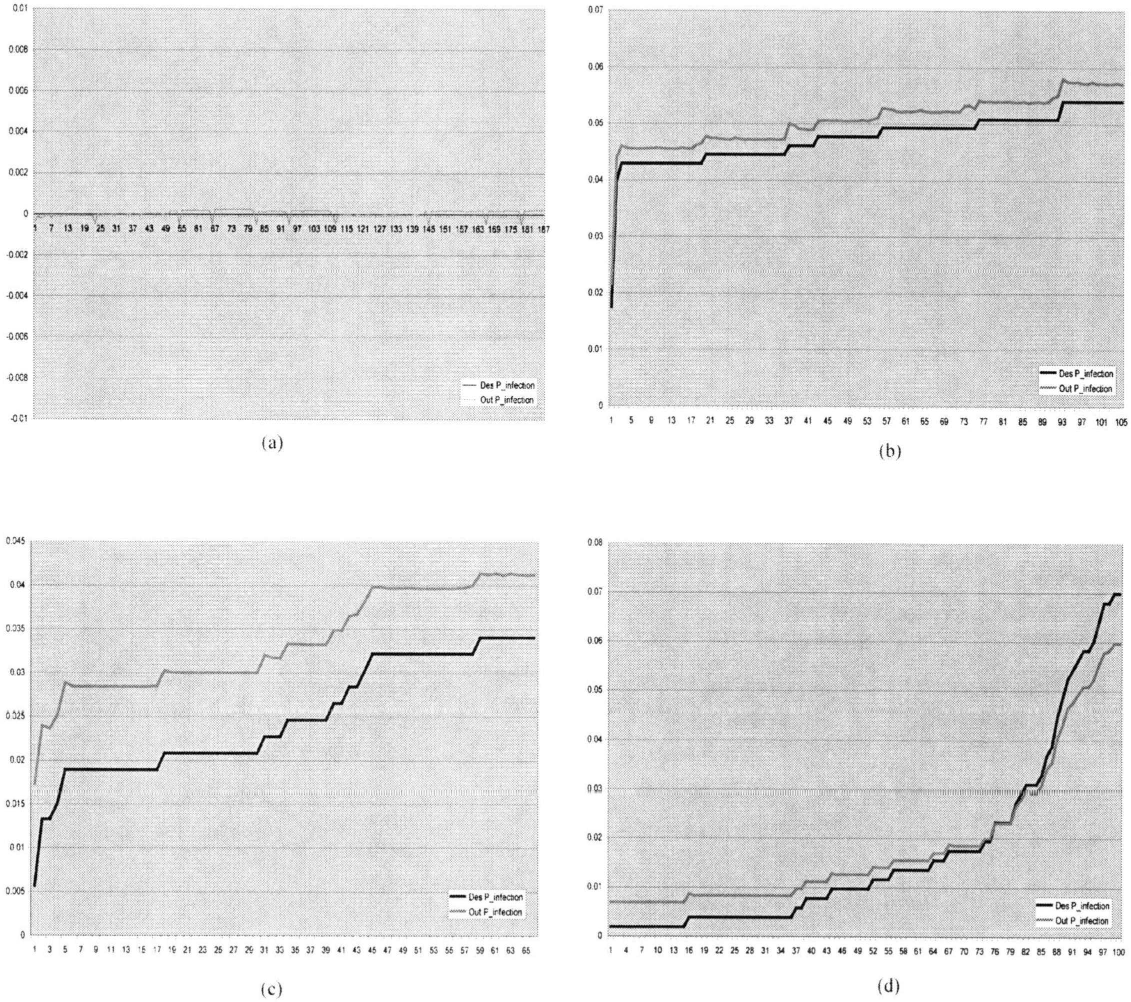

Results of the Second Model

Experiment 3

This experiment is a repetition of experiment 2 using the second model. MSE of percentage of infection is 7.59E-04; MSE of classification is 8.15E-04. Figure (10) shows the results of tests done with code red II repeated four times with the second model.

Comparison between the two Models

The results of the comparison between two models are done by studying these models. The relation between the error in prediction and other parameters are evaluated. The result of this comparison cannot be presented because the lack of space, so some of these results are shown here in Figure 8. Table (1) produces the TPR, FPR and the accuracy of the worm detecting in the two models. Although that the second model has better

Figure 9. Prediction of percentage of code red ii infection in the network by the first model

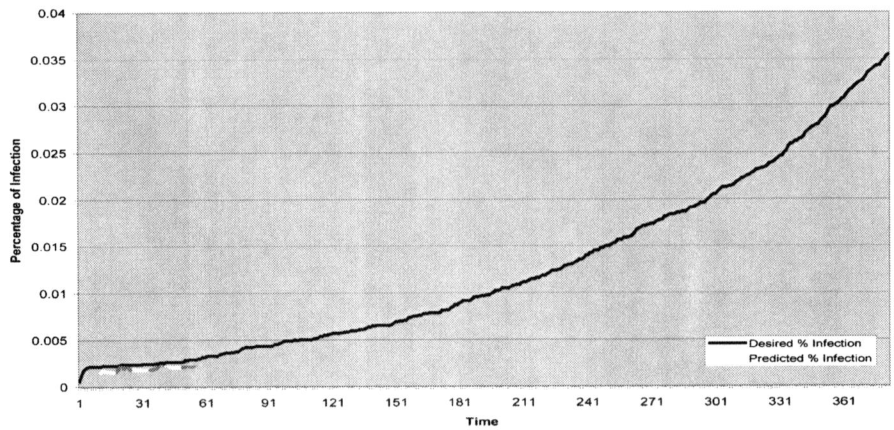

Figure 10. Comparison between four Codered II tests

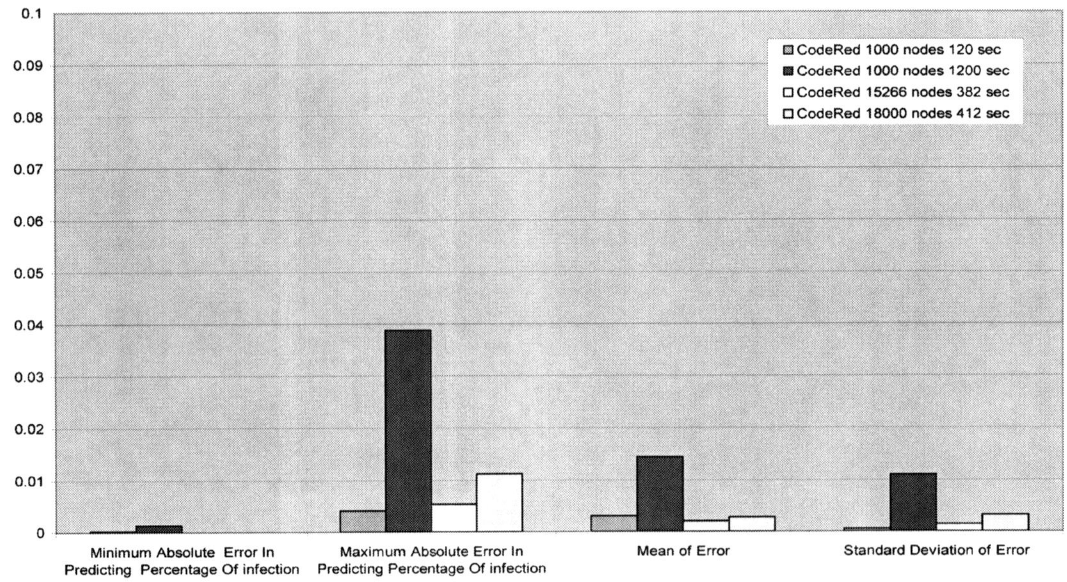

performance than the first one, the difference is not significant. The comparison between errors in prediction of infection between the two models is shown in Table (2). Figure 11-a show the relation between number of threads in TCP worms and error in predicting the percentage of infection in the network. Figure 11-b shows the relation between scan rate in UDP worms and error in predicting the percentage of infection in the network. Figure 11-c shows the relation between payload size of

Table. 1. Comparison between accuracy of the two models

	(Experiment 1) First Model	(Experiment 2) First Model	(Experiment 3) Second Model
TPR	1	99.10%	99.85%
FPR	undefined	0.07%	0%
Total Accuracy	1	99.71%	99.96%

Table 2. Comparison between absolute error in the experiments in two models

	First Model	Second Model
Mean of Error	8.78E-02	4.52E-03
Standard Deviation of Error	3.47E-02	2.37E-03
Minimum Absolute Error In Predicting Percentage Of infection	7.20E-05	3.00E-06
Maximum Absolute Error In Predicting Percentage Of infection	5.55E-01	4.02E-02

the worm and error in predicting the percentage of infection in the network. Figure 11-d shows the relation between worm target vector and error in predicting the percentage of infection in the network. All these comparisons indicate that the second model has better performance.

CONCLUSION

In this chapter we first presented the concepts and recent techniques of worms' infection, as

Figure 11. (a) Relation between absolute error in infection percentage and threads for TCP worms; (b) Relation between absolute error in infection percentage and scan rate for UDP worms; (c) Relation between absolute error in infection percentage and worm payload; (d) Relation between absolute error in infection percentage and worm target vector.

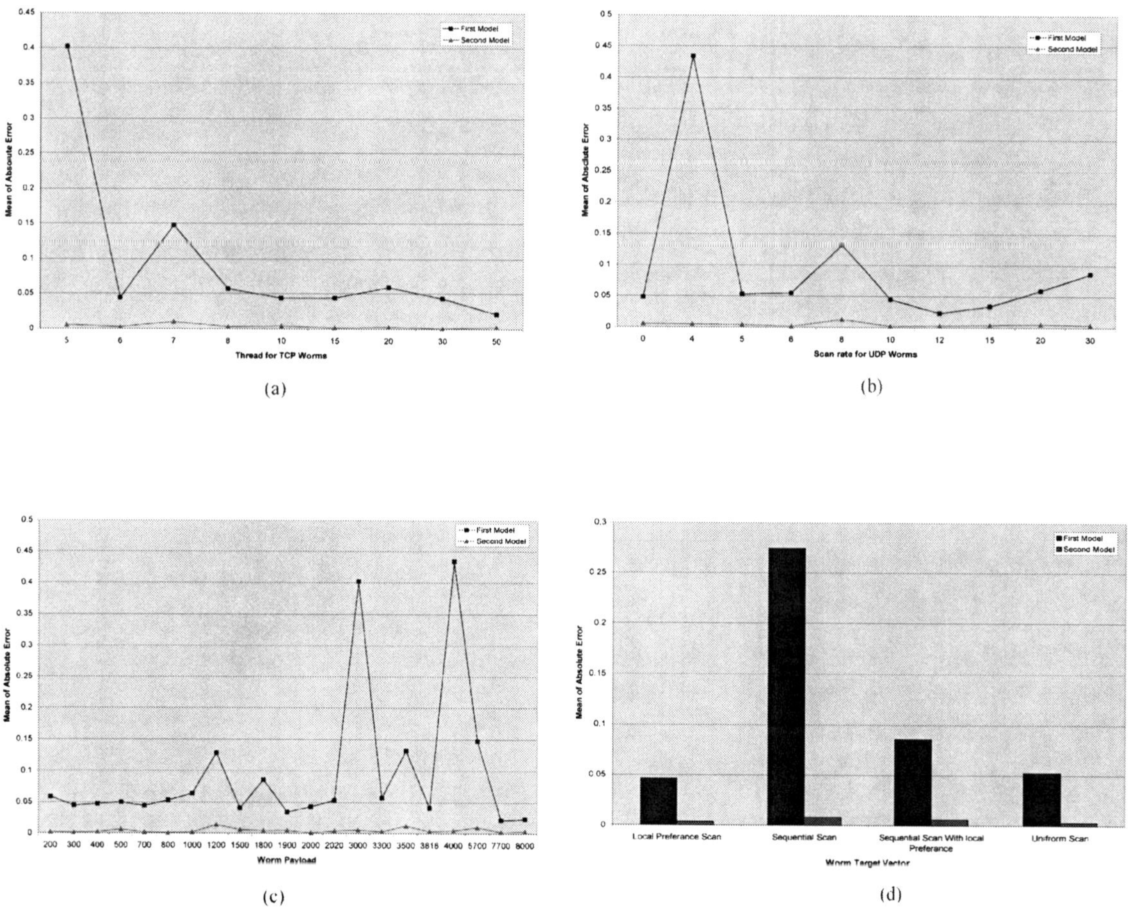

(a) (b) (c) (d)

well as worm function components and execution mechanisms. Then we describe a model for minimizing the damage due to worm infection in e-service networks. It introduces a model for detecting and predicting the number of infected nodes in order to minimize the damage. It can protect internal hosts from internal and external worm attacks. It can be used to notify other networks about worms attack.

The proposed model produces good results in worm detection. The advantage of the ANN method over other techniques is its ability to classify correctly a worm not used in the training. The proposed system produces perfect result with accuracy of %99.96 in detecting the presence of worm in the network even for unknown worms.

The prediction of percentage of infection has better performance in the CPS Model than in the CPC Model. Average of the error in prediction is 4.52E-03. When testing system in different states. The system has good performance for both small and large network. The drawback of this system is that when the system become highly infected, the error in prediction increases slightly. Thus it is recommended in future work to modify the learning of ANN module to include more training set in for the conditions of high infection.

REFERENCES

Bielecki, A., & Hajto, P. (2004). A Neural-Based Agent for IP Traffic Scanning and Worm Detection . In *Proceedings of Artificial Intelligence and Soft Computing* (p. 816). ICAISC.

CERT. (2008). *Advisory CA-1999-04 Melissa Macro Virus*. Retrieved from http://www.cert.org/advisories/CA-999-04.html

CERT. (2008). *Advisory CA-2000-04 Love Letter Worm*. Retrieved from http://www.cert.org/advisories/CA-2000-04.html

CERT. (2008). *Advisory CA-2001-26 Nimda Worm*. Retrieved from http://www.cert.org/advisories/CA-2001-26.html

Chen, X., & Heidemann, J. (2004). Detecting Early Worm Propagation through Packet Matching. In *Proceedings of ISI-TR-2004-585, USC Information Sciences Institute.*

Chen, Z. (2007). *Modeling and Defending Against Internet Worm Attacks*. School of Electrical and Computer Engineering, Georgia Institute of Technology.

Chen, Z., Gao, L., & Kwiat, K. (2003). Modeling the spread of active worms.In *Proceedings of Twenty-Second Annual Joint Conference of the IEEE Computer and Communications Societies INFOCOM, IEEE.*

Dagon, D., et al. (2004). HoneyStat: LocalWorm Detection Using Honeypots. In *Proceedings of Seventh International Symposium on Recent Advances in Intrusion Detection* (RAID).

Dantu, R., Cangussu, J. W., & Patwardhan, S. (2007). Fast Worm Containment Using Feedback Control. *IEEE Transactions on Dependable and Secure Computing*, *5*(2), 119–136. doi:10.1109/TDSC.2007.1002

David, W., Paul, C. O., & Evangelos, K. (2005). Detecting Intra-Enterprise Scanning Worms Based on Address Resolution. In *Proceedings of the 21st Annual Computer Security Applications Conference*, IEEE Computer Society.

Erbschloe, M. (2005). *Trojans, Worms, and Spyware: A Computer Security Professional's Guide to Malicious Code*. Elsevier Inc.

George, F. R. (2003). The Georgia Tech Network Simulator. In *Proceedings of the ACM SIGCOMM workshop on Models, methods and tools for reproducible network research*. Karlsruhe, Germany: ACM.

George, F. R., Monirul, I. S., & Wenke, L. (2004). Simulating Internet Worms. In *Proceedings of 12th Annual International Symposium on Modeling, Analysis, and Simulation of Computer and Telecommunications Systems* (MASCOTS'04), IEEE Computer Society.

Guofei, G., et al. (2004). Worm Detection, Early Warning and Response Based on Local Victim Information. In *Proceedings of the 20th Annual Computer Security Applications Conference* (ACSAC'04), IEEE Computer Society.

Hanxun, Z., Yingyou, W., & Hong, Z. (2007). Detecting early worm propagation based on entropy. In *Proceedings of the 2nd international conference on Scalable information systems, ICST* (Institute for Computer Sciences, Social-Informatics and Telecommunications Engineering): Suzhou, China.

Jacob, G., Debar, H., & Filiol, E. (2008). *Behavioral detection of malware: from a survey towards an established taxonomy*. Journal in Computer Virology.

Kabiri, P., & Ghorbani, A. A. (2005, September). Research on intrusion detection and response: A survey. *International Journal of Network Security*, *1*(2), 84–102.

Kephart, J. O., & White, R. S. (1991). Directed-graph epidemiological models of computer virus prevalence. In *Proceedings of the IEEE Symposium on Security and Privacy* (pp. 343-359).

Kienzle, D., & Elder, M. (2003). Recent Worms: A Survey and Trends. In *Proceedings of the ACM Workshop on Rapid Malcode*. Washington DC: ACM Press.

Kim, J. (2005). *Reducing Worm Detection Time and False Alarm in Virus Throttling* (p. 297). Computational Intelligence and Security.

Li, P., Salour, M., & Su, X. (2008). A survey of internet worm detection and containment. *Communications Surveys & Tutorials, IEEE, 10*(1), 20. doi:10.1109/COMST.2008.4483668

Michael, L., et al. (2003). Simulating realistic network worm traffic for worm warning system design and testing. In *Proceedings of the ACM workshop on Rapid malcode*. Washington, DC: ACM.

Moore, D., Paxson, V., & Savage, S. (2003). Inside the Slammer Worm. *IEEE Security and Privacy Archive*, *1*(4), 33–39. doi:10.1109/MSECP.2003.1219056

Moore, D., Shannon, C., Voelker, G., et al. (2003). Internet Quarantine: Requirements for Containing Self-Propagating Code. In *Proceedings of the IEEE Infocom conference*, San Francisco, CA.

Moskovitch, R., Elovici, Y., & Rokach, L. (2008). Detection of unknown computer worms based on behavioral classification of the host", Computational Statistics and Data Analysis, ElSevier, 2008.

Nathanael, P. (2005). A Closer Look at Viruses and Worms. *IEEE Security and Privacy*, *3*(4), 7. doi:10.1109/MSP.2005.86

Nazario, J. (2004). Defense and Detection Strategies against Internet Worms, *Artech House, Inc.*,290.

Nazario, J., Anderson J., Wash, R., et al. (2001). The Future of Internet Worms, *Crimelabs research*.

Nicholas, W., Vern, P., Stuart, S., et al. (2003). A Taxonomy of Computer Worms. In *Proceedings of the ACM workshop on Rapid Malcode*. Washington, DC: ACM Press.

Qing, S., & Wen, W. (2005). A Survey and Trends on Internet Worms. *Computers & Security*, *24*(4), 334–346. doi:10.1016/j.cose.2004.10.001

Sanguanpong, S., & Kanlayasiri, U. (2007). Worm damage minimization in enterprise networks . *International Journal of Human-Computer Studies*, *65*(1), 3–16. doi:10.1016/j.ijhcs.2006.09.001

Spafford, E. (1988). *The Internet Worm Program: An Analysis*(Technical report CSD-TR-823) Department of Computer Science, Purdue University, (pp. 1-29).

Staniford, S., Paxson, V., & Weaver, N. (2002). How to Own the Internet in Your Spare Time. In *Proceedings of 11th Usenix Security Symposium*, San Francisco, USA.

Stoppel, D., et al. (2006). Improving Worm Detection with Artificial Neural Networks through Feature Selection and Temporal Analysis Techniques. In *Proceedings of International Conference on Neural Networks ICNN 2006: International Journal of Applied Mathematics and Computer Sciences.*

Stoppel, D., et al. (2006)Application of Artificial Neural Networks Techniques to Computer Worm Detection. In *Proceedings of International Joint Conference on Neural Networks IJCNN '06.*

Symantec (2008). *W32.Benjamin.Worm*. Retrieved from http://securityresponse.symantec.com/avcenter/venc/data/w32.benjamin.worm.html

Wang, J. (2007). Internet worm early detection and response mechanism. *Journal of China Universities of Posts and Telecommunications, 14*(3), 79. doi:10.1016/S1005-8885(07)60153-8

Weaver, N., Staniford, S., & Paxson, V. *Very Fast Containment of Scanning Worms*. Revisited, in Malware Detection (p. 113).

Yaneza, J. L. (2006). *The trend of threats today: 2006 Annual Roundup and 2007 Forecast.* Trend Micro.

Yaneza, J. L. (2007). 1H 2007 Threat Roundup and 2H 2007 Forecast . In *Securing Your Web World.* Trend Micro.

Yaneza, J. L. (2008). 2007 Threat Report | 2008 Threat and Technology Forecast . In *Securing Your Web World.* Trend Micro.

Yaneza, J. L., Thiemann, T., & Drake, C. (2008). 2007 Threat Report | 2008 Threat and Technology Forecast . In *Securing Your Web World.* Trend Micro.

Yang, W., & Chenxi, W. (2003). Modeling the Effects of Timing Parameters on Virus Propagation. In Proceedings of the ACM workshop on Rapid Malcode, Washington, DC: ACM Press.

Zou, C. C., et al. (2003). Monitoring and Early Warning for Internet Worms. In *Proceedings of the 10th ACM conference on Computer and communications security*. Washington DC: ACM Press.

Zou, C. C., Gong, W., & Towsley, D. (2002). Code red worm propagation modeling and analysis. In*Proceedings of the 9th ACM conference on Computer and communications security*. Washington, DC: ACM Press.

Zou, C. C., Towsley, D., & Gong, W. (2003). On the Performance of Internet Worm Scanning Strategies. *Performance Evaluation, 63*(7), 700–723. doi:10.1016/j.peva.2005.07.032

Chapter 28
Towards a Dynamic Font Respecting the Arabic Calligraphy

Abdelouahad Bayar
Cadi Ayyad University, Morocco

Khalid Sami
Cadi Ayyad University, Morocco

ABSTRACT

To justify texts, Arabic calligraphers use to stretch some letters with small flowing curves; the kashida instead of inserting blanks among words. Of course, such stretchings are context dependent. An adequate tool to support such writing may be based on a continuous mathematical model. The model has to take into account the motion of the qalam. The characters may be represented as outlines. Among the curves composing the characters outlines, some intersections are to be determined dynamically. In the Naskh style, the qalam's head behaves as a rigid rectangle in motion with a constant inclination. To determine the curves delimiting the set of points to shade when writing, we have to find out a mathematical way to compare plane curves. Moreover, as the PostScript procedure to produce a dynamic character, should be repeated whenever the letter is to draw, the development of a font supporting a continuous stretching model, allowing stretchable letters with no overlapping outlines, without optimization would be of a high cost in CPU time. In this chapter, some stretching models are given and discussed. A method to compare curves is presented. It allows the determination of the character encoding with eventually overlapping outlines. Then a way to approximate the curves intersection coefficients is given. This is enough to remove overlapping outlines. Some evaluations in time processing to confirm the adopted optimization techniques are also exposed.

DOI: 10.4018/978-1-61520-789-3.ch028

INTRODUCTION

The justification of texts written in an Arabic alphabet based script, is based on stretching letters instead of the ordinary insertion of spaces (blanks) among words. This concept called the kashida is almost mandatory in cursive writings such as Arabic.

Many typesetting systems such as TeX/LaTeX (Knuth, 1984 & Lamport, 1985), WYSWYM systems such as LyX (LyX Team, 2004) and WYSIWYG systems such as TeXMacs (Joris, 2003) provide support to typeset documents in latin alphabet based scripts in a quite good quality. Some extensions of TeX and LaTeX like ArabTeX (Lagally, 2004), Ω (Haralambous, 1997) and RydArab (Lazrek, 2001) allow typesetting lines in Arabic alphabet based scripts. As the stretching of characters, according to the rules of Arabic calligraphy, is *curvilinear*, the encoding languages are to support what can be called "dynamic fonts" as PostScript language does (Adobe Systems Incorporated, 1999). Instructions used in coding characters in TrueType fonts (Weise, 1992) also allow such support. Unfortunately, this support is not offered by Metafont (Knuth, 1986). That's the reason why extensions of (La)TeX don't support the dynamism needed by an Arabic font. Big improvements had been provided in the CurExt system proposed by A. Lazrek (2003). When the system is called with RydArab it allows typesetting documents with stretchable characters. With this package, the variable sized character, in the suitable size, is produced via repeated calls of Metafont in TeX. A certain number of stretchings in different sizes can so be used in a document. But in some cases, much more than this amount of stretchings can be necessary.

The dynamic fonts have been studied first by J. André and B. Borghi (1990). Daniel Berry used the concept in (André & Borghi, 1990) and developed a type 3 PostScript font to be used with the dittroff/ fforttid system to typeset documents in right-to-left alphabet based scripts (Berry, 1999). This system offers a good support for the characters dynamism even though it contains some flaws. Actually, in (Berry, 1999), the stretching is performed in the horizontal direction only and the stretching model don't take into account the motion of the nib's head. This fact leads to some lost of quality in big stretching. Solutions to fix such flaws have been proposed in (Bayar & Sami, 1999). The actual chapter extends the results already published in (Bayar, 2008).

The suitable extent to which characters in an Arabic alphabet script based text are to be stretched is context dependent. The stretching model may be continuous. In a dynamic PostScript font, the procedure to produce a character is repeated whenever the character is to be drawn. So, introducing a program to support the kashida in the font, without taking into account some optimizations, would be of a high cost in CPU. We have then to find out an alternative way to develop a stretching model. The natural way to represent stretching in PostScript can be based on parameterized *cubic* Bézier curves. Such model introduces a big amount of calculations in comparison to a *quadratic* stretching model. A study and evaluation of the cubic and quadratic models is proposed in this chapter.

Due to cursivity of the Arabic script, the qalam characteristics and the kashida, writing words based on stretched outlined letters implies taking into account some particular properties and requirements. Intersections of some curves are to be determined dynamically in the font. Unless some optimizations are done, the use of such font would slow the typesetting.

The chapter follows the plan: the second section highlights the kashida notion, the requirements of writings in outlined letters and the classification of characters in term of dynamism. The third section presents the geometrical representation and therefore the notion of qalam's motion. In the fourth section, the stretching models are presented and compared for optimization. In the fifth section, we show how static letters are implemented in the font. The way to implement the dynamic letters, in filled in or outlined version, is the main part of the chapter. The sixth and seventh parts provide more extensions. Implementations based on the different concepts are compared and evaluated.

ON SOME CHARACTERISTICS AND REQUIREMENTS OF ARABIC CALLIGRAPHY

Kashida

In Arabic alphabet based scripts, the calligraphic rules can be considered as almost mandatory as grammar. In such writing, stretching letters is used instead of the ordinary insertion of spaces (blanks) between words, to justify the lines. There are two kinds of kashida stretching: between two connected letters and inside the same letter. The stretching between two connected letters doesn't mean that the kashida is a curve or a character that we add between the letters but it implies directly the two connected letters. For clarity, the two kinds of stretching are presented with bounding boxes of characters in Figure 1. In the first line, there are stretchings in different sizes between the two connected letters C and B in the word BCD. In the following line, the last letter E of the word EF is stretched in four different sizes.

Kashida and Outlined Letters

One goal of this chapter is to provide a support for developing a PostScript font that allows typesetting Arabic texts, in characters represented as outlines, according to the basic calligraphic rules. The existing systems don't offer such support. In the first line, in Figure 2 (from right to left), the word BCD is displayed in outlines, in two options: with and without limits between two consecutive characters. Most of the systems allowing writing Arabic script in outlines, such as Microsoft Word, can produce only the first sample (in the right). Of course, The cursivity is observed better in the second way of writing in Figure 2.

Managing stretchability is better shown with fonts that provide characters in outlines. An example of stretched outlines is presented in Figure 3. This characters stretchability needs a mathematical formalization. So, the stretching letters model presented in (Bayar & Sami, 1999) would be deeply improved.

Figure 1. Inter-curvilinear and intro-curvilinear stretching's in Arabic calligraphy

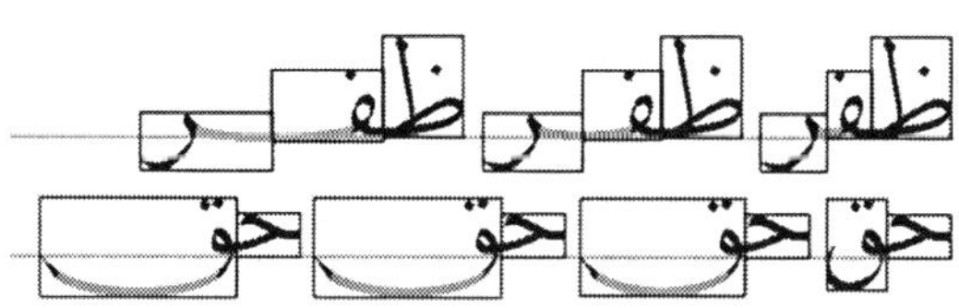

Fixed and Variable Sized Letters

Let us recall that there are fixed and variable sized letters. Fixed letters have static shapes as the letter G (standalone DEL) and H (standalone REH) in Figure 4(a). Variable sized letters have stretchable parts. The first line of Figure 4(b) shows the letter A (BEH connected after) with three different curvilinear stretchings whereas the second line presents the letter B (REH connected before).

Figure 2. Possibilities of outlines writing in Arabic

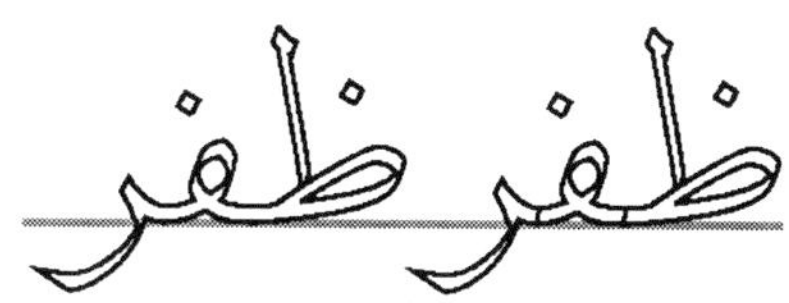

Figure 3. Stretchable outlines in Arabic

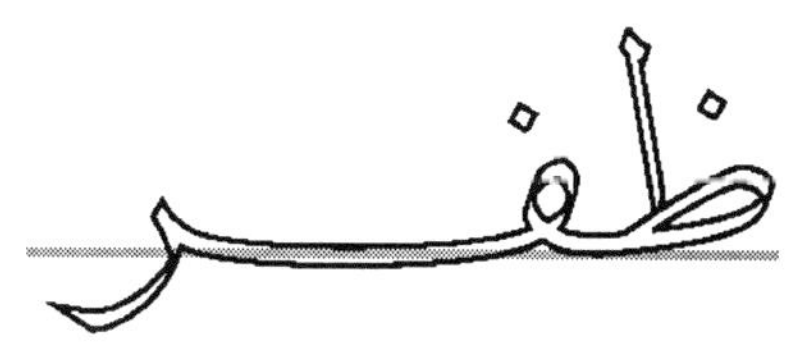

Figure 4. (a) Examples of static letters, (b) Examples of variable sized letters

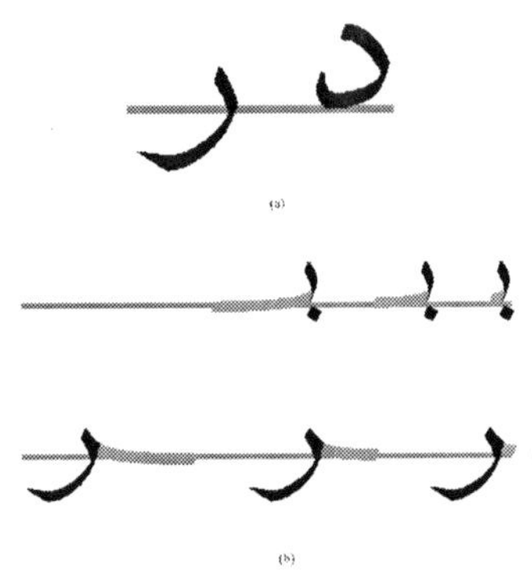

Variable sized letters are composed of a static part (in terms of shape; the shape is kept as it is after a shifting transformation) and a dynamic one. In Figure 4(b), the dynamic parts are in gray. For the letter A, this part is used to connect the letter to the following one in the left, since the Arabic writing is a right-to-left. In the same context, the stretchable part in the other letter is the preceding connection in the letter B (this is also used to connect it to the preceding letter in its right).

NIB'S HEAD MOTION-RAZING MODELING AND DECOMPOSITION

There are different styles in Arabic writing. Among the most popular ones, we can mention: Farsi, Koufi, Maghrebi, Naskh, Thuluth, Rouqaa, Dywani. Samples of such styles are presented in Figure 5. For the present purpose, let us consider the Naskh style (the framed one in Figure 5) since it is the most widely used in digital typography. So, in this chapter, we'll develop mathematical tools to help in the development of a stretchable Naskh font. Of course, this font will support writing in outlines.

Now, let's give some characteristics of the nib's head motion under Arabic calligraphy rules.

Qalam's Motion Modeling

In the Naskh style, the nib's head or simply the qalam (the pen, calligraphers use to write with) behaves as a rectangle of width l and thickness $e = {}^{l}\!/_{6}$. This rectangle moves with a constant inclination angle of about 70° with regard to the baseline. A nib's head with l=12*mm* (and e=2*mm*) is presented in Figure 6.

In the following, let us consider the general case where the pen's head motion can be represented by a polygonal shape with n+1 vertices, in translation. For more clarity, examples are given with rectangles with sizes and inclinations different from the Naskh qalam's ones. Let's represent a pen's head with n+1 vertices $M_0, M_1, \ldots, M_n$ by B(M_0,F) where $F = \left(\vec{u}\right)_{i=0,\ldots,n}$ is a family of n+1 vectors such that $\vec{u}_i = \overrightarrow{M_0M_i}$. The point M_0 stands for an origin for the pen's head in motion. Whenever particular values are associated to that point and to the vectors, all the vertices, and therefore positions, of the pen's head can be determined precisely. When the trajectory of the origin vertex is the parametric curve f defined on [0,1], the motion of a pen B(M_0,F) will be denoted by **M(B(**M_0,F**)**,f,[0,1]/ In Figure 7, the motion is characterized by the start position of the pen's head and a Bézier curve (Bézier, 1977) B_0 representing the trajectory of the vertex M_{00}. In the case

Figure 5. Most popular Arabic writing styles

Figure 6. Nib's head in Naskh style with 12 mm width

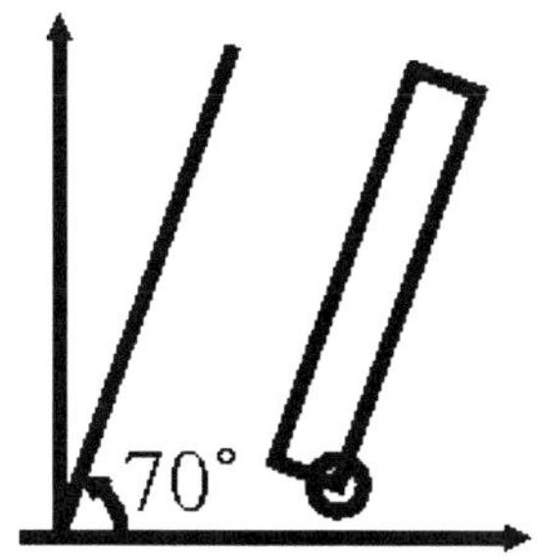

of the qalam, the origin is the vertex with a circle in Figure 6.

Motion-Razing

The razing of a qalam motion is the set of points darken by the qalam in the plane. Of course, this set is delimited by external curves corresponding to the trajectories of the qalam's vertices and some edges of the qalam. Therefore, we need a mean to help comparing the shifting transforms of curves in order to find out the external curves of a razing. For this, it is necessary to define the notion of the *orthogonal range associated to a parametric function according to a vector*.

Consider:

- the affine space $\mathbb{R}^3$ with the orthonormal basis $R\left(O,\vec{i},\vec{j},\vec{k}\right)$,
- an affine plane $\mathbb{R}^2$ in $\mathbb{R}^3$ containing the origin o with a direct orthonormal basis $\left(\vec{i},\vec{j}\right)$. Let's denote $\overrightarrow{\mathbb{R}}^2$ the vector plane associated to $\mathbb{R}^2$.
- a parametric function f defined on $[0,1]$ with values in $\mathbb{R}^2$. Suppose that f is continuous on $[0,1]$ and differentiable on $]0,1[$.
- and the vectors $\vec{u}$, $\vec{u_1}$ and $\vec{u_2}$ in $\overrightarrow{\mathbb{R}}^2$.

Figure 7. Example of motion

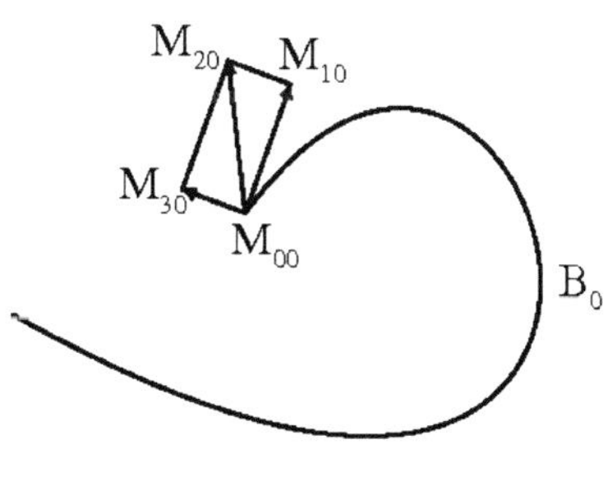

Definition 1 (Direct orthogonal range with respect to a vector): *The Direct orthogonal range associated to f, according to the vector* $\vec{u}$, is the scalar function $\mathbf{R}_{\left(f,\vec{u}\right)}$ defined from $[0,1]$ *onto* $\mathbb{R}$ such that $\mathbf{R}_{\left(f,\vec{u}\right)}\left(t\right)=\left(\vec{u}\wedge\overrightarrow{Of\left(t\right)}\right)\cdot\vec{k}.$

The derivative verify $\mathbf{R}'_{\left(f,\vec{u}\right)}\left(t\right)=\mathbf{R}_{\left(f',\vec{u}\right)}\left(t\right)$.

Now, we can define the way to compare the shifting transform of a curve.

Definition 2 (Comparison of shifted curves): *We have* $t_{\vec{u_1}}\left(f\right)\leq t_{\vec{u_2}}\left(f\right)$ on $[0,1]$ *(respectively* $t_{\vec{u_1}}\left(f\right)\geq t_{\vec{u_2}}\left(f\right)$) if and only if $\mathbf{R}'_{\left(f,\vec{u_1}-\vec{u_2}\right)}\left(t\right)<0$ *(respectively* $\mathbf{R}'_{\left(f,\vec{u_1}-\vec{u_2}\right)}\left(t\right)\geq 0$) $\forall t\in\left[0,1\right]$).

The comparison between $t_{\vec{u_1}}\left(f\right)$ and $t_{\vec{u_2}}\left(f\right)$ on $[0,1]$ can be done through the study of the monotony of $\mathbf{R}_{\left(f,\vec{u_1}-\vec{u_2}\right)}$ on $[0,1]$.

Now, we have the tools necessary for studying the nib's head motions and their associated razings. Before doing that, let's present a particular type of motions, the *normal* motions, and their associated razings.

Consider the motion M such that M=M(B(M_{00},F),f,[0,1]) and $F=\left(\vec{u}\right)_{i=0,\ldots,n}$.

Definition 3 (Normal Motion): *M is said to be normal on* $[0,1]$ *if and only if* $\exists i\in\{0,\ldots,n\}$ and $\exists j\in\{0,\ldots,n\}$ such that: $t_{\vec{u_k}}\left(f\right)\leq t_{\vec{u_i}}\left(f\right)$ *and* $t_{\vec{u_k}}\left(f\right)\geq t_{\vec{u_j}}\left(f\right)$ on $[0,1]$ $\forall k\in\{0,\ldots,n\}$.

In this definition, $t_{\vec{u}_i}(f)$ is the maximal curve whereas $t_{\vec{u}_j}(f)$ is the minimal one among the set $\{t_{\vec{u}_k}(f), \vec{u}_k \in \mathbf{F}\}$. A normal motion and its corresponding razing are presented in Figure 8. The razing is delimited by the two segments $[M_{30},M_{00}]$, $[M_{00},M_{10}]$, the Bézier curve B_1, the two segments $[M_{11},M_{21}]$, $[M_{21},M_{31}]$ and the Bézier curve B_3.

Lemma 1: *If* $\forall i \in \{0,\ldots,n\}$, $\mathbf{R}_{\left(f,\vec{u}_{(i+1) \bmod n}-\vec{u}_i\right)}$, *is monotone on* $[0,1]$ *then M is a normal motion.*

The lemma can be proved through considering the motion in Figure 8. In general, the razing associated to a motion is determined via its decomposition into normal sub-motions. Then, we have the theorem.

Theorem 1 (Decomposition into normal sub-motions): *The motion M can be decomposed into normal sub-motions on* $[0,1]$ *so that the concatenation of their associated razings constitute exactly the global razing associated to M.*

Proof:

Let $F = \left(\vec{u}\right)_{i=0,\ldots,n}$ $(\vec{u}_0 = \vec{0})$, studying the sign of $\mathbf{R}'_{\left(f,\vec{u}_{(i+1) \bmod n}-\vec{u}_i\right)}$ on]0.1[for $i\in\{0,\ldots,n\}$ gives the set of extrema of $\mathbf{R}_{\left(f,\vec{u}_{(i+1) \bmod n}-\vec{u}_i\right)}$ on]0,1[.

Figure 8. (a) Normal motion, (b) The corresponding normal razing

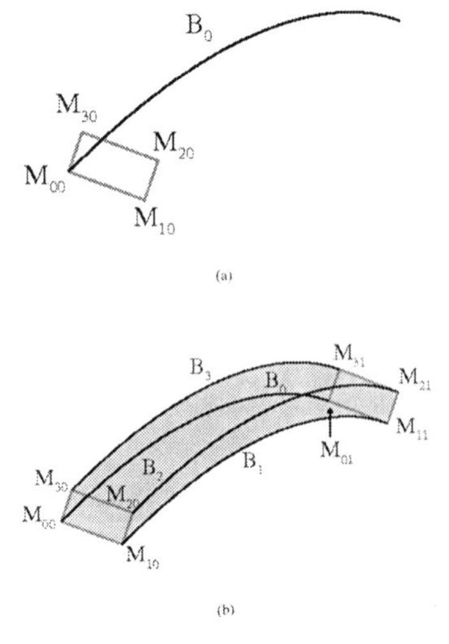

Let $E_i = \left\{T_{i,1}, T_{i,2}, \ldots, T_{i,\varphi(i)}\right\}$ be the set of extrema of $\mathbf{R}_{\left(f,\vec{u}_{(i+1) \bmod n}-\vec{u}_i\right)}$, ordered in an increasing order ($\varphi(i)$ reverses the cardinal of E_i).

The restrictions of the direct orthogonal range $\mathbf{R}_{\left(f,\vec{u}_{(i+1) \bmod n}-\vec{u}_i\right)}$ to the segments $[0,T_{i,1}[,[T_{i,1},T_{i,2}[,\ldots$ $[T_{i,\varphi(i)=1},Ti_{,\varphi(i)}[,[Ti,_{\varphi(i),1}]$ are monotone.

Now, let us consider E={T1,T2,...,Tm} the union of the sets Ei, ordered in an increasing order.

According to the previous reasoning, $\mathbf{R}_{\left(f,\vec{u}_{(i+1) \bmod n}-\vec{u}_i\right)}$ is monotone on $[0,T_1[,[T_1,T_2[,\ldots$ $[T_{m-1},T_m[,[T_m,1]$ for $i\in\{0,\ldots,n\}$

By the lemma 1, The qalam's motion is normal on $[0,T_1[,[T_1,T_2[,\ldots,[T_{m-1},T_m[,[T_m,1]$.

The restrictions considered together constitute the exact trajectories of the vertices of the qalam's head. So, the concatenation of the razings gives the exact razing of the pen's head.

In order to illustrate the study of motions, we consider a concrete example. Let us consider the motion of a qalam of extremities M_{00}, M_{10}, M_{20} and M_{30} (see Figure 7). The trajectory of the origin M_{00} is the cubic Bézier curve B_0. The control points of B_0 are M_0=(135,80), M_1=(180,140), M_2=(220,0) and M_3=(100,65). The point M_0 coincides with M_{00}. The family of the motion vectors is $F = \left(\vec{u}\right)_{i=0,\ldots,3}$ such that $\vec{u}_0 = \vec{0}$,

$$\vec{u}_1 = \overrightarrow{M_{00}M_{10}} = \overrightarrow{(6.83116, 18.7972)},$$

$$\vec{u}_2 = \overrightarrow{M_{00}M_{20}} = \overrightarrow{(-2.5696, 22.2069)} \text{ and}$$

$$\vec{u}_3 = \overrightarrow{M_{00}M_{30}} = \overrightarrow{(-9.40076, 3.40964)}.$$

Studying $\mathbf{R}'_{\left(B_0,\vec{u}_{(i+1) \bmod 3}-\vec{u}_i\right)}$ on]0,1[for $i\in\{0,\ldots,3\}$ shows that $\mathbf{R}'_{\left(B_0,\vec{u}_1-\vec{u}_0\right)}$ vanishes at t_0=0.580246and the sign changes in the neighborhood of t_0 Whereas, $\mathbf{R}'_{\left(B_0,\vec{u}_2-\vec{u}_1\right)}$ is null at t_1=0.238061 and t_2=0.919186 and changes in sign near these two real numbers.

$\mathbf{R}'_{\left(B_0,\vec{u}_3-\vec{u}_2\right)}$ and $\mathbf{R}'_{\left(B_0,\vec{u}_0-\vec{u}_3\right)}$ have the same roots and opposite sign as $\mathbf{R}'_{\left(B_0,\vec{u}_1-\vec{u}_0\right)}$ and $\mathbf{R}'_{\left(B_0,\vec{u}_2-\vec{u}_1\right)}$ respectively.

The function $\mathbf{R}_{\left(B_0,\vec{u}_{(i+1)\bmod 3}-\vec{u}_i\right)}$ is monotone on [0, 0.238061], [0.238061, 0.580246], [0.580246, 0.919186] and [0.919186, 1].

Then, we get that the motions restricted to the intervals [0, 0.238061], [0.238061, 0.580246], [0.580246, 0.919186] and [0.919186, 1] are normal.

Let $B_{0,j}, j\in\{0,1,2,3\}$ be the curves obtained by successive Bézier refinement according to t_0, t_1 and t_2, the four curves are represented in Figure 9.

Let $B_{ij} = t_{\vec{u}_i}\left(B_{0j}\right), i\in\{0,1,2,3\}, j\in\{0,1,2,3\}$. $t_{\vec{u}}$ stands for the shifting transformation trough the vector $\vec{u}$.

- On the interval [0,0.238061], the maximum is B_{00} and the minimum is B_{20} (see Figure 10(a)).
- On [0.238061,0.580246], the maximum is B_{31} and the minimum is B_{11} (see Figure 10(b)).
- On [0.580246,0.919186], the maximum is B_{22} and the minimum is B_{02} (see Figure 10(c)).
- On [0.919186,1], the maximum is B_{13} and the minimum is B_{33} (see Figure 10(d)).

Figure 9. Decomposition of the origin trajectory

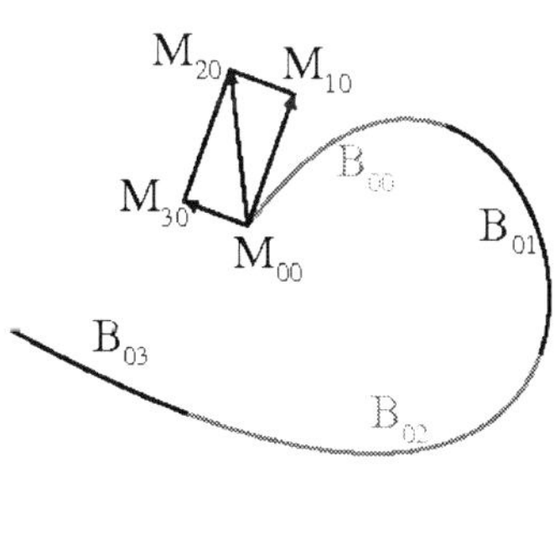

When the normal sub-razings are superposed, we get exactly the set of points that are really razed with the polygonal pen (see Figure 13). Some parts are painted twice. They are in middle gray in Figure 11.

We can reduce this redundancy through considering the outline with overlapping parts in Figure 12. It is obtained by considering the external edges of the polygonal pen in the start position, laying the maximum curves with segments (that are really edges of the pen), doing the same thing for the minimum curves and in the final position, the external edges are considered. Filling in this outline with overlapping with respect to the winding odd algorithm, we get exactly the real razing of the motion.

We can determine the outline that suggests a minimal effort through filling in the interior with determining intersection between B_{00} and B_{31}, the

Figure 10. Normal sub-razings

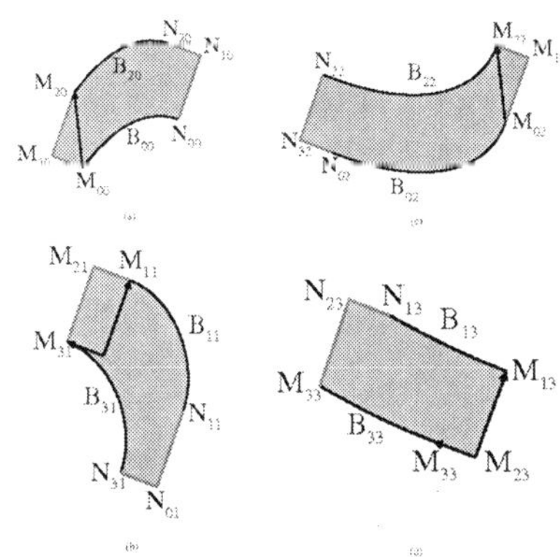

Figure 11. Superposed normal sub-razings

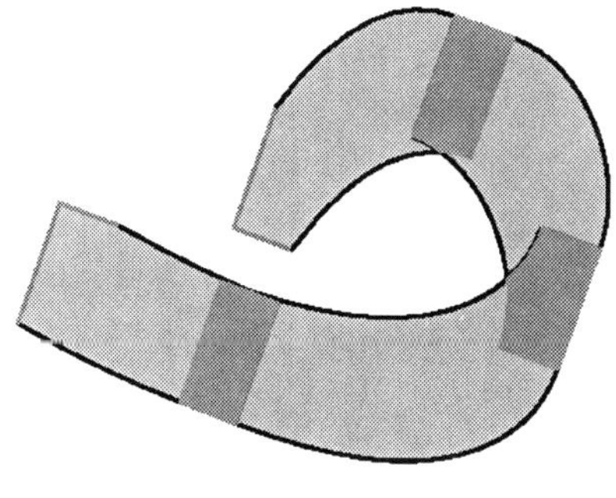

Figure 12. The razing in outline with overlapping

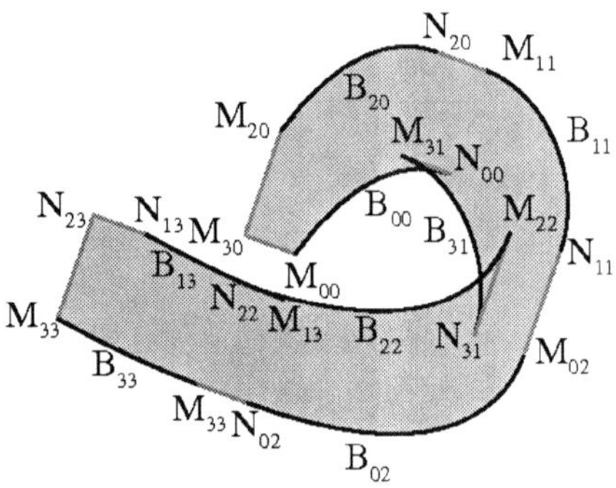

intersection between the curves B_{31} and B_{22} and the intersection between B_{22} and B_{13} (see Figure 13).

STRETCHING MODEL

Now, the way to reconstitute the envelope of the set of the qalam motion is built, we can find out the stretching model. In the following, we present the stretching model based on *cubic* curves (this model has been already developed in (Bayar & Sami, 2009). Next, a *quadratic* stretching model will also be presented as improvement of the previous one. A time processing evaluation for the two models will be done through tests on the preceding connection of the letter B.

Cubic Stretching Model

As mentioned previously, the trajectory of one of the vertices of the qalam determines the other ones. So, the model will be defined through considering the vertex surrounded with a circle in Figure 6. Before presenting the stretching models, some kinds of curves are to be defined.

Let $[M_0,M_1,\ldots,M_n]$ be a Bézier curve of degree n and control points M_0, M_1, …, M_n. In the cubic stretching model, the dynamic parts in variable sized letters, (for example, the preceding connection in the case of B and the following connection in the case of the letter A) are cubic Bézier curves. The preceding connections are curves belonging to the set $\mathbf{B}_1^c$ and the succeeding ones belong to $\mathbf{B}_2^c$. The sets $\mathbf{B}_1^c$ and $\mathbf{B}_2^c$ are defined as follows. Consider the curve $B=[M_{10},M_{11}M_{12},M_{13}]$, then:

Figure 13. The razing in true outline

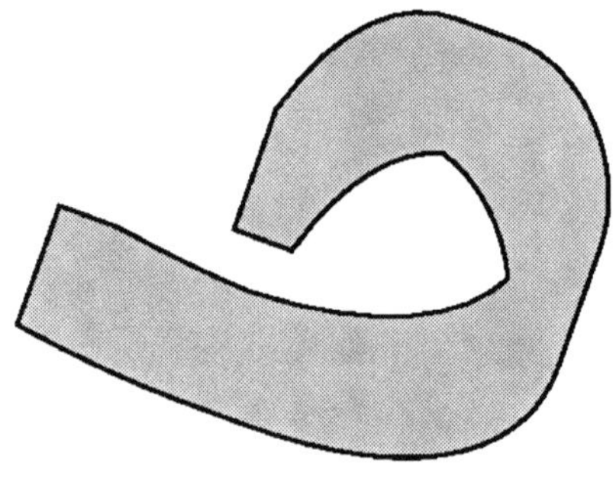

- The curve $B \in \mathbf{B}_1^c \Leftrightarrow \overrightarrow{M_{10}M_{11}} = \lambda\vec{i}$, $\lambda \in \mathbb{R}_*^-$ and $0 \leq \widehat{\left(\overrightarrow{M_{13}M_{12}}, \vec{i}\right)} \leq \frac{\pi}{2}$ (see Figure 14(a)) where $\widehat{\left(\vec{w_1}, \vec{w_2}\right)}$ stands for the angle between the two vectors $\vec{w_1}$ and $\vec{w_2}$. The vector $\vec{i}$ is the axis X vector director.
- The curve $B \in \mathbf{B}_2^c \Leftrightarrow \overrightarrow{M_{12}M_{13}} = \lambda\vec{i}$, $\lambda \in \mathbb{R}_*^-$ and $0 \leq \widehat{\left(-\vec{i}, \overrightarrow{M_{10}M_{11}}\right)} \leq \frac{\pi}{2}$ (see Figure 14(b)).

Now, how can we stretch the curves in $\mathbf{B}_1^c$ and $\mathbf{B}_2^c$. Let $B_1=[M_{10},M_{11}M_{12},M_{13}]$ be a cubic Bézier curve with control points M_{10}, M_{11}, M_{12} and M_{13} and $B_2=[M_{20},M_{21}M_{22},M_{23}]$ be a stretched version of B_1 with an horizontal stretching value *h* and a vertical one *v*. We have:

- If $B_1 \in \mathbf{B}_1^c$, then: $M_{20}=M_{10}-(0,v)$, $M_{23}=M_{13}-(h,0)$, $M_{21}=(1-c_1)M_{20}+c_1J$ and $M_{22}=(1-c_2)$

Figure 14. (a) Cubic curve in $\mathbf{B}_1^c$*, (b) Cubic curves in* $\mathbf{B}_2^c$

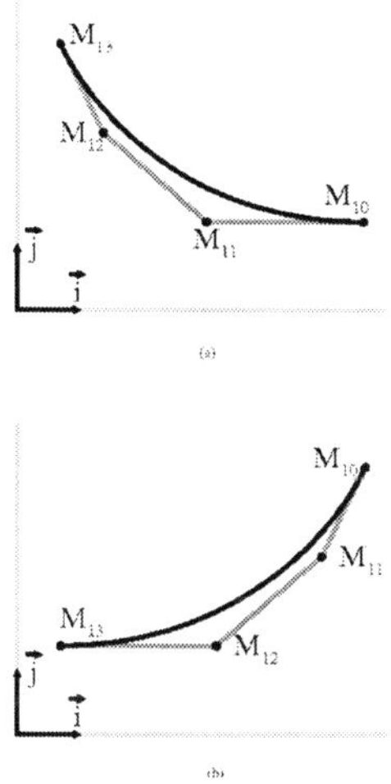

J+c_2M_{23} with c_1,c_2∈[0,1] satisfying the equations: M_{11}=(1-c_1)M_{10}+c_1I and M_{12}=(1-c_2)I+c=2$_M$13 where $\{I\}=(M_{10}M_{11})\cap(M_{12}M_{13})$ and $\{J\}=\Delta_1\cap\Delta_2$ where Δ_1 is the parallel to $(M_{10}M_{11})$ passing through the point M_{20}. Δ_2 is the parallel to $(M_{12}M_{13})$ passing through the point M_{23}.

An illustration of this case is presented in Figure 15(a).

- If $B_1 \in \mathbf{B}_2^c$, then: $M_{20}=M_{10}$, $M_{23}=M_{13}-(h,v)$, $M_{21}=(1-c_1)M_{20}+c_1J$ and $M_{22}=(1-c_2)J+c_2M_{23}$ with c_1,c_2∈[0,1] satisfying the equations: $M_{11}=(1-c_1)M_{10}+c_1I$ and $M_{12}=(1-c_2)I+c_2M_{13}$ where $\{I\}=(M_{10}M_{11})\cap(M_{12}M_{13})$ and $\{J\}=\Delta_1\cap\Delta_2$where Δ_1 is $(M_{10}M_{11})$. Δ_2 is the parallel to $(M_{12}M_{13})$ passing through the point M_{23}.

An illustration of this case is shown in Figure 15(b).

We can remark that the cubic stretching model is based on the conservation of a barycentric relation.

Figure 15. (a) Stretching of a curve belonging to the set $\mathbf{B}_1^c$*, (b) Stretching of a curve belonging to the set* $\mathbf{B}_2^c$

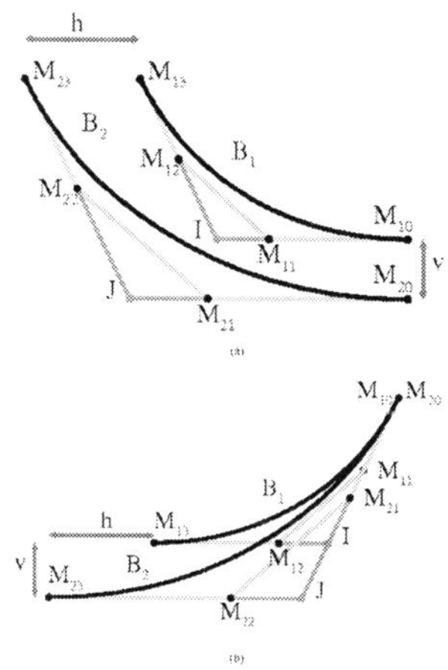

Since the PostScript procedure to produce the dynamic letter should be executed every time the letter has to be drawn, the calculus has to be minimized. The procedure to stretch curves belonging to $\mathbf{B}_1^c$ (respectively $\mathbf{B}_2^c$) is called *ebe* (respectively *eaf*) and has as inputs M_{10}, M_{13}, I, c_1, c_2, h and v. Thus, I, c_1 and c_2 are computed out of the font (they would not be computed by the PostScript interpreter). Whereas, J is determined and so, for M_{20}, M_{21}, M_{22} and M_{22} into the font and every time the procedure to draw the letter is called.

Quadratic Stretching Model

In the sequel, we present a model based on quadratic curves. The dynamic parts of the letters are now quadratic curves. PostScript doesn't support quadratic curves but every quadratic curve can be presented as a cubic one. When a quadratic curve is a contribution to a drawing, it will be transformed into the corresponding cubic one. In the encoding of the letter for example, we determine a quadratic curve to replace the cubic one so that the visual accuracy is satisfied (Reeves, 1981).

As in the case of the cubic model, we consider two sets $\mathbf{B}_1^q$ and $\mathbf{B}_2^q$ such that for all $B=[M_{10},M_{11},M_{12}]$ we have:

- $B \in \mathbf{B}_1^q \Leftrightarrow \overrightarrow{M_{10}M_{11}} = \lambda \vec{i}, \quad \lambda \in \mathbb{R}_*^-$ and $0 \le \left(\widehat{\overrightarrow{M_{12}M_{11}}, \vec{i}}\right) \le \frac{\pi}{2}$ (see Figure 16(a)).
- $B \in \mathbf{B}_2^q \Leftrightarrow \overrightarrow{M_{11}M_{12}} = \lambda \vec{i}, \quad \lambda \in \mathbb{R}_*^-$ and $0 \le \left(\widehat{-\vec{i}, \overrightarrow{M_{10}M_{11}}}\right) \le \frac{\pi}{2}$ (see Figure 16(b)).

Now, let's present the way to stretch curves in $\mathbf{B}_1^q$ and $\mathbf{B}_2^q$. Let $B_1=[M_{10},M_{11},M_{12}]$ be a quadratic Bézier curve with control points $M_{10}=(x_{10},y_{10})$, $M_{11}=(x_{11},y_{11})$, and $M_{12}=(x_{12},y_{12})$ and let $B_2=[M_{20},M_{21},M_{22}]$ be a stretched version of B_1 with an horizontal stretching value h and a vertical one v. We have:

- If $B_1 \in \mathbf{B}_1^q$ then $M_{20}=(x_{10},y_{10}-v)$, $M_{22}=(x_{12}-h,y_{12})$ and
$$M_{21} = \left(x_{12} - h + \frac{(y_{10} - y_{12} - v)(x_{11} - x_{12})}{y_{11} - y_{12}}, y_{10} - v\right).$$
- If $B_1 \in \mathbf{B}_2^q$ then $M_{20}=(x_{10},y_{10})$, $M_{22}=(x_{12}-h,y_{12}-v)$ and
$$M_{21} = \left(x_{10} + \frac{(y_{12} - y_{10} - v)(x_{11} - x_{10})}{y_{11} - y_{10}}, y_{12} - v\right).$$

Figure 16. (a) Quadratic curve in $\mathbf{B}_1^q$, (b) Quadratic curve in $\mathbf{B}_2^q$

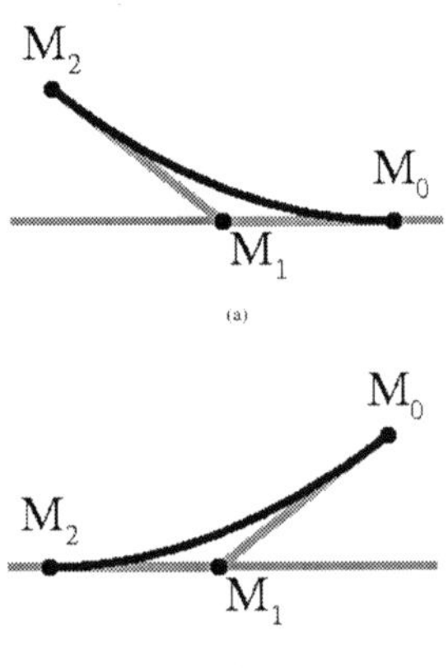

An example of stretching for the two types is presented in Figure 17. The procedure to perform the stretching in the quadratic case is called *qebe* (in the case of $\mathbf{B}_1^q$) and has as input parameters M_{10}, M_{11}, M_{12}, h, and v.

In particular, in the font, the vertical stretching value v depends on h. Let us write $v = \frac{V}{H}h$ where V and H stand respectively for the maximal values of the vertical and horizontal stretchings. We can remark that the type of the curve (type 1 or 2, quadratic or cubic) to stretch is preserved after stretching.

Time Processing for Each Model

It's obvious that the quadratic model requires less time processing than the cubic one, but after stretching a quadratic curve the result can't be used to draw the curve before its transformation into a cubic curve. This transformation is done through a procedure that we call "*quadToCub*". To compare the two models, we have to compare the time necessary to execute "*ebe*" with the time to compute "*qebe*" and "*quadToCub*". The compari-

Figure 17. (a) Example of stretching a quadratic curve in $\mathbf{B}_1^q$, (b) Example of stretching a quadratic curve in $\mathbf{B}_2^q$

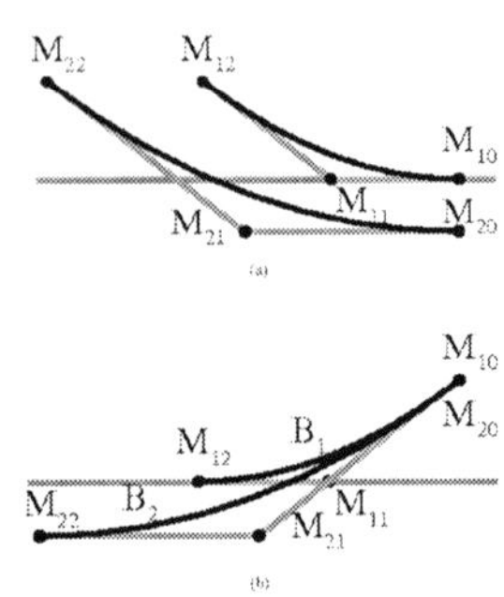

son can be done through considering the trajectory of the origin vertex of the preceding connection of the letter B in both cases of the models. We have programmed a PostScript document named "cubicReh.ps" in which a loop runs *n* times the ebe procedure applied to the connection of the letter B and strokes this curve where *n*=100000. In the end of the document (just after the loop) the "quit" operator is called to quit the PostScript interpreter and give the control to the shell process. We get the time necessary to run this document through executing the Linux command "time -p gs cubicReh.ps". In the same way, we constituted another document "quadReh.ps" but in the loop body, the procedure "*qebe*" is executed with the same values of stretching followed by "*quadToCub*". The number of iterations is also 100 000 (a big number to solve the problem of rounding values). The observed times for the two cases are presented in Table 1 (these values in Table 1 can change from a computer to another but the order will always be kept). So, we can conclude that the quadratic model is better than the cubic one.

IMPLEMENTATION OF STATIC LETTERS

When a letter is static, it is directly implemented in the font with the true outline drawn by the qalam's motion (Outlines without overlapping parts, see Figure 18). The true outline is determined with a mean external to the font applying the mathematical notions studied in the section 3.

Table 1. Comparison in time of the cubic and quadratic models

h	*v*	*n*
145.207425	12.100619	100000
Procedure	useful time	
ebe	6.182 s	
qebe+quadToCub	5.898 s	

OPTIMIZED IMPLEMENTATION OF FILLED IN DYNAMIC LETTERS

Implementation of the Static Part

In the case of variable sized letters, the encoding can be implemented in PostScript exactly as in the following example of the letter B. For the static part of the letter B, a non closed outline without overlapping parts is implemented in the font (see Figure 19). The outlines are then determined out of the font.

Implementation of the Stretchable Part

The stretchable part of a letter implementation can be illustrated once again through considering the preceding connection of the letter B. Whether we use a cubic or quadratic curve, the reconstitution of the set of points razed in the plane with the qalam in the preceding connection of the letter B is the same. The motion of the nib's head is shown in Figure 20(a). Let's denote by B^h the trajectory of the motion's origin. For all values

Figure 18. The Qalam's motion and the corresponding true outlines of the standalone DEL

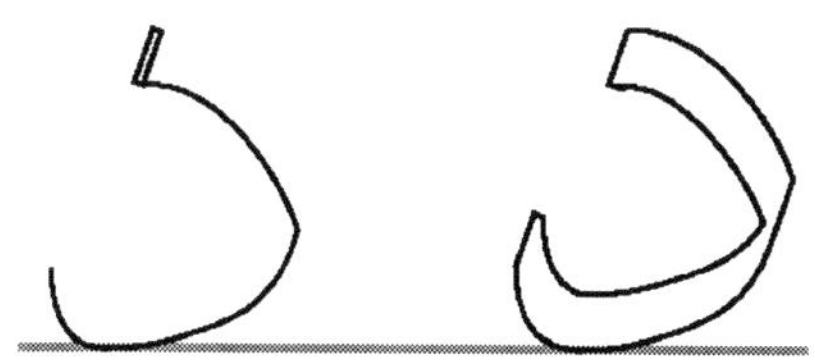

Figure 19. Non closed outline of the static part of End REH

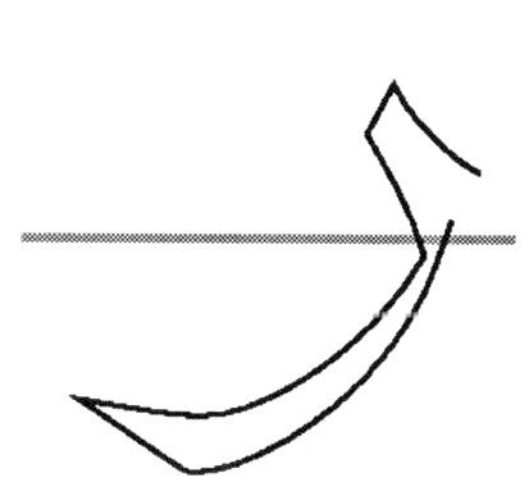

of h, the scalar function $\mathbf{R}_{\left(B^h,\vec{u_3}\right)}$ have an extrema on]0,1[(note that $\vec{u_2} - \vec{u_1} = \vec{u_3}$). Let t^h be this extrema (h here is not an exponent. It only means that t depends on h). The direct orthogonal ranges $\mathbf{R}_{\left(B^h,\vec{u_1}-\vec{u_0}\right)}$ and $\mathbf{R}_{\left(B^h,\vec{u_3}-\vec{u_2}\right)}$ are strictly monotone over [0,1]. So, the motions on $[0,t^h]$ and $[t^h,1]$ are normal. Consider the following notations:

- t^h is the extrema of $\mathbf{R}_{\left(B^h,\vec{u_3}\right)}$ on]0,1[,
- B_1^h and B_2^h are the curves obtained by the decomposition of B^h, applying the generalized Bézier algorithm of refinement (Barsky, 1985) with respect to t^h (see Figure 20(b)),
- $B_{1i}^h = t_{\vec{u_i}}\left(B_1^h\right),\ i \in \{0,1,2,3\} \quad (\vec{u_0} = \vec{0})$ and
- $B_{2i}^h = t_{\vec{u_i}}\left(B_2^h\right),\ i \in \{0,1,2,3\}$.

Then, we have the results:

- On $[0,t^h]$, the maximal curve is B_{12}^h and the minimal one is B_{10}^h
- On $[t^h,1]$, the maximal curve is B_{21}^h and the minimal one is B_{23}^h.

Figure 20. Motion of the stretchable part of End REH

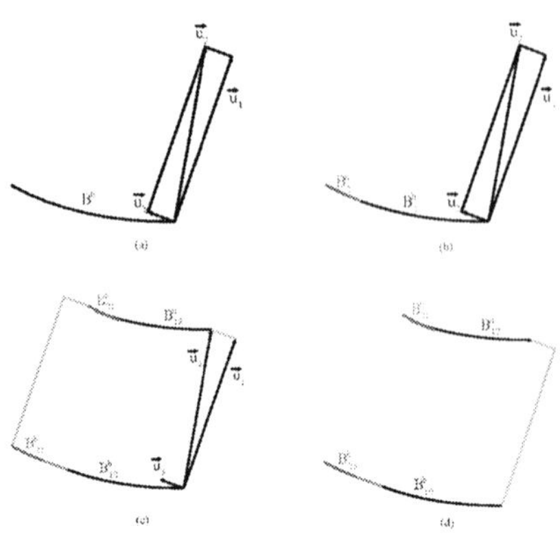

These results are illustrated in Figure 20 with h=0.

Figure 20(c) presents the overlapped outline corresponding to the set razed by the qalam in the preceding-connection when filled. But in the font, we use a non closed overlapping outline (see Figure 20(d)) to be fitted to the non closed static part of the letter B (presented in Figure 19).

As t^h changes as the value of h varies, this parameter must be computed in the font. Consequently, the Bézier refinement process should be incorporated to the procedure of drawing stretchable B.

Let's recall that the goal here is to optimize the implementation of the kashida in the font. In the sequel, we give the time necessary, in a procedure, to write the stretchable filled in letter REH through applying a quadratic and cubic stretching model.

Denote by t_q^h the parameter t^h in the case of the quadratic model (respectively t_c^h the same parameter in the cubic model). The expressions of t_q^h and t_c^h are in the Formulas 1 and 2 respectively:

$$t_q^h = \frac{47.79081298 + h}{63.67851945 + 1.0887286138 \cdot h} \qquad (1)$$

$$t_c^h = \frac{1412.000904 \cdot h + 82586.35211}{.0002 \cdot h + .0125202406} - \frac{22766.53323\sqrt{.003846591162 \cdot h^2 + .4499656282 \cdot h + 13.15899317}}{.0002 \cdot h + .0125202406} \qquad (2)$$

So, it is clear that the computing of the quadratic t_q^h requires less time than the cubic t_c^h. Also, the time used to refine a quadratic curve is less than the one we need in the case of a cubic curve. The same comparison holds in the case of shifting curves. In the case of a quadratic model, of course, the quadratic curves are to transform into cubic ones but the time to do so is less than the difference got for the compared previous operations. We have used a daily newspaper to find out the occurrences number of the letter B. We've found 5684 occurrence. In a first PostScript document, a font containing only the letter B is developed with a preceding-connection based on a quadratic model. In the second, the same is done with a cubic model. The preceding connection is parametrized in h, in the font to support the stretching. So, with a null value of stretching, the computing necessary for the stretching operation is also executed. The evaluation has been done only with null values of stretching. The amount of operations relative to the stretching is independent of the value of h. In the two documents, we've written the letter 5684 times. Then, we have an evaluation of the time to execute in the two cases. The results of such evaluation are presented in Table 2.

The daily newspaper was chosen in our study only because we have it in its electronic format what simplified the counting of the number of occurrences of B. This daily newspaper produces 90 000 copies (of course in one day) but the saved time 0.049 (0.88-0.831) using the quadratic model than the cubic for the letter REH will take place only in the first copy since the result of the first copy would be reused to produce the thousands of copies needed using the offset printing techniques. We should recall that this time is saved only for one letter and there are a lot of stretchable letter others than B. So, the quadratic model seems to be better than the cubic one. The case becomes more important when we have to print a big document (in term of pages) in more than one copy with a laser printer (printing some courses at some universities for example with laser copier-printers). The time saved with the quadratic model would be surely very important.

Table 2. Comparison between the complete implementation of the end REH in cubic and quadratic models

h	v	n
0	0	5684
Model	Time	
Quadratic	0.831 s	
Cubic	0.880 s	

OPTIMIZED IMPLEMENTATION OF OUTLINED DYNAMIC LETTERS

In this section we will show how can we get a font allowing to write Arabic with stretchable outlined letters. The letters should be implemented with non closed outlines to get writings like those in Figure 3. Samples of letters in this form are showed in Figure 21. In the same way, the concepts of implementation are illustrated with the letter B. The static part of the letter B is encoded in the same way as for the filled in version studied in the section 6.

Now what about the preceding connection. In this case, only the top and bottom parts of the connection are considered as it is presented in Figure 22. Figure 22 is obtained from Figure 20(d) through deleting the two edges of the qalam on the right. The connection is not on its final state because we have to remove the overlapping parts representing the intersection between the curves B_{12}^h and B_{21}^h (see Figure 22 with a big scaling factor).

The non overlapping curves of the preceding connection can't be directly determined because there is an intersection between B_{12}^h and B_{21}^h.

Figure 21. Letters with non closed and non overlapping outlines

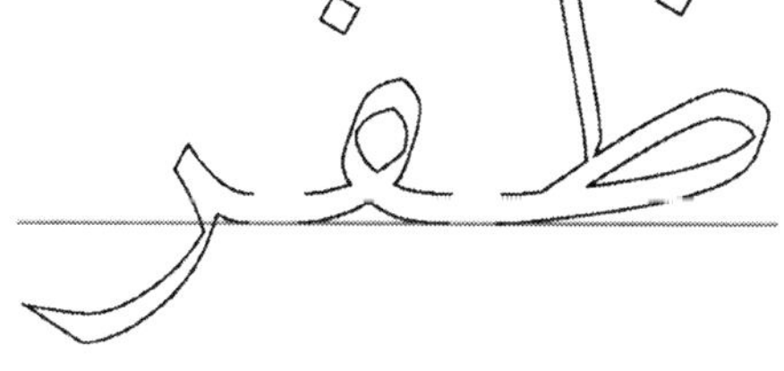

Figure 22. Opened overlapping of stretchable part of End REH

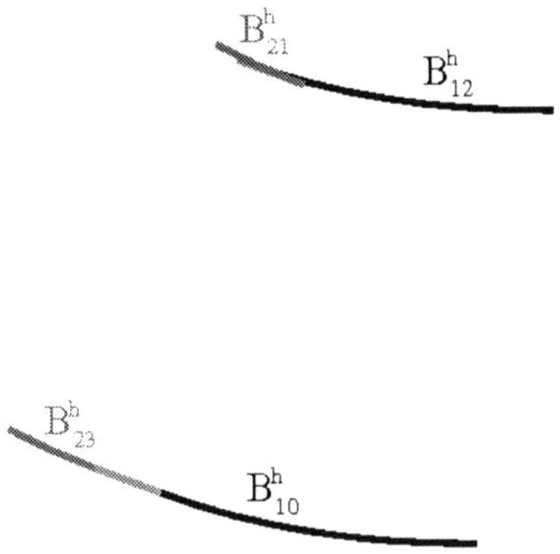

Note that this intersection is unique. Let r^h and s^h be the two variables on [0,1] characterizing the intersection coefficients of B^h_{12} and B^h_{21} respectively. Their values are solutions of the Equation 3.

$$B^h_{12}\left(r\right) - B^h_{21}\left(s\right) = \left(0,0\right) \quad (3)$$

The values of t^h, r^h and s^h change as h changes. The values are to be computed dynamically in the font. As B^h is a quadratic curve, the orthogonal range $\mathbf{R}'_{\left(B^h,\vec{u_3}\right)}$ is a linear function of t. Then, it is easy to determine explicitly t^h in function of h. The formula is given on the Equation 4. It was in order to get an easy and explicit determination of t^h that we were to represent the stretchable parts in letters with quadratic curves instead of cubic ones. The function t^h is a monotone increasing function of h.

$$t^h_q = \frac{47.79081298 + h}{63.67851945 + 1.0887286138 \cdot h} \quad (4)$$

In general, the determination of the intersection between two quadratic or cubic Bézier curves is done through iterations (there is no explicit solution). Since the PostScript procedure to produce a character, in a dynamic font, is repeated whenever the letter is to draw, the determination of the curves intersections coefficients in the procedure, applying an iterative algorithm is of a high cost. So, we have to find out a way to minimize the time necessary to compute r^h and s^h.

In order to implement a font in stretchable outlines, we use approximations. So, we need to consider some precisions or tolerances. In the following; we define the notions of digital equivalence and tolerance.

Definition 4 (Digital Equivalence): *Let $M_1=(x_1,y_1)$ and $M_2=(x_2,y_2)$ be two points in $\mathbb{Z}^2$. M_1 is digitally equivalent to M_2 if and only if* $|x_1-x_2|\leq 1$ and $|y_1-y_2|\leq 1$. *The digital equivalence is then denoted by $M_1 \equiv M_2$.*

So, for the visual aspect, a point in $\mathbb{Z}^2$ and points in his direct neighbor would then be considered as the same.

To each point in $\mathbb{R}^2$ to draw corresponds an image in $\mathbb{Z}^2$ by a function denoted N. The tolerance of a Bézier curve can then be defined as follows:

Definition 5 (Tolerance of a Bézier Curve): *Let B a Bézier curve and* $\tau = \frac{1}{n}$, $n \in \mathbb{N}^*$. τ is a tolerance of B if and only if for all t_1 *and* t_2 *in* [0,1] *we have:*

$|t_1 - t_2| < \tau \Rightarrow N(B(t_1)) \equiv N(B(t_2))$.

The notions of digital equivalence and the tolerance are tools toward the formalization of the visual accuracy. We can define the notion of the optimal tolerance.

Definition 6 (Optimal Tolerance): *Let B a Bézier curve. The optimal tolerance of B is the greater element of the set* $\left\{\frac{1}{m} \,/\, m \in \mathbb{N}^*,\ \frac{1}{m} \text{ is a tolerance of } B\right\}$.

We have the property:

Property 1: *Let us consider the Bézier curves* B_1, B_2 *and* B_3. *Let* τ_1, τ_2 and τ_3 their optimal tolerances respectively, then we have the properties:

- *if* B_2 *is a stretched version of* B_1 *then* $\tau_2 \leq \tau_1$,
- *if* B_2 *and* B_3 *are curves obtained from* B_1 *by a Bézier refinement according to a parameter t in* [0,1], *then we have* $\tau_2 \geq \tau_1$ *and* $\tau_3 \geq \tau_1$.

We can now continue the presentation of the method to determine he intersection coefficients. Let us consider once again the notations:

- τ_{12}^h the tolerance of B_{12}^h depending on *h*.
- τ_{21}^h the tolerance of B_{21}^h depending on *h*.

In the Naskh style, the stretching variable *h* can vary from 0 to *H*, where *H* is 6 diacritic points (12 dp for all the kashida and 6 dp for each of its components). Consider a font in 1000 points size, *H*=580.829699. The determination of the coefficients r^h and s^h would be based on approximations as follows.

The system Maple can be used to get the following properties:

Property 2:

- *The function* r^h *is monotone increasing of h on* [0,*H*], (1)
- *The function* s^h *is monotone increasing of h on the left edge of* [0,*H*] *and monotone decreasing of h on the right edge of* [0,*H*], (2)
- *The functions* τ_{12}^h and τ_{21}^h are monotone decreasing on [0,*H*], (3)
- *and* $\tau_{12}^h \leq \tau_{21}^h$ on [0,*H*]. *This means that for* $h \in [0,H]$. τ_{12}^h is an optimal tolerance of B_{12}^h and a tolerance of B_{21}^h. (4)

Now, we have all the properties necessary to build the function giving the approximated values of r^h and s^h.

Let $r_{\min}=r^0, r_{\max}=r^H$. Consider the sequence $R=(r_i)_{i=0,\dots,n}$ such that $r_i = r_{\min} + \frac{r_{\max} - r_{\min}}{n} i$, where $n = \left[\frac{r_{\max} - r_{\min}}{\tau_{12}^H}\right] + 1$. [*x*] stands for the integer part of *x*. Let's also consider the two sequences H=$(h_i)_{i=0,\dots,n}$ and $S=(s_i)_{i=0,\dots,n}$ such that $\{r_i, s_i\}_{i=0,\dots,n}$ are solutions of the Equation 3 where *h* and *s* are the unknown and *r* is given taking r_i as value. The system Maple can help to solve all the equations. In some cases, some of these equations can require some minutes when B^h is quadratic and even some hours when B^h is cubic. That's another reason to choose quadratic curves to encode dynamic parts. We get the following results:

- $r_{i+1} - r_i < \tau_{12}^H \ \forall i = 0,\dots,n-1$,
- $r_{i+1} - r_i < \tau_{12}^h \ \forall i = 0,\dots,n-1 \ \forall h \in [0,H]$ (according to the property 2(3)). This means that $\mathbf{N}(B_{12}^h(r_i)) \equiv \mathbf{N}(B_{12}^h(r_{i+1})) \ \forall h \in [0,H]$.
- $|s_i - s_{i+1}| < \tau_{21}^h \ \forall i = 0,\dots,n-1 \ \forall h \in [0,H]$ (according to the property 2(2,4)). This means that $\mathbf{N}(B_{21}^h(s_i)) \equiv \mathbf{N}(B_{21}^h(s_{i+1})) \ \forall h \in [0,H]$.

Finally, we have a property useful for the determination of the approximation function, $\forall i \in \{0,\dots,n-1\}$, $\forall h, h_i \leq h \leq h_{i+1}$ we have:

- $r_i \leq r^h \leq r_{i+1}$ and $\mathbf{N}(B_{12}^h(r^h)) \equiv \mathbf{N}(B_{12}^h(r_i))$ and so, $\mathbf{N}(B_{12}^h(r^h)) \equiv \mathbf{N}(B_{12}^h(r_{i+1}))$.
- ($s_i \leq s^h \leq s_{i+1}$ or $s_{i+1} \leq s^h \leq s_i$) and $\mathbf{N}(B_{21}^h(s^h)) \equiv \mathbf{N}(B_{21}^h(s_i))$ and so, $\mathbf{N}(B_{21}^h(s^h)) \equiv \mathbf{N}(B_{21}^h(s_{i+1}))$.

Then, we know very well the tolerant values of $B_{12}^h(r^h)$ and $B_{21}^h(s^h)$.

Now, consider the sequence $P=(P_i)_{i=0,\dots,n}=(r_i,s_i)_{i=0,\dots,n}$. Let's approximate the set of points P_i by a quadratic Bézier curve A such that $A(0)=P_0=(r_0,s_0)$ and $A(1)=P_n=(r_n,s_n)$. In order to approximate a set of points $\{P_0,\dots,P_n\}$ by a curve parametrized on [0,1], we may associate to every point P_i a coefficient t_i in [0,1] such that the sequence $(t_i)_{i=0,\dots,n}$ is strictly monotone increasing and $t_0=0$ and $t_n=1$.

First, let us determine $(t_i)_{i=0,\dots,n}$.

Recall that t^h (defined in the Equation 4) is a monotone increasing function of h. Since r^h is monotone increasing, the sequence $(h_i)_{i=0,\dots,n}$ deduced through the sequence $(r_i)_{i=0,\dots,n}$ is monotone increasing. Consider $(t_i)_{i=0,\dots,n}$ such that $t_i = \frac{t^{h_i} - t^0}{t^H - t^0}$. $(t_i)_{i=0,\dots,n}$ is a strictly monotone increasing sequence with $t_0=0$ and $t_n=1$.

Consider that the quadratic Bézier curve to be determined has the control points (r_0,s_0), (x_1,y_1) and (r_n,s_n). We have to determine (x_1,y_1) in order to minimize the value D (see Equation 5).

$$D = \sum_{i=0}^{n} \left(P_i - A\left(t_i\right)\right)^2 \tag{5}$$

D can be minimal if the following mandatory conditions are satisfied:

- $\frac{\partial D}{\partial x_1} = 0$ and
- $\frac{\partial D}{\partial y_1} = 0.$

$\frac{\partial D}{\partial x_1} = 0$ and $\frac{\partial D}{\partial y_1} = 0$ imply that:

- $x_1 = \frac{\sum_{i=0}^{n} t_i\left(1-t_i\right)\left(r_i - \left(1-t_i\right)^2 r_0 - t_i^2 r_n\right)}{2\sum_{i=0}^{n} t_i^2\left(1-t_i\right)^2}$

and

- $y_1 = \frac{\sum_{i=0}^{n} t_i\left(1-t_i\right)\left(s_i - \left(1-t_i\right)^2 s_0 - t_i^2 s_n\right)}{2\sum_{i=0}^{n} t_i^2\left(1-t_i\right)^2}.$

Suppose that $A(t)=(r(t),s(t))$. Then A is a good approximation if the condition in the Formula 6 is satisfied.

$$\left|r\left(t_i\right) - r_i\right| < \tau_{12}^{H} \; \forall i = 0,\dots,n \tag{6}$$

If the condition 6 isn't satisfied the sequences H and P are subdivided in two pairs of subsequences $\{(h_i)_{i=0,\dots,k},(P_i)_{i=0,\dots,k}\}$ and $\{(h_i)_{i=0,\dots,n},(P_i)_{i=0,\dots,n}\}$ such that k verify the Formula 7 and the process is repeated.

$$\left|r\left(t_k\right) - r_k\right| = \max_{i=0}^{n} \left|r\left(t_i\right) - r_i\right| \tag{7}$$

For a more concrete view, we give in some details the method used to determine the approximated outline of the stretchable part of the letter B i.e. the preceding connection. We recall that the preceding connection is a curve in $\mathbf{B}_1^q$ that is parameterized (respecting the stretching model given in the chapter) to take into account the stretching. As we know, the fonts in PostScript are designed in the size 1000 pt (PostScript point unit). The basic (i.e. the curve with a null stretching) preceding connection curve B has as control points in this size:

- $M_0=(0,0)$,
- $M_1=(-40.4367,0)$ and
- $M_2=(-67.99062, 14.92163)$

Let h be the horizontal stretching amount and v the vertical corresponding one. v verify that $v = \frac{V}{H}h$ where H and V are maximal amounts of stretching in horizontal and vertical directions respectively. Since H is six diacritic points and V is a half of a diacritic point then $v = \frac{h}{12}$. The control points of the preceding connection of the letter B^h when parameterized on h ($B^0=B$) become:

- $M_0 = \left(0, -\frac{h}{12}\right)$,
- $M_1 = \left(-40.43770052 - .8461247196 \cdot h, -\frac{h}{12}\right)$

  and
- M_2=(-67.99062-h, 14.92163).

The vectors defining the motion of the qalam in the size 1000 pt are:

- $\vec{u_0} = \overrightarrow{(0,0)}$,
- $\vec{u_1} = \overrightarrow{(24.2376, 66.5923)}$,
- $\vec{u_2} = \overrightarrow{(13.1389, 70.6320)}$ and
- $\vec{u_3} = \overrightarrow{(-11.0987, 4.0396)}$.

Solving the equation $\mathbf{R}'_{\left(B^h, \vec{u_3}\right)} = 0$ gives us the formula of the extrema t^h (h means here that t^h depends of h, it is not an exponent) in function of h such that

$$t^h = \frac{47.79081298 + h}{63.67851945 + 1.0887286138 \cdot h}.$$

In the size 1000 pt, the width of the diacritic point is 96.8049 and so H=580.829699. The variable h then describes the interval [0, 580.829699].

We have:

- t^0=.750501 and
- t^H=.903133,

We get the results concerning the Tolerances of B^h_{12} and B^h_{21} when h=H:

- $\tau^H_{12} = .00106952$ and
- $\tau^H_{12} = .0344828$.

Using Maple or other tools, we solve the Equation 3 for h=0 and h=H. So, we determine the following values:

- $r_{\min}$=r^0=.879858,
- $r_{\max}$=r^H=.980454.

We obtain:

- $n = \left\lceil \frac{r_{\max} - r_{\min}}{\tau^H_{12}} \right\rceil + 1 = 95$,
- $r_i = .879858 + \frac{.100596}{n} i = .879858 + .001058 \cdot i$

Getting the sequence $R=(r_i)_{i=0,\ldots,n}$, we use once again a computer algebra system such as Maple to solve the equation with r, taking r_i as value and considering s and h as variables. We get the table in Appendix A containing h_i, s_i and other values:

- $t_i = \frac{t^{h_i} - t^{h_0}}{t^H - t^{h_0}} = \frac{t^{h_i} - t^0}{t^H - t^0} = \frac{t^{h_i} - .750501}{.152632}$.

  $(t_i)_{i=0,\ldots,n}$ are real numbers in [0,1] to be as sociated to $P_i=(r_i,s_i)_{i=0,\ldots,n}$ for approximation.
- $r(t)$ and $s(t)$ are component functions of a quadratic Bézier curve $A(t)$ where:
  - $r(t)=(1-t)^2r_0+2t(1-t)x_1+t^2r_{95}$
  - $s(t)=(1-t)^2s_0+2t(1-t)y_1+t^2s_{95}$

To minimize D, we get (x_1,y_1)=(0.912975, 0.494131).

Then we have,

- $\Delta_r = \operatorname{Max}_{i=0}^{n} \left| r(t_i) - r_i \right| = .002442$ and
- $\Delta_s = \operatorname{Max}_{i=0}^{n} \left| s(t_i) - s_i \right| = .0388$

We have $\Delta_r > \tau^H_{12}$, so the sequences would be subdivided at index i=72 (see the red slanted bold line on the table of Appendix A).

The process is repeated with the two sub-sequences obtained in Appendix B and C. In Appendix B and C, we remark that $\Delta_r < \tau_{12}^H$ and automatically, due to the construction of the sequence R, $\Delta_s < \tau_{21}^H$.

We get then a curve A_1, with using the Appendix B, of control points M_{10}=(0.879858, 0.361504), M_{11}=(0.911133, 0.413212) and M_{12}=(0.956099, 0.313817).

In the same way, we get a curve A_2, with using Appendix C, with control points M_{20}=(0.956099, 0.313817), M_{21}=(0.966307, 0.282649) and M_{22}(0.980454, 0.182371).

These two curves allow us to approximate the intersection coefficients. For more clarity let's give an abstract algorithm. Let h be a stretching amount, then we have:

```
IF h is in [0, 179.595499[THEN
BEGIN
  t = (t^h -.750501) / (.877231-.750501);
  A1(t);
END
ELSE
 IF h is in [179.595499,
580.818536[THEN
 BEGIN
  t = (t^h -.877231) / (.903132-.877231);
  A2(t);
 END
```

We conclude that for the preceding connection of the letter B, the determination of the intersection coefficients are computed with the evaluation of a curve A_1 where h is in [0, 179.595499[and another curve A_2 if h is in [179.595499, 580.818536[.

The approximation has been tested with arbitrary values of h and we got intersection coefficients with respect of the curves tolerances.

With this mechanism, we can encode the preceding connection to get the stretchable letter B with non closed outline to be used to write words in outlines (see Figure 23).

Now, the process to determine the intersection coefficients can be more improved. Actually, instead of a quadratic approximation of the sequence of points $P=(P_i)_{i=0,...,n}=(r_i,s_i)_{i=0,...,n}$, we would use a cubic one. The reason why we do this is explained in the following.

Let's approximate the set of points P_i respecting the same way and constraints but with a cubic Bézier curve B of control point (r_0,s_0), (x_1,y_1), (x_2,y_2) and (r_n,s_n). We have to determine (x_1,y_1) and (x_2, y_2) in order to minimize D (see equation 5).

D can be minimal if the following mandatory conditions are satisfied:

- $\dfrac{\partial D}{\partial x_1} = 0,$
- $\dfrac{\partial D}{\partial y_1} = 0,$
- $\dfrac{\partial D}{\partial x_2} = 0$ and
- $\dfrac{\partial D}{\partial y_2} = 0.$

We get a system with four equations and x_1, x_2, y_1 and y_2 as unknowns. Solving the system through considering the preceding connection of the letter B, the values of the unknown control points are as follows:

- (x_1,y_1)=(0.910238, 0.328969)
- (x_2,y_2)=(0.927859, 0.501073)

Now, let us consider the Bézier curve B of control points (r_0,s_0)=(0.879858, 0.361504),

Figure 23. Opened non overlapping outline of End REH

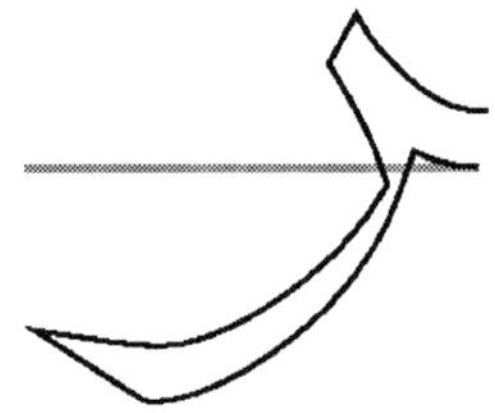

(x_1,y_1)=(0.910238, 0.328969), (x_2,y_2)=(0.927859, 0.501073) and (r_{95},s_{95})=(0.980454, 0.182371). The intersection coefficients are $r(t)$ and $s(t)$ components of $B(t)=(r(t),s(t))$. As presented in Appendix D, we have:

- $\Delta_r = \operatorname{Max}_{i=0}^{n} \left| r\left(t_i\right) - r_i \right| = .000501$ and so $\Delta_r < \tau_{12}^H$.
- $\Delta_s = \operatorname{Max}_{i=0}^{n} \left| s\left(t_i\right) - s_i \right| = .011959$ and then $\Delta_s < \tau_{21}^H$.

We conclude that only one cubic curve approximates the sequences of points $(P_i)_{i=0,\ldots,n}=(r_i,s_i)_{i=0,\ldots,n}$.

A comparison between the quadratic approximation and the cubic one seem to be necessary. It is obvious that the evaluation of a cubic Bézier curve requires more time than a quadratic one. But in our case, the set of points $(P_i)_{i=0,\ldots,n}$ is approximated by two quadratic curves. So, we have to do some alternative tests about the value of h, when it is in [0, 179.595499[or in [179.595499, 580.818536[. We know that in algorithmic theory, tests are generally big CPU time consumers especially in PostFix programming languages. So, a comparison of the two approximation models would help to determine the better one. We have developed two PostScript files where we write the letter in opened non overlapping outlines (as in Figure 23) 1000 times based on the quadratic approximation in first one and on the cubic approximation in the second one. The time necessary in the two cases is presented in Table 3. We remark that the cubic approximation of the intersection coefficients calculation is better (tests in PostScript are of high cost in CPU time).

For the stretchable version of letter E in the end of a word, the corresponding generated sequences of points $(P_i)_{i=0,\ldots,n}$ can be approximated only by one quadratic Bézier curve. So, it has been implemented with a quadratic Bézier curve approximation. But for the letter B, the approximation process is based on a cubic Bézier curve.

In the section 6, we have implemented the letter to be filled in with overlapping outlines. A part will be painted twice when filling in the closed path defining this letter. With reference to the section 7, we can encode the letter B with true outlines, in other words with outlines without any overlapping. This is possible because we can determine the intersection and remove the overlapping. What would require less time when we have to draw a filled in B, encoding with overlapping outlines or outlines without overlapping. An evaluation of the two methods is shown in Table 4.

We conclude that when we have to write filled in letters, we don't need to take into account the intersection since that will not optimize the processing.

CONCLUSION

Drawing stretchable, variable sized outlined or darken Arabic letters needs the development of techniques to optimize the implementation of such letters and PostScript seem not to be directly suit-

Table 3. Comparison in time of the cubic and quadratic approximations

h	*v*	*n*
145.20742	12.100619	1000
Approximation	Time	
Quadratic	2.18 s	
Cubic	1.22 s	

Table 4. Filled End REH, overlapping outlines versus non overlapping outlines

h	*v*	*n*
145.20742	12.100619	1000
Outlines	Time	
overlapping	6.74 s	
Non overlapping	7.03 s	

able for dynamic Arabic fonts. On the other hand, to typeset an Arabic document, with all kinds of Arabic letters, a unique font is not enough. The availability of various fonts and the variety of letters inside the same font contribute significantly to improve the rendering of Arabic documents respecting the rules of Arabic calligraphy. Only the Naskh style, where the nib's head keep in a constant inclination, has been studied here. This approach will be extended next to styles where the nib's head can be in translation and/or in rotation. This can also help to compose calligraphic mathematical formulas. So, until Now, we only developed some pieces of the dynamic font. The concepts presented here are suitable for other letters because the preceding connections have the same general shape. Nevertheless, developing the whole dynamic font in a reasonable time requires also the development of other specific graphical tools. That will be done in coming works.

REFERENCES

Adobe Systems Incorporated. (1999). *PostScript Language Reference Manual*. Reading, MA: Addison-Wesley.

André, J., & Borghi, B. (1990). Dynamic Fonts. *PostScript Language Journal*, *2*(3), 4–6.

Barsky, B. A. (1985). *Arbitrary Subdivision of Bézier Curves (Technical Report UCB.CSD 85/265)*. Computer Science Division, University of California.

Bayar, A., & Sami, K. (2008). *An Optimal Way to Encode the Outlines of Variable Sized Arabic Letters in a PostScript Font*. Presented at The 16th International Conference in Central Europe on Computer Graphics, Visualization and Computer Vision, Full Papers Proceedings (pp.57-64), University of West Bohemia, Plzen Czech Republic.

Bayar, A., & Sami, K. (2008). Optimization of the curvilinear stretching in a PostScript font with quadratic Bézier curves. Presented at The International Arab Conference of e-Technology. In [Arab Open University, Amman, Jordan.]. *Proceedings of IACe-T, 2008*, 97–104.

Bayar, A., & Sami, K. (2009). How a font can respect rules of Arabic calligraphy. *The International Arab Journal of e-Technology, 1*(1).

Bézier, P. E. (19770. *Essai de Définition Numérique des Courbes et des Surfaces Expérimentales*. Ph.D. dissertation, Université Pierre et Marie Curie, Paris. Berry, D. M. (1999). Stretching Letter and Slanted-Baseline Formatting for Arabic, Hebrew and Persian with dittroff/fforttid and Dynamic PostScript Fonts. *Software-Practice and Experience, 29*(15), 1417-1457.

Haralambous, Y., & Plaice, J. (1997). *Multilingual Typesetting with \Omega, a Case Study: Arabic.* Presented at the International Symposium on Multilingual Information Processing'97, Tsukuba, Japan.

Joris, V. H. (2003). *The TeXmacs User Manual, Version 1.0.6.6*. Retrieved from http://www.texmacs.org

Knuth, D. E. (1984). *The TeXBook, Computers and Typesetting*. Reading, MA: Addison-Wesley.

Knuth, D. E. (1986). *The MetafontBook, Computers and Typesetting*. MA: Addison-Wesley.

Lagally, K. (2004). *ArabTEX User Manual*. Universitat Stuttgart, Fakultat Informatik.

Lamport, L. (1985). *LaTeX-A Document Preparation System*. Reading, MA: Addison Wesley.

Lazrek, A. (2001). A package for typesetting Arabic mathematical formulas. *Die TeXnische Komodie, DANTE e.V., 13*(2), 54-66.

Lazrek, A. (2003). *CurExt, Typesetting variable-sized curved symbols*. Presented at EuroTeX 2003 Pre-prints: 14th. European TeX conference (pp. 47-71), Brest, France.

LyX Team. (2004). *The LyX User Manual*. Retrieved fromhttp://www.LyX.org

Reeves, W. T. (1981). *Quantitative Representations of Complex Dynamic Shapes for Motion Analysis*, PhD thesis, University of Toronto, Canada.

Weise, D., & Adler, D. (1992). *TrueType and Microsoft Windows 3.1*. Redmond, WA: Technical Report, Microsoft Corporation.

APPENDIX A

Quadratic Approximation: First Stage

i	h_i	t^{h_i}	r_i	s_i	t_i	$r(t_i)$	$\|r(t_i)-r_i\|$	$s(t_i)$	$\|s(t_i)-s_i\|$
0	0.000000	0.750501	0.879858	0.361504	0.000000	0.879858	0.000000	0.361504	0.000000
1	0.673936	0.752415	0.880917	0.362009	0.012538	0.880694	0.000223	0.364760	0.002751
2	1.365277	0.754333	0.881976	0.362514	0.025107	0.881543	0.000433	0.367884	0.005370
3	2.074384	0.756256	0.883035	0.363018	0.037701	0.882404	0.000631	0.370873	0.007855
4	2.801842	0.758181	0.884094	0.363519	0.050317	0.883278	0.000816	0.373726	0.010207
5	3.548259	0.760110	0.885153	0.364018	0.062955	0.884164	0.000989	0.376442	0.012424
6	4.314267	0.762042	0.886211	0.364514	0.075613	0.885063	0.001148	0.379020	0.014506
7	5.100522	0.763977	0.887270	0.365007	0.088287	0.885973	0.001297	0.381459	0.016452
8	5.907705	0.765914	0.888329	0.365494	0.100978	0.886897	0.001432	0.383758	0.018264
9	6.736524	0.767853	0.889388	0.365977	0.113681	0.887832	0.001556	0.385915	0.019938
10	7.587715	0.769793	0.890447	0.366453	0.126396	0.888779	0.001668	0.387932	0.021479
11	8.461604	0.771734	0.891506	0.366921	0.139113	0.889737	0.001769	0.389804	0.022883
12	9.360083	0.773678	0.892565	0.367383	0.151847	0.890708	0.001857	0.391536	0.024153
13	10.282207	0.775620	0.893624	0.367834	0.164570	0.891689	0.001935	0.393121	0.025287
14	11.231929	0.777566	0.894683	0.368277	0.177321	0.892683	0.002000	0.394566	0.026289
15	12.207061	0.779510	0.895742	0.368708	0.190058	0.893688	0.002054	0.395865	0.027157
16	13.209627	0.781454	0.896800	0.369127	0.202791	0.894703	0.002097	0.397020	0.027893
17	14.240595	0.783396	0.897859	0.369533	0.215520	0.895729	0.002130	0.398030	0.028497
18	15.300972	0.785338	0.898918	0.369924	0.228240	0.896765	0.002153	0.398896	0.028972
19	16.391803	0.787278	0.899977	0.370300	0.240950	0.897812	0.002165	0.399617	0.029317
20	17.514181	0.789216	0.901036	0.370658	0.253646	0.898869	0.002167	0.400194	0.029536
21	18.669243	0.791151	0.902095	0.370998	0.266326	0.899935	0.002160	0.400628	0.029630
22	19.858172	0.793084	0.903154	0.371318	0.278988	0.901011	0.002143	0.400918	0.029600
23	21.082201	0.795013	0.904213	0.371617	0.291628	0.902096	0.002117	0.401066	0.029449
24	22.342619	0.796939	0.905272	0.371892	0.304244	0.903190	0.002082	0.401072	0.029180
25	23.640767	0.798860	0.906331	0.372144	0.316833	0.904293	0.002038	0.400936	0.028792
26	24.978048	0.800777	0.907390	0.372368	0.329392	0.905403	0.001987	0.400661	0.028293
27	26.355926	0.802689	0.908448	0.372565	0.341918	0.906522	0.001926	0.400247	0.027682
28	27.775924	0.804595	0.909507	0.372732	0.354409	0.907648	0.001859	0.399695	0.026963
29	29.239645	0.806496	0.910566	0.372867	0.366860	0.908781	0.001785	0.399007	0.026140
30	30.748755	0.808390	0.911625	0.372969	0.379270	0.909921	0.001704	0.398184	0.025215
31	32.305002	0.810277	0.912684	0.373035	0.391636	0.911068	0.001616	0.397227	0.024192
32	33.910209	0.812157	0.913743	0.373064	0.403954	0.912221	0.001522	0.396140	0.023076
33	35.566291	0.814030	0.914802	0.373053	0.416222	0.913379	0.001423	0.394923	0.021870
34	37.275256	0.815894	0.915861	0.372999	0.428437	0.914543	0.001318	0.393578	0.020579

continues on following page

Appendix A. continued

i	h_i	t^{h_i}	r_i	s_i	t_i	$r(t_i)$	$\|r(t_i)-r_i\|$	$s(t_i)$	$\|s(t_i)-s_i\|$
35	39.039201	0.817750	0.916920	0.372902	0.440596	0.915711	0.001209	0.392107	0.019205
36	40.860332	0.819597	0.917979	0.372759	0.452696	0.916884	0.001095	0.390514	0.017755
37	42.740959	0.821434	0.919037	0.372566	0.464735	0.918061	0.000976	0.388799	0.016233
38	44.683515	0.823262	0.920096	0.372323	0.476709	0.919241	0.000855	0.386965	0.014642
39	46.690556	0.825079	0.921155	0.372025	0.488616	0.920425	0.000730	0.385016	0.012991
40	48.764762	0.826886	0.922214	0.371672	0.500453	0.921611	0.000603	0.382953	0.011281
41	50.908965	0.828682	0.923273	0.371260	0.512218	0.922800	0.000473	0.380779	0.009519
42	53.126142	0.830466	0.924332	0.370787	0.523908	0.923990	0.000342	0.378498	0.007711
43	55.419434	0.832238	0.925391	0.370249	0.535520	0.925182	0.000209	0.376111	0.005862
44	57.792151	0.833999	0.926450	0.369645	0.547053	0.926375	0.000075	0.373622	0.003977
45	60.247801	0.835746	0.927509	0.368972	0.558503	0.927568	0.000059	0.371033	0.002061
46	62.790070	0.837481	0.928568	0.368227	0.569869	0.928762	0.000194	0.368349	0.000122
47	65.422883	0.839203	0.929627	0.367406	0.581148	0.929955	0.000328	0.365572	0.001834
48	68.150378	0.840910	0.930685	0.366508	0.592337	0.931147	0.000462	0.362705	0.003803
49	70.976950	0.842604	0.931744	0.365529	0.603436	0.932338	0.000594	0.359751	0.005778
50	73.907257	0.844284	0.932803	0.364466	0.614442	0.933528	0.000725	0.356714	0.007752
51	76.946252	0.845950	0.933862	0.363316	0.625353	0.934715	0.000853	0.353596	0.009720
52	80.099208	0.847600	0.934921	0.362077	0.636168	0.935901	0.000980	0.350402	0.011675
53	83.371720	0.849236	0.935980	0.360745	0.646884	0.937083	0.001103	0.347135	0.013610
54	86.769758	0.850856	0.937039	0.359318	0.657500	0.938262	0.001223	0.343797	0.015521
55	90.299714	0.852461	0.938098	0.357792	0.668015	0.939437	0.001339	0.340393	0.017399
56	93.968376	0.854050	0.939157	0.356164	0.678427	0.940608	0.001451	0.336925	0.019239
57	97.783034	0.855624	0.940216	0.354432	0.688735	0.941775	0.001559	0.333396	0.021036
58	101.751486	0.857181	0.941274	0.352592	0.698937	0.942938	0.001664	0.329811	0.022781
59	105.882105	0.858722	0.942333	0.350641	0.709033	0.944095	0.001762	0.326172	0.024469
60	110.183864	0.860247	0.943392	0.348576	0.719022	0.945247	0.001855	0.322483	0.026093
61	114.666422	0.861755	0.944451	0.346394	0.728903	0.946393	0.001942	0.318746	0.027648
62	119.340180	0.863246	0.945510	0.344093	0.738675	0.947533	0.002023	0.314965	0.029128
63	124.216353	0.864721	0.946569	0.341668	0.748337	0.948666	0.002097	0.311143	0.030525
64	129.307075	0.866179	0.947628	0.339117	0.757889	0.949793	0.002165	0.307283	0.031834
65	134.625430	0.867620	0.948687	0.336437	0.767330	0.950913	0.002226	0.303389	0.033048
66	140.185658	0.869044	0.949746	0.333625	0.776659	0.952026	0.002280	0.299462	0.034163
67	146.004674	0.870451	0.950805	0.330678	0.785880	0.953132	0.002327	0.295505	0.035173
68	152.096321	0.871841	0.951864	0.327593	0.794987	0.954230	0.002366	0.291523	0.036070
69	158.480296	0.873214	0.952923	0.324368	0.803982	0.955320	0.002397	0.287517	0.036851
70	165.176589	0.874570	0.953982	0.320998	0.812866	0.956402	0.002420	0.283491	0.037507
71	172.207011	0.875909	0.955041	0.317483	0.821637	0.957476	0.002435	0.279446	0.038037
72	*179.595499*	*0.877231*	*0.956099*	*0.313817*	*0.830298*	*0.958541*	*0.002442*	*0.275386*	*0.038431*

continues on following page

Appendix A. continued

i	h_i	t^{h_i}	r_i	s_i	t_i	$r(t_i)$	$\lvert r(t_i)-r_i\rvert$	$s(t_i)$	$\lvert s(t_i)-s_i\rvert$
73	187.368344	0.878535	0.957158	0.310000	0.838847	0.959597	0.002439	0.271312	0.038688
74	195.554501	0.879823	0.958217	0.306028	0.847284	0.960645	0.002428	0.267228	0.038800
75	204.185960	0.881094	0.959276	0.301898	0.855612	0.961684	0.002408	0.263135	0.038763
76	213.298038	0.882348	0.960335	0.297608	0.863829	0.962714	0.002379	0.259036	0.038572
77	222.930039	0.883586	0.961394	0.293154	0.871936	0.963734	0.002340	0.254933	0.038221
78	233.125610	0.884807	0.962453	0.288535	0.879934	0.964746	0.002293	0.250828	0.037707
79	243.933484	0.886011	0.963512	0.283748	0.887824	0.965747	0.002235	0.246723	0.037025
80	255.408273	0.887199	0.964571	0.278791	0.895606	0.966740	0.002169	0.242620	0.036171
81	267.611167	0.888370	0.965630	0.273660	0.903281	0.967722	0.002092	0.238520	0.035140
82	280.611343	0.889525	0.966688	0.268353	0.910849	0.968695	0.002007	0.234426	0.033927
83	294.486893	0.890664	0.967747	0.262869	0.918312	0.969659	0.001912	0.230340	0.032529
84	309.326515	0.891788	0.968806	0.257204	0.925671	0.970613	0.001807	0.226262	0.030942
85	325.231603	0.892895	0.969865	0.251357	0.932926	0.971556	0.001691	0.222194	0.029163
86	342.317952	0.893986	0.970924	0.245325	0.940078	0.972490	0.001566	0.218138	0.027187
87	360.719117	0.895063	0.971983	0.239106	0.947128	0.973415	0.001432	0.214095	0.025011
88	380.589646	0.896123	0.973042	0.232698	0.954078	0.974329	0.001287	0.210067	0.022631
89	402.109227	0.897169	0.974101	0.226098	0.960929	0.975233	0.001132	0.206054	0.020044
90	425.488075	0.898200	0.975160	0.219305	0.967680	0.976128	0.000968	0.202059	0.017246
91	450.974391	0.899215	0.976219	0.212316	0.974335	0.977013	0.000794	0.198081	0.014235
92	478.861844	0.900216	0.977278	0.205130	0.980893	0.977888	0.000610	0.194122	0.011008
93	509.502026	0.901203	0.978336	0.197745	0.987356	0.978753	0.000417	0.190184	0.007561
94	543.318879	0.902175	0.979395	0.190159	0.993725	0.979609	0.000214	0.186266	0.003893
95	580.818536	0.903132	0.980454	0.182371	1.000000	0.980454	0.000000	0.182371	0.000000
			x_1:	0.912975		Δ_r:	0.002442	Δ_s:	0.038800
			:	0.494131					

APPENDIX B

Quadratic Approximation: Second Stage, First Part

i	h_i	t^{h_i}	r_i	s_i	t_i	$r(t_i)$	$\lvert r(t_i)-r_i\rvert$	$s(t_i)$	$\lvert s(t_i)-s_i\rvert$
0	0.000000	0.750501	0.879858	0.361504	0.000000	0.879858	0.000000	0.361504	0.000000
1	0.673936	0.752415	0.880917	0.362009	0.015101	0.880806	0.000111	0.363031	0.001022
2	1.365277	0.754333	0.881976	0.362514	0.030239	0.881762	0.000214	0.364493	0.001979
3	2.074384	0.756256	0.883035	0.363018	0.045406	0.882726	0.000309	0.365888	0.002870
4	2.801842	0.758181	0.884094	0.363519	0.060602	0.883699	0.000395	0.367216	0.003697

continues on following page

Appendix B. continued

i	h_i	t^{h_i}	r_i	s_i	t_i	$r(t_i)$	$\|r(t_i)-r_i\|$	$s(t_i)$	$\|s(t_i)-s_i\|$
5	3.548259	0.760110	0.885153	0.364018	0.075823	0.884679	0.000474	0.368477	0.004459
6	4.314267	0.762042	0.886211	0.364514	0.091067	0.885668	0.000543	0.369669	0.005155
7	5.100522	0.763977	0.887270	0.365007	0.106332	0.886664	0.000606	0.370792	0.005785
8	5.907705	0.765914	0.888329	0.365494	0.121616	0.887668	0.000661	0.371846	0.006352
9	6.736524	0.767853	0.889388	0.365977	0.136916	0.888679	0.000709	0.372831	0.006854
10	7.587715	0.769793	0.890447	0.366453	0.152229	0.889697	0.000750	0.373745	0.007292
11	8.461604	0.771734	0.891506	0.366921	0.167546	0.890722	0.000784	0.374589	0.007668
12	9.360083	0.773678	0.892565	0.367383	0.182882	0.891755	0.000810	0.375363	0.007980
13	10.282207	0.775620	0.893624	0.367834	0.198206	0.892794	0.000830	0.376065	0.008231
14	11.231929	0.777566	0.894683	0.368277	0.213564	0.893841	0.000842	0.376698	0.008421
15	12.207061	0.779510	0.895742	0.368708	0.228903	0.894893	0.000849	0.377259	0.008551
16	13.209627	0.781454	0.896800	0.369127	0.244239	0.895952	0.000848	0.377749	0.008622
17	14.240595	0.783396	0.897859	0.369533	0.259569	0.897016	0.000843	0.378167	0.008634
18	15.300972	0.785338	0.898918	0.369924	0.274889	0.898087	0.000831	0.378514	0.008590
19	16.391803	0.787278	0.899977	0.370300	0.290197	0.899163	0.000814	0.378790	0.008490
20	17.514181	0.789216	0.901036	0.370658	0.305488	0.900244	0.000792	0.378995	0.008337
21	18.669243	0.791151	0.902095	0.370998	0.320760	0.901330	0.000765	0.379129	0.008131
22	19.858172	0.793084	0.903154	0.371318	0.336010	0.902421	0.000733	0.379193	0.007875
23	21.082201	0.795013	0.904213	0.371617	0.351234	0.903516	0.000697	0.379186	0.007569
24	22.342619	0.796939	0.905272	0.371892	0.366428	0.904616	0.000656	0.379110	0.007218
25	23.640767	0.798860	0.906331	0.372144	0.381590	0.905720	0.000611	0.378964	0.006820
26	24.978048	0.800777	0.907390	0.372368	0.396716	0.906827	0.000563	0.378750	0.006382
27	26.355926	0.802689	0.908448	0.372565	0.411802	0.907938	0.000510	0.378467	0.005902
28	27.775924	0.804595	0.909507	0.372732	0.426845	0.909051	0.000456	0.378116	0.005384
29	29.239645	0.806496	0.910566	0.372867	0.441842	0.910168	0.000398	0.377699	0.004832
30	30.748755	0.808390	0.911625	0.372969	0.456788	0.911287	0.000338	0.377215	0.004246
31	32.305002	0.810277	0.912684	0.373035	0.471681	0.912408	0.000276	0.376665	0.003630
32	33.910209	0.812157	0.913743	0.373064	0.486517	0.913530	0.000213	0.376052	0.002988
33	35.566291	0.814030	0.914802	0.373053	0.501293	0.914654	0.000148	0.375374	0.002321
34	37.275256	0.815894	0.915861	0.372999	0.516004	0.915779	0.000082	0.374634	0.001635
35	39.039201	0.817750	0.916920	0.372902	0.530648	0.916905	0.000015	0.373833	0.000931
36	40.860332	0.819597	0.917979	0.372759	0.545221	0.918031	0.000052	0.372971	0.000212
37	42.740959	0.821434	0.919037	0.372566	0.559720	0.919158	0.000121	0.372049	0.000517
38	44.683515	0.823262	0.920096	0.372323	0.574142	0.920283	0.000187	0.371070	0.001253
39	46.690556	0.825079	0.921155	0.372025	0.588483	0.921409	0.000254	0.370034	0.001991
40	48.764762	0.826886	0.922214	0.371672	0.602739	0.922533	0.000319	0.368942	0.002730
41	50.908965	0.828682	0.923273	0.371260	0.616909	0.923656	0.000383	0.367796	0.003464
42	53.126142	0.830466	0.924332	0.370787	0.630988	0.924777	0.000445	0.366597	0.004190

continues on following page

Appendix B. continued

i	h_i	t^{h_i}	r_i	s_i	t_i	$r(t_i)$	$\|r(t_i)-r_i\|$	$s(t_i)$	$\|s(t_i)-s_i\|$
43	55.419434	0.832238	0.925391	0.370249	0.644974	0.925896	0.000505	0.365347	0.004902
44	57.792151	0.833999	0.926450	0.369645	0.658863	0.927013	0.000563	0.364047	0.005598
45	60.247801	0.835746	0.927509	0.368972	0.672654	0.928127	0.000618	0.362699	0.006273
46	62.790070	0.837481	0.928568	0.368227	0.686343	0.929238	0.000670	0.361303	0.006924
47	65.422883	0.839203	0.929627	0.367406	0.699927	0.930345	0.000718	0.359863	0.007543
48	68.150378	0.840910	0.930685	0.366508	0.713404	0.931449	0.000764	0.358378	0.008130
49	70.976950	0.842604	0.931744	0.365529	0.726771	0.932549	0.000805	0.356852	0.008677
50	73.907257	0.844284	0.932803	0.364466	0.740026	0.933644	0.000841	0.355285	0.009181
51	76.946252	0.845950	0.933862	0.363316	0.753168	0.934735	0.000873	0.353679	0.009637
52	80.099208	0.847600	0.934921	0.362077	0.766192	0.935821	0.000900	0.352035	0.010042
53	83.371720	0.849236	0.935980	0.360745	0.779099	0.936901	0.000921	0.350357	0.010388
54	86.769758	0.850856	0.937039	0.359318	0.791885	0.937976	0.000937	0.348644	0.010674
55	90.299714	0.852461	0.938098	0.357792	0.804548	0.939045	0.000947	0.346898	0.010894
56	93.968376	0.854050	0.939157	0.356164	0.817088	0.940107	0.000950	0.345123	0.011041
57	97.783034	0.855624	0.940216	0.354432	0.829503	0.941164	0.000948	0.343318	0.011114
58	101.751486	0.857181	0.941274	0.352592	0.841791	0.942214	0.000940	0.341485	0.011107
59	105.882105	0.858722	0.942333	0.350641	0.853951	0.943256	0.000923	0.339627	0.011014
60	110.183864	0.860247	0.943392	0.348576	0.865981	0.944292	0.000900	0.337745	0.010831
61	114.666422	0.861755	0.944451	0.346394	0.877882	0.945321	0.000870	0.335840	0.010554
62	119.340180	0.863246	0.945510	0.344093	0.889650	0.946342	0.000832	0.333913	0.010180
63	124.216353	0.864721	0.946569	0.341668	0.901287	0.947355	0.000786	0.331968	0.009700
64	129.307075	0.866179	0.947628	0.339117	0.912791	0.948360	0.000732	0.330004	0.009113
65	134.625430	0.867620	0.948687	0.336437	0.924162	0.949357	0.000670	0.328024	0.008413
66	140.185658	0.869044	0.949746	0.333625	0.935399	0.950346	0.000600	0.326028	0.007597
67	146.004674	0.870451	0.950805	0.330678	0.946504	0.951327	0.000522	0.324019	0.006659
68	152.096321	0.871841	0.951864	0.327593	0.957473	0.952299	0.000435	0.321998	0.005595
69	158.480296	0.873214	0.952923	0.324368	0.968306	0.953262	0.000339	0.319966	0.004402
70	165.176589	0.874570	0.953982	0.320998	0.979005	0.954217	0.000235	0.317924	0.003074
71	172.207011	0.875909	0.955041	0.317483	0.989570	0.955162	0.000121	0.315874	0.001609
72	179.595499	0.877231	0.956099	0.313817	1.000000	0.956099	0.000000	0.313817	0.000000
			x_1:	0.911133		Δ_r:	0.000950	Δ_s:	0.011114
			y_1:	0.413212					

APPENDIX C

Quadratic Approximation: Second Stage, Second Part

i	h_i	t^{h_i}	r_i	s_i	t_i	$r(t_i)$	$\lvert r(t_i)-r_i \rvert$	$s(t_i)$	$\lvert s(t_i)-s_i \rvert$
0	179.595499	0.877231	0.956099	0.313817	0.000000	0.956099	0.000000	0.313817	0.000000
1	187.368344	0.878535	0.957158	0.310000	0.050376	0.957137	0.000021	0.310501	0.000501
2	195.554501	0.879823	0.958217	0.306028	0.100097	0.958182	0.000035	0.306885	0.000857
3	204.185960	0.881094	0.959276	0.301898	0.149167	0.959232	0.000044	0.302981	0.001083
4	213.298038	0.882348	0.960335	0.297608	0.197587	0.960287	0.000048	0.298802	0.001194
5	222.930039	0.883586	0.961394	0.293154	0.245361	0.961345	0.000049	0.294361	0.001207
6	233.125610	0.884807	0.962453	0.288535	0.292491	0.962408	0.000045	0.289672	0.001137
7	243.933484	0.886011	0.963512	0.283748	0.338983	0.963472	0.000040	0.284745	0.000997
8	255.408273	0.887199	0.964571	0.278791	0.384839	0.964539	0.000032	0.279592	0.000801
9	267.611167	0.888370	0.965630	0.273660	0.430064	0.965608	0.000022	0.274226	0.000566
10	280.611343	0.889525	0.966688	0.268353	0.474663	0.966677	0.000011	0.268657	0.000304
11	294.486893	0.890664	0.967747	0.262869	0.518641	0.967747	0.000000	0.262897	0.000028
12	309.326515	0.891788	0.968806	0.257204	0.562002	0.968817	0.000011	0.256956	0.000248
13	325.231603	0.892895	0.969865	0.251357	0.604753	0.969886	0.000021	0.250844	0.000513
14	342.317952	0.893986	0.970924	0.245325	0.646899	0.970954	0.000030	0.244571	0.000754
15	360.719117	0.895063	0.971983	0.239106	0.688445	0.972021	0.000038	0.238147	0.000959
16	380.589646	0.896123	0.973042	0.232698	0.729399	0.973086	0.000044	0.231581	0.001117
17	402.109227	0.897169	0.974101	0.226098	0.769766	0.974149	0.000048	0.224882	0.001216
18	425.488075	0.898200	0.975160	0.219305	0.809552	0.975208	0.000048	0.218060	0.001245
19	450.974391	0.899215	0.976219	0.212316	0.848764	0.976265	0.000046	0.211121	0.001195
20	478.861844	0.900216	0.977278	0.205130	0.887409	0.977318	0.000040	0.204076	0.001054
21	509.502026	0.901203	0.978336	0.197745	0.925494	0.978368	0.000032	0.196930	0.000815
22	543.318879	0.902175	0.979395	0.190159	0.963024	0.979413	0.000018	0.189692	0.000467
23	580.818536	0.903132	0.980454	0.182371	1.000000	0.980454	0.000000	0.182371	0.000000
			x_1:	0.966307		Δ_r:	0.000049	Δ_s:	0.001245
			y_1:	0.282649					

APPENDIX D

Cubic Approximation

i	h_i	t^{h_i}	r_i	s_i	t_i	$r(t_i)$	$\|r(t_i)-r_i\|$	$s(t_i)$	$\|s(t_i)-s_i\|$
0	0.000000	0.750501	0.879858	0.361504	0.000000	0.879858	0.000000	0.361504	0.000000
1	0.673936	0.752415	0.880917	0.362009	0.012538	0.880995	0.000078	0.360375	0.001634
2	1.365277	0.754333	0.881976	0.362514	0.025107	0.882123	0.000147	0.359429	0.003085
3	2.074384	0.756256	0.883035	0.363018	0.037701	0.883242	0.000207	0.358660	0.004358
4	2.801842	0.758181	0.884094	0.363519	0.050317	0.884353	0.000259	0.358059	0.005460
5	3.548259	0.760110	0.885153	0.364018	0.062955	0.885456	0.000303	0.357619	0.006399
6	4.314267	0.762042	0.886211	0.364514	0.075613	0.886551	0.000340	0.357333	0.007181
7	5.100522	0.763977	0.887270	0.365007	0.088287	0.887639	0.000369	0.357193	0.007814
8	5.907705	0.765914	0.888329	0.365494	0.100978	0.888720	0.000391	0.357192	0.008302
9	6.736524	0.767853	0.889388	0.365977	0.113681	0.889794	0.000406	0.357320	0.008657
10	7.587715	0.769793	0.890447	0.366453	0.126396	0.890863	0.000416	0.357571	0.008882
11	8.461604	0.771734	0.891506	0.366921	0.139113	0.891925	0.000419	0.357934	0.008987
12	9.360083	0.773678	0.892565	0.367383	0.151847	0.892982	0.000417	0.358403	0.008980
13	10.282207	0.775620	0.893624	0.367834	0.164570	0.894033	0.000409	0.358968	0.008866
14	11.231929	0.777566	0.894683	0.368277	0.177321	0.895082	0.000399	0.359622	0.008655
15	12.207061	0.779510	0.895742	0.368708	0.190058	0.896125	0.000383	0.360355	0.008353
16	13.209627	0.781454	0.896800	0.369127	0.202791	0.897164	0.000364	0.361158	0.007969
17	14.240595	0.783396	0.897859	0.369533	0.215520	0.898200	0.000341	0.362022	0.007511
18	15.300972	0.785338	0.898918	0.369924	0.228240	0.899233	0.000315	0.362939	0.006985
19	16.391803	0.787278	0.899977	0.370300	0.240950	0.900264	0.000287	0.363900	0.006400
20	17.514181	0.789216	0.901036	0.370658	0.253646	0.901292	0.000256	0.364895	0.005763
21	18.669243	0.791151	0.902095	0.370998	0.266326	0.902318	0.000223	0.365917	0.005081
22	19.858172	0.793084	0.903154	0.371318	0.278988	0.903342	0.000188	0.366956	0.004362
23	21.082201	0.795013	0.904213	0.371617	0.291628	0.904366	0.000153	0.368003	0.003614
24	22.342619	0.796939	0.905272	0.371892	0.304244	0.905388	0.000116	0.369050	0.002842
25	23.640767	0.798860	0.906331	0.372144	0.316833	0.906410	0.000079	0.370088	0.002056
26	24.978048	0.800777	0.907390	0.372368	0.329392	0.907432	0.000042	0.371109	0.001259
27	26.355926	0.802689	0.908448	0.372565	0.341918	0.908454	0.000006	0.372104	0.000461
28	27.775924	0.804595	0.909507	0.372732	0.354409	0.909476	0.000031	0.373065	0.000333
29	29.239645	0.806496	0.910566	0.372867	0.366860	0.910499	0.000067	0.373984	0.001117
30	30.748755	0.808390	0.911625	0.372969	0.379270	0.911523	0.000102	0.374854	0.001885
31	32.305002	0.810277	0.912684	0.373035	0.391636	0.912548	0.000136	0.375666	0.002631
32	33.910209	0.812157	0.913743	0.373064	0.403954	0.913575	0.000168	0.376413	0.003349
33	35.566291	0.814030	0.914802	0.373053	0.416222	0.914603	0.000199	0.377088	0.004035
34	37.275256	0.815894	0.915861	0.372999	0.428437	0.915634	0.000227	0.377684	0.004685

continues on following page

Appendix D. continued

i	h_i	t^{h_i}	r_i	s_i	t_i	$r(t_i)$	$\|r(t_i)-r_i\|$	$s(t_i)$	$\|s(t_i)-s_i\|$
35	39.039201	0.817750	0.916920	0.372902	0.440596	0.916666	0.000254	0.378194	0.005292
36	40.860332	0.819597	0.917979	0.372759	0.452696	0.917701	0.000278	0.378613	0.005854
37	42.740959	0.821434	0.919037	0.372566	0.464735	0.918738	0.000299	0.378933	0.006367
38	44.683515	0.823262	0.920096	0.372323	0.476709	0.919778	0.000318	0.379149	0.006826
39	46.690556	0.825079	0.921155	0.372025	0.488616	0.920820	0.000335	0.379256	0.007231
40	48.764762	0.826886	0.922214	0.371672	0.500453	0.921866	0.000348	0.379248	0.007576
41	50.908965	0.828682	0.923273	0.371260	0.512218	0.922914	0.000359	0.379120	0.007860
42	53.126142	0.830466	0.924332	0.370787	0.523908	0.923965	0.000367	0.378869	0.008082
43	55.419434	0.832238	0.925391	0.370249	0.535520	0.925019	0.000372	0.378490	0.008241
44	57.792151	0.833999	0.926450	0.369645	0.547053	0.926076	0.000374	0.377979	0.008334
45	60.247801	0.835746	0.927509	0.368972	0.558503	0.927136	0.000373	0.377333	0.008361
46	62.790070	0.837481	0.928568	0.368227	0.569869	0.928199	0.000369	0.376549	0.008322
47	65.422883	0.839203	0.929627	0.367406	0.581148	0.929265	0.000362	0.375624	0.008218
48	68.150378	0.840910	0.930685	0.366508	0.592337	0.930334	0.000351	0.374556	0.008048
49	70.976950	0.842604	0.931744	0.365529	0.603436	0.931406	0.000338	0.373343	0.007814
50	73.907257	0.844284	0.932803	0.364466	0.614442	0.932480	0.000323	0.371983	0.007517
51	76.946252	0.845950	0.933862	0.363316	0.625353	0.933557	0.000305	0.370474	0.007158
52	80.099208	0.847600	0.934921	0.362077	0.636168	0.934637	0.000284	0.368817	0.006740
53	83.371720	0.849236	0.935980	0.360745	0.646884	0.935719	0.000261	0.367011	0.006266
54	86.769758	0.850856	0.937039	0.359318	0.657500	0.936803	0.000236	0.365055	0.005737
55	90.299714	0.852461	0.938098	0.357792	0.668015	0.937889	0.000209	0.362949	0.005157
56	93.968376	0.854050	0.939157	0.356164	0.678427	0.938977	0.000180	0.360693	0.004529
57	97.783034	0.855624	0.940216	0.354432	0.688735	0.940067	0.000149	0.358290	0.003858
58	101.751486	0.857181	0.941274	0.352592	0.698937	0.941158	0.000116	0.355738	0.003146
59	105.882105	0.858722	0.942333	0.350641	0.709033	0.942251	0.000082	0.353040	0.002399
60	110.183864	0.860247	0.943392	0.348576	0.719022	0.943345	0.000047	0.350197	0.001621
61	114.666422	0.861755	0.944451	0.346394	0.728903	0.944439	0.000012	0.347211	0.000817
62	119.340180	0.863246	0.945510	0.344093	0.738675	0.945534	0.000024	0.344084	0.000009
63	124.216353	0.864721	0.946569	0.341668	0.748337	0.946630	0.000061	0.340818	0.000850
64	129.307075	0.866179	0.947628	0.339117	0.757889	0.947725	0.000097	0.337415	0.001702
65	134.625430	0.867620	0.948687	0.336437	0.767330	0.948821	0.000134	0.333878	0.002559
66	140.185658	0.869044	0.949746	0.333625	0.776659	0.949916	0.000170	0.330210	0.003415
67	146.004674	0.870451	0.950805	0.330678	0.785880	0.951011	0.000206	0.326413	0.004265
68	152.096321	0.871841	0.951864	0.327593	0.794987	0.952105	0.000241	0.322491	0.005102
69	158.480296	0.873214	0.952923	0.324368	0.803982	0.953197	0.000274	0.318448	0.005920
70	165.176589	0.874570	0.953982	0.320998	0.812866	0.954289	0.000307	0.314286	0.006712
71	172.207011	0.875909	0.955041	0.317483	0.821637	0.955378	0.000337	0.310008	0.007475
72	179.595499	0.877231	0.956099	0.313817	0.830298	0.956466	0.000367	0.305619	0.008198

continues on following page

Appendix D. continued

i	h_i	t^{h_i}	r_i	s_i	t_i	$r(t_i)$	$\|r(t_i)-r_i\|$	$s(t_i)$	$\|s(t_i)-s_i\|$
73	187.368344	0.878535	0.957158	0.310000	0.838847	0.957551	0.000393	0.301122	0.008878
74	195.554501	0.879823	0.958217	0.306028	0.847284	0.958635	0.000418	0.296520	0.009508
75	204.185960	0.881094	0.959276	0.301898	0.855612	0.959715	0.000439	0.291818	0.010080
76	213.298038	0.882348	0.960335	0.297608	0.863829	0.960793	0.000458	0.287019	0.010589
77	222.930039	0.883586	0.961394	0.293154	0.871936	0.961868	0.000474	0.282126	0.011028
78	233.125610	0.884807	0.962453	0.288535	0.879934	0.962939	0.000486	0.277144	0.011391
79	243.933484	0.886011	0.963512	0.283748	0.887824	0.964007	0.000495	0.272077	0.011671
80	255.408273	0.887199	0.964571	0.278791	0.895606	0.965071	0.000500	0.266928	0.011863
81	267.611167	0.888370	0.965630	0.273660	0.903281	0.966131	0.000501	0.261700	0.011960
82	280.611343	0.889525	0.966688	0.268353	0.910849	0.967187	0.000499	0.256399	0.011954
83	294.486893	0.890664	0.967747	0.262869	0.918312	0.968239	0.000492	0.251027	0.011842
84	309.326515	0.891788	0.968806	0.257204	0.925671	0.969286	0.000480	0.245588	0.011616
85	325.231603	0.892895	0.969865	0.251357	0.932926	0.970328	0.000463	0.240087	0.011270
86	342.317952	0.893986	0.970924	0.245325	0.940078	0.971366	0.000442	0.234526	0.010799
87	360.719117	0.895063	0.971983	0.239106	0.947128	0.972398	0.000415	0.228909	0.010197
88	380.589646	0.896123	0.973042	0.232698	0.954078	0.973425	0.000383	0.223239	0.009459
89	402.109227	0.897169	0.974101	0.226098	0.960929	0.974446	0.000345	0.217521	0.008577
90	425.488075	0.898200	0.975160	0.219305	0.967680	0.975462	0.000302	0.211757	0.007548
91	450.974391	0.899215	0.976219	0.212316	0.974335	0.976473	0.000254	0.205951	0.006365
92	478.861844	0.900216	0.977278	0.205130	0.980893	0.977477	0.000199	0.200107	0.005023
93	509.502026	0.901203	0.978336	0.197745	0.987356	0.978476	0.000140	0.194226	0.003519
94	543.318879	0.902175	0.979395	0.190159	0.993725	0.979468	0.000073	0.188313	0.001846
95	580.818536	0.903132	0.980454	0.182371	1.000000	0.980454	0.000000	0.182371	0.000000
			x_1:	0.910238		Δ_r:	0.000501	Δ_s:	0.011960
			y_1:	0.328969					
			x_2:	0.927859					
			y_1:	0.501073					

Chapter 29
Building Semantic Webs for E-Government with Wiki Technology

Mohammed Abdula Saleh Al-helali
Al- Rafedain University, Iraq

ABSTRACT

E-government webs are among the largest webs in existence, based on the size, number of users and number of information providers. Thus, creating a Semantic Web infrastructure to meaningfully organize e-government webs is highly desirable. At the same time, the complexity of the existing E-government implementations also challenges the feasibility of Semantic Web creation. We therefore propose the design of a two-layer semantic Wiki web, which consists of a content Wiki, largely identical to the traditional web and a semantic layer, also maintained within the Wiki, that describes semantic relationships. This architectural design promises several advantages that enable incremental growth, collaborative development by a large community of non-technical users and the ability to continually grow the content layer without the immediate overhead of parallel maintenance of the semantic layer. This chapter explains current challenges to the development of a Semantic Web, identifies Wiki advantages, illustrates a potential solution and summarizes major directions for further research.

INTRODUCTION

The effectiveness of any governments is reflected by its efficiency, better services to citizens and improved governmental processes. Many governments therefore have embarked on aggressive campaigns to vastly increase the number of online interactions with citizens, and to provide large amount of online information and knowledge to citizens (as well as to government employees). A review of government pages available through the Google search engine demonstrates this reality, as shown in Figure 1.

The largest contingent of government pages, from the USA and represented by the.gov top-level domain, accounts for 368 million pages. No other government comes close. But even smaller e-government sites, such as.gov.uk (9.28 million

DOI: 10.4018/978-1-61520-789-3.ch029

Figure 1. Page count of selected e-government sites available through Google (June, 2005)

Country	*Government domain*	*Number of web pages*
USA	.gov	368,000,000
Canada	.gc.ca	12,100,000
UK	.gov.uk	9,280,000
Australia	.gov.au	7,200,000
China	.gov.cn	2,630,000
New Zealand	.gov.nz	1,290,000
South Africa	.gov.za	816,000
Hong Kong	.gov.hk	887,000
Thailand	.gov.th	728,000
Slovenia	.gov.si	388,000

pages) or.gov.au (7.2 million pages) exceed the size of major company sites such as IBM (3.93 million for ibm.com), eBay (3.14 million for ebay.com) and dwarf sites of companies such as Ford (55,700 for ford.com) or Barclays Bank (24,200 for barclays.co.uk).

Even Slovenia, a country with only 2 million citizens, maintains a vastly larger e-government website of over 380,000 pages.

To encourage usage of all this information and knowledge, an e-government must be able to provide a convenient way for its citizens to access and obtain the information and knowledge they desire, without having to manually filter out too much content that is not needed. Some governments try to do this by building aggregator sites or portals to capture the content created by multiple government sources. For example, Hong Kong's government has individual portal solutions (ESDLife) for almost every government department, as well as a portal for electronic content and service delivery to citizens (http://ESDlife.com.hk and http://esd.gov.hk).

Other than portals, as in the case of ESDlife, there are several technologies governments can use to provide useful information to its citizens through the internet, such as special KM portals, CRM software, content management systems, e-mail broadcasts, listservs or discussion forums. All these solutions can help to disseminate and exchange information, each of which with its own strengths and weaknesses. Overall however, they face the same difficulties, namely the management of too much information, created by too many heterogeneous, distributed sources. Resulting issues such as inconsistent terminologies, information overload and too little maintenance of outdated knowledge are only too frequent.

Hence, to handle knowledge organization and access in a more feasible way, an e-government needs to add some 'logic', a semantic structure, to organize its knowledge offerings. Hyperlinks can be used to provide information to citizens by allowing them to access information with a relatively little effort. However, to organize the links in a manageable way is a great challenge to the websites developers, and hyperlinks in conventional HTML do not have a definable meaning.

One approach to solve this problem is the development of a Semantic Web for e-government. Such a web can be used to develop a more effective and transparent e-government. As with any Semantic Web, site developers would annotate the web pages with semantic markup, semantic links and metadata so as to enable machines to follow the links and ideally to facilitate the integration of knowledge and information from many different sources. Semantic markup refers to a markup language whose name spaces, vocabulary and relationships are meaningfully definable. Semantic links are pointers between web objects, which can be meaningfully interpreted because of their labeling elsewhere in the system, and because they may have properties or methods associated with them. The metadata adds further well-defined, meaningful information so as to facilitate machine readability even more and to enable better web analysis to furnish best results to citizen users.

Semantic Web technology has been used for Knowledge Management (KM) in e-government, with ontologies to provide a well-defined means for users to structure and access the knowledge effectively. For instance, Klischewski launched a project at Hamburg University to apply Semantic Web technology to enable the contextualization of DiBIS (www.dibis.de), a web information service for Hamburg's citizens. Another project, conducted by Fraser et al., developed the Smart-Gov e-government ontology to provide the public authority with a knowledge-based core repository for government transaction services. Daddieco developed an ontology for the subject domain of export controls in the US government for effective knowledge retrieval and sharing.

An obvious starting point for these projects has been the development of ex ante ontologies, with the objective to provide an authoritative framework, which could then structure all contents subsequently added to the web. Unfortunately, the practical application is not as easy as the theoretical concept suggests. As has been recognized in the research on schema integration in database design, or knowledge integration among just a few experts, creating a common vocabulary or a common terminology is a difficult task even at a relatively small scale. In a large environment with multiple, heterogeneous knowledge sources, and fast changing content, maintaining such a 'clean' ontology appears highly challenging, if not impossible. Furthermore, since the knowledge resources on e-government websites consist of different electronic objects such as files for downloads (e.g. forms and customer applications), transactions processed by back end applications, links and services that require further interaction (e.g. authentication), it is difficult to identify which objects are the candidate objects that need semantic markup. The more markup, the more effort required for creation and maintenance of the semantic links. An analysis of a large online encyclopedia, the Wikipedia (wikipedia.org), for instance shows that inter-web hyperlinks grow linear with the number of web pages ($R2 = 0.997$, based on 38 observations). In the Wikipedia's case, each page contained on average more than 22 links, resulting in over 10 million links for over 500,000 web pages. By comparison, an e-government web with millions of web pages and possibly tens of millions of links between them would require formidable maintenance capability.

Clearly then, both the challenge of creating and maintaining a semantic e-government web with different name spaces, formats and structures for the same kind of knowledge, and the challenge of integrating knowledge represented at different levels of granularity, refinement, or precision by multiple heterogeneous sources demand novel solutions. We will discuss the main challenges and their treatment through existing approaches more systematically in Section 2. In Section 3, we explain our proposed solution, the creation of a two-layer semantic Wiki web. Section 4 illustrates our solution with an example, while Section 5 reviews strengths and weaknesses, and identifies possible extensions to this research. Section 6 draws conclusions.

CHALLENGES OF EXISTING TECHNOLOGY SOLUTIONS

Overview

The application of Semantic Web technology has promising results in e-government and other applications, such as e-commerce and search engines.

However, designing and developing a Semantic Web for an application such as an e-government web is also a daunting task. The following points highlight major challenges.

Difficulty in Extracting Knowledge

It is difficult to extract the knowledge and information from documents and people.

Extracting knowledge from documents requires some form of data or text mining, which is difficult when documents are unstructured. Knowledge extraction from people is often hindered by the fact that people tell less than they know, a phenomenon often explained by the term "tacit knowledge". Yet, it is even more difficult to identify the semantic relationships between these knowledge objects. Semantic relationships are evolving, and thus it is impossible to know all of them upfront. This creates a problem in updating, interpreting and navigating the information.

Heterogeneous Knowledge Sources

Knowledge Management in e-government services has to address at least three areas:

in relationship to the public, within government departments and in the coordination between government departments. A large amount of diverse knowledge is required, with knowledge sources being located in different departments, often spread out over the entire country or state. Yet we need to build linkages across, to meaningfully connect the separate knowledge offerings from various sources.

For example, a citizen who wishes to run a liquor store may have to deal with one government department that issues business licenses, one that issues liquor licenses, with the tax department, labor department and so on. All will be involved, but neither one will provide the 'big picture', unless their knowledge is semantically linked. Furthermore, different sources will represent knowledge at different levels of granularity, with different points of view, and thus possibly inconsistencies or contradictions.

Limit to Expertise

With large size and heterogeneity of knowledge sources comes the difficulty in maintaining a common, consistent truth. Yet, with even a smaller government having hundreds of thousands of web pages, no single individual or group may have the necessary knowledge to verify the entire Semantic Web, both content and the semantic links. Hence, having an e-government Chief Knowledge Officer (CKO) dictate what is correct or incorrect knowledge may not at all work, due to the limits of the CKO's offices own knowledge.

Non-Technical End User Contributions

Given the size of the e-government Semantic Web, it cannot be developed by a group of programmers. Non-technical 'end users' will be the ones who need to specify the semantic knowledge. Yet they commonly lack the technical knowledge to understand the implicit semantic links between web documents in the format and notation that is typically part of Semantic Web development. In fact many of these non-technical users may not even be able to write web documents in HTML.

Mistakes Made in Semantic Web Development

Given the size of e-government Semantic Webs, and the involvement of non-technical users, mistakes will be made. Semantic Web developers require training in the Semantic Web language. End users will not have such training, and thus, even though they possess the domain knowledge, will make mistakes in representing it, usually by choosing inefficient or wrong representations to describe a concept in the ontology.

Difficulty in Maintaining Knowledge

The government is one of the largest online knowledge providers for citizens. In fact, as Figure 1 demonstrates, many government websites are an order of magnitude larger than those of big corporations. As the knowledge volume grows, KM, including links management and maintenance becomes increasingly difficult, error prone and costly.

Ambiguous Web

As web documents change rapidly, so does their semantic relationship. If one page, say exp.htm, previously served as an explanation to another page, qp.htm, but now contradicts it, the semantic relationship is no longer one of explanation. Moreover, web documents will invariably combine or 'couple' multiple knowledge components, which makes a unique classification in a Semantic Web ambiguous. For example, a single page may raise a question, answer that question, describe conditions under which the answer is true and give counter examples. Hence, such a page cannot be classified as a question, or an answer, or by any other single classifier. This requires extra attention and cost to update and maintain the knowledge base.

Research Question

Can we build a semantic knowledge repository that deals with all these challenges?

Attempting to find a solution alternative to overcome the challenges is the purpose of this paper. In the previous section, we have discussed the significant challenges faced by a semantic e-government web. These challenges are present in the entire KM cycle, from knowledge elicitation to formalization, to Semantic Web design, implementation and maintenance of the knowledge. A new paradigm is needed which recognizes these inherent limitations, and defines a sufficiently robust development approach to address the challenges.

Figure 2 summarizes the challenges and their corresponding possible remedies. Given all the challenges faced by a semantic e-government web, we propose to develop a semantic Wiki web, details of which are discussed in Section 3.

Figure 2. Challenges and potential remedies

Challenge	*Suggested remedies*
Difficulty in extracting knowledge	Develop a mechanism to capture and maintain evolving knowledge using Wiki technology
Heterogeneous knowledge sources	Involve multiple users across departments and outside government
Limit to expertise	Collaboratively aggregate the knowledge of multiple experts and non-experts
Non-technical end user contributions	Make the semantic relationships accessible to the end users, by making them independent of the content web in a separate layer
Mistakes made in Semantic Web development	Create a semantic knowledge repository that represents Semantic Web definitions explicitly, scrutinisable by many 'eyeballs' (users)
Difficulty in maintaining knowledge	Use Wiki technology to enable a community to openly create and maintain the knowledge in the Semantic Web. Allow changes in content web and semantic relationships to be made separately from each other
Ambiguous web	Remove ambiguities through iterative refinements and distributed knowledge refactoring

SOLUTION PROPOSAL: SEMANTIC WIKI WEB

Proposed Solution Overview

The conceptualization of a knowledge resource, which can address the challenges of e-government semantics webs, will be the purpose of this section. Fundamentally, the proposed solution relies on the following key elements:

1. use a many-to-many technology for free and open knowledge sharing, with a few technical demands on the user; namely Wiki technology and the Wiki way.
2. create a two-layer design, one layer being the traditional web, the second layer being semantic relationships, also *explicitly written* and maintained as Wiki web pages using simplified syntax; namely Notation 3
3. rely on a community of users to maintain the semantic relationships in the form of a Wiki web.

Each of these elements will be discussed in the following subsections. Taken together, we surmise, they will enable the design of a Semantic Web architecture for e-government that is not only technologically possible, but also socially feasible.

Wiki Technology and the Wiki Way

Wiki Definition

A Wiki (from *WikiWiki*, meaning 'fast' in Hawaiian) is a set of linked web pages, created through the incremental development by a group of collaborating users (Leuf and Cunningham, 2001), as well as the software used to manage the set of web pages. Ward Cunningham developed the first Wiki in 1995, as the PortlandPatternRepository, to communicate specifications for software design. The term Wiki (from the Hawaiian *WikiWiki* meaning 'fast') gives reference to the speed with which content can be created with a Wiki. According to the Wikipedia (www.wikipedia.org), an online encyclopedia written as a Wiki, its key characteristics are as follows:

1. it enables web documents to be authored collectively
2. it uses a simple markup scheme (usually a simplified version of HTML)
3. Wiki content is not published instantly, once the author submits the Wiki page to the Wiki engine
4. new web pages are created when users create a hyperlink that points nowhere (usually simply by writing a term in 'CamelCase', concatenating two or more words and capitalizing them).

Wiki Design Principles

Wiki design is based on 11 principles originally formulated by Cunningham (e.g. http://c2.com/cgi/wiki?WikiDesignPrinciples), shown in Figure 3. These principles describe, in part, what has been termed the 'Wiki way', namely a form of collaborative web writing. As such, the principles describe how web creation, maintenance and access should take place, as well as the features the technology has to provide, so as to enable this form of collaboration.

Why are these principles important? Previously we described that the design and maintenance of a knowledge-based system is a difficult task for those who have domain knowledge expertise, but who are usually not technical experts. This calls for a web technology whose effort and cost of web page creation is very low, whose technology is forgiving towards mistakes, whose errors are easily detected and where detected errors can be instantly repaired.

Figure 4 overviews the desired web benefits, and the Wiki principles that support them. For instance, low effort in creation and maintenance is realized through an interface that requires very

Figure 3. Wiki design principles

Principle	*Explanation*
Open	If a page is found to be incomplete or poorly organised, any reader can edit it as he/she sees fit
Incremental	Pages can cite other pages, including pages that have not been written yet
Organic	The structure and text content of the site is open to editing and evolution
Mundane	A small number of (irregular) text conventions will provide access to the most useful (but limited) page markup
Universal	The mechanisms of editing and organising are the same as those of writing so that any writer is automatically an editor and organiser
Overt	The formatted (and printed) output will suggest the input required to reproduce it (e.g. location of the page)
Unified	Page names will be drawn from a flat space so that no additional context is required to interpret them
Precise	Pages will be titled with sufficient precision to avoid most name clashes, typically by forming noun phrases
Tolerant	Interpretable (even if undesirable) behaviour is preferred to error messages
Observable	Activity within the site can be watched and reviewed by any other visitor to the site
Convergent	Duplication can be discouraged or removed by finding and citing similar or related content

little technical knowledge to write and publish content. Using plain text, or a simplified ('mundane') markup language, even non-technical users can create text (albeit not necessarily RDF syntax). The principle of incrementalism allows contributors to add a little or a lot, even links to non-existing pages, which the Wiki identifies as such. Web pages typically come with an edit button as part of Wikis' organic nature, allowing anyone to edit.

Inevitable mistakes can be easily corrected, as Wikis are open for edit by anyone, and even incorrectly written pages will be rendered. This process is further simplified by the fact that results of any page creation or maintenance are instantly visible ('observable'), and accessible by a

Figure 4. Wiki principles and benefits

Desired web benefit	*Supporting Wiki principles*
Low effort of development and maintenance	Open, mundane, incremental, organic
Forgiving towards mistakes	Tolerant, open
Ease of error detection and repair	Open, observable, universal

standard user interface for content creation and maintenance throughout ('universal').

Other principles, such as precision or unified naming describe less the technology and more the way in which Wikis should be used. In addition to these, there are further conventions for content creation and maintenance, as can be found for instance in the Wikipedia (http://wikipedia.org). One such convention describes 'refactoring' of content, that is, the decomposition and recomposition of web pages to create a single semantic unit as a single page, with pointers (links) being used rather than content being duplicated ('convergence').

As previously identified, in a Semantic Web environment, where both the content and the semantic knowledge will be evolving, being able to easily refactor the content appears to be a high priority, one that can be realized by Wiki technology.

Given the benefits of Wiki technology in the representation of Semantic Web content, one would expect that there are already Wiki implementations. In fact, the Platypus Wiki (Tazzoli et al., 2004) is one such solution. Its main difference to the solution proposed here, however, is the representation of semantic content 'behind' the rendered web pages, as will be explained in the next subsection.

Two-Layer Design

One of the proposed design elements is an explicit representation of Semantic Web links, as a separate layer of web pages themselves. Instead of hiding the semantic information 'behind' the rendered pages, one layer of the Semantic Web would consist of explicitly visible and maintainable pages, expressing the semantic relationships.

Using a multi-layer design is a concept borrowed from database systems.

Within database systems, the bottom layer involves the raw data containing the data or information itself, whereas on top of the raw data layer additional indexes are used for fast access to specific data according to an index-specific search criterion. Whenever multiple different search criteria shall be supported, multiple indexes must be defined. A database index, however, is always stable in the sense that the criterion used to search data with a given index cannot change. This non-flexible behavior is an advantage in database systems. In knowledge bases for e-government it is not, because the criteria used to search for knowledge or to follow a link are likely to vary over time. Thus, an adaptive indexing approach is needed as part of the solution. It is incorporated in our two-layer design.

Using a two-layer approach in the web means that the traditional web pages that contain the content can be developed independently from a semantic structure overlaid on it, thus enabling the incremental growth of either, if necessary, independently. In other words, a group of content creators would be able to develop new web pages, without having to resolve all the semantic relationships between the new web pages and existing ones. Hence, content creation would not be stifled. In addition, semantic relationships could be built incrementally, growing the reasoning capability of the Semantic Web incrementally.

Making semantic links explicit is another approach borrowed from relational database design. The relational data model models relationships by so-called foreign-key constraints that require the use of identical values in related attributes of the key and the foreign key. In comparison, other data models (the hierarchical, network, object-oriented or XML data model) hide meaning within their implicit structures such as parent–child hierarchies, pointer sets or network sets. Within these data models, database users and maintainers use the implicit (semantic) structures in queries. We consider explicit semantic relationships a significant advantage whenever flexible semantic-based search has to be supported, as for instance in KM for e-government. A further advantage is that once relationships are made explicit, they can be more easily managed (e.g. updated), interpreted and navigated. For the Semantic Web, an explicit representation of the semantic structure enables the separation of the document web itself from the semantic relationships and a separate maintenance of each.

Note however that our concept of making links explicit is less restrictive than the foreign-key concept of relational databases in the following sense. In the relational data model, a reference to a data record can only be defined when the referred-to data record already exists (otherwise a foreign key constraint violation error occurs). In comparison, our concept of modeling semantic relationships by Wikis has the same advantage of making the relationship explicit, but, additionally allows a content provider to define a link to a piece of knowledge that has not yet been created. We consider this way of representing semantic relationships advantageous compared to foreign key constraints, because it allows Wiki web knowledge bases to grow dynamically, rapidly and without global coordination.

Our semantic overlay also draws on lessons from P2P networks, where overlay network structures are defined on top of a given network structure. As in P2P systems, our two-layer architecture provides a semantic view of a network of nodes (or pieces of information in our case), which is independent of the nodes' physical location. Another property that our two-layer architecture has in common with P2P overlay networks is that the links followed in the network depend on the task and may change over time. However, in P2P systems the optimization criterion that selects the appropriate links is fixed and implemented as part of an algorithm. In comparison, in our approach the criteria to follow a link depend on the Wiki specifications in the overlay layer, which are modifiable on demand by the users that manage the overlay layer. This enables our overlay structure to adapt its search structure with the help of the community users and according to the requirements of the community users, which we consider to be a significant contribution to community-supported KM for e-government.

Multi-User Network

Maintaining the Semantic Web for an e-government site invariably becomes a large-scale project, with many heterogeneous data sources, separated both physically and semantically from each other. No individual or small group of people will be able to maintain such a web. It has to rely on the resources of a large, possibly volunteer, network to create and maintain meaning relationships.

As the case of the Wikipedia demonstrates, a volunteer network was able to create the world's largest encyclopedia (now with over 500,000 concepts in the English language), within only a few years. This result has been achieved by a volunteer network, that as of May 2005 counts more than 25,000 members, with more than 1000 of them making more than 100 edits per month each, equaling the full-time efforts of a staff of over 200 researchers (estimate based on Wikipedia Statistics). See http://en.wikipedia.org/wikistats/EN/TablesWikipediaEN.htm for details.

Not only can such a network provide the needed manpower to maintain a large Semantic Web, it can also provide the multiple points of view needed to create a multitude of semantic relationships, and can provide, following Linus' Law, the needed 'many eyeballs' that would identify mistakes in the existing Semantic Web structure and enable their correction.

Implementation and Illustration

In this section, we will explore how a semantic Wiki web might work in an actual problem scenario. The example will illustrate a 'help facility', a simplified expert system (Hayes-Roth et al., 1983) implemented as a semantic Wiki web. The illustration makes use of the MediaWiki software, which has no embedded RDF or Notation 3 interpreter. Hence we will not demonstrate the actual knowledge processing, but the conceptual structure, web content and navigation structure.

'Help Facility' Wiki

One important class of software applications today is KM systems that provide interactive help. These include, for instance, embedded systems, such as the help function of applications software, as well as helpdesk applications that exist in many companies to facilitate customer support. Frequently, these systems analyze a problem by traversing through a hierarchical or network search tree, ruling out irrelevant nodes through question and answer dialogue and then relay the most appropriate response for the given condition. In the past, such systems were implemented through a range of technologies. During 1980s, expert systems emerged as a technology particularly suited for this task type. Expert systems were successful in a number of well-publicised applications, but also suffered from several weaknesses, such as their brittleness at the limits of expert system knowledge, narrow domain focus, maintenance difficulty and the role conflict between domain expert and knowledge engineer.

Semantic Wiki webs promise an opportunity to acquire the expertise needed for help system development in a less rigid, incremental manner. The resulting system might be able to answer questions based on expert knowledge, but with a less formal knowledge base than traditional expert systems. In fact, the knowledge base could emerge from previously disconnected or only loosely connected web pages. For example, a forward looking government requires its citizens to save part of their income in a self-managed 'mandatory provident fund', maintained by a non-government financial institution. Citizens who are not skilled in making investment decisions may then look towards the government to provide guidance on how best to invest. Similarly, government and civil service will have an interest in citizens making good investment decisions, so as to avoid large social welfare payments or social unrest in case of delinquencies.

Hence, a citizen might approach a government information site with the following question: "I have money in my mandatory provident fund, presently in a savings account, earning almost no interest. I want to invest this money. What is my best choice?" Traditionally, a response would have been furnished in form of stand-alone hard copy documents, or in an e-government site as flat web pages, pages such as 'Investing in Real Estate' or 'How to Invest in Stocks?', logically not connected and with overlapping content. Figure 5 shows one such example.

Working towards the development of a semantic Wiki web, a first step would be the refactoring of individual web pages into a more loosely coupled, internally a more cohesive set of information components, which together would provide the needed information. The conceptual structure of such a system is shown in Figure 6. The system depicts a content web, with pages shown as rectangular boxes, and arrows depicting the (semantic) relationships between the pages.

The system consists of pages of different types, question pages, condition pages and explanation pages.

Question pages state questions together with a list of potential answer links (multiple options). Options might be sequenced by likelihood or other meaningful criteria. Answer links point to condition pages. See Figure 7 for an example.

Condition pages list the conditions under which the answer is appropriate. Condition pages have an explanation page link (if properly refactored) or contain the explanation of the discussed answer condition on the page. Condition pages also list one or more conditions that need to be fulfilled. For instance, the page shown in Figure 8 depicts three conditions associated with 'investing in stocks' (e.g. 'InvestorAge is young or middle'). Condition pages link to further condition pages, so as to explore complex conditions in a breadth-first manor. Finally, condition pages have an

Figure 5. 'Flat' page 'how to invest in stocks'

Figure 6. Wiki help facility argument flow (old- replace CW)

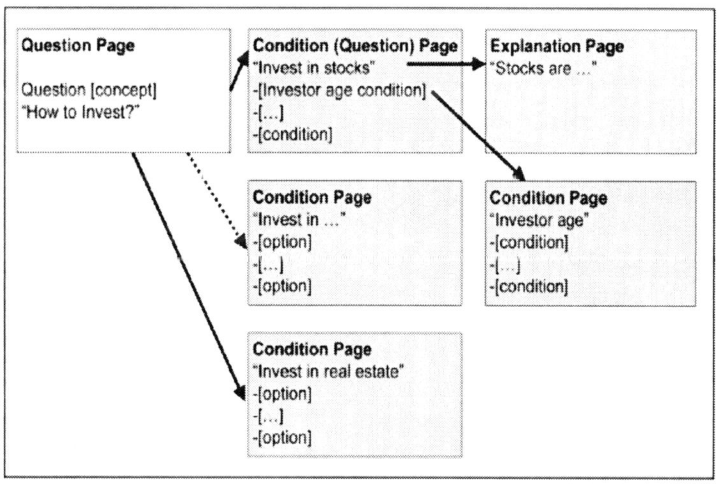

Figure 7. Question page

Figure 8. Condition page

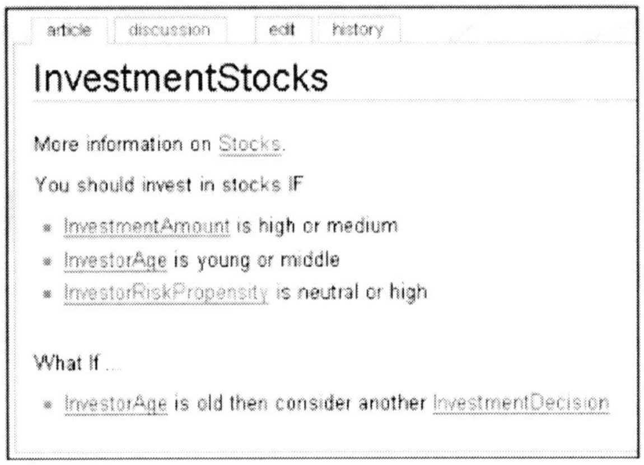

off-link that points elsewhere, possible to the previous condition or to the next option, in case the condition is not fulfilled. This enables the citizen to explore another condition or the next answer option.

Explanation pages provide explanatory content for each complex condition, explaining the concept (answer option) that is reflected in the complex condition. They remain as 'flat' documents, possibly with a 'back' button to redirect the user to the page that linked to the explanation. Figure 9 shows an example. The document is somewhat similar to that shown in Figure 5, but purposely lacking the conditional logic and question.

A system with this structure, even without an overlaid Semantic Web framework can already be useful as a question answering system or helpdesk system. However, in building a Semantic Web, we envision that such a helpdesk structure is not envisioned by the original page designers, but that a logic of question – condition – explanation can be overlaid over existing pages, thus allowing a previously not associated set of pages to be meaningfully queried. Such a system can be developed incrementally, adding more content options, conditions and explanations as they are created, or as they are found within the available web content. Semantically, the structure is relatively simple, which also makes it suitable for citizen users to structure Semantic Webs accordingly which could then be machine interpreted and furnished to other users in a more expert system-like fashion.

Semantic Wiki Web Help Desk

The overlaid semantic Wiki web would identify the semantic relationships, here question – condition – explanation, and explicitly express them in a separate structure, also within easily modifiable Wiki pages that are people- and machine-readable. A suitable organization would separate name space definitions and 'logic' pages, as illustrated in Figures 6 and 7. Name space definitions would define the basic terms of the e-government Semantic Web; logic pages would describe the vocabulary and relational concepts.

We envision numerous 'logic' pages, such as the special purpose page E-govHelpDesk that contains an (incomplete) logic for an e-government help desk (Figure 10).

The illustrated example defines the pages as questions, conditions and so on, and furthermore defines the relationships existing between them. Generic rules denote general relationships, while specific rules identify relationships between specific pages. Hence, the rule 'InvestmentStocks: requires: InvestorAge', processed by a query

Figure 9. Explanation page

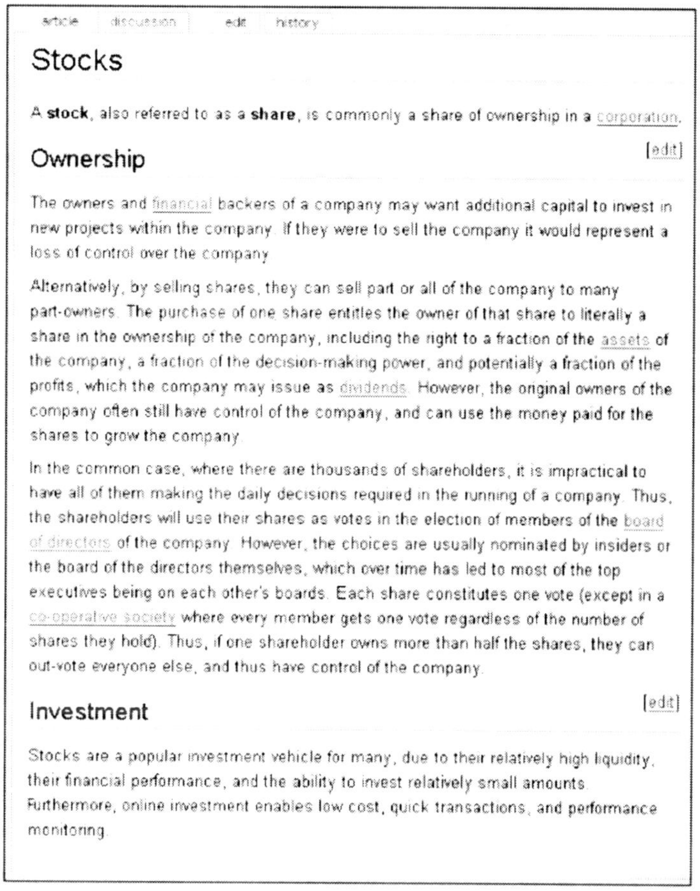
article | discussion | edit | history

Stocks

A **stock**, also referred to as a **share**, is commonly a share of ownership in a corporation.

Ownership [edit]

The owners and financial backers of a company may want additional capital to invest in new projects within the company. If they were to sell the company it would represent a loss of control over the company.

Alternatively, by selling shares, they can sell part or all of the company to many part-owners. The purchase of one share entitles the owner of that share to literally a share in the ownership of the company, including the right to a fraction of the assets of the company, a fraction of the decision-making power, and potentially a fraction of the profits, which the company may issue as dividends. However, the original owners of the company often still have control of the company, and can use the money paid for the shares to grow the company.

In the common case, where there are thousands of shareholders, it is impractical to have all of them making the daily decisions required in the running of a company. Thus, the shareholders will use their shares as votes in the election of members of the board of directors of the company. However, the choices are usually nominated by insiders or the board of the directors themselves, which over time has led to most of the top executives being on each other's boards. Each share constitutes one vote (except in a co-operative society where every member gets one vote regardless of the number of shares they hold). Thus, if one shareholder owns more than half the shares, they can out-vote everyone else, and thus have control of the company.

Investment [edit]

Stocks are a popular investment vehicle for many, due to their relatively high liquidity, their financial performance, and the ability to invest relatively small amounts. Furthermore, online investment enables low cost, quick transactions, and performance monitoring.

Figure 10. Name space definitions

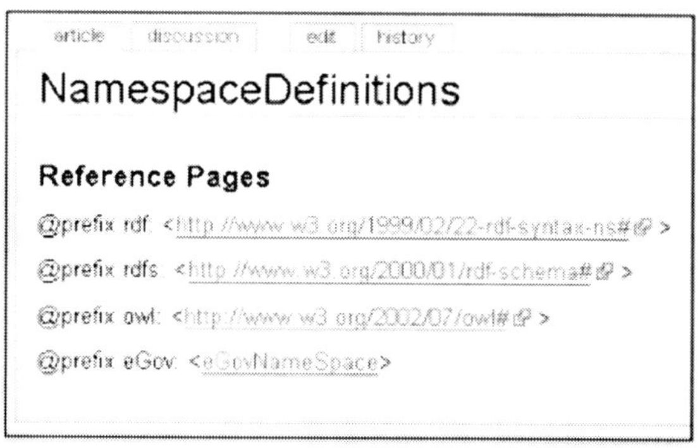
article | discussion | edit | history

NamespaceDefinitions

Reference Pages

@prefix rdf: <http://www.w3.org/1999/02/22-rdf-syntax-ns# >

@prefix rdfs: <http://www.w3.org/2000/01/rdf-schema# >

@prefix owl: <http://www.w3.org/2002/07/owl# >

@prefix eGov: <eGovNameSpace>

Semantic Web processor should furnish the InvestorAge page in conjunction (as condition for) the InvestmentStocks page.

Generic rules, in this example, would result in any explanation page being provided as explanation to any condition page, without selectivity.

They would hence only be useful in conjunction with links embedded in the content web. In other words, if the content web depicted a normal hyperlink from page InvestmentStocks to page Stocks, while the Semantic Web identified page Stocks as an explanation and InvestmentStocks as a condition, plus 'Explanation: explains: Condition' (see Figure 11), then the Semantic Web query processor could still select Stocks as the most appropriate explanation in the context.

This incremental approach to building Wikis, with a content web layer and a semantic layer, would enable the creation of an incrementally growing system containing the shared knowledge of multiple sources. Thus, a group of helpdesk experts can jointly create a helpdesk knowledge base that covers a wide range of conditions and answers.

Figure 11. Defining semantic relationships (excerpt only)

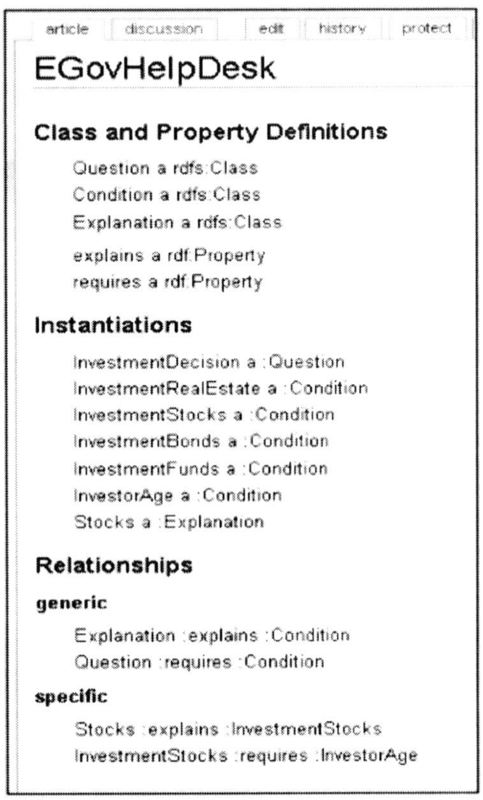

ASSESSMENT AND DISCUSSION

Previously, we identified seven challenges to the feasibility of Semantic Web development. In this section, we will revisit these challenges and assess how our proposed solution would tackle them, as well as identify new challenges that our solution would create.

Feasibility Challenges Addressed Significantly Easier Extraction of Knowledge

As the help desk overlay application illustrates, knowledge extraction is made easier as the user can be guided by questions to fulfill his or her specific information requirements. Note that different overlay networks may coexist, allowing each user to select the most suitable overlay network for his or her knowledge requirements. Some may want to query the web as a help desk, while others may want to structure workflows, to name just two alternatives.

Integration of Heterogeneous Knowledge Sources

As the architecture does not require the knowledge to be stored in a specific format and because the storage format of one piece of knowledge is independent from the storage format of another piece of knowledge, it is possible to integrate heterogeneous knowledge sources under the common interface of an overlay layer.

Limit to Expertise and Non-Technical End User Contribution

A key design aspect is the use of Wiki technology that can easily adopted by end users. End user can use the same technology to contribute to both the content web and the – usually hidden and complicated – overlay network.

Repair Mistakes Made in Semantic Web Development and to Knowledge Maintenance

The participation of users of the community in all levels including the structuring and the organization of knowledge has several significant benefits. One advantage is that not only the knowledge itself but also its organization can be adapted continuously according to the users' needs. Unlike in most other systems, errors can be repaired by any users who detect them. Similarly, pages that are difficult to read or use can be improved by exactly those who detect them.

To summarise, one of the main advantages is that Wiki technology used in both layers turns many normal users into experts for some details, and if they volunteer to contribute their expertise, they can significantly improve the entire knowledge base. Ambiguous Web Ambiguity remains in the knowledge base; however, the choice between multiple independent overlay layers allows the user to select that access path that best fits the user's requirements.

Challenges for the Two-Layer Wiki Web Solution and Further Research Directions

Although we envision the two-layer semantic Wiki web as a beneficial architecture for E-government websites, the following new challenges may arise when this technology is used by a large community of users.

As individual preferences and application behaviors will differ, one challenge is to provide individual users with the most appropriate overlay layer for their task and knowledge needs. There are multiple directions how this challenge can be addressed, ranging from user profiling to ranking of Wiki pages to providing a special search engine for overlay layers over large Wiki structures.

Another challenge is security of and public trust into such a publicly developed and maintained Wiki web knowledge base. This includes quality aspects of specific content, such as for information about investment opportunities. Additionally, it includes transparency of the authorship of a piece of knowledge as well as for the overlay layer that guides users to specific knowledge. Finally, it includes guarantees that such information cannot be falsified. Future research in security and trust guarantees may include search for information and security models which allow for multiple or mixed authorship models that nevertheless provide knowledge users with a transparent minimum of the above-mentioned guarantees. One such model could have the government provide trusted versions of Wikis, with all elements of an overlay structure and the information contained in content pages being government-checked and verified. Obviously, such a solution would lead to several other interesting questions concerning verification and ongoing version control, as well as to questions on how to enable careful authorship checking and trust management, while still maintaining the ease and efficiency of user contributions that Wikis are made to provide. Another challenge and therefore a topic for further research may be, how to integrate the Wiki way of organizing knowledge with a search engine in such a way that the appropriate mix or integration of overlay layer and search engine can be used.

CONCLUSION

E-government encompasses the largest amount of web documents worldwide, and is still rapidly growing. The organization of this knowledge in a user-friendly, efficiently usable and widely accepted way will be one of the major hurdles of the communication between government and the e-government users who are citizens and voters.

Our research suggests that the development of feasible e-government Semantic Webs is as much a technical as a social challenge. The enormous complexity of such webs Requires a paradigm shift in the design that enables large numbers of citizens to Participate in the development. These are citizens whose technical expertise is not Guaranteed. The scenario therefore calls for the creation of a knowledge web, which is easy to develop and maintain. In reviewing the challenges, a two-layer Semantic Web Based on Wiki architecture and explicit representation of semantic information offers Numerous benefits.

While such an architecture can address several existing challenges, other still remain and new ones emerge. Trading off accuracy of the web and trust in it against broad and easy participation remains an unanswered question. Managing a multitude of semantic overlays may become a task of unmanageable size and complexity; while the design of hybrid search engines that combine content search and Semantic Web analysis creates a new research challenge.

Overall our analysis suggests that the development of e-government Semantic Webs Will create a multitude of difficult research questions and application issues for a long Time to come. These questions and issues will increase in difficulty, as citizen demands For larger and better e-government sites grow.

REFERENCES

Amaravadi, C. S. (2005). Digital repositories for e-government. *Electronic Government, 2*(2), 205–218. doi:10.1504/EG.2005.007095

Bergamaschi, S., & Guerra, F. (2002). Peer-to-peer paradigm for a Semantic Search Engine. In *Agents and Peer-to-Peer-Computing*, Bologna, Italy.

Berners-Lee, T., & Miller, E. (2002). The Semantic Web lifts off'. *Special Issue of ERCIM News, 51*, 9–11.

Daddieco, R. J. (2004). Retrieving knowledge in e-government: the prospects of ontology for regulatory domain record keeping systems. In Wimmer (Ed.), *Building Semantic Webs for e-government with Wiki technology 55*

Fraser, J., Adams, N., Macintosh, A., McKay-Hubbard, A., Lobo, T. P., Pardo, P. F., et al. (2003). Knowledge Management applied to e-government service: the use of an ontology. In Wimmer (Ed.), *Building Semantic Webs for e-government with Wiki technology 55*

Gaines, B. R., & Shaw, M. L. G. (1993). Eliciting knowledge and transferring it effectively to a knowledge-based system. *IEEE Transactions on Knowledge and Data Engineering, 5*(1), 4–14. doi:10.1109/69.204087

Garcia-Molina, H., Ullman, J. D., & Widom, J. (2002). *Database Systems. The Complete Book.* Upper Saddle River, NJ: Prentice Hall.

Grönlund, Å. (2004). Introducing e-gov: history, definitions, and issues. *Communications of the Association for Information Systems, 15*, 713–729.

Hayes-Roth, F., Waterman, D. A., & Lenat, D. (1983). *Building Expert Systems*. Reading, MA: Addison-Wesley.

Holsapple, C. W., & Joshi, K. D. (1999). Description and analysis of existing knowledge management frameworks. In *Proceedings of the 32nd Hawaii International Conference on System Sciences*, (pp.1–15).

Klischewski, R. (2003). Semantic Web for e-government. In Traunmuller, R. (Ed.), *EGOV 2003, Springer Lecture Notes No. 2739.*

Leuf, B., & Cunningham, W. (2001). *The Wiki Way: Collaboration and Sharing on the Internet.* Reading, MA: Addison-Wesley.

Liebowitz, J. (2004). Will Knowledge Management work in the government? *Electronic Government, 1*(1), 1–7. doi:10.1504/EG.2004.004133

Metaxiotis, K., & Psarras, J. (2005). A conceptual analysis of Knowledge Management in e-government. *Electronic Government, 2*(1), 77–86. doi:10.1504/EG.2005.006649

Nonaka, I., & Takeuchi, H. (1995). *The Knowledge-Creating Company: How Japanese Companies Create the Dynamics of Innovation*. Oxford, UK: Oxford University Press.

Polanyi, M. (1966). *The Tacit Dimension*. New York: Doubleday and Company.

Storey, V. C., Chiang, R. L., Dey, D., Goldstein, R. L., & Sundaresan, S. (1997). Database design with common sense business reasoning and learning. *ACM Transactions on Database Systems, 22*(4), 471–512. doi:10.1145/278245.278246

Tazzoli, R., Castagna, P., & Campanini, S. E. (2004, November 7-11). Towards a Semantic Wiki Wiki Web. In *Proceedings of the Third International Semantic Web Conference*, Hiroshima, Japan.

Wagner, C. (2000). End-users as expert system developers. *Journal of End User Computing, 12*(3), 3–13.

Wagner, C., Cheung, K., Lee, F., & Ip, R. (2003). Enhancing e-government in developing countries: managing knowledge through virtual communities. *Electronic Journal of Information Systems in Developing Countries, 14*(4), 1–20.

Waterman, D. A. (1986). *A Guide to Expert Systems*. Reading, MA: Addison-Wesley.

Wimmer, M. (Ed.). (2003). Knowledge Management in e-government. In *Proceedings of the KMGov 2003*, Springer Lecture Notes No. 2645.

Wimmer, M. (Ed.). (2004). Knowledge Management in e-government. In *Proceedings of the KMGov 2004*, Springer Lecture Notes No. 3035.

Chapter 30
Design Principles for E-Government Architectures

Alain Sandoz
Université de Neuchâtel, Switzerland

ABSTRACT

This chapter describes a holistic approach for the design of e-government platforms. It defines principles for architecting a system which must sustain the entire e-government activity of a mid-level public authority (Geneva). The four principles are: Legality, Responsibility, Transparency, and Symmetry. The principles speak to policymakers and to users. They also lead to usable and coherent architectural representations at all levels of responsibility of a project, i.e. the client, the designer and the builder. The approach resulted in deploying multipartite, distributed public services, including legal delegation of roles and the outsourcing of non mandatory tasks through PPP on an e-Government platform that will support a threefold increase in services yearly until 2012. In this sense, as well as in its daily operation, the system is a success.

INTRODUCTION

The paper's subject is *architecting a system capable of sustaining the entire e-government activity of a mid-level public authority.*

The example we consider is the State of Geneva, where the results were elaborated and are currently applied in the e-government program [Secrétariat, 2008]. This corresponds to a population basin in the order of 1 million residents and 100'000 local businesses and non-government organizations (*NGO*'s). The number of lower level authorities depending on this mid-level authority is in the order of 100. There is a sequence of higher-level authorities (national and international) above it. Each authority defines a jurisdiction under which lower-level authorities as well as residents, businesses and *NGO*'s live or operate. Neighbor authorities can interact with our referential mid-level authority at the same level and at different levels, in particular in Geneva which is a center for

DOI: 10.4018/978-1-61520-789-3.ch030

international organizations and shares its borders with France and the European Union.

A government is a working model of society: every regulatory aspect of society pertaining to the level of the referential is modeled, implemented and operated in the referential. There are many interactions between the referential and the world.

The standard repository of procedures of Swiss public administrations [e-Government, 2007] describes *ca.* 800 official procedures for our referential.

The components of society interact with the referential authority over technical and organizational channels, using specific rules and procedures. Organizational channels, rules and procedures change regularly under social evolution and new legislation, whereas the set of technical channels (teller, postal mail, telephone, fax) has recently been extended by ICT's and the internet. Integrating this new *channel* into the activities of an authority is called e-government. E-government requires resources, interfaces, procedures, and other components that were not present or not instantiated for the purpose of interacting with society, in the absence of e-government. Identifying necessary components, and implementing and integrating them in order to sustain *parts of* or *the whole of* e-government activities is the task of building an e-government platform (noted *EGP*). There is a fundamental difference between the "parts of" and the "the whole of" approaches. The former considers an *EGP* as the juxtaposition of components that deal each with some part of e-government, the sum of these parts and of their effects being the expected result. This leads to the definition of incremental strategies for e-government: projects "start small" with easy to deliver services; one might emphasize communication with citizens and develop a portal; etc. Over time, most incremental projects encounter difficulties.

The latter considers an *EGP* from the start as a system. Architecting complex systems is a delicate and risky task: because of the greater importance of component *interactions*, it is impossible to foresee how well the design will work, if at all, before an initial version of the system is completed and tested. We chose this approach in the Geneva project, confident in an earlier success with e-voting through internet [Chevallier M., 2006] between 2002 and 2005, which at that time achieved world-class recognition.

Architecting Complex Systems

In complex systems, the definition of system components and of interactions between components is important from the start. Architecting the system ("architecture" comes from the Greek words for "principle" and "construction") consists in designing abstractions and representations of structural characteristics which will enable to understand, build, repair, and reproduce the system effectively and efficiently all through its life cycle. Modern systems architecting [Maier M., 2000] relies on six foundations, the first of which is a *systems approach*, and considers that "the architect is principally an agent of the client, not the builder". These elements are central in our approach and we will come back to them in section 5. Because governments are builders of their own information infrastructure, they tend to build e-government infrastructures as an Appendix to existing IT platforms –without "C". These are often juxtapositions of legacy applications, loosely connected through an intranet exhibited as proof that the systems interoperate. Initiatives, like the US Defense Information Infrastructure Common Operating Environment [Frazier G, 2001], define *Enterprise Architecture Frameworks* (*EAF*) [CIO Council, 1999] and standardization processes [NIH Enterprise Architecture Standards Development Process] for government information systems (see [Zachmann J., 1987] on information system and enterprise architectures). It is uncommon to approach the design of an *EGP* from the client's side. This is however necessary, because the client, *i.e.* society as a whole, *is not an enterprise*. Therefore, building an *EGP* is both *new* and *complex*. The difference between designing this new system *vs.* adding a feature to the old one is comparable to the one between "designing systems safety" *vs.* "reliability engineering" in aeronautics [Leveson N. G., 2005].

Objective and Structure of the Chapter

The objective of the chapter is to define a small set of design principles for e-government architectures. The principles are called *Legality*, *Responsibility*, *Transparency* and *Symmetry*. The names and statements of the principles speak to policymakers, *i.e.* the people confronted with the real problems of e-government (complexity and scale, *i.e.* costs; trust and expectations of citizens, *i.e.* choice and added value; dissemination and impact of technology *i.e.* change in society), and to users.

Section 2 presents the principles and simple consequences on the architecture. Section 3 examines the consequences at the systems level. Examples are given in section 4. Section 5 comes back to the issue of architecting an *EGP* in this manner and briefly compares the principles with those of the Federated Architecture of the Government of Canada [Government of Canada].

Principles for Architecting an *EGP*

The following paragraphs state each principle, describe the situation in the absence of e-government, and examine some simple consequences on the organization of the *EGP* under consideration of the principle. Consequences (corollaries) are superficially justified.

The baseline of e-government is the possibility for an actor external to an administration to interact with that administration through the internet. An external actor can be a citizen, a non-resident, a business, a *NGO*, an association, another administration, but also a machine or any identified or unidentified entity which can interact through the internet with the considered *EGP*. We call such an actor a *user*. We *do not assume* existence of any contract between the administration and the user.

Legality

The first principle aims at protecting the user's legal and civil rights, if any, in the jurisdictions under which the referential operates. It is related to two fundamental differences between web-based interaction *vs.* the absence of e-government. The differences are real-time *vs.* differed operation and automatic *vs.* manual treatment.

Statement of the Legality principle (LP). Any operation suggested to a user on an interface of the *EGP* and all the consequences of the execution *by the user* of this operation must be legal and respect the users legal and civil rights within the jurisdictions under which the referential operates. In the absence of e-government, interfaces between user and administration all go through at least one human operator who is basically instructed to respect the users' rights *at the interface*. The operations requested from a user are of the type "make a declaration", "sign a document", "deliver information". After this entry point, every operation is executed inside the authority's domain, either manually or semi-automatically under the authority's responsibility. Traceability is enforced in an *ad hoc* manner using a *file* of paper or electronic records for each *business case*. Files are used to reconstruct procedures when a decision is contested, *e.g.* in front of the judiciary. In this case, it is usually a legal right of the user to access this file. The usage of files, their copying and dissemination through administrations, and their conservation over time, can lead to legal or civil rights violations.

Comment. We are not considering the situation where some ignorant or malevolent user attempts to violate another person's legal or civil rights, *e.g.* by using counterfeit identity or documents. This can arise with or without e-government. This situation and its consequences relate to the question of security, which is not considered *per se* in this paper. In our approach, security relies on the *ultraquality implementation* and *certification* foundations [Maier M., 2000] of systems architecting and is a systemic consequence of the application of the four principles.

Corollary 1. Under *LP* a user cannot be lead to execute an interactive operation on the *EGP* if the underlying application is not certified for *LP*. Consequently, in practice, it is impossible to authorize interactive access by users to legacy applications on the *EGP*. Interactive operations must be simple and traceable (*e.g.* upload a file, trigger a transition in a workflow). Expected effects must be certified. The systematic application of *Corollary 1* in the design of the architecture is an aspect of the architecture which raises a bitter emotional rejection from builders. *Ultraquality implementation* as an architecting foundation implies that if there is any chance that *LP* will not be respected because of a loophole in the design, then the design must be scrapped. For example, if a user is brought to execute online some old segment of code that everyone had forgotten, but that violates some legal or civil rights. This might happen by the implementation of the 543rd procedure, when all initial developers are off on their careers. For that reason, interactive operations of users are deliberately confined to the *EGP* (see Figure 1) and their consequences on the legacy infrastructure of the administration are executed *asynchronously* by the authority after the passing of a token in the way of a handshake protocol. *Corollary 1* breaks *de facto* the stovepipe model (see Figure 1), which raises opposition from builders.

Corollary 2. At any time, the user must be able to reconstruct the trace of operations executed on the *EGP*.

This implies that traceability is not just about keeping records in the basement, but that each user must be provided with a *service* to trace his or her actions easily and meaningfully.

Responsibility

The second principle deals with the question "Who is the user?". This is a delicate question, often oversimplified by security technicians who treat the problem at the identification and authentication level of *enterprise directories*, using logins of physical persons as a basis for profile and role management. In e-government this is not

Figure 1. Articulation of the EGP according to LP

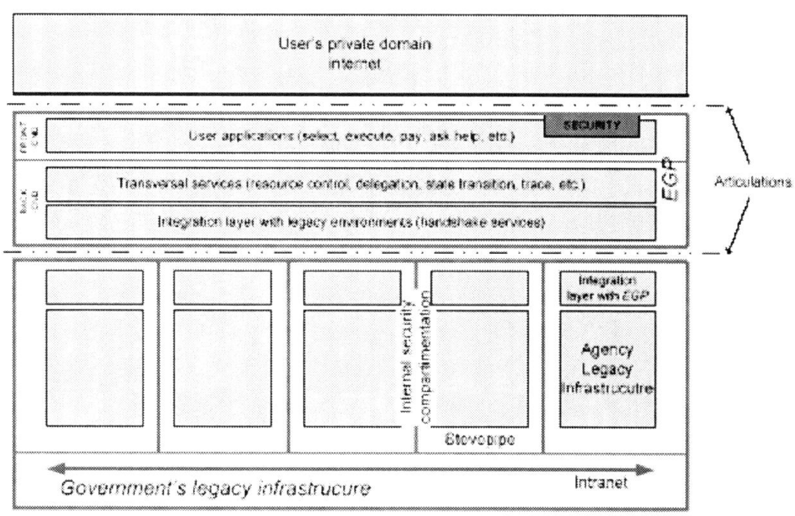

possible for several reasons. First, *society is not an enterprise* and e-government is no reason to impose a contract on every citizen. Next, people move, change jobs and companies, sometimes quit for intervals and come back, etc. The process of managing logins, profiles and roles for all the people interacting with an administration through the web in their own name, in the name of their employers or of their customers, or of the *NGO*'s they are active in, etc. is meaningless, expensive, and insecure for an administration, and furthermore doesn't respect *LP*.

Statement of the Responsibility principle (RP). Each *operation* executed on the *EGP* can be attributed to a unique identified legal personality. This legal personality is legally responsible for the execution of the considered operation and for all its publicized and certified consequences.

The legal personality can be a physical person (*i.e.* a resident within a jurisdiction where the authority can legally file a claim against the user in relation to the execution of the operation) or a moral person (company, *NGO*, etc.), or the government itself which is usually a legal personality in its own jurisdiction. If the user is untraceable, the responsible personality will be the state.

In the absence of e-government, this is a baseline of public administrative interaction. If a person files a tax reduction request for herself and one for her company, in one case she is legally responsible and in the other her company is. Even though the people at each end of the communication channel can be the same in both cases, they distinguish the responsibilities from one case to the other.

Comment. *RP* sets the basis to solve the delegation problem, *e.g.* a fiduciary that deposits a tax declaration in the name of a customer is responsible legally towards the customer according to the contract binding these two entities, whereas the customer is responsible towards the state for matters concerned with the tax declaration, *i.e.* all for operations executed by the fiduciary.

Corollary *3*. For each operation executed on the *EGP*, it is necessary to identify the legal personality assuming responsibility.

From a design point of view, this draws a line between operations executed under legal responsibility of the state (*e.g.* decision steps in e-administrative processes, notifications, etc., and everything that runs on legacy systems) and operations executed out of the state's scope of legal responsibility, *i.e.* operations executed on infrastructures out of the administration's control (user PC's, company mainframes), and operations executed under the *control of the administration* but under the *responsibility of the user* (*e.g.* upload of a form). Operations of the latter type, in particular, will have to be certified.

Transparency

In the absence of e-government, the knowledge a government employee uses to answer a request is usually very detailed: from terminology, to regulatory and organizational aspects, along with the knowledge of the people and services to forward demands and records and of the legacy applications used during the procedure, an employee might need years of training to be efficient, and usually in only one service.

If one takes the human actor out of the process, this missing knowledge becomes a problem. Shifting the *necessity to know* to the user is not only disloyal (though some e-government programs start out with the idea of shifting the administration's workload to the user over the web), but also impossible in practice. Consequently, the *EGP* must be architected so that this knowledge becomes unnecessary. This seems impossible, but in fact it is not. Because the complexity of working organizations is often due to organic growth [Mintzberg H, 1989], IT and process re-engineering help make large portions of this knowledge oblivious. This design step is comparable to what deploying ATM's was for the banking industry.

Our task is to make it possible on the *EGP*.

Statement of the Transparency principle (TP). Organizational characteristics (of actors) which are not explicitly necessary to perform an operation on the *EGP* are not reflected in that operation.

Here, the actors are all the partners in the execution of an e-government process, like filing a tax reduction request for a family. For the tax agency, some characteristics of the demander might be necessary (number of newborn children in the household); others might not (number of parking lots in the garage). Therefore the number of parking lots is not reflected in the operation, whereas the number of newborn children is. Similarly, *for the demander*, organizational characteristics of the taxing agency should not be reflected in the operation (name of the agency, taxpayer *id* in the agency's database, redundant information on the demander himself, etc.).

Corollary 4. Any function which is used by more than one agency (*e.g.* login, payment, trace, geo-localization, directory, support, delegation, etc.) is seen by users as one service instance. Such services are called *transversal.*

Corollary 5. All transversal services are implemented in the *EGP*.

This corollary is far reaching, because it establishes the *EGP* as the central locus for dematerializing administrative processes inside the administration. We will see an example in section 4.

Symmetry

The last principle, *Symmetry*, is the least intuitive and the farthest reaching. Basically it states that anything the government is not mandated to do, it should be able not to do. In other words:

Statement of the Symmetry principle (SP). Any function that is necessary for an *EGP* to operate correctly, but that is not directly determined by a mandate of the state, should be implemented on the *EGP*, if at all, in a way that an external service provider can furnish the service.

As a simple example, take the function of completing e-forms. A service is necessary to display form frames with fields that users fill in. A set of rules is applied to verify online that the syntax and low level semantics of information provided are correct. The service provides backup for partially completed forms that the user can come back to later (also in case of a failure), and for archiving completed forms. If any *EGP* is to operate correctly, this kind of service is necessary. *If* the service is provided by the *EGP* itself, it should be unique (by *TP*) and furnish every form the administration requires from its users. However, the mandatory characteristic of the state with regards to this service is not to enable users to *complete forms* online, but to enable users to *transfer data* online.

According to *SP* the e-forms service should be implemented on the *EGP* so that an external service provider can do the *same*. This comprises technical aspects like invocation of the service from the *EGP* and data transfer to the *EGP*, as well as functional aspects like publishing verification rules and data or file structures. Prior to e-government, public services were specifically tailored to the needs of organizational units according to the evolution of constraints (*e.g.* Switzerland had 3 federal employees in 1848 and 30'000 in 2008) and corporate identity was a theme at the inter-agency level. A typical public administration manages thousands of forms and a maze of procedures. Auxiliary manpower is employed to type the content of paper forms into legacy applications. Everything is repeatedly done everywhere with small variations that are insignificant from the point of view of the state's mandate, which means basically that any administration could provide many of its services to many counterparts.

Corollary 6. A service which is built according to *SP* can be shared among *administrations.*

The principle of symmetry sets the path for low-level authorities to *share services on the internet without losing sovereignty.* It enables administrations to overcome the small-scale syndrome which is a killer for local governments seeking a presence on the web.

CONSEQUENCES ON THE DESIGN OF THE EGP

Basic Articulation

Any *EGP* relies on a foundation of information and computer systems which compose an administration's IT infrastructure. In the absence of e-government, this core is isolated from the internet. It is organized in stovepipes, either for legal or for historical reasons. Due to pressure on costs, more and more functions on this foundation are shared among agencies, services and systems, what over time leads to define an *EAF* for the administration. Interoperability [Gov. of the Hong Kong SAR,2007] among sub-systems becomes an internal goal, but is fundamentally not a requirement of e-government (according to *TP*, the government is free to organize as it wishes, as long as internal organizational characteristics are not reflected unduly to external users.) Every operation executed on the infrastructure is under the legal responsibility of the authority. On the other hand, the external user (citizen, business, *NGO*) of e-government also possesses an infrastructure operated under his/her sole legal responsibility.

When considering these two zones (government core infrastructure and external user's infrastructure), we remark that the *LP* does *not* apply to either. Not that there exists a good excuse not to apply the principle there. The principle only applies to operations executed through an *EGP* interface, and this applies *a priori* to neither of these zones. This is represented in Figure 1. As a first consequence, the *EGP* (where *LP* will systematically be applied) must be properly articulated with the two other "platforms", which are each a zone of exclusive legal responsibility. These articulations in turn define the mechanisms which will be used to interact between zones and implement *LP*. These mechanisms must be certified according to all four architecting principles.

Platform Organization

When discussing *TP*, we noted that the users must be given simple functions to invoke. This goes like "Select", "Execute", "Complete form", "Pay", "Ask for help", "Read trace".

Figure 2 represents the platform organization at the application level. The "Select" application should enable the user to select two things: first, *in the name of whom* an interaction takes place (this is delegation –see below); second, *what* has to be done. So "Select" deals with managing *authorizations*. It must quickly bring a user to a business case he or she wants to consult and correctly manage authorized operations before and after interactions. Controlling access with fine granularity and in conformity to the dynamics of transactions is delicate [Sandoz A., 2005].

Given the scale and complexity of the underlying information system and the relatively small number of protected resources *per* user, a capability based [Miller M., 2003] approach to access control, centralized in the *EGP* seems a good design choice for globally solving this problem. On one side, the justification of this choice is technical (the web basically functions with low-level capability addressing); on the other it relies on the *insights and heuristics* foundation of systems architecting.

After a business case has been selected, it can be presented to the user with its different *components*. In administrative processes, information must be exchanged and operations must be executed. The process evolves according to the execution of formal steps by actors, what leads other actors to proceed in turn.

Here it is important to briefly dwell on the nature of public administrative procedures. Some are linear and only concern one user and the

Figure 2. Platform organization

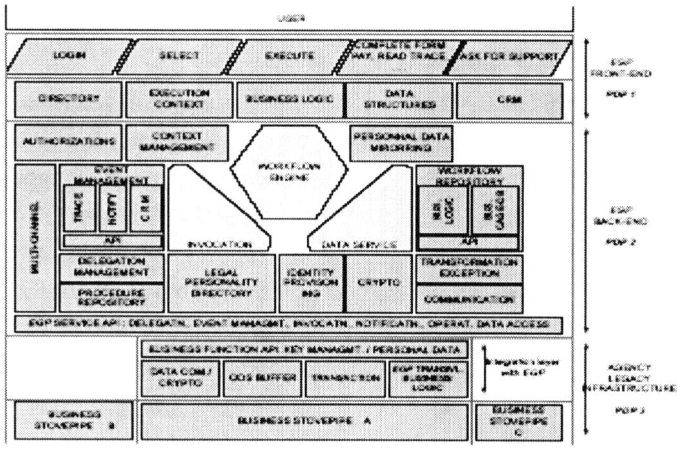

authority (*e.g.* declaring taxes, see §4.1). Other procedures implicate several parties, and in each party, several users. For example, a building construction-request can implicate two levels of authority, several services within each authority, the demander and his representatives (lawyers, architects, insurance and commodities companies, banks, etc.), plus stakeholders concerned with the environment or the town's historical and tourist values, etc. Each actor intervenes when required and at the moment he or she chooses according to personal dispositions and interests.

Therefore the nature of e-government interactions is *multipartite*, *distributed* and *asynchronous*. At any moment, all actors should see consistent *views* of the business case state. The *execution context* of a user contains different kinds of elements like workflow instances, documents, partially or fully completed forms, attributes, messages, invoices, etc. To some extent, this is independent of the administration's organization and depends more on society's. The application that manages the execution context of a user is designed according to *TP*. It contains a workflow engine, and mechanisms to implement different kinds of mailboxes for the management and communication of e-documents, in particular *among* the actors in one party (*e.g.* the demander and his hired staff, or the authority and its multiple agencies) and according to dynamic access control rules (*e.g.* maybe the banker shouldn't know the *NGO*'s claims until the lawyer has finished negotiating under the patronage of the city council).

In this situation, there are several reasons for letting the user choose a service provider for functions like completing e-forms or storing documents. A user might not want the administration to access partially completed forms, for example a tax declaration. Depositing a form is a formal act, like committing a transaction, and anything that happens before commit should be undoable without leaving a trace.

How can an administration credibly guarantee this if it provides safe e-forms? This generalizes to any kind of data residing on or transiting through the *EGP*.

Where should data persist when the user is not online? Applying design principles enables to solve this problem in a globally ordered and manageable way using *predicates* on the locality of data persistence.

We distinguish between two types of data: *personal data* describe *what the user is*; *operational data* describe *what the user does*. The following predicates on data persistence determine where these data persist when the user is not connected.

Here also, the *ultraquality implementation* approach to platform design (using predicates) enables to guarantee properties intrinsically.

PDP1: no personal data and no operational data persist in the front-end of the *EGP* when the user is off-line; *PDP2*: no personal data and all operational data persist in the back-end of the *EGP* when the user is off-line; *PDP3*: all personal data and no operational data persist in the government's legacy infrastructure when the user is off-line.

Predicate *PDP2*, is a guideline for robust user support systems, guaranteeing that their personal data are not accessible to first level support staff. The trace service is designed as an application that the user can choose to subscribe to or not. According to *SP*, it is integrated in the *EGP* in such a way that an external service provider can furnish the service. In this case, the external trace service (as well as the *EGP*'s own) must be certified so that a logged trace can be used as proof in a legal case. In this manner, a user can subscribe to a unique trace service for using the e-services of *different* administrations.

Examples

Simple Transaction

The first example is the deposit of a tax declaration. The transaction is implemented through the *EGP* vertically above the tax agency's stovepipe legacy system, but respects the four principles. In particular, *EGP* applications implement a handshake protocol between user and legacy systems which respects *LP*, *RP* and *TP*. The user can subscribe to an external e-forms service or use the platform's own. In this sense, *SP* is respected. These elements are illustrated in Figure 3.

The workflow used to implement the transaction depends on the underlying functionality (depositing a tax declaration). However this consists in a few simple steps:

A. opening the case (except for new taxpayers, most of the information will be furnished by the tax service itself using the *data service* to present it to the user's execution context);
B. completing the forms and uploading documents;
C. C)formally committing the case;
D. receiving an acknowledgement; and

Figure 3. Tax declaration transaction

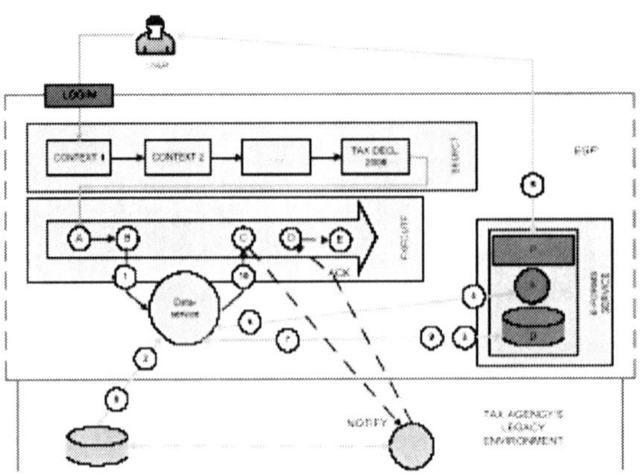

E. receiving the tax decision and invoice. Further steps (opposing the decision, paying taxes online, etc.) are implemented in other generic workflows. Implementing this instance of a procedure in the *EGP* gives a generic solution to most administrative procedures of the "declaration" type.

The numbered steps in the figure indicate progress in the handshake protocol between the *EGP*'s data-service and the legacy application. This requires an integration effort between the *EGP*'s back-end system and the legacy environment. It must be furnished by every agency for any transaction to be put online, but is done using a uniform model. We are currently working on the extension of the referential *EAF* development framework so that new legacy applications can be integrated with the *EGP* during their development. To summarize: the *EGP* furnishes the transversal functions (resource control, delegation, state transition, traceability, etc.); an external service provider can furnish e-forms; and the public agency furnishes the forms' specifications, the transactions' workflow specification, the integration with the legacy system through the implementation of the handshake protocols on the side of the agency.

Delegation

Delegation has two aspects. One is to *register* the fact that a user authorizes another to execute some transaction *T* in his or her name. The latter plays the role of a contractual representative like a lawyer, an architect or a fiduciary. This action is a tripartite transaction where the actors are the user, the representative and the administration. All three must be informed and must agree, and any one must be able to skip out of the deal at once. If this is the case, the previous situation must be immediately re-established and access authorizations managed in consequence. This is a transversal function of the administration (it works the same and uses the same legal basis for any public procedure). It can be implemented centrally in the *EGP* for all transactions (on- or offline), using all possible communication channels (*e.g.* delegation by letter or by fax).

The second aspect of delegation is to manage the *execution* of *T* according to this situation (see §3.2).

Complicated Transaction

Once vertical integration, delegation, and other transversal functions have been implemented, complicated transactions consist basically in dynamically controlling access to components of a business case instance.

We are currently implementing the execution context for the authorization of demonstrations (sports tournaments, open-air concerts, political rallies, etc.). The transaction implicates more than ten actors (demander, city, state, public transport company, airport authorities, security, fire department, health department, alcohol control and patent service) and requires the on line transformation of a chapter process that uses eight forms (a header request and seven appendices).

The interesting aspect of this case is that the implementation will enable an effective dematerialization of the procedure inside the administration, since any case filed over the paper channel will be transferred to the *EGP* and sharing of documents among all actors (except the demander if the request was filed on paper) will be accomplished over the *EGP*'s execution context for this procedure.

Re-Engineering Government Processes through *PPP*

The last example concerns using external services in public-private partnerships (*PPP*) in order to drive the re-engineering of administrative processes. In [Sandoz A., 2008] we use a *PPP* to reduce the payment delays of the administration to its furnishers (the process is implanted on the *EGP*).

Why develop *PPP* in e-government? The reason is related to hard metrics.

France has 63'000'000 inhabitants and over 35'000 towns with less than 10'000 inhabitants, each one running its own administration with hundreds of procedures. This reflects the general situation in Western Europe. For most of these administrations, there is a very small limit (0 to 50) to the number of transactions that they can put online, moreover through integration portals of higher authorities or private providers, what blurs development with interests and competition.

The internet however is a place where *communities* can be founded, driven by common goals and methods of their members, sharing tools, results and successes, with mutual respect of individuals. If communities are to emerge that enable fullfledged e-government, with all the added value that can be expected from ICT, securely, and without rejection or outbreaks of anti-big brother syndrome from the client, then *EGP*'s must be built and interlinked using an approach that relies on these characteristics from the beginning (*i.e.* that makes them intrinsic to the system's architecture).

Figure 4. Modular

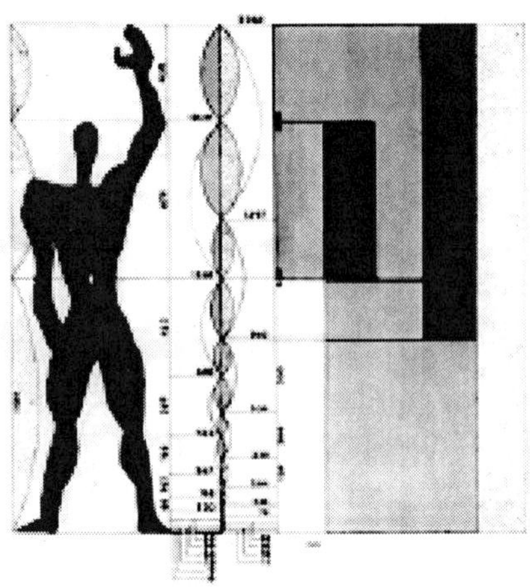

Discussion

Implementing the four principles, or any others, in the *EGP*'s architecture is a choice. Platforms that don't respect *LP*, *RP*, *TP* or *SP* exist, operate and are correct. However, in our experience, this set of design principles applies to most architectural representations [Zachmann J., 1987] that pertain to the client, the designer and the builder of an *EGP*. The principles enable to systematically check their conformity and to maintain a global coherency in the development and parallel operation of a complex e-government system.

Our approach uses the foundations of systems architecting:

1. *a systems approach*, as we started out with in §1;
2. *a purpose orientation*, *i.e.* to include all forces of society to implement all possible administrative procedures on the web and bring complexity and waste in administrations down to a minimum over time;
3. *a modeling methodology*: identifying and formalizing design principles for the architecture of the system;
4. *ultraquality implementation*: an *EGP* may not seem as critical as an airplane or a nuclear power plant, but the consequences, on the life and health of individuals or the success of businesses, of failures in the management of information must be considered seriously when the systems we build apply to society as a whole;
5. *certification*: a basis for quality, for credibility, for fairness, also for the courage needed by policymakers to delegate the execution of day to day information management tasks to external parties;
6. *insights and heuristics*: this last foundation is the more delicate, and [Maier M., 2000] dedicates its entire second chapter to its presentation.

The Conceptual Architecture of the Federated Architecture of the Government of Canada (Iteration one) [Government of Canada] defines 13 principles: Reduce integration complexity; Holistic approach; Business event-driven systems; Defined authoritative sources; Security, confidentiality, privacy and protection of information; Proven technologies; Total cost of ownership; Plan for growth; Adopt formal methods of engineering; Extended information and services environment; Multiple delivery channels; Accessible government; and Robustness.

Canada's e-government initiative is successful (it is used as a model in the Geneva project), so this paragraph is not critic with regards to this achievement. Examining the 13 principles' statements and their rationale, however reveals differences between the two approaches of the architecture paradigm, Canada's being traditional and analytic, ours taking a systems perspective.

A parallel out of the field of traditional civil architecture is Le Corbusier's [fr.wikipedia] Modulor [Le Corbusier, 1950] system for modern housing. Modulor relies on the principle that *the place people live in should be built along lines proportional to the dimensions of ahuman body*. Many famous constructions were realized in the 20th century based on this system. The principle seems natural, though the consequences for multistory housing are far-reaching. On the other hand, designing the Modulor system was close to an act of faith because system design principles are far from being only equations derived from an analytical breakdown of their abstract subject.

CONCLUSION

We define four principles for the design of e-government architectures: *Legality*, *Responsibility*, *Transparency* and *Symmetry*, which respect the client's understanding of a complex problem, not *a priori* the builder's.

The principles are declined into structural constraints of *EGP*'s, like articulations or predicates on the locality of data persistency. Transactions from simple (*i.e.* vertical) to complex (*i.e.* multipartite, distributed and asynchronous) illustrate how the Geneva e-government platform functions.

The possibilities for an administration to provide services to others (*i.e.* hosting services for other authorities) and to subscribe to external services (public, or private through *PPP*) without losing sovereignty are discussed. This enables to position an *EGP* as a member of a community on the web which can contribute to deliver exhaustive e-government services on a large scale.

REFERENCES

Chevallier, M., Warynski, M., & Sandoz, A. (2006). Success Factors of Geneva's e-Voting System. *Electronic. Journal of E-Government*, *4*(2). Retrieved from http://www.ejep.com.

Council, C. I. O. (1999, September). *Federal Enterprise Architecture Framework*. Retrieved from http://www.cio.gov/Documents/fedarch1.pdf

e-Government Standards (2007, July). *eCH0070 Inventory of Public Services, Ver. 2.5*. Retrieved from http://www.ech.ch

Frazier, G. (2001, October). The DII COE: An Enterprise Framework. *Journal of Defense Software Engineering*. Retrieved from http://www.stsc.hill.af.mil/CrossTalk/2001/10/frazier.html

Gov. of the Hong Kong SAR (2007, December). *The HKSARG Interoperability Framework*. Hong Kong, China: HKSARG.

Government of Canada. (n.d.). *Federated Architecture, Conceptual Architecture*. Retrieved from http://www.tbs-sct.gc.ca/fap-paf/documents/iteration/iteration05-eng.asp

Le Corbusier. (1950). *Le Modulor, Architecture d'Aujourd'hui*. New York: Springer.

Leveson, N. G., (2005, November). *Safety in Integrated Systems Health Engineering and Management*, draft paper for the NASA AISHEM Forum.

Maier, M., & Rechtin, E. (2000). *The Art of Systems Architecting*. Boca Raton, Fl: CRC Press, 2nd Edition.

Miller, M., Yee, K.-P., & Shapiro, J. (2003). *Capability Myths Demolished*. Baltimore, MD: Systems Research Laboratory, Johns Hopkins University.

Mintzberg, H. (1989). *Inside Our Strange World of Organizations*. New York: Free press.

NIH. (n.d.). *Enterprise Architecture Standards Development Process*. Retrieved from http://enterprisearchitecture.nih.gov/

Sandoz, A., Eudes, J.-R., & Prévot, R. (2008, January). *Public-Private Partnership in e-Government: a Case Implementation*, MCETECH, Montreal. Retrieved from http://fr.wikipedia.org/wiki/Le_Corbusier

Sandoz, A., Haenni, N., & Eudes, J.-R. (2005). *Addressing and Protecting Distributed Resources in e-Government Architectures using Multiple Digital Identities*. Presented at theEuropean Conference on E-Government.

Secrétariat du Grand conseil (2008). *Projet de loi ouvrant un crédit d'investissement de 30 850 000 F pour le développement de l'administration en ligne. Geneva*. Retrieved from http://www.ge.ch/grandconseil/data/texte/PL10177.pdf

Zachmann, J. A. (1987). A Framework for Information Systems Architecture. *IBM Systems Journal*, *26*(3). doi:10.1147/sj.263.0276

Chapter 31

Learning from Failure:
Braving the Multifaceted Challenges to E-Government Development

Fadi Salem
Dubai School of Government, UAE

Yasar Jarrar
Dubai School of Government, UAE

ABSTRACT

Large-scale electronic government projects had mixed results over the past decade. A considerably large percentage of such projects effectively failed. The over-ambitious promise of e-governance positively transforming public sectors in developing nations didn't fully materialize. The actual causes of e-government failures are still to be explored in more detail to improve the understanding of the phenomenon by practitioners and scholars alike. This chapter explores the causes of e-government failures within the context of Arab states and discusses prevailing views of such failures in earlier literature. Based on a survey of senior e-government practitioners in nine Arab countries, our findings indicate that the underlying roots of failure in e-government projects in Arab countries (which we classify in nine main categories) are entwined with multifaceted social, cultural, organizational, political, economic and technological factors. We argue that, despite their many similarities, e-government initiatives in the Arab states would be better equipped for avoiding failure when a local 'fit' is established between leadership commitment, sustainable cross-government vision, appropriate planning, rational business strategy, suitable regulatory framework, practical awareness campaigns and rigorous capacity building for the public administrators and society at large. Based on our findings, we argue that replicable "best practices" in a complex and developing field of e-government rarely exist. We conclude with a proposal to nurture a culture more tolerant to risk-taking and failure in the relatively new area of e-government in the Arab states. Until a local maturity level is reached, such culture should be accompanied with home-grown e-government risk management approaches as well as effective mechanisms of knowledge management to enable extracting relevant local lessons from failed projects and partial successes.

DOI: 10.4018/978-1-61520-789-3.ch031

INTRODUCTION

By the turn of the century, an ever increasing interest in electronic government was building-up globally; a digital government revolution was in the making. The advocates of this revolution were cheering e-government as the panacea; a solution to all public sector predicaments. Most Arab states joined the e-excitement euphoria that swept regional governments. The promise that electronic government (hereafter e-government) initiatives will address public administration dilemmas captured the imaginations of policy makers and attracted citizens and businesses alike. Very few years later and after massive public investments, many of the promises put forward by e-government advocates to obliterate corruption, cut red-tape, reduce government costs and deliver more participatory governance systems have cooled down (Ciborra, 2003).

Debates started and the core question was 'what went wrong?' e-Government projects failures are not limited to Arab states. They have been documented almost in every region around the globe, see for example: (Akther et al., 2005; AP, 2004; Ciborra & Navarra, 2005; Cloete, 2004; Davenport & Horton, 2004; Eynon & Dutton, 2007; Pardo & Scholl, 2002; Salem, 2007; Titah & Barki, 2006).

There is a wide agreement that e-government projects fail in high percentages worldwide. For example, an earlier estimate by UNDESA suggested that more than 60% of e-government projects in developing countries fail (UNDESA, 2003). The World Bank estimate was even more alarming. One lead information specialist at the bank put the percentage of failed e-government projects in developing countries at 85%, from which 35% are total failures (AP, 2004). There is no solid estimate on the percentage of failed e-government projects in the Arab countries, but one could safely argue that the failure ratio had followed the same trend.

Following the general trend in the information systems body of knowledge, information systems research focusing on the public sector has primarily followed a positivist approach (Pardo & Scholl, 2002). The result has arguably been unsatisfactory in explaining failure in complex social, cultural and technical environment. However, literature viewing e-government from a socio-technical perspective managed to explore these predicaments from an arguably more realistic point of view. For example, Heeks categorized success and failure in government information systems into total failures, partial failures and successes (Heeks, 2002). A total failure in e-government projects would be described as a planned initiative that never gets implemented or an implemented e-government project that is directly abandoned almost immediately after implementation. Partial failure in the same context would describe the case in which a system is successfully implemented without achieving its key objectives. Partial failure also could describe e-government projects that achieve the intended goals but also deliver considerable undesirable results with significant implications. Success of e-government projects on the other hand is widely perceived as the case where most stakeholders would achieve most of the main objectives of the project without major unwanted outcomes. Given the many stakeholders with usually conflicting interests, assessment of total or partial failure of e-government initiatives and implementations as well as their success tends to be an issue of subjectivity (OECD & DSG, 2007; Salem, 2007). e-Government barriers have also been explored from various cultural and social perspectives. For example, cultural barriers to e-government were discussed in the literature, including the common "myths" among public administrators regarding technology, which could contribute to creating actuality gaps between expectations and realities (Eynon & Dutton, 2007; Margetts & Dunleavy, 2002). The researchers categorized cultural e-government barriers into supply side and demand side barriers within European societies. While such exercises are generally useful for extracting lessons from different cultural orientations, their applicability to other societies and cultures require rigorous cultural contextualization (Hofstede, 2004). From social science perspective, Dunleavy et al. evaluated e-government implementations failures on three fronts: the extent of project failure, competitiveness of IT government contracts and the status of public sector information technology systems compared to the private sector. Such research highlights the dynamics of the relationship between powerful IT corporations and the public sector in which governments are weakly placed, which in turn can foster an environment where e-government failure is more probable (Dunleavy et al., 2004; Heeks, 2006).

There is a general agreement however, that the consequences of e-government projects failures are usually immense but are mostly intangible. Arguably, the less developed the country's public administration system is, the more damaging the consequences of failed e-government projects to citizens' trust, economic development prospects and to the potential contribution of the private sector to public good. The tangible consequences of e-government projects failure incorporate direct financial losses, such as the investments made for consultancies, equipments, managerial and technical systems and training. In addition, there are indirect losses, such as the lost costs and efforts of public administrators involved in the failed e-government project.

Other than just losing the promised benefits of the e-government project, losses would most likely incorporate political or reputational damage to individuals and organizations involved and to government at large. There is also the cost of the lost opportunity of alternatively spending the funds on development projects badly needed in developing countries. Perhaps the most overlooked loss of a failed e-government project is when political leadership looses faith in future transformative initiatives as well as citizens losing trust in government promises. This damage to government credibility usually has even more severe implications, the clearest of which is the migration of e-government champions and skillful human resources to the private sector or to other countries (Heeks, 2006). In the absence of rigorous ex-post analysis to such failed projects, the opportunities created by the failure usually attract opportunistic behavior and contribute to the increase of corruption levels (Ciborra & Navarra, 2005). It may also strengthen the position of the "old guards" in government and those who have vested interest in the status quo. Most public administrators and e-government practitioners are less aware of the intangible costs of a failed e-government project.

The aim of the paper is twofold: Firstly, it contributes to the relatively limited body of research on e-government projects failures in developing countries by exploring the perceptions held by e-government practitioners on the roots of failure. Secondly, it seeks to enrich the literature focusing on e-government in the Arab states from a critical perspective, with the end goal of contributing to discussions on reform and modernization in the region. Based on our findings, the discussions section explores the following research questions:

- Why do e-government projects repeatedly fail in the Arab states?
- What are the key barriers and constraints to e-government development?

Methodology and Framework

The research was conducted through a combination of a survey and semi-structured interviews. Invitations to take part in the survey were sent through email and followed up by phone calls to a specifically selected list of respondents. The intended survey audience consisted of the senior government officials in fifteen Arab governments; namely: Algeria, Bahrain, Egypt, Iraq, Jordan, Lebanon, Libya, Morocco, Palestinian Authority,

Qatar, Sudan, Syria, Tunisia, UAE and Yemen. The list of respondents included directors of e-government initiative at the national level as well as advisors to ministers directly involved in the national e-government development in those countries.

Part of the findings of this paper is based on a survey conducted under the "Good Governance for Development in the Arab Countries Initiative" (GfD); an initiative launched in collaboration between the OECD and the UNDP since 2005. One of the six working groups in this initiative focuses primarily on "e-Government and Administrative Simplification" and consists of practitioners and country experts from the OECD and Arab countries. The findings are also partially based on the proceedings of a series of high level forums for e-government practitioners held in Dubai between September 2005 and March 2007 under the GfD initiative as well as other e-government focused policy forums held in the Dubai School of Government during the same period (OECD & DSG, 2007). However, the findings in this paper are mainly based on the results related to nine of the participating countries, where the targeted response rate was achieved; namely: Algeria, Bahrain, Egypt, Jordan, Lebanon, Morocco, Palestinian Authority, Tunisia and the UAE. Follow-up semi-structured interviews with the same respondents were conducted during forums and meetings held in Dubai in 2006 and 2007. Data collected through the discussions, presentations, transcripts and proceedings of the meetings were also considered as a quality control method.

Barriers to E-Government in Arab States

The main findings of the research indicate that Arab governments viewed e-government as one of the key focus areas for achieving public sector reform objectives. However, e-government is viewed with different levels of importance in Arab countries. For example, while its urgency is still debated in some Arab states, the Palestinian government officials considered e-government development as almost the only way for businesses and citizens to interact with the government (because of the Israeli-built segregation wall and travel difficulties inside the occupied territories as well as between the two separated population areas of Gaza and West Bank). Another main outcome of the study was the broad realization among Arab states that they, as most developing countries, face common barriers and challenges in e-government initiatives design, implementation and development. There was also vast acknowledgment among participants that there is no single "right" approach to e-government development. We categorized the common challenges faced by e-government directors in the Arab countries in nine main areas. The following paragraphs present the findings of each category in more detail.

Government Instability

The Middle East is one of the most politically turbulent regions in the world. Most Arab states face numerous external and internal challenges as well as increasing threats to their stability and security. As is the case of most other national development projects, e-government initiatives suffer greatly from the prevailing unstable political environment in the region. Furthermore, e-government is widely viewed in many Arab states as a complimentary governance trend rather than an essential reform and modernization approach. Many governments adopt e-government as a form of a cosmetic tool; sometimes in response to international pressure (Ciborra, 2003). It is this view of e-government that makes it one of the first government projects to be "sacrificed" when major security or financial threats pressure the government. In our research, e-government practitioners confirmed that lack of political stability and security are a key barrier to e-government development in several Arab countries. For example, the governments in Lebanon and Palestine considered regional conflicts as the key barriers to e-government development. Frequent government changes and reshuffles and politically motivated commercial or technological embargos are few other examples of the political factors that contributed to e-government failures in many Arab states. Many Arab governments lack sustainable planning and development during government changes, which in many cases take an abrupt form. While this impact is not limited to Arab states, changes in senior government positions closely related to the e-government development plan usually hinder its development severely, or worse, halt it all together. The notion of "handing-over" the management of government projects is lacking in many Arab governments. This causes development projects to abruptly end without reaching the designated objectives. However, despite their agreement on the damaging effect of abrupt governments change in the Arab states to e-government development, officials referred to this barrier differently. Some referred to it as an excuse for the modest status of e-government development in the country. Others put the blame on external political factors for government instability which hampered e-government development as an outcome. A third group acknowledged the disruptive effect of government changes and reshuffles in the Arab region on e-government development as one cause for failure complimenting other challenges.

Development Strategies

The unbefitting positioning of e-government initiatives in the national reform or development plan is one main barrier to e-government progress in the Arab states Several Arab countries have hastily developed their national e-government strategies and visions during the past decade. Since then, many countries have revised and re-launched them over the last few years (for example: Jordan and Bahrain). The main cause of this planning "disappointment" was missing the link in the first place between the e-government plans and the national public sector reform or modernization plans. This was most obvious in countries where public sector reform was under a specialized Ministry of Public Sector Development (or its equivalent) while e-government was under the Ministry of ICT (or its equivalent), with little or no coordination. Since then, some governments have bridged that gap, but some are yet to do so. For example, in Palestine, officials highlighted the lack of coordination between the ministerial administrative reform committee and the e-government committee, while in Egypt both responsibilities fall in the jurisdiction of the Ministry of State for Administrative Development. Our findings also highlight two related factors:

- **Lack of e-government authority:** In earlier plans, several governments placed the e-government portfolio in the hands of a single ministry or government department that lacked the overall authority required for national level e-government development (for example: Jordan, Lebanon and Morocco).
- **Single-sided view of e-government:** Initially, e-government was merely perceived as a "technological mission." This made several earlier unrealistic e-government plans being deemed "null and void." In contrast, many new plans realize the socio-technical nature of e-government and view it as a policy tool for advancing effectiveness and efficiency of the public sector.

Newer -and the renewed- e-government plans in Arab states established this missing link and position the e-government national plan in the core of the overall public sector modernization and reform plan. The findings also highlight different views and levels of acceptance of e-government among different government departments and ministries. For example, despite its advanced e-government initiative, Bahrain's e-government directors viewed the "completion of building a common (e-government) vision and strategy" as the key requirement for e-government development. In Jordan and Lebanon, resistance to change, lack of single e-government authority and low acceptance levels are perceived as the main barriers to e-government dissemination. Similarly, ineffective change management is seen in Bahrain as one of the areas posing key challenge to the e-government development. In most countries, the majority of e-government plans are set centrally for different departments. Occasionally, different departments have different agendas that trigger resistance to changes presented by e-government plans. In many cases, this is usually caused by lack of adequate inter-governmental communication. Concluding his answer, an e-government official in Bahrain confirmed this, indicating the need to have a nationwide concerted e-government effort: "If we had begun with this concerted effort [of involving all the parties in building the e-government strategy] then much more progress could have been realized".

Underdeveloped Institutional Frameworks

e-Government development in most Arab states has so far been largely project-based. The findings indicate that the lack of appropriate e-government institutional structure, sometimes coupled with inadequate financial resources, construct a major barrier to e-government development in the Arab region. For example, participants indicated that one of the most important challenges to e-government implementation in Bahrain is the lack of "inter-ministry partnership and alignment on objectives", a view also shared in Lebanon. In Jordan, e-government practitioners acknowledged the need for common inter-government technological standards. In Morocco, Palestine and Lebanon, e-government practitioners highlighted the fractioned or limited political support for e-government initiatives on certain political levels which hinders the e-government development. Even in more successful examples like the UAE, the lack of such intra-governmental coordination and joint planning mechanisms have caused miss-alignment in systems and approaches and wasted valuable resources as each individual local or federal department built their own system separately (Salem & Jarrar, 2009).

Poor Technical Infrastructure and Lack of Interoperability

Proper ICT infrastructure in the public sector is a key prerequisite for e-government dissemination. The absence of efficient telecommunication infrastructure is a global barrier to e-government development (UNDESA, 2005). Despite a few good performers, most Arab countries suffer from inadequate ICT infrastructure within their public sector agencies. Our research highlights different approaches to IT infrastructure development followed by regional governments and the lack of interoperability among different systems. While all countries in the region have established Internet access at different levels of sophistication, majority of countries are still in the early stages of developing other components of their infrastructure (WEF & INSEAD, 2007; WEF & INSEAD, 2009). Furthermore, most governments in the region are facing challenges to developing a collaborative approach for facilitating interoperable ICT infrastructure among government departments (for example: Jordan, Palestinian Authority, Tunisia, Algeria and Morocco.) A collaborative approach to the public IT infrastructure would ensure setting common standards for critical infrastructure components such as digital signature and authentication, secure data exchange and shared applications.

Legislative and Regulatory Frameworks

Establishing proper legislative and regulatory e-government frameworks is an integral part of successful e-government initiatives (OECD,

2005). Replacing paper-based processes with their legally-accepted electronic counterparts is still in its early stages in most Arab countries. Collectively, participants widely agreed that the lack of appropriate legal frameworks has slowed down the provision of many e-government services in their respective countries.

The levels of available regulatory frameworks differ among the Arab states. For example, Egypt identified regulatory constraints as the top challenge to e-government implementation in the country, a common view shared in Algeria. In Jordan, e-government related laws are all "temporary laws" that lack sufficient authority. E -Government directors in Morocco and Lebanon considered the slow processing and application of e-government related decrees a main barrier. Interestingly, challenges caused by administrative processes that become norms by convention (without regulation) and the problems that arise from changing them through legally accepted e-government processes were highlighted by several countries.

Digital Divide

The digital divide is one of the key global barriers to e-government development and adoption (Cloete, 2004, EC, 2006, OECD, 2005). In developing countries, low internet and PC penetration levels have even more impact on e-government adoption because of the wider digital divide and the more urgent need for reform in the public sector. In general, Arab states suffer from low PC and Internet penetration. UNDESA put the number of Arab Internet users at 10 million (UNDESA, 2005) while other reports put the number at around 26.3 million with 8.5 penetration rate in 2005 (Madar, 2006b).

According to UNCTAD's Digital Divide report, the average ranking of Arab states in the Middle East is 105 among 180 countries while Arab states in North Africa rank 123rd on average (UNCTAD, 2006). Annual internet growth rate is relatively high (55%) and the number of internet users in the Arab states was estimated to reach 52 million by the end of 2008, with 15% penetration rate (Madar, 2006a). Nonetheless, computer illiteracy and low Internet and PC penetration are still relatively widespread.

The findings of our study indicate that all Arab states realize the gravity of the problem. For example, Algeria considers PC and internet penetration the primary priority for e-government development, while Egypt considers it one of the top three key challenges to e-government development. Similarly, Jordan considers low internet penetration a key barrier to e-government development. While in Lebanon, the "society's unwillingness to learn ICT skills" is seen as a main challenge. Given these findings, most Arab governments' officials interviewed have indicated that priority would be given to increasing internet accessibility and the effective development of essential ICT skills among the citizens.

Capacity Deficit

According to our finding, a vast percentage of civil servants in the Arab countries lack the proper ICT knowledge required for successful e-government implementation. In addition to ICT skills, key skills acknowledged as a required for successful e-government development are project management and business process redesign. For example, the UAE government considers capacity building the "biggest constraint (for e-government development) on both federal and local levels". The key skills required for successful e-government implementation in the UAE (as underlined by the UAE government) are project management, business process redesign and technology related skills, a view shared in part by Jordan, Algeria and Tunisia. Additionally, despite the broad realization of the importance of capacity building in the public sector, resistance to change is a common problem that hinders such efforts, thus posing one major barrier to e-government development.

Brain drain is another related constraint for most Arab governments, specifically in sectors closely associated with e-government. While Arab governments with more developed economies, such as the UAE, suffer from the migration of "significantly knowledgeable employees from public to private sectors due to better compensation packages" (a problem also highlighted by Morocco), other Arab countries such as Lebanon, Iraq and the Palestinian Authority suffer from brain drain on a wider national level. A phenomenon not limited to e-government and ICT sectors. The main deterrents for public sector talented workers are perceptions of widespread favoritism, patronage networks, the prevalent rent-seeking model and the general lack of meritocracy (Solimano, 2006). These are national problems rather than e-government specific ones and they should be dealt with on a national level.

Funding Shortage

Financial resource are required for planning and coordinating projects, building infrastructure, developing and managing new information systems as well as for training and capacity building projects. All respondents other than those in the Gulf Cooperation Council (GCC) countries identified funding as a main barrier to their e-government plans (For example, Egypt, Palestinian Authority, Jordan, Morocco, Tunisia and Lebanon).

Some countries also depend on aid from international donors for most of their development projects, which is usually fragmented and heavily dependent on political decisions by international powers. The international donor community has identified e-government as a valid area for aid to assist public sector reform in the many countries in the Arab world. Many of these initiatives have not been successful in driving e-government development, even in countries that managed to secure sustainable funding for their e-government projects. For example, Jordan has received a relatively substantial amount of aid for e-government development in comparison to other countries in the Arab world. Nonetheless our findings confirm earlier research suggesting that the approach that international development agencies followed so far is not necessarily helping in accelerating the development of the e-government initiatives (Ciborra & Navarra, 2005). As a result, many funding initiatives in Arab countries have not been successful in driving e-government development, primarily because they tend to dictate e-government "best practices" from developed countries, ignoring the specific context of Arab states. Additionally, our findings indicate that only few countries have conducted analysis and evaluation of their e-government investments in terms of costs and benefits.

Take-Up of Services

Ensuring the take-up of e-government services by citizens and businesses is one of the most common barriers to e-government dissemination (Eynon & Dutton, 2007, Titah & Barki, 2006). This is clear even in leading e-government initiatives in the Arab states such as the UAE's which ranks highly worldwide in terms of e-government readiness (UNDESA, 2008) and even in cities such as Dubai which usually even rank higher on e-government development (Geray & Al-Bastaki, 2005; Holzer & Kim, 2008; Salem, 2003). In Bahrain, officials stated that changing "public perception on the value of e-government" is perceived as one of the main challenges. Similarly, one of the top priorities in Egypt's e-government development objectives is to provide innovative incentives to encourage current internet users to become "heavy users of e-government online services". The Egyptian government indicated a need to increase public awareness and trust of e-government services as the "usage of e-government services is less than expected", a view shared also by Morocco. As an incentive, the Egyptian government decided to make the cost of many online services less than their manual versions, but citizens kept opting for the manual ones. In another example, officials in Jordan stated that despite the low level of public awareness of e-government advantages, financial resources allocated to e-government development do not take into consideration "marketing" of e-government services adequately.

Our findings confirm that in majority of Arab states, citizens and businesses are provided with limited information on the services available online. They also have limited understanding of the ways to access these services and make use of them. Our research also indicates that electronic service development in the Arab states has not followed a uniform approach. Some countries have followed the quantitative approach of making available as many online services as possible, while others focused mainly on utilizing ICT primarily for reducing the costs and increasing efficiency of back office government procedures. Such approaches have been dubbed as "narrow" as they not take into consideration the information flows in government, which arguably could lead to wider impact of e-government investments and take-up (Mayer-Schönberger & Lazer, 2007).

CONCLUSION AND DISCUSSIONS

On an international level, key outcomes of government programs and initiatives aimed to transform government and society through innovative adoption of information and communication technology include nurturing a culture of innovation in society and public sector and rewiring information flows within government and with society (Mayer- Schönberger & Lazer, 2007). In addition, e-government can potentially promote a more participatory and transparent government model, increase the accessibility to government information, and increasing the levels of trust, satisfaction and interaction of citizens with the government (Salem & Jarrar, 2009). These objective are added to the direct intended outcomes of creating a more responsive and efficient government by cutting red-tape and decreasing the negative side-effects of bureaucracy in public agencies. The overall societal value of e-government development on a national level is to nurture economic growth by reducing corruption, the costs of government transactions and the costs of doing business both between the public and private sector and on the intra-governmental level (Lau, 2007).

Today, understanding societal and government innovative transformations through information and communication technology in the Arab countries is gaining unprecedented importance for public policy makers, the business community and civil society at large due to the paradigm shift in innovation in governance approaches.

However, the existing research on ICT, innovation and government transformation in developed countries is often less relevant in the context of developing nations, and even more so in the Arab world. Applying practices based on experiences and research conducted in developed nations had mostly resulted in vast actuality gaps between expectations and realities in developing countries.

Based on our regional study findings and consistent with prior e-government research, we argue that "replicable best practices" in a complex and developing field such as e-government rarely exist in the regional context of the Arab countries. Such practices are always helpful tools for triggering ideas and developing innovative ways of overcoming e-government barriers and avoiding failures, but good practices should not be copied or cloned. In many cases, the "if it works for them, it will work for us" approach would be the formula of failure in e-government projects (Ciborra & Navarra, 2005, Heeks, 2002). Instead, studying failed e-government projects in countries sharing similar public sector environment on the cultural, political and social levels might be a better learning approach for avoiding such pitfalls.

Based on our regional research findings, we conclude that e-government projects in the Arab states would have a higher probability of success and would be better equipped for avoiding repeated failure only when the "right fit" is achieved between leadership commitment, sustainable development, a clear cross-government vision, appropriate planning, rational business strategy, suitable regulatory framework, practical awareness campaign and rigorous capacity building for the public administrators and society at large. This "right fit" is very much contextual. Despite the many similarities and the common constraints and barriers to e-government development in the Arab countries, each state has its unique combination of political, regulatory, economic and social constraints that affect the e-government development efforts differently. Finally, we call for nurturing a culture for learning from failures as an imperative for development in the Arab states. In the rapidly developing e-government field where failures are more probable, such culture should be promoted. This would have to go hand in hand with a systematic assessment of the hidden costs of failures of e-government projects. Country-specific e-government risk assessment and management approaches could also be developed and implemented throughout the design and implementation phases of e-government projects. This should limit the impact of failed projects as well as make the process of learning from failure more systematic. Senior public managers in the Arab states should accept the high probability of partial and total failures in e-government projects more openly as a first step for overcoming them and understanding the associated challenges. Moving forward, if this is accompanied with a vision for knowledge management where failed projects are perceived as valuable learning processes, failures would be increasingly perceived as common risks that could be alleviated in advance.

REFERENCES

Akther, M. S., Onishi, T., & Kidokoro, T. (2005). *E-Government Practice: What One Country Could Learn from Other Electronic Government*. Berlin, Heidelberg: Springer.

AP. (2004). E-Governance Failures Abound. *The Associated Press.*

Ciborra, C. (2003). E-government: Between Development and War. In Järvi, T., & Reijonen, P. (Eds.), *People and Computers*. Tuscon, Arizona: TUCS Publications.

Ciborra, C., & Navarra, D. D. (2005). Good governance, development theory, and aid policy: Risks and challenges of e-government in Jordan. *InformationTechnology for Development*, *11*(2), 141–159. doi:10.1002/itdj.20008

Cloete, F. (2004). *Maximising the potential of transforming policy failure into policy success: E-government, the digital divide and e-development.* Annual Congress of the International Institute of Administrative Sciences (IIAS). Seoul, South Korea.

Davenport, E., & Horton, K. (2004) A Social Shaping Perspective on an e-Governmental System(ic) Failure. In Traunmuller, R. (Ed.), *Electronic government: Third International Conference, EGOV.* Berlin: Springer.

Dunleavy, P., Margetts, H., Bastow, S., & Tinkler, J. (2004) Government IT Performance and the Power of the IT Industry: A Cross-National Analysis. *Annual Meeting of American Political Science Association.* Chicago, IL.

EC. (2006). *Breaking Barriers to e-government - Overcoming Obstacles to Improving European Public Services. e-government Unit.* Oxford, UK: DG Information Society and Media, European Commission.

Eynon, R., & Dutton, W. H. (2007). Barriers to Networked Governments: Evidence from Europe. *Prometheus*, *25*(3), 225–242. doi:10.1080/08109020701531361

Geray, O., & Al-Bastaki, M. (2005). *Dubai e-government initiative: Concepts, achievements, and future pillars of success. (UNDP Report). Dubai.* UAE.

Heeks, R. (2002). Information Systems and Developing Countries: Failure, Success, and Local Improvisations. *The Information Society, 18*(2), 101–112. doi:10.1080/01972240290075039

Heeks, R. (2006). *Implementing and Managing e-government: An International Text*. London: Sage publications.

Hofstede, G. (2004). *Cultures and Organizations: Software for the Mind*. New York: McGraw-Hill.

Holzer, M., & Kim, S.-T. (2008). Digital Governance in Municipalities Worldwide. In *The E-Governance Institute, National Center for Public Performance*. Newark, NJ:Rutgers, the State University of New Jersey

Lau, E. (2007). Electronic Government and the Drive for Growth and Equity. In Mayerschönberger, V., & Lazer, D. (Eds.), *Governance and Information Technology: From Electronic Government to Information Government*. Cambridge, Massachusetts: MIT Press.

Madar (2006a). Arab ICT Use Index, 2005. *Madar Research Journal, 4*(1).

Madar (2006b). Arab Internet users exceed 26 million in 2005. *Arab Knowledge Economy Newsletter, 1*(2), 1-8.

Margetts, H., & Dunleavy, P. (2002). *Cultural Barriers to E-Government*. London: National Audit Office.

Mayer-Schönberger, V., & Lazer, D. (2007). *Governance and Information Technology: From Electronic Government to InformationGovernment*. Cambridge, Massachusetts: MIT Press.

OECD. (2005) *e-Government for Better Government*. Paris: OECD.

OECD & DSG. (2007). Measuring and Evaluating e-Government in Arab Countries. In *Governance for Development in Arab Countries Initiative: 3rd WG2 High Level Seminar on e-Government and Administrative Simplification*. Dubai: OECD.

Pardo, T. A., & Scholl, H. J. (2002). Walking Atop the Cliffs: Avoiding Failure and Reducing Risk in Large Scale E-Government Projects. In *Proceedings of the 35thAnnual Hawaii International Conference on System Sciences (HICSS)*, 1656- 1665.

Salem, F. (2003). Evaluating Dubai Government e-Services (Against EU States). In Kamli, A. K. (Ed.), *Dubai Knowledge Economy 2003-2008. Dubai, UAE: Madar Research*.

Salem, F. (2007). Benchmarking the e-government bulldozer: beyond measuring thetread marks. *Journal of Measuring Business Excellence, 11*(4), 9–22. doi:10.1108/13683040710837892

Salem, F., & Jarrar, Y. (2009). *Cross-agency Collaboration in the UAE Government: The Role of Trust and Impact of Technology*. Dubai, UAE: Dubai School of Government.

Solimano, A. (2006) *The International Mobility of Talent and its Impact on Global Development*. New York: United Nations University - World Institute for Development Economic Research (UNU-WIDER).

Titah, R., & Barki, H. (2006). E-Government Adoption and Acceptance: A Literature Review. *International Journal of Electronic Government Research, 2*(3), 23–57.

UNCTAD. (2006) *The Digital Divide Report: ICT Diffusion Index 2005*. New York and Geneva: United Nations Conference on Trade and Development.

UNDESA. (2003). *World Public Sector Report 2003*. New York: United Nations Department of Economic and Social Affairs.

UNDESA. (2005). *Global E-government Readiness Report 2005 - From E-government to E-inclusion*. New York: United Nations Department of Economic and Social Affairs.

UNDESA. (2008) *UN E-Government Survey 2008: From E-Government to Connected Governance.* New York: United Nations Department of Economic and Social Affairs (UNDESA), Division for Public Administration and Development Management.

WEF & INSEAD. (2007). *World Economic Forum and INSEAD,* The Global Information Technology Report 2006-2007. Genevea, Switzerland.

WEF & INSEAD. (2009) *Mobility in a Networked World World Economic Forum*, The Global Information Technology Report 2008–2009. Geneva, Switzerland.

Chapter 32
A Secure Electronic Voting

Mohammed Abdula Saleh Al-helali
Al- Rafedain University, Iraq

Wamedh Wadood Abdoul Hameed
Al- Rafedain University, Iraq

ABSTRACT

This chapter presents a security framework architecture for electronic voting that permits the avoidance of problems occasioned by interposing computer system and technical personnel between the voter and the electoral board. The architecture is based on replicating the conventional security mechanisms and in segregating all critical functions into very simple systems that are audited, monitored and physically secured. This security architecture minimizes the number of components that must be trusted to only two, namely, the software generating the encrypted ballot and the software opening the digital ballot boxes and the envelopes there in. This addresses one of the main causes of trouble in electronic voting systems, namely, the need to trust overly-complex systems like DREs, web browsers, operating systems or Internet servers.

INTRODUCTION

Electronic voting (also known as e-voting) is a term encompassing several different types of voting, embracing both electronic means of casting a vote and electronic means of counting votes.

Electronic voting technology can include punch cards, optical scan voting systems and specialized voting kiosks (including self-contained Direct-recording electronic (DRE) voting systems). It can also involve transmission of ballots and votes via telephones, private computer networks, or the Internet. Electronic voting technology can speed the counting of ballots and can provide improved accessibility for disabled voters. However, there has been contention, that electronic voting especially DRE voting could facilitate electoral fraud. Electronic voting systems for electorates have been in use since the 1960s when punch card systems debuted. The newer optical scan voting systems allow a computer to count a voter's mark on a

DOI: 10.4018/978-1-61520-789-3.ch032

ballot. DRE voting machines which collect and tabulate votes in a single machine.

The last fifteen years following the wider trend of ICT adoption in government (e-government) some countries have started slowly adopting and in some cases fully substituting traditional voting systems with electronic voting systems (e-voting).

E-Voting comes in different forms and shapes. A general distinction could be made between electronic machine voting (eMV), which is voting on an election controlled device, and electronic distance voting (eDV), which allows voting remotely using mediums such as the Internet, Short Message Service (SMS), and interactive TV.

Chapter-Based Electronic Voting System

Sometimes called a "document ballot voting system," chapter-based voting systems originated as a system where votes are cast and counted by hand, using paper ballots. With the advent of electronic tabulation came systems where paper cards or sheets could be marked by hand, but counted electronically. These systems included punch card voting, mark sense and later digital pen voting systems.

Most recently, these systems can include an Electronic Ballot Marker (EBM), that allow voters to make their selections using an electronic input device, usually a touch screen system similar to a DRE. Systems including a ballot marking device can incorporate different forms of assistive technology.

Direct-Recording Electronic (DRE) Voting System

A *direct-recording electronic* (DRE) voting machine records votes by means of a ballot display provided with mechanical or electro-optical components that can be activated by the voter (typically buttons or a touch screen).

They were introduced in the 1970s. DREs are somewhat analogous to (although more sophisticated than) lever machines. The voter chooses candidates from a posted ballot. Depending on the equipment used, the ballot may be printed and posted on the DRE, as it is with a lever machine, or it may be displayed on a computer screen. Voters make their choices by pushing buttons, touching the screen, or using other devices. The voter submits the choices made before leaving the booth, for example by pushing a "vote" button, and the votes are then recorded electronically. that processes data by means of a computer program; and that records voting data and ballot images in memory components. After the election it produces a tabulation of the voting data stored in a removable memory component and as printed copy. The system may also provide a means for transmitting individual ballots or vote totals to a central location for consolidating and reporting results from precincts at the central location.

Like all voting machines DRE systems increase the speed of vote counting. They can also incorporate the most broad assistive technologies for the largest classes of handicapped people, allowing them to vote without forfeiting the anonymity of their vote. These machines can use headphones and other adaptive technology to provide the necessary accessibility. DRE's can also provide the most robust form of immediate feedback to the voter detecting such possible problems as undervoting and overvoting which may result in a spoiled ballot. This immediate feedback can be helpful in successfully determining voter intent.

Additionally, with DRE voting systems there is no risk of exhausting the supply of paper ballots, and remove the need for printing of paper ballots, a significant cost. When administering elections in which ballots are offered in multiple languages, DRE voting systems can be programmed to provide ballots in multiple languages on a single machine.

Smartcards

While it is true that one can design secure systems around the use of smartcards, merely the use of smartcards in a system does not imply that the system is secure. The system must use the smartcards in an intelligent and security-conscious way. Unfortunately, the Diebold system's use of smartcards provides very little (if any) additional security and, in fact, opens the system to several attacks.

Public Network DRE Voting System

A public network DRE voting system is an election system that uses electronic ballots and transmits vote data from the polling place to another location over a public network. Vote data may be transmitted as individual ballots as they are cast, periodically as batches of ballots throughout the election day, or as one batch at the close of voting. This includes Internet voting as well as telephone voting. Public network DRE voting system can utilize either precinct count or central count method. The central count method tabulates ballots from multiple precincts at a central location. Internet voting can use remote locations (voting from any Internet capable computer) or can use traditional polling locations with voting booths consisting of Internet connected voting systems.

Corporations and organizations routinely use Internet voting to elect officers and Board members and for other proxy elections. Internet voting systems have been used privately in many modern nations.

Security Concerns about DREs

One thing that distinguishes DREs from document ballot systems is that with DREs, the voter does not see the actual ballot, but rather a representation of it on the face of the machine. With few exceptions, current DREs do not provide a truly independent record of each individual ballot that can be used in a recount to check for machine error or tampering. The ballot itself consists of redundant electronic records in the machine's computer memory banks, which the voter cannot see. This is analogous to the situation with mechanical lever voting machines, where casting the ballot moves counters that are out of view of the voter. In a lever machine, if the appropriate counters do not move correctly when a voter casts the ballot, the voter will not know, nor would an observer. Similarly, with a DRE, if the machine recorded a result in its memory that was different from what the voter chose, neither the voter nor an observer would know.

The same is true with a computerized counting system when it reads punchcards or optical scan ballots. Even if the ballot is tabulated in the precinct and fed into the reading device in the presence of the voter, neither the voter nor the pollworker manning the reader can see what it is recording in its memory. However, with such a reader, the ballot documents could be counted on another machine or by hand if there were any question about the results.

Lever machines also do not have an independent document ballot. That has led some observers to distrust those machines, but most who use them appear confident that tests and other procedural safeguards render them sufficiently safe from tampering. Is the same true for DREs? Some computer experts think not, arguing that the software could be modified in ways that could alter the results of an election and that would be very difficult to detect. This concern appears to stem largely from three factors:

- Malicious computer code, or malware, can often be written in such a way that it is very difficult to detect.
- DRE software is moderately complex, and it is generally accepted that the more complex a piece of software is, the more difficult it can be to detect unauthorized modifications.

- Most manufacturers of DREs treat their software code as proprietary information and therefore not available for public scrutiny. Consequently, it is not possible for experts not associated with the companies to determine how vulnerable the code is to tampering.

Accessibility

Electronic voting machines can be made fully accessible for persons with disabilities. Punchcard and optical scan machines are not fully accessible for the blind or visually impaired, and lever machines can be difficult for voters with limited mobility and strength. Electronic machines can use headphones, sip and puff, foot pedals, joy sticks and other adaptive technology to provide the necessary accessibility. Organizations such as the Verified Voting Foundation have criticized the accessibility of electronic voting machines and advocate alternatives. Some disabled voters (including the visually impaired) could use a tactile ballot, a ballot system using physical markers to indicate where a mark should be made, to vote a secret paper ballot. These ballots can be designed identically to those used by other voters. However, other disabled voters (including voters with dexterity disabilities) could be unable to use these ballots.

Cryptographic Verification

Electronic voting systems can offer solutions that allow voters to verify their vote is recorded and tabulated with mathematical calculations. These systems can alleviate concerns of incorrectly recorded votes. One feature to mitigate such concerns could be to allow a voter to prove how they voted, with some form of electronic receipt, signed by the voting authority using digital signatures. This feature can conclusively prove the accuracy of the tally, but any verification system that cannot guarantee the anonymity of voter's choice, can enable voter intimidation or vote selling. Some cryptographic solutions aim to allow the voter to verify their vote personally, but not to a third party. One such way would be to provide the voter with a digitally signed receipt of their vote as well as receipts of other randomly selected votes. This would allow only the voter to identify her vote, but not be able to prove her vote to anyone else. Furthermore, each vote could be tagged with a randomly generated voting session id, which would allow the voter to check that the vote was recorded correctly in a public audit trail of the ballot.

Requirements for E-Voting

Traditional voting systems have been developed to ensure that the principles required for democratic elections and referendums are met, namely the guarantee of the freedom to vote, the secrecy of the vote, the non modification of the expressed intention of the vote and lack of intimidation during the vote operation. It is essential that these principles are not undermined by the introduction of new voting methods and, accordingly, e-voting systems must be so designed and operated as to ensure the reliability and security of the voting process.

In sum: E-voting has to be as free, secret, reliable and secure as voting systems that do not involve the use of electronic means.

An e-voting system therefore should consider the following minimum requirements:

1. To ensure that only persons with the right to vote are able to cast a vote.
2. To ensure that every vote cast is counted and that each vote is counted only once.
3. To maintain the voter's right to form and to express his or her opinion in a free manner, without any coercion or undue influence.
4. To protect the secrecy of the vote at all stages of the voting process.

5. To guarantee accessibility to as many voters as possible, especially with regard to persons with disabilities.
6. To increase voter confidence by maximising the transparency of information on the functioning of each system.

FUNCTIONAL REQUIREMENTS

Enhancement to the online voting system will primarily provide a more precise vote management tool that will establish accountability and improve data accuracy, and thus allowing voters to feel a greater level of confidence in the reported data. The majority of the precinct managers, who will benefit from these enhancements, currently use their professional judgment and expertise to anticipate the voter's needs when making decisions. They also rely on outside vendor data and poorly captured metrics from the current state of traditional voting system.

Appropriate behavior constitutes the functionality of a system and there is often a tight correspondence between particular requirements and particular functions of the solution system [*Analysis of an Electronic*]. The following represents a partial list of functional requirements for the **Online Voting System:**

1. The system must provide voters with accurate data
2. Metric reports of current/live votes must be provided
3. The system should make use of tools available for users on the internet
4. It must adhere to government requirements
5. Ease of GUI use that can be accessed via web browser must be established
6. The system must follow technical development standards supported on known operating systems such as Windows, Linux, and UNIX, in addition to future operating systems versions
7. The system must grant technician/customer general communications and training documents
8. The system must supply a prototype or process to approve site customization
9. Backup data restore capabilities should be granted
10. The system must send a notification to administrator if an onsite workstation is classified as inoperative or unusable
11. The system should send a notification to administrator of updates from Verification popup windows
12. The system must supply standard reports for decision making
13. Audit trails of who made changes to the database must be maintained
14. The system should allow voting administrators to make updates to the voter information database
15. The system must verify on a daily basis responsible users ID and location
16. The system must provide standard error checking
17. The system must provide data integrity checks to ensure data remains consistent and updated

MAJOR CONSTRIANTS

When dealing with requirements engineering for any systems, there are some constraints that must be considered. The major constraints for the Online Voting System are:

1. Voting is carried out from many consoles on the internet.
2. All voting is done in one day.
3. Many interfaces exist including Windows Explorer, Netscape, and Mozilla browsers.
4. The operating system in use are, but not limited to, Windows, Linux, and UNIX.

5. Many different levels of expertise in the system use will be prevalent.
6. Each state can administer the system differently depending on state laws.
7. Each state can have unique election and proposals, needing many different administrative interfaces.

NONFUNCTIONAL REQUIREMENTS

Nonfunctional requirements are requirements that are not specifically concerned with the functionality of a system. They normally place restrictions on the product being developed and the development process. Nonfunctional requirements may be regarded as parameters of functionality in that they determine how quickly, how accurately, how reliably, how securely, etc., functions must operate. Some of the Online Voting System's nonfunctional requirements are as follows.

Response and net processing time must be acceptable by user and by application Defects in the local voting database file must be less than 0.0001% Defects contained in the collection server must be less than 0.0001% Defects in the database must be less than 0.0001% Number of collection failures per voting process must be at six sigma, or better. Taking the entire state of Michigan, with a population of about 9.9M citizens (if all voted), as an Example, this works out to be 33 errors When checking the database for errors, a 100% scan of the data is required, rather than selecting a sample set.

The system must be working at 100% peak efficiency during the voting process. Transfer of existing and future data to an Voting Management Data Center must be Granted The system should be allow adding more voters to allow a greater connectivity rate A process must be devised to support normal precinct business hours The system should support response time for addressing severe issues in less than 5 minutes, due to the shortness of the voting timeframe. The system should provide documentation to inform users of system functionality and any change to the system. The system should provide friendly graphical Interface to ensure ease of use when end users utilize system functionality

Electronic Voting Risks and Challenges

As explained in the previous section, electronic voting has the potential to improve our electoral processes in many ways. This sort of technology also promises to enable efficient participatory (e-consultation or e-participation) platforms with the objective of building trust in governments by allowing people to have their say in the decision-making process.

Electronic voting and electronic consultation therefore become exemplary tools for enhancing democracy. However, electronic voting is not problem-free. A whole new set of risks and challenges is created by this new voting scenario that is based on the use of electronic voting systems. These risks and challenges can be broadly classified in three categories: legislative, socio-political and technological. Legislative challenges appear as a consequence of the introduction of new electoral legislation, as current electoral laws do not usually allow for electronic voting procedures. Socio-political challenges and risks are consequences of the impact on the electorate of new ways of voting and in particular of ICT-based voting systems. The *digital divide* is often referred to as the primary socio-political issue. With respect to technological risks and challenges, the most important relate to security and confidence. An analysis of several socio-political and technical concerns with electronic voting can be found in. This chapter focuses on the currently most debated risks and challenges that relate to security, trustworthiness and confidence. Electronic voting systems are in their nature very different from traditional, physical voting methods. Because of these differences, four main sources of risks can be encountered:

- The digital nature of the ballots.
- The complexity of the systems used.
- The lack of transparency – to the voters and electoral authorities – of the Systems used.
- The existence of people that have special abilities and/or privileges in the systems used.

These four factors act as the source of a whole range of particular threats and attacks. To name a few, electronic equipment may malfunction, software may contain intentional or unintentional programming errors, ballots may be deleted or manipulated by privileged actors, and voters' privacy may be undermined. All of these problems are very serious and can threaten the integrity of elections and undermine confidence in democratic processes as well. As the final range of problems is extensive, there are a large number of publications detailing security and integrity risks that can be found in electronic voting. From the above, it is clear that an electronic voting system not suitably protected will face a large list of security problems. In the past few years, and especially after 2000, a debate at many levels – academic, governmental and industrial – has taken place to discuss both the advantages and the security risks of electronic voting. Although most of the hype was initially placed on remote voting over the internet, this debate has been recently extended to all kinds of electronic voting, and it is currently including DRE-based poll-site voting systems. In the context of this debate, some computer scientists have championed the need to complement computerised electoral systems with a physical record (usually chapter) of each vote that can be visually verified by the voter before being cast.

The call for a voter verifiable physical trail has recently received much attention and publicity in the USA as witnessed by the "Resolution on Electronic Voting" that has been endorsed by over one thousand people so far. In line with their arguments, in which a voter verifiable paper trail is required. The above resolution demands the incorporation of a paper trail in DRE machines. According to the resolution, DRE systems, although superficially attractive to both voters and election officials, hide many dangerous problems that can only be solved by the addition of a paper printer. The objective of such printer is to create a physical record of each vote, verifiable by voters in real-time, and useful for recount purposes. Without printers, they argue, DRE machines must not be used in elections in the US. In our opinion, there is room for improvement in current electronic equipment used in elections worldwide, although we believe that other solutions are possible that do not rely on the extensive use of paper. We believe that the ultimate goal is to have secure, reliable and auditable voting systems, rather than to have paper-centred voting systems.

Security, reliability and auditability of electronic voting may be achieved without a paper trail. Although the inclusion of printers in electronic voting systems is possible and gives an additional layer of confidence, it involves its own list of problems. Printers often have paper jams and they run out of paper. There are high costs in printing, securing and transporting paper ballots. The extensive use of paper poses, in general, administrative headaches for election officials. From our point of view, putting a paper trail in an electronic voting system is like removing the engine from a brand-new automobile and pulling it around by a horse. It is possible, but it is senseless. We believe that adequate solutions must be devised to bring trust to pure electronic voting systems.

Threats

Kinds of Attacks and Attackers. The best known type of attack on a voting system is one that changes the vote totals from what voters actually cast such as adding, dropping, or switching votes.

Many of the features of modern voting systems such as secret balloting and the use of observers are designed to thwart such threats. The impact of such vote tampering depends on several factors. Two of the most important are the scale of an attack and the competitiveness of the contest. An attack would have to have sufficient impact to affect the outcome of the election. For that to happen, scale is critical. If tampering impacts only one ballot or one voting machine, the chances of that affecting the election outcome would be small. But tampering that affects many machines or the results from several precincts could have a substantial impact, although it might also be more likely to be detected. The scale of attack needed to affect the outcome of an election depends on what proportion of voters favor each candidate. The more closely contested an election is, the smaller the degree of tampering that would be necessary to affect the outcome.34 While attacks that added, subtracted, or changed individual votes are of particular concern, other kinds of attacks also need to be considered. One type of attack might gather information that a candidate could use to increase the chance of winning. For example, if vote totals from particular precincts could secretly be made known to operatives for one candidate before the polls closed, 35 the results could be used to adjust get-out-the-vote efforts, giving that candidate an unfair advantage.

Another type of attack might be used to disrupt voting. For example, malware could be used to cause voting machines to malfunction frequently. The resulting delays could reduce turnout, perhaps to the benefit of one candidate, or could even cause voters to lose confidence in the integrity of the election in general. The latter might be of more interest to terrorists or others with an interest in having a negative impact on the political system generally.

An Evolving Threat Environment

The kinds of attacks described above are potential threats against any voting system. However, the growing use of information technology in elections has had unique impacts on the threat environment. It provides the opportunity for new kinds of attacks, from new kinds of attackers. As information technology has advanced and cyberspace has grown, so too have the rate and sophistication of cyberattacks in general

- The number of reported computer-security violations has grown exponentially in the past decade, from about 100 in 1989 to more than 100,000 in the first three quarters of 2003.
- Potential threats may now come from many sources — amateur or professional hackers using the Internet, insiders in organizations, organized crime, terrorists, or even foreign governments. With respect to election tampering, some such attackers could benefit in traditional ways, but some, such as terrorists, might be interested instead in disrupting elections or reducing the confidence of voters in the electoral process.
- New and more ingenious kinds of malware are constantly being invented and used. There are now tens of thousands of known viruses, and the sophistication of tools used to develop and use new ones has increased.

Malware in a voting system could be designed to operate in very subtle ways, for example, dropping or changing votes in a seemingly random way to make detection more difficult. Malware can also be designed to be adaptive — changing what it does depending on the direction of the tally. It could also potentially be inserted at any of a number of different stages in the development and implementation process — from the precinct all the way back to initial manufacture — and lie in wait for the appropriate moment.

Several other kinds of attack could also be attempted in addition to malware.

Among them are electronic interception and theft or modification of information during transport or transmission, modifications or additions of hardware, and bypassing system controls or misuse of authority to tamper with or collect information on software or election data.

Enabling Trustworthy Electronic Voting

Traditional paper-based voting systems obtain their confidence through the direct, face-to-face interaction between voters and election authorities, as well as the physical evidence (paper ballots) that remains after the polling places close. Ballot secrecy and integrity is preserved by paper envelopes and physical ballot boxes. The fairness of the tallying process relies on the fact that electoral boards are composed of (and/or monitored by) people of opposing interests (e.g. members of different parties), which presumably prevents any collusion to alter the election results. Moreover, independent third parties and observers supervise the entire electoral process.

In contrast, pure electronic voting introduces a totally new interface between voters and election authorities and it removes the physical audit trails. The straight human-to-human interaction of traditional systems is substituted by a variety of hardware and software components, whose inner workings are not easily accessible or understandable. A new and complex technological infrastructure is interposed between the voters and the election authorities who in the end will tally the votes, obscuring the transparency of the ballot casting process. In addition, to create and administer this new infrastructure, technicians control the computer systems that are between the voters and the electoral board. Through their positions and functions, these technical people have many privileges that could be used to corrupt the electoral process. Therefore, naively implemented electronic voting systems can pose very serious threats to election integrity and shake the public's confidence in elections.

We propose a security architecture for electronic voting that replicates the conventional security measures found in traditional elections. The principal objective of this architecture is to avoid putting all of one's trust on the computing infrastructure and on the technical people operating between the voters and the electoral authorities. The group of systems that compose the front-end of an electronic voting system (the systems that capture the ballots, be they web servers or DRE machines) are by definition complicated machines and difficult to protect or to certify. These are usually closed proprietary systems that are exposed to some extent to the risk of internal attacks by privileged operators. In the case of servers connected to the internet, the number of risks clearly grows. This means that the effort to protect such machines becomes an extremely difficult task, and trusting them is not a good policy. We feel that opponents of electronic voting are correct on this point. Our focus consists in maintaining a clear separation of critical and non-critical modules. In this way, it is only necessary to trust the two modules located at the extremes of the system (at the beginning with the voter and at the end with the electoral board). By means of end-to-end, application-level cryptographic protocols, a direct "secured voting dialog" can occur between the voter and the corresponding electoral board. In this way, the electoral process integrity is no longer exposed to the rest of the electronic voting infrastructure, systems, components and technical personnel interposed in between. These two modules at the extremes are very simple, auditable, open and protected with physical and/or logical security.

All the critical functions described below are realised in these two extremely simple modules. The first module is the *voting agent* used by voters. It is a light-weight piece of software that can take the form of a digitally-signed applet of a couple hundred kilobytes, running either in the voter's browser or as an add-on to DRE software. The certification of such an applet avoids all of the complexity associated with the host operating system, the ballot presentation software, the network interface and so on. For improved security in remote electronic voting, the voting agent could run on a "clean" operating system version loaded from a bootable CDROM provided by the electoral authorities. In the case of DRE-based poll-site voting, maximum security would be attained if the voting agent ran on a simple hardware device attached to the DRE machine.

The second module is the *electoral board agent*. It consists of software, which is used to generate sensitive cryptographic keys and other critical data, and perform the critical process of opening digital ballot boxes. This software should be open and extensively audited by several parties. It runs on a very simple specific-purpose hardware system, directly operated by election authorities and constantly monitored by several parties. It is connected to a dedicated network or, even better, totally disconnected from any network at all. Physical security is extremely important to protect this module.

At this point it may be noticed that the main principle of this security architecture changes the current paradigm of electronic voting, in which the DREs or in many cases the remote voting platforms group the casting, recording and counting of ballots in a unitary, complex system, more easily accessed by technicians than by electoral board members. We propose a new paradigm that permits a secure and trustworthy use of such complex proprietary DRE devices or remote voting platforms that offer the advantages of usability, flexibility, and support for multiple languages and for the disabled.

Let us provide an overview of how our two key software modules operate in order to circumvent the problems that plague unprotected electronic voting systems. During the ballot casting period, after the voter has been properly authenticated, the voting agent performs security functions on his/her behalf. For instance, the voting agent becomes the hands of the voter, cryptographically sealing the virtual ballot for him/her.

This takes place when the voter makes his/her choices on a virtual personalized ballot that is presented through the DRE device or the web pages that constitute the remote voting platform. Once the choices are made, the virtual ballot is not directly recorded by the DRE nor sent back to a ballot collecting server. Instead, the virtual ballot is passed to the voting agent, which seals it in a digital envelope. The digital envelope protects the confidentiality and integrity of the ballot, as it is created by using a public (encryption) key for which the private (decryption) key does not exist.

Other additional tasks performed by the voting agent include attaching a proof of authorship to the digital envelope (to ensure its authenticity) and obtaining a validated voting receipt. The voting receipt contains a unique identifier for the ballot. This unique identifier is not known by anyone as its creation and subsequent validation take place in a blind cryptographic process. A copy of the identification number is placed into the digital envelope along with the virtual ballot, while the voter keeps a copy of the voting receipt (it can be saved to disk or printed on paper if desired). When the election outcomes are published the voting receipt will allow the voter to check whether his/her ballot has successfully reached the electoral board. If not, the receipt will allow the voter to complain with irrefutable proof, as it incorporates a digital signature proving its validity. It is important to stress that the voting receipt does not allow for systemic coercion or vote-selling, as it does not show who the voter voted for.

This voting protocol enables the creation of ballot boxes that are secure even from privileged personnel that have programmed and/or are operating the systems that manage the ballots and the ballot boxes. At the end of the election, the digital ballot boxes are securely transferred to the second critical software module, the electoral board agent. In the most secure scenario, this electoral board agent runs on secure and simple hardware completely disconnected from any network. This would require that the transfer of the digital ballot boxes is done by physical means in such cases. To open up the digital ballot boxes, a predetermined threshold of electoral board members must present their cryptographic credentials to the electoral board agent. This replicates the distribution of trust principle used in conventional elections in the digital domain. The collaboration of the members of the electoral board allows the reconstruction of the private key needed to open the digital envelopes that protect ballots.

This is done simultaneously with a cryptographic mixing process, which breaks the correlation between the voters and the contents of their ballots, eliminating any possibility of the violation of their privacy. Moreover, as the ballots collected during the ballot casting period can only be decrypted with a non-existent key, this also ensures the secrecy of intermediate results (an important issue if the election takes place over several time zones or in the case of extended periods of voting).

The voting receipts that we described above fulfill the important mission of improving the voter's confidence in the system: the immediate reassurance that every ballot has been taken into account, that occurs when paper-based ballots are physically cast in front of the electoral board, is lost in electronic voting. In our proposed security architecture, all the unique ballot identifiers are published at the end of the election, electronically and/or in newspapers or official bulletins. Since each identifier is protected into the same digital envelope that contains the actual ballot, the publication of an identifier guarantees that the corresponding ballot has been received and processed by the electoral board (and therefore has not been lost or manipulated at any point between the voter and the electoral board). This is at least the same degree of assurance as that provided in conventional elections systems when the voter sees the paper envelope being placed into the urn that is controlled by the electoral board. Therefore, these voting receipts are an essential part of electronic voting that establish voter confidence in the system.

Conventional voting processes also provide an additional physical audit trail that allows verifying the fairness of the election by any trusted third party. The main component of this verifiable audit trail is paper-based and consists of the ballots themselves. In principle, electronic voting eliminates this well-known audit token (although it is also subject to threats, fraud and errors). Therefore, electronic voting systems must provide alternative means of independent verification. This issue has raised well-founded concerns (Mercury, 2002), regarding specifically how to demonstrate after the election that all valid ballots (and only valid ballots) have been counted.

As explained previously, one proposed solution for DRE systems is the generation of printed ballots as a back-up paper trail. We feel that the current technology can and must go further, and provide audit trails that are safer and more dependable than paper-based ones. In the proposed security architecture, as every valid ballot incorporates a proof of authenticity that only the legitimate voter is able to create, this prevents privileged personnel from adding invalid ballots or from modifying the valid ballots. All the critical system operations are logged (using trusted, auditable software subsystems devoted to handling the voting protocol) and cryptographically protected with the aid of chained digital signatures created in tamperresistant cryptographic hardware modules. The counting of ballots is a very sensitive process, and so it should take place in a very simple, tightly monitored, and physically-protected device.

The software in this device must be subject to the highest software certification standards, and possibly including the requirement of being open-source (at least open to the proper certifying institutions). In addition to being constantly monitored, the device cannot initiate the opening of the ballots' digital envelopes until the members of the electoral board gather together.

We believe that electronic audit trails can totally substitute paper trails if so desired, but by no means prevent their use; in a way they can be an excellent complement to paper trails, reinforcing and enhancing them with the addition of the digital signatures validating the ballots in the printed records (properly encoded, e.g. using bar codes).

An implementation of the proposed architecture is already available and it is currently being integrated in governmental systems and in ASP platforms providing voting to the private and public sectors. In this system, the voting agent is implemented as a small Java applet that can run in a wide range of client platforms, including the vast majority of desktop computer browsers, PDAs and interactive TV set-top boxes. The product can also be deployed in poll-site systems, providing a much needed trust boost to DRE-based electronic voting systems.

System Accountability

A voting system should be able to detect malfunctions and possible manipulations, reconstruct the result and be capable of identifying its causes. Auditing the election process in terms of its electronic and physical processes help towards that goal. Auditing though presents a major challenge in e-voting systems. The fact that voter anonymity needs to be maintained disallows the voter from receiving a receipt, like in financial transactions, that shows how he or she voted. Such a receipt could have then been checked against the actual results in order to verify their correctness.

In an attempt to adjust the financial receipt in the voting context the concept of voter-verified paper trail has been suggested. This only works in eMV as it requires the voter to get a printed receipt from the voting machine then check its correctness and place it in a ballot box. This allows for an end-to end audit since both input verification and reliable recount becomes possible, Luck of such receipts makes auditing less reliable. Suggestions to better this reliability concern propose recounts using a third party software mechanism that are different from the original in order to verify the result.

System Disclosability

On systems that voter-verified paper trails are not used, trust for the validity of the election outcome is shifted towards the software vendors and any possible subcontractors. Such trust is not sufficient so standards for the external scrutiny of the vendors in terms of software and processes are put forward. E-Voting systems need to be tested and certified by experts both in terms of code and functionality. There is a growing debate on whether these systems should be tested only on government approved specialised laboratories or whether they should be open source so that anyone could examine and critique them.

Open source supporters claim that open systems result in greater transparency, trust and confidence since there is universal scrutiny. They also suggest that such the oversight increases the incentive of the vendor to produce more secure code and fix errors in order to avoid negative publicity. Open source opponents on the other hand claim that most open source projects are usually maintained by a single person and that the popular ones (for which public scrutiny really works) are only those that are actually used by the developers themselves. Since e-voting systems belong to the first category opening their source will not provide any benefits in terms of security. They also claim that even if the code developed is open source it's hard to ensure that the code used on election day has not been altered as was the case with the Diebold e-voting scandal in the US. In terms of the procedural measures suggestions have been made for public observers to monitor the process either through specially created computer monitors or through a series of logic and accuracy tests of the machines on Election

Day. Other researchers have though disregarded them as inadequate and contributing more towards feeling rather being secure.

Internal Components

Registration Server (RS): It's responsible for monitoring and controlling the first stage of the election process, which will be the registration and identification stage. The registration server allows only eligible persons to participate in the election process. Any person can participate in the election process by providing his identification data to the registration sever. The registration server will be responsible to confirm the correctness of the identification data, and use it to check if the person is eligible to participate in the election according to the rules of the election authority, these rules could be some restrictions for example the age of the person, etc. Usually different kind of election (local people's council elections, president elections, etc) will have its private rules and restrictions. If the person is eligible to practicable in the election the registration server will generate an electronic voting certificate to that person and send it to the person, this voting certificate will allow its holder to cast his vote, and he will use it to prove that he is an eligible voter. The registration server records the identification data of the voter and his voting certificate.

Privacy Server (PS): The privacy server plays a principle role in the election process, by allows eligible voters to create an anonymous identity (anonymous voter ID) for themselves so they can freely cast their votes. The privacy server authenticate the voter identity by confirming his election certificate, and if the voter hold a valid election certificate the privacy server will accept and validate the anonymous identity generated by the voter himself. After the privacy server validate the anonymous identity of the voter the voter can easily use it to cast his vote, with a high level of privacy and guarantee that it is impossible to any other party to trace his vote or figure his identity.

Voting Server (VS): The voting server is responsible for the second stage of the election process. The voting server manages the vote casting stage. It receives the voters' anonymous ID validated from the privacy server, and use it to authenticate the legality of voter, but not the voter identity, which mean the voting server can only check if the voter have the rights to cast a vote or not, but it will be never able to figure the real identity of the voter who cast the vote in the time of the voting or after the end of the voting session. The voting server also keeps tracking the voting process to ensure that each eligible voter will vote only once.

Votes Counting Server (VCS): The counting server is responsible for the last and final stage of the election process which is votes counting also known as election post, the counting server collects the vote's ballots, counts the votes, and finally professes the election result.

External Components

E-Token: Is a national public key infrastructure (National PKI) based on smart card and USB technologies. E-token includes a full suite of security and authentication methods. Voters will use e-token for authentication purpose in the registration stage and also to store their election certificate, and to execute other security and cryptology computing required by the e-voting system. The use of e-token in our scheme provides a high level of security, and introduces a new feature which is the mobility of the scheme, which allows voters to cast their vote from any place and on any computer (it slides into a common USB port).

Certificate Authority (CA): Is responsible to confirm the person identification data received by the registration server in the registration and identification stage and to provides personal information about the voter where the registration server can use this information to take a decision about the state of the voter if he/she is eligible or not.

E-Voting Scheme Interactions

Different components in the scheme are interacting together in order to provide a secure modern e-voting system that satisfy the needs of the public and democracy. Figure 1 gives an abstract view of the interactions between different components and their distributions in the scheme. The scenario of these interactions runs through three main stages: registration/identification, votes casting, and votes counting.

The Registration and Identification Stage

Normally the election committee will start the election process by define the time interval for the registrations phase, and start accepting people to register and participate in the election. Every person wish to participate in the election must hold a national digital certificate assigned by the certificate authority CA and stored on his e-token (smart USB token). A person will need to contact to the registration server to register himself in the election process. The registration phase can be summarized in the following steps:

Figure 1. Abstract view of the scheme's interaction

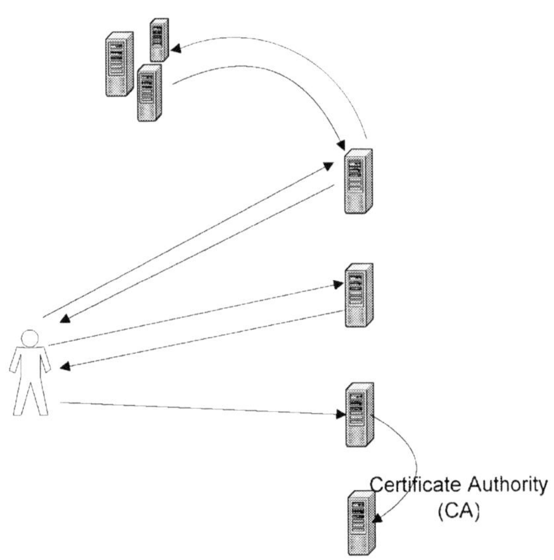

1. A person sends his public key (the public key of his digital certificate stored on e-token) to the registration server (RS).
2. The RS authenticate that the person who send this public key is the real owner of the key by using challenge/response message (if the sender of the key fail to pass the challenge/response message test, or his public key was founded in the ineligible list the registration session will be ended, otherwise the session will continue to the next step). The RS check whether that person is already registered in the election process or not (if he is already registered the RS send to him an election certificate and end the registration session)
3. The RS contact the CA to request the persons' credentials.
4. The CA replies the RS with the voters' credentials.
5. The RS review and check the current rules of the election process to figure weather the person is an eligible and can become a voter or not (if the person is not an eligible voter the RS end the session and records this person in the Ineligible list). The RS issues the voter a valid election certificate and records the voter as eligible registered voter in the registered list.
6. The RS send the voter his/her certificate (the most important information in the election certificate are the certificate serial number, unique pair of public/private keys, digital stamp of the current election, and the public key of the election committee).
7. The person who becomes an eligible registered voter will store the received election certificate on his e-token.

The Voting Stage

The beginning of the voting stage will be directly after the end of the registration and identification stage. The most important process in the voting stage is the generation of the voters' anonymous

ID, which allows him to cast his vote in untraceable voting system, while in the same time the voting system guarantee that a voter can cast his vote only once. The voting phase continues after the registration and identification phase in the following steps:

8. The voter using his e-token security suite and some data founded in his stored election certificate to generate a unique identification number, a simple process to generate this number is by encrypting the digital stamp of the election certificate by the voter private key and hashing the result with one way hash function (the digital stamp is a public information stored in each election certificate generate by the RS).
9. The voter uses blind signature to blind his unique identification number and, sign the output with the private key of his election certificate.
10. The voter encrypts the output of the preview step by the public key of the election committee, and sends it to the privacy server (The voter uses his election certificate to authenticate his identity to the PS).
11. The PS decrypts the received message using the election committee private key and blindly signs the voters' unique identification number using the election committee private key.
12. The PS then encrypts the signed voter's unique identification number by the voters' election certificate public key.
13. The PS sends the encrypted signed unique identification number to the voter, and records the voter as authentic voter so he can't request another blind signature.
14. The voter receives the blindly signed unique identification number and decrypts it using his private key and reverse the blinding signature to obtain his signed unique identification number, which he will use as his anonymous ID (now we can see that the voter hold an authentic an valid ID from the PS and in the same time no one can link his real identity to this ID).
15. The voter contacts to the voting sever, and authenticate himself by his anonymous ID.
16. The VS check if the received anonymous ID is a valid ID, by decrypts it using the election committee private key, and if the voter is an eligible voter the VS allows him to cast his vote.
17. Finally the VS record the anonymous ID as a voted voter (so at most a voter can vote only once.) The privacy server ensures that a voter can only get a blindly signed ID only once, and the voting server ensures that blindly signed ID can cast a vote only once.

Using Electronic Voting Systems in Lectures

- Voting systems are best understood as a tool rather than a teaching approach. They do not 'cause' good learning – in fact, if poorly prepared or used for their own sake, students were extremely critical of them. However, when lecturers used these tools as part of a wider effort to support active engagement with learning there is evidence that they can support increased motivation and attainment, at least in part as a result of their ability to provide rapid feedback on the learning process.
- Such systems represent an opportunity to improve lecturing. The requirement to emphasise engagement and interaction with students prompts lecturers to reflect on qualities elieved to characterise good teaching.
- Such systems build on work already undertaken in college, in areas such as technology and lecturing, confidence assessment and objective testing.
- The introduction of such a system has resource implications. there are indirect

costs in terms of lecturers' time (to learn how to use the system and reflect on how it will change their teaching), support staff time (including Media Resources and Information Services) and for staff time to provide pedagogic support (e.g. involvement in a SCILTA project or a secondment to Education & Professional Development).
- In addition, practical issues such as the installation and mobility of the resource would need to be addressed.

In summary, voting systems do appear to have the potential to enhance learning and motivation, as well as providing variety and engagement within lectures. Based on this review, it is recommended that:

- Provided adequate resources can be made available (for the initial purchase and for supporting use) such a would be an asset to learning at teaching at UCL
- If purchased, the system should be installed in a single location, with a priority system in the room bookings process to allow the optimum use of this resource.

It is also important to note that a system of this type is already in use at UCL. The Discourse system has been used within lectures at the Royal Free campus for several years; it offers the full functionality of most other systems but is also able to support bi-directional free text exchanges. The system has been installed in nine classrooms on the Royal Free site, is available in a browser-supported format suitable for use in cluster rooms and a site licence has been purchased that also covers the Whittington and Bloomsbury campuses. It is currently being developed so that it can be used via wireless network enabled laptops or Personal Digital Assistants (PDAs), removing the need for specialist handsets to be purchased. Students' access to suitable laptops could be provided under the Student Notebook Initiative currently being considered by the Academic Systems Steering Group, if wireless networking for selected lecture rooms was considered viable by EISD. For these reasons, it is recommended that Discourse be considered as a first choice for a system of this type, although it is recognised that such a purchase may need to be delayed until an appropriate wireless infrastructure is in place within college.

General Description

This section will outline the basic process involved in using a voting system, and illustrate the common features of voting systems as considered in this study.

The basic process during the lecture, the lecturer poses a question. This can be done verbally, or could be displayed using presentation technology on a computer, overhead transparencies (OHTs) or from within the voting software. Each student has a handset that allows him or her to select the preferred option for the answer. The handsets transmit this information to a receiver, which in turn transmits it to the voting software on a computer in the theatre. After the allotted time, the software produces a histogram or bar-chart of the results, which is displayed to the students using a data projector connected to the computer. The lecturer then chooses a course of action to respond to the results.

Equipment Features and Functionality

Each voting system has its own specific set of features and functionality. However, the common features of the major systems currently in use are summarised below. Handset usually one handset is used by one student, but it is feasible for each to be used by a group working together.

Handsets can have one or multiple buttons (which are usually marked numerically).

The single button handset is best used to answer simple binary question, for example by pressing to indicate a 'yes' response to question. There are advantages in this simplicity: it requires little effort to understand the system, there is no possibility of the wrong button being pressed, and it causes minimal disruption and distraction when used. However, if the one-button system is used for multiple choice questions, it requires each response option to be offered in sequence rather than in parallel, thus lengthening the time for response. Most handsets allow multiple choice responses (and sometimes multiple selections), with up to ten answers available.

As well as transmitting the preferred option, with some systems (e.g. PRS) the handsets have buttons where the student can record low, medium or high confidence in the accuracy of their answer. This is helpful in analysing whether correct answers were chosen through luck or based on knowledge. (The ability to assess confidence about multiple choice assessment is another interest of staff at UCL The handsets can be used anonymously so that only the number of the handset is known, not the individual students' name. However, the handsets have an ID number that can be mapped to a student's name. This allows the lecturer to see an individual's answer, either within the lecture or when reviewing responses at a later stage, also identifies other desirable developments that may become available in future systems, including:

- The use of Personal Digital Assistants (PDAs) rather than handsets;
- The ability to enter multi-digit numbers;
- The ability to enter a sequence of digits rather than exactly one as an answer; and
- Free text entry.

The ability to use free text is available in the Discourse system. Using this system in the lecture theatre (it can also be used in a computer laboratory with PCs), the student has a wireless portable terminal (known as a Study.com) and not a handset with buttons. Importantly, however, this dedicated terminal is now being phased out in favour of PDAs or laptops that have been configured to transmit information to the lecturers' computer over a wireless local network. Discourse allows bi-directional free text: students can respond to the lecturer's question in their own words and the lecturer can share a response with the whole class by sending it to each student's computer, or to send a message to just one student.

Free text is also possible to a limited extent using the Series 8 system. Each handset has a small LCD panel that can display automated information (e.g. count down of time left for response). Text can also be sent to all, some, or individual handsets but the system does not allow the student to send a free-text message to the lecturer.

Voting software Information from the handsets is sent to a local computer, where it is processed using a dedicated application. This software can display the number of the question being asked, the time allowed in which to answer and the number of attempts allowed. It can also be used to display the questions in a plain text format, thus obviating the need for additional presentation software if required.

Once the timer is started, students can then register their response. Acknowledgement of each response can be done in several ways. For example, using the PRS system, a series of cells are displayed on the data projector which then change colour as each answer is registered. If the students have been assigned a handset, it can also display their name; if used anonymously, it will just display the handset number. Responses can be revealed as they are made, or else hidden until all or a majority of students have responded. With the Reply system, acknowledgement is via the handset: a light comes on when the response is made and switched off when the response is received.

With all systems, the software can then display a summary of the responses in a variety of ways such as bar-charts, histograms or a simple percentage. The different software available provides additional functionality in a variety of ways. For example, the PRS software can record information, including the number of attempts made, the time taken to register an answer and the confidence levels. These results can be saved and used later, using standard software such as Microsoft Office to view the results. If the handsets have been used in named mode, then an individual's performance can be recorded, but in anonymous mode, only a summary is recorded. The differences in functionality would need to be considered when selecting a voting system.

CONCLUDING REMARKS

When technology is carelessly applied to elections, it can create several risks and challenges that will shake the public's confidence in elections. However, the technology itself can offer proper solutions. It is necessary to raise the bar of security standards to maintain the integrity and confidence of elections, and in this work electoral authorities, the election industry and experts should participate. We should take advantage of the current momentum as well as the funding available in some countries to improve election equipment properly.

The opportunity exists now, and we should not let it go by. We should also be wary of precipitating towards the first available solution that is offered which will probably tend to be reactionary and as such not well-thought out; the purchase of election equipment is a decision for the long term. We should therefore pay attention to the questions relating to security to maintain or even increase the public's confidence in elections while at the same time improving the speed of the recount and the convenience for the voters.

For our part, we have presented a security architecture for electronic voting that permits the avoidance of the problems occasioned by interposing computer systems and technical personnel between the voter and the electoral board. The architecture is based on replicating the conventional security mechanisms and in segregating all critical functions into very simple systems that are audited, monitored and physically secured. This security architecture minimises the number of components that must be trusted to only two, namely, the software generating the encrypted ballot and the software opening the digital ballot boxes and the envelopes there in. This addresses one of the main causes of trouble in electronic voting systems, namely, the need to trust overly-complex systems like DREs, web browsers, operating systems or Internet servers.

The cryptographic voting protocol that is part of this security architecture allows voters to independently verify that the electronic voting system correctly delivers their ballots to the electoral board. Third parties (such as candidates or observers) have reliable means to gain confidence in the accuracy of the election. A conundrum is solved; voter privacy is ensured while every voter is properly identified before casting their ballot.

In our opinion, this architecture relaxes the need to use paper trails to have confidence in electronic voting. Nevertheless, if paper is to be used, the architecture allows improving the security offered by the physical chapter trail by introducing cryptography to it.

REFERENCES

Al-Shalabi, H. (n.d.). *E-Voting Scheme over internet.* Retrieved from http://74.125.113.132/search?q=cache:izHh8ng4EVcJ:academic-papers.org/ocs2/session/Papers/E6/215-1540-2-DR.doc+E-Voting+Scheme+over+internet&cd=1&hl=en&ct=clnk&gl=us

Fisher, E. A. (2003, November 4). *Election Reform and Electronic Voting Systems (DREs): Analysis of Security Issues.* (Congressional Research Service Report No. RL32139). Washington, DC: Library of Congress.

Kohno, T., Stubblefield, A., Ruben, A. D., & Waalach, D. S. (2004, February 27). *Analysis of an Electronic Voting System.* Presented at the IEEE Symposium on Security and Privacy. Paolo Alto, CA.

Simpson, V., & Oliver, M. (n.d.) *Using electronic voting systems in lectures.* Retrieved from http://www.ucl.ac.uk/learningtechnology/assessment/ElectronicVotingSystems.pdf

Wiki (n.d.). *Wikipedia.com.* Retrieved from http://www.wikipedia.com

Chapter 33

E-Business:
Concepts and Context with Illustrative Examples of E-Business and E-Commerce in Education

Raid Al Dabbagh
Mosul University, Iraq

ABSTRACT

This chapter outlines the important of e-business in today's world and how one thinks it affects decision making. In today's world e-business is extremely important for many reasons, some of which are due to the fact that it can speed up the whole process of ordering. This means that the lead time can be decreased because the ordering of products can be done much more quickly because the Internet is a fast running wide area network. This chapter shows how better procurement and supply chains make sales teams more effective. The ability to outsource functions such as, accounting, remote access to systems, linking management teams in different locations, being able to locate the lowest cost supplier improve customer services, improved collection of customer information for databases and more effective management of remote manufacturing sites.

INTRODUCTION

The daily growth of the internet and e-commerce has changed the way of marketing and selling products and services. As a result of development in electronic information resources and the evolution of the "digital age" product sellers and information service providers face many new challenges. Internet is changing the way corporations conduct business with their consumers who are increasingly expecting higher services, becoming time saved, and wanting more convenience. In addition e-service quality is an essential strategy to gain success, according to the results of previous literatures, probably more important than a low price for online companies. Since one of the main duties of the internet as a communication channel is how to manage service quality, which holds a significant importance to customer satisfaction, the purpose of this research is to gain a better understanding of the impact of web site quality factors on customer satisfaction.

DOI: 10.4018/978-1-61520-789-3.ch033

On the above idea, we explore the theoretical foundations of value creation in e-business, *Electronic Business*, commonly referred to as "*eBusiness*" or "*e-Business*", may be defined as the utilization of information and communication technologies (ICT) in support of all the activities of business. Commerce constitutes the exchange of products and services between businesses, groups and individuals and hence can be seen as one of the essential activities of any business. Hence, electronic commerce or eCommerce focuses on the use of ICT to enable the external activities and relationships of the business with individuals, groups and other businesses.

Electronic business methods enable companies to link their internal and external data processing systems more efficiently and flexibly, to work more closely with suppliers and partners, and to better satisfy the needs and expectations of their customers.

Information Technology and Business

When computer and communications technologies are combined, the result is information technology, or "infotech". Information Technology (IT) is a general term that describes any technology that helps to produce, manipulate, store, communicate, and/or disseminate information. Presumably, when speaking of Information Technology (IT) as a whole, it is noted that the use of computers and information are associated.

This has been contributed to make all business process available to all beneficiaries possible. As such, The United States Census Bureau defines e-business as "any process that a business organization conducts over a computer mediated network. Business organizations include any for profit, governmental, non-profit entity. Their processes include production-, customer-, and internal or management-focused business processes." In a shorter broader sense, e-business is the process of conducting business electronically or over the internet. Electronic mail is e-mail, electronic commerce is e-commerce, and following this formula, electronic business is e-business. Every time business is conducted over the internet, e-business takes place and as the internet grows, so grows e-business.

Considerations in Defining E-Business and E-Commerce

As discussed in the sections above, contemporary definitions of e-business and e-commerce are problematic. They create confusions and hinder advancements in the discipline. Porter (2001) and Tapscott (2001) presented two different views on impacts of the Internet on business. Porter (2001) suggested that organizations should integrate the application of the Internet to their traditional business process while Tapscott (2001) advocated changes to business process based on applications of the Internet. Porter focused on existing organizations that use technologies to enhance business processes while Tapscott was concerned about new organizations that use technologies to create value in new ways. They provided valuable insight on impacts of the Internet from different perspectives. However, under contemporary definitions of e-business and e-commerce, all organizations using the Internet to perform similar functions are considered the same irrespective of their strategies of Internet usage. Porter and Tapscott would be considered as discussing e-business (or e-commerce) in the same context and confusion might arise from the apparently contradictory conclusions.

Creating another set of definitions using the perception-based approach does not help to improve the situation. Individual perceptions cannot provide a solid ground in explaining the rationale of the definitions. A more rigorous approach should be adopted in defining ebusiness and e-commerce. Definitions should be derived through logical reasoning rather than individual perceptions.

Defining e-business and e-commerce is more than explaining the terms. It is a process that allows people to reflect and express their views on the discipline. The outcome of defining process should include not only the definitions but also an explanation of how the definitions are derived. The definitions should enable readers to recognize the scope of the discipline. The relationship between e-business and e-commerce should be clearly stated. If e-business and e-commerce are considered as two different concepts, the difference between the two terms should be clearly identified and the rationale of the difference should be expressed. By applying the definitions, readers should be able to identify whether a particular entity or activity is e-business or e-commerce and provide the reason of the classification. (Michael, 2005)

NEW DEFINITIONS OF E-BUSINESS AND E-COMMERCE

The Value-Centric Approach

In this chapter, a new value-centric approach is proposed to redefine e-business and ecommerce. E-business and e-commerce are considered as two different entity concepts. They represent two types of organizations that adopt different strategies in applying computing and telecommunication technologies in value creation.

The new definitions include companies that use any form of open or proprietary networks which incorporate computers and/or other computing devices. While the use of computing and telecommunication technologies in business operations is facilitated by widespread adoption of the Internet, organizations can apply these technologies in their operations without involving the use of the Internet. Therefore, the use of the Internet is not a criterion in deciding whether an organization is an e-business organization or an e-commerce organization.

Under the value-centric approach, the ultimate objective of all organizations is to create value. Organizations create value by producing valuable outputs in the form of goods, services or information and delivering the outputs to consumers.

Part of the value created in the value creation process is captured by organizations as revenue and others are captured by consumers. Revenue may be sourced from consumers of outputs or from independent third parties such as government. The ones who consume the outputs may not be the ones who pay for them. For example, a high proportion of public hospital revenue comes from the government.

In considering the nature of an organization, two fundamental questions are asked: (1) what value can an organization create and, (2) how can an organization create and transfer value. Two concepts, value proposition and value chain, are employed to address the questions.

Value proposition is one of the key components of an organization's business model. It is a specification of an organization's choice of target segment(s), choice of focal customer benefits and rationale of competitive edge in delivering value to its target customers (Rayport & Jaworski, 2001). It represents an organization's view on what value can be created and how it can differentiate itself from others.

Value chain refers to the set of activities through which products or services are created and delivered to customers (Porter, 2001). It includes activities that are directly related to transactions like marketing and sales as well as support activities such as accounting and human resources. An organization creates value through performing activities in the value chain.

The application of computing and telecommunication technologies in business activities can improve the efficiency of the value chain, thus enhancing the value created by an organization. Amit and Zott (2001) suggested that using the Internet to conduct business can enhance value creation in four dimensions, namely efficiency, complementarities, lock-in and novelty. The application of technologies also allows an organization to create new value by performing business activities in a manner that may not be feasible without application of the technologies and hence establish a new value proposition. (Michael, 2005)

E-Business

Under the value-centric approach, e-business is defined as an organization that applies computing and telecommunication technologies jointly to any of its activities that is a component of the entity's value chain. The application of computing and telecommunication technologies in the organization is not limited to business transactions. However, the technologies must be applied in an activity that forms a part of the value chain. For instance, a convenience store that uses a computer to play music downloaded from the Internet is not an e-business as playing music in the store is not related to its value chain activities. On the other hand, a record shop that plays music on the records it sells from a system that is linked to its corporate intranet is an e-business. Playing music is part of the shop's promotional activities and the promotional activities constitute a part of the shop's value chain.

E-Commerce

For some organizations, the application of computing and telecommunication technologies plays a critical role in their value propositions. Without applying the technologies, their value propositions cannot be sustained. Under the value-centric approach, these organizations are considered as e-commerce. Accordingly, e-commerce is defined as an *organization with a value proposition that relies on joint applications of computing and telecommunication technologies*.

Under this definition, all Internet-based organizations that perform operational activities without physical interactions with their clients are e-commerce organizations as their value propositions are based on their virtual operations. Nevertheless, physical presence itself does not preclude an organization from being an e-commerce organization. An organization can integrate its physical presence with its virtual operations through the Internet and become an e-commerce.

As e-commerce organizations rely on computing and telecommunication technologies in their operations, they are all e-business organizations. The key differentiator of e-business organization and e-commerce organization is value proposition. Every organization has its own value proposition. Applying technologies in similar ways does not necessarily mean that value propositions are the same. Therefore, an organization operating in a way identical to an e-commerce organization can be an e-business organization.

For instance, a computer shop that sells computers through both physical storefront and the Internet can either be an e-business organization or e-commerce organization. If the Internet operations are considered as supplementary to physical operations then the company is an e-business. If the physical storefront is operated to support and facilitate Internet operations, then the company is an e-commerce. In both scenarios the shop can use similar technologies in its Internet operations. (Michael, 2005)

Where Does E-Business Take Place?

E-business is offered to all users via the internet, to internal users via an intranet (similar to the internet, an intranet is a smaller network of computers usually within a single organization), and to specified users via an extranet (an intranet partially accessible to specified users from outside an organization via a valid username and password).

MAIN TYPES OF E-BUSINESS

Business to Consumer (B2C)

The most widely recognized form of e-business, B2C is the exchange of information, products or services taking place between a business and a consumer over the internet. As the internet develops, B2C is continually changing the way consumers acquire information, the way products are compared against one another and the way in which they are purchased.

An example of a B2C only site is amazon.com. Ae.com is an example of a B2C site housing a physical location as well.

Business to Business (B2B)

The largest form of e-business in terms of money spent is B2B. Business-to-business allows trading to take place between businesses, using a low-cost sales channel for the sale of goods and services and is responsible for constantly changing corporate buying habits.

An example of a B2B site would be a car part company selling parts to a car dealership, another company, rather than directly to consumers.

Business to Government (B2G)

B2G is the online exchange of information and transactions between businesses and government agencies, also known as e-government. B2G allows government agencies and businesses to use electronic means to conduct business and interact with each other over the internet.

An example of a B2G site would be one that offers electronic tax filing.

E-Commerce and its Relation to E-Business

In practice, e-business is more than just e-commerce. While e-business refers to more strategic focus with an emphasis on the functions that occur using electronic capabilities, e-commerce is a subset of an overall e-business strategy. E-commerce seeks to add revenue streams using the World Wide Web or the Internet to build and enhance relationships with clients and partners and to improve efficiency using the Empty Vessel strategy. Often, e-commerce involves the application of knowledge management systems.

E-business involves business processes spanning the entire value chain: electronic purchasing and supply chain management, processing orders electronically, handling customer service, and cooperating with business partners. Special technical standards for e-business facilitate the exchange of data between companies. E-business software solutions allow the integration of intra and inter firm business processes. E-business can be conducted using the Web, the Internet, intranets, extranets, or some combination of these.

The United States Census Bureau defines e-commerce as "any transaction completed over a computer mediated network that involves the transfer of ownership or rights to use goods and services. Transactions occur within selected e-business processes (e.g., selling process) and are 'completed' when agreement is reached between buyer and seller to transfer ownership or rights to use goods or services." So while e-business covers the entire range of online business dealings (from customer service to selling), e-commerce refers specifically to one entity paying for goods or services from another entity via the internet. With this in mind, remember that e-commerce can relate to all types of e-business involved in the transfer of goods or services, including but not limited to B2C, B2B and B2G.

Marketing Significance of E-Business vs. E-Commerce

Having a successful business in the real world is more than just simply opening a storefront or factory. The same holds true in that conducting business online is more than having just a web site. There are other fundamental variables to consider for a business to succeed.

It is paramount to have a solid infrastructure with great products, superior customer service, effective marketing strategies, real-time information systems, and efficient product fulfillment processes. The proper planning, implementation and execution of these functions are the foundation of any successful business. Unfortunately however, when it comes to the Internet, many companies forgo their business plans, strategies and infrastructure and treat the World Wide Web like a crapshoot. Many brick-and-mortar companies get a web site simply because their competition has one, and thus put little forethought into making the web work for them.

For most companies the Internet is an untapped resource. However, of the companies that do have an Internet presence, only a small fraction will actually utilize the Internet to it's full potential.

The reason why is quite simple. Most companies mistakenly make use of the Internet for just basic e-commerce, not actual e-business. In doing so, other intrinsic and critical business functions found in a true e-business platform are neglected. The use of an exclusive e-Commerce platform is a common and understandable mistake. If you were to survey a room full of senior corporate executives, almost all questioned would not be able to tell you the difference between e-commerce and e-business. But make no mistake about it; there is a difference between e-commerce and e-business, a tremendous difference.

E-commerce is the concept of buying and selling on the Internet. However, the infrastructure of any business is more than just buying and selling and this is where e-business begins. A strong e-business platform enables a company to provide quality customer service, prompt delivery, a strong marketing presence, maintain flexibility, have reliable inventory control mechanisms and access to real-time information. Let's take an example of a fictitious company that sells widgets to distributors as well as the general public worldwide. Widgets, Inc. has been very successful selling their widgets for many years in which they contribute their success to a combination of a solid product, prompt delivery, efficient management, and excellent customer service. These variables add up to a satisfied customer base and a profit margin to be proud of.

The president of Widgets, Inc. decides to expand business by creating an Internet presence. However, instead of approaching the Internet division of the business as it did the brick-and-mortar division, with planning and careful consideration to business process management, marketing and quality customer service, the company as an alternative puts together a web site with just a "shopping cart" and without the necessary tools needed to maintain Widgets, Inc.'s dominance in its industry.

The biggest mistake Widgets, Inc. made was not taking into consideration that although their web site at first glance is only a portion of their corporation, their site is a very visible and therefore, influential representation of their corporation. If the site is not able to fulfill the duties of its brick-and-mortar counterparts, then it does not properly represent the qualities that it should. Such a faux pas can also ruin the possibility of increased profits that Widgets, Inc. would make, from a quality and efficient Internet division of their business.

In actuality with the right implementation, the e-business faction of a company can be more profitable than their brick-and-mortar counterparts without comprising the same "real world" philosophies that helped propel the company to success in the first place. All you need are the right tools and how to make the most of them.

Now, imagine being able to maintain and manage every aspect of your traditional business, but have access to it anywhere in the world. Imagine expanding your business without having to build expensive storefronts. Imagine running elaborate, expansive, intricate marketing campaigns in hours rather than weeks and at the fraction of the cost. Imagine your RMA and CRM satisfaction levels being either at par or higher online in comparison to your brick-and-mortar division. In today's e-business world, these concepts are not possibilities, but a reality and need to be implemented in every Internet business structure as such.

These are just a few examples of how an expansion into the Internet via e-business can vastly increase your profits without conceding the very idiosyncrasies that made you successful in the first place.

E-Business and Global Issue: Entrepreneurship

Entrepreneurship is currently undergoing a fundamental transformation that reflects the rapid and radical changes that are affecting the global market place. The emergence of the Internet and developments in Information and Communication Technologies (ICTs) have opened new markets and considerably altered existing ones (Brynjolfsson & Kahin, 2002). From an entrepreneurship perspective, the full economic impact of the Internet and related ICT is yet to be fully understood or empirically tested (Martin & Matlay, 2003). Nevertheless, it is increasingly obvious that a shift in entrepreneurial equilibrium is taking place (Matlay & Addis, 2003). Although some of the traditional entrepreneurial concepts still apply, much of the context in which related activities are taking place has changed dramatically over a relatively short period of time (Matlay, 2003b). Consequently, and in order to capture the economic value that is created within rapidly evolving e-Markets, a new and highly adaptable brand of e-Entrepreneurs has emerged (Matlay, 2003a).

Afuah and Tucci (2003) recommend that all organisations that are affected by the Internet should have a dedicated "business model". The authors justify their suggestion by pointing at the complexity, speed and uncertainty of Internet trading. Matlay (2004) agrees with this advice. An effective business model often depends upon organisational aims, human and physical resources as well as market orientations. Bakker (2005) does the simple observation that an increasing number of people are not only using the Internet, but who are relying on the Internet for social contacts, purchasing goods and being informed on what is happening in the world. The Internet is becoming a significant factor in today's society.

Because the internet has become mature and new simple techniques make it possible for everyone to use the internet new aspects of e-Business and e-entrepreneurship become more important. Although much has been written about these developments, scientifically research about the underlying value drivers of this next stage is missing. This research attempts to fill this theoretical gap by seeking to identify the (most important) value drivers, features and underlying business models in Web 2.0.

In Gartner's 2006 Emerging Technologies Hype Cycle (see Figure 1), which assesses the maturity, impact and adoption speed of 36 key technologies and trends during the next ten years, three major themes that are experiencing significant activity and which include new or heavily hyped technologies, where organisations may be uncertain as to which will have most impact on their business, are argued. One of the three key technology themes identified by Gartner, and the corresponding technologies for enterprises to examine closely within them, is Web 2.0 and represents a broad collection of recent trends in Internet technologies and business models. Particular focus has been given to user-created content, lightweight technology, service-based access and shared revenue models. Technologies rated by Gartner as having transformational, high or moderate impact include: Social Network Analysis, Marsh-ups, AJAX and Collective Intelligence. Web 2.0 and it's concepts and technologies are now at its peak of the Hype and will be adopted within 2 years (Gartner, 2006).

(*) The "Hype Cycle for Emerging Technologies, 2006" report is one of 78 hype cycles released by Gartner in 2006. More than 1,900 information technologies and trends across more than 75 industries, technology markets, and topics are evaluated by more than 300 Gartner analysts in the most comprehensive assessment of technology maturity in the IT industry. Gartner's hype cycles assess the maturity, impact and adoption speed of hundreds of technologies across a broad range of technology, application and industry areas. It highlights the progression of an emerging technology from market over enthusiasm through a period of disillusionment to an eventual understanding of the technology's relevance and role in a market or domain (Gartner, 2006).

The scarce e-business theory on value creation, the increasing use and importance of the Internet, and the emergence of Web 2.0 ask for a close look at features of the New Internet and its underlying value drivers.

With this research a contribution to value creation theories and business model theories in the field of a combination of entrepreneurship and strategic management is delivered. This research does not only contains value drivers derived from Strategy theories, e.g. Strategic Network Theory (Dyer, 1998), but also focuses on Innovation and Entrepreneurship theories, e.g. Schumpeter's theory of creative destruction (Schumpeter, 1942). This research also contributes to the scarce theories of e-businesses by looking at new developments within the Internet, particularly Web 2.0.

Research on e-business value drivers are useful but probably not up-to-date anymore with the emergence of Web 2.0. The research of Amit and Zott (Amit, 2001) for instance deals with companies before the Internet bubble of 2001. With Web 2.0 new features of the Internet transactions and participations are taking place. More and different stakeholders add value in e-business. This raises questions which (new) value drivers we can find in Web 2.0 and which ones are more important. By looking at these factors we are indirectly looking at the business models that are important in the New Internet. Providing more insight in value drivers and business models in Web 2.0 enables companies and entrepreneurs to adopt and prepare

Figure 1. The Gartner Hype Cycle for emerging technologies 2006(*) (Gartner 2006)

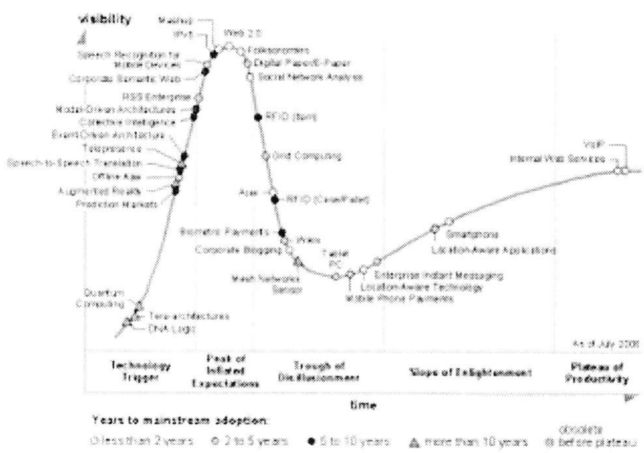

to take advantage of opportunities in this next stage of the Internet.

ILLUSTRATIVE EXAMPLES OF E-BUSINESS AND E-COMMERCE

Charles Sturt University

Charles Sturt University (CSU) is the largest regional university in New South Wales, Australia. It has four major campuses at Albury-Wodonga, Bathurst, Dubbo and Wagga Wagga and operates centres at Broken Hill, Canberra, Goulburn, Morpeth and Manly (AVCC, 2004). CSU offers its course through its own campuses and partner institutions in Australia and other countries. Students can complete their studies through traditional on-campus mode, distance education mode or a mixture of both.

In 2003, CSU offered more than 300 courses to 40,694 students. 29,325 students were enrolled in pure distance education mode and another 3,911 students undertook their studies through mixed mode (CSU, 2003).

As the leading distance education provider in Australia, CSU had considered the use of Internet in distance education in the mid-1990s (Bisman, 1996). CSU recognized two key values to its students as flexibility in delivery of higher education and well-established network of partner institutions. To capitalize on these strengths, CSU decided to maintain its traditional distance education system. Computing and telecommunication technologies are applied to complement rather than replace the traditional system.

All students who enrolled in distance education subjects receive their study materials in printed form. At the same time, same material is available through CSU's online portal, my.csu. Students can access the material through the Internet anywhere, at anytime. To communicate with their lecturers, students can use telephone, fax, e-mail as well as online forums. They can submit their assignments by mail, by fax or by EASTS, an online assignment submission system.

On-campus students also benefit from the application of technologies. My.csu is available to all students and online forums can be accessed by on-campus students, subject to lecturer approval. On-campus students are also allowed to enroll in subjects offered by distance education mode. This is particularly useful for students who want to undertake subjects that are not available at their host campus.

In addition to the delivery of education, CSU also uses computing and telecommunication technologies in its support functions. For example, staff members can access their personnel records and file leave applications through the university website. Video conferencing is used extensively to support administrative functions such as selection and promotion of academic staff.

CSU is a successful example of transforming an existing business into e-business. The university recognized its strengths in creating value and used computing and telecommunication technologies to reinforce these strengths. Technology-enabled systems co-exist with traditional system and enhance each others' value.

E-Business as an ISP Case Study (IST –Africa Consortium 2005-2006, E-Business: Case Studies)

We have defined e-business not just as basically the act of selling and buying goods and services through the Internet, but also as the conduct of business over the Internet including collaborating with business partners. We have also presented two major emerging business models that consist in business built on the Internet and business providing the infrastructure. The second major category of e-business model comprises *businesses that provide the platform* upon which digital businesses are built and operated:

- Create and package technology-based products, services, and solutions;
- Enable consumers and business to access online services and information;
- Enable technology buyers and sellers to transact business.

In this case study we present a successful case of business providing the infrastructure that has started from scratch by a University Computer Center (UCC).

Case Background and Narrative

The computer center is this case study is an autonomous institution within the public University in an African country. The UCC was established in 1979. In 1982, it became a formal computer centre. Its purpose is to spearhead the introduction of information and communication technologies (ICTs) in the university and in the community at large. The Centre also functions as a commercial Internet Service Provider (ISP)1, providing Internet services, training courses and research, supports national information technologies (IT) policy development, software analysis and design, including hardware installation and maintenance, web design and hosting for private clients as well as for the University. The UCC provides access not only to students but also to NGOs, businesses, government and members of the international community. It also operates the largest Internet service.

The UCC, for example provides a course on Networking for CISCO systems; web pages are developed for government institutions, public institutions and the public in general. Students and the university teachers use e-mail provided by UCC free of charge.

The UCC was the first public ISP for the country. It initially provided free Internet accounts for the first one hundred users in order to build awareness about the Internet. Today, UCC has more than 2000 e-mail clients registered on the web as email users and around 600, those who pay for email use.

Analyzing UCC as an ISP, it provides e-mail and Internet access to individual citizens and organizations, including the University, to conduct their business. These services are part of the core business of UCC. The question that arises is how UCC became one of the major ISPs in the country?

The basic premise of running an e-business is the creation of a good infrastructure to run the business. In the beginning, UCC relied on the telecommunication infrastructures provided by the local public telecommunications provider, however, afterwards, the UCC drew up and implemented its own plans concerning the improvement of the infrastructure connecting them to the Internet to become a full- Internet Service Provider.

The UCC's first Internet connection was in 1992 through a dial-up link of 9.6Kb to Rhodes University in Natal, South Africa, through UNINET, paying $14,000 USD/month. In 1993, the Center moved to a leased line of 14.4 Kb, then to 28 Kb and then 33 Kb. Its first VSAT link was through transtel in South Africa (64 Kb connection).

It was finally upgraded in 1997 to a 1 MB shared connection with Tanzania and the Seychelles. This upgrade was funded through the Leland Initiative. The Leland Initiative is a US AID project that funded five Internet Service Providers from the private sector. The quality was very low for the demand (less than 128 Kb), so a decision was made to move to a dedicated link in October 2000.

This is a 2-way link (394 down and 128 up). The second VSAT link (through the World Bank's satellite channel) is from the US. It is a 512 Kb link to be strictly used for educational purposes (such as video conferencing) and not for commercial purposes. This link was funded through the World Bank. The UCC is licensed to provide Internet services, which maintains its license through payment. The UCC also has a license for a wireless metropolitan network, which costs the same as the ISP license.

Objective Analysis

The UCC has done an excellent job in supplying people and organizations with email and Internet access. Although it has not satisfied the needs of the whole country, due to many constraints, such as funds, infrastructures, regulations, human resources capacity, the selected strategy of finding the right partners to fund the infrastructures and interested in the same business as UCC was one of the major issue to the success of the business provided to the clients in a very a low costs.

We have to underline that, Internet is the basic requirement for running an e-business, and, UCC was the first organization in country to provide this important tool – access to the Internet. Today the country has more than ten ISPs under the umbrella of the UCC vision. Therefore, we have to eulogize UCC, an institution that is not business oriented but has opened windows for other business institutions either as ISPs or as just Internet users for e-business.

Lessons Learnt

Critical Success Factors

UCC was always led by many bright minds who are tirelessly striving to lay the foundations and building blocks of an economy that can compete in the new world order, an economy that has only recently ended two wars, one civil and the other of independence, not so long ago. The team lead is characterized by:

- Good management skills
- Vision
- Intensive work by people at the UCC and their foreign partners
- Willing to win and to be useful for the whole society
- Innovation.

Alternative and Conclusions

Within a set of objectives of UCC, the provision for access to the Internet and e-mail was one of them. However, the existing infrastructure, funds available and willingness were not compatible, so the UCC had to draw its own strategies for acquiring the appropriate infrastructures for data in order to provide effective and cheap services. Another alternative adopted by the UCC would be to rely and work within the existing telecommunications infrastructures. Probably, with this alternative UCC would have achieved less customers and the reputation than today. For other

companies willing to provide platforms for e-mail and internet services for business, and do not have infrastructures for data telecommunications, it seems to be feasible to use the same strategy as that of the UCC, by getting partners or making a joint venture with big telecommunications companies or funding.

CONCLUSION

We conclude from the above interpretation and discussions, that how important is the e-business in today's world and how do you think it effects decision making in business? In today's world e-business is extremely important for many reasons. Some of which is due to the fact it can speed the whole process of ordering etc. up. This then means that the lead time can be decreased because the ordering of products can be done much more quickly, particularly because the Internet is a fast running wide area network. However, despite this, the question should be asked, what does e-business mean? E-business actually means: Better procurement and supply chain, making sales teams more effective, the ability to outsource functions such as accounting, remote access to systems, linking management teams in different locations, being able to locate the lowest cost supplier, improve customer services, improved collection of customer information for databases and more effective management of remote manufacturing sites.

On the other side, the Internet is now a thriving industry. With the knowledge advancing at a quick pace, more and more people are exposed to computers and internet. Increasingly they are learning to utilize the Internet for their day to day needs. Here e-commerce websites take a front seat, moving out to the millions of people looking for your kind of product or services online.

E-commerce or electronic commerce is actually trading of, either goods or services on the internet.

Before making any decision in business, it is worth taking into consideration the benefits, the company would reap on implementation of the new strategy of Ecommerce. Therefore, the most important thing that you must consider here is whether your business actually needs ecommerce?

In recent years, interest in studying issues in the application of computing and telecommunication technologies in business activities has been accelerated by the growth of Internet-based business activities. However, practitioners and academics have little interest in defining the scope of the field. This paper examines contemporary definitions of e-business and e-commerce and problems associated with these definitions. The need of a new approach in defining the two terms is highlighted and a new value-centric approach is proposed.

To managers, the value-centric approach represents a new view on the relationship between technology and business strategies. The distinction between e-business and e-commerce is based on an organization's strategy in applying computing and telecommunication to its operations rather than the types of operations that the technologies are applied. The choices of technologies and their applications are made in accordance to the organization's value proposition. These decisions constitute an organization's technology strategy. The choice of being an e-business organization or e-commerce organization is a strategic decision, not a technical one.

An organization's technology strategy should be based on its unique value proposition rather than its competitors' actions. A particular strategy may be useful for one organization but not for the others. For instance, CSU has a strong network of partner institutions. Therefore, a completely online education delivery model may not be the best model for CSU as such model does not allow CSU to utilize its partner institutions network. In contrast, the University of Phoenix is highly successful with its Internet based education delivery model. Differences in organizational resources between two institutions result as different value propositions for them. Consequently the two institutions are better off with their respective education delivery model.

REFERENCES

Amit, R. A. Z. C. (2001). Value Creation in E-Business. *Strategic Management Journal*, *22*, 493–520. doi:10.1002/smj.187

AVCC. (2004). *Australia's universities: individual universities - Charles Sturt University*. Retrieved October 12, 2004, from http://www.avcc.edu.au/news/public_statements/publications/Uni_Facts/csu.htm

Bisman, J. (1996). Integrating the Internet into distance education in accounting at Charles Sturt University: an assessment of potential. *Occasional Papers in Open and Distance Learning*.

Brynjolfsson, E., & Kahin, B. (2002). *Understanding the Digital Economy: Data, Tools and Research*. Cambridge, MA: MIT Press.

Dyer, J., & Singh, H. (1998). The relational view: cooperative strategy and sources of interorganizational competitive advantage. *Academy of Management Review*, *23*, 660–679. doi:10.2307/259056

Gartner, L. (2006). *Hype Cycle for Emerging Technology*. Retrieved from.http://www.gartner.com/it/page.jsp?id=495475

Martin, L., & Matlay, H. (2003). Innovative use of the Internet in established small firms: The impact of Knowledge Management and Organisational learning in accessing new opportunities. *Qualitative Market Research*, *6*(1), 18–26. doi:10.1108/13522750310457348

Matlay, H. (2003). Small Tourism Firms in e-Europe: Definitional, Conceptual and Contextual Considerations. In Thomas, R. (Ed.), *Small firms in Tourism: International perspectives* (pp. 297–312). Oxford, UK: Pegamon.

Matlay, H. (2003, March). *e-Babel: in Search of a Theory of e-Everything*. Paper presented at the UCE Business School Research Seminar, Birmingham, UK.

Matlay, H., & Addis, M. (2003). The value of E-Commerce for high growth SME's. *International Small Business Journal*, *23*(3), 279–302. doi:10.1177/0266242605052074

Rayport, J., & Jaworski, B. (2001). *e-Commerce. International Edn*. New York: McGraw-Hill.

Schumpeter, J. (1942). *Capitalism, Socialism, and Democracy*. New York: Harper Collins.

WEBSITES

www.buseco.monash.edu.au

www.iskiv.net

www.seeta.com

www.tanzaniagateway.org

www.unpan1.un.org

www.witiger.com

Compilation of References

Abugu, I. (2007, June): *SME: Issues, Challenges and Prospects*, An invited presentation at the International Conference on Financial System Strategy (FSS) 2020 Organized by the Central Bank of Nigeria. Retrieved February 2007, from http://www.cenbank.org/fss/wed/sme_issues,%20challenges%20and%20prospects_ike%20abugu.pdf

Accenture (2003) eGovernment Leadership: Engaging the Customer, *The Government Executive Series*. Retrieved from http://www.accenture.com/xdoc/en/industries/government/gove_capa_epa_leadership.pdf

Accenture (n.d.). *High Performance Government*. Retrieved May 25, 2008, from http://www.accenture.com

Adaptive (2005). Adaptive and assistive technologies in e-learning. Retrieved February 20, 2009, from http://www.adcet.edu.au/StoredFile.aspx?id=1353&fn=adptve_assstv_techn_elearning.pdf

Adobe Systems Incorporated. (1999). *PostScript Language Reference Manual*. Reading, MA: Addison-Wesley.

Advance Healthcare Group Limited. (2005). *Advance and IBA enter online pharmacy and electronic prescribing collaboration and convertible note Investment*. Retrieved May 25, 2008 from, http://www.ahgl.com.au/files/document/9_Collab.pdf

Affairs, C. (2005, January) *Webseals of Approval/final Report*. Retrieved June 26, 2008, from http://www.consumer.vic.gov.au/CA256902000FE154/Lookup/CAV_Publications_Computers_Internet_Discussion_Papers/$file/WebSealsFinalReport.pdf

AFIGEO, (1998, May). *L'information géographique française dans la société de l'information: état des lieux et propositions d'action*, p. 35.

Afrique en ligne (2008). *Afrique en ligne*. Retrieved September 10, 2008, from http://www.afriquenligne.fr/nigeria's-gsm-operator,-globacom,-hits-20m-subscribe-base-2008082911686.html

Agarwal, A., & Ramana, V. V. (Eds.). (2008). Foundations of E-Government. Naidoo, G. (ed.), *An overview of eGovernment policy initiatives in the South African government*. New Delhi. India.

Agunloye, O. (2004): *e-Government strategies for west Africa: public-private-partnership*. Retrieved from www.enigeria.org

Aio (2008). *e-Learning in Local government: A briefing paper*. Retrieved February 10, 2009, from http://www.idea.gov.uk/idk/aio/1702668

Ajayi, G. O. (2005). *e-Government in Nigeria's e-strategy*. Retrieved from http://www.nitda.gov.ng/papers

Akther, M. S., Onishi, T., & Kidokoro, T. (2005). *E-Government Practice: What One Country Could Learn from Other Electronic Government*. Berlin, Heidelberg: Springer.

Al-Adawi, Z., Yousafzai, S., et al. (2005). *Conceptual Model of Citizen Adoption E-Government*, the Second International Conference on Innovations in Information Technology, Dubai, U. Retrieved from http://citeseerx.ist.psu.edu/viewdoc/download?doi=10.1.1.92.2165&rep=rep1&type=pdf

Alessandro, M. (2005). Borsa Lavoro Lombardia: e-Gov Interoperability in the labour market. In*Proceedings of e-Gov-Interop'05 conference*, Geneva, Switzerland.

Alimadhi, F. (2002, September). *Mobile Internet: Wireless access to Web-based interfaces of legacy simulations, Master of Science Thesis.* Amsterdam: University of Amsterdam, Faculty of Science, Informatic Institute, Section Computational Science

Ally, M. (2008). *e-Learning Solutions and Innovations*, Workshop Presented at the E-Learning Excellence in the Middle East 2008, Learning Excellence.

Al-Shalabi, H. (n.d.). *E-Voting Scheme over internet.* Retrieved from http://74.125.113.132/search?q=cache:izHh8ng4EVcJ:academic-papers.org/ocs2/session/Papers/E6/215-1540-2-DR.doc+E-Voting+Scheme+over+internet&cd=1&hl=en&ct=clnk&gl=us

Amaravadi, C. S. (2005). Digital repositories for e-government. *Electronic Government*, *2*(2), 205–218. doi:10.1504/EG.2005.007095

America Telemedicine Association. (n.d.). *America Telemedicine Association.* Retrieved May 25, 2008, from http://www.atmeda.org

Amin, H. (2000), *Internet in the Arab African World.* Retrieved from www.highwayafrica.org.za/archive/2000/pages/monamin.doc

Amit, R. A. Z. C. (2001). Value Creation in E-Business. *Strategic Management Journal*, *22*, 493–520. doi:10.1002/smj.187

Anantraman, V., Mikkelsen, T., Khilnani, R., Kumar, V. S., Machiraju, R., Pentland, A., & Ohno-Machado, L. (2002). Handheld computers for rural healthcare, experiences in a large scale implementation. In*Proceedings of the 2nd Development by Design Workshop (DYD02).*

Anderson, J. G. (2007). Social, ethical and legal barriers to E-health. *International Journal of Medical Informatics*, *76*, 480–483. doi:10.1016/j.ijmedinf.2006.09.016

André, J., & Borghi, B. (1990). Dynamic Fonts. *PostScript Language Journal*, *2*(3), 4–6.

Andreassen, H. K., Bunjnowska-Fedak, M., Chronaki, C. E., Dumitru, R. C., Pudule, I., & Santana, S. (2007). European citizens use of E-health services: A study of Seven Countries'. *BMC Public Health*, *7*(53), 1–7.

Angaye, C. (2007, November 26). NeGST has no monopoly on e-Government. *Financial Standard*, pp. 46.

ANSI/ISO/IEC. (1999). *International Standard (IS). Database Language SQL—Part 2: Foundation (SQL/Foundation).* Stockholm: Swedish Trade Council.

Anstead, N., & Chadwick, A. (2008). Parties, election campaigning, and the Internet: Toward a comparative institutional approach. In Chadwick, A. (Eds.), *The Routledge Handbook of Internet Politics* (pp. 56–73). London: Routledge.

Anttiroiko, A. (2008). *An Effective E-Governance Framework: The Key to Enhanced E-Government Services.* Retrieved February 18, 2009, from http://www.uta.fi/laitokset/yhdt/artikkelit/um_ict4dev_anttiroiko_2008-5.doc

Arthur, W. B. (1994). *Increasing returns and path dependence in the economy.* Ann Arbor, MI: University of Michigan Press.Barnard, C. I. (1938). *The Functions of the Executive.* Cambridge, MA: Harvard University Press.

Asgarkhani, M. (2005). Digital Government and its Effectiveness in Public Management Reform: A Local Government Perspective. *Public Management Review*, *7*(3), 465–487. doi:10.1080/14719030500181227

Asgarkhani, M. (2002, December 5-7). *E-governance in Asia Pacific.* International Conference on Governance in Asia. Retrieved from Http://www.cityu.edu.hk/garc/conference/Asgarkhani,Mehdi.doc

Ashworth, L., & Free, C. (2006). Marketing Dataveillance and Digital Privacy: Using Theories of Justice to Understand Consumers' Online Privacy Concerns. *Journal of Business Ethics*, *67*(2), 107–123. doi:10.1007/s10551-006-9007-7

Asian Development Bank Institute (ADBI). (2009). *Legal aspects of e-government.* Retrieved June 14, 2009, from http://www.adbi.org/book/2004/11/05/725.implementing.egovernment.book/1.2.j.legal.aspects.of.egovernment/

Aussenac-Gilles, N., Biébow, B., & Szulman, S. (2000). *Modélisation du domaine par une méthode fondée sur l'analyse de corpus*. Actes de la conférence IC'2000, Journées Francophones d'Ingénieurie des connaissances, pp. 93-103.

Australian Bureau of Statistics. (1998). *1291.0 - A Guide to Major ABS Classifications*. Canberra: Commonwealth of Australia.

Australian Government Portal. (n.d.). *Australian Government Portal*. Retrieved May 8, 2009, from http://www.australia.gov.au/States_and_Territories

Australian Government. (2008). *Australian Government - Department of Health and Aging*. Retrieved May 25, 2008, from http://www.health.gov.au/internet/ministers/publishing.nsf/Content/mr-yr08-je-je023.htm

Australian Government. (n.d.). *Australian Government- Medicare Australia*. Retrieved May 8, 2009, from http://www.medicareaustralia.gov.au/provider/aged-care/online-claiming/index.jsp

Australian Institute of Health and Welfare. (n.d.). *Australian Institute of Health and Welfare*. Retrieved May 25, 2008, from http://www.aihw.gov.au/publications/age/oag04/oag04.pdf

AVCC. (2004). *Australia's universities: individual universities - Charles Sturt University*. Retrieved October 12, 2004, from http://www.avcc.edu.au/news/public_statements/publications/Uni_Facts/csu.htm

Ayo, C. K., Babajide, D. O. (2007). Design and Implementation of a Secure i-Voting System. *Journal of Computer Science and its Applications, 14*(2), 38-51.

Azeta, A. A., Ikhu-Omoregbe, N. A., Ayo, C. K., & Atayero, A. A. (2008b, June). "Development and Deployment of VoiceXML-Based Banking Applications," *Journal of Computer Science & Its Application*. [NCS]. *An International Journal of the Nigeria Computer Society, 15*(1), 59–72.

Azeta, A. A., Ayo, C. K., Atayero, A. A., & Ikhu-Omoregbe, N. A. (2008a November 18-20). Development of a Telephone-based e-Learning Portal, *1st International Conference on Mobile Computing, Wireless Communication, e-Health, M-Health and TeleMedicine* (FICMWiComTelHealth '08), Ladoke Akintola University of Technology, Ogbomosho, Nigeria.

Ba, S., & Pavlou, P. A. (2002). Evidence of the Effect of Trust Building Technology in Electronic Markets: Price Premiums And Buyer Behavior. *Management Information Systems Quarterly, 26*, 243–268. doi:10.2307/4132332

Bachimont, B. (2000). Engagement sémantique et engagement ontologique: conception et réalisation d'ontologies en ingénierie des connaissances. In R. Teulier, J. Charlet & P. Tchounikine (eds.), *Coordinateurs, Ingénierie des connaissances*, chapitre 19. Paris: L'Harmattan.

Backhouse, J. (2007). e-Democracy in Australia: the Challenge of Evolving a Successful Model, *The Electronic. Journal of E-Government, 5*(2), 107–116. Retrieved from www.ejeg.com.

Baier, A. (1986). Trust And Antitrust. *Ethics, 96*, 231–260. doi:10.1086/292745

Bajkowski, J. (2007, November 24). Online Face-offs and Spoofs Win Viewers. *MIS Financial Review*

Baker, D. W., Wolf, M. S., Feinglass, J., Thompson, J. A., Gazmararian, J. A., & Huang, J. (2007). Health literacy and mortality among elderly persons. *Archives of Internal Medicine, 167*(14), 1503–1509. doi:10.1001/archinte.167.14.1503

Baker, L., Wagner, T. H., Singer, S., & Bundorf, M. K. (2003). Use of the Internet and e-mail for health care information. *Journal of the American Medical Association, 289*, 2400–2406. doi:10.1001/jama.289.18.2400

Baldoni, M., Baroglio, C., & Henze, N. (2005). Personalization for the Semantic Web. In *Proceedings of the 1st international Summer School. Reasoning Web., Malta*, pp.173-212.

Bamford, W., Coulton, P., & Edwards, R. (2006). Location-based Mobile Blogging. In *Proceedings of the 2nd IEEE International Conference on Information & Communication Technologies: from Theory to Applications (ICTTA'06)*, (vol. 1, pp. 39 – 40). Damascus, Syria.

Baneyx, A. (2007). *Construire une ontologie de pneumologie*. Thèse de doctorat, Université Paris6 page 61; 85. Février.

Barber, B. (1983). *Logic And Limits Of Trust*. East Rutherford, NJ: Rutgers University.

Baresi, L., Morasca, S., & Paolini, P. *Estimating the Design Effort of Web Applications*. Presented at the Ninth International Software Metrics Symposium (METRICS'03)(p. 62)

Baron, R., & Kenny, D. (1986). The moderator-mediator variable distinction in social psychological research: Conceptual, strategic, and statistical considerations. *Journal of Personality and Social Psychology*, *51*, 1173–1182. doi:10.1037/0022-3514.51.6.1173

Barry, D. K. (2003). *Web Services and Service-Oriented Architectures: The Savvy Manager's Guide*. San Francisco: Morgan Kaufmann.

Barsky, B. A. (1985). *Arbitrary Subdivision of Bézier Curves (Technical Report UCB.CSD 85/265)*. Computer Science Division, University of California.

Bayar, A., & Sami, K. (2008). Optimization of the curvilinear stretching in a PostScript font with quadratic Bézier curves. Presented at The International Arab Conference of e-Technology. In [Arab Open University, Amman, Jordan.]. *Proceedings of IACe-T*, *2008*, 97–104.

Bayar, A., & Sami, K. (2008). *An Optimal Way to Encode the Outlines of Variable Sized Arabic Letters in a PostScript Font*. Presented at The 16th International Conference in Central Europe on Computer Graphics, Visualization and Computer Vision, Full Papers Proceedings (pp.57-64), University of West Bohemia, Plzen Czech Republic.

Bayar, A., & Sami, K. (2009). How a font can respect rules of Arabic calligraphy. *The International Arab Journal of e-Technology*, *1*(1).

Belhadef, H., Ouafek, N., & Kholladi, M. K. (2008). *A Set of Mapping Rules E/R and Relational Schema Database towards an Ontology*. First IEEE International Conference on the Applications of Digital Information and Web Technologies (ICADIWT 2008). Retrieved from http://ieeexplore.ieee.org/xpl/freeabs_all.jsp?arnumber=4664361

Bello, S. (2003): *The Impact of the Wire Nigeria (WiN) Project on Universal Service Provision*. Retrieved February 2007, from http://www.ncc.gov/Workshop%20Papers/Consultative%20Workshop-August%202003/bello's%20presentation%20at%20presentation%20at%20consultative%20forum2.pdf

Bentham, J. (1787). *The Panopticon Writings*. London: Verso.

Bergamaschi, S., & Guerra, F. (2002). Peer-to-peer paradigm for a Semantic Search Engine. In *Agents and Peer-to-Peer-Computing*, Bologna, Italy.

Bernard, J. G., Rivard, S., & Aubert, B. A. (2004). L'exposition au risque d'implantation d'ERP: éléments de mesure et d'atténuation. *Systèmes d'Information et Management*, *9*(2), 25–50.

Berners-Lee, T., & Miller, E. (2002). The Semantic Web lifts off'. *Special Issue of ERCIM News*, *51*, 9–11.

Bernerth, J. (2004). Expanding our understanding of the change message. *Human Resource Development Review*, *3*(1), 36–52. doi:10.1177/1534484303261230

Bettaz, M., & Maouche, M. (1993). How to specify non determinism and true concurrency with algebraic term nets. *Lecture Notes in Computer Science*, *655*, 164–180.

Bettaz, M. D. (1996). Performance comparison of high level algebraic nets distributed simulation protocols. *Winter Simulation Conference*.

Bézier, P. E. (19770. *Essai de Définition Numérique des Courbes et des Surfaces Expérimentales*. Ph.D. dissertation, Université Pierre et Marie Curie, Paris. Berry, D. M. (1999). Stretching Letter and Slanted-Baseline Formatting for Arabic, Hebrew and Persian with dittroff/fforttid and Dynamic PostScript Fonts. *Software-Practice and Experience*, *29*(15), 1417-1457.

Bieber,, C. (2007, November 21-25). Open Source Campaigning? How Online Innovations Trigger Offline Changes in Political Organizations. *ESF-LiU Conference. Electronic Democracy: Achievements and Challenges*, Vadstena, Sweden.

Bielecki, A., & Hajto, P. (2004). A Neural-Based Agent for IP Traffic Scanning and Worm Detection. In *Proceedings of Artificial Intelligence and Soft Computing* (p. 816). ICAISC.

Biriwasha, M. (2007). *15% Now! Campaign: Africa Must Invest in Public Health*. Retreived April 29, 2008, from http://www.rhrealitycheck.org/node/4363/print

Bisman, J. (1996). Integrating the Internet into distance education in accounting at Charles Sturt University: an assessment of potential. *Occasional Papers in Open and Distance Learning*.

Bloom, B. S. (Ed.). (1956). *Taxonomy of Educational Objectives, the classification of educational goals – Handbook I: Cognitive Domain*. New York: McKay.

Bloor Research. (2006). *ILOG Jrules 6.0, Analysts Rave About JRules6! White Paper.* Retrieved April 2009, from http://www.ilog.com/products/jrules/whitepapers/index.cfm

Bomba, D. (2005). Evaluating the Quality of Health Web Sites: Developing a Validation Method and Rating Instrument. In*Proceedings of the 38th Hawaii International Conference on System Sciences*.

Bontis, N. (1998). Intellectual Capital: An exploratory Study that Develops Measures and Models. *Management Decision*, *36*(2), 63–76. doi:10.1108/00251749810204142

Borras, J. (2003). International Technical Standards for e-Government, *The Electronic. Journal of E-Government*, *2*(2), 75–80. Retrieved from www.ejeg.com.

Borsboom, D., Mellenbergh, G. J., & Heerden, J. V. (2003). The Theoretical Status of Latent Variables. *Psychological Review*, *110*, 203–219. doi:10.1037/0033-295X.110.2.203

Bouaziz, (2006, December 14-16), Managing e-government projects failure and risks, *Internet & Information Systems in the Digital Age: Challenges & Solutions, 7th International Business Information Management (IBIMA) Conference*. Brescia Italy.

Bourigault, D. (2002). *Upery: un outil d'analyse distributionnelle étendue pour la construction d'ontologies à partir de corpus. Actes de la 9ème conférence annuelle sur le Traitement Automatique des Langues* (pp. 75–84). TALN.

Boutin, P. (2004). *Is E-voting Safe*. Retrieved June 2006, from http://www.pcworld.com/resource/

Boutin, P. (2006, April 26). A Grand Unified Theory of YouTube and MySpace: Point and Click Sites That Don't Tell You What To Do. Retrieved from http://www.slate.com/id/2140635/

Bozsak, E., et al. (2002)KAON - Towards a large scale Semantic Web. In Proceedings *of the ThirdInternational Conference on E-Commerce and Web Technologies (ECWeb)*, Springer-Verlag LNCS, pages 304–313.2002.

Brannigan, C. (2003). Online *Dispute Resolution: Resolving in Cyberspace*. Retrieved February 3, 2008, from http://www.mediate.ca/onlineresolution.html

Brauckmann, P. (2009). Why Obama would not have succeeded in Germany. *Sound Off*, Mar 2, Politics. Retrieved from http://www.politicsonline.com/content/main/soundoff/soundoff.asp?id=444

Brayshaw, M., & Gordon, N. (2008). Inquiry based Learning in Computer Science teaching in Higher Education. *Innovations in Teaching And Learning in Information and Computer Sciences*, *7*(1), 22–33.

Brayshaw, M., & Gordon, N. (2009). Inquiry based learning in computer science: a natural approach to learning. In: P. Levy & P. McKinney (eds), *Proceedings of the 3rd Learning Through Enquiry Alliance Conference*, 25-27 June 2008, Sheffield, UK: Centre for Inquiry-based Learning in the Arts and Social Sciences (CILASS): University of Sheffield, pp 31-39.

Breindl, Y., & Francq, P. (2008, November 16). Can Web 2.0 applications save e-democracy? A study of how new internet applications may enhance citizen participation in the political process online. *International Journal of Electronic Democracy*, *1*(1), 14–31. doi:10.1504/IJED.2008.021276

Bremer, A. A., & Prado, L. A. L. (2006). Municipal m-Services using SMS,Euro mGov 2006.

BRG. (2003). *The Business Rules Manifesto*. Retrieved April 2009, from http://www.businessrulesgroup.org/brmanifesto.htm

BRG. (2009). *Business Rules Group*. Retrieved April 2009, from http://www.businessrulesgroup.org/home-brg.shtml

Briscoe, T., & Carroll, J. (2002). *Robust accurate statistical annotation of general tex*. In LREC.

Brown, S. R. (1997). *The History And Principles Of Q Methodology In Psychology And The Social Sciences*. Kent, Ohio.

Bruegge, B., & Dutoit, A. H. (n.d.). *Object-Oriented Software Engineering: Using UML, Patterns and Java*. Upper Saddle River, NJ: Prentice Hall.fff

Brusilovsky, P. (2001). Adaptive Hypermedia. *User Modeling and User-Adapted Interaction*, *11*, 87–110. doi:10.1023/A:1011143116306

Brusilovsky, P., & Paylo, C. (2003). Adaptive and intelligent Web-based educational systems. *International Journal of Artificial Intelligence in Education*, *13*, 159–172.

Brynjolfsson, E., & Kahin, B. (2002). *Understanding the Digital Economy: Data, Tools and Research*. Cambridge, MA: MIT Press.

Brynjolfsson, E., & Hitt, L. (2002). *Digital organization: preliminary results from an MIT study of Internet organization, culture and productivity*, MIT Working Paper.

Buckhout, S., Frey, E., & Nemec, J. (1999). Making ERP Succeed: Turning Fear into Promise. *Technology (Elmsford, N.Y.)*, *15*, 60–71.

Building VoiceXML applications (2005). *Building VoiceXML applications*. Retrieved May 20, 2008, from https://studio.tellme.com/vxml2/ovw/applications.html.

Bushry, M. (2005). *E-Commerce*. Firewall Media.

California Internet Voting Task Force. (2000). *A report on the feasibility of Internet Voting*. Retrieved August 2006, from http://www.ss.ca.gov/

Cape Gateway Portal. (2008). *Cape Gateway Portal*. Retrieved June 10, 2008, from http: www.capegateway.gov.za

Cardoso, J., Bostrom, R. P., & Sheth, A. (2004). Workflow management systems and ERP systems: differences, commonalities, and applications. *Information Technology Management*, *5*, 319–338. doi:10.1023/B:ITEM.0000031584.14039.99

Cardoso, J., Mendes, M., Figueiredo, A., Kamada, A., Monte, R., Hoepner, P., & Bolliger, S. (2004) *Implementing Electronic Government: The eGOIA Project*. In: 3o. EU-LAT Workshop on e-Government and e-Democracy, Santiago do Chile, Chile.

Carr, D., & Stelter, B. (2008). Political campaigns in a Web 2.0 world. *The New York Times*, pp. B1, B11.

Carrizales, T. (2004). Citizen Driven Government Performance, *Public Performance &. Management Review*, *28*(1), 123–129.

Carrizales, T. (2008). Critical Factors in an Electronic Democracy: A Study of Municipal Managers, *The Electronic. Journal of E-Government*, *6*(1), 23–30. Retrieved from www.ejeg.com.

Carrizales, T., Holzer, M., Kim, S.-T., & Kim, C.-G. (2006). Digital Governance Worldwide: A Longitudinal Assessment of Municipal Web Sites. *International Journal of Electronic Government Research*, *2*(4), 1–23.

Carter, L., & Bélanger, F. (2005). The utilization of e-government services: citizen trust, innovation and acceptance factors. *Information Systems Journal*, *15*(1), 5–25. doi:10.1111/j.1365-2575.2005.00183.x

Castells, M. (2000). *The Rise of the Network Society*. London: Blackwell Publishing Ltd.

Cats-Baril, W., & Jelassi, T. (1994). The French Videotex System Minitel: A Successful Implementation of a National Information Technology Infrastructure. *Management Information Systems Quarterly*, *18*(1), 1–20. doi:10.2307/249607

Cellary, W. (2008) Strategic impact of e-government on economy and society In *Proceedings of the 2nd International Conference on Theory and Practice of Electronic Governance, 351*, 149-153.

Central Government. (2000). *Green Paper on Electronic Commerce*. Retrieved from http://www.polity.org.za/govdocs/green_papers/greenpaper/index.html

Central Intelligence Agency. (2007, June 14). *The World Factbook2007*. Retrieved June, 19, 2007, from https://www.cia.gov/library/publications/the-world-factbook/geos/sf.html

CERT. (2008). *Advisory CA-2001-26 Nimda Worm*. Retrieved from http://www.cert.org/advisories/CA-2001-26.html

Chadwick, A. (2009) Web 2.0: new challenges for the study of e-democracy in an era of international exuberance, *I/S: A journal of Law and Policy for the Information Society, 5*(1), 1-32.

Chaffey, D. (2002). *Enterprise Resource Planning and E-Commerce Management*. Upper Saddle River, NJ: Prentice Hall.

Chafkin, M. (2007, June). How to Kill a Great Idea. *Inc.com*. Retrieved from http://www.inc.com/magazine/20070601/features-how-to-kill-a-great-idea.html

Chamberlin, D. D., & Boyce, R. F. (1974). Sequel: a structured English Query Language. In *Proceedings of the 1974 ACM SIGFIDET Workshop on Data Description, Access and Control* (pp. 249–264). Association for Computing Machinery.

Charfi, A., & Mezini, M. (2004). *Hybrid Web Service Composition: Business Processes Meet Business Rules*. New York: ICSOC'04.

Chau, P. Y. K., Hu, P. J.-H., Lee, B. L. P., & Au, A. K. K. (in press). Examining Customers' Trust in Online Vendors And Dropouts: An Empirical Study. *Electronic Commerce Research and Applications*.

Chen, Z. (2007). *Modeling and Defending Against Internet Worm Attacks*. School of Electrical and Computer Engineering, Georgia Institute of Technology.

Chen, X., & Heidemann, J. (2004). Detecting Early Worm Propagation through Packet Matching. In *Proceedings of ISI-TR-2004-585, USC Information Sciences Institute*.

Chen, Z., Gao, L., & Kwiat, K. (2003). Modeling the spread of active worms. In *Proceedings of Twenty-Second Annual Joint Conference of the IEEE Computer and Communications Societies INFOCOM, IEEE*.

Cheniti-Belcadhi, L., Henze, N., & Braham, R. (2008). Assessment Personalisation on the Semantic Web. *Special issue: Intelligent Systems and Knowledge Management. Journal of Computational Methods in Sciences and Engineering, 8*, 1–20.

Cheniti-Belcadhi, L., Braham, R., Henze, N., & Nejdl, W. (2005). A Generic Framework for Assessment in Adaptive Educational Hypermedia. *IADIS International Journal on WWW/Internet, 3*, 17-28.

Cheung, C. M. K., & Lee, M. K. O. (2006). Understanding consumer trust in Internet shopping: a multidisciplinary approach. *Journal of the American Society for Information Science and Technology*, *57*(4), 479–492. doi:10.1002/asi.20312

Chevallier, M., Warynski, M., & Sandoz, A. (2006). Success Factors of Geneva's e-Voting System. *Electronic. Journal of E-Government*, *4*(2). Retrieved from http://www.ejep.com.

Chin, C. C., Hock, G. T., & Veerappan, C. M. (2006). VoiceXML as Solution for Improving Web accessibility and Manipulation for e-Education. *School of Computing and IT, INTI College Malasia*. Retrieved July 2008, from, http://intisj.edu.my/INTISJ/InfoFor/StaffResearch/10.pdf

Chisholm, M. (2004). *How to Build a Business Rules Engine - Extending Application Functionality through Metadata Engineering*. New York: Elsevier Inc.

Choi, D. (2003). Online dispute resolution: Issues and Future directions. In. *Proceedings of the UNECE Forum on ODR, 2003*, 1–3.

Chong, J. L. L., Singh, M., & Teoh, S. Y. (2008). *An Exploration of E-Health in the Public Sector: the Australian Perspective*. International Conference on e-Government, Australia, October 23-24.

Ciborra, C., & Navarra, D. D. (2005). Good governance, development theory, and aid policy: Risks and challenges of e-government in Jordan. *InformationTechnology for Development, 11*(2), 141–159. doi:10.1002/itdj.20008

Ciborra, C. (2003). E-government: Between Development and War. In Järvi, T., & Reijonen, P. (Eds.), *People and Computers*. Tuscon, Arizona: TUCS Publications.

Clark, B. (2002, November). ODR: the new kid in town. *The New Law Journal, 152*(7050), 1710–1711.

Clark, T. H., Croson, D. C., & Schiano, W. T. (2001). A hierarchical model of supply-chain integration: information sharing and operational interdependence in the US grocery channel. *Information Technology Management, 2*, 261–288. doi:10.1023/A:1011497025090

Clarke, E., Grumberg, O., & Peled, D. A. (1999). *Model Checking*. Cambridge, MA: MIT Press.

Clavel, M., Durán, F., Eker, S., Lincoln, P., Marti-Oliet, N., Meseguer, J., & Quesada, J. F. (2002, August). MAUDE: specification and programming in rewriting logic. *Theoretical Computer Science, 285*(2), 178–243. doi:10.1016/S0304-3975(01)00359-0

Clavel, M., Durán, F., Eker, S., Lincoln, P., Martí-Oliet, N., Meseguer, J., & Talcott, C. (2007). *Maude Manual (Version 2.3)*. Retrieved fromhttp://maude.cs.uiuc.edu

Cloete, F. (2004). *Maximising the potential of transforming policy failure into policy success: E-government, the digital divide and e-development*. Annual Congress of the International Institute of Administrative Sciences (IIAS). Seoul, South Korea.

Cloud, J. (2006, December 16). The Gurus of YouTube. *Time*.

Coase, R. H. (1937). The Nature of the Firm. *Economica, 4*(16), 386–405. doi:10.1111/j.1468-0335.1937.tb00002.x

Cohen, J. (1960). A Coefficient of Agreement For Nominal Scales. *Educational and Psychological Measurement, 20*, 37–46. doi:10.1177/001316446002000104

Coleman, S. (2001). Online Campaigning. *Parliamentary Affairs, 54*(4), 679–688. doi:10.1093/parlij/54.4.679

Coleman, K. (2002). Internet Voting- Issues and Legislation in CRS Report for Congress. Retrieved November 2008, from http://www.ipmall.info/hosted_resources/crs/RS20639.PDF

Coleman, N., Rousseau, N., & Carpenter, H. (2004). *Jobcentre Plus Service Delivery Survey* ((IAD Social Research Division Research Report No. 223). London.

Colton, D., & Covert, R. W. (2007). *Designing And Constructing Instruments For Social Research And Evaluation*. San Francisco: Jossey-Bass.

Commonwealth Centre for Electronic Governance. (2001). Electronic Governance in Context In *Electronic Governance and Electronic Democracy: Living and Working in the Connected World*. Retrieved May 27, 2008, from http://www.electronicgov.net/pubs/research_papers/eged/chapter1.shtml#introduction

Compton, K., Huggins, J. K., & Shen, W. (2000). A semantic model for the state machine in the Unified Modeling Language. *In Proceeding of Dynamic Behavior in UML Models: Semantic Questions, UML 2000 workshop*Crane, M. D. (2005). *On the Semantics of UML State Machines: Categorization and Comparison*. Ontario,Canada: School of Computing, Queen's University.

Cookey, P.(2005, September): Corruption Stall Nigeria Development – World Bank. *Financial Standard*, pp. 9

Corbitt, B. J., Thanasankit, T., & Yi, H. (2003). Trust and e-commerce: a research of consumer perceptions. *Electronic Commerce Research and Applications, 2*(3), 203–215. doi:10.1016/S1567-4223(03)00024-3

Cordella, A. (2006). Transaction costs and information systems: does IT add up? *Journal of Information Technology, 21*, 195–202. doi:10.1057/palgrave.jit.2000066

Cordella, A. (2001, June 27-29). *Does Information Technology Always Lead to Lower Transaction Costs?* Presented at The 9th European Conference on Information Systems, Bled, Slovenia.

Cordella, A., & Simon, K. A. (1997, August 9-12). *The Impact of Information Technology on Transaction and Coordination Cost*. Presented at theConference on Information Systems Research in Scandinavia (IRIS 20), Oslo, Norway.

Corporate Technology Group. (2008). *The threat within: is your company safe from itself?* Retrieved February 2009, from http://www.ctgyourit.com/newsletter.php

Council, C. I. O. (1999, September). *Federal Enterprise Architecture Framework*. Retrieved from http://www.cio.gov/Documents/fedarch1.pdf

Coursey, D., & Norris, D. F. (2008, May-June). Models of E-Government: Are They Correct? An Empirical Assessment. [PAR]. *Public Administration Review, 68*(3), 523–536. doi:10.1111/j.1540-6210.2008.00888.x

Cox, P. T., & Song, B. (2001). A Formal Model for Component-Based Software. *IEEE 2001 Symposium on Human Centric Computing Languages and Environments (HCC'01)*.

Crnkovic, I., & Larsson, M. (2002). *Building Reliable Component-based Software Systems*. London: Artech House.

Cronbach, L. J., & Meehl, P. E. (1955). Construct Validity In Psychological Tests. *Psychological Bulletin, 52*, 281–302. doi:10.1037/h0040957

Cross, R. M. (2004). Exploring Attitudes: The Case For Q Methodology. *Health Education Research, 20*, 206–213. doi:10.1093/her/cyg121

Cuecent. (2008). *Standard based Framework*, Cuecent BPMS. Retrieved April 2000, from http://www.bahwancybertek.com/cuecentBpms.html

Curtis, R. (2007). What is e-health and why is it important? *ADF Health, 8*, 82–83.

Dada, D. (2006). *The Failure of E-Government in Developing Countries* (pp. 39–43). The Electronic Journal on Information Systems in Developing Countries.

Daddieco, R. J. (2004). Retrieving knowledge in e-government: the prospects of ontology for regulatory domain record keeping systems. In Wimmer (Ed.), *Building Semantic Webs for e-government with Wiki technology 55*

Dagon, D., et al. (2004). HoneyStat: LocalWorm Detection Using Honeypots. In *Proceedings of Seventh International Symposium on Recent Advances in Intrusion Detection* (RAID).

Dalziel, D. (2004) Government Online-A multi-country Study of e-government usage, *The World Association of Research Professionals*. Retrieved from http://www.tns-global.com/corporate/Doc/0/MJHPECQDDJ94195OMMQKECDBC0/GovernmentOnline-ESOMAR_Paper2004.pdf

Daniel, E. M. (2003). The role of dynamic capabilities in e-business transformation. *European Journal of Information Systems, 12*(4), 282–296. doi:10.1057/palgrave.ejis.3000478

Dantu, R., Cangussu, J. W., & Patwardhan, S. (2007). Fast Worm Containment Using Feedback Control. *IEEE Transactions on Dependable and Secure Computing, 5*(2), 119–136. doi:10.1109/TDSC.2007.1002

Dasgupta, P. (1998). Trust as a Commodity. In Gambetta, D. (Ed.), *Trust: Making And Breaking Cooperative Relations. Electronic Edition*. London: Basil Blackwell Ltd.

Davenport, T. (1998). Putting Enterprise into the Enterprise System. *Harvard Business Review, 76*(4), 121–131.

Davenport, E., & Horton, K. (2004) A Social Shaping Perspective on an e-Governmental System(ic) Failure. In Traunmuller, R. (Ed.), *Electronic government: Third International Conference, EGOV*. Berlin: Springer.

David, W., Paul, C. O., & Evangelos, K. (2005). Detecting Intra-Enterprise Scanning Worms Based on Address Resolution. In *Proceedings of the 21st Annual Computer Security Applications Conference*, IEEE Computer Society.

Davies, V., Taylor, J., Hartfree, Y., & Kellard, K. (2004). *Delivering the Jobcentre Plus vision: Qualitative research with staff and customers (Phase 3)* (Research Report No. 222). IAD Social Research Division. London.

Davis, F. D. (1989). Perceived Usefulness, Perceived Ease Of Use, And User Acceptance of Information Technology. *Management Information Systems Quarterly*, *13*, 319–340. doi:10.2307/249008

Davis, F. D., Bagozzi, R. P., & Warshaw, P. R. (1989). User Acceptance of Computer Technology: A Comparison Of Two Theoretical Models. *Management Science*, *35*, 982–1003. doi:10.1287/mnsc.35.8.982

Dawes, S., Pardo, T. A., & Jiang, Y. (2008) A holistic framework for understanding government information access initiatives. In *Proceedings of the 2nd International Conference on Theory and Practice of Electronic Governance, 351*, 83-89.

DCSF. (2008). *GCSE and equivalent results in England, 2007/09*, Department for Children, Schools and Families. Retrieved March 2009 from http://www.dcsf.gov.uk/rsgateway/DB/SFR/s000815/index.shtml

De Blomac F, (2005). *Les systèmes d'information géographique territoriaux-La mise en ligne des données géographiques: principes et expériences*, Cybergeo: European Journal of Geography, n°318, p. 123.

De Blomac F, (2009, June 01). *Publier des cartes sur Internet: ces solutions qui nous viennent du graphique*. SIG La Lettre, n°108, p. 3.

De Blomac, F. (2001). *L'open source, véritable alternative pour les SIG?* p. 4.

De Geus, A. (1997). *The Living Company*. Cambridge, MA: Harvard Business School Publishing.

De, R. (2005). E-Government Systems in Developing Countries: Stakeholders and Conflict. In Wimmer, M. A. (Eds.), *EGOV 2005, LNCS 3591* (pp. 26–37).

Decker, M. (2006) Generalized Notification Services: A Simple but Versatile Paradigm for the Implementation of Mobile Data Services, *Euro mGov 2006*. Retrieved from http://www.mgovernment.org/resources/euromgvo2006/PDF/10_Decker.pdf

Delaney, C. (2006). Social Media: Promising Tool, Double-Edged Sword. In Germany, J. B. (Ed.), *Person-to-Person-to-Person: Harnessing the Political Power of Online Social Networks and User-Generated Content* (pp. 7–11). Institute for Politics Democracy & the Internet.

DeLone, W. H., & McLean, E. R. (2003). The DeLone and McLean Model of Information Systems Success: A ten-Year Update. *Journal of Management Information Systems*, *19*(4), 9–30.

Demegre, J., & Salge, F. (2004). *Que sais-je? Les SIGs*, p. 84.

Department of Economic and Social Affairs - Division for Public Administration and Development Management United Nations. (2008). *e-Government Survey 2008 From e-Government to Connected Governance*. Retrieved Novermber 4, 2008, from http://unpan1.un.org/intradoc/groups/public/documents/UN/UNPAN028607.pdf

Department of Human Services. (1997). *Department of Human Services: Public Health in Australia*. Retrieved May 8, 2009, from http://www.dhs.vic.gov.au/nphp/publications/broch/contents.htm

Department of Human Services. (2008) *National E-health Strategy Summary*, Paper presented to Australian Health Ministers Conference.

Deutsch, M. (1960). The Effect Of Motivational Orientation Upon Trust And Suspicion. *Human Relations*, *13*, 123–139. doi:10.1177/001872676001300202

Devlin, J., Guerrieri, P., & Page, J. (n.d.). *MENA and the WTO: a post Seattle agenda*. Retrieved from www.worldbank.org/mdf/mdf3/papers/global/Devlin.pdf

Dhillon, G., & Hackney, R. (2000) IS/IT and dynamic business change. In *Proceedings of the 33rd Annual* HICSS, Maui, Hawaii. eGOIA (2006) Electronic Government Innovation and Access. Retrieved April 2000, from http://www.egoia.sp.gov.br/portugues/project.htm

Di Maio, A. (2006). *E-government strategies Highlight key focus areas*. Stamford, CT: Gartner Inc.

Don Libes, D. F., Wallace, E., Steves, M., Feeney, A. B., & Barkmeyer, E. (2004). *The challenges of automated methods for integrating systems*. Innsbruck, Austria: Software Engineering.

Donaldson, T., & Preston, L. (1995). The stakeholder theory of the corporation - Concepts, evidence, and implications. *Academy of Management Review*, *20*(1), 65–91. doi:10.2307/258887

Dong, W., Wang, J., Qi, X., & Qi, Z. (2001). Model Checking UML Statecharts. In *Proceedings of the Eighth Asia-Pacific Software Engineering Conference (APSEC.01)*.

Dowson, L., House, S., & Sanderson, I. (2004). *Jobcentre Plus Customer Satisfaction 2003: Findings from qualitative research* (DWP Research Report No. 191). Leeds, UK.

Duford, S. (2004). Building a Wireless Web Solutions: Tools and Justifications for Building a Wireless Web Solutions. In Purba, S. (Ed.), *Architecture for E-business System* (pp. 263–286). Oxford, UK: Auerbach.

Dunleavy, P., Margetts, H., Bastow, S., & Tinkler, J. (2004) Government IT Performance and the Power of the IT Industry: A Cross-National Analysis. *Annual Meeting of American Political Science Association*. Chicago, IL.

Dupasque X, (2004, April). *Etats des lieux des solutions Internet de diffusions des données géographiques*, Géo événement.

Dupont G, (2004, January 23). *L'IGN cartographie la France en numérique*, Journal: Le Monde, p. 2.

Durand H, (2003, April). *Du SIG à la donnée sur internet: Quel mode de diffusion pour quel public*. Journée professionnelle SIG-LR.

Dyer, J., & Singh, H. (1998). The relational view: cooperative strategy and sources of interorganizational competitive advantage. *Academy of Management Review*, *23*, 660–679. doi:10.2307/259056

Ebrahim, Z., & Irani, Z. (2005). e-Government adoption: architecture and barriers. *Business Process Management Journal*, *11*(5), 589–611. doi:10.1108/14637150510619902

EC. (2006). *Breaking Barriers to e-government - Overcoming Obstacles to Improving European Public Services. e-government Unit*. Oxford, UK: DG Information Society and Media, European Commission.

EFA Global Monitoring Report (2008). *Educational, Scientific and Cultural Organization. Regional Overview: Sub-Saharan Africa.*

e-Gov (2002). Roadmap for E-Government in the Developing World", *10 Questions E-Government Leaders Should Ask Themselves,* The Working Group on E-Government (2002, April). *Government in the Developing World.* Retrieved February 20, 2009, fromhttp://www.pacificcouncil.org/pdfs/e-gov.paper.f.pdf

E-government Act of 2002 (2002). *US-Public Law 107–347, 107th Congress, 116 STAT. 2899*. Retrieved from http://frwebgate.access.gpo.gov/cgi-bin/getdoc.cgi?dbname=107_cong_public_laws&docid=f:publ347.107.pdf

eGovernment Research Center (2008). UK: SMS to help track nearest health services. Retrieved from http://www.epractice.eu/document/4405

e-Government Standards (2007, July). *eCH0070 Inventory of Public Services, Ver. 2.5*. Retrieved from http://www.ech.ch

eGovt (2005). *An Effective E-Governance Framework: The Key to Enhanced E-Government Services*. Retrieved 20th February 2009 fromhttp://www.cito.gov.jm/files/E-Gov%20Framework%20-%20JCS%20BizTech%20Forum%202005%20paper.pdf

Eisenberg, M. (2008). Information Literacy: Essential Skills for the Information Age. *DESIDOC Journal of Library & Information Technology, 28*(2).

Ekpiwhire, G. (2008, March 3). Meeting MDGs Safe Water Target, *Financial Standard, 9*(96), 12.

E-Learning Glossary, meaning of e-Learning (2008). *Cipherion Translation*. Retrieved February 25, 2009, from http://www.cipherion.com/glossaryelearn.php

El-Kiki, T., & Lawrence, E. (2006). Mobile User Satisfaction and Usage Analysis Model of mGovernment Services, *Euro mGov 2006*. Retrieved from http://www.mgovernment.org/resources/euromgvo2006/PDF/11_El-Kiki.pdf

Elrad, T., Aksit, M., Clarke, S., & Filman, R. E. (2004). *Introduction to Aspect-Oriented Software Development*. Reading, MA: Addison Wesley Professional.

ElShenawi, N. (2001). *E-commerce in Egypt*. International Telecommunication Union Regional Seminar on E-commerce for the Arab Region IDSC, Egypt.

Encyclopaedia, A. C. E. (2008). *Requirements for e-Voting, Accessed date: Nov. 2008*. Retreived from http://aceproject.org/ace-en/focus/e-voting/e-voting-requirements

Eng, T. R. (2001). *The EHealth Landscape -A Terrain Map of Emerging Information and Communication Technologies in Health and Health Care*. Princeton, NJ: The Robert Wood Johnson Foundation.

ENISA. http://www.enisa.europa.eu/doc/pdf/deliverables/enisa_measuring_awareness.pdf, May 2008

epractice.eu. (2008). Retrieved August 11,2008, from http://www.epractice.eu/home

Erbschloe, M. (2005). *Trojans, Worms, and Spyware: A Computer Security Professional's Guide to Malicious Code*. Elsevier Inc.

ETSI. (2000). *GSM 03.40 v7.4.0, Digital cellular telecommunications system (Phase 2+). Technical realization of the Short Message Service (SMS)*. ETSI.

Euromonitor International. (2007). No end in sight for Africa's mobile telephone boom. Retrieved April 23, 2008, from http://www.euromonitor.com/No_end_in_sight_for_Africas_mobile_telephone_boom

European e-Business Market Watch, (2005). *Overview of International e-Business Developments*.

European Union MEDA Programme, (2002). *ICT Solutions for Mediterranean SMEs*.

Evangelidis, A. (2004). FRAMES-A Risk Assessment Framework for e-Services, *Electronic. Journal of E-Government, 2*(1), 21–30.

Executive Training Programme, C. E. S. P. A. M. (2003, February 26-28). Implementing *e-government in Public Sector Organisations*. Cape Town, South Africa e-Gov News (2006). e-government In *South Africa*, (Oct/Nov) e-Gov News (2007). e-government In *South Africa*, (Oct/Nov) e-Gov News (2008). e-government In *South Africa*, (Oct/Nov) eNatis (2007). eNatis to have a major impact on traffic law enforcement. Retrieved June 14, 2008. From http://www/enatis.com/content/view/85/2

Eynon, R., & Dutton, W. H. (2007). Barriers to Networked Governments: Evidence from Europe. *Prometheus, 25*(3), 225–242. doi:10.1080/08109020701531361

Eysenbach, G. (2001). What is e-health? *Journal of Medical Internet Research, 3*(2), 20. doi:10.2196/jmir.3.2.e20

Ezigbo, O.(2007, February).Nigeria Image still not Good, says World Bank. *This Day*.

Fair Isaac Corp. (2007). *Achieving Decision Consistency Across the SOA-based Enterprise: Using Business Rules Management Systems in an SOA*, White Paper. Retrieved April 2009, from http://researchlibrary.theserverside.net/detail/RES/1129644089_373.html

Fair Isaac. (2007b). Enterprise Software for Business Rules Management, Fair Isaac Corp. Retrieved March 2007, from http://www.fairisaac.com/fic/en/product-service/product-index/blaze-advisor/blaze-advisor.htm

Falchuk, B., & Leob, S. (2007). Mobile Healthcare: Technologies and Architectures. *Life Science Systems and Applications Workshop, 2007*, 180–183.

Feng, Y., Ng, S.-L., & Schwiderski-Grosche, S. (2006). *An Electronic Voting System Using GSM Mobile Technology*. Retrieved November 2008, fromhttp://www.ma.rhul.ac.uk/static/techrep/2006/RHUL-MA-2006-5.pdf

Fernandez, M., Gómez-Pérez, A, & Juristo, N. (1997). *Methontology: from ontological art towards ontological engineering*, Actes de AAAI, 1997.

Fischer, E. A. (2003).*Election reform and electronic voting system (DREs): Analysis of security issues*. CRS report for congress. Retrieved August 2006, from http://www.amcham.co.nz/Newsletters/Elections20041.pdf

Fishbein, M., & Ajzen, I. (1975). *Belief, Attitude, Intention, and Behavior: An Introduction To Theory And Research*. Reading, MA: Addison-Wesley.

Fisher, E. A. (2003, November 4). *Election Reform and Electronic Voting Systems (DREs): Analysis of Security Issues*. (Congressional Research Service Report No. RL32139). Washington, DC: Library of Congress.

Flak, L. S., & Dertz, W. (2007). Stakeholder Theory and Balanced Scorecard to Improve IS Strategy Development in Public Sector, In *Balanced Scorecard - Multi Sector Perspectives*. Hyderabad, India: Icfai University Press. Retrieved Janurary 22, 2009, from wwwold.hia.no/iris28/Docs/IRIS2028-1109.pdf

Flak, L. S., & Nordheim, S. (2006). Stakeholders, Contradictions and Salience: An Empirical Study of a Norwegian G2G effort. In *Proceedings of the 39th Hawaii International Conference on System Sciences*.

Flak, L. S., Nordheim, S., & Munkvold, B. E. (2008). Analyzing Stakeholder Diversity in G2G Efforts: Combining Descriptive Stakeholder Theory and Dialectic Process Theory. *e-Service Journal, 6*(2), 3-23.

Foley, P. (2005). Does the Internet help to overcome social exclusion? *The Electronic. Journal of E-Government, 2*(2), 139–146. Retrieved from www.ejeg.com.

Forder, J., & Quirk, P. (2001). *Electronic Commerce and the Law*. New York: John Wiley and Sons Australia Ltd.

Forsythe, S., & Shi, B. (2003). Consumer patronage and risk perceptions in Internet shopping. *Journal of Business Research, 56*, 867–875. doi:10.1016/S0148-2963(01)00273-9

France, R., Evans, A., Lano, K., & Rumpe, B. (1998). The UML as a formal modeling notation. *Computer Standards & Interfaces, 19*, 325–334. doi:10.1016/S0920-5489(98)00020-8

Fraser, J., Adams, N., Macintosh, A., McKay-Hubbard, A., Lobo, T. P., Pardo, P. F., et al. (2003). Knowledge Management applied to e-government service: the use of an ontology. In Wimmer (Ed.), *Building Semantic Webs for e-government with Wiki technology 55*

Fraser-Moleketi, G. (2003, August 4). *Post-Cabinet Lekgotla briefing on Governance and Administration*. Issued by the Department of Public Service and Administration.

Fraunholz, B., & Unnithan, C. (2008, November 16). Anti-apathy approaches in representative democracies: e-governance and web 2.0 – facilitating citizen involvement? *International Journal of Electronic Democracy, 1*(1), 51–84. doi:10.1504/IJED.2008.021278

Frazier, G. (2001, October). The DII COE: An Enterprise Framework. *Journal of Defense Software Engineering*. Retrieved from http://www.stsc.hill.af.mil/CrossTalk/2001/10/frazier.html

Freeman, R. E., Wicks, A. C., & Parmar, B. (2004, May-June). Stakeholder Theory and The Corporate Objective Revisited. *Organization Science, 15*(3), 364–369. doi:10.1287/orsc.1040.0066

Friedman-Hill, E. (2003). *Jess in Action*. Greenwich, CT: Manning Publication Co.

FrontLine. (n.d.). www.frontlinedefenders.org. Retrieved May 2008, from http://www.frontlinedefenders.org/manual/en/esecman/chapter1_2.html

Fukuyama, F. (1999). *The Great Disruption*. Bury St Edmunds, UK: St Edmundsbury Press.

Gaines, B. R., & Shaw, M. L. G. (1993). Eliciting knowledge and transferring it effectively to a knowledge-based system. *IEEE Transactions on Knowledge and Data Engineering*, *5*(1), 4–14. doi:10.1109/69.204087

Galindo, F. (2002). E-Government Trust Providers. In Gronlund, A. (Ed.), *Electronic Government: Design, Applications And Management*. Hershey, PA: Idea Group Publishing.

Gallivan, P., Hong, Q., Jordan, L., Li, E., Mathew, G., Mulyani, Y., et al. (2002). VoiceXML Absentee System. In*Proceedings of MASPLAS'02*. The Mid-Atlantic Student Workshop on Programming Languages and Systems Pace University, USA.

Gambetta, D. (1988). Can We Trust Trust? In Gambetta, D. (Ed.), *Trust: Making And Breaking Cooperative Relations*. London: Basil Blackwell Ltd.

Garcia-Molina, H., Ullman, J. D., & Widom, J. (2002). *Database Systems. The Complete Book*. Upper Saddle River, NJ: Prentice Hall.

Gartner, L. (2006). *Hype Cycle for Emerging Technology*. Retrieved from.http://www.gartner.com/it/page.jsp?id=495475

Gefen, D. (2000). E-Commerce: The Role of Familiarity and Trust. *The International Journal of Management Science*, *28*, 725–737.

Gefen, D., Karahanna, E., & Straub, D. (2003a). Trust and Tam in Online Shopping: An Integrated Model. *Management Information Systems Quarterly*, *27*, 51–90.

Gefen, D., & Straub, D. W. (2004). Consumer Trust in B2c E-Commerce and the Importance of Social Presence: Experiments in E-Products and E-Services. *The International Journal of Management Science*, *32*, 407–424.

Gefen, D., Rao, V. S., & Tractinsky, N. (2003b). The Conceptualization Of Trust, Risk And Their Relationship In Electronic Commerce: The Need For Clarifications. *Proceedings of The 36th Hawaii International Conference On System Sciences*. Hawaii, Usa.

Geminiuc, K. (2006). *A Services-Oriented Approach to Business Rules Development, SOA Best Practices: The BPEL Cookbook*. Oracle Technology Network.

Genda, Y., & Maganuma., M. (2004). NEET – *Freeter demo naku Shitsugyo-sha demo naku* (NEET – Neither Freeters nor Unemployed). Togen-sha.

George, F. R. (2003). The Georgia Tech Network Simulator. In *Proceedings of the ACM SIGCOMM workshop on Models, methods and tools for reproducible network research*. Karlsruhe, Germany: ACM.

George, F. R., Monirul, I. S., & Wenke, L. (2004). Simulating Internet Worms. In *Proceedings of 12th Annual International Symposium on Modeling, Analysis, and Simulation of Computer and Telecommunications Systems* (MASCOTS'04), IEEE Computer Society.

Geray, O., & Al-Bastaki, M. (2005). *Dubai e-government initiative: Concepts, achievements, and future pillars of success. (UNDP Report). Dubai*. UAE.

Getting Started with VoiceXML. (n.d.). Retrieved May 20, 2008 fromhttp://developer.voicegenie.com/tutorials_VoiceGenie.php

Giampiero, E. G. (2008). Secure and Easy Internet Voting. *IEEE Press, February*, 52-56.

Gifford, F. (1999). *Internet GIS Architecture - Which Side Is Right for You?* p. 11.

Gillen, M. (2007, November). Managing Virtual Communities: Time to turn to the Whetstone? *International Review of Law Computers & Technology*, *21*(3), 211–220. doi:10.1080/13600860701701371

Glaister, D. (2007, March 20). US: YouTube a Test Tube for US Politicians. *AsiaMedia*, Los Angelas: UCLA Asia Institute.

Goldkuhl, G. (2007). Towards a Practical Theory Founded in Socio-instrumental Pragmatism. [Retrieved fromhttp://www.ijpis.net]. *International Journal of Public Information Systems*, *3*, 135–159.

Goldstuck, A. (2002). *The Goldstuck Report: Internet Access in South Africa*. Pinegowrie, South Africa: World Wide Worx.

Goldstuck, A. (2006). *PC user base in South Africa reaches 5 million*. Pinegowrie, South Africa: World Wide Worx.

Goldstuck, A., Whitford, S., & Super, R. (2006). *The Goldstuck Report: Online Retail in South Africa*. Pinegowrie, South Africa: World Wide Worx.

Gomes, R. C. (2006). Stakeholder Management in the Local Government Decision-Making Area: Evidences from a Triangulation Study with the English Local Government. *Brazilian Administration Review*, *3*(1), 46–63.

Gonzalez, D. (2003). *A roadmap to wireless: The state of the technology, Air2Web*. Retrieved June 2006 from http://www.air2web.com/pdf/roadmap.pdf

Gordon, R. (2001, February-April). The Electronic Personality and Digital Self. *Dispute Resolution Journal*, *56*(1), 9–19.

Gordon, N., & Brayshaw, M. (2006). E-commerce And E business: A New Paradigm Or Old Business In New Clothes? *E-Society*, 178-182.

Gov. of the Hong Kong SAR (2007, December). *The HKSARG Interoperability Framework*. Hong Kong, China: HKSARG.

Government of Canada. (n.d.). *Federated Architecture, Conceptual Architecture*. Retrieved from http://www.tbs-sct.gc.ca/fap-paf/documents/iteration/iteration05-eng.asp

Gowon, Y. (2006, July 27). *Issues of Government for Nations State of African: Pathways for Leadership Development*, Presented at the first Convocation Lecture of Covenant University, Ota.

Grace, O. M., & Lee, M. W. (2002). Labour-market policies in Shanghai and Hong Kong: A study of "one country, two systems" in Greater China. *International Journal of Manpower*, *23*(6), 505–526. doi:10.1108/01437720210446379

Graf, S. & Kinshuk (2006). An Approach for Detecting Learning Styles in Learning Management Systems. ICALT 06, 161-163

Graham, P. (2005). *Web 2.0*. Retrieved from http://www.paulgraham.com/web20.html

Grant, D., Hall, R., Wailes, N., & Wright, C. (2006). *The false promise of technological determinism: the case of enterprise resource planning systems'; New Technology, Work and Employment*. Oxford, UK: Blackwell Publishing Ltd.

Grant, D., & Hardy, C. (2004). Struggles with Organizational Discourse. *Organization Studies*, *25*(1), 5–13. doi:10.1177/0170840604038173

Gray, V. (2001). *Barriers to Internet penetration in the Arab World*. Muscat, Oman: Arab Region Internet and Telecom Summit.

Grimsley, M., & Meehan, A. (2008). Attaining Social Value from Electronic Government. *The Electronic. Journal of E-Government*, *6*(1), 31–42. Retrieved from www.ejeg.com.

Grisedale, S., Graves, M., & Grunsteidl, A. (1997). *Designing a Graphical User Interface for Healthcare Workers in Rural India*. ACM CHI.

Grönlund, Å. (2004). Introducing e-gov: history, definitions, and issues. *Communications of the Association for Information Systems*, *15*, 713–729.

Grossman, L. (2005, December 13). Time's Person of the Year: You. *Time*.

Gruninger, M., & Fox, M. (1995). The logic of enterprise modelling. In Brown, J., & O'Sullivan, D. (Eds.), *Reengineering the Enterprise* (pp. 83–98). Chapman and Hall.

Guardian (2009). *Facebook and Bebo risk 'infantilising' the human mind*, The Guardian Online. Retrieved March 2009, from http://www.guardian.co.uk/uk/2009/feb/24/social-networking-site-changing-childrens-brains

Gueorguieva, V. (2007). *Voters, MySpace, and YouTube: The Impact of Alternative Communication Channels on the 2006 Election Cycle and Beyond. Social Science Computer Review Online First*. Thousand Oaks, CA: SAGE Publications.

Gulati, G. J., & Williams, C. B. (2007). Closing the Gap, Raising the Bar: Candidate Web Site Communication in the 2006 Campaigns for Congress. *Social Science Computer Review, 25*(4), 443–465. doi:10.1177/0894439307305624

Guofei, G., et al. (2004). Worm Detection, Early Warning and Response Based on Local Victim Information. In *Proceedings of the 20th Annual Computer Security Applications Conference* (ACSAC'04), IEEE Computer Society.

Guomundsdottir, G. B. (2005, December 5-7). *Approaching the Digital Divide in South Africa.* Paper presented at the NETREED Conference, Beitostolen, Norway.

Gupta, M. P., & Jana, D. (2003). E-government evaluation: a framework and case study. *Government Information Quarterly, 20*(4), 365–387. doi:10.1016/j.giq.2003.08.002

Gupta, M. P. (2004a). Towards E-governance Management Challenges. InNaidoo, G. (ed.), *Introduction of E-governance and its implications for developing countries*. New York: McGraw Hill Publishing Company.

Gupta, M. P. (2004b). Towards E-governance Management Challenges. In Naidoo G. & Van Jaarsveldt (eds.),*Electronic government: Strategies and Implementations: E-governance in South Africa: A perspective on initiatives, readiness and development issues.*New York: McGraw Hill.

Haas, J. (2001). Mobile Security: SMS (& a little WAP), ITSX. Retrieved from http://72.14.205.104/search?q=cache:kJbYby7zyp8J:www.itsx.com/hal2001/hal2001-itsx.ppt+SMS+security&hl=en&ct=clnk&cd=1&gl=auIDASingapore (2006). *Innovative Projects Showcased At the Building Our Singapore - The*

Hagel, J. III, & Armstrong, A. G. (1997). *Net Gain: Expanding Markets Through Virtual Communities*. New York: McKinsey and Co Inc.

Halle, B. V. (2001). *Business Rules Applied* (1st ed.). New York: Wiley.

Han, S.-R. (1996). Present and future of non-store retailing. In *Proceedings of Korea Marketing Association Spring Conference* (pp.49–59).

Hanxun, Z., Yingyou, W., & Hong, Z. (2007). Detecting early worm propagation based on entropy. In *Proceedings of the 2nd international conference on Scalable information systems, ICST* (Institute for Computer Sciences, Social-Informatics and Telecommunications Engineering): Suzhou, China.

Haralambous, Y., & Plaice, J. (1997). *Multilingual Typesetting with \Omega, a Case Study: Arabic.* Presented at the International Symposium on Multilingual Information Processing'97, Tsukuba, Japan.

Hasan, S. (2003). Introducing E-Government in Bangladesh: Problems and Prospects. *International Social Science Review*, 78.

Hassinen, M., & Laitinen, P. (2005). End-to-end Encryption for SMS Messages in the Health Care Domain. *Studies in Health Technology and Informatics*, 316–321.

Havey, M. (2005). *Essential Business Process Modeling*. Newton, NJ: O'Reilly.

Hayek, F. (1945, September). The Use of Knowledge in Society. *The American Economic Review, 35*, 519–530.

Hayes-Roth, F., Waterman, D. A., & Lenat, D. (1983). *Building Expert Systems*. Reading, MA: Addison-Wesley.

He. H. (2003) What is Service-Oriented Architecture?. *O'Reilly WebServices.XML.com.*

Healthcare, I. D. S. (n.d.). *Ehealth History, Real Time Data Transfer, Advised Therapy, Distant Sufferer, Telephony, Videoconferencing*. Retrieved March 24, 2009, from http://www.com/hospital _management/global/UK_EHealth_Association /EHealth_History_Telephony_Videoconferencing/5_0/g_supplier_5.html

HealthConnect – A Health Information network for all Australians (2005a). About HealthConnect', June 2005.

Healy, P. (2007, February 2). US: Web Plays Key Role in Elections. *AsiaMedia*, Los Angelas: UCLA Institute.

Heeks, R. (2002). Information Systems and Developing Countries: Failure, Success, and Local Improvisations. *The Information Society, 18*(2), 101–112. doi:10.1080/01972240290075039

Heeks, R. (2006). *Implementing and Managing e-government: An International Text*. London: Sage publications.

Heeks, R. (2003) eGovernment for Development: eGovernment Success/Failure: Definitions.University of Manchester, UK: IDPM. Retrieved from http://www.egov4dev.org/.

Henderson, J., Britt, H. C., & Miller, G. (2006). Extent and Utilisation of Computerisation in Australian Practice. *The Medical Journal of Australia, 185*(2), 84–87.

Hertz, D., & Thomas, H. (1984). *Practical Risk Analysis: An Approach through Case Histories*. Chichester, UK: Wiley.

Hesse, B. W., & Shneiderman, B. (2007). e-Health Research from the User's Perspective. *American Journal of Preventive Medicine, 32*, 97–103. doi:10.1016/j.amepre.2007.01.019

Hildreth, S. (2005). *Rounding Up Business Rules*. ComputerWorld Software. IDG.

Hill, H. (2004) Transformation of the Administration by e-government German Journal of Urban Studies, *45*(2). Retreived September 5, 2008, from http://www.difu.de/publikationen/dfk/en/04_2/04_2_hill.shtml

Hill, R. (2003, May 20). *Network Centric Warfare*. Presented at theAddress to the ADF Network Centric Warfare Conference, Australian War Memorial, Australian Government.

HMSO, *Better Public Services through e-government*, REPORT BY THE COMPTROLLER AND AUDITOR GENERAL, HC 704-I Session 2001-2002: 4 April 2002.

Hoepner, P., Agune, R., & Mendes, M. (2005). (eGOIA)), A joint Latin American and European Project. In *IV Fórum Global de Combate à Corrupção (IV FG)*. Brasília, Brazil: Electronic Government Innovation and Access.

Hofstede, G. (2004). *Cultures and Organizations: Software for the Mind*. New York: McGraw-Hill.

Hogg, C. (2007, July 12). Japan's Old-fashioned Campaigning. *BBC News (Asia-Pacific)*. Retrieved from http://news.bbc.co.uk/1/hi/world/asia-pacific/6292602.stm

Holliday, I., & Tam, W. K. (2004). E-health in the East Asian tigers. *International Journal of Medical Informatics, 73*, 759–769. doi:10.1016/j.ijmedinf.2004.08.001

Holsapple, C. W., & Joshi, K. D. (1999). Description and analysis of existing knowledge management frameworks. In *Proceedings of the 32nd Hawaii International Conference on System Sciences*, (pp.1–15).

Holzer, M., & Kim, S.-T. (2004). *Digital Governance in Municipalities Worldwide, 2003*. Newark, NJ: National Center for Public Productivity, Rutgers University.

Hornle, J. (2002) *Online Dispute Resolution- The Emperor's New Clothes? Benefits and Pitfalls of Online Dispute Resolution and its Application to Commercial Arbitration*. Retrieved April 1, 2005, from http://www.bileta.ac.uk/02papers/hornle.html

Horwitz, B., & Currie, W. (2007, September-October). Another instance where privatization trumped liberalization: The politics of telecommunications reform in South Africa —A ten-year retrospective. *Telecommunications Policy, 31*(8-9), 445–462. doi:10.1016/j.telpol.2007.05.008

Hsiu-Fen, L., & Gwo-Guang, L. (2005). Impact of organizational learning and knowledge management factors on e-business adoption. *Management Decision, 43*(2), 171–188. doi:10.1108/00251740510581902

Huang, M. J., & Chen, M. Y. (2007). Integrated design of the intelligent web-based Chinese Medical Diagnostic System (CMDS) – Systematic development for digestive health. *Expert Systems with Applications, 32*, 658–673. doi:10.1016/j.eswa.2006.01.037

Huang, W., Siau, K., & Woi, K. K. (2004). Electronic government Strategies and Implementation. In Naidoo, G. & Singh S. (eds.), *Towards an E-governance Solution-A South African perspective*. Ohio. USA.

Hughes, B., & Cotterell, M. (n.d.). *Software Project Management, 2nd Edition*. New York: McGraw-hill international

Humphery, J., & Schmitz, H. (1998). Trust and Inter Firm Relations in Developing and Transition Economies. *The Journal of Development Studies*, *34*, 32–61. doi:10.1080/00220389808422528

Humphreys, P., Mcadam, R., & Leckey, J. (2005). Longitudinal evaluation of innovation implementation in SMEs. *European Journal of Innovation Management*, *8*(3), 283–304. doi:10.1108/14601060510610162

Hunter, L. M., Kasouf, C. J., Celuch, K. A., & Curry, K. A. (2004). A classification of business-to-business buying decisions: risk importance and probability as a framework for e-business benefits. *Industrial Marketing Management*, *33*, 145–154. doi:10.1016/S0019-8501(03)00058-0

ICC International Court of Arbitration. (2004). *Using Technology to Resolve Business Disputes-Special Supplement*. New York: ICC.

ILOG. (2007). *Deploying Rule Applications with ILOG Jrules*, White Paper. Retrieved April 2009, from http://www.ilog.com/products/jrules/whitepapers/index.cfm?filename=WP-JRules6Deployment.pdf

ILOG. (2009). *ILOG Business Rule Management Systems*. Retrieved April 2009, from http://www.ilog.com/products/businessrules/

IMS Learning Design Information Model. (2009). *Version 1.0 Final Specification*. Retrieved March 3, 2009, from http://www.imsproject.org/learningdesign/ldv1p0/imsld_infov1p0.html

Info-Tech. (n.d.). *The project Estimation Workbook*. London, Canada. *Info-Tech Research Group*.

INSEAD. (2008). *Global Technology Information Report 2007 – 2008*. Retrieved from http://www.insead.edu/v1/gitr/wef/main/explore/framework.cfm

International Chamber of Commerce. (2003). *Resolving disputes online: Best practices for online dispute resolution in B2C and C2C transaction*. New York: ICC.

International Telecommunication Union. (2005). *Internet Indicators: Hosts, Users and Number of PCs*. Retrieved March 20, 2005, fromhttp://www.itu.int/ITU-D/ict/statistics/

Internet World Statistics. (2008). *Internet World Statistics*. Retrieved from http://www.Internetworldstats.com/stats5.htm

Internetworldstats.com. (2007). *Internet Usage and Marketing Report*. Retrieved June 11, 2007, from http://www.internetworldstats.com/af/za.htm

Isaac, A. (2005, December). *Conception et utilisation d'ontologies pour l'indexation de documents audiovisuels*.Thèse de doctorat, l'université paris iv – Sorbonne, page 131.

ISF. (n.d.). *Security Forum*. Retrieved June 2008, from https://www.securityforum.org/index.htm

ISoun. T. (2004): *Nigeria: Government/Private Sector Partner to deliver e-government*. Retrieved from http://www.e-lo-go.de/html/

Istepanian, R. S. H., Jovanov, E., & Zhang, Y. T. (2004). M-health: Beyond Seamless Mobility for Global Wirless Healthcare Connectivity – Editorial paper. *IEEE Tans. Information Technology in Biomedicine*, *8*(4), 405–412. doi:10.1109/TITB.2004.840019

Istepanian, R. S. H., & Lacal, J. C. (2003). *Emerging mobile communication technologies for health: some imperative notes on m-health*, Paper presented to Engineering in Medicine and Biology Society, 2003. Proceedings of the 25th Annual International Conference of the IEEE.

ITU. (2007). Retrieved from http://www.itu.int/ITU-D/ict/statistics/ict/

itwire (2008). *SMS Voting*. Retrieved fromhttp://www.itwire.com/content/view/15481/1105/1/2/

Ives, B. (2008). How Barack Obama is Using the Web to Further Engage Voters. *EContent*, *31*(5), 12–13.

Iyayi, F. (2004). *The Conduct of Elections and electoral practices in Nigeria*. Retrieved from http://nigerianbar.com/papers3.htm

Jacob, G., Debar, H., & Filiol, E. (2008). *Behavioral detection of malware: from a survey towards an established taxonomy*. Journal in Computer Virology.

Jacquemin, C., Klavans, J. L., & Tzoukermann, E. (1997). *ACL-EACL'97*. Expansion of Multi- Word Terms for Indexing and Retrieval Using Morphology and Syntax.

James, P. (2005). *How BPEL and SOA Are Changing Web Services Development. IEEE computer society*. May/June.

Jan, K. T. (2001). *Information Security architecture – An Integrated approach to security in the organization*. Boca Raton, FL: CRC press LLC.

Janack, J. A. (2006). Mediated Citizenship and Digital Discipline: A Rhetoric of Control in a Campaign Blog. *Social Semiotics*, *16*(2), 283–301. doi:10.1080/10350330600664862

Janssen, M., & Kuk, G. (2009). *E-Government Business Models: Theory, Challenges and Research issues*. Hershey, PA: IGI Global.

Janssen, M., Kuk, G., & Wagenaar, R. (2008). A Survey of e-Government Business Models in the Netherlands. *Government Information Quarterly*, *20*(4), 353–363.

Jarvenpaa, S. L. (1989). The Effect Of Task Demands And Graphical Format On Information Processing Strategies. *Management Science*, *35*, 285–303. doi:10.1287/mnsc.35.3.285

Jarvenpaa, S. L., Tractinsky, N., & Vitale, M. (2000). Consumer Trust In An Internet Store. *Information Technology Management*, *1*, 45–71. doi:10.1023/A:1019104520776

Jason, L. (2003). *The business of E-voting and how it can put wrong candidate in office*. Retrieved June 2006, from http://www.dissidentvoice.org/Articles8/Leopold_E-Voting.htm

Java community Process (2006). *JSR-94 Java Rule Engine API*. Retrieved April 2009, from http://jcp.org/en/jsr/detail?id=94

Jefferson, D., et al. (2004).A security analysis of the secure electronic registration and voting experiment (SERVE). Retrieved August, 2006 from http:// www.servesecurityreport.org

Jongler D. & Lestrat L, (2001, February). *Dossier technique: les SIG et Internet*, Signature n°20, CERTU, p. 11.

Jongler, D., & Lestrat, L. (2002). *Cartographie sur Internet*, Fiche technique du CNIG (Aide à la Maîtrise d'Ouvrage) n°64, p. 8.

Joris, V. H. (2003). *The TeXmacs User Manual, Version 1.0.6.6*. Retrieved from http://www.texmacs.org

Joseph, B. (2006). Service Oriented Architecture (SOA): A New Paradigm to Implment Dynamic E-business Solutions. *ACM-Ubiquity*, *7*(30).

Judd, C., & Kenny, D. (1981). Process analysis: Estimating mediation in treatment evaluations. *Evaluation Review*, *5*, 602–619. doi:10.1177/0193841X8100500502

Kaaya, J. (2004). Implementing e-Government Services in East Africa: Assessing Status through Content Analysis of Government Websites. *The Electronic. Journal of E-Government*, *2*(1), 39–54. Retrieved from www.ejeg.com.

Kabiri, P., & Ghorbani, A. A. (2005, September). Research on intrusion detection and response: A survey. *International Journal of Network Security*, *1*(2), 84–102.

Kalakota, R., & Whinston, B. (1997). *Electronic Commerce, A Manager's Guide*. Reading, MA: Addison Wesley, Pearson Education.

Kamada, A., & Mendes, M. (2007). *Web Services Composition based on Business Rules*. Cambridge, MA: IASTED/SEA Software Engineering and Applications.

Kamada, A. (2006) *Service Execution based on Business Rules*, PhD Thesis in Computing Engineering, Unicamp, Campinas, Brazil.

Kant, I. (1781). *Critique of Pure Reason*. London: Norman Kemp Smith, MacMillan.

Karnjanatawe (2002). ICT Ministry pushes e-Government plans - will help agencies to offer e-Services, *Bangkok Post*.

Karnjanatawe (2003). Gateway to govt sites - single access point to public e-Services, *Bangkok Post*.

Kassel, G. (2002)Ontospec: une méthode de spécification semi-formelle d'ontologies. In *13e journées francophones d'Ingénierie des Connaissances (IC)*, Rouen, France. pp. 75–87.

Katsh, E. (1995). *Law in a Digital World.* Oxford, UK: Oxford University Press.

Katsh, E. (1996). Dispute Resolution in Cyberspace-Symposium: Legal Regulation of the Internet. *Connecticut Law Review*, 1–18.

Katsh, E. (2004). Bringing online dispute resolution to virtual worlds: Creating processes through code. *New York Law School Review*, *49*, 271–291.

Katsh, E. (2007). Online Dispute Resolution: Some Implications for the Emergence of Law in Cyberspace. *International Review of Law Computers & Technology*, *21*(2), 97–107. doi:10.1080/13600860701492096

Katsh, E., & Rifkin, J. (2001). *Online Dispute Resolution: Resolving Conflicts in Cyberspace.* San Francisco: Jossey-Bass Publishers.

Katsh, E., & Wing, L. (2006, Fall). Ten years of inline dispute resolution: Looking at the past and constructing the future. *University of Toledo Law Review. University of Toledo. College of Law*, *38*, 19–46.

Katsh, E. (2000, Winter) The new frontier: Online ADR becoming a global priority *Dispute Resolution Magazine* pp.6-8.

Katsh, E. (2008) Dispute resolution and e-government In *Proceedings of the 2nd International Conference on Theory and Practice of Electronic Governance*, Vol. 351, pp.494-495.

Katsh, E., Rifkin, J., & Gaitenby, A. (2000). E-Commerce, E-Disputes and E-dispute Resolution: In the Shadow of eBay law *Ohio State Journal on Dispute Resolution, 15*(3), 705-734.

Kaufmann-Kobler, G., & Schultz, T. (2004). *Online Dispute Resolution, Challenges for Contemporary Justice.* Amsterdam: Kluwer Law International.

Kaylor, C., Deshazo, R., & Eck, V. D. (2001). Gauging E-Government: A Report on Implementing Services Among American Cities. *Government Information Quarterly*, *18*, 293–307. doi:10.1016/S0740-624X(01)00089-2

Kelly, P. (2003). *E-government must offer value for money: Report.* Retrieved September 3, 2008, from http://www.electricnews.net/story/show/9379230

Kenny, D., Kashy, D., & Bolger, N. (1998). Data analysis in social psychology. In Gilbert, D., Fiske, S., & Lindzey, G. (Eds.), *The Handbook of Social Psychology, 1* (pp. 233–265). New York: McGraw-Hill.

Kephart, J. O., & White, R. S. (1991). Directed-graph epidemiological models of computer virus prevalence. In *Proceedings of the IEEE Symposium on Security and Privacy* (pp. 343-359).

Keskinen, A. (2004). MIDEM. Models for Interactive Decision Making. *The Electronic. Journal of E-Government*, *2*(1), 55–64. Retrieved from www.ejeg.com.

Khalil, M. M. & Jones, R. (2007, November 18). Electronic Services – An Introduction to Theory and Application. *Libyan Journal of Medicine, 2*(4).

Khin, T. W., & Cooper, J. (2004). Information Age. Electronic Health Record and Australia Healthcare. *International Journal of The Computer, the Internet and Management, 12*(3), 14-21.

Khoja, S., Scott, R., Ishaq, A. F. M., & Mohshin, M. (2007). Testing Relibility of eHealth readiness Assessment Tools for Developing Countries. *eHealth. International Journal (Toronto, Ont.)*, *3*(1), 31–37.

Kholladi M. K, (1999a, November 15-17). *Mécanismes de raisonnement spatiaux sur des objets géographiques*, Séminaire International sur les SIGs, « AL-SIG'99 » organisé par le Conseil National de l'Information Géographique « CNIG », Alger, p. 9.

Kholladi M. K, (1999b, November 15-17). *Modèle Numérique de Terrain par la Méthode de Triangulation de Delaunay avec Contraintes*, Séminaire International sur les SIGs, « AL-SIG'99 » organisé par le Conseil National de l'Information Géographique « CNIG », Alger, p. 21.

Kholladi M. K, (2004a, September). *Raisonnement et Manipulation Spatial sur des Objets Urbains « RMSOU »*, CISC'2004: Conférence Internationale des Systèmes Complexes, Jijel, p. 13.

Kholladi, M. K. (2004b, December). *Geographical Information System for Urban Spatial Analysis*, ACIT'2004: The International Arab Conference on Information Technology, Mentouri University of Constantine, Algeria, pp. 188-193, ISSN: 1812-0857.

Kholladi, M. K. (2008, October 15-16). *Carto Web Solution for the Web Mapping*, IACET: International Arab Conference of e-Technology, Arab Open University, Amman, Jordan, pp. 105-113.

Kienzle, D., & Elder, M. (2003). Recent Worms: A Survey and Trends. In *Proceedings of the ACM Workshop on Rapid Malcode*. Washington DC: ACM Press.

Kim, H., & Bracha, Y., & Tipnis. (2007). Automated Depression Screening in Disadvantaged Pregnant Women in an Urban Obstetric Clinic. *Archives of Women's Mental Health, 10*(4), 163–169. doi:10.1007/s00737-007-0189-5

Kim, L. H., Kim, D. J., & Leong, J. K. (2005). The Effect Of Perceived Risk On Purchase Intention In Purchasing Airline Tickets Online. *Journal of Hospitality & Leisure Marketing*, *13*, 33–53. doi:10.1300/J150v13n02_04

Kim, J. (2005). *Reducing Worm Detection Time and False Alarm in Virus Throttling* (p. 297). Computational Intelligence and Security.

Kim, Y. H., & Kim, D. J. (2005). A Study Of Online Transaction Self-Efficacy, Consumer Trust, And Uncertainty Reduction In Electronic Commerce Transaction. In *Proceedings Of The 38th Hawaii International Conference On System Sciences.*

Kim, Y., Bhattarai, M., & Ayyad, M. (2008). Electronic Governance in Post-Conflict Countries In *Proceedings of the 2nd International Conference on Theory and Practice of Electronic Governance, 351*, 489.

Klischewski, R. (2003). Semantic Web for e-government. In Traunmuller, R. (Ed.), *EGOV 2003, Springer Lecture Notes No. 2739.*

Knapp, A., & Merz, S. (2002). Model checking and code generation for UML state machines and collaborations. In *Proceeding of the 5th Workshop on Tools for System Design and Verification.*

Knuth, D. E. (1984). *The TeXBook, Computers and Typesetting*. Reading, MA: Addison-Wesley.

Knuth, D. E. (1986). *The MetafontBook, Computers and Typesetting*. MA: Addison-Wesley.

Kohno, T., Stubblefield, A., Ruben, A. D., & Waalach, D. S. (2004, February 27). *Analysis of an Electronic Voting System.* Presented at the IEEE Symposium on Security and Privacy. Paolo Alto, CA.

Komito, L. (2005). e-Participation and Governance: Widening the net. *The Electronic Journal of e Government, 3*(1), 39-48, available online at www.ejeg.com

Koper, R., & Tattersall, C. (2005). *Learning Design: A handbook on Modelling and Delivering Networked Education and Training*. New York: Springer.

Korper, S., & Ellis, J. (2001). *The E-Commerce Book: Building the E-Empire*. San Francisco: Morgan Kaufmann, Academic Press.

Koufaris, M., Kambil, A., & Labarbera, P. A. (2001). Consumer Behavior In Web-Based Commerce: An Empirical Study. *International Journal of Electronic Commerce*, *6*, 115–138.

Kranish, M. (2007, May 10). *Internet and Politics an Uneasy Fit*. Retrieved from http://www.politicsonline.com/coverage/boston2007/boston.html

Krueger, A. (1974). The Political Economy of the Rent-Seeking Society. *The American Economic Review*, *64*, 291–303.

Kruger, H.A., Drevin, L., & Steyn T. (n.d.). *A framework for evaluating ICT security awareness*. Retrieved May 2008, from http://www.computer.org/portal/site/security/menuitem.6f7b2414551cb84651286b108bcd45f3/index.jsp?&pName=security_level1_article&TheCat=1001&path=security/2006/v4n5&file=bsi.xml&

Kuhn, H. W., & Nasar, S. (Eds.). (2002). *The Essential John Nash*. Princeton, NJ: Princeton University Press.

Kuster, M., Dekkers, M., & Moore, G. (2008). Draft final report of the project team of the CEN/ISSS eGovernment focus group on the *eGovernment standards roadmap*

Kyama, G. W. (2005, June 28-29). *e-Government: A view from South Africa*. East African e-government consultative workshop. Grand Regency Hotel. Nairobi, Kenya.

Kyriacou, E., Pavlopoulos, S., Berler, A., Neophytou, M., Bourka, A., & Georgoulas, A. (2003). Multi-purpose HealthCare Telemedicine Systems with mobile communication link support. *Biomedical Engineering Online*, 2.

Lagally, K. (2004). *ArabTEX User Manual*. Universitat Stuttgart, Fakultat Informatik.

Lal, K. (2005). Determinants of the adoption of e-business technologies. *Telematics and Informatics*, *22*(3), 181–199. doi:10.1016/j.tele.2004.07.001

Lallana, E. (2008). *eGovDev4Dev cases on mGovernment*. e. f. Development. Manchester, UK: University of Manchester's Institute for Development Policy and Management.

Lallana, E. L. (2004). SMS, business and Government in the Philippines, ICT4D.ph (a project of the Department of Science and Technology and IDRC). Retrieved from http://unpan1.un.org/intradoc/groups/public/documents/Other/UNPAN024834.pdf

Lallana, E. L. (2007). mGovernment and eDemocracy. *eDevelopment*. Retrieved from http://web.worldbank.org/wbsite/external/topics/extinformationandcommunicationandtechnologies/extedevelopment/0,contentMDK:21534706~pagePK:210058~piPK:210062~theSitePK:559460,00.html

Lamport, L. (1985). *LaTeX-A Document Preparation System*. Reading, MA: Addison Wesley.

Landis, R., & Koch, G. G. (1977). The Measurement Of Observer Agreement For Categorical Data. *Biometrics*, *33*, 159–174. doi:10.2307/2529310

Lane, C., & Bachmann, R. (1996). The Social Constitution Of Trust: Supplier Relations In Britain And Germany. *Organization Studies*, *17*, 365–395. doi:10.1177/017084069601700302

Langer, G. (2008). Politics and the Internet Meet in the Rise of the Wired Electorate. *ABC News/Facebook Poll: The Election and The Internet*. Retrieved from http://abcnews.go.com/images/PollingUnit/1055a1TheElectionandtheInternet.pdf

Lasker, R. D., Weiss, E. S., & Millers, R. (2001). Partnership Synergy: A Practical Framework for Studying and Strengthening the Collaborative Advantages. *The Milbank Quarterly*, *79*(2), 179–205. doi:10.1111/1468-0009.00203

Latella, D, Majzik, I., & Massink, M. (1999). Automatic verification of UML statechart diagrams using the SPIN model-checker. *Formal Aspects of Computing, 11*(6), 637/664.

Lau, A., & Ornaghi, M. (2001). *A Formal Approach to Software Component Specification*. Montreal, Canada: OOPSLA Workshop.

Lau, E. (2007). Electronic Government and the Drive for Growth and Equity. In Mayerschönberger, V., & Lazer, D. (Eds.), *Governance and Information Technology: From Electronic Government to Information Government*. Cambridge, Massachusetts: MIT Press.

Laughlin, S. (1999). An ERP Game Plan. *The Journal of Business Strategy*, *20*(1), 32–37. doi:10.1108/eb039981

Laurini, R., & Milleret-Raffort, F. (1993). *Les bases de données en géomatique*. Paris, France: Editions Hermès.

Laurini, R., & Thompson, D. (1992). *Fundamentals of Spatial Information Systems, the APIC*. Series Academic Press.

Lawley, B. (2007, November 19). Hey, Pollies, You're in My Space. Get Out! *ONLINE Opinion*. Retrieved from http://onlineopinion.com.au/view.asp?article=6646

Layne, K., & Lee, J. (2001). Developing Fully Function E-Government: A Four Model. *Government Information Quarterly*, *18*, 122–136. doi:10.1016/S0740-624X(01)00066-1

Lazrek, A. (2001). A package for typesetting Arabic mathematical formulas. *Die TeXnische Komodie, DANTE e.V., 13*(2), 54-66.

Lazrek, A. (2003). *CurExt, Typesetting variable-sized curved symbols*. Presented at EuroTeX 2003 Pre-prints: 14th. European TeX conference (pp. 47-71), Brest, France.

Le Corbusier. (1950). *Le Modulor, Architecture d'Aujourd'hui*. New York: Springer.

Leadbeater, C. (2007, July). Social Software for Social Change. *Discussion Paper for the Office of the Third Sector*.

Lee, M. K. O., & Turban, E. (2001). A trust model for consumer Internet shopping. *International Journal of Electronic Commerce*, *6*(1), 75–91.

Lee, A., Neilson, J., Tower, G., & Van Der Zahn, J. - L.W., Mitchell. (2007). Is Communicating Intellectual Capital Information Via the Internet Viable: Case of Australian Private and Public Hospitals. *Journal of Human Resource Costing & Accounting*, *11*(1), 53–78. doi:10.1108/14013380710746401

Lee, H. Y., Ahn, H., & Han, I. (2006). Analysis of trust in the e-commerce adoption. In *Proceedings of the 39th Hawaii International Conference on System Sciences*, Big Island, HI.

Lee, K. J., & Hong, J. H. (2002). Development of An E-government Service Model: A Business Model Approach, *International Review of Public Administration* 2002, *7*(2).

Leitner, C. (2003), *eGovernment in Europe: The State of Affairs* EIPA (European Institute of Public Administration). Retrieved September 5, 2008, from http://www.eipa.eu/files/repository/product/20070214113429_egoveu.pdf

Leitner, K. (2003, July 7-8). *eGovernment in Europe: The State of Affairs. European Institute of Public Administration*, Presented at the eGovernment 2003 Conference Como, Itlay.

LeMay, M. (n.d.). *E-health: Australia's $5bn black hole*. Retrieved March 2009, from http://www.zdnet.com.au/news/software/soa/E-Health-Australia-s-5bn-black-hole/0,130061733, 339293816,00.htm

Leuf, B., & Cunningham, W. (2001). *The Wiki Way: Collaboration and Sharing on the Internet*. Reading, MA: Addison-Wesley.

Leveson, N. G., (2005, November). *Safety in Integrated Systems Health Engineering and Management*, draft paper for the NASA AISHEM Forum.

Lewis, J. D., & Weigert, A. J. (1985). Trust as A Social Reality. *Social Forces*, *63*, 967–985. doi:10.2307/2578601

Li, P., Salour, M., & Su, X. (2008). A survey of internet worm detection and containment. *Communications Surveys & Tutorials, IEEE*, *10*(1), 20. doi:10.1109/COMST.2008.4483668

Liebermann, Y., & Stashevsky, S. (2002). Perceived Risks as Barriers to Internet and E-Commerce Usage. *Qualitative Market Research: An International Journal*, *5*, 291–300. doi:10.1108/13522750210443245

Liebowitz, J. (2004). Will Knowledge Management work in the government? *Electronic Government*, *1*(1), 1–7. doi:10.1504/EG.2004.004133

Lilius, J., & Paltor, I. P. (1999). vUML: A tool for verifying UML models. In *Proceedings of the 14th IEEE International Conference on Automated Software Engineering (ASE'99)*, pp. 255-258.

Lim, E., Tan, C. W., & Pan, S. L. (2007). E-Government Implementation: Balancing Collaboration and Control in Stakeholder Management. *International Journal of Electronic Government Research*, *3*(2), 1–28.

Lodder, A. R. (2006, June). The Third party and Beyond. *Information & Communications Technology Law*, *15*(2), 143–153. doi:10.1080/13600830600676438

LOM. (2007). *LTSC Learning Object metadata standard*. Retrieved March 10, 2007, from http://ltsc.ieee.org.http://ltsc.ieee.org/wg12/index.html

Low Literacy Equals Early Death Sentence. (2008). *Low Literacy Equals Early Death Sentence*. Retrieved June 24, 2008 from http://www.northwestern.edu/newscenter/stories/2007/07/health.html

Luhmann, N. (1979). *Trust and Power*. New York: John Wiley & Sons Ltd.

Luhmann, N. (1988). Familiarity, Confidence, Trust: Problems And Alternatives. In Gambetta, D. (Ed.), *Trust: Making and Breaking Cooperative Relations*. London: Basil Blackwell Ltd.

Luo, M. (2008, February 20). Small Online Contributions Add Up to Huge Fund-Raising Edge for Obama, *New York Times*.

Lusoli, W., & Ward, S. (2005). Logging On or Switching Off? The Public and the Internet at the 2005 General Election. In Coleman, S. (Eds.), *Spinning the Web: Online Campaigning in the 2005 General Election* (pp. 13–21). London: Hansard Society.

Lusoli, W. (2007, May 18). Internet Winner of the French Presidential Election? Retrieved from http://www.esri.salford.ac.uk/ESRCResearchproject/blog/index.php/2007/05/18/internet-winner-of-the-french-presidential-election/

LyX Team. (2004). *The LyX User Manual*. Retrieved fromhttp://www.LyX.org

Madar (2006a). Arab ICT Use Index, 2005. *Madar Research Journal, 4*(1).

Madar (2006b). Arab Internet users exceed 26 million in 2005. *Arab Knowledge Economy Newsletter, 1*(2), 1-8.

Madden, M., & Fox, S. (2006, October 5). *Riding the Waves of Web 2.0. More than a Buzzword, but Still Not Easily Defined.* PEW Internet & American Life Project.

Maedche, A., & Staab, S. (2001). Ontology Learning for the Semantic Web. *IEEE Intelligent Systems, 2001*, 1–16.

Mahmoud, M., & Ugur, Y. (2007). An analysis of E-business practices in the Arab culture. *Cross Cultural Management, 14*(1), 68–73. doi:10.1108/13527600710718840

Mahmoud, Q. H. (2005, April) Service-Oriented Architecture (SOA) and Web Services: The Road to Enterprise Application Integration (EAI), SDN - Sun Developer Network. Retrieved from http://java.sun.com/developer/technicalArticles/WebServices/soa/

Maier, M., & Rechtin, E. (2000). *The Art of Systems Architecting*. Boca Raton, Fl: CRC Press, 2nd Edition.

Mail and Guardian. (2007). *Traffic-system chaos: Minister was warned.* Retrieved from Http://www.mg.co.za/article.aspx?articleid=308615&area=/breaking_news/breaking_news_national

March, J. G., & Shapira, Z. Managerial perspectives on risk and risk taking. *Management Science, 33*(11), 1404–1418. doi:10.1287/mnsc.33.11.1404

Margetts, H., & Dunleavy, P. (2002). *Cultural Barriers to E-Government.* London: National Audit Office.

Marshall, J. (2001). *Developing Internet-Based GIS Applications*, p. 11.

Martin, L., & Matlay, H. (2003). Innovative use of the Internet in established small firms: The impact of Knowledge Management and Organisational learning in accessing new opportunities. *Qualitative Market Research, 6*(1), 18–26. doi:10.1108/13522750310457348

Martin, L. (2007, July 23). MySpace Impact. *The Age*.

Marti-Oliet, N., & Meseguer, J. (1996). Rewriting logic as a Logical and Semantic framework. In *1st International Workshop on Rewriting Logic and its Application (WRLA'96), Electronic Notes in Theoretical Computer science vol4.*

Matlay, H., & Addis, M. (2003). The value of E-Commerce for high growth SME's. *International Small Business Journal, 23*(3), 279–302. doi:10.1177/0266242605052074

Matlay, H. (2003). Small Tourism Firms in e-Europe: Definitional, Conceptual and Contextual Considerations. In Thomas, R. (Ed.), *Small firms in Tourism: International perspectives* (pp. 297–312). Oxford, UK: Pegamon.

Matlay, H. (2003, March). *e-Babel: in Search of a Theory of e-Everything.* Paper presented at the UCE Business School Research Seminar, Birmingham, UK.

Matthews, I. (2002). *Feasibility study for criminal justice strengthening project.* A feasibility study. Retrieved May 15, 2008, from http://www.ipt.co.za/cjs%20study.pdf

Matthewson, J. A. (2001). *Enterprise Resource Planning a jargon-free practical guide*. Boston: Butterworth Heineman.

Mauvière, E. (1999). *La cartographie sur le web*. p. 40.

Mayer, R. C., Davis, J. H., & Schoorman, F. D. (1995). An Integrative Model Of Organizational Trust. *Academy of Management Review*, *20*, 709–734. doi:10.2307/258792

Mayer-Schönberger, V., & Lazer, D. (2007). *Governance and Information Technology: From Electronic Government to InformationGovernment*. Cambridge, Massachusetts: MIT Press.

McAlindon, A. (2007). A window on the world of health ICT, HIMSS AsiaPac07. Retrieved April 15, 2009, from http://www.chik.com.au/files/HIMSSAsiaPacDel07.pdf

Mcallister, D. J. (1995). Affect- And Cognition-Based Trust as Foundations For Interpersonal Cooperation. *Academy of Management Journal*, *38*, 24–59. doi:10.2307/256727

McCarthy, C. (2007, December 5) Facebook's Zuckerberg: 'We simply did a bad job' handling Beacon, *The Social*. Retrieved from http://news.cnet.com/8301-13577_3-9829526-36.html

McGregor, D. (1960). *The Human Side of Enterprise*. New York: McGraw Hill.

Mcknight, D. H., Kacmar, C. J., & Choudhury, V. (2004). Dispositional Trust And Distrust Distinctions In Predicting High- And Low-Risk Internet Expert Advice Site Perceptions. *E-Service Journal*, *3*, 35–55. doi:10.2979/ESJ.2004.3.2.35

McKnight, H. D., Choudhury, V., & Kacmar, C. (2002). Developing and validating trust measures for e-commerce: an integrative typology. *Information Systems Research*, *13*(3), 334–359. doi:10.1287/isre.13.3.334.81

Mcknight, D. H., & Chervany, N. L. (2001). Conceptualizing Trust: A Typology and E-Commerce Customer Relationships Model. *34th Hawaii International Conference on System Sciences*.

McNiven, J. D., & Marche, S. (2003). E-government and e-governance: The future isn't what it used to be. *The Canadian Journal of Administrative Sciences*. Retrieved May 21, 2008, from http://findarticles.com/p/articles/mi_qa3981/is_200303/ai_n9178064

Medical Library Association. (2008). *A User's Guide to Finding and Evaluating Health Information on the Web*. Retrieved May 25, from http://www.mlanet.org/resources/userguide.html

Melitski, J., Holzer, M., Kim, S.-T., Kim, C.-G., & Rho, S.-Y. (2005). Digital Government Worldwide: An e-Government Assessment of Municipal Web-sites. *International Journal of E-Government Research*, *1*(1), 1–19.

Mentzas, G., Apostolou, D., Kafentzis, K., & Georgolios, P. (2006). Inter-organizational networks for knowledge sharing and trading. *Information Technology Management*, *7*, 259–276. doi:10.1007/s10799-006-0276-8

Meseguer, J. (1992). Conditional Rewriting logic as unified model of concurrency. *Theoretical Computer Science*, *96*, 73–155. doi:10.1016/0304-3975(92)90182-F

Meseguer, J. (2002). *Software specification and verification in rewriting logic*. Lectures at the Marktoberdorf Summer School.

Metaxiotis, K., & Psarras, J. (2005). A conceptual analysis of Knowledge Management in e-government. *Electronic Government*, *2*(1), 77–86. doi:10.1504/EG.2005.006649

Metherell, M. (2007, November 28). Internet Activists Claim Role in Howard's End. *The Sydney Morning Herald*.

Metropolitan Ambulance Service. (n.d.). *Metropolitan Ambulance Service*. Retrieved May 25, 2008, from http://www.oracle.com/customers/snapshots/metropolitan-ambulance-service-ebs-casestudy.pdf

Michael, L., et al. (2003). Simulating realistic network worm traffic for worm warning system design and testing. In *Proceedings of the ACM workshop on Rapid malcode*. Washington, DC: ACM.

Microsoft. (n.d.). *Cyber Security Month*. Retrieved May 2008, from http://www.microsoft.com/protect/promotions/us/cybersecuritymonth_us.mspx

Middleton, B., & Brennan, P. F. (2005). Accelerating U.S EHR Adoption: how to get there from here recommendations based on the 2004 ACMI Retreat. *Journal of the American Medical Informatics Association*, *12*(1), 13–19. doi:10.1197/jamia.M1669

Milford, S. (2000). Racing to e-government: using the Internet for citizen service delivery. *Government Finance Review*, *16*(5), 21–22.

Millard, J. (2009, March) eParticipation, *European Journal of ePractice, 2009*(7).

Miller, M., Yee, K.-P., & Shapiro, J. (2003). *Capability Myths Demolished*. Baltimore, MD: Systems Research Laboratory, Johns Hopkins University.

Milosevic, Z. (2006). *Addressing interoperability in e-health: an Australian approach*. Paper presented to 10th IEEE International Enterprise Distributed Object Computing Conference Workshops. Paolo Alto, CA.

Min, D. S., Lee, B. W., Yoon, S. W., Lee, Y. B., Kim, J. K., & Park, M. C. (2007). Actual Condition of Korea e-Health: What Do Enterprisers Want for developing e-health Industry? *E-Health Networking, Application and Services*, 9th International Conference 2007, pp 304-307.

Ministry of Health (MOH). (n.d.). *Transforming Healthcare*. Retrieved on May 25, 2008, from http://www.moh.gov.sg/mohcorp/speeches.aspx? id=12394

Mintzberg, H. (1989). *Inside Our Strange World of Organizations*. New York: Free press.

Mirza, F., & Norris, T. (2007). Opportunities and Barriers for Mobile Health in NewZealand,'. *Medinfo*, *2*(1), 102–106.

Mitchell, R. K., Agle, B. R., & Wood, D. J. (1997). Toward a theory of stakeholder identification and salience: Defining the principle of who and what really count. *Academy of Management Review*, *22*(4), 853–886. doi:10.2307/259247

Mitchell, K. J., Becker-Blease, K. A., & Finkelhor, D. (2005). Inventory of Problematic Internet Experiences Encountered in Clinical Practice. *Professional Psychology, Research and Practice*, *36*, 498–509. doi:10.1037/0735-7028.36.5.498

Mohamad A., Michael C., Dan, H., Kevin C., & Vishram, P. (2007, May). *SOA Governance Framework and Best Practices, version 1.1*. Redwood Shores, CA: Oracle.

Molla, A., & Licker, P. S. (2005). e-Commerce adoption in developing countries: a model and instrument. *Information & Management*, *42*(6), 877–899. doi:10.1016/j.im.2004.09.002

MOODLE. (2009). *Open source community based tools for learning*. Retrieved February 25, 2009, from http://moodle.org

Moon, M. J. (2002). The Evolution of E-government Among Municipalities: Rhetoric or Reality? *Public Administration Review*, *62*(4), 424–433. doi:10.1111/0033-3352.00196

Moon, M. J., & deLeon, P. (2001). Municipal Reinvention: Municipal Values and Diffusion Among Municipalities. *Journal of Public Administration: Research and Theory*, *11*(3), 327–352.

Moore, G. C., & Benbasat, I. (1991). Development of An Instrument To Measure The Perceptions Of Adopting An Information Technology Innovation. *Information Systems Research*, *2*, 192–222. doi:10.1287/isre.2.3.192

Moore, D., Paxson, V., & Savage, S. (2003). Inside the Slammer Worm. *IEEE Security and Privacy Archive*, *1*(4), 33–39. doi:10.1109/MSECP.2003.1219056

Moore, D., Shannon, C., Voelker, G., et al. (2003). Internet Quarantine: Requirements for Containing Self-Propagating Code. In *Proceedings of the IEEE Infocom conference*, San Francisco, CA.

Moore, M. (2007, March 30). French Politics in 3-D on Fantasy Web Site. *The Washington Post*.

Moses, A. (2007, September 13). Australia: the Election's New Front is Online. *AsiaMedia*, Los Angeles: UCLA Asia Institute.

Moses, A. (2007, September 14). Pollies Embrace Google for the 'E-Election'. *The Age*.

Moskovitch, R., Elovici, Y., & Rokach, L. (2008). Detection of unknown computer worms based on behavioral classification of the host", Computational Statistics and Data Analysis, ElSevier, 2008.

Mount, C. D., Lelman, L. R., & Douglas, R. M. (2000). An integrated electronic health record and information system for Australia. *Med J.*, *172*(1), 25–27.

Mukherjee, A., & McGinnis, J. (2007). E-healthcare: an analysis of key themes in research. *International Journal of Pharmaceutical and Healthcare*, *1*(4), 349–363. doi:10.1108/17506120710840170

Mundt, J. C., Ferber, K. L., Rizzo, M., & Greist, J. H. (2001). Automated Dementia Screening Using a Touch-Tone Telephone. *Archives of Internal Medicine*, 161.

Mundt, J. C., Moore, H. K., & Greist, J. H. (2005). A Novel Interactive Voice Response (IVR) System for Dementia Screening, Education and Referral:One-Year Summary *Alzheimer Disease and Associated Disorders*, *19*(3), 143–147. doi:10.1097/01.wad.0000174992.68332.0d

Munshi, V. (2008). E-government in Developed Nations: An Insight, *ICFAI Press*. OASIS LegalXML *Online Dispute Resolution TC*. Retrieved May 20, 2009, fromhttp://www.oasis-open.org/committees/tc_home.php?wg_abbrev=legalxml-odr

Murray, S., William, G., & Huges, M. (2004). *Implementation strategies for e-government: a stakeholder analysis approach*. Retrieved November 4, 2008, from http://is2.lse.ac.uk/asp/aspecis/20040151.pdf

Murugesan, S. (2007, July-August). Understanding Web 2.0. *IT Professional*, *9*(4), 34–41. Retrieved from http://ieeexplore.ieee.org/stamp/stamp.jsp?arnumber=04287373. doi:10.1109/MITP.2007.78

Musso, J., Weare, C., & Hale, M. L. (2000). Designing Web Technologies for Local Governance Reform: Good Management or Good Democracy. *Political Communication*, *17*(1), 1–19. doi:10.1080/105846000198486

Nagl, C., Rosenberg, F., & Dustdar, S. (2006) ViDRE – A Distributed Service-Oriented Business Rule Engine based on RuleML. In*Proceedings of the 10th IEEE International Enterprise Distributed Object Computing Conference*. Hong Kong.

Nahm, A. Y., Solis-Galvan, L. E., Rao, S. S., & Ragu-Nathan, T. S. (2002). The Q-Sort Method: Assessing Reliability And Construct Validity Of Questionnaire Items At A Pre-Testing Stage. *Journal of Modern Applied Statistical Methods; JMASM*, *1*, 114–125.

Nathan, R. J., Yeow, P. H. P., & Murugesan, S. (2008). Key Usability Factors of Service-Oriented Websites for Students: An Empirical Research. *Online Information Review*, *32*(3). doi:10.1108/14684520810889646

Nathanael, P. (2005). A Closer Look at Viruses and Worms. *IEEE Security and Privacy*, *3*(4), 7. doi:10.1109/MSP.2005.86

National Bureau of Statistics. (2005). *The Nigerian Fact Sheets on Economic & Social Development*. Nigeria: National Bureau of Statistics.

National Research Council. (2002). *Information Technology Research, Innovation, and E-Government*. Washington, DC: National Academy Press.

National, E. -Health Transition Authority (2000). *Connecting Australia*. Retrieved on May 25, 2008, from http://www.nehta.gov.au

National, E. -Health Transition Authority (2008). Retrieved on May 25, 2008, from http://www.nehta.gov.au/nehta-news/473-aust-govt-national-e-health-strategy

National, E. -Health Transition Authority (n.d.). *Clinical Communications*. Retrieved on May 25, 2008, from http://www.nehta.gov.au

Nazario, J. (2004). Defense and Detection Strategies against Internet Worms, *Artech House, Inc.*,290.

Nazario, J., Anderson J., Wash, R., et al. (2001). The Future of Internet Worms, *Crimelabs research*.

NEEDS. (2004). *Nigeria- National Economic Empowerment Development Strategy*. Retrieved February 2007, from http://www.cenbank.org/out/publications/communique/guidelines/rd/2004/needs.pdf

Negroponte, N. (1998, January). The Third Shall be First: The Net Leverages Latecomers in the Developing World, *Wired Magazine*.

Nicholas, W., Vern, P., Stuart, S., et al. (2003). A Taxonomy of Computer Worms. In *Proceedings of the ACM workshop on Rapid Malcode*. Washington, DC: ACM Press.

Nigeria, D. F. I. D. (2007): *Country Profile: Africa*. Retrieved August 2007 from, http://www.dfid.gov.uk/countries/africa/nigeria.asp

NIH. (n.d.). *Enterprise Architecture Standards Development Process*. Retrieved from http://enterprisearchitecture.nih.gov/

Nilsson, A. (2008). Management of Technochange in an Interorganizational e-Government Project. In *Proceedings of the 41st Hawaii International Conference on System Sciences*.

Nkanga, N. (2007). *Nigeria: UN Endorses Nigeria's E-Government Model*. Retrieved from http://www.egovnews.org/?p=2965

Nokia (2001). *Sending Content over SMS to Nokia Phones, Version 1.0*. Forum Nokia.

Nonaka, I., & Takeuchi, H. (1995). *The Knowledge Creating Company*. New York: Oxford University Press.

Nonaka, I., & Takeuchi, H. (1995). *The Knowledge-Creating Company: How Japanese Companies Create the Dynamics of Innovation*. Oxford, UK: Oxford University Press.

Norris, P. (2001). *Digital Divide: Civic Engagement, Information Poverty, and the Internet worldwide*. Cambridge, UK: Cambridge University Press.

Nsuangani, N. M., & Pérez, M. A. (2006). Accessing Web-Based Health Related Information by College Students: An Exploratory Study. *Californian Journal of Health Promotion*, *4*(1), 64–74.

Ntiro, S. (2000). *eGovernment in Eastern Africa*. Dar-es-Salaam, Tanzania: KPMG.

Nwabueze, B. (2003). *Constitutional Democracy in Africa*. Nigeria: Spectrum Books.

O'Neill, O. (2002a). *Trust and Technology. Presented atThe Reith Lectures 2002, BBCi*. The Open University.

O'Neill, O. (2002b). *Trust*. Presented at The Reith Lectures 2002, BBCi, The Open University. Park, N. K., Mezias, J. M., & Song, S. (2004). A Resource-based View of Strategic Alliances and Firm Value in the Electronic In Park, P. (Ed.), People, Knowledge, and Change in Participatory Research. *Management Learning, 30*(2), 141-157.

OASIS Group. (2006), *Reference Model for Service Oriented Architecture 1.0, Public Review Draft 1.0*. Retrieved from http://www.oasis-open.org/committees/download.php/16628/wd-soa-rm-pr1.pdf

OCDE. (2003). *The e-Government imperative*. Retrieved from www1.worlbank.org/publicsector/egov/e-GovernmentImperative.pdf

Odedra-Straub, M. (2003). E-commerce and Development: Whose Development? *Electronic Journal on Information Systems in Developing Countries*, *11*(2), 1–5.

OECD & DSG. (2007). Measuring and Evaluating e-Government in Arab Countries. In *Governance for Development in Arab Countries Initiative: 3rd WG2 High Level Seminar on e-Government and Administrative Simplification*. Dubai: OECD.

Oh, H., Rizo, C., Enkin, M., & Jadad, A. (2005). What is eHealth? (3): A Systematic Review of Published Definitions. *Journal of Medical Internet Research*, *7*(1). doi:10.2196/jmir.7.1.e1

Olu Ogunrin, F., Ogunrin, O., & Akerele, A. (2007). Motivating Nigerian Doctors for Improved Healthcare Delivery. *International Journal of Health Care Quality Assurance*, *20*(4), 290–306. doi:10.1108/09526860710754361

Olubamise, B., & Awe, J. (2007). *NIGERIA: ICT4D Annual Review 2007.* Retrieved September 21, 2007, from http://www.jidaw.com/itsolutions/ict4dreview2007.html

OMG. (2003) *MDA Guide Version 1.0.1*. Retrieved April 2009 from http://www.omg.org/docs/omg/03-06-01.pdf

OMG. (2005) *MOF 2.0/XMI Mapping Specification, v2.1.1*. Retrieved April 2009, from http://www.omg.org/docs/formal/05-09-01.pdf

OMG. (2008) Semantics of Business Vocabulary and Business Rules (SBVR), v1.0 *OMG Available Specification*. Retreived April 2009, from http://www.omg.org/docs/formal/08-01-02.pdf

Orabuchi, A. (2005). *Poor Healthcare System: Nigeria's moral difference*. Retrieved April 28, 2008 from http://www.kwenu.com/publications/orabuchi/poor_healthcare.htm

Oracle (2009) *Oracle WebLogic Server*. Retrieved April 2009, from http://www.oracle.com/technology/products/weblogic/index.html

O'Reilly, T. (2005, September 30). *What is Web 2.0. Design Patterns and Business Models for the Next Generation of Software*, O'Reilly Media. Retrieved from http://www.oreillynet.com/pub/a/oreilly/tim/news/2005/09/30/what-is-web-20.html

Orriens, B., & Yang, J. (2006). *Specification and Management of Policies in Service Oriented Business Collaboration*. The Netherlands: Tilburg University.Schmidt, R. (2002). *Web Services Based Execution of Business Rules*, RuleML 2002 - International Workshop on Rule Markup Languages for Business Rules on the Semantic Web. Sardinia, Italy.

Osimo, D. (2008, August) Benchmarking eGovernement in the Web 2.0 era: what to measure, and how, *European Journal of ePractice, 4*, August.

Osimo,, D. (2008, May 14) *Web 2.0 in government: why and how?* Institute for Prospective Technological Studies Report.

OECD. (2000). In Outlook, I. T. (Ed.), *The Economic and Social Impacts of Electronic Commerce: Preliminary Findings and Research Agenda* (pp. 1–50).

Oyelaran-Oyeyinka, B. (2007, June). *SME: Issues, Challenges and Prospects*, An invited presentation at the International Conference on Financial System Strategy (FSS) 2020 Organized by the Central Bank of Nigeria. Retrieved February 2007, from http://www.cenbank.org/fss/wed/sme_issues,%20challenges%20and%20prospects_oyeyinka%20banji.pdf

Panagopoulos, C. (2007). Technology and the Transformation of Political Communications. *Social Science Computer Review, 25*(4), 423–424. doi:10.1177/0894439307305622

Paquette, G., Aubin, C., & Crevier, F. (1999). MISA, A Knowledge-based Method for the Engineering of Learning Systems. *Journal of Courseware Engineering, 2.*

Paquette, G., Crevier, F., & Aubin, C. (1997). *Méthode d'ingénierie d'un système d'apprentissage (MISA)*, Centre de recherche LICEF, Télé-université. Revue Informations In Cognito, In French, Retrieved from http://www.licef.teluq.uquebec.ca/gp/docs/pub/ingenierie/misa.doc

Pardo, T. A., & Scholl, H. J. (2002). Walking Atop the Cliffs: Avoiding Failure and Reducing Risk in Large Scale E-Government Projects. In *Proceedings of the 35th Annual Hawaii International Conference on System Sciences (HICSS)*, 1656- 1665.

Parisopoulos, K., Tambouris, T., & Tarabanis, K. (2007) Analyzing and Comparing European eGovernment Strategies, In *Proceedings of the 3rd International Conference on e-Government (ICEG)* (pp.179-188).

Parker, M. (2007, November 3). It Takes a Brave New Politician to Step Online. *The Canberra Times.*

Pascual, P. J. (2003, MAY). *"e-Government" e-ASEAN Task Force*. New York: UNDP-APDIP

Pattichis, C. S., Kyriacou, E. C., Pattichis, M. S., Panayides, A., Mougiakakou, S., Pitsillides, A., & Schizas, C. N. (2007). A brief overview of m-health e-Emergency Systems. *6th International Special Topic Conference on ITAB*, 2007, vol. 44, (pp.143- 153). Tokyo, Japan.

Paul, D. (2003). Speech recognition for students with disabilities. *Nisbet, CALL Centre, University of Edinburgh* pp. 1 - 6. Retrieved January 18,2009, from http://callcentre.education.ed.ac.uk/downloads/speech_recognition/hitmesse2003.pdf

Pavlopoulos, S., Kyriacou, E., Berler, A., Dembeyiotis, S., & Koutsouris, D. (1998). A novel emergency telemedicine system based on wireless communication technology – Ambulance. *IEEE Transactions on Information Technology in Biomedicine*, *2*(4), 261–267. doi:10.1109/4233.737581

Pavlopoulos, S., Kyriacou, E., Berler, A., & Koutsouris, D. (1998). A mobile system for emergency health care provision via telematics support-'AMBULANCE. In *Proceedings of the IEEE International Conference on Information Technology Applications in Biomedicine 1998 (ITAB 98)* (pp. 150–154).

Pavlou, P. A., & Gefen, D. (2004). Building Effective Online Marketplaces With Institution-Based Trust. *Information Systems Research*, *15*, 37–59. doi:10.1287/isre.1040.0015

Pavlou, P. A. (2003). Consumer acceptance of electronic commerce: integrating trust and risk with the technology acceptance model. *International Journal of Electronic Commerce*, *7*(3), 101–134.

Pavlou, P. A., Tan, Y.-H., & Gefen, D. (2003) The Transitional Role Of Institutional Trust In Online Interorganizational Relationships. In *Proceedings of The 36th Hawaii International Conference On System Sciences (Hicss '03).*

Pavlovski, C. HeeSam, K., & Wood, D. (2004). Ubiquitous mobility in clinical healthcare. In *Proceedings of the IDEAS Workshop on Medical Information Systems: The Digital Hospital (IDEAS-DH '04)* (pp. 147-153).

Personal Reader Framework. (2007). *Personal Reader Framework*. Retrieved January 11, 2007, from http://www.personal-reader.de

Peterson, S., & Michael, M. (2008, March 2). Loser generated content: From participation to exploitation. *First Monday*, *13*(3). Retrieved from http://firstmonday.org/htbin/cgiwrap/bin/ojs/index.php/fm/article/view/2141/1948.

Peterson, R. A. (2000). *Constructing Effective Questionnaires*. Thousand Oaks, CA: Sage Publications.

PEW (2008, January 11). *Internet's Broader Role in Campaign 2008: Social Networking and Online Videos Take Off*. PEW Research Center for the People and the Press.

Pierre, R. (2006). Mobile e-Government Options: Between Technology-driven and User-centric. *Journal of E-Government*, *4*(2), 79–89. Retrieved from http://www.ejeg.com.

Piers, M. (2004, November). -January 2005) How EU law affects arbitration and the treatment of consumer disputes: The Belgian example. *Dispute Resolution Journal*, *59*(4), 77–85.

Plans Review and Monitoring Office. (2008). *Report on National Government Agencies (NGAs) with Short Messaging Service (SMS) Facility*, National Computer Center-Commission on Information and Communications Technology. Retrieved from http://www.ncc.gov.ph/files/sms_report1208.pdf

Plauche, M., Nallasamy, U., Pal, J., Wooters, C., & Ramachandran, D. (2006). Speech Recognition for Illiterate Access to Information and Technology. In *Proceeding of International Conference on Information and Communications Technologies and Development.*

Polanyi, M. (1966). *The Tacit Dimension*. New York: Doubleday and Company.

Popkin, S. L. (2007, April). Changing Media and Changing Political Organization: Delegation, Representation and News. *Japanese Journal of Political Science*, *8*(1), 71–93. doi:10.1017/S1468109907002484

Porter, M. E. (2001). Strategy and the Internet. *Harvard Business Review*, *79*(3), 62–78.

Pottier, P. (2000). *La sémiologie et communication cartographique*, Fiche technique du CNIG n°40, p. 6.

Public Service in Action Exhibition. Retrieved from http://www.ida.gov.sg/InSG/Dec06/egov.html

QAA. (2007). *Quality Assurance Agency, Code of Practice for the Assurance of Academic Quality and Standards in Higher Education*. Retrieved June 5, 2007, from http://www.qaa.ac.uk/public/cop/codesofpractice.htm

Qing, S., & Wen, W. (2005). A Survey and Trends on Internet Worms. *Computers & Security*, *24*(4), 334–346. doi:10.1016/j.cose.2004.10.001

QTI. (2007). *IMS Question & Test Interoperability Specification, V1.2*. Retrieved March 10, 2007, from http://www.imsglobal.org/question/index.cfm

Qureshi, R. (2007). *Building a Telephony Web Application*. Retrieved August 15, 2008, from http://www.hunzatechnologies.com/telephony-web-tutorial/

Qureshi, S. (2007). *Information Technology for Development*. Retrieved February 2007, from http://www.wmin.ac.uk/wbs/pdf.ITD-Presentation_for_WBS_June_20_2007.pdf

Ramamoorthy, C. V., & Ho, G. S. (1980). Performance Evaluation of Asynchronous Concurrent systems Using Petri Nets. *IEEE Transactions on Software Engineering*, 440–449. doi:10.1109/TSE.1980.230492

Rannu, R., & Semevsky, M. (2005, December). *Mobile Services in Tartu*, Mobi Solutions Ltd, Tartu, Estonia. Retrieved from http://www.mobisolutions.com

Ratchford, B. T., Talukdar, D., & Lee, M. (2001). A model of consumer choice of the Internet as an information source. *International Journal of Electronic Commerce*, *5*(3), 7–21.

Rayport, J., & Jaworski, B. (2001). *e-Commerce. International Edn*. New York: McGraw-Hill.

Reddick, C. (2004). Empirical Models of E-Government Growth in Local Governments. *E-service Journal*, *3*(2), 59–84. doi:10.2979/ESJ.2004.3.2.59

Reeves, W. T. (1981). *Quantitative Representations of Complex Dynamic Shapes for Motion Analysis*, PhD thesis, University of Toronto, Canada.

Report, I. M. F. (2007). *Nigeria- Poverty Strategy Paper- Progress Report*. Retrieved February 2007, from http://siteresources.worldbank.org/INTPRS1/Resources/Nigeria-PRSP-PR(August2007).pdf

Ricketson, M. (2007, October 15). Cyberspace Democracy. *The Age*.

Ridder, R. (2008). Transatlantic relations under the Obama Administration. *Centre for European Studies*. Retrieved from http://www.thinkingeurope.eu/content.php?hmID=17&smID=43&ssmID=114

Rifkin, J. (2000). *The Age of Access*. London: Penguin Books Limited.

Robert, E. M. (1995). *Diffusion of Innovations*. New York: The Free Press.

Robert, J., Van, E., Gerwen, N., & Graave, J. (2005). Art Lighthart, Ron van Rooij, Service Oriented Architecture, ICT-bibliotheek Den Haag.

Ross, C., Parkinson, L., Bates, L., Green, S., & Aye Thida, H. (2005). Pilot of a Novel Cervical Screening Intervention: Interactive Voice Response. *Australian and New Zealand Journal of Public Health*, *29*(3), 261–264. doi:10.1111/j.1467-842X.2005.tb00765.x

Ross, R. G. (2003). *Principles of Business Rule Approach*. Reading, MA: Addison-Wesley.

Rotter, J. B. (1971a). Generalized Expectancies For Interpersonal Trust. *The American Psychologist*, *26*, 443–452. doi:10.1037/h0031464

Roullard, J. (2007). Web services and speech-based application around VoiceXML. *Journal of networks, 2*(1).

Rousseau, D. M., Sitkin, S. B., Burt, R. S., & Camerer, C. (1998). Not So Different After All: A Cross-Discipline View Of Trust. *Academy of Management Review*, *23*, 393–404.

Rudnicky, A., Thayer, E., Constantinides, P., Tchou, C., Stern, R., Lenzo, K., et al. (1999). Creating natural dialogs in the Carnegie Mellon Communicator System. In*Proceedings of Eurospeech,* 1531-1534.

Rule, C. (2002). *ODR is Alive and Kicking*. San Francisco: Jossey-Bass Publishers.

Rule, M. L. (2006) *The Rule Markup Initiative*. Retrieved April 2009, from http://www.ruleml.org/

Rumbaugh, J., Jacobson, I., & Booch, G. (1999). *The Unified Modeling Language Reference Manual*. Reading, MA: Addison-Wesley.

Sachs, J. (2000, June). A New Map of the World, *The Economist*.

Sæbø, O., Sein, M. K., & Flak, L. S. (2008). *The need for a Cumulative Tradition in eGovernment Research: Conceptualizing the fundamental entities*, Retrieved from www.electronicgovernment.se/SIGeGOV/7_Sabo.pdf

Salam, A., Iyer, L., Palvia, P., & Singh, R. (2005). Trust in e-commerce. *Communications of the ACM*, *48*(2), 72–77. doi:10.1145/1042091.1042093

Salem, F. (2007). Benchmarking the e-government bulldozer: beyond measuring thetread marks. *Journal of Measuring Business Excellence*, *11*(4), 9–22. doi:10.1108/13683040710837892

Salem, F. (2003). Evaluating Dubai Government e-Services (Against EU States). In Kamli, A. K. (Ed.), *Dubai Knowledge Economy 2003-2008. Dubai, UAE: Madar Research.*

Salem, F., & Jarrar, Y. (2009). *Cross-agency Collaboration in the UAE Government: The Role of Trust and Impact of Technology*. Dubai, UAE: Dubai School of Government.

Salisbury, W., David, R. A., Pearson, A., Pearson, W., & Miller, D. W. (2001). Perceived security and World Wide Web purchase intention. *Industrial Management & Data Systems*, *101*(4), 165–176. doi:10.1108/02635570110390071

Sandoz, A., Eudes, J.-R., & Prévot, R. (2008, January). *Public-Private Partnership in e-Government: a Case Implementation*, MCETECH, Montreal. Retrieved from http://fr.wikipedia.org/wiki/Le_Corbusier

Sandoz, A., Haenni, N., & Eudes, J.-R. (2005). *Addressing and Protecting Distributed Resources in e-Government Architectures using Multiple Digital Identities*. Presented at theEuropean Conference on E-Government.

Sanguanpong, S., & Kanlayasiri, U. (2007). Worm damage minimization in enterprise networks. *International Journal of Human-Computer Studies*, *65*(1), 3–16. doi:10.1016/j.ijhcs.2006.09.001

Sarikas, O. D., & Weerakkody, V. (2007). Realising integrated e-government services: a UK local government perspective. *Transforming Government: People. Process and Policy*, *1*(2), 153–173.

SARS. (2002). *File PAYE and Skills Development Levies Online! File Vat and Diesel Refunds Online!* Retrieved November 1, 2002, from http://www.sars.gov.za/commerce

Satriyantono, T. (2002). *Tantangan Aplikasi Mobile Generasi 3 (3G)*, Seminar MTI-ITB. Retrieved from http://satriyantono.net/blogs2.php?id=1&parameter=1

Sauger, N. (2007, November). The French Legislative and Presidential Elections of 2007. *West European Politics*, *30*(5), 1166–1175. doi:10.1080/01402380701617548

Schatz, A. (2007, March 19). In '08 Race, Web Tactics are Even More Integral. Retrieved from http://www.politicsonline.com/coverage/wsj2007/wsj.htm

Schein, E. H. (1988). *Organisational Culture and Leadership*. San Francisco: Jossey-Bass.

Schiavetta, S. (2005, April) *Online Dispute Resolution, E-Government and Overcoming the DigitalDivide*. Retrieved April 16, 2008, from http://www.bileta.ac.uk/Document%20Library/1/Online%20Dispute%20Resolution,%20EGovernment%20and%20Overcoming%20the%20Digital%20Divide.pdf

Schlenker, B. R., Helm, B., & Tedeschi, J. T. (1973). The Effects Of Personality And Situational Variables On Behavioral Trust. *Journal of Personality and Social Psychology*, *25*, 419–427. doi:10.1037/h0034088

Schmidt, R., Lyytinen, K., Keil, M., & Cule, P. (2001). Identifying software project risks: An international Delphi study. *Journal of Management Information Systems*, *17*(4), 5–36.

Schneider, G. P. (2003). *Electronic Commerce*. Boston, MA: Thomson Learning Inc.

Scholl, H. J. (2001). *Applying Stakeholder Theory to E-Government: Benefits and Limits*. Retrieved from http://projects.ischool.washington.edu/jscholl/Papers/Scholl_IFIP_2001.pdf

Scholl, H. J. (2005). Interoperability in e-Government: More than Just Smart Middleware, In *Proceedings of the 38th Hawaii International Conference on System Sciences*.

Schreiber, G., Wielinga, B., & Jansweijer, W. (1995). The kactus view of the 'o' word. *IJCAI'1995, Workshop on Basic Ontological Issues in Knowledge*.

Schultz, T. F. (2004, Fall). Does online dispute resolution need governmental intervention? The case for architectures of control and trust *North Carolina. The Journal of Law and Technology*, *6*(1), 71–106.

Schumpeter, J. (1942). *Capitalism, Socialism, and Democracy*. New York: Harper Collins.

Scott, D. T. (2005). *Tempests of the Blogosphere: Presidential Campaign Stories that Failed to Ignite Mainstream Media*. IlyaMEDIA. Retrieved from http://ilyagram.org/media/fetch/scott.pdf

Secrétariat du Grand conseil (2008). *Projet de loi ouvrant un crédit d'investissement de 30 850 000 F pour le développement de l'administration en ligne. Geneva*. Retrieved from http://www.ge.ch/grandconseil/data/texte/PL10177.pdf

Senecal, S. (2000). Stopping variables in Online buying processes: An innovation diffusion approach, Proceedings of the 6th Americas Conference on Information Systems, pp. 1380-1385.

Shaheen, A.-H. (2000, June 19).*The Utilization of the World Wide Web for Decision-Making in the United Arab Emirates (U.A.E) Business Settings: The Case of Dubai*. Tallahassee, FL: Graduate School of Information Studies, Florida State University.

Shahlook, K. A., Saghafi, F., & Abdollahi, A. (2008) Retrieved March 2009, from http://www.ieee.org/portal/site

Shahri, A. M., Norouzi, M., & Paikan, A. (2005). RoboCupRescue - Robot League Team MRL (IRAN). In *Rescue Robot League Competition, RoboCup 2005*. Osaka, Japan.

Shahzad, B., Iqbal, J., & Aslam, S. (n.d.). *Phase wise risk estimation through relative Impact technique* Pressman (n.d.). *Software Engineering: A Practitioner's Approach*. Boca Raton, FL: R.S. Pressman & Associates. *Inc*.

Shannon, M. (2007). Shaking hands, kissing babies, and blogging. *Communications of the ACM*, *50*, 21–24. doi:10.1145/1284621.1284639

Shapiro, S. P. (1987). The Social Control of Impersonal Trust. *American Journal of Sociology*, *93*, 623–658. doi:10.1086/228791

Sharma, S. K. (2006). Electronic healthcare: issues and challenges. *International Journal Healthcare*, *2*(1).

Shen, W., Compton, K., & Huggins, J. K. (2002). A toolset for supporting UML static and dynamic model checking. In *Proceedings of the 26th International Computer Software and Applications Conference COMPSAC 2002*, pp. 147-152.

Sherwani, J., Ali, N., Mirza, S., Fatma, A., Memon, Y., Karim, M., et al. (2007). HealthLine: Speech-based Access to Health Information by Low-literate Users. In *Proceedings of IEEE/ACM Int'l Conference on Information and Communication Technologies and Development*, Bangalore, India.

Shim, S., Eastlick, M. A., Lotz, S. L., & Warrington, P. (2001). An Online prepurchase intentions model: the role of intention to search. *Journal of Retailing*, *77*, 397–416. doi:10.1016/S0022-4359(01)00051-3

Shirali-Shahreza, M. (2006). Emergency SMS. In *Proceedings of the SICE - ICASE International Joint Conference 2006 (SICE - ICCAS 2006)* (pp. 1139-1142). Busan, KOREA.

Shirali-Shahreza, M. H., & Shirali-Shahreza, M. (2007). Finding a Person with Amnesia's Disease by Mobile Phone. In *Proceedings of International Conference on Robotics, Vision, Information and Signal Processing 2007 (ROVISP07)* (pp. 681-682). Penang, Malaysia.

Shirali-Shahreza, M., & Shirali-Shahreza, S. (2006). Rescue SMS. In *Proceedings of the SICE - ICASE International Joint Conference 2006 (SICE - ICCAS 2006),* (pp. 1300-1303). Busan, KOREA.

Shiroma, N., et al. (2004). Development of rescue robotic systems for both daily and emergency use. In *Proceedings of First IEEE Technical Exhibition Based Conference on Robotics and Automation, (TExCRA '04)* (pp. 85-86).

Signo, S. M. (2006). Pnp Text 2920 Service: A Communication Perspective on M-Government In Philippine Context. *Asian Culture Forum 2006*. Retrieved from http://64.62.231.21:8080/dspace/bitstream/123456789/233/1/cprs2_CS_P.pdf.

Silcock, R. (2001). What is e-Government? *Parliamentary Affairs*, *54*(1), 88–101. doi:10.1093/pa/54.1.88

Sillanpaa, A. (2001) Mobile Asset Security and How to Make Money on It. *Seminar on Network Security, Publications on Telecommunications Software and Multimedia*. Helsinki University of Technology. Retrieved from http:// www. tml.hut.fi/Studies/T-110.501/2001/papers/index.html

Simpson, V., & Oliver, M. (n.d.) *Using electronic voting systems in lectures*. Retrieved from http://www.ucl.ac.uk/learningtechnology/assessment/ElectronicVotingSystems.pdf

Sinclair, L. (2007, September 13). Web Gears Up for Election. *Australian IT*.

Singh, M., Sarkar, P., Dissanayake, D., & Pittayachawan, S. (2008, June). Diffusion of E-Government Services in Australia: Citizens' Perspectives. In *Proceedings of the European Conference on Information Systems (ECIS)* 2008, Galway, Ireland.

Singh, M., & Byrne, J. (2005). Performance Evaluation of e-Business in Australia. *The Electronic Journal of Information Systems Evaluation, 8*(1), 71-80. Retrieved from www.ejise.com

Singh, S. (2002). *Unravelling the Chaos in E-Commerce Land: A Preliminary Framework for Auditors for Systemactically Dealing with Processing of Electronic Transactions.* Paper presented at the International Economic and Management Science Conference: Transformation on South Africa: Management Improvements and Best Practicesin Accountability. Productivity and Customer Service Quality, Vanderbijlpark, South Africa.

Sirkemaa, S. (2007). The Role of Partnerships in Development of E-Services - Highlighting Public Sector Organizations. *International Journal of Public Information Systems*, *3*, 201–212.

Skinner, H., Biscope, S., Poland, B., & Golberg, E. (2003). How adolescents use technology for health information: Implications for health professionals for focus group studies. *Journal of Medical Internet Research*, *5*(32).

Smith, H. A., McKeen, J. D., & Staples, D. S. (2001). Risk Management in Information Systems: Problems and Potentials. *Communications of AIS*, *7*(13), 1–29.

Smith, J. (April 2005). Cutting the wires: why Asian governments are going mobile, *Public Sector Technology & Management*.

So, W. C. M., Wong, T. N. D., & Sculli, D. (2005). Factors affecting intentions to purchase via the Internet. *Industrial Management & Data Systems*, *105*(9), 1225–1244. doi:10.1108/02635570510633275

Sohm, J. C. (2003). *Image et graphique pour le web*, p. 5.

Sohn, Y.-S., & Ahn, K. H. (1999). Theoretical and empirical research on the impacts of consumer knowledge on adoption of e-commerce market. *Korean Marketing Review*, *14*(1), 75–91.

Solimano, A. (2006) *The International Mobility of Talent and its Impact on Global Development*. New York: United Nations University - World Institute for Development Economic Research (UNU-WIDER).

Soludo, C. C. (2007). *Nigeria's Financial System Strategy 2020 Plan OUR DREAM*, A paper presented at the International Conference on Financial System Strategy (FSS) 2020 Organized by the Central Bank of Nigeria. Retrieved February 2007, from http://www.cenbank.org/fss/mon/FSS2020---Presentation%20at%20International%20Conference.ppt

Song, C-S., & Shin, J-C. (1999). Adoption of Internet shopping In *Proceedings of Korean Academy of Commodity Science and Technology*, 27–53.

Soussain, G. (2001). *Publier des cartes sur internet: Les repères*. p. 64.

Soussain, G. (2003). *Cartographie sur Internet: synthèse à l'usage d'une maîtrise d'œuvre*. p. 7.

South Africa Yearbook 2007/08 (2008). *Integrated Justice System (IJS)*. Retrieved June 20, 2008, from http://www.info.gov.za/aboutgov/justice/system.htm#transform

South African Government Gateway Portal. (2003). *South African Government Gateway Portal*. Retrieved October 17, 2003,http://www.gov.za/structure/pubserv.html

South African Revenue Services. (2008). Retrieved June 20, 2008, from http://www.sars.gov.za

Spafford, E. (1988). *The Internet Worm Program: An Analysis*(Technical report CSD-TR-823) Department of Computer Science, Purdue University, (pp. 1-29).

Stanberry, B. (2001). Legal ethical and risk issues in telemedicine. *Computer Methods and Programs in Biomedicine*, *64*, 225–233. doi:10.1016/S0169-2607(00)00142-5

Staniford, S., Paxson, V., & Weaver, N. (2002). How to Own the Internet in Your Spare Time. In *Proceedings of 11th Usenix Security Symposium*, San Francisco, USA.

Stanyer, J. (2005). Political Parties, the Internet and the 2005 General Election: From Web Presence to E-Campaigning? *Journal of Marketing Management*, *21*(9), 1049–1065. doi:10.1362/026725705775194094

Starfield, B., Shi, L., & Macinko, J. (2005). Contribution of Primary Care to Health Systems and Health. *The Milbank Quarterly*, *83*(3), 457–502. doi:10.1111/j.1468-0009.2005.00409.x

Stephen, J. R., and Vivienne, J., (2003). eGovernment Leadership: Engaging the Customer, The Government executive series, Accenture Innovation delivered.

Stephens, R. T. (2004). *A Framework For The Identification Of Electronic Commerce Visual Design Elements That Enable Trust Within The Small Hotel Industry. School Of Computer and Information Sciences*. Fort Lauderdale, FL: Nova Southeastern University.

Stephenson, W. (1953). *The Study Of Behaviour: Q-Technique And Its Methodology*. Chicago: University Of Chicago Press.

Steve, M. (2004). *E-Democracy: stealing the Election in 2004*. Retrieved June 2006 from http://www.globalresearch.ca/articles/ MOO407A.html.

Stewart, K. A., & Segars, A. H. (2002). An empirical examination of the concern for information privacy instrument. *Information Systems Research*, *13*(1), 36–49. doi:10.1287/isre.13.1.36.97

Stodder, D. (2006). Loosen Up, *Intelligent Enterprise*. Retrieved from http://intelligent-enterprise.informationweek.com/showArticle.jhtml;jsessionid=PHDMLI3MGM4FJQE1GHPSKHWATMY32JVN?articleID=181503583

Stoppel, D., et al. (2006). Improving Worm Detection with Artificial Neural Networks through Feature Selection and Temporal Analysis Techniques. In *Proceedings of International Conference on Neural Networks ICNN 2006: International Journal of Applied Mathematics and Computer Sciences*.

Stoppel, D., et al. (2006)Application of Artificial Neural Networks Techniques to Computer Worm Detection. In *Proceedings of International Joint Conference on Neural Networks IJCNN '06*.

Storey, V. C., Chiang, R. L., Dey, D., Goldstein, R. L., & Sundaresan, S. (1997). Database design with common sense business reasoning and learning. *ACM Transactions on Database Systems*, *22*(4), 471–512. doi:10.1145/278245.278246

Studio Archetype/Sapient & Cheskin Research (1999) Ecommerce Trust Study.

Sujansky, W. V. (1998). The benefits and challenges of an electronic medical record: much more than a "word-processed" patient chart. *The Western Journal of Medicine*, *169*(3), 176–183.

Sukasame, N. (2002). *The development of e-service in Thai government*. BU Academic Review.

Sunday Times. (2007). Mortgage fraudsters have been stealing homeowners' identities by using the internet, *The Sunday Times online*. Retrieved October, 2008, from http://property.timesonline.co.uk/tol/life_and_style/property/article2830910.ece

Susanto, T. D., & Goodwin, R. (2006 June). Opportunity and Overview of SMS-based eGovernment in Developing Countries. *The Internet Society II: Advances in Education, Commerce & Governance*. The New Forest, UK, WIT Press.

Susanto, T. D., & Goodwin, R. (2006, December) Implementing SMS-based eGovernment Model, 8th *International Conference on Information Integration and Web-based Applications & Services (iiWAS2006)*, Yogyakarta, Indonesia.

Susanto, T. D., & Goodwin, R. (2007 June). Content Presentation and SMS-based e-Government, *International Conference on Electrical Engineering and Informatics (ICEEI)*, Bandung, Indonesia.

Symantec (2008). *W32.Benjamin.Worm*. Retrieved from http://securityresponse.symantec.com/avcenter/venc/data/w32.benjamin.worm.html

Sztompka, P. (2003). *Trust: A Sociological Theory*. Cambridge: Cambridge University Press.

Tabuchi, H. (2008, February 4). Japan Prime Minister Debts on YouTube. *ABC News: Technology & Science*. Retrieved from http://abcnews.go.com/Technology/wireStory?id=4073578

TADO. M. (1989). Petri Nets: Proprieties, analysis and applications. In *Proceedings of the IEEE, 77*(4).

Tadokoro, S. (2005). Special Project on Development of Advanced Robots for Disaster Response (DDT Project). In *Proceedings of the 2005 IEEE Workshop on Advanced Robotics and its Social Impacts* (pp. 66-72).

Takemura, F., et al. (2004). Proposition of a human body searching strategy using a cable-driven robot at major disaster. In *Proceedings of 2004 IEEE/RSJ International Conference on Intelligent Robots and Systems (IROS 2004)* (pp. 1456 – 1461).

Tallinn (2005). *E-Voting System Overview*. Retrieved November 2008 from http://www.vvk.ee/elektr/docs/Yldkirjeldus-eng.pdf

Tan, C. W., Pan, S. L., & Lim, E. (2007). Managing Stakeholder Interests in E-Government Implementation: Lessons Learned from a Singapore E-Government Project. *International Journal of Electronic Government Research*, *3*(1), 61–84.

Tan, F. B., & Sutherland, P. (2004). Online consumer trust: a multi-dimensional model. *Journal of Electronic Commerce in Organizations*, *2*(3), 40–58.

Tan, S. J. (1999). Strategies for reducing consumers? risk aversion in Internet shopping. *Journal of Consumer Marketing*, *16*(2), 163–180. doi:10.1108/07363769910260515

Tan, Y.-H., & Thoen, W. (2001). Toward a generic model of trust for electronic commerce. *International Journal of Electronic Commerce*, *5*(2), 61–74.

Tang, T. W., & Chi, W. H. (2005). The Role of Trust In Customer Online Shopping Behavior: Perspective Of Technology Acceptance Model. In *Proceedings of Naacsos Conference 2005*. Indiana, USA.

Tapscott, D., & Williams, A. D. (2006). *Wikinomics: How Mass Collaboration Changes Everything*. New York: Portfolio.

Tarnas, R. (1991). *The passion of the western mind: Understanding the ideas that have shaped our world view*. New York: Harmony Books.

Taylor, M., & Murphy, A. (2004). SMEs and e-business. *Journal of Small Business and Enterprise Development*, *11*(3), 280–289. doi:10.1108/14626000410551546

Tazzoli, R., Castagna, P., & Campanini, S. E. (2004, November 7-11). Towards a Semantic Wiki Wiki Web. In *Proceedings of the Third International Semantic Web Conference*, Hiroshima, Japan.

Tell Editorial. (2006). *Standing Up Against Corruption* (pp. 18–19). Tell Magazine.

Thailand, Ministry of Information and Communication Technology (2006) *Thailand e-Government Interoperability Framework Version 1.0*.

The e-Business Handbook (2005). The 2005 review of innovation at work in South African business. An ITweb informatica Publication. Creda Communication (Pty) Ltd

The Times. (2008). Google could be superseded, says web inventor, *The Times Online*. Retrieved March 2009, from http://technology.timesonline.co.uk/tol/news/tech_and_web/article3532832.ece

Thomazeau, J. *(1997)*. Le Web support d'applications client/serveur, une voie suivie par la DSI pour le système d'information de gestion du CNRS, *p. 12*.

Thomson, J. D. (1996). *Australian Department of Defence Purchasing Statistics Bulletin 1989/90 to 1995/96*. Canberra: Commonwealth of Australia.

Titah, R., & Barki, H. (2006). E-Government Adoption and Acceptance: A Literature Review. *International Journal of Electronic Government Research*, *2*(3), 23–57.

Todd, P., & Benbasat, I. (1993). An Experimental Investigation of The Relationship Between Decision Makers, Decision Aids And Decision Making Effort. *Information Systems Research*, *31*, 80–100.

Tojanović, Z. (2005). *A Method for Component-Based and Service-Oriented Software Systems Engineering", Doctoral Dissertation, Delft University of Technology, The Netherlands 2005*. The Netherlands: Doctoral Dissertation, Delft University of Technology.

Trunick, P. (1999). ERP: Promise or Pipedream. *Transport and Distribution*, *40*(1), 1–39.

Turban, E., King, D., McKay, J., Lee, J., & Viehland, D. (2008). *Electronic Commerce A Managerial Perspective* (International Edition). Upper Saddle River, NJ: Prentice Hall.

Turban, E., King, D., Lee, L., Warkentin, M., & H, M. C. (2002). *Electronic Commerce: A Managerial Perspective*, Upper Saddle River, NJ: Prentice Hall.

Turner, J. R., & Muller, R. (2003). On the nature of the project as a temporary organization. *International Journal of Project Management*, *21*, 1–8. doi:10.1016/S0263-7863(02)00020-0

UN, (2005) *From e-Government to E-inclusion*, UN Global e-Government Readiness Report. Retrieved September 21, 2007, from unpan1.un.org/intradoc/groups/public/documents/un/unpan021888.pdf

UN, (2008). United Nations e-Government Survey 2008: From e-Government to Connected Governance. Retrieved February 2008, from unpan1.un.org/intradoc/groups/public/documents/UN/UNPAN028607.pdf, access: 02-2008

UN. (2005). *UN Global E-government Readiness Report 2005: From E-government to E-inclusion*. Retrieved from http://unpan1.un.org/intradoc/groups/public/documents/un/unpan021888.pdf

UN. (2008). *E-Government Survey 2008, From E-Government to Connected Governance*. http://unpan1.un.org/intradoc/groups/public/documents/UN/UNPAN028607.pdf

UN/CEFACT CCTS. (2006). *Core Component Technical Specification, Part 8 of the ebXML Framework*. Retrieved from http://www.unece.org/cefact/ebxml/CCTS_V2-01_Final.pdf

UN/CEFACT XML. (2006). *UN/CEFACT XML Naming and Design Rules Version 2.0*. Retrieved from http://www.unece.org/cefact/XML-Naming-and -Design-Rules-V2.0pdf

UNCTAD. (2006) *The Digital Divide Report: ICT Diffusion Index 2005*. New York and Geneva: United Nations Conference on Trade and Development.

UNDESA. (2003). *World Public Sector Report 2003*. New York: United Nations Department of Economic and Social Affairs.

UNDESA. (2005). *Global E-government Readiness Report 2005 - From E-government to E-inclusion*. New York: United Nations Department of Economic and Social Affairs.

UNDESA. (2008) *UN E-Government Survey 2008: From E-Government to Connected Governance*. New York: United Nations Department of Economic and Social Affairs (UNDESA), Division for Public Administration and Development Management.

UNDP. (2000). *Millennium Development Goals*. Retrieved from http://www.undp.org/mdg/basics.shtml

Unhelkar, B. (2003, November 24-25). *Understanding the Impact of Cultural Issues in Global e-Business Alliances*, 4th International We-B Conference, Perth, Western Australia.

United Nations Department of economic and Social Affairs (2005). *Global E-government Readiness Report: From E-Government to E-inclusion*. Retrieved on May 8, 2008, from http://unpan1.un.org/intradoc/groups/public/documents/un/unpan021888.pdf

United Nations Division for Public Economics and Public Administration (UNPAN) and American Society for Public Administration. (ASPA) (2002) *Benchmarking E-government: A Global Perspective - Assessing the UN Member States*. Retrieved September 5, 2008, from http://unpan1.un.org/intradoc/groups/public/documents/UN/UNPAN021547.pdf

US. (2008). *University of Sousse*. Retrieved from http://www.uc.rnu.tn/ (can also be accessed via http://www.mes.tn)

UVT. (2008). *Virtual University of Tunis*. Retrieved from http://www.uvt.rnu.tn

Van der Merwe, C. (2008). *Fundamental shifts on the cards for SA e-government strategy*. Engeneering news.

Van Os, R., & Hagermann, C. (2007). The Netherlands: Party and Candidate Web Sites during the 2004 European Parliament Election Campaign. In Kluver, R. (Eds.), *The Internet and National Elections: A Comparative Study of Web Campaigning* (pp. 23–59). London: Taylor and Francis.

Vasilyeva, E. (2006). The Challenge of Feedback Personalization to Learning Styles in a Web-Based Learning Systems. *ICALT*, *06*, 1143–1144.

Vassilios, L. (2004). *Information Society Policy link initiative*. Retrieved from http://europa.eu.int/information_society/activities/policy_link/index_en.htm

Veblen, T. (1899). The Theory of the Leisure Class: An Economic Study of Institutions. *American Journal of Sociology*.

Venkatesh, V., & Morris, M. G. (2003). User Acceptance of Information Technology: Toward a Unified View. *Management Information Systems Quarterly*, *27*(3), 425–478.

Ventor, D. (2003, March 13). IT at the Heart of Shock and Awe: With US Invasion, Era of Network Centric Warfare has dawned, *Computer World*.

Vijayakumari, K. (2001). International migration and labour market adjustments in Malaysia: The Role of Foreign Labour Policies. *Asia-Pacific Migration Journal, 10*(3-4).

Vijayasarathy, L. R., & Jones, J. M. (2000). Print and Internet catalogue shopping: assessing attitudes and intentions. *Internet Research: Electronic Networking Applications and Policy*, *10*(3), 191–202. doi:10.1108/10662240010331948

Voice, E. M. L. (VoiceXML) Version 2.0 (2004). *VoiceXML*. Retrieved May 24, 2008 from http://www.w3.org/TR/2004/REC-voicexml20-20040316/

Voice, X. M. L. 2.x Essentials (2005). *VoiceXML 2.x Essentials*. Retrieved May 20, 2008, from https://studio.tellme.com/vxml2/ovw/essentials-p.html

Volz, R., Handschuh, S., Staab, S., Stojanovic, L., & Stojanovic, N. (2003). *Unveiling the hidden bride: deep annotation for mapping and migrating legacy data to the Semantic Web* (pp. 187–206). Elsevier BV.

W3C (2004) *Web Services Architecture*, Working Group Note 11. Retrieved April 2009, from http://www.w3.org/TR/ws-arch/

Wagner, C. (2000). End-users as expert system developers. *Journal of End User Computing*, *12*(3), 3–13.

Wagner, C., Cheung, K., Lee, F., & Ip, R. (2003). Enhancing e-government in developing countries: managing knowledge through virtual communities. *Electronic Journal of Information Systems in Developing Countries*, *14*(4), 1–20.

Wang, J. (2007). Internet worm early detection and response mechanism. *Journal of China Universities of Posts and Telecommunications*, *14*(3), 79. doi:10.1016/S1005-8885(07)60153-8

Wang, Y. (1999). *A General Analysis of the Impact of Electronic Commerce on Small Businesses and Entrepreneurships in the U.S.* Retrieved March, 10, 2002, from http://www.cs.wits.ac.za/~philip/SAICSIT/SAICSIT-99/electronic/exp/Wang.pdf

Wangpipatwong, S. Chutimaskul, W., & Papasratorn, B. (2008). Understanding Citizen's Continuance Intention to Use e-Government Website: a Composite View of Technology Acceptance Model and Computer Self-Efficacy. *The Electronic Journal of e-Government, 6*(1), 55–64. Retrieved from www.ejeg.com

Warkentin, M., Gefen, D., Pavlou, P. A., & Rose, G. M. (2002). Encouraging Citizen Adoption of E-Government By Building Trust. *Electronic Markets*, *12*, 157–162. doi:10.1080/101967802320245929

Warrior, J., McHenry, E., & McGee, K. (2003). They know where you are [location detection]. *Spectrum, IEEE,* 40(7), 20 - 25.

Wateridge, J. (1998). How can IS/IT projects be measured for success? *International Journal of Project Management*, *16*(1), 59–63. doi:10.1016/S0263-7863(97)00022-7

Waterman, D. A. (1986). *A Guide to Expert Systems*. Reading, MA: Addison-Wesley.

Weare, C., Musso, J., & Hale, M. L. (1999). Electronic Democracy and the Diffusion of Municipal Web Pages in California. *Administration & Society*, *31*(1), 3–27. doi:10.1177/00953999400935475

Weaver, N., Staniford, S., & Paxson, V. *Very Fast Containment of Scanning Worms*. Revisited, in Malware Detection (p. 113).

WEF & INSEAD. (2007). *World Economic Forum and INSEAD,* The Global Information Technology Report 2006-2007. Genevea, Switzerland.

WEF & INSEAD. (2009) *Mobility in a Networked World World Economic Forum*, The Global Information Technology Report 2008–2009. Geneva, Switzerland.

Weise, D., & Adler, D. (1992). *TrueType and Microsoft Windows 3.1*. Redmond, WA: Technical Report, Microsoft Corporation.

Welch, E. W., Hinnant, C. C., & Moon, M. J. (2005). Linking Citizen Satisfaction With E-Government and Trust In Government. *Journal of Public Administration: Research and Theory*, *15*, 371–391. doi:10.1093/jopart/mui021

Western Australian Local Government Association. (2009). *Productivity Commission Health Workforce Study*. Retrieved on April 6, 2009, from http://www.pc.gov.au/_data/assets/file/0003/10596/sub086.rtf

Whitney, Q. (2000). Voting for usability: Background on the issue. Retrieved June 2006 from http://www.wqusability.com/articles/voting-background2000.html

Wickramasinghe, N., Fadlalla, A. M. A., Geisler, E., & Schaffer, J. L. (2005). A Framework for accessing e-health preparedness. *International Journal of Electronic Healthcare, 1*(3), 316–334. doi:10.1504/IJEH.2005.006478

Wikipedia (2007). Web 2.0. *Wikipedia, the Free Encyclopedia*. Retrieved from http://en.wikipedia.org/wiki/Web_2.0

Wikipedia (2008). *Electronic Voting*. Retreieved December 2008, from http://en.wikipedia.org/wiki/Electronic_voting

Willcocks, L., & Margetts, H. (1994). Risk assessment and information systems. *European Journal of Information Systems, 3*(2). doi:10.1057/ejis.1994.13

William, A. E. (2003, December). An evaluation framework for deploying Web Services in the next generation manufacturing enterprise. *Robotics and Computer-integrated Manufacturing, 19*(6), 509–519. doi:10.1016/S0736-5845(03)00061-9

Williams, P. D. (2008). The 2007 Australian Federal Election: the Story of Labor's Return from the Wilderness. *The Australian Journal of Politics and History, 54*(1), 104–125. doi:10.1111/j.1467-8497.2008.00487.x

Williams, M. (2000). The World Bank, the World Trade Organization and the Environmental Social Movement. In Higgot, R., Underhill, G., & Bieler, A. (Eds.), *Non-State Actors and Authority in the Global System 2000*. New York: Routledge.

Williamson, O. E. (1991, June). Comparative Economic Organization: The Analysis of Discrete Structural Alternatives. *Administrative Science Quarterly, 36*, 269–296. doi:10.2307/2393356

Williamson, O. E. (1991). Economic Institutions: Spontaneous and Intentional Governance. *Journal of Law Economics and Organization, 7*(Special Issue), 159–187.

Williamson, O. E. (1996). *The Mechanisms of Governance*. New York: Oxford University Press.

Williamson, O. E. (2002). Empirical Microeconomics: Another Perspective. In Augier, M., & March, J. (Eds.), *The Economics of Choice, Change and Organization*. Brookfield, VT: Edward Elgar.

Williamson, O E. (2002b, January). *The Theory of the Firm as Governance Structure: from Choice to Contract*. Berkley, CA: University of California.

Williamson, O. E. (2002a, January). *The Lens of Contract: Private Ordering*. Berkley, CA: University of California.

Wimmer, M. (Ed.). (2004). Knowledge Management in e-government. In *Proceedings of the KMGov 2004*, Springer Lecture Notes No. 3035.

Wittmann, C., & Cullen, M. (2000). *B2B Internet*. Philadelphia: First Union Securities.

Won-sup, Y. (2007, November 21). Unlike in 2002, Campaigners Fail to Attract Netizens. *Korea Times*.

World Bank. (2006). *World Bank*. http://www.worldbank.org/edevelopment

World Health Organization. (n.d.). S*trategy 2004-2007 health for Health-care Delivery*. Retrieved on May 25, 2008, from http://www.who.int/eht/en/eHealth_HCD.pdf

WSIS. (2003): *World Summit on the Information Society Declaration of principles*. Retrieved from www.itu.int/dms_pub/itu_s/md/03/wsis/

Wu, J., Wang, S., & Lin, L. (2005). What Drives Mobile Health Care? An Empirical Evaluation of Technology Acceptance. In *Proceedings of the 38th Annual Hawaii International Conference on System Sciences (HICSS '05)*, (pp.150–159)

Wu, L., Meng, X., & Liu, S. (2007). *Service-oriented encapsulation of manufacturing resources*, IEEE International Conference on Services Computing (SCC 2007).

Wyld, D. C. (2007). *The Blogging Revolution: Government in the Age of Web 2.0*. IBM Center for the Business of Government. Retrieved from http://www.businessofgovernment.org/pdfs/WyldReportBlog.pdf

Xu, Z., Cao, X., Dong, Y., & Su, W. (2004). Formal Approach and Automated Tool for Translating ER Schemata into OWL Ontologies. In *Advances in Knowledge Discovery and Data Mining* (pp. 464–475). Berlin, Heidelberg: Springer-Verlag.

Yaneza, J. L. (2006). *The trend of threats today: 2006 Annual Roundup and 2007 Forecast*. Trend Micro.

Yaneza, J. L. (2007). 1H 2007 Threat Roundup and 2H 2007 Forecast. In *Securing Your Web World*. Trend Micro.

Yaneza, J. L. (2008). 2007 Threat Report | 2008 Threat and Technology Forecast. In *Securing Your Web World*. Trend Micro.

Yaneza, J. L., Thiemann, T., & Drake, C. (2008). 2007 Threat Report | 2008 Threat and Technology Forecast. In *Securing Your Web World*. Trend Micro.

Yang, K., & Callahan, K. (2005). Assessing Citizen Involvement Efforts by Local Governments. *Public Performance & Management Review*, *29*(2), 191–216.

Yang, W., & Chenxi, W. (2003). Modeling the Effects of Timing Parameters on Virus Propagation. In Proceedings of the ACM workshop on Rapid Malcode, Washington, DC: ACM Press.

Yildiz, M. (2007). E-government research: Reviewing the literature, limitations, and ways forward. *Journal of Government Information Quarterly*, 646-665.

Yusuf, A. (2008, March 17). Nigerian Hospitals-Corridors of Death. *Tell Magazine*, pp 18-23.

Zachmann, J. A. (1987). A Framework for Information Systems Architecture. *IBM Systems Journal*, *26*(3). doi:10.1147/sj.263.0276

Zand, D. E. (1972). Trust and Managerial Problem Solving. *Administrative Science Quarterly*, *17*, 229–239. doi:10.2307/2393957

Zappen, J. P., Harrison, T. M., et al. (2008). A new paradigm for designing e-government: web 2.0 and experience design. In *Proceedings of the 2008 international conference on Digital government research*, Montreal, Canada.

Zeghib, N., Barkaoui, K., & Bettaz, M. (2006). Contextual ECATNets Semantics. *IEEE*, 36-943.

Zhang, J., Ghorbani, A. A., & Cohen, R. (2007). A Familiarity-Based Trust Model For Effective Selection of Sellers In Multiagent E-Commerce Systems. *International Journal of Information Security*, *6*, 333–344. doi:10.1007/s10207-007-0025-y

Zou, C. C., Towsley, D., & Gong, W. (2003). On the Performance of Internet Worm Scanning Strategies. *Performance Evaluation*, *63*(7), 700–723. doi:10.1016/j.peva.2005.07.032

Zou, C. C., et al. (2003). Monitoring and Early Warning for Internet Worms. In *Proceedings of the 10th ACM conference on Computer and communications security*. Washington DC: ACM Press.

Zou, C. C., Gong, W., & Towsley, D. (2002). Code red worm propagation modeling and analysis. In *Proceedings of the 9th ACM conference on Computer and communications security*. Washington, DC: ACM Press.

Zucker, L. G. (1986). Production of Trust: Institutional Sources Of Economic Structure. In Staw, B. M., & Cummings, L. L. (Eds.), *Research In Organizational Behavior*. London: Jai Press Inc.

Zue, V., Seneff, G. J., Polifront, J., & Pao, C., HAZEN, T. J., & Hetherington, I. (2000). JUPITER: A Telephone-Based Conversqtional Interface for Weather Information. *IEEE Transactions on Speech and Audio Processing*, *8*(1). doi:10.1109/89.817460

About the Contributors

Abid Thyab Al Ajeeli received his BSc degree from University of London – Queen Mary College, MSc in Operational Research from University of Southampton, UK and a PhD degree in Software Engineering from University of Keele, UK. Dr. His research interests are Optimization, Computer-Aided Manufacturing, Software Engineering, Distance Education, and e-government strategies and implementation.

Yousif Al-Bastaki received a BSc degree from University of Bahrain, MSc from University of Leeds, UK and a PhD degree from University of Nottingham, UK. Recently he has been appointed as an IT advisor at the Deputy Prime Minster at the Kingdom of Bahrain and previously worked as the Dean of College of IT at the University of Bahrain. Currently he is an associate professor and the Dean of Admission and Registration at the University of Bahrain. His research interests are Neural Networks, genetic algorithms E-Learning, Distance Education and e-government strategies and implementation.

* * * *

Mohammed Saeed Abdo Ahmed grew up in Yemen. He received his early education in Hodeida, Yemen and later went to Malaysia to pursue his degree in business. He received his Bachelors in Marketing Management (Hons) from Multimedia University, Malaysia in 2008. Currently Mr. Ahmed works for an MNC based in Dubai, UAE. Mr.Ahmed is active in academic research activities, particularly in conducting marketing research in the area of internet marketing and online consumer behaviour research.

Hisham M. Alsaghier holds a Master of e-Commerce, PhD candidate, Griffith University, Australia. Research interest and expertise: e-Government adoption, e-Commerce and e-Government trust.

Aderemi Aaron Anthony Atayero holds a BSc degree (summa cum laude) in Radio Engineering and M.Sc. in Satellite Communication Systems (1992, 1994 respectively) both from the Moscow Institute of Technology, and a PhD in Technical Sciences (Speech Processing / Satcom, 2000) from the Moscow State Technical University of Civil Aviation, Moscow, Russia. His current areas of research interest are: Speech Processing, Information theoretic analysis of written languages, FPGA Implementation of Digital Speech Processors. He is a member of a number of academic and professional organisations including the Institute of Electrical and Electronic Engineers (IEEE). Atayero is a Senior Lecturer in the department of Electrical and Information Engineering at Covenant University.

Charles K. Ayo holds a BSc, MSc and PhD in Computer Science. His research interests include: mobile computing, Internet programming, e-business and government, and object oriented design and development. He is a member of the Nigerian Computer Society (NCS), and Computer Professional Registration Council of Nigeria (CPN). He is currently the Head of Computer and Information Sciences Department of Covenant University, Ota, Ogun state, Nigeria, Africa. Dr. Ayo is a member of a number of international research bodies such as the Centre for Business Information, Organization and Process Management (BIOPoM), University of Westminister. http://www.wmin.ac.uk/wbs/page-744; the Review Committee of the European Conference on E-Government, http://www.academic-conferences.org/eceg/; and the Editorial Board, Journal of Information and communication Technology for Human Development.

A. A. Azeta is a PhD student in the Department of Computer and Information Sciences, Covenant University, Ota, Nigeria. He holds BSc and MSc in Computer Science from University of Benin and Lagos respectively. His current research interests are in the following areas: Software Engineering, Algorithm Design and Mobile Computing. He currently lectures at Covenant University. He is a member of the Nigerian Computer Society (NCS) and Computer Professional Registration Council of Nigeria (CPN).

Jenny Backhouse is an academic at the Australian Defence Force Academy campus of the University of New South Wales in Australia. Jenny has been teaching in a wide range of IT technologies over many years. Currently she has a special interest in the emerging developments and social role of Information and Communication Technologies. This includes the e-government arena with particular reference to democratic processes, the digital divide and accessibility issues.

Tatiana Balikhina received her MSc. In computer engineering from Electrical Engineering Institute, St. Petersburg, Russia, 1989 on her research in image processing. Since graduation she has been involved in developing software for business applications. She was a database administrator and main developer for finance department at Petra University (PU) from 1998 – 2002. She joined the Faculty of Information Technology 2004 as teacher assistant. She was awarded a PhD in computer science in 2005 for her work on network architectures for large scale distributed virtual environments. Since 2005 she is an assistant professor in the Faculty of Information Technology at PU. She is involved in research relating to network architectures, distributed virtual environments, image processing, network performance, computer and internet security awareness.

Abdelouahad Bayar is professor of mathematics and computer science at Cadi Ayyad University (école Supérieure de Technologie) in Safi, Morocco since 1996. He gets a CEUS (Certificat d'Etudes Uinversitaire Supérieures) in applied mathematics and computer science in 1996. He integrates then the university as a research-teacher. He holds his Doctorate of the thirth cycle in 1999 in Computer science in communication networks. Since 2007, Bayar is a member of the group of Information Systems and Communication Networks LSNC in Information Systems Engineering Laboratory ISIL. His actual investigations deal especially with dynamic fonts and calligraphic rules formalization.

Lilia C. Belcadhi is an assistant professor of Computer Science at the University of Sousse, Tunisia, and a graduate of the University of Braunschweig in Germany where she received an MS degree in Computer Sciences. She holds a PhD from Faculty of Sciences of Tunis (2008). She is a member of the PRINCE Research group at the University of Sousse and her doctoral research was conducted in collaboration with the Semantic Web group at the Institute of Information Systems of the University of Hannover in Germany. Her research interests include personalisation and reasoning on the semantic web, web-based assessment and e-learning. She is involved, as part of her ongoing research, in several e-learning projects and has co-authored various online courses for graduate students. She can be reached at lilia.belcadhi@infcom.rnu.tn and ISITC, GP1, Hammam Sousse, 4011 Tunisia.

Fatma Bouaziz is PhD student in Management at the Faculty of Economics and Management of Sfax, Tunisia. Her researches treat in the use of ICT by public administration, their organisational impacts and abilities to enhance services quality. Her thesis concerns the risk management of e-government projects.

Rafik Braham is currently a professor of computer science at ISITC of Hammam Sousse, the University of Sousse. He is the head of the research group PRINCE. He received a PhD degree from Georgia Institute of Technology in 1990. His research interests include learning technologies, neural networks, wireless networking (MAC and PHY), Internet-based services and automatic processing of Arabic language. R. Braham is a member of IEEE and IEEE Computer and Education societies.

Allaoua Chaoui is with the department of computer science, Faculty of Engineering, University Mentouri Constantine, Algeria. He received his Master degree in Computer science in 1992 (in cooperation with the University of Glasgow, Scotland) and his PhD degree in 1998 from the University of Constantine (in cooperation with the CEDRIC Laboratory of CNAM in Paris, France). He has served as associate professor in Philadelphia University in Jordan for five years and University Mentoury Constantine for many years. During his career he has designed and taught courses in Software Engineering and Formal Methods. Dr. Allaoua Chaoui has published many articles in International Journals and Conferences. He supervises many Master and PhD students. His research interests include Mobile Computing, formal specification and verification of distributed systems, and graph transformation systems.

Narjess T. Chebaane is a doctoral student in computer science at Faculty of Sciences of Tunis. She is currently a lecturer at ISITC of Hammam Sousse, the University of Sousse. Her research interests include e-leraning, pedagogical scenarios and tutoring. She is a member of the PRINCE Research group.

Raid Al-Dabagh holds (MSc) in Electronic and communication Engineering since (1991) from Mosul University – Iraq. Mr. Raid has been taught many subjects in Computing, Hardware, Software, Programming, Computer Programming Languages, Office Programs, and management information system with many related Subjects in Iraq and other countries. He holds many administrative work beside an academic teaching tasks, he promoted to different academic ranks and by 2005 have promoted to Associate Professor in Computer & Communication Engineering. He attended many national and International conferences and has spoken at conferences nationwide.

J.O. Daramola is currently a PhD research candidate in Computer Science of the Department of Computer and Information Sciences, Covenant University, Nigeria where he is also Lecturer. He also holds a temporary research fellowship of the Centre for Mobile e-Services for Development, University of Zululand, South Africa. His research interest includes software architecture, software tools development, Artificial Intelligence and Knowledge Engineering.

Pasquale Del Vecchio PhD in e-business at eBusiness Management Section of Scuola Superiore ISUFI - University of Salento, Italy. After a degree in Economics at LUISS University of Rome, he had job experiences as junior consultant in marketing field and as coordinator of CRM services for utilities. His research field concerns the Customers Knowledge Management and Relational Marketing with a special interest to the social phenomenon of users virtual communities enabled by the web 2.0 technologies. Currently, he is involved in a project for the development of an Interdisciplinary Approach at the Educational Learning and of a New Competency Model in Management Education.

Heba Zaki El-Fiqi is a Teaching Assistant in IT Dept, Faculty of Computers & Informatics, Zagazig University. She received her MSc degree in 2008 from Computer Science Department, Faculty of Computers & Information, Cairo University. She is a member of Software Engineers Association (ESEA). Also, she is certified as CCNA Instructor and certified as MCSE +Security. Her research of interest includes computer networks, security systems, and intelligent systems.

Gianluca Elia - Researcher at University of Salento. After his degree in Computer Science Engineering and a Master of Science in e-Business Management, he is strongly involved in his research field, focusing on methodological and technological aspects of knowledge management and web learning processes and platforms. In his field he published many papers and he led many complex research projects, also with multinational companies. In October 2006, he also received an award from "Brandon Hall Research" in "Learning Technology" category, for "Virtual eBMS", a knowledge management and e-learning integrated system. He is also responsible for a research program in the Mediterranean countries, focused on experimenting innovative approaches to diffuse digital and organizational innovation in traditional industries, including education sector. Finally, he teaches at the Faculty of Engineering at the University of Salento (Italy).

I.T. Fatudimu holds a BSc in Engineering Physics and MSc in Computer Science. She is currently a PhD student in the Department of Computer and Information Sciences, Covenant University, Ota, Nigeria. Her research interest is in the field of Data Mining. She is an Assistant Lecturer in the Department of Computer and Information Sciences, Covenant University, Ota, Nigeria. She enjoys reading and engages in creative arts.

Adriana Figueiredo is a software engineer at Centro de Tecnologia da Informacao Renato Archer (CTI). She received a BS from Universidade Federal de Minas Gerais in 1983 and a M.S. from Universidade de Campinas in 2004, all in Computer. Adriana joined CTI in 1984. For many years she worked in software development, transfering software technology to Brazilian industry. In 2002, she changed her focus to research, which interests include metadata for distributed systems and trust mechanisms for online communities.

Marilyn Ford is an associate professor in the School of Information and Communication Technology. She has extensive publications in the areas of reasoning, sentence perception, production, linguistics, and education.

Robert Goodwin is a senior lecturer at School of Computer Science, Engineering, and Mathematics (CSEM), The Flinders University of South Australia. He is a research coordinator for Enterprise Information Technology Research Group at CSEM. Dr. Goodwin's research interests relate to the application of information technology in business and education (e-business, e-government, and e-learning). His articles appeared in various journals and international conferences. He has published four Information Technology books for the school. Areas of lecturing include: Business Information Systems and Computer Security.

Francesca Grippa - Researcher in Knowledge Management at the eBusiness Management Section, Scuola Superiore ISUFI, University of Salento, Italy. Her current research interest is in applying Social Network Analysis to monitoring learning communities. She holds a PhD in e-Business, discussing a thesis on a methodology to measure social networks implied by different communication media. She got her Master's Degree in Business Management at eBMS-ISUFI, Italy. She is also interested in integrating Knowledge Management and e-Learning Strategies.

Rene Hexel has been an active researcher in the area of real-time communication environments and time-triggered systems. His recent research has been on ubiquitous computing environments, particularly networked mobile and autonomous systems. A strong focus of his research has been human-computer interaction with such systems, particularly investigating privacy and security. He has been instrumental in the development of robust, secure, and dependable architectures and communication protocols for safety-critical systems that affect people's everyday lives. Dr Hexel is currently supervising two PhD students in the area of privacy, security, and trust into computing environments.

Marc Holzer is Dean and Board of Governors Professor at the School of Public Affairs and Administration at Rutgers University, Newark. He is also the director of the National Center for Public Performance (NCPP). His research addresses issues of public performance, e-governance, comparative public administration, and the influence of culture on management. He is a Fellow of the National Academy of Pubic Administration.

Yasar Jarrar is a Partner at PricewaterhouseCoopers, UAE and leads its ME Government and Public Sector Group. Prior to joining PwC, Yasar was the Executive Dean of Dubai School of Government and a Fellow at Harvard Kennedy School. Yasar also served as the Strategy Advisor at The Executive Office of HH Sheikh Mohammed Al Maktoum in Dubai (UAE). Yasar also worked as the Director of the Government Performance Directorate in the Prime Ministry of Jordan, and as the Head of Policy and Strategy in the Executive Council of the Dubai Government. Prior to moving to Dubai, Yasar was a Research Fellow in Cranfield School of Management in the UK. He is the author of numerous reports and papers on strategy and performance management. He is also a Visiting Fellow, Cranfield School of Management, an Adjunct Professor, Lee Kuan Yew School of Public Policy, and Advisor, Harvard International Negotiation Initiative, Harvard University.

Aqueo Kamada is a software engineering researcher at CTI – Centro de Tecnologia da Informacao Renato Archer and a part-time lecturer at Faculty of Technology, Unicamp – University of Campinas. He holds PhD and MSc in Computer Engineering at FEEC – School of Electrical and Computer Engineering, Unicamp, Campinas, Brazil; Specialization in Database Systems at SUNY - State University of New York, Binghamton, U.S.A.; Specialization in Software Development Environmen at SMU - Southern Methodist University, Dallas, U.S.A.; and BSc in Computer Science at IC – Institute of Computing,

Unicamp, Campinas, Brazil. His research and development experience are focused in areas, such as, business rules, semantic web, service modeling, service oriented architecture, services composition, electronic government systems and model driven architecture/engineering. Currently, he is also a lecturer in programming languages and database systems. In the past, he worked in areas, such as, database management systems, object oriented development, software engineering environment, industry automation, bank automation, languages and compilers. Besides, he also was a lecturer in Operating Systems and Computer Architecture.

Maha Khemaja is an assistant professor of computer science and director of the Higher Institute of Management and Computer Science of Kairouan (ISIGK), University of Kairouan, Tunisia. She received a PhD in computer science from the University of Tunis in 2000. Her research interests include ontologies, semantic web, e-learning and e-services. She is a member of the PRINCE Research group.

Mohamed-Khireddine Kholladi is a Doctor of state in data processing (graduate Doctor of the INSA of Lyon). He is currently a head of Computer science Department of the Faculty of Science of the engineer of the university Mentouri Constantine and president of association sciences and development of the university. He is member of the network Cassini in France and member of network ACIT International and IACET International. Its work concerns the geographical information systems, the computer graphics, the treatment and synthesis of image, national's archives, knowledge bases, the new technology of information and communication "NTIC", etc.

Niall Levine is a communications researcher and currently assists at the School of Computing, UNISA. He can be contacted at levinn@unisa.ac.za

Marco De Maggio - PhD in "e-business" at eBusiness Management Section of Scuola Superiore ISUFI - University of Salento, Italy. Bachelor Degree in Economics at University of Lecce, and Chartered Accountant. His research field concerns the development of Methodologies for the analysis and management of Organizational Learning Patterns inside Organizations and Communities of Practice. His focus is mainly on the development of tools and methodologies for the monitoring of the organizational behavior responsible for Social Capital creation. Visiting Scholar at MIT – Boston, MA, he experimented the application of Content and Social Network analysis supported by computer-aided systems for the improvement in the analysis of Virtual Communities.

Raida El Mansouri is with the department of computer science, Faculty of Engineering, University Mentouri Constantine, Algeria. She received a Master degree in Computer science in 1997 and a PhD degree in 2009 at the same University. Her research interests include formal specification and verification of distributed information systems.

Ali Maqousi received his PhD in computer science from Oxford Brookes University, UK, 2003 for his work on providing Quality of Service (QoS) in packet switched networks. He was a network administrator and part-time teacher assistant at Petra University (PU) from 1993 – 1997 and full-time teacher assistant from 1999 - 2003. Since 2003 he is an assistant professor in the Faculty of Information Technology at PU and currently he is the head of computer science department and computer networks department. He is ITSAF Secretary - General (Information Technology Students Activity Fair, ITSAF is a yearly event for all Jordanian Universities since 2005). He is the university liaison officer for European Union 7th framework program (FP7) to support and fund R&D since 2007. He is involved in research relating to multi-service networking, network performance, computer and internet security awareness, and network architectures for large scale distributed virtual environment.

Robert Jeyakumar Nathan received his Bachelors in Marketing with Multimedia from Multimedia University, Malaysia and Masters of Philosophy (Research in Ergonomics and Internet Marketing) from the same university. Prior to joining the academia, he worked for Infineon Technologies AG, a semi-conductor manufacturing company based in Munich, Germany as a System Analyst. He specializes in Manufacturing Statistics and Data Analysis and has conducted statistical, data mining and enterprise document and knowledge management system trainings in various Infineon plants in Asia, Europe and North America. He is currently working for Multimedia University Malaysia under the Faculty of Business and Law. He conducts Marketing, Research Methodology and Leadership courses. Mr. Nathan is active in various research projects in Malaysia, Singapore, Australia and in the Middle East. His research interests include Marketing and Information Technology, Electronic Commerce, Social Networks Technologies, Student Internet Users, Usability and Ergonomics, and Occupational Safety & Health Research. Mr. Nathan is an active member of the National Institute of Occupational Safety and Health (NIOSH) Malaysia. He currently holds an Adjunct Lecturer position with the University of Newcastle Australia (Singapore Campus) where he delivers modules on Marketing and Research Methodologies.

Oyelami Olufemi Moses holds both BSc and MSc in Computer Science and currently teaches the same in Covenant University, Ota, Ogun State, Nigeria. He is a member of both Computer Professional Registration Council of Nigeria (CPN) and Nigerian Computer Society (NCS). He is a PhD student of Computer Science in the Department of Computer and Information Sciences, Covenant University, Ota. E-Learning, Algorithms, Programming Languages and Mobile Computing are his current research interests.

Goonasagree Naidoo was born in South Africa (SA). She pursued her studies at the University of Kwa-Zulu Natal (Honours and MA degrees in Public Administration), University of Edinburgh (MBA), University of Pretoria and Gonzaga University-Washington State (PhD in Public Affairs). She is currently employed as a senior lecturer by the University of South Africa.

Nicholas Ikhu-Omoregbe, has a BSc degree in Computer science from the University of Benin, Benin city, an M.Sc degree in Computer Sciences from the University of Lagos, and a PhD degree in Computer Science from Covenant University, Ota, Nigeria. His research interests include: Software Engineering, Mobile Computing, Mobile Healthcare and Telemedicine Systems, and Soft Computing. He currently lectures at Covenant University. He is a member of the Institution of Electrical and Electronics Engineers (IEEE).

Norma M. Riccucci is professor of public administration at the School of Public Affairs and Administration at Rutgers University, Newark. Her research focuses on broad issues of public management and improving government performance. She is a fellow of the National Academy of Public Administration and is President of the Public Management Research Association.

Sarah Afzal Safavi (Islamabad) secured her Masters in Computer Science degree in year2000 from Hamdard University Karachi. She worked in local software industry from year 2000 to 2002. Then she joined a public sector university as Lecturer in IT department. There she engaged herself in teaching and research activities for the period of 5 years. In year 2006 she further admitted herself in MS-Computer Science specializing in Software Engineering in COMSATS Institute of Information Technology, Islamabad Campus, Pakistan. She successfully completed this degree in year 2008. During this period she produced number of local and international publications. Ms. Safavi is currently undertaking her research work in the area of e-government, cloud computing and service driven architecture. In 2007, Ms. Sara Afzal Safavi is joined Electronic Government Directorate (i.e. a division of Ministry of Information Technology and Telecommunication) as Director Systems. She is serving in strategic planning and architecture wing where she is experiencing her skill set for monitoring and evaluation of ongoing automation projects in different ministries of Government of Pakistan. Further she gives her input in policy making, standardization of process in different areas of electronic governance.

Mohammed Abdullah Saleh al-Hilali Bachelor of Statistics and Computer Science, Faculty of Rivers University in 1998. He worked in the field of computer programming and software, maintenance and repair for the period 1998-2003 in the private sector. Teaching at the Higher Institute of Administrative Development in the field of computers 2001-2003. Employee in the Ministry of Higher Education and Scientific Research in the Iraqi Board of Medical Specialties, in a section of the Computer and the Internet in 2004 - until now.

Fadi Salem is the Director of the Governance and Innovation Program at the Dubai School of Government. He is also a Fellow with the I+I Policy Research Center, Lee Kuan Yew School of Public Policy, National University of Singapore; and previously a Research Associate with the Belfer Center for Science and International Affairs, Harvard University. His expertise and research focus areas include ICT's transformational impact on governance and society as well as electronic government and development. His current research interests also include new media, information security, measurement and evaluation in the knowledge economy, and societal implications of online social networking services. He advises several governments in the Middle East and North Africa and is the author of articles published in journals, print and new media. He publishes in Arabic and English and frequently contributes to media programs and international conferences.

Khalid Sami is professor of mathematics at Cadi Ayyad university (Faculté des Sciences) in Marakech, Morocco since 1983. Since years, he's interested in multilingual scientific text formatting. Some of the work relevant to this area is presented in the url www.ucam.ac.ma/fssm/rydarab.

Giustina Secundo - Researcher in Management Education at the e-Business Management Section (eBMS) of the Scuola Superiore ISUFI– University of Salento (Italy). Her current research concerns the emerging trends in management education and the human capital creation process in Business Schools, with a special interest to the learning processes supported by the Information and Communication Technologies. These research fields are strictly connected to her activities related to the Management of the Advanced education programs of the eBMS, with a particular focus on the programs devoted to people coming from the Mediterranean Countries.

Maqbool Uddin Shaikh received his MSc as well as PhD degrees from the University of Liverpool, Liverpool, UK. He served as faculty member in different universities in different countries such as Jordan, UK, Kuwait, Sultanate of Oman, Malaysia, Bahrain and UAE. Currently, he is Professor at department of Computer Science in COMSATS Institute of Information Technology (CIIT), Islamabad, Pakistan. During his job in CIIT he had supervised seventeen (17) MS / M. Phil students and at present he is supervising two PhD and five MS students. His major research interests are Business Intelligence (Data warehousing, Web Warehousing, Data mining, etc.), Decision support Systems, Knowledge Base Systems, and e-Systems. He has published many research articles in international conferences /journals. He is in the list of Higher Education Commission (HEC) Govt. of Pakistan, approved supervisor of MS/ PhD. Further information is available on the following link http://sc.hec.gov.pk/aphds/submit.asp?supid=2016

Mohammad Shirali-Shahreza is an undergraduate student in computer science at Sharif University of Technology in IRAN. He got his diploma from Allameh Helli high school, Tehran, IRAN, that is a school for exceptional talents students. He is selected as "Iranian Distinguished University Student" by the Ministry of Science, Research and Technology of Iran in 2008. His project on Steganography won the best prize of 5th Iranian Khwarizmi young festival. He has 90 accepted papers in international conferences, 16 published papers in journals, three book chapters, one book and one Iranian patent. He won the "Best Undergraduate Researcher Award" from Iranian Society of Cryptology (2006), the "Young Researcher Award" of IEEE ICTTA 2006 conference and the "Young Researcher Award" of the 11th International CSI Computer Conference (CSICC'2006). He is a student member of IEEE and Iranian Computer Society. His research interest includes Steganography, CAPTCHA, mobile programming, and e-learning.

Sajad Shirali-Shahreza received Bachelor of Science and Master of Science in Software Engineering from Computer Engineering Department of Sharif University of Technology in 2006 and 2007. Currently, he is a PhD candidate at Computer Engineering Department of Sharif University of Technology. He ranked second in the 2006 Iranian Scientific Olympiad in Computer Engineering and also has the silver medal of 2002 National Iranian Olympiad in Informatics. He was the only student who finished B.Sc in computer engineering in 3 years among 200 undergraduate students of his department in 2007. He is the first student in the history of Computer Engineering Department of Sharif University who finished MSc in 1 year. He published 7 journal and 53 conference papers. He is a member of IEEE Computer Society, IEEE Signal Processing and ACM. His research interests are Human Interactive Proofs (HIP), Optical Character Recognition, Image Processing and Machine Learning.

Panagiota-Aikaterina (Katerina) Sidiropoulou is an advocate (Athens Bar Association) and Doctoral candidate at the Business School of Middlesex University in London in the area of Online Dispute Resolution (ODR). She is also an Associate Lecturer in the Law Department. Aikaterina holds a Bachelor of Laws (LLB), a Master of Laws (LLM) in International Commercial Law and a Master in Research Methods for Business and Management (MSc). Her research interest and knowledge is in International Trade Law, International Arbitration and Online Arbitration, Conflict Management, International Commercial Law, Consumer Protection, European Single Market, Employment Relations and Organizational Behavior. She has published over a dozen of research outcomes in academic conferences procedures and business reviews internationally.

Shawren Singh is a PhD candidate at the University of South Africa and a senior lecturer in the School of Computing. His research interest include: Problem-Based Research in Information Systems, Human Computer Interaction (HCI), Web-based Courseware Tools, Internet Applications, Blended Education, E-commerce, E-government and Accounting Information Systems.

Tony Dwi Susanto is a PhD candidate at School of Computer Science, Engineering, and Mathematics (CSEM), The Flinders University of South Australia. He is one of Australia Leadership Award (ALA) awardees. Before joining the PhD program, he has held positions as visiting researcher at CSEM-South Australia and King Saud University-Saudi Arabia, and a representative of Indonesia at IATSS Forum-Japan. His research interests include technology adoption, e-government and mobile technology. His papers in the fields of e-government and mobile services have been published and presented at several international conferences and journal.

Tarek Salah Sobh received his BSc degree in computer engineering from Military Technical College, Cairo, Egypt in 1987. Both MSc and PhD degrees from Computer and System Engineering Department, Faculty of Engineering, Al-Azhar University, Cairo, Egypt. He has managed, designed and developed several package for business applications and security systems. He has authored/co-authored of many refereed journal/conference papers and booklet. Some of the articles are available in the ScienceDirect Top 25 hottest articles. His research of interest includes computer networks, security systems, distributed systems, knowledge discovery, data mining, and software engineering.

Akinwale Adio Taofeek was born in Abeokuta, Ogun State, Nigeria. He attended Mac-Job Grammar School from 1975 to 1980. Lodz University, Lodz, Poland from 1984 t0 1985. Oscar Lange University, Wroclaw, Polan from 1985to 1990 where he bagged an MSc in Cybernetics and informatics. He earned his PhD in Economics Informatics in the same university in 2005. He started his teaching career in Oscar Lange University as an Assistant Lecturer. He joined the services of University of Agriculture, Abeokuta in 1998 and is currently a senior lecturer and the head of the department of Computer Science. His current areas of interest are knowledge database and algorithm optimization for database operations.

Say Yen Teoh is a Lecturer of Business Information Technology in the RMIT University, Australia. Dr. Teoh's primary research interests are in the areas of design, implementation, and evaluation of the Health Informatics, E-Health and Enterprise Systems. In particular, she focuses on Health Informatics research in Asia: Singapore, China and Australia. Currently, her publications have appeared in the Journal of Systems and Information Technology, Journal of Enterprise Information Management, with a few book chapters published by ICEG Publisher, World Scientific Publisher, IRM Press. She has also attended conferences such as European Conference on Information Systems (ECIS), Information Resource Management Association (IRMA) Conference, Pacific Asia Conference on Information Systems (PACIS), and Australasian Conference on Information Systems (ACIS).

John Douglas Thomson PhD has been with the RMIT University, Melbourne, Australia since 2002. From Sep 2005 to Sep 2007 he was the MBA Programs Manager for the Graduate School of Business and is currently a Lecturer and Course Coordinator. He has extensive global experience in the application of e-business in the private and public sectors, and worked in Vietnam for four months in 2007 at the RMIT IUV's Ha Noi campus. He has more than 20 years international experience and published extensively in ICT and e-business policy development, public and private sector e-business management, e-entrepreneurship and project management.

Okba Tibermacine has received a Master degree in Computer science in 2009 from the University of Batna, Algeria. He received his BS degree in Computer science from Biskra University. Okba had worked for three years as a computer engineer at a financial company, and for two years as a lecturer. His research interests include Compilers, Formal Methods, and programming.

Charles Onuwa Uwadia attended St. Charles Grammar School, Osogbo (1970 – 1974) and holds a BSc. Degree honours in Computer Science from the University of Ibadan in 1979. He served at the Polytechnic Ibadan for his NYSC programme. He had his MSc. In 1983 and PhD in 1990 both at the University of Lagos. Professor Uwadia joined the services of the University of Lagos as an Assistant Lecturer in 1983, and rose steadily to the post of a full Professor of Computer Science in the year 2004. His major area of specialization is Software Engineering with emphasis on Compiling Techniques and Systems Software. He is also actively involved in teaching and research work in networking, congestion control and management aspects of Information Technology. With over 40 publications in both local and international journals, he has three books to his name. He is an active member of the Nigeria Computer Society (NCS), and the Computer Professionals Registration Council of Nigeria. He is the current President of the Society. Besides his enviable service in Nigeria, Professor Uwadia has been a visiting Fellow to Universities and Institutions in the United States of America, Europe, Asia, and Australia.

Wamedh Wadood Abdul Hameed (Baghdad), Bachelor of Science in Software Engineering from the Faculty of the University of Baghdad, Iraq / Iraq in 2001. He worked in the design and manufacture of computer systems from 2001 to 2004 in the Iraqi private sector and in 2005 I enrolled as an employee to the Department of Computer and the Internet in the Iraqi Board of Medical Specialties formations and one of the Ministry of Higher Education and Scientific Research in Iraq.

Amer R. Zerek is with the Department of Electric and Electronic Engineering, Engineering Academy, Tajura, Libya. He is associate professor. His research interests include formal methods and image processing.

Tarek Zernadji has received a Master degree in Computer science in 2009 from the University of Batna, Algeria. He received his Bachelor degree in Computer science from the University of Biskra. His research interests include Formal Methods and software engineering.

Index

D

E

F

G

H

I

J

K

L

M

N

O

Breinigsville, PA USA
10 November 2010
249029BV00003B/4/P